Studia Fennica
Historica 24

The Finnish Literature Society (SKS) was founded in 1831 and has, from the very beginning, engaged in publishing operations. It nowadays publishes literature in the fields of ethnology and folkloristics, linguistics, literary research and cultural history.

The first volume of the Studia Fennica series appeared in 1933. Since 1992, the series has been divided into three thematic subseries: Ethnologica, Folkloristica and Linguistica. Two additional subseries were formed in 2002, Historica and Litteraria. The subseries Anthropologica was formed in 2007.

In addition to its publishing activities, the Finnish Literature Society maintains research activities and infrastructures, an archive containing folklore and literary collections, a research library and promotes Finnish literature abroad.

Studia Fennica Editorial Board
Editors-in-chief
Pasi Ihalainen, Professor, University of Jyväskylä, Finland
Timo Kallinen, University Lecturer, University of Helsinki, Finland
Taru Nordlund, Professor, University of Helsinki, Finland
Riikka Rossi, Title of Docent, University Researcher, University of Helsinki, Finland
Katriina Siivonen, Title of Docent, University Teacher, University of Turku, Finland
Lotte Tarkka, Professor, University of Helsinki, Finland

Deputy editors-in-chief
Anne Heimo, Title of Docent, University of Turku, Finland
Saija Isomaa, Professor, University of Tampere, Finland
Sari Katajala-Peltomaa, Title of Docent, Researcher, University of Tampere, Finland
Eerika Koskinen-Koivisto, Postdoctoral Researcher, Dr. Phil., University of Helsinki, Finland
Laura Visapää, Title of Docent, University Lecturer, University of Helsinki, Finland

Tuomas M. S. Lehtonen, Secretary General, Dr. Phil., Finnish Literature Society, Finland
Tero Norkola, Publishing Director, Finnish Literature Society, Finland
Virve Mertanen, Secretary of the Board, Finnish Literature Society, Finland

oa.finlit.fi

Editorial Office
SKS
P.O. Box 259
FI-00171 Helsinki
www.finlit.fi

Pasi Ihalainen

The Springs of Democracy

National and Transnational Debates on Constitutional Reform in the British, German, Swedish and Finnish Parliaments, 1917–1919

Finnish Literature Society • SKS • Helsinki • 2017

STUDIA FENNICA HISTORICA 24

The publication has undergone a peer review.

The open access publication of this volume has received part funding via
a Jane and Aatos Erkko Foundation grant.

© 2017 Pasi Ihalainen and SKS
License CC-BY-NC-ND 4.0 International

A digital edition of a printed book first published in 2017 by the Finnish Literature Society.
Cover Design: Timo Numminen
EPUB: eLibris Media Oy

ISBN 978-952-222-918-2 (Print)
ISBN 978-952-222-929-8 (PDF)
ISBN 978-952-222-928-1 (EPUB)

ISSN 0085-6835 (Studia Fennica)
ISSN 1458-526X (Studia Fennica Historica)

DOI: http://dx.doi.org/10.21435/sfh.24

This work is licensed under a Creative Commons CC-BY-NC-ND 4.0 International License.
To view a copy of the license, please visit http://creativecommons.org/licenses/by-nc-nd/4.0/

 A free open access version of the book is available at http://dx.doi.org/10.21435/sfh.24
or by scanning this QR code with your mobile device.

BoD – Books on Demand, Norderstedt, Germany 2017

Table of contents

Acknowledgements 10

List of abbreviations 12

1. **Introduction 13**
   1.1 The reform debates of the revolutionary era 1917–19 in inter- and transnational comparisons 13
   1.2 Towards a comparative and transnational history of political discourse 23
   1.3 Discourse-oriented political history based on parliamentary sources 37
   1.4 The structure of the analysis 41

2. **National backgrounds of constitutional disputes from spring 1917 to summer 1919 44**
   2.1 The standstill in the British constitutional reform before and during the war 44
   2.2 Universal male suffrage in Germany. Prussian executive power and scepticism about parliamentarism 50
   2.3 Prolonged disputes on suffrage and parliamentary government in Sweden 57
   2.4 Finland – a grand duchy of the Russian Empire with exceptionally broad suffrage but no parliamentary government 62

3. **The spring of democracy in 1917: The new constitutional scene created by the prolonged war, the Russian Revolution and the American intervention 72**
   3.1 Britain: The wartime situation used to force through a postponed reform 72
       3.1.1 A continuing constitutional crisis 72
       3.1.2 Creating 'a new Britain' consensually in a time of war and revolution 75
       3.1.3 Cautious Labour and Liberal democrats versus patently democratic Conservatives 85

- 3.1.4 Creating a 'Parliament of the people' while avoiding a 'constitutional revolution' 92
- 3.1.5 A new Parliament – 'a mirror of the nation' engaging the citizens and placing its trust in the masses 97
- 3.1.6 The committee stage during a campaign for amendments 104
- 3.2 Wartime demands for the democratisation and parliamentarisation of Imperial Germany 108
    - 3.2.1 The German polity in a profoundly transformed world 108
    - 3.2.2 Implications of the war, the Russian Revolution and the British reform for the German constitution 113
    - 3.2.3 The Western democracies and a new democratic order in Germany 124
    - 3.2.4 The role of a 'free' German people and the masses in a new era 131
    - 3.2.5 What would the co-sovereignty of parliaments mean? 134
- 3.3 Sweden: Renewed reform demands under the threat of revolution 139
    - 3.3.1 The situation created by a repeatedly postponed suffrage reform 139
    - 3.3.2 Building 'dams of ice' or welcoming the spring in the midst of transnational change 143
    - 3.3.3 A global breaking-up of the ice for the forces of democracy? 154
    - 3.3.4 The role of the Swedish people in the reformed polity 162
    - 3.3.5 Should parliamentarism be seen as the established system, an instrument for creating a better society through debate, or a system to be taken over by the people? 166
- 3.4 Finland: The legitimacy of the parliament deteriorates at the moment of democratisation and parliamentarisation 173
    - 3.4.1 Sovereignty in the former grand duchy: in the parliament, the government or a Russian-style 'democracy'? 173
    - 3.4.2 The international, imperial and national political order changed by the war and revolution 185
    - 3.4.3 International democracy or the vernacular 'rule by the people'? 197
    - 3.4.4 Defining the position of the people within the Finnish polity 205
    - 3.4.5 Prospects for a parliamentary Finland: opposing Social Democratic and bourgeois views 207

4. The autumn of 1917: A completed, a suspended and a partial reform – and a failed reform leading to a civil war 214

- 4.1 Britain: The rising politisation of democracy 214
    - 4.1.1 A final confrontation on extended suffrage between the two chambers 214
    - 4.1.2 'This Bill is a revolution': The reform in relation to British constitutional history and foreign examples 219

  4.1.3 The increasingly contested definition of 'democracy' 225
  4.1.4 'Women in Parliament, in Governments': The widening involvement of the people in politics 232
  4.1.5 The future of a democratic parliamentary polity after the war 236
 4.2 Germany: Democratisation and parliamentarisation come to a halt 240
 4.3 Sweden: The introduction of parliamentary government as a safeguard against domestic upheaval 251
 4.4 Finland: Discursive struggles over democracy and parliamentarism turn into an attempted revolution 256
  4.4.1 The Bolshevik Revolution and the questioned legitimacy of Finland's disputatious new parliament 256
  4.4.2 Reforms to be implemented by a national parliament or by an international revolution? 259
  4.4.3 The Finnish 'rule by the people' in the shadow of Bolshevism 273
  4.4.4 A people divided by class and parliamentary discourse 281
  4.4.5 Diminishing trust in parliamentary government escalates the crisis 282

5. The Spring of 1918: Western and Prussian versions of 'parliamentarism' clash in the Swedish and Finnish parliaments 292

 5.1 Britain after of the Representation of the People Act 292
 5.2 Germany: All quiet on the reform front 297
 5.3 Sweden: A parliamentarised ministry introduces its first reform proposal 298
  5.3.1 Anti-reformism bolstered by a civil war next door 298
  5.3.2 Surrounding wars and revolutions as transnational agents of political change 302
  5.3.3 An attempted democratic breakthrough 306
  5.3.4 Bypassing the political rights of the Swedish people 310
  5.3.5 All parties on the side of parliamentarism – but different kinds of parliamentarism 312
 5.4 Finland reconstructed to resemble a little Prussia 315
  5.4.1 The attempt to restrict reform by restoring the monarchy 315
  5.4.2 A counter-revolution built on an assumed German victory 321
  5.4.3 Redescribed rightist or principled centrist democracy – or no democracy at all? 326
  5.4.4 Disappointment with the Finnish people or continuing confidence in it 331
  5.4.5 Limited debates on parliamentarism in the Rump Parliament 337

6. **The autumn of 1918: German, Swedish and Finnish constitutional debates in the face of a democratic turn 340**
    6.1 Democratic suffrage applied in Britain for the first time 340
    6.2 Germany loses the war, introduces parliamentary government and experiences a revolution 349
        6.2.1 The course of the German Revolution up to the fall of the Kaiser 349
        6.2.2 Comparing the German Revolution with the Bismarckian system and the Finnish counterrevolution 351
        6.2.3 Divergent understandings of German democracy 355
        6.2.4 The German people as a political agent 357
        6.2.5 Crypto-parliamentarism comes into the open 359
        6.2.6 The radical phase of the revolution in November and December 1918 363
    6.3 Sweden introduces an electoral reform: No revolution like those in Russia, Finland or Germany 367
        6.3.1 A reluctant rightist opposition gives in after the fall of the German monarchy 367
        6.3.2 The war and revolution as agents of domestic reform 373
        6.3.3 Optimistic and pessimistic visions of a democratic Sweden 381
        6.3.4 The relationship between the will of 'the people' and the interests of 'the realm' is problematised 392
        6.3.5 Parliamentarism under democratised suffrage 399
    6.4 The monarchist majority of the Finnish Rump Parliament in search of a stable polity 401
        6.4.1 The strange logic of Finnish constitutional politics in late summer and autumn 1918 401
        6.4.2 A controversy over the excessive transnational influence of Germany 403
        6.4.3 Monarchical vs. republican democracy 407
        6.4.4 'The will of the people' interpreted for and against a republic 411
        6.4.5 Parliamentarism redefined or endangered by the monarchists? 417

7. **The spring of 1919: The beginning of an era of democracy and parliamentarism? 422**
    7.1 Britain: Parliamentary democracy established or a bureaucratic state reinforced? 422
    7.2 The construction of a democratic and parliamentary Germany in the Weimar National Assembly 428
        7.2.1 Expert planning for a new constitution 428
        7.2.2 A revolution against dictatorship 432
        7.2.3 Defining 'the most democratic democracy in the world' 435
        7.2.4 'Power in the state belongs to the people' 445
        7.2.5 Extolling, limiting and ignoring parliamentarism 450

7.3 Sweden: Adjusting the principles of a future democracy 455
    7.3.1 Swedish parties after the suffrage reform 455
    7.3.2 Internationalism after war and revolution 457
    7.3.3 Further prospects for democracy and parliamentarism 458
    7.3.4 Politics of the people in a democratic Sweden 461
    7.3.5 A glance across the Gulf of Bothnia 463
7.4 Finland: Moving towards a compromise on a presidential parliamentary republic 465
    7.4.1 Re-orienting the polity after the war 465
    7.4.2 Rethought international comparisons and transnational connections after the war and the revolutions 475
    7.4.3 Searching for a compromise between Socialist, centrist and rightist democracy 481
    7.4.4 Popular sovereignty recognised by all but one parliamentary party 488
    7.4.5 The remaining limits on parliamentarism 495

8. The entangled parliamentary revolutions of 1917–19: Comparison, discussion and conclusion 504

Appendix: Selected key events in national politics 534

Bibliography 536
    Primary sources 536
    Newspapers 537
    Literature 537

Abstract 555

Subject and Place Index 556
Index of Names 577

Acknowledgements

It took seven years to complete this book, and it is hardly possible to thank all the people who have contributed to the process. I made the move from the comparative study of eighteenth-century political cultures to transnational research on early twentieth-century politics in spring 2010 during a research stay in Uppsala at the Swedish Collegium for Advanced Studies whose fellows and Director Björn Wittrock were highly supportive of the idea. The intention was to complete research at the Freiburg Institute for Advanced Studies in spring 2012, and colleagues there and especially Director Jörn Leonhard were equally supportive of my work, but this study turned out to be much more extensive and demanding than foreseen so that I had to go on writing parallel with my position as a professor of comparative European history at the University of Jyväskylä. The teams of two Academy of Finland projects on parliamentary means of conflict resolution and supra- and transnational foreign policy as well as the research group on the comparative study of political cultures have supported my work and so have several colleagues at the Departments of History and Ethnology, Applied Language Studies and Social Sciences and Philosophy. Unable to name everyone I would like to thank especially research assistants Ville Häkkinen, Emilia Lakka, Lauri Niemistö, Jukka Nissinen and Adrian Steinert as well as my language copy-editor Gerard McAlester. The Department of History and Ethnology, the Academy of Finland Project 'Supra- and Transnational Foreign Policy versus National Parliamentary Government, 1914–2014' (decision 275589) and the Faculty of Humanities (led by Minna-Riitta Luukka) funded copy-editing, and Finnland-Institut in Berlin (led by Laura Hirvi) provided a site for proof-reading. I would also like to thank Pertti Ahonen, Stuart Ball, Tapio Bergholm, Richard Bessel, Benjamin Beuerle, Marnix Beyen, Linda Colley, Martin Conway, Gustavo Corni, Seikko Eskola, Anna Friberg, Norbert Götz, Christopher Gusy, Mia Halonen, Jonas Harvard, Irène Herrmann, Mary Hilson, Janne Holmén, Antero Holmila, Teemu Häkkinen, Cornelia Ilie, Joanna Innes, Theo Jung, Miina Kaarkoski, Petri Karonen, Jukka Kekkonen, Pauli Kettunen, Tiina Kinnunen, David Kirby, Laura Kolbe, Michael Koß, Jussi Kurunmäki, Ilkka Liikanen, Marcus

Llanque, Laura-Mari Manninen, Jani Marjanen, Satu Matikainen, Henrik Meinander, Ola Mestad, Jeppe Nevers, Jari Ojala, Kari Palonen, Tuija Parvikko, Onni Pekonen, Rolf Petri, Mark Philp, Markus Prutsch, James Retallack, Matti Roitto, Taina Saarinen, Robert Saunders, Andreas Schulz, Paul Seaward, Alexander Semyonov, Willibald Steinmetz, Henk te Velde and Jouni Tilli for their helpful comments on various parts and versions of the manuscript. Finally, I would like to thank Sari Katajala-Peltomaa for guiding the manuscript through the referee process and the Finnish Literature Society and the Finnish Historical Society for including the volume in their open access history list.

Jyväskylä, 15 March 2017,
the centennial anniversary of the abdication of Nicholas II

Pasi Ihalainen

List of abbreviations

AK: Documents of the Lower Chamber of the Riksdag (Sweden)
DDP: German Democratic Party
DVP: German People's Party
FK: Documents of the Upper Chamber of the Riksdag (Sweden)
Hansard: Official Reports of the Houses of Parliament
SDP: Social Democratic Party (Finland)
SPD: Social Democratic Party of Germany
USPD: Independent Social Democratic Party of Germany
Verhandlungen: Documents of the Lower Chamber of the Reichstag (Germany)
VP: Documents of the Eduskunta (Finland)
WSF: Worker's Suffrage Federation

1. Introduction

*1.1 The reform debates of the revolutionary era 1917–19
in inter- and transnational comparisons*

The First World War was a transnational tragedy the effects of which crossed boundaries and led to the questioning of established truths. This unprecedented tragedy, which made peoples suffer without the prevailing political systems responding to their views, also provided an unexpected impetus for reforms that extended democratic suffrage and increased the parliamentary responsibility of governments. The total war, consequent revolutions in Russia and Germany, suffrage reforms, declarations of independence and modifications of constitutions affected and were affected by changing understandings of 'democracy', the political role of 'the people' and 'parliamentarism'. These terms and related concepts became objects of constant debate, redefinition and contestation within, and at times between, European political cultures as part of constitutional and political struggles. The dynamics of the discursive processes related to the transformation catalysed by the war is the subject of this book.

Unlike in previous revolutionary eras, 'democracy' (or 'the power or rule by the people' in various vernacular translations) was widely used of in parliaments and newspapers in the years 1917–19 as nearly all political groups wished to identify themselves with democracy and view themselves as democrats. Especially among socialists and liberals, the experiences of the war, turns in political discourse and constitutional shifts after spring 1917 gave rise to redefinitions of the political order that were of historic importance. The understandings of democracy were inherently diverse, however, and tended to get more so in the ideological heat of reform demands and constitutional debates that often led to the expression of radicalised stances before ending up with compromises with which few would be completely happy. Attitudes towards parliamentarism were also becoming more positive in that parliaments came to be regarded as providing a proper medium for the representation of the will of the people in the political process, though parliamentarism remained an object of even greater dispute than democracy. Many European political cultures were, as a result of the devastating war, entering a new stage of nationally multi-sited and transnationally connected debates on democracy, the political role of the people and parliamentarism.

This transformative period will be explored comparatively and transnationally on the basis of parliamentary and media sources in what follows. Such an exploration relativises any simplifying narratives of popular sovereignty and representative democracy as having emerged already among the English revolutionaries or Dutch authors in the seventeenth century or as a result of the French Enlightenment thought, innovative political practices in mid-eighteenth-century Sweden or the American or French Revolutions in the eighteenth century.[1] It also relativises narratives on democracy being straightforwardly related to the rise of capitalism[2] or having made linear progress under liberal constitutionalism in the course of the nineteenth century.

Recent research suggests, after all, that Europe that went to war in 1914 was far from democratic in either a French revolutionary or any post-First World War sense. As Bo Stråth has pointed out, the century that followed the French Revolution had been characterised by competing and contradictory definitions of the nation and the people and their relations to sovereignty – and hence increasingly also of democracy.[3] Volker Sellin has argued that Europe had experienced since 1814 a century of restorations, all of them aimed at countering the revolutionary principle of popular sovereignty and solving crises of legitimacy of monarchies by introducing reactionary constitutions, Russia of 1906 being an extreme case.[4] Researchers in the project 'Europe 1815–1914: Between Restoration and Revolution' have likewise demonstrated that no linear development from absolute monarchies to representative democracy existed but that authoritarian regimes had rather introduced constitutions and parliaments for anti-revolutionary purposes.[5] By the early 1910s, the Habsburg Empire and the Russian Empire – and to a great extent also states such as Britain, Germany, Sweden and Finland – were experiencing a domestic political crisis in which there was a parliament but also widespread disappointment with what it had to offer in terms of popular representation. While conservatives reacted by supporting extra-parliamentary politics, leftists looked for ways to replace parliaments

---

1 A summary of the conventional narrative can be found in Eley 2002, 18. Contemporary parliamentary and public as well as later historiographical debates on democracy in the late eighteenth century have been discussed by Ihalainen 2010, 1–28. Teleological narratives of nineteenth-century progress from absolutism to parliamentary democracy on the basis of the values of the Enlightenment and the French Revolution has been questioned by Stråth 2016, 1–2, 5, 17. Inspired by Reinhart Koselleck's emphasis on discursive struggles in politics he emphasises contingency, human agency and imagination in and the connected fragility of democratic projects instead.
2 This is questioned also by Geoff Eley who rather links the rise of democracy to the socialist analysis of capitalism and calls for societal reorganization. Eley 2002, 4, 18, 109.
3 Stråth 2016, 7.
4 Sellin 2014, 7–11, 135.
5 Grotke & Prutsch (eds) 2014, 4, 13.

as 'bourgeois' institutions with more democratic political bodies. Both ways of thinking increased potential for the radicalisation of political debate and expectations of major political changes once a major was encountered.[6]

The transforming effects of the First World War on political systems have been aptly summarised in recent research inspired by its centennial, though without particular attention to parliamentary debates. Jan-Werner Müller, Jay Winter, Richard Bessel and Jörn Leonhard have characterised the Great War as a test of the credibility and legitimacy of the principles, hierarchies and institutions of the states involved in it. The war and the connected revolutions challenged all previous conceptions of the state and society, intensifying and reorienting postponed processes of reform. The old categories of those entitled to participate in the political process tended to lose relevance as everyone was required to participate in the defence of the state. The experiences of the war and the revolutions separated the old world from the new, opening new visions for the future. Prevailing political structures and connected political concepts were transformed by new, often more optimistic conceptions of the proper relationship between the people and the state, formulated in new constitutions and reinterpretations of old ones. The demands placed on the people during the war often also led to the strengthening of parliamentarism. At the same time, the pervasive war potentially vindicated violence not only in international relations but also in domestic politics.[7] Violence could be used to replace dialogical means of political action, including parliamentary deliberation, as a way to resolve conflicts of interest. In addition to their democratising and parliamentarising effects, the war and the revolutions also inspired attempts to use extra-parliamentary methods to force through societal change that voting and the parliamentary framework seemed unable to produce.

State interventions in various areas of societal life increased drastically during the war. Richard Bessel has pointed out the risks that such interventions entailed: the rulers might lose their credibility and the legitimacy of their power if they failed to fulfil the rising expectations of the people. Especially in countries whose political systems did not care much about popular opinion, wartime sacrifices and shortages tended to give rise to popular discontent. There followed calls for political reforms that would strengthen the participation of the people at large in politics in a way that corresponded to their participation in fighting the war or their contribution to the wartime economy. However, the combination of poor economic conditions and postponed reforms could have similar effects in countries that were not directly involved in the war as well. Without the military disasters of the war, there would hardly have been revolutions in Russia and Germany, Bessel argues.[8] And without these revolutions and the German defeat, there would

---

6   Lieven 2015. I am grateful for Alexander Semyonov for pointing at this pan-European pattern.
7   Leonhard 2008; Müller 2011, 16–19; Winter 2014, 1; Becker 2014, 32; Bessel 2014, 126–7, 144. On the totality of the war and political changes, see also Müller 2002, 289, and Leonhard 2014, 11, 14.
8   Bessel 2014, 128–30, 136, 139–44.

not have been such clear political transformations in Sweden and Finland, for instance, I argue in this book. Pan-European experiences of massive violence led to brutality finding its way into domestic political conflicts also in countries that were not directly involved in the war,[9] most famously in Finland. International wartime debates on national and popular sovereignty and revolution, furthermore, had global effects, awakening expectations for autonomy and independence in various national contexts.[10]

The war internationalised (in the sense of producing references to relations and comparisons between nation states) and transnationalised (in the sense of creating political discourses that crossed frontiers through networks and individual contacts) debates on political reform. While the reform processes took place, and have been studied, primarily at the level of nation states, I argue that they were also more transnationally linked than has been customarily recognised. Wartime propaganda increasingly presented the battle as concerning the basic character of the states involved. However, the political elites and the press had been transnationally connected before the war and remained so during it. Furthermore, as Richard Bessel has pointed out, national and transnational interaction between people of various social backgrounds caused by the war led to the dissemination of revolutionary ideas and contributed to the rise of a shared understanding of the necessity of an immediate political transformation. Individuals acted as micro-level agents, transferring a revolutionary mood from one national context to another;[11] conversely, individuals might also reinforce reactionary views held in one country in other national contexts, as this book will show. The reform debates became entangled both on the macro and micro levels, and their transnational connections deserve more analytical attention. I have hence paid particular attention to revolution as a transnational phenomenon. As Robert Gerwarth has put it, the Russian Revolution redefined international politics and provoked anti-revolutionary action to counter real and imagined Bolshevik threats. It led to brutal civil wars inspired by the Bolshevik conception of foreseeable resistance from the old elites and a class war as thus unavoidable – Finland being a case in point. This new type of revolution also extended the practitioners of revolutionary agitation from intellectuals and activists to self-educated revolutionaries who were ready to use both radical rhetoric and radical action.[12] By focusing on these phenomena I wish especially to provide a complementary interpretation on the background of the Finnish Civil War. I am not interested in questions of 'guilt' but aim at understanding national

9   Gerwarth 2014, 640–1.
10 Leonhard 2014, 655, 706, 937, 940–2.
11 Bessel 2014, 141–3.
12 Gerwarth 2014, 642, 644–9. Robert Gerwarth concludes on the basis of the numbers of Russian volunteers and the assumption that the moderate Social Democrats controlled the revolutionary movement that there was no real Bolshevik threat in Finland. However, he does not consider the revolutionary discourse of the left and its implications on both sides of the conflict; Leonhard 2014, 940.

and transnational discursive processes that led to the use of violence instead of parliamentary deliberation to solve conflicts of interest.[13]

In early 1917, political leaders on both sides of the Western Front shared an understanding that the war had made it necessary to look for better ways to take the will of the people into consideration and that the best way to do this was through universal suffrage and parliamentary representation. In both the great powers engaged in the war and in countries not directly involved in it, people came out onto the streets in the spring weather. Following an exceptionally cold winter that had brought hunger, the spring of 1917 became an experience that was both real and psychological. This happened first in Petrograd on 8 March 1917.[14] Thereafter references to a spring of democracy – as a powerful metaphor emphasising the irresistibility of the political changes that were to follow – were also heard in reform debates in London, Berlin, Stockholm and Helsinki, and such metaphors have also provided the starting hypothesis for this book. Once the revolutionary process had started, many, especially on the left, believed that a new age of revolution was beginning and that it would change societies and the entire world in ways that would allow of no turning back.[15]

By the autumn of 1917 and the spring of 1918 – after the postponement of reforms in Germany, the outbreak of the Bolshevik Revolution in Russia, the continuation of the warfare with evident German successes in the east, and fatal failures of reform processes as exemplified by the Finnish Civil War – the atmosphere both internationally and nationally would already be very different. Instead of a permanent spring of democracy, an autumn of parliamentarism seemed to have come, which caused especially the right side of the political spectrum in several countries to take up anti-reformist stances.

By autumn 1918 and spring 1919, the international situation had again changed completely – with Western parliamentary democracies victorious in the war, the Germans beginning to construct what was to become the first democratic system in that country and the Swedes and Finns, too, reconstructing their polities, trying to reconcile native traditions, alternative foreign models and ideologically motivated rival understandings

---

13   Cf. Liikanen 1993, 562, 567–79, according to whom interwar literature on 'a war of liberty' denied the existence of national socio-political confrontations and emphasised Russian Bolshevist influence on the labour movement instead. While Juhani Paasivirta (1957) pointed at the Red Guards having adopted Bolshevik revolutionary examples, Hannu Soikkanen (1975) concluded on the basis of party documents (not parliamentary debates) that the labour leaders remained Kautskyist rather than became Leninists, attempting to confine readiness for an armed rising among the unorganised and spontaneous 'masses' led by a few activists influenced by Bolshevism (also Kettunen 1986). Marja Leena Salkola (1985) failed to find Bolshevik impulses at this micro level either. Liikanen hence concluded that no new interpretation on the political background of the Civil War had emerged and hence the emphasis remained on 'social or structural conflicts'. See also Haapala 2014.
14   Hobsbawm 1994, 60.
15   Bessel 2014, 127.

of democracy, the people and parliamentarism. Autumnal metaphors were used in several national contexts to describe the unavoidability of constitutional reform.

The spring of 1919 consequently arrived with promises of the beginning of a new global democratic era – only to be superseded by a further international change of climate in the summer of that year, manifested in the Treaty of Versailles. The course of reform and revolution was changeable like the four seasons in the period of roughly two years between the outbreak of the Russian Revolution in March 1917 and the adoption of the Weimar Constitution in August 1919. Many contemporaries nevertheless believed, or at least wanted to believe, in a transnationally changed political atmosphere.

In this book I reconstruct and analyse the discursive processes of reform and revolution, as catalysed by the First World War and the two Russian Revolutions, in four national parliaments and presses, aiming at a synthesis written from a new perspective of combined parliamentary and conceptual history. I do this not only in national but also comparative and transnational contexts. This work aims at a deeper understanding of the dynamics of nationally multi-sited and to a great extent transnationally interconnected debates, in which democracy, the political role of the people and parliamentarism came to be defined in conflicting ways by various actors and groups involved in political processes. The book explores how the participants construed, defined and redescribed these concepts through political use in particular arguments, why certain conceptual redefinitions took place and with what consequences. It does not build on any normative definitions of analytical concepts such as 'democracy' or 'parliamentarism'.[16]

The research for this book consists in a textual and comparative conceptual analysis of the contents of the most important plenary constitutional debates[17] and related press debates in four interconnected countries that experienced different versions of democratisation and parliamentarisation almost simultaneously: Britain, Germany,[18] Sweden and Finland.[19] Democratisation refers here simply to the process of extending the possibilities for the political participation of the people mainly through universal suffrage (as opposed to

---

16   On the historical nature of the concept of democracy, see Ihalainen 2010, 15; Friberg 2012, 16, 42, and Kurunmäki 2015, 32.
17   Only debates explicitly related to constitutional reforms have been analysed as the parliamentary records are extensive and digitised ones allowing a big data approach are not yet available from all four countries. Alternative uses of the key concepts may of course have appeared in the context of other debates.
18   An earlier version of a comparative analysis of British and German constitutional debates of spring 1917 has been presented in Ihalainen 2014, 423–48.
19   I have analysed the parliamentary discursive processes related to constitutional reform in the four countries side by side, paying attention to the specific linguistic resources available in the various national contexts and to the fact that none of the key political concepts was simply translatable into another language. The national contexts and occasionally phrases in the original languages have thus been retained, although English has been used as the medium of the comparative and transnational analysis. Unfortunately, full original citations cannot be provided owing to space limitations.

alternative applications in late twentieth-century political science[20]), while parliamentarisation refers to a transformation that gave representative institutions influence on the formation and control of government.[21] I intend to show, furthermore, how and why transnational transfers in debates on democracy, the people and parliamentarism occurred or were blocked and what their political implications were. I propose a thesis on the existence of competing ideologically motivated transnational theoretical and ideological networks, in the period studied, most clearly those of the socialist left and the conservative right but to some extent also of the reformist liberals.

Why should we focus on parliamentary debates and not on executive actions or academic discussions to uncover these? Philip Norton has pointed out that the British unwritten constitution has experienced considerable 'organic evolution' *within* Parliament.[22] The same is true of states with written constitutions: various constitutions represent stages in long-term discursive processes that define the values of political communities, customarily in transnational interaction. Parliaments have provided the forums in which proposed constitutions have been most extensively and publicly debated, a high variety of political views expressed and the meanings of concepts disputed, even in cases in which the decision had already been made by cabinets, parties or committees. This discursive action needs to be taken seriously,[23] which has not always been the case in older political history. The fact that parliament was simultaneously a national and a transnational institution and the process of legislating on constitutions common to the states in question together with transnational contacts between MPs calls for an analysis of the cross-border circulation of ideas, including transnational communication, borrowings, importations, transfers, imitation, selective applications and dissemination. As I shall argue in subsection 1.3, it is helpful to analyse parliamentary debates as nexuses of multi-sited political discourses and academic and public debates so that the previous and simultaneous activities of parliamentarians in other national and transnational forums are taken into consideration.[24] National parliaments and their members have often had extensive transnational connections in the form of official contacts between representative institutions, participation in inter-parliamentary conferences, the exchange of parliamentary records, foreign news in the national press and political literature. Learning from abroad could take place by reading newspaper reports and literature, visiting foreign countries and contacting politicians and experts there or applying foreign models in parliamentary practice.[25] Socialist parties had their Internationals, while conservative parties were interconnected through established academic

20   For contemporary definitions of democracy, see also Ihalainen 2018, which sets the debates of 1917–19 in the context of European debates on 'democracy' over the long term.
21   Schönberger 2001, 624; Kühne 2005, 311–12.
22   Norton 2011, 1, 12.
23   Bollmeyer 2007, 41; Ihalainen 2010, 19; Friberg 2012, 68; Galembert, Rozenberg & Vigour 2013, 9–10.
24   The methodological background is explained in Halonen, Ihalainen & Saarinen 2015 and is also based on Ihalainen, Ilie & Palonen 2016.
25   Pekonen 2014, 28, 34, 38.

contacts as a result of the significant number of professors in various fields who were leading rightist politicians. Many liberals, too, entertained internationalist ideas. While measuring their exact 'impact' is difficult, considering the significance of explicit and implicit transnational transfers is important.

Both official and informal individual links could be activated when necessary to gain support in political battles at home, possibly leading to transfers in political discourse. International comparisons and the activation of transnational links tended to be highly variable: foreign models were always selected, often tendentiously interpreted and deliberately applied in the discursive processes of constitutional decision-making to win arguments and extend political power at home rather than to introduce unmodified transfers between political cultures. The seemingly transnational character of parliamentary discourse may thus also be misleading: foreign parliaments and political events provided parliamentarians with a never-ending source of examples from a variety of temporal and spatial contexts that could be used in arguments to advance particular points in particular domestic debates and do not necessarily reflect a deeper knowledge, understanding or even a genuine interest in a foreign case as a model to be followed.[26] As Kari Palonen has emphasised, when translated and thereby transferred, concepts are simultaneously often changed, either intentionally or unintentionally.[27] Onni Pekonen has shown how Finnish journalists and parliamentarians made use of foreign examples and concepts to advance particular goals in Finnish political disputes, to support differing interpretations of domestic political questions and to provide competing contexts in order to dispute suggestions by political rivals. A foreign example could be used to introduce an innovation but also to support an established practice or to demonstrate why a reform should not be adopted because of its obvious disadvantages.[28] Henk te Velde has noted that, while elements of political culture or discourse are often transformed when transferred from one national context to another, their foreign origin may also be intentionally concealed.[29] The covert use of foreign examples thus also needs to be considered, and this is facilitated by an awareness of the prevailing links between political cultures in the period studied. Transfers were much more likely from the German to the Swedish or Finnish political cultures than the other way around or than from Britain – at least until 1919.

Transnational discursive interaction between parliaments and the press deserves attention as it has tended to be neglected in nation-state-centred research on post-First World War reforms,[30] although it was of course only

---

26   See Leonhard 2011 and Ihalainen 2016a and national case studies in the volume *Parliament and Parliamentarism* (2016).
27   Palonen 2014, 145.
28   Pekonen 2014, 29, 44.
29   te Velde 2005, 208.
30   See Alapuro 1988, Andræ 1998, Brusewitz 1964, Carlsson 1985, Gerdner 1966, Gruhlich 2012, Gusy 1997, Haapala 2010b, Kirby 1986b, Lindman 1968, Machin 2001, Mylly 2006, Nyman 1965, Olsson 2002, Pohl 2002, Polvinen 1987, Seils 2011, Turner 1992, Upton 1980, Vares 1998 and Vares 2006, for instance.

one aspect of the discursive processes of reform: national contexts were often decisive. Parliamentary debates on constitutions in 1917–19 were often to a great extent comparative, but the genuine understandings of foreign contexts was often lacking. Each national debate built on a selection of arguments and discursive practices borrowed from other national contexts and made an abundant use of deliberate comparisons between similar constitutions and political events in other countries. Foreign examples were used selectively – rhetorically – to support particular arguments and goals in current domestic political struggles, alternative interpretations from foreign countries providing a means to redefine the prospective future of the speaker's own political community.

Transnational transfers, as far as they occurred, were based to a great extent on pre-war connections. They were restricted but not prevented by the war, however. The German press was dependent on news in the press of the Entente or that of neutral states.[31] Even the British press was subject to censorship as far as copy sent via post or cable was concerned, but the control did not concern leading articles, and the editors were skilful in circumventing attempts by the authorities to stop 'Bolshevik propaganda', for instance. The British parliament was expected to avoid risky topics, but even though some discussion about the violation of parliamentary privilege emerged, its reports were not subject to censorship, and parliamentary reports continued to be published with a degree of self-censorship by the major papers throughout the war.[32] This was true of all countries: debates in both national and foreign parliaments were reported more extensively than in any medium in the twenty-first century, even though sometimes very selectively and with a bias.

The press debates in Germany, Sweden and Finland[33] cannot yet be so extensively analysed using digitised databases as those in Britain; in the British case it is easier to complement reform debates with a longer-term analysis of press debates (sections 6.1. and 7.1). Three groups of politically oriented newspapers representing predominantly conservative (*The Times, Neue Preußische Zeitung* [also known as *Kreuz-Zeitung*], *Aftonbladet, Hufvudstadsbladet*), liberal (*The Manchester Guardian, Berliner Tageblatt, Dagens Nyheter, Helsingin Sanomat*) and socialist (*The Herald, Vorwärts, Social-Demokraten, Työmies/Suomen Sosialidemokraatti*) points of view in all four countries have been consulted on relevant dates before and after major constitutional debates in the parliaments. These do not cover all parties or points of view, of course, but they provide sufficiently representative samples of parliamentary reporting and commentary. As Onni Pekonen has pointed out, newspapers constituted a forum in which parliamentary debates were prepared and subsequently extended. Arguments presented in newspapers could be taken up in parliamentary debates and the arguments presented in

---

31   Fuchs 2008, 33.
32   Rose 1995, 20, 27–30.
33   Finnish newspapers of 1917–20 became available online only after the referee round of this book.

these elaborated in press articles.³⁴ However, in wartime public discourse, it was governments that first set the parliamentary agenda,³⁵ which then governed the press debates to a great extent; there was little public debate that was independent of ministries and parliaments going on in the media in the period studied. This fact also supports the prioritisation of parliamentary over journalistic sources in this study.

The constitutional reforms in different European countries and related conceptualisations of democracy, the people and parliamentarism increased considerably in inter- and transnational interaction between historically related and competing political cultures with diverse experiences of parliamentary government. The Russian Revolution catalysed this transnational debate. Despite translations published in the press discursive transfers from Russia remained limited and depended on the intensity of transnational links with Petrograd. The Russian Revolution at first intensified and inspired national debates on democracy especially on the left and was then used by all political groups to define what democracy should stand for in national contexts by providing an example of an undesirable kind of democracy. The Russian Revolution also played an indirect role in redefinitions of parliamentarism by openly challenging – in the form that Lenin gave to it since April 1917 – 'bourgeois' and 'Western' parliamentarism with a soviet system initially invented by anarchists and syndicalists. As Eric Hobsbawm has argued and this volume empirically demonstrates, the Russian Revolution advanced parliamentary democracy in Western Europe by transforming most Social Democratic parties from oppositional to governmental forces that emphasised their moderation in order to distinguish themselves from the Bolsheviks. Social Democratic participation was, furthermore, increasingly accepted by the older elites in order to contain revolutionary trends.³⁶

The parliamentary models of countries other than Russia were much more influential, certainly. Comparisons between Sweden and Germany and Finland and Germany were particularly frequent in the smaller national parliaments. For Finland, eighteenth-century rather than contemporary Sweden was a major point of comparison as result of the entangled history of the two polities; for Sweden, the failure of the Finnish democratic parliament provided an essential warning example. After the Entente won the war, both countries turned increasingly to the British model. By 1919, however, the national constitutional debates of the four studied countries, interconnected by the impulses created by the war and the Russian Revolution after 1917,

---

34 Pekonen 2014, 30.
35 Archival sources related to the executive preparation of draft constitutions, ministerial preparation for debates, or the activities of individual politicians would be worth studying but fall outside the scope of this project as result of the large number of discussed cases, the extent of the parliamentary and public debates analysed and the focus on the comparative and transnational elements rather than the details of national processes of decision-making. Cf. Roitto 2015, 48, 392.
36 Hobsbawm 1994, 84.

had ended up with transfers from Russia being consciously limited and a decrease in comparisons with other parliamentary democracies as well. The debates and the applied vocabularies were increasingly nationalised, which left the impression (also expressed in later national historiographies[37]) that each reform had been a national affair only marginally influenced by what was happening at the same time elsewhere. This interconnectedness and variation between the national and transnational deserves more attention.

The research strategy applied in this study will be explained in more detail in section 1.3, after a review of the state of the art in comparative and transnational history and further justification for the selection of the four countries studied here in the following section. Lastly, the structure of the study will be explained in section 1.4.

1.2 Towards a comparative and transnational history of political discourse

Nation states have traditionally been regarded as natural units for historical analysis. By contrast, comparative – let alone transnational – analyses of past political processes have remained rare, especially in the field of the history of ideas. After comparative, international and transnational turns in recent decades, however, historians increasingly agree that research should be extended beyond national histories to include a consideration of the similarities and differences between various national contexts and of human interaction across national frontiers together with the common and particular conditions of historical phenomena.[38]

The nation-state-oriented nature of much historical research has affected the study of the formation of national constitutions; indeed, many such studies are rather dated, written before the above-mentioned methodological turns and often authored by non-historians such as law scholars.[39] Newer comparative approaches to the history of European political and legal cultures, too, have continued to favour nation states as units of comparison.[40] This is wholly justified given that nation states have

---

37   Grotke & Prutsch 2014, 8.
38   Paulmann 1998, 649, 684; Kocka 2003, 40; Cohen & O'Connor 2004, ix–xii; Baldwin 2004, 3; Sluga 2004, 103; Grew 2006, 105; Friberg, Hilson & Vall 2007, 717–37; Neunsinger 2010, 3. For comparative and historical sociology, see Ragin 1987.
39   See Bogdanor 2003, Botzenhart 1993, Brusewitz 1964, Gerdner 1946, Grosser 1970, Gusy 1997, Huldén 1989, Jyränki 2006, Kluxen 1985, Lindman 1935, Nyman 1965, Rauh 1977, Sihvonen 1997, Stjernquist 1993, Trippe 1995, von Sydow 1997, for instance.
40   Leonhard 2001; Müller 2002; Ihalainen 2005; Koselleck, Spree & Steinmetz 2006; Leonhard 2008; Ihalainen 2010; Kekkonen 2016; cf. Kari Palonen's study in political theory of the comparative conceptual and rhetorical history of politics as an activity based on the analysis of nine *topoi*. Such an analysis views national contexts as 'secondary' and enables the comparison of parallel cases originating in different national and linguistic contexts. Palonen 2006, 10–11, 23, 83–4; Ihalainen, Ilie & Palonen 2016.

determined the political conditions of the past to a great extent.[41] The comparative history of constitutions, although it supports the selection of nation states as objects of analysis,[42] may however lead to the deconstruction of some of their assumed particularity. Comparisons between simultaneous nation-state-level debates carried out by the same historian on the basis of parallel primary sources and taking into consideration their mutual links can challenge ways of thinking that have been considered self-evident in national historiographies.[43] The comparative and transnational history of ideas may reveal similarities and differences in attitudes and ideologies, explaining why certain political concepts were interpreted similarly or differently in different national contexts and regimes. The study of the communication, diffusion, crossing, importation, translation, borrowings, transfers, appropriation, imitation and rejection of ideas between nations also helps us to understand the circulation of ideas between political cultures and across national borders,[44] and increases our awareness of the entangled nature of national pasts.

Transnational history emphasises history beyond nations, analysing links between them and interaction across boundaries and complementing comparative history;[45] it is argued here that one cannot be studied without another. While interest in the transnational history of concepts has increased, motivated by a growing awareness of the transnational nature of political debates and the practice of translating political concepts in the modern world, empirical studies in conceptual history often still focus on individual nation states. A previous comparative study of eighteenth-century debates on democracy and popular sovereignty in Britain and Sweden has led the present author to conclude that the parliamentary and public debates studied here and the connected intellectual changes were to a considerable extent transnational, each national debate building on conceptual innovations introduced in other national contexts and making an abundant use of explicit comparisons between similar constitutions.[46] It has been suggested that various versions of parliamentarism began to influence each other at the constitutional level more extensively in the post-Second-World-War period,[47] but interaction between parliamentary institutions and constitutional debates had clearly already existed in the eighteenth century and was particularly significant in the late 1910s as well, as will be demonstrated in this volume.

41 Fredrickson 1995, 5690; Cohen & O'Connor 2004, xvii; Cohen 2004, 61; Kocka & Haupt 2009, 19.
42 Kocka 2003, 41; Green 2004, 46; Sluga 2004, 103–4, 108, 111; Grew 2006, 102; Neunsinger 2010, 3–4, 9, 12; see Ihalainen at al. 2011; On the danger that the focus on nations determined the results, see Werner & Zimmermann 2006, 46, or reinforces national differences, see Friberg, Hilson & Vall 2007, 717–37.
43 Cohen & O'Connor 2004, xx; Haupt 2007, 709–10; Steinmetz 2007, 19; Ihalainen & Palonen 2009; Kocka & Haupt 2009, 4.
44 Cohen 2004, 59; Sluga 2004, 108, 112; O'Connor 2004, 140, 142; Petrusewisz 2004, 153–4; Grew 2006, 110; Saunier 2012, 81.
45 Sluga 2004, 109; Miller 2004, 126; Armitage 2004, 171; Saunier 2013, 2.
46 Ihalainen 2010.
47 von Sydow 1997, 13.

The comparative and transnational (related, transfer, connected, shared or entangled) history of parliaments and transfers between them has its methodological challenges and limitations. The challenges include the prevailing emphasis on the temporal uniqueness of historical topics and the strictly context-bound understanding of meaning in historical research. Historians are suspicious of abstractions, generalisations and theories, seeing them (often with good reason) as misrepresentations or simplifications of the complexity of the past. It is difficult to define categories that are valid through time and space without overemphasizing similarities at the cost of particularities. Historians working on comparative history consequently often focus on just two or three cases in order to allow sufficient consideration of national contexts and discussion of details that are unique to the cases being studied.[48] Comparative research should, furthermore, lead to the discovery of new information about both national histories and larger inter- or transnational phenomena.

The sources used may frequently have been produced differently in the countries of comparison, or parallel sources may not even exist in the first place – parliamentary sources and the party press being important exceptions. In the presentation of the findings, argumentation about broad historical phenomena and more general patterns must be reconciled with sufficient references to contexts and details, in the way that historians working on national cases alone would expect. At the same time, however, the temptation to reinforce orthodox interpretations of national historiographies needs to be avoided[49] and something substantial must be said about the inter- and transnational aspects.

In this study, the key categories of the political discourse of the studied period are subjected to semantic, pragmatic, textual and discourse analysis on the basis of uniform sources in their appropriate political contexts instead of attempting any universally valid definitions. The four cases here are limited in terms of time, topics and sources and analysed mostly in their national contexts so that generalisations can be based on a sufficient number of empirical cases.

Some abstraction and decontextualisation is needed in comparative history, but in this work it is mainly postponed to the conclusion. As common, long-term and coherent patterns of historical development emerge, generalisations become possible as long as they are based on several 'empirical' individual cases. It is worth considering how and why these general patterns vary from one society to another. Similarities and differences between national cases are discussed in order to clarify and understand historical phenomena in single cases better – to deepen our understanding of what is central in each case and to reveal attitudes, meanings and developments that would otherwise go unnoticed or be

---

48 Kocka 2003, 44; Haupt & Kocka 2004, 24–6; Cohen & O'Connor 2004, xx; Baldwin 2004, 1–3; Yengoyan 2006, 3, 7, 9; Grew 2006, 100, 106; Haupt 2007, 703; Neunsinger 2010, 14.
49 Paulmann 1998, 651; Cohen & O'Connor 2004, x, xvi–xvii; Green 2004, 50; Pedersen 2004, 91–2; Miller 2004, 124; Grew 2006, 102; Neunsinger 2010, 14.

considered natural. Seemingly peripheral and less known national cases – such as the Finnish – offer alternative narratives that help to understand discursive processes that contribute to the rise of crises of legitimacy and the reconstruction of that legitimacy after crisis in other political cultures as well. This leads to reflections on causal explanations as well,[50] suggesting critical factors or autonomous variables that explain differences between nations and possibly help to refine interpretations of national history.[51]

A major benefit of transnational comparative history is that it permits one to distance oneself from the 'self-evident facts' of national history in a way that enables new conceptualisations, demonstrates the relevance of sources, methods and interpretations applicable elsewhere and perhaps explains differences and particularities, including connections and entanglements between the cases.[52] Historical phenomena can be identified more clearly and then analysed so that similarities and differences and possibly causal explanations may be discovered.[53] The choice of particular units of comparison must be justified, differences in historiographical traditions understood and the logic of the comparison problematised. Causal explanations can be sought from a variety of perspectives, including alternatives that were not considered by contemporaries or by later historians but which can be pointed to in other parallel national cases.[54] This implies an ability to break away from conventional (nationalist) interpretations[55] and perhaps a move towards post-nationalist history. Working comparisons customarily challenge assumptions that have been taken as self-evident (for national, ideological or other reasons), pointing (counterfactually) at contingency and alternative paths of development and relativising national narratives that tend to overemphasise differences. Institutions that national history takes as self-evident – including constitutions – can be problematised through parallel histories that add to our understanding of the transnational aspects of development.[56]

Comparative history has been sometimes criticised for being excessively analytical in viewing the compared cases as independent units and dismissing their interconnections.[57] The originally French study of the history of cultural transfer may help to explicate how transnational links and networks – as manifested for instance in the presence of linguistic minorities in parliaments, for example Swedish-speakers in the Finnish parliament, or in the transnational networks of radical socialists or leading academics – led to the transmission and translation of concepts and ideas from one

50 Kocka 2003, 40–1; Baldwin 2004, 11, 14–15, 18; Green 2004, 42; see also Miller 2004, 115–16; Petrusewisz 2004, 149; Grew 2006, 105–6, 126; see also Yengoyan 2006, 4.
51 Fredrickson 1995, 587.
52 Kocka 2003, 41; Miller 2004, 124; Grew 2006, 105; Kocka & Haupt 2009, 20–1.
53 Haupt 2007, 700; see also Grew 2006, 104.
54 Haupt 2007, 700, 703; Grew 2006, 104; Miller 2004, 115.
55 Grew 2006, 105.
56 Cohen & O'Connor 2004, xvi, xvii; Cohen 2004, 64, 66; Petrusewisz 2004, 149; Grew 2006, 113.
57 Kocka 2003, 43.

national context to another. Interdependence, transnational influences and similarities among the national cases are considered throughout this study and are dealt with in separate subsections. *Histoire croisée*, entangled history, with its emphasis on the multiple points of view available to contemporaries, reminds us of the existence of interaction between the objects of comparison, such as shared legal systems (in Sweden and Finland) or common academic tenets (manifested in criticism of parliamentarism in all the countries studied) and direct connections between the institutions of various states,[58] and of course between cosmopolitan individuals who could focus on similarities or differences between societies in order to support particular historical trajectories in their national context.[59] Even if comparative history and entangled history have had slightly different interests, the interrelations between the cases need to be considered as possible factors in explaining discovered similarities and differences.[60] Entangled history helps us to avoid explaining developments by means of purely indigenous factors without paying proper attention to wider historical contexts and transnational networks.[61] Transnational history has an obvious contribution to make to the study of interconnected parliamentary discourses and constitutional debates. An example of the solutions adopted here is the comparison of constitutional disputes in Sweden and Finland – two historically related smaller nation states with long traditions of representative government and emerging parliamentary cultures – over a relatively brief period within which not only the national contexts but also the transfers between these political cultures, as well as between them and two leading great powers, Britain and Germany, are taken into consideration while still bearing wider European patterns in mind. Swedish and Finnish national histories become thereby integrated to general European history.[62]

Constitutions – like nation states – are not natural units but the results of long-term processes of discursive construction and state building that have taken place in inter- and transnational interaction between related political cultures, centres and peripheries. Following Andreas Wirsching, we can talk about a constitutional culture as 'the sum of the subjective attitudes, experiences, values, expectations and thought as well as the (objective) actions of the citizens and groups, the bodies of the state etc. in relation to the constitution as a public process'.[63] Constitutions as 'public processes' have been reformulated by national communities, often as a result of dramatically changing internal and/or external political circumstances. To understand definitions of 'democracy', 'the people' and 'parliamentarism' in the context of the late 1910s, the processes of the discursive construction of these concepts need to be studied not only at national levels but also with

---

58   Haupt & Kocka 2004, 31–4; Werner & Zimmermann 2006, 32, 35; Haupt 2006, 147–8; Haupt 2007, 712–14.
59   Saunier 2013, 5.
60   Kocka 2003, 44; Neunsinger 2010, 17.
61   Neunsinger 2010, 6–7.
62   See Saunier 2013, 139.
63   Wirsching 2008, 372–3.

regard to inter- and transnational connections. This also involves an attempt to deduce how the transfers between constitutional debates took place, were used for differing purposes in different argumentative contexts or were denied or obstructed.

Comparative or transnational studies in parliamentary history[64] or constitutional history[65] have been few, though an awareness of the importance of taking transnational perspectives into account and focusing on transfers between political cultures has been on the rise.[66] In Germany, Reinhart Koselleck and his pupils have published some works on comparative constitutional and political history from the point of view of conceptual history. In these, they pay particular attention to the unique political processes in various national contexts. The history of transfers, translations, imports, further developments, exports and implicit comparisons within the past language of politics play a role in their analyses, but the national contexts continue to be seen as primary.[67]

Existing studies on the constitutional reforms of the late 1910s often focus on the course of events in national cases without analysing related discursive processes or making comparisons between thematically, synchronically and ideologically linked constitutional debates in various national parliaments. Transitions to parliamentary government based on democratic suffrage have been seen as nation-specific, even though the transitions in 1917–19 took place simultaneously in several north-western European polities.[68] Instead of a mere comparison of separately treated national contexts, the transnational

---

64 An older tradition of comparing the structures and functions of parliamentarism, though not its language, is represented by Schmidt 1977, 137–87, and Kluxen 1985; Schönberger 2001 has focused on structural comparisons between British, French and German parliamentarism. The more recent works Möller & Kittel (eds) 2002, and Recker (ed.) 2004, do not analyse parliamentary discourse. Nor does Dittmar Dahlmann 2014, 33–65, which discusses the political role of parliament in the political process of each warring great power in an enlightening way but lacks any deeper comparison and only refers to parliamentary discourse at a general level. Kari Palonen's comparison of procedural texts represents a novel approach to the political theory of parliaments. Palonen 2014, 55. One of the first attempts to analyse parliamentary history comparatively and with the consideration of language is provided by Ihalainen, Ilie & Palonen 2016. Further volumes are under preparation by Henk te Velde and Tobias Kaiser.

65 A good example of comparative constitutional history is Gusy 2008 (ed.), 417–18, though one written by legal scholars rather than historians, which often implies a normative perspective, as pointed out by Grotke & Prutsch 2014, 8. Finnish and Russian revolutionary legislative practices have been compared from the perspective of legal studies, without an interest in long-term constitutional discourses, parliaments or transnational links, in Borisova & Siro, 2014, 84–113. Kurunmäki, Nevers & te Velde 2018 will provide a longer-term comparison with regard to the concept of democracy.

66 te Velde 2005, 206; Pombeni 2005; Marjanen 2009, 240, 243; Pekonen 2014. Recent illustrations of a comparative history that includes transnational elements are Grotke & Prutsch 2014, 8–9, Leonhard 2011, Leonhard 2014 and Stråth 2016.

67 Koselleck, Spree & Steinmetz 2006, 412–14; Steinmetz 2007, 23–5; Steinmetz et al. 2013.

68 See, for instance, Gusy 2008a, 418; Schönberger 2009, 43, 45.

character of the transition towards democratic parliamentarism calls for historians to carry out a transnational analysis as well.[69]

Previous evolutionary developments towards democracy and parliamentarism at the national level were significantly accelerated by the First World War, the first global catastrophe of the twentieth century.[70] The war experience became a force that mobilised and politicised the public in an unprecedented way, and this politicisation turned into calls for extended political participation. Most European societies were exhausted by the war and began to reconsider older loyalties, identities and conceptions of the proper political order. Difficulties in the war efforts gave rise to demands for increased democratisation and parliamentary involvement in the scrutiny and implementation of policies – sometimes including foreign policy and the notion of parliamentary representation in international relations as well.[71] Major transnational influences followed in spring 1917: the Russians provided an example of a revolution against a monarchy and then of a world revolution in the Bolshevik sense. At the same time, the Western powers, with US President Woodrow Wilson in the lead, increasingly adopted 'democracy' as their unifying war aim, declaring that the Allies were 'making the world safe for democracy' with their struggle, emphasising the right of self-determination and finally demanding democratisation from the Germans before agreeing to a ceasefire. This unifying war aim and fears of revolution gave momentum to democratisation and parliamentarisation in many countries, including the Western powers themselves (Britain), neutral states (Sweden and Finland) and Germany. Even the British and French adopted the American concept of democracy,[72] which constituted a major transnational discursive turn. When a ceasefire was agreed in November 1918, a unique moment for the reorganisation of the political order was at hand, and these nation-state-centred reforms concerned not only Germany but many smaller European states as well. The years 1918 and 1919 consequently appeared for contemporaries major advances in parliamentary democracy. Britain introduced an electoral reform in 1917–18, providing a model for countries in which reforms had been debated

---

69   In the field of transnational history, the closest recent project has been Geyer 2011, 187, 192, but Geyer focuses on the revolutionary process and not on constitutional questions or parliaments as potentially transnational arenas. What is relevant here is that the German Revolution, too, should be seen as part of a global wave of unrest, strikes and revolutions. Correspondingly, the fragmentation of the European constitutional reforms of 1917–19 also deserve attention. An older tradition of structural comparisons between social systems in Britain and Germany is represented by Schmidt 1977. Congleton 2011, bypasses the analysis of political discourse and applies rational-choice models and quantitative data connected with generalising overviews of constitutional history to interpret (not very convincingly) rule-based governance in England, Sweden, Germany, and some other countries. Colley forthcoming will provide an analysis of constitutional development within the British Empire.
70   Möller 2002, 5, building on George F. Kennan.
71   Götz 2005, 273.
72   Dodd 1923, 120.

but not yet realised. In post-war Europe, almost every new constitution recognised popular sovereignty as a foundation for political power, introduced universal and equal suffrage, emphasised parliamentarism in the field of legislation and increased the responsibility of the government to parliament.[73] The constitutional choices made in the aftermath of the First World War had many far-reaching consequences: they would determine for a considerable time (especially in the cases of Britain, Sweden and Finland) the basic structure and rules of each polity and thereby affect future legislation and political development. In Germany, the development would not be so straightforward, but democratisation and parliamentarisation nevertheless took place with the introduction of the Weimar Constitution.

Comparative constitutional history ideally starts with phenomena which the people of the age being studied themselves regarded as comparable. The original international (and potentially transnational) nature of discussions on similarities and differences between political systems can then be reconstructed and analysed.[74] Interrelations between Germany, Sweden and Finland (and increasingly also between these countries and Britain from late 1918 onwards) are shown by the primary sources to have played major roles especially in the Swedish and Finnish debates. Comparisons between Britain, Germany, Sweden and Finland were incorporated on the basis of explicit references in parliamentary debates to constitutional circumstances in another of these countries or the potential relevance of the other country as the source of cultural and political models (or of warning examples) as suggested by secondary literature. Recent historiography (especially German) on constitutional debates in the immediate aftermath of the First World War was also used as a source of methodological inspiration.

While the German case of transition to parliamentary democracy in 1917–19 has been analysed with some attention being paid to parliamentary debates as well,[75] this is not the case with the other three countries. German research, inspired by the historical trauma of the failure of the Weimar, provides a starting point for analysing similar debates on democracy, the people and parliamentarism in the other three countries. Such comparisons bring new light to the German case as well, showing which ways of thinking were common to the Germans on the one hand and the Swedes, the Finns and even the British on the other and which were indeed particular to Germany. For instance, how did the discursive strategies of the leading political parties differ in countries with longer representative traditions from those in Germany, which experienced a more radical transformation in the period studied here? Comparative history, which is more established in Germany than in any other European country, has tended to focus on comparisons between Germany, Britain and France, often leading to conclusions that Germany was either different from or similar to the other

---

73 Kaelbe 2001, 49–53; Wirsching 2007, 9, 16; Gusy 2008b, 16–17; Pyta 2008, 86, 93; Wirsching 2008, 371; Geyer 2011, 188, 194, 196, 218. Cf. Kaelbe's claim that a common European concept of democratisation was lacking.
74 Cohen 2004, 65.
75 Pohl 2002; Bollmeyer 2007.

two Western great powers with established parliamentary democracies.[76] Alternatively, Germany could well be compared with political cultures that were historically more closely connected to Germany, namely Sweden and Finland, which in the late 1910s were in many respects German cultural 'hinterlands'. Sweden and Finland shared with Germany intellectual currents starting from the Lutheran Reformation and continuing with the Protestant Enlightenment[77] through to nineteenth-century national romanticism, nationalism and academic trends in most fields of the human sciences. In the early twentieth century, a community of Germans and Swedes was constructed in many fields through the joint rejection of British or French culture.[78] Moreover, the landowners in Sweden formed a dominant conservative political group not unlike the Junkers – even to the extent that Sweden was sometimes called 'the Mecklenburg of the North',[79] and there was a movement supportive of German warfare during the First World War both in Sweden and in Finland.[80] Some long-term cultural similarities and connections, which were at their strongest in the aftermath of the Civil War, were manifested in both the Finnish parliament and in Reichstag debates, which justifies the appellation of Finland as 'a little Prussia'. Both of these Nordic countries were either about to ally themselves with Germany during the war, as the king and the right in Sweden had long contemplated doing, or actually did so, like Finland in 1918 when accepting a German intervention. The anti-Russian panic connected with Bolshevism and the anti-American criticism with regard to excessive internationalism that were seen as typical of Germany,[81] were common in Sweden and Finland, too.

On the other hand, there were also major long-term differences between the German and the Swedish and Finnish political cultures, the most obvious being the tradition of the representation of the free peasantry in the Swedish and Finnish parliamentary institutions since early modern times, and the potential for arguments based on political history that this created, the consequent higher political awareness of the lower orders, the strong traditions of constitutionalism and legalism and the established legitimacy of a government in which the representatives of the citizenry had at least nominally participated.[82] How these convergent and divergent features of German, Swedish and Finnish political cultures functioned in the revolutionary period of 1917–19 deserves further attention. In German research, similarities between the simultaneously formulated Finnish constitution and the Weimar constitution as republican, democratic and based on the duality of power have sometimes been recognised.[83]

Even independently of obvious diachronic and synchronic connections and frequent explicit references to Germany in the Swedish and Finnish

76 Kocka & Haupt 2009, 5.
77 Ihalainen 2009.
78 Muschick 2001, 180.
79 Brandt 2008, 166.
80 Schuberth 1981.
81 Geyer 2011, 189.
82 See Ihalainen 2015 for details.
83 Endemann 1999, 15.

constitutional debates, the inclusion of the German case is important because of the extensive secondary literature on the background and content of the Weimar Constitution that German historians and constitutional lawyers have produced over the past few decades.[84] Germany has been frequently included in comparative studies in a number of fields of historical research – because of a strong German awareness of the need to explain the national history in the European context.[85] No such research offering comparative perspectives and an emphasis on the post-First-World-War constitutional debates in a parliamentary context is available from the other countries – not even for the otherwise much studied British parliament.[86] Wartime, exceptionally consensual attempts to strengthen the legitimacy of parliament and limited reformulations of British 'democracy' become visible in the international comparative context. This context includes the uses of 'democracy' and 'Prussianism' in the war propaganda of the Entente and international comparisons carried out by the contemporaries. The German research provides methodological inspiration and some ready objects of comparison. On the other hand, this study places German constitutional debates within a broader European and more particularly northern European context. It shows how the pressures of Western propaganda played a role in attempts to democratise and parliamentarise the Prussian political order. Yet such influence turned the key concepts party-political, potentially treasonous or in need of nationalisation. Germany has been rarely compared with the Scandinavian countries,[87] and even comparisons with Britain have often concerned areas such as industrialisation, classes and political movements – i.e. structures and processes rather than experiences of political change and ideological transfers.[88] Britain and Germany have been contrasted in some previous studies on parliamentarism, though not from the perspective of parliamentary discourse.[89] Contrasting them continues to be worthwhile provided that Britain is not seen merely as a normative model,[90] particularly as its regime differed from the continental ones. In some respects, however, the two countries were perhaps not so different, and there were also transnational links between their debates that relativise Britain's status as a model (see section 7.1).

Comparative studies should not halt at merely contrasting the great powers as major parties of the First World War. Alternative, internationally less well known but equally interesting, ways to parliamentary democracy

---

84 Rauh 1977; Gusy 1991; Gusy 1993; Gusy 1997; Beyme 1999; Llanque 2000; Mergel 2002; Pohl 2002; Bollmeyer 2007; Wirsching 2007; Gusy 2008 (ed.); Schöne & Blumenthal (eds) 2009.
85 Paulmann 1998, 652; Cohen 2004, 57. This is especially true of social history.
86 See Close 1977, Lenman 1992, Musolf 1999, Machin 2001, Seaward 2002, Bogdanor 2003 and Lyon 2003.
87 See, however, Götz 2001.
88 Kocka 1996, 54, 57.
89 Möller & Kittel (eds) 2002; Recker (ed.) 2004; Wirsching (ed.) 2007.
90 For a related application of *Begriffsgeschichte*, see Reimann 2000, 10–12, 24, which has used the press and the field post to compare British and German wartime discourses.

existed. The units of comparison in this study therefore include two separate, albeit connected in multiple ways, nation states, Sweden and Finland, which experienced constitutional crises to differing degrees. The comparability between these two political cultures is often considered self-evident as result of their obvious historical links.[91] However, their comparability was not always explicitly stated by those who lived in the era studied here and has also been overlooked by later scholars who focus on the late 1910s.[92] The continuous connection between the Swedish and Finnish legal traditions, political semantics and political cultures after 1809 – and the status of the Finnish state as a descendant of early modern Sweden – have been emphasised by several Swedish and Finnish historians who work with a long-term perspective.[93] In the Swedish and Finnish cases, the comparison here focuses on language use in two representative institutions that had a common historical background, similarities in procedures and highly parallel political roles.[94] The goal is to understand both similarities in conceptualising constitutional issues in a revolutionary era – arising from the trajectories of common early-modern experiences and continuing cross-national connections – and differences arising from the two countries' separate national experiences after 1809, divergent transnational connections and the different national contexts in the late 1910s. A long-term diachronic survey provided a hint about what would be an appropriate research period,[95] but it also turned out to be necessary to extend the synchronic analysis by roughly two years to enable both sufficient contextualisation and the consideration of diachronic change.[96]

The selection of Britain, Germany, Sweden and Finland for comparison unavoidably affects the conclusions that are drawn.[97] However, only countries that went through major constitutional transformations that were actively debated in their parliaments in the studied period are worth comparing. Other national parliaments could, of course, have been included were there no limits to time and resources. For the British, as we shall see, the dominions constituted major objects of comparison, and the Germans certainly looked towards France. In the Swedish debates, references to Denmark and Norway occurred as a result of the fact that these, too, were Scandinavian monarchies with representative and parliamentary governments and had recently implemented constitutional reforms – in Norway with the introduction of universal suffrage in 1913 and in Denmark with the introduction of female

91 Junila, & Westin (eds) 2006; Jansson 2009; Halonen, Ihalainen & Saarinen 2015.
92 See von Sydow 1997, 17, who emphasises parallel developments in Danish, Norwegian and Swedish parliamentarism and recognises the related nature of the Nordic constitutions but bypasses Finland. Cf. Eskola 2011 and Jakobsen & Kurunmäki 2016 who recognise comparability.
93 See especially Jansson 2009, 10–11, 244–6, 330; Ihalainen & Sundin 2011, 192.
94 Institutions are easier to compare than many other objects, but they may still have different functions in different countries. Grew 2006, 100. This is as true of parliaments as of any other institution.
95 Ihalainen 2013.
96 See also Haupt & Kocka 2004, 26–7.
97 Baldwin 2004, 17.

suffrage in 1915.[98] Norway was an object of comparison mainly for Swedish reformists, whereas the right was disappointed with the way Norway had been parliamentarised in the course of the nineteenth century and the fact that it had left the personal union between the two countries in 1905. In Finland, the eighteenth-century Swedish constitution was a natural starting point for the debates.[99] Contemporary Sweden was avoided as result of a regional dispute over the Åland Islands, whereas Norway served as an alternative source of examples both for the reformists and the conservatives. The republican models of France and sometimes the United States were referred to mainly in spring 1919 as alternatives to the German-oriented monarchical discourse of the autumn of 1918. Switzerland provided a further model of an original republican constitution that was favoured by the far left in both countries, but its form of direct democracy appeared to most as inapplicable in other national contexts.

There were not many other objects of comparison, and from the Swedish and Finnish point of view Germany and Britain provided the major external rival political models. For both Swedish and Finnish parliamentarians, the original representative government of Britain and the restricted parliamentary element within the constitution of imperial Germany had long been relevant for constitutional comparisons.[100] While Sweden and Finland remained culturally connected with Germany, there had also been sources of alternative political trends from France and the economically increasingly important – and politically similar (as some liberals suggested) – British model, even though the British case was still often seen as too exceptional.[101] By 1919, however, Britain had won the war, and this increased the appeal of its polity among the Scandinavians. A rapid (if not always very well informed) re-evaluation of the Anglo-American model and the reduction of references to Germany followed. Sweden moved from German to Western political models after fierce ideological confrontations over democracy. Though Swedish and Finnish constitutional solutions depended to a great extent on the course of the war and on German debates, they differed from them as for the readiness of the right to experiment with democratisation. However, even in the interwar period Germany remained culturally the most influential external power.

Britain provided the best-known model for parliamentary government globally and an object of comparison with the Age of Liberty of the mid-eighteenth century that was used in Sweden to construct a narrative of ancient Swedish democracy, the continuities of which are challenged by this study.[102] Despite newspaper reports on British parliamentary proceedings in the late nineteenth century,[103] Britain remained politically and culturally remote to most Swedes and Finns. Even though there were Anglophiles among the

---

98   Jakobsen & Kurunmäki 2016.
99   Ihalainen 2015.
100 Ihalainen 2010; Pekonen 2015.
101 Ihalainen 2016a.
102 See Ihalainen 2010 on the historiography of eighteenth-century 'democracy'.
103 Pekonen 2014; Jakobsen & Kurunmäki 2016.

political elites and even though Anglophone examples were sometimes cited in Swedish and Finnish debates on parliamentary reform, fewer politicians possessed a command of the English language than of German or French. Furthermore, as Vesa Vares has pointed out, the Finnish political elite could choose between several alternative objects of political identification: there was the British and Scandinavian model of a monarchy combined with a gradual introduction of parliamentarism, the German monarchical model of controlled democracy and the eastern European alternative of outright authoritarian rule.[104] I argue in this book that radical political discourses adopted from Revolutionary Russia and legalist responses contributed to a more fierce confrontation on democracy and parliamentarism in Finland than in the other countries and to the rise of a crisis of independence: the legitimacy of parliamentary government deteriorated, a cycle of violent parliamentary discourse, civil war and Prussian reaction followed, and finally a republican compromise was made under external pressures. While Finland became internationally a warning example of a failed democracy in spring 1918, foundations for what would much later be called a 'very sustainable' polity were nevertheless laid in spring 1919.

The British model rose in favour in Sweden and Finland from 1918 onwards, but it did not supplant the German one. The elites of the three countries remained connected by similar educational backgrounds, shared German as an international language and were linked by travel, studies, work and ideological trends. The people of the time in Finland and Sweden, especially on the right, admired German culture and regarded their own countries and Germany as comparable. The shared cultural background allowed translations and the transfer of terms and values from German to Swedish and Finnish. Even Finnish, despite belonging to a different linguistic group, to a great extent gave the same semantic values to key cultural, social and political concepts as German did. Furthermore, in 1917 all three political systems were still characterised by the duality of government, an overwhelmingly monarchical constitution and doubts about excessive parliamentarism.[105] Even many Swedish and Finnish leftists were influenced by the German debates. For many Social Democrats especially in Finland, Karl Kautsky's uncompromising and 'orthodox' version emphasising the inevitability of a revolution and transition to socialism was the original model.[106] His democratic justification of parliamentarism as an instrument for advancing the cause of socialism also mattered. It was based on hopes that a transition to socialism would be realised through universal suffrage, as a result of which a well-organised Social Democratic working class would rise. The revolution would come when the circumstances were suitable for it; there was no need to actively make one. The workers would be able to control the administration and carry on their class struggle through the parliament. In Eduard Bernstein's revisionist socialism, followed especially by the Swedish Social Democrats, democracy was both a means and an

---

104   Vares 1998, 324–5.
105   Ihalainen 2016a.
106   Hentilä 2015, 151–2.

end. Rosa Luxemburg, on the other hand, rejected parliamentarism as an historical form of class rule by the bourgeoisie. Participation in such politicking hindered the transition to a socialist society as it ignored the revolutionary potential of the masses. Parliament could hence be no more than a forum for socialist agitation that would with time be removed as a result of an intensified class struggle inside and outside the parliament.[107]

Peter Baldwin has urged Scandinavian historians to replace conventional histories of Nordic particularity with such comparisons with Germany, which, he argues, has been deliberately excluded from the Scandinavian historical consciousness since the Second World War. An alternative national (or even Anglophone) research orientation has followed not only as a result of methodological nationalism but also for ideological reasons. According to Baldwin, the exclusion of the German connection has been part of 'the welfare whiggery of a Social Democratic reading of history', which sees modern Sweden as the teleological goal of a national historical progress and even as a universal target of historical development. Comparisons with Germany would not only reveal similarities but also the insular and particular nature of many Scandinavian developments that arose out of unique and not universally valid circumstances, Baldwin suggests.[108] Comparisons between Sweden and Britain indicate both similarities and differences,[109] as the historical experiences of these two countries have been so different; comparisons with Germany, by contrast, might show considerable similarities.[110] This study puts Baldwin's suggestion into practice not only by comparing two Nordic countries with Germany but also by making Finland a point of comparison for Swedish history. The comparison needs to work both ways so that Sweden is not simply seen as a norm followed by Finland after a delay; rather, the Finnish case is used for a deeper understanding of political development in Sweden. Finland as 'another Sweden' after 1809 shows that the development of Sweden proper was not the only possible one; that Sweden, too, remained traditional in many ways; and that Finnish developments mattered more in Sweden in 1917–19 than has been generally recognised.

The following chapters will show that the combination of Britain, Germany, Sweden and Finland works extremely well in the comparative and transnational analysis even though the inclusion of four cases has produced a more extensive and comprehensive study than was first intended. Before proceeding to the analysis, some further explanation of the methodology used will help to show how the analysis has been focused and delimited.

---

107   Kirby 1986b, 7; Hewitson 2001, 760; Jörke & Llanque 2016.
108   Baldwin 2004, 3, 5–6; see also Neunsinger 2010, 11 for a comparison between Germany and Sweden between the world wars; Ihalainen 2010 and Ihalainen 2015 on Swedish particularity in the eighteenth century; Ihalainen et al. 2011.
109   Friberg, Hilson & Vall 2007.
110   See Götz 2001.

1.3 Discourse-oriented political history based on parliamentary sources

The research for this book has been inspired methodologically by a new type of political history that analyses communication and a variety of interlinked discourses as central elements of political processes, institutions, events and actions.[111] I have considered the connections between words and deeds in politics[112] and the related mobility and physical experiences of the historical agents. In the interpretation of the use of language as political action I have paid considerable attention to the biographies and the psycho-physical experiences of the parliamentarians. I have analysed politics primarily (though not solely) as discursive processes taking place simultaneously on different horizontally and vertically linked planes and forums and in different times (historical trajectories) and places (multi-sitedness) – so that a variety of actors are seen as constructing, reproducing and contesting policies in interaction with each other and with the political process.[113] In practice, this means contextualising and comparing content, and conducting a textual and conceptual analysis of parliamentary and press debates on constitutional reforms, the goal being to reconstruct competing and ideologically motivated understandings of the constitutional implications of the war and the revolutions as well as alternative conceptualisations of democracy, the people and parliamentarism. Instead of a mere comparison between separately treated national histories, I have also paid attention to transnational aspects of constitutional discourse, in which parliamentarians as nationally and internationally connected political actors contributed to transfers between political cultures. I shall now proceed to explain these methodological starting points in further detail.[114]

This study is based on a soft version of social constructivism that analyses language and discourse but does not see them as determining what could be thought, said or done. The linguistic, cultural, discursive, spatial, mobile, material and transnational turns in the human sciences are all seen as reconcilable with a new political history whose central starting point has been the incorporation into research of political discourse as a form of political action. The linguistic and discursive turns have emphasised the significant role of the use of language side by side with structures, institutions and practices in most aspects of politics and have called for an analysis of the actual language of past political discourse in its proper contexts and with appropriate attention to agency. They suggest that the social world is to a great extent (though not solely) constructed and constituted by symbolic

---

111   Bollmeyer 2007, 18–19; Steinmetz 2011, 4–5; Leonhard 2011; Steinmetz 2013.
112   See Palonen 2014, 11, on Quentin Skinner's intellectual history, and 126 on rhetorical studies of parliamentary debates.
113   For a more extensive discussion, see Halonen, Ihalainen & Saarinen 2015. On an application to conceptual history, see Friberg 2012, 21.
114   A more extensive discussion will be provided in Ihalainen & Saarinen forthcoming.

systems, and above all by language. Politics in general and parliaments in particular can hence be approached as being based primarily on the use of language and communication.[115] These approaches to political and parliamentary history do not claim to be all-embracing or to deny the need to simultaneously study agency, events, structures, institutions and practices; rather, they emphasise an aspect of politics that is essential for an understanding of political processes. Their analyses are built to a great extent on the results of more conventional political history. In this study, data from national biographies have been used to contextualise all speech acts but are not explicitly referred to in order to avoid an excessive number of references to mainly background information.

The seeming methodological gap between the study of political action (as traditionally studied in political history) and political discourse (as conventionally studied in the history of ideas) can be overcome when politics in the past is seen as essentially (though not exclusively) discursive and competing understandings of politics viewed as being reflected by discursive tensions.[116] Instead of the mere analysis of the causes and consequences of past political change, we should also be interested in the discursive processes that gave rise to differing and ideologically contested views of policy questions[117] and sometimes explain the course of more physical political action as well. This kind of history of argumentation concentrates on the processes of development in the meanings of political terms and concepts as applied in a number of arguments by representatives of several political groups when they encounter new political situations, as Jörn Leonhard has put it.[118]

Such a process-like understanding of political discourse is particularly applicable to the parliament, which, according to Kari Palonen, should be seen as 'the paradigmatic institution for political deliberation'[119] and as offering 'options ... for political action by means of speech, debate and procedure'.[120] Markku Peltonen has emphasised the rhetorical and adversarial nature of the English tradition of parliamentary speaking.[121] According to Cornelia Ilie, as well, power relations in parliaments are discourse-shaped so that 'the struggle over the use of language' should be taken 'as a concrete manifestation of the struggles for power': power can be gained, challenged, competed for, defended and consolidated through the use of language. Facts

---

115 On political culture, see Ihalainen & Sennefelt 2011 and Leonhard 2011, 245. In Germany, 'the cultural history of the political' has been discussed by Stollberg-Rilinger 2005, 10–11, 22, 24. A linguistic turn in English-language research on German political history was suggested by Childers 1990, 335–6, 358. Recent developments in parliamentary history towards conceptual history include Ihalainen, Ilie & Palonen 2016. See also Ihalainen & Palonen 2009, 33.
116 Leonhard 2011, 249; Halonen, Ihalainen & Saarinen 2015, 14; Ihalainen and Saarinen 2015, 34.
117 Ihalainen and Saarinen 2015, 33.
118 Leonhard 2008, 18.
119 Palonen, Rosales & Turkka 2014, 3.
120 Palonen, Rosales & Turkka 2014, 5.
121 Peltonen 2013, 7.

tend to be shaped by language, whereas language change is based on the real situation. This is to say that parliamentary language affects and is affected by ongoing political transformations elsewhere in society.[122]

Politics is analysed here as a discursive process that has taken place on different horizontally and vertically linked levels and forums simultaneously and in different times and places,[123] the focus being on national parliaments but with press debates (and through research literature other potentially connected debates) also being considered. This entails particular attention to historical trajectories and to the multi-sitedness of past political debates. Different layers of political discourse (historical trajectories) may have come together and merged at the same time into a point, a nexus, which has given rise to new political discourses.[124] Policies have taken shape as a variety of actors have reinforced and potentially reformulated them in interaction with each other and the political process.[125]

The physical life experiences and recollections of past political actors as 'historical bodies' formed in particular social spaces, as well as their mobility between different spaces, call for particular attention in the analysis as they may have conditioned the use of language.[126] Attention is paid here to the role of individuals as political agents by taking into account the simultaneity and reflexivity of all of their psycho-physical experiences and ongoing actions. Individual political agents often created concrete links between two or more discourses at the national level as well as between different national discourses transnationally.[127] The most obvious examples are provided by Hjalmar Branting of the Swedish Social Democrats and some Finnish Social Democrats who had contacts with the Bolsheviks, but equally noteworthy are scholarly networks of conservative professors and Swedish and Finnish liberals sharing a world-view with British, French or German liberals.

Spatiality and mobility refer to the simultaneity of a large number of contexts, practices and concepts moving in time and space. The notion of multi-sitedness supports the transnational turn in this field of historical research:[128] multi-sited and potentially transnational debates, and constitutional debates in particular, have been typical of parliaments. The focus on the process-like nature of parliamentary discourse invites attention to interaction within and between political parties and the movement of discourses in time and space, including trajectories from the past, links with other debates and references to the future. An individual contribution to a parliamentary debate can be seen as a nexus of historically layered, multi-sited and transnational policy discourses so that different ideological, national, international and transnational historical and current discourses come together and give rise to new discourses in a parliamentary debate.

---

122 Ilie 2016, 134, 143.
123 Halonen, Ihalainen & Saarinen 2015, 3.
124 Halonen, Ihalainen & Saarinen 2015, 17, inspired by Scollon & Scollon 2004.
125 This is an application of Hornberger & Johnson 2007, 509–32.
126 Scollon & Scollon 2004.
127 Halonen, Ihalainen & Saarinen 2015, 17.
128 Halonen, Ihalainen & Saarinen 2015, 15.

The debaters, through their active use of language, participate in a variety of discursive processes.

This multi-sitedness and multi-layeredness of parliamentary debates calls for a longer-term and parallel analysis of parliamentary debates and the consideration of a variety of forums within one national debate, in other words the inclusion of a selection of extra-parliamentary debates. Even if the focus is on parliamentary discourse as a form of political activity, other discourses moving in time and space and potentially interlinked with this as well as physical political actions need to be considered. This also leads to a focus on individual parliamentarians as political agents linking political discourses that have taken place in various forums. These connections have been created by ideologies, religions, parties, the press, associations, academic traditions, visits abroad, family ties, friendships etc. Typical instances would be a Swedish MP with work experience in Germany, France and Britain and another who knew the Archbishop of Canterbury, or a Finnish MP born in Ingria and fluent in Russian attending revolutionary assemblies in Petrograd and then taking the train to Helsinki to speak in the Finnish parliament about the future constitution.

The production of a new political history in this study has entailed writing comparative and transnational histories of political discourses. It consists in the study of the multi-sited and potentially interconnected contributions to political discourse made by individuals and political groups in several European countries with comparable and partly entangled national histories. Attention is paid to spatiality and mobility in discourse – in addition to historical semantics, conceptual history (as represented by Reinhart Koselleck[129] and his pupils), historical pragmatics and the analysis of speech acts in the history of political thought (as advocated by Quentin Skinner[130] and 'the Cambridge School' in general). Whereas Anglophone research on the history of political thought emphasises the role of individuals in doing things in unique speaking situations, continental conceptual historians pay more attention to the functioning of communities, continuities in the contexts of political speaking and the recycling of political language. These slightly diverging conventional styles of studying the history of political discourse are seen here as complementing rather than competing with each other as they merely focus on different aspects of the multidimensional phenomenon of the language of politics.

The comparative and transnational analysis of constitutional discourse in this study focuses on the very essence of representative government – parliamentary sources, which record institutionalised debates between political actors. Due to multiple contemporary perspectives included by them they provide fruitful sources for the analysis of the alternative definitions of the values of political communities. Speaking is a major form of political action in parliaments, which are founded on the rhetorical principle of dissensus and argument *in utramque partem* or *pro et contra* about every item on the agenda. The debaters can 'parliamentarise' any

---

129   Koselleck 1972, xvi–xvii.
130   Skinner 2002.

political concept, construct alternatives and discuss various definitions. Parliamentary debates contain concrete conceptualisations carried out by political agents themselves in connection with decision making on constitutions and reactions from fellow parliamentarians. They clarify opposite alternatives rather than lead to consensus. They can be analysed by focusing on conceptual moves, innovations and interventions as well as on references to past examples, the application of different historical layers of concepts and selective comparisons with contemporary political systems.[131]

Speaking for and against issues on the agenda often led to the expression of strongly contrasting understandings of the political reality. Teun van Dijk has argued that parliamentary debates on alternative political solutions – especially in historical moments characterised by the polarisation of politics and ongoing shifts of paradigms – are revealing about the diverse party-political agendas of the time. According to Cornelia Ilie, parliamentarians, when trying to influence the audience's beliefs and opinions, discursively problematise and potentially reshape prevailing conceptualisations of political values on which decision making in the polity is based.[132] While conceptual innovations can be borrowed from outside the parliamentary chamber (from media debates, for example – and may also be introduced back into these so that parliamentary discourse extends beyond the representative institution),[133] they may also arise out of the acute needs of the actual moment of speaking in parliament, sometimes even being coined without advance planning as a reaction to an interjection, for example. Parliamentary debates nevertheless remain linked to physical political realities outside the chamber in a number of ways.

1.4 The structure of the analysis

This study of the understandings and conceptualisations of transitions towards parliamentary democracy aims at reconstructing and analysing in a synthetising way the prevailing values and alternative solutions held by the British, German, Swedish and Finnish parliamentary elites and reflected in their use of language between March 1917 and July 1919. In a close reading of the major constitutional debates in the four countries, I have paid attention to both general historical semantics and to distinct speech acts in which the basic values of the political community and its future prospects as a (potential) parliamentary democracy were defined through the use of the terminology of democracy, the people and parliamentarism. Explicit disputes about the meanings of related key concepts have received further attention. Technical questions concerning elections such as the limits of suffrage were left outside the study (including the concepts of

---

131 Palonen 2008; Ihalainen & Palonen 2009, 19–21, 32–3; Ihalainen 2010; Palonen 2010, 1, 3, 5 156–72; Palonen 2012, 21; Palonen 2014, 13, 24, 106–7, 139; Ihalainen 2014; Ihalainen & Saarinen 2015; Ihalainen 2015.
132 Van Dijk 2003; Ilie 2016.
133 Ilie 2016; Harvard 2016.

representation, mandate, election, suffrage, the electorate, voting, majority, minority, government, opposition, party and faction).[134] In order to grasp contemporary understandings of the influence of the war and revolution on political life, uses of these key concepts were also analysed. References to foreign examples were registered to enable the analysis of inter- and transnational interaction.

Even though in Britain, Germany and Sweden (and in many other European countries, though not in Finland, where it already existed) the period 1917–19 involved the introduction of women's suffrage as well, a conscious choice was made not to focus specifically on the gender aspects of constitutional reforms here. Many contemporaries, after all, did not automatically associate women's suffrage with democracy.[135] This study rather considers possibilities for political participation in parliamentary polities for both men and women on equal terms. Such a choice does not stand for any deprecation of the gender aspect; it arises from a desire to avoid the repetition of already existing analyses of the introduction of women's suffrage into national parliaments,[136] which cannot be deepened within the confines of this study. Gender is considered as an analytical category in cases where the parliamentarians themselves explicitly associated it with the war, revolution, democracy, the political role of the people or parliamentarism – at times quite extensively especially in the British and Swedish parliaments (see subsections 3.1.2, 3.1.5, 3.1.6, 3.3.4, 3.3.4, 4.1.3, 4.1.4 and 7.3.4), occasionally also in German and Finnish parliaments.

The structure of this book has three dimensions: time, national contexts, and the debates surrounding a key concept (democracy, the people, parliamentarism). Chronologically, the book is divided into seven chapters, the central five each discussing constitutional debates over roughly half a year – although there is flexibility in the timings so that thematically and contextually coherent series of debates have not been split up. The basic structure runs so that British, German, Swedish and Finnish debates are discussed (always in this order) for the first and second half of 1917, the first and second half of 1918 and the first half of 1919. There were differences in the timing and intensity of the debates, and hence the extent and source basis of the sections differ. Comparisons and cross-references are made throughout the text when appropriate, while generalisations and abstractions have mainly been saved for the conclusion. Each country-specific section is opened with (i) a subsection reviewing the state of research in each country

---

134 See Palonen 2010.
135 Kurunmäki 2015, 32, 48.
136 See Purvis & Stanley Holton (eds) 2000, Gullace 2002 (who has also made use of parliamentary debates and the press), Smith 2005 (who has studied 'suffrage discourse' as concerning women's suffrage from the point of view of women only) and Gottlieb & Toye (eds) 2013 for the British case. See Sulkunen, Nevala-Nurmi & Markkola 2009 and Adams 2014 for historiographical reviews of the field and comparative studies. Adams argues that nationalism rather than feminism gave rise to women's suffrage.

and contextualising the debates at the national level. This is followed by up to four subsections discussing (ii) debates on the political impact of the war and revolutions as well as the principal international comparisons and transnational connections of the debates, (iii) competing conceptualisations of democracy, (iv) alternative arguments on the political role of the people and (v) rival understandings of parliamentarism. In the conclusion, this division is followed by an explication of similarities and differences and a discussion of causal factors. Here, generalisations are formulated and some nation-specific findings rising from the comparison and the consideration of transnational aspects pointed out.

2. National backgrounds of constitutional disputes from spring 1917 to summer 1919

2.1 The standstill in the British constitutional reform before and during the war

Considerable constitutional tensions on the need for a further widening of suffrage and the parliamentarisation of the government (in the sense of increasing the powers of the lower house) were typical of British politics at the beginning of the twentieth century. The key issues concerned the extension of manhood suffrage beyond 60 per cent as legislated in 1884, female suffrage as demanded by a militant suffragist movement and opposed by equally principled anti-suffragists, proportional representation as applied in a growing number of other countries and the need to reform or restore the House of Lords. Women's suffrage dominated the debate as unenfranchised men were passive in claiming their political rights in comparison with the vocal and well-to-do suffragettes. Later research[137] has also prioritised the gender perspective from the women's point of view. Proportional representation was supported by some MPs from all parliamentary parties. The Lords had already passed a bill on its introduction in local elections and was ready to extend it to the national level in 1918, but the Commons did not adopt these reforms. Most importantly, the Liberal government had forced through a Parliament Act in 1911, cutting the political power of the upper house. On the other hand, it preferred to avoid any technical changes in the electoral system that would benefit the Labour Party, the prospective competitor of the Liberals, preferring to focus on welfare reforms to obviate Labour advances rather than on the extension of parliamentary government through increased proportionality of representation – a tactic not entirely unlike that used by German governments. The Liberal government did introduce a compensation for MPs,[138] which of course made the post more accessible. The Conservatives, for their part, were uninterested in a suffrage reform as it did not suit to their elitist understanding of the British nation, and as they willingly opposed any Liberal reform.[139]

137 See note 136.
138 Machin 2001, 125–6.
139 Müller 2002, 320.

In the Parliament Act, the constitutional relationship between the two Houses of Parliament was radically redefined so that the possibilities for the House of Lords to postpone legislation were considerably decreased. The length of parliaments was reduced from seven to five years and the relationship between the Crown and the government more clearly defined. Some politicians even regarded these changes as a transition from an unwritten to a written constitution, but in reality this was just a further stage in the constitutional evolution that was typical of Britain. The reform of 1910–11 in any case constituted a major precedent for that of 1917–18 as it demonstrated the growing self-confidence of the Commons in relation to the Lords. With its unilateral bill of April 1910, the Commons had declared that the Lords would no longer be able to reject or make amendments to economic bills or postpone legislation already passed by the lower house for longer than three parliamentary sessions or two years. The 1910 general election and the Liberal ministry's threat to create hundreds of pro-reformist peers by making use of the royal prerogative forced the Lords to accept this reform against their will. The compromise solution saw the veto rights of the Lords limited but its composition untouched – one proposal having been that it should be replaced with a chamber elected by a popular vote. Suffrage in elections for the Commons was not reformed either, so that forty per cent of adult males and all women remained outside the franchise.[140]

Despite its limitations, Vernon Bogdanor has argued that the Parliament Act made the British parliamentary system increasingly unicameral. Representative government became associated with the House of Commons, and the political role of the Lords tended to be marginalised,[141] though the upper house retained its status as a forum for value debates. The consequences of the act were soon felt in parliamentary decision-making: the Lords rejected three bills in 1912–13 but rarely intervened thereafter, recognising the new power-sharing realities. The peers would continue to challenge governments in more limited fields, often related to specific issues concerning the countryside. Otherwise they would adopt the role of examining and revising bills passed by the Commons.[142] As we shall see, some vestiges of the old system would still be heard in 1917 and 1918, however, with the speakers in both houses either lamenting the radicalisation of the Parliament Act or calling for its further radicalisation.

The transition to 'lower house parliamentarism' was difficult for many Conservatives to accept. The reform, despite its limits, gave rise to considerable constitutional tension, many Conservatives opposing the changes to the bitter end, claiming that the Lords (rather than the Commons) constituted the real representatives of the people. Some even threatened, at least rhetorically, a civil war in support of the former parliamentary system.[143] This political crisis concerning the legitimacy of parliamentary

---

140   Close 1977, 893; Machin 2001, 130–3; Walters 2003, 197, 228; Bogdanor 2003a, 4–5, 23; Dahlmann 2014, 55.
141   Bogdanor 2003b, 690.
142   Walters 2003, 210–13.
143   Müller 2002, 48; Saunders 2013b, 76–80.

government was further deepened by the extensive strikes that preceded the outbreak of the First World War in Britain, the ongoing violent campaign of the suffragettes and plans for Home Rule for Ireland.[144] Previous research shows that when it entered the war in 1914, Britain was by no means a stable parliamentary polity that the Continentals would readily imitate.

Even the British participation in the war was not so self-evident as that of most Continental powers: the Liberal ministry and party, which had ruled since 1910 with support from minority parties, were divided during the war, and there was opposition in Parliament to involvement in the Continental troubles. The ministry lost two of its left-wing Liberal members to an extra- and intra-parliamentary peace opposition when the war broke out. This opposition was also supported by the Union of Democratic Control (founded in September 1914 to oppose secret diplomacy and to advance peace negotiations, national self-determination and free trade) and the small Independent Labour Party, which emerged as a part of the transnational division of the labour movement into revisionist social democrats, who supported involvement in the war and were generally willing to cooperate with bourgeois reformist forces, and future communists, who rejected parliamentarism as an outdated strategy and expected support from the Russian Revolution. Views on the democratisation of Germany would become a further issue dividing the Labour Party after 1917. However, the British Labour Party, unlike most Continental labour parties, was not split as a consequence of the war. Despite disagreements the radical influence within it remained modest. For the Conservatives, by contrast, the war gave a new patriotic motivation, enabling them to move on from their heated anti-Home Rule campaign and disagreements surrounding the reform of the Lords. In order to ensure that the Continental war would not directly reach Britain, the British government received extensive wartime powers and the support of a party truce that allowed it to intervene in the economy and civil liberties in unprecedented ways, including the oppression of the pacifist opposition.[145] All in all, the British political system of the late 1910s was not that different from those of the other war-faring nations, discourse on nation legitimating wartime politics such as in Germany,[146] the major exception being the principal controlling position of the Commons over the government, a feature that was lacking especially in Germany.

In the spirit of a political truce, the Liberal government sought a broader parliamentary basis and managed to recruit Conservative and Labour ministers in May 1915. A general election, which should have been held in accordance with the Parliament Act by December 1915, was postponed, and the Commons elected in 1910 – insofar as its members were not on military service – continued to work. As German critics of parliamentary government of the British and French type also implied, Parliament had

---

144 Dahlmann 2014, 56; Leonhard 2014, 212.
145 Webber 1988, x; Cook 1988, 63; Weckerlein 1994, 15; Berger 1994, 8; Ball 1995, 58–9; Smith 1997, 61; Collette 1998, 2; McCrillis 1998, 10; Thorpe 2001, 37; Wrigley 2009, 91; Pugh 2011, 100; Dutton 2013, 64–78; Leonhard 2014, 213.
146 Müller 2002, 353–4.

little actual influence in making major political decisions during the war: the British ministry dealt with wartime problems through administrative measures. Things became more complicated, however, when no major military victory was won and the Coalition failed to restore peace. In the meantime, the Conservatives were becoming the leading party in Parliament through gains in by-elections and consequently became the decisive force in the new coalition. Together with an awareness of unenfranchised men and women serving patriotically in the army and armaments industry, this development tended to make both the Conservatives and the Liberals more interested in the possibility of an electoral reform. Such a reform was debated in the Commons from 1915 onwards, but a clear turning point was only reached in late 1916, when bad electoral successes in by-elections had made it impossible for the Liberal Prime Minister H. H. Asquith to continue. In the so-called 'Nigeria Debate' of November 1916, Conservative backbenchers withdrew their support for the Coalition, which forced the Conservative leader Bonar Law to look for alternative solutions for the ministry. King George V asked Law to take over the premiership, but he declined in the lack of sufficient cross-party support. As an election would have been very difficult to organise in the midst of escalating fighting, and as Asquith refused to join a government led by Law, the King nominated a government of all parties under the leadership of David Lloyd George (Liberal).[147] Only some of the Liberals and Labour supported Lloyd George, but he could count on Conservative backing instead[148] – once again a state of affairs that affected the course of the reform and subsequent elections. In these circumstances, however, a suffrage reform introduced by the Coalition would not be simply a party-political manoeuvre as all parties were to some extent divided over the war, support for the current ministry and the nature of the reform.

In Parliament, Unionists (Conservatives) and Liberals now both had 272 seats, Labour 42 and the Irish National Party 84. In Lloyd George's coalition government, the Conservatives had a majority, headed by Chancellor of the Exchequer and Deputy Prime Minister A. Bonar Law. They also held the Foreign Office, Home Office, War Office, Admiralty and other important ministries. The Liberal prime minister had won the support of the majority of the Conservatives through his proven resoluteness in decision-making and his abilities as a public speaker. Such broad support was decisive for a successful electoral reform. A determination to introduce constitutional changes, too, was easier to demonstrate in wartime with only a few men coordinating decision-making within the war cabinet and the special circumstances justifying extraordinary measures in this field as well. The good working relationship between Lloyd George and Bonar Law made it easier to agree even on previously controversial questions like this one. In practice, however, the Conservatives were the stronger partner, thanks to their unanimous support for total warfare. There was

---

147 Ball 1995, 55, 58, 60; Cook 1988, 66; Pugh 2002, 153, 155; Lyon 2003, 398–9; Morrow 2004, 154, 224; Dahlmann 2014, 58.
148 Becker 2014, 25.

also a rising conception among them that the party might actually benefit from a wartime reform. The Liberals, by contrast, were split, with Asquith as Leader of the Opposition, even though he did not actively oppose the government on issues such as electoral reform. The Labour Party, headed by William Adamson, remained rather marginal in comparison with Social Democrats in many other countries,[149] and the Irish Nationalists frequently concentrated on Irish affairs only.

An electoral reform enfranchising soldiers and female workers seemed possible under the wartime coalition as a means of encouraging the war effort. It was far from clear, however, that the reform would be launched in the name of 'democracy', a term that was not yet generally used to define the British political system. It was more common to talk about popular or parliamentary government. Democracy, when not rejected as the unrealisable power of the masses, had been generally considered no more than one of the three elements of a balanced mixed constitution, and the notion of popular sovereignty had emphasised the origins rather than the active use of power. In popular radical discourse 'democracy' had nevertheless been used since the 1830s and 1840s to challenge the degree of reforms.[150] Only the late nineteenth century had seen the rise of a broader understanding of democracy as an essential part of British parliamentarism, partly through the influence of the USA, the political system of which had become increasingly characterised by the term in the course of that century. In Britain, a turn towards a more positive understanding of democracy took place from the 1880s onwards,[151] though no agreement about Britain being a democracy emerged, and the concept with its multiple meanings became an object of controversy and rhetorical redescriptions especially by those Conservatives who remained unhappy with the reforms of the early 1910s.[152] This battle over definitions continued in 1917–18 and was intensified by the trans-Atlantic Wilsonian 'democratic' turn in war propaganda.

The British political elite talked about democracy during the first half of the war quite differently from the way they did in the second. Scepticism rather than optimism about the functioning of democratic institutions had been typical of British discourse before the war – something that Continental anti-parliamentary politicians readily echoed. Britain was 'free' and 'constitutional', no doubt, but was it a 'democracy'? Only the war, and especially the discursive turn of 1917 in war propaganda, supported a change in the attitudes of the political elite as to the desirability of democracy. According to Lloyd George himself, the cause of democracy had not originally been among the reasons for British involvement in the war, but democracy had become a goal of future policies during the war. He himself had rather used the phrase 'popular government' in accordance with

149   Ball 1995, 60–1; Pugh 2002, 155–6.
150   Ihalainen 2010; Innes & Philp 2013, 2–3; Philp 2013, 102; Innes, Philp & Saunders 2013, 115.
151   Saunders 2013a.
152   Saunders 2013; Saunders 2013b, 74, 77.

British traditions of defining the political system and would continue to do so until he was assured of an election victory in late 1918. Ernest Barker, on the other hand, had already justified the alliance between Britain and France in 1914 by appealing to democracy as a basic political attitude and arguing: 'France, like England, is a democracy. France is one of the greatest democracies in the world.' German war propaganda was, at the same time, challenging 'Western' democracy (see section 3.2 for details). Lloyd George and his colleagues gradually began to defend democracy internationally after the entry of the United States into the war, which suggests that the discourse on democracy gained popularity in Britain as a pragmatic means of finding a common denominator with the United States, the engagement of which in the war was eagerly hoped for and the current president of which favoured the rhetoric of democracy. In March 1916, Richard Haldane, 1st Viscount Haldane and a former Lord Chancellor, had given an interview to American journalists urging America, as a *democratic* country, to involve itself in a war that was expected to produce 'a great democratic advancement' in Europe and the world more generally. In 1917, the United States, having made the decision to join the war as a reaction to total submarine warfare by Germany, came forward using a similar vocabulary and speaking about a joint fight for democracy. The breakthrough of this discourse in war propaganda gradually caused the British to proceed towards an increasing use of references to democracy[153] also in connection with domestic reforms that had not been initially conceptualised in that way, and, in time, to sometimes question the correspondence of existing political structures with the principles of 'democracy' – however that term might be defined.

Despite long traditions of parliamentary rule and the development of parliamentarism in relation to sovereignty, representation, responsibility and deliberation,[154] no clear doctrine of parliamentarism either existed in Britain before the First World War. The war therefore contributed significantly to redefining the essentially contested concepts of democracy and parliamentarism in Britain as well,[155] as part of the continuing discursive processes of constructing democracy and parliamentarism.[156] The constitutional change of 1917–18 originated to a great extent from domestic debates about the necessity to finally hold the postponed general election, to create an electoral register for that purpose and to proceed to a proper electoral reform as well.[157] The special circumstances of the war, however, enabled the achievement of a unique cross-party consensus on constitutional changes. This was foreign to the usual British government-versus-opposition divisions.[158] In the sections on Britain, we shall analyse the dynamics of parliamentary debate on reform[159] in these circumstances

153 Llanque 2000, 106–107, 110–11; Jefferys 2007, 8.
154 Seaward & Ihalainen 2016.
155 Llanque 2000, 112.
156 Ihalainen, Ilie & Palonen 2016, 6, 12; Ihalainen 2016a, 19–20.
157 Blackburn 2011, 38–40.
158 Norton 2011, 7, 15–16.
159 Debates on women's suffrage have been analysed in a helpful way by Gullace 2002.

from a conceptual, comparative and transnational points of view unlike those of previous research.

2.2 Universal male suffrage in Germany. Prussian executive power and scepticism about parliamentarism

The degree of democratisation and parliamentarisation of the German polity before the First World War has long been the subject to scholarly debate (see section 4.2 for details); the unified country had already introduced equal and universal male suffrage in national elections in 1867 – long before Britain, Sweden or Finland – but had distinguished between democracy in that sense and the parliamentarisation of government both in theory and in practice.[160] Despite the seemingly democratic suffrage and a federal national parliament side by side with regional state parliaments, the German constitution, dominated under Wilhelm II by the conservative Prussian political culture, did not support a parliamentary or democratic regime. This differs from the ideal of governmental responsibility to parliament as sometimes expressed in the liberal Frankfurt Parliament (1848–9)[161] but such a critical attitude to parliaments was mainstream in Northern Europe, including Sweden and Finland until 1917.

James Retallack has argued that all areas of German political life were regulated by authoritarian structures, practices and ways of thinking that obstructed political reform,[162] whereas Margaret Lavinia Anderson has maintained that the German electoral culture was gradually becoming more participatory and democratic in comparison with Western powers. This happened, according to her, thanks to prevalent legalism,[163] a further feature linking Germany to Sweden and Finland. The majority vote in federal elections nevertheless limited the representation of the Social Democrats in the Reichstag, and their influence had also been suppressed with anti-socialist and social security legislation, measures that were widely admired among conservatives in the north of Europe. The other parties were doubtful about reforms, wishing to retain their seats in the Reichstag. The Chancellor was only to a limited extent accountable to the Reichstag, while the heads of governmental departments remained responsible to the Kaiser only. The Kaiser led the army, decided on war and peace, appointed civil servants, convened the Reichstag and promulgated laws. The Bundesrat, in which the regional states were represented and which had executive powers as well, bypassed the Reichstag as the supreme authority of the Reich, and within this body Prussia alone could veto any decision. Within Prussia itself, the continuance of a three-class franchise based on the amount of taxes paid by the voters (often compared in the Swedish debate with their 40-grade franchise scale) and the use of the federalist system to prevent

---

160 Gusy 2008a, 421.
161 Botzenhart 1974, 790–3.
162 Retallack 2006, 10.
163 Anderson 2000, 19–20.

reforms maintained a conservative political order. While Prussia had been the leader in modernisation in the mid-nineteenth century, by the 1910s its political system, which included an upper house (Herrenhaus) consisting of noblemen and lacking equal popular representation,[164] appeared as a barrier to political reform in Prussia and the extension of the powers of the Reichstag in Germany as a whole – even more so because not only Prussian conservatives but also many liberals were sceptical about the rule of the masses[165] and parliamentarism. As Andreas Biefang has pointed out, parliamentary government was rejected by the bourgeois parties as not serving their power-political interests, and even by the Social Democrats, who, though recognising the progressive features of parliamentarisation, would have rather seen the parliament replaced with a system that would not so clearly serve the interests of the bourgeoisie as they considered it to be doing.[166] Even moderate socialists in the north of Europe thus found support to their scepticism about parliamentarism from Germany.

The Prussian political culture remained dominant since the Kaiser was also the King of Prussia, the Chancellor was the Prussian Prime Minister, and Prussian ministers prepared proposals for the federal Reichstag. The Prussian political elites were nationalistic and militaristic and generally admired the former chancellor Otto von Bismarck, who had prioritised the use of sheer power over discussion in politics – all attitudes shared by the 'conservative international' in Sweden and Finland. Kaiser Wilhelm II himself despised parliamentarism and preferred to have around him officers, civil servants and noblemen who shared his views. The inhabitants of the smaller states, liberals and Catholics did not necessarily identify themselves with this Prussian order,[167] but their influence in the Reich was limited as a result of the established political structures.

At the same time, the voter turnout in elections had risen from the 51% in 1871 to 85% in 1912, which reflects the rising mobilisation and politicisation of the electorate: there was clearly an interest in politics among the public. A working relationship between the parliament and the public sphere was also gradually emerging. The legitimacy of the Reichstag was based on its broad popular basis and increasing publicity through debates and interpellations in which diverse interests could be expressed and which were widely reported in the press. Nevertheless, in concrete policy decision-making, the role of the Reichstag remained marginal. It participated in the legislative process and in the approval of the budget, which grew rapidly in these years, but not in decisions concerning the actual governing of the country. No governmental responsibility to the parliament or efficient parliamentary control of government existed. Furthermore, the German

---

164   The debates of the Prussian parliament have not been analysed in this study, which focuses on the national levels. However, British, Finnish and Swedish observers were aware of the debates of that important representative institution as well. For Prussia, see Müller 2002.
165   Spenkuch 1998, 551–2.
166   Biefang & Schulz 2016.
167   Ullrich 2010, 161–5; Winkler 2006; Dahlmann 2014, 43–4.

public debate did not esteem the representatives' work very highly, nor indeed did they themselves. Parliamentary matters were often seen as secondary to the administration and the army.[168]

The prospects for the parliamentarisation of government were thus poor in pre-war Germany. In 1912, an article in a National-Liberal paper complained about concealed parliamentarism (*Kryptoparlamentarismus*), criticising what it saw as the growing role of the parliament in German politics. According to its author, the political parties of the Reichstag did not really aim at the common good but rather advanced the particular interests of trusts, cartels and syndicates.[169] Since parliamentary government was lacking, parties had no need for compromises, which tended to support the advancement of particular interests and the use of violent rhetoric in parliamentary debates. This was an understanding of parliamentarism that many members of the Swedish and Finnish political elites also shared, both on the left and on the right.

The nature of German parliamentary life had nevertheless changed to some extent as a consequence of the parliamentary election of 1912, which made the Social Democrats the largest parliamentary group for the first time. Their share of the votes reached 34.8%, giving them 110 representatives out of 397. In the eyes the old elite, the growing strength of the socialists appeared as a threat to the established balance of power. As a reaction, the political influence of extra-parliamentary forces tended to increase further.[170] It was difficult for the conservatives and liberals to rethink their conception of the Social Democrats as being potentially revolutionary even though most Social Democratic leaders had already rejected the Marxist revolutionary goals of the original party programme. Eduard Bernstein, for instance, wished to see socialism as a constant process of negotiation in which parliamentary cooperation with other parties was needed. A change in the attitudes of the other parties only started when they saw the cooperative, even patriotic, stance of the Social Democrats during the war.[171] On the other hand, some radicalism survived among the left-wingers of the party, and so did old prejudices among the right and centre parties.

The attitudes of the German (and Swedish and Finnish) old elites can be contrasted with those of their counterparts in Britain, where the aristocracy and bourgeoisie may have paid more attention to the demands of the (numerically fewer) socialists as a result of the sovereign status of Parliament in the political system in order to prevent a rise in electoral support for the Labour Party, a common call for all conservatives. In the German polity, where the Reichstag did not play a decisive role in the political system and bureaucracy dominated, it was easier for the aristocracy and bourgeoisie just to disregard the socialists,[172] even though counter-measures were also taken there. The political influence of the Reichstag was, in any case, not

---

168 Pohl 2002, 6; Bollmeyer 2007, 60–1; Ullrich 2010, 161–5.
169 Seils 2011, 68–9.
170 Bollmeyer 2007, 67; Seils 2011, 70; Dahlmann 2014, 44.
171 Berger 1994, 41; Seils 2011, 58–9; Gerwarth & Horne 2013, 67–8.
172 Seils 2011, 21.

increased or the chancellor made more accountable to it before or during the war.[173] This more authoritarian, non-parliamentary political tradition is also reflected in the fact that while in Britain the civil government retained supremacy over the armed forces in wartime, no clear supremacy over, or even parliamentary supervision of, the armed forces existed even in peacetime Germany. The majority of the Reichstag once called for a vote of no confidence in the government of Theobald von Bethmann Hollweg concerning the way in which army matters were handled, but the Chancellor did not resign.[174] This situation differs particularly from British conceptions of parliamentary government. The only pre-war innovation strengthening the nominal importance of the German parliament was the introduction of the right of interpellation in 1912,[175] which activated parliamentary debate to some extent.

The older hypothesis of a silent process of parliamentarisation in German politics before the First World War has been questioned in more recent research. While some scholars continue to find evidence of such a development (see sections 4.2 and 6.2), others have concluded that support for a stronger political role for the Reichstag remained limited. The left-liberals supported parliamentarisation but they, too, were unwilling to join the pre-war demands of the Social Democrats for a reform that would change the constitutional monarchy into parliamentary government. For many German liberals, a 'truly' constitutional government implied that the emperor chose the chancellor after taking the will of the parliament into consideration. A proposal to make the chancellor accountable to the parliament was consequently rejected by the centre and right parties. Illustrative of the attitudes of these parties is a tendency within not only the Conservatives but also the Zentrumspartei (Catholic Centre) and the National-Liberals to use the term *Parlamentsherrschaft*[176] (parliamentary supremacy) in parliamentary debates with a highly negative connotation. All these groups and constitutional lawyers were reluctant to reject constitutional monarchy (which was widely admired outside Germany) and wanted especially to prevent any development towards a parliamentarism of the abhorred French or British types. In pre-war Germany, the socialists were left practically alone with their demands for constitutional changes.[177] Some of them were strongly pro-parliamentary and were suspected of aiming at a British or French type of parliamentarism. On the other hand, for many socialists parliamentarism provided only the means to bring about reform and perhaps even revolution rather than any ultimate goal in its own right.[178]

The attitudes of the German parties of the centre differed not only from those of most British Liberals but also from the stances of the Swedish

---

173   Dahlmann 2014, 44.
174   Seils 2011, 73; Dahlmann 2014, 44.
175   Seils 2011, 73.
176   A very similar term was repeatedly used by the Finnish conservative Kaarle Rantakari in 1917. See section 3.4.5.
177   Kühne 2005, 314; Seils 2011, 72; Biefang & Schulz 2016, 69.
178   Hewitson 2001, 754, 776; Biefang & Schulz 2016, 9.

and Finnish centre groups. In Sweden, the Liberals and Social Democrats cooperated consistently for years to extend suffrage and to parliamentarise government. In Finland, the Social Democrats and the majority of the liberals and the centrist Agrarian League turned out to be republicans in their constitutional views but became divided in their understandings of the proper extent of parliamentarism during 1917. In Germany, the Social Democrats and the liberals voiced some related constitutional reform demands from spring 1917 onwards, and some of the parties would cooperate in the Weimar Coalition, but not consistently or whole-heartedly in the case of the Catholic Centre and many right-liberals. Unifying features between Germany, Sweden and Finland include the consistent Social Democratic call for the introduction of parliamentary government (with the exception of the Finnish Social Democrats, who turned to anti-parliamentary discourse in November 1917 and to extra-parliamentary violence in January 1918) and the fear of the dominance of the parliament, which was very strong among the monarchist right in all countries. As we shall see, the links between the groups in each of the two ideological camps justify the claim that there existed two, even three, competing transnational ideological networks in this period.

The outbreak of the First World War in early August 1914 was not a matter for the parliament in Germany: war and peace remained for the emperor to decide. The Reichstag never debated the reasons for Germany's entry into the war; it rather debated loans needed to finance the war.[179] Nevertheless the events of August 1914 constituted a watershed in domestic politics: before the outbreak of the war, the German population had been divided by class, regional and denominational conflicts, but after the general mobilisation such divisions mostly went underground, and the population was taken over by the feeling of being of a united 'community of the people' *(Volksgemeinschaft,* discussed in section 7.2) engaged in a common battle. A party truce, known as the *Burgfrieden,* between the political parties and within the Reichstag was proclaimed. While the political debate in pre-war Germany had been shaped to some extent by calls for constitutional reforms and disagreements over the proper nature of the polity, such issues were now pushed aside.[180] The Kaiser welcomed the members of all political parties but the Social Democrats to his palace, symbolically convening a national community inspired by patriotism.[181] However, the exclusion of the Social Democrats is evidence of the continuing ideological divisions, which would not be removed by the war or even by the peace and the construction of a new polity after it.

Nevertheless, even the excluded socialists and those liberals who had been calling for the parliamentarisation of government, the introduction of female suffrage and the abolition of the three-class franchise in Prussia aligned themselves in August 1914 with the prevailing mood of support for the war effort. The *Burgfrieden* received concrete expression in the Reichstag

---

179 Seils 2011, 138.
180 Llanque 2000, 12.
181 Seils 2011, 132–5.

session of 4 August 1914, when Hugo Haase, the parliamentary party leader of the Social Democrats and ideologically inclined to the left, declared the support of the Social Democrat MPs for the defence of the fatherland against 'Russian despotism'.[182] This 'spirit of 1914' caused some reformists to deplore the party truce, claiming that it was tantamount to 'waging war for the Prussian franchise'.[183]

The Reichstag approved the loans for financing the war by an overwhelming majority. In practice, it transferred much of its limited constitutional rights to the Bundesrat, which was controlled by the princes of the German regional states. The Bundesrat was empowered to issue emergency laws that were binding on all levels of civil government. The Reichstag no longer held public plenaries, and a new election could not be expected as long as the war continued. Even though it retained its parliamentary control in principle, the Reichstag only met twice a year to approve war credits and did not veto any of the over 800 orders issued by the upper house during the war.[184] Despite restrictions, some parliamentary publicity continued to be maintained by the press, and this news was also followed in countries such as Britain, Sweden and Finland; this maintained transnational links in political debate across the front lines of the war.

Civil politics tended to become brushed aside in the German wartime system. Not even the chancellor had much say concerning the conduct of the war as political power was to a great extent taken out of the hands of the civil government and transferred to the General Headquarters. The leaders of the army, in late 1916 Paul von Hindenburg and Erich Ludendorff, exclusively coordinated the military effort. However, there did emerge some pressure for the government to take over the command of the military in 1916. Chancellor Bethmann Hollweg was more prepared than the General Headquarters to negotiate with the Entente, but he was unable to prevent the launching of total submarine warfare in early January 1917 – a measure that was predicted to provoke the United States into joining the war.[185] Outside Germany, such military leadership would be interpreted either as a demonstration of the admirable strength of the Prussian system or as a further aspect of its boundless militarism.

As a result of the deliberate transition of power to other political, or rather military, institutions, the Reichstag was a peripheral arena during the first half of the war. However, its importance began to rise as a result of two factors: Firstly, the strengthening involvement of the German state in social policies called for legislation to be passed by the Reichstag. Secondly, the visibility of the Reichstag in the public sphere continued to increase,[186] which gave the impression that the institution was nevertheless actively involved in the political process. Its formal budgetary power was retained. In December 1916, the originally planned slogan *Dem deutschen Volke* (To

---

182 See Huber (ed.) 1990, 138. Becker 2014, 27; Dahlmann 2014, 45.
183 Wehler 2003, 45.
184 Chickering 2004, 34; Dahlmann 2014, 45.
185 Becker 2014, 27; Leonhard 2014, 207.
186 Bollmeyer 2007, 60.

the German People) was added to the pediment of the Reichstag building.[187] All these suggested to the public that the Reichstag really mattered.

Nor was the constitutional debate at a complete standstill. Already in autumn 1914, the left had begun to call for a constitutional reform that would increase governmental responsibility and improve the representation of the people. Eduard David of the SPD then suggested that the working class deserved reforms as compensation for its wholehearted support for the war effort[188] – a point heard at some stage in most European combatant countries. Some Social Democrats protested outspokenly from June 1915 onwards: Eduard Bernstein, Hugo Haase and Karl Kautsky questioned the war goals of the government as irreconcilable with a defensive war. Little by little this peace opposition within the Social Democrats grew from 15 to 40 per cent of the parliamentary group. Some, like Georg Ledebour, also sympathised with the radical Zimmerwald International, which convened in Switzerland in September 1915. In this meeting of radicals, V. I. Lenin advocated turning the inter-state war into an international revolution and civil war for the rights of the oppressed.[189] He did not initially find many supporters, but these began to emerge in all the countries studied here during the years that followed.

Discursively, the political role of the people was being activated in Germany. Reinhart Koselleck has pointed at how *Volk* tended by 1918 to become an agreeable and uniting concept for all parties independently of their otherwise conflicting ideologies reflected by concepts such as 'fatherland' and 'patriotism', 'nation' and 'democracy' or 'social democracy', 'revolutionary masses' and 'international'.[190] According to Heiko Bollmeyer, *Volk* continued to have specific connotations in Reichstag debates during the war. It was not so much connected with the term 'nation', which for many Germans had a foreign, French, connotation. The MPs rather spoke about 'the German people' (*das deutsches Volk*) in the sense of a national fellowship or collective community united by a common language and cultural ties.[191] In the German (and likewise the Swedish and Finnish) debates on the constitution, *das Volk* (and correspondingly *folket* and *kansa* respectively) was a dominant term. Speakers of all political groups referred to *das Volk* to legitimise their goals or delegitimise political demands made by other politicians. Many speakers also liked to refer to 'our people' (*unseres Volk*).[192] While this concentration on the unity of the political and the ethnic, linguistic and cultural community may appear as a specifically German phenomenon when compared with French and British slightly more pluralistic concepts of the nation and the people, it does find resemblances in other northern European states, including Sweden and Finland. And in the wartime political discourse, even some British references to a unified people were not so different from it.

187   Ullrich 2010, 161–5.
188   Dahlmann 2014, 45.
189   Leonhard 2014, 385–6.
190   Koselleck 1992, 396.
191   Bollmeyer 2007, 74–8.
192   Bollmeyer 2007, 74–5.

As long as the German political parties believed in victory and approved the war finances, emphasising the unity of *das Volk*, Chancellor Bethmann Hollweg and the General Staff had nothing to fear from the Reichstag. However, this wartime consensus was fragile and deteriorated from 1916 onwards as a result of the continuing unsuccessful war effort. By the end of that year, a fundamental conflict between the parliament and the government was emerging. There were general strikes in Berlin, Bremen and Stuttgart after Karl Liebknecht, a radical socialist leader, had been convicted and sent to prison in June 1916. Continuous food shortages also led to a weakening fighting spirit throughout the population.[193]

With the people's motivation for waging the war apparently waning, the relationship between the Reichstag and the government also became more confrontational as liberals and Social Democrats started to cooperate in challenging the executive power. In October 1916, they demanded more say in foreign policy decision-making. Hans Sivkovich of the Progressivists asked whether foreign policy should continue to be conducted in secret cabinet meetings or instead controlled by the elected representatives.[194] The Main Committee (Hauptausschuss) of the Reichstag was then made into a decreased plenum, which was supposed to control the running of the war.[195] The Social Democrats started to openly express their desire for a transition to a parliamentary system based on universal suffrage.[196] Noteworthy are the simultaneity of the activation of the constitutional debate in Britain and Germany and the initiation of their reform processes well before the external impulses created by the Russian Revolution and the American entry into the war. Further national and transnationally linked disputes would follow during the first half of 1917. In the sections on Germany they will be analysed in a comparative context, Germany being contrasted with not only Britain but also Sweden and Finland.

2.3 Prolonged disputes on suffrage and parliamentary government in Sweden

The joint interest of the Social Democratic Labour Party (SAP) and the Liberals in demands for universal suffrage, the parliamentarisation of government and the redefinition of the relationship between the two chambers of the parliament was characteristic of early twentieth-century Swedish domestic politics. In all these questions they had The Right (*Högern*) as their common opponent.[197] The Social Democratic Labour Party, established in 1889 and closely linked to the trade unions, had retained its original socialist programme, but in practice it turned under the leadership of Hjalmar Branting, the first MP of the party, towards reformist, revisionist,

---

193   Seils 2011, 189.
194   Bollmeyer 2007, 93–4.
195   Brandt 1998, 174.
196   Botzenhart 1993, 132.
197   Nilsson 2004.

non-revolutionary and parliamentary strategies supportive of the state. In this respect, it resembled its German and even its British counterparts rather than its Finnish sister party. The party enjoyed growing support among workers and less affluent people more generally. It campaigned especially for universal suffrage to advance reforms and was ready to cooperate with reformist bourgeois parties for that purpose.[198] From the 1890s onwards the Social Democrats began to increasingly aim at democracy in a representative form. Yet Jussi Kurunmäki and Anna Friberg have shown that only the First World War led to a breakthrough of the rhetoric of democracy in the Swedish parliament,[199] which suggests dependence on transnational influences from Germany and the Entente also in this respect.

The Swedish Liberals, ready to cooperate with the Social Democrats despite the fact that the parties competed for some of the electorate, found most of their supporters among the middle class, the free churches, the temperance movement and much of the urban press. The Right, supported by the traditional elite – much like the British Conservatives, the Prussian right and the Finnish Party and Swedish Peoples' Party in Finland combined – consistently opposed extensions of suffrage as irreconcilable with the established political system and its party interests. It has been argued, however, that their leader Arvid Lindman would prevent more conservative forces within the party from continuing to block reforms, the impetus for which gained speed in Sweden, too, in the immediate aftermath of the First World War – though, as we shall see, this was to a greater extent than generally recognised due to external factors related to the German defeat in the war. Because The Right had previously been ready to make only very limited concessions on the extension of suffrage, the Social Democrats had twice used a general strike to advance reform. The failure of these attempts and the cooperative and parliamentary line of the Social Democratic leaders, not unlike that of their counterparts in Germany, led to a division of the Swedish labour movement into moderates and radicals, the more leftist socialists being increasingly ready for a revolution to achieve immediate democratisation and transition to a republican constitution. The war, too, strengthened the division into the left and the right within the Swedish Social Democrats. Zeth Höglund of the leftists attended the Zimmerwald conference in 1915, and the radicals socialised with Russian revolutionaries staying in Stockholm, including the famous Alexandra Kollontai, who later had close contacts with Finnish radical socialists as well. The left-socialist press turned to unashamedly revolutionary, even Bolshevik, language at times, emphasising the class struggle and predicting the outbreak of a proletarian revolution.[200] In this respect, far-left discourse in Sweden resembled that of mainstream Social Democracy in Finland. At the same time, according to Aleksander Kan, not only the radicals but

198 Hentilä 1979, 303–6; Molin 1992, xviii.
199 Kurunmäki 2008; Friberg 2012, 82–3.
200 Birgersson, Hadenius, Molin & Wieslander 1984, 87–9; Molin 1992, xxi; Kan 1999b, 97; Hadenius 2008, 26–8, 30–3, 35. For the major arguments of the debate on universal suffrage during the preceding twenty years, see Möller 2007, 51–61.

also the moderate Swedish Majority Social Democrats remained better connected with Russian socialists than any other socialists outside Russia – including the Finnish socialists. They were becoming increasingly divided ideologically, with the radical Swedish far-left supporting the Bolsheviks and the Finnish Reds, the mainstream Swedish party associating itself with the opponents of such radical groups.[201]

Much as in Finland, where universal suffrage had been implemented in 1906 but social reforms mostly postponed, revolutionary radicalism arose among the Swedish far left as a reaction to reform proposals being repeatedly voted down by the parliament and as a result of inspiration from German and Russian revolutionary radicalism.[202] The degree of radicalisation and ideological confrontation in parliamentary debate remained lower in Sweden than in Finland, however. Ever since 1911, the Majority Social Democrats had successfully cooperated with reformist bourgeois forces to advance their goals, distancing themselves from Kautskyist doctrines other than the expectation that the revolution would arrive once the time was ripe.[203] Their language was socialist, but moderately so.

In 1909, Arvid Lindman's conservative government had given in to demands for a limited suffrage reform that introduced universal male suffrage and proportional representation for the lower chamber but kept the nomination of the upper chamber by regional assemblies elected through regulated suffrage with forty categories of voters. The point of the reformist conservatives had been to retain the political influence of the conservatives by conserving this electoral system and the old constitution, although some hardliners had been ready for extra-parliamentary action to oppose compromises,[204] rather as in Britain at that time. The Liberals, who had often regarded the British parliamentary system as their model, had failed to carry out such a reform even though they had planned to introduce universal suffrage and cut the power of the upper chamber.[205] The rightist leaders, though they opposed democratic suffrage and admired the political system of Williamite Germany, possibly already understood in 1909 that universal suffrage would need to be introduced sooner or later. However, as the analysis that follows will show, their anti-reformist discourse in the parliament continued almost unchanged until late 1918. In the established system of suffrage based on taxation, the number of the enfranchised was growing automatically thanks to increased incomes among large sectors of the population and high inflation – a point often made by conservative circles. Aware of the long-term risks of the exclusion of the working class from politics, the leaders of The Right have been viewed as having looked for ways to abolish limitations on suffrage in a controlled way that would benefit their party, just as in Britain. This would explain their readiness for proportional representation: it would hinder the rise of radicalism.

201   Kan 2005.
202   Möller 2007, 55.
203   Hentilä 1979, 306–8.
204   Molin 1992, xix; Nilsson 2004, 79.
205   Molin 1992, xx; Stjernquist 1993, 138.

Universal suffrage had applied to men over 24 in the election for the Second Chamber since 1909, though legislation continued to limit the right to vote in many ways. Different rules for the First Chamber ensured the continuity of the dominance of the conservatives there, The Right gaining 60 per cent of seats as opposed to only 25 per cent in the Second Chamber, the composition of which already reflected the election results reasonably well and guaranteed the left (including the Liberals in the case of Sweden) a majority there. A modest step towards parliamentarism had also been taken before the war when a Liberal government headed by Karl Staaff had been nominated against the express wishes of King Gustaf V, an obdurate critic of parliamentarism.[206]

The reform of 1909 had obviously been a partial one, and confrontations between the left and right over electoral reform continued until the outbreak of the war. The monarchy, army and administration all felt themselves threatened by the demands of the left, very much as in Germany. As the international situation became tenser, electoral reforms appeared less timely, with the bourgeois parties focusing on questions of defence. In February 1914, the King addressed a peasant demonstration in a speech authored by rightist army officers and urged the government to strengthen the army, thereby challenging the policy of the current ministry. This extra-parliamentary action provoked a demonstration by the workers, calling for 'democratic reforms' so that the will of the Swedish people would be realised.[207] Hjalmar Branting defined democracy in this context (anachronistically) as the central element of the Swedish tradition of representative government, which suggests a connection to national historiographical debates and not merely to wartime transnational ones. Disagreement on defence spending developed into a constitutional conflict on parliamentarism when the left questioned the legitimacy of the monarchical intervention. This confrontation further led to the resignation of Staaff's ministry,[208] a demonstration of the continuing force of non-parliamentary practices.

An extraordinary election of the First Chamber was held in March 1914 to settle the dispute, which led to the parties confronting each other on constitutional issues and defence spending. The Right won seats, but the Social Democrats also made progress despite some intra-party disagreement on parliamentary cooperation with the bourgeoisie. The election of the Second Chamber in September 1914, when much of Europe was already at war, confirmed this result, but no government with a clear parliamentary majority was nominated. Sweden was governed until 1917 by Hjalmar Hammarskjöld's rightist ministry, which consisted of civil servants and lacked party backing, The Right being unwilling to get more directly engaged in governing the country, and the left not wishing to support an openly rightist government. During the first three years of the world war, Sweden thus continued to be governed in traditional ways, emphasising the role of the monarch and keeping delicate matters secret, in the spirit of

---

206   Molin 1992, xx; Möller 2007, 54–5, 57, 59, 63–4, 72; Hadenius 2008, 31, 34.
207   von Sydow 1997, 108; Möller 2007, 65; Hadenius 2008, 35–7.
208   von Sydow 1997, 109; Möller 2007, 66; Ihalainen 2015.

the Instrument of Government of 1809 and not unlike the contemporary German constitutional monarchy. As Rudolf Kjellén, a political scientist and active Rightist parliamentarian put it, 'the true will of the people' was best interpreted by an autocratic ruler who remained in close symbiosis with his people. After the election of autumn 1917, however, the king would be forced to nominate a government supported by a parliamentary majority, which meant the rejection of the monarchical interpretation of the old constitution in favour of the parliamentarisation of government.[209]

Despite the seeming consensus within the Swedish political elite during the war, there were disagreements on foreign policy, especially after 1916, when a quick German victory appeared increasingly unlikely. The Prime Minister and the King were known to sympathise with German policies, and Rightist intellectuals such as Carl Hallendorf, Karl Hildebrand, Rudolf Kjellén and many others insisted that Sweden should support the Germanic cultural battle against the Slavic peoples in the east and reject American, British and French propaganda concerning democratisation and parliamentarism. The increasingly Anglophile Social Democrats and Liberals, by contrast, challenged the pro-German trade policies of the Swedish ministry, denounced the possibility of Sweden allying itself with Germany and had nothing against exploring the possibilities offered by the democratic and parliamentary ideals of the West, seeing them as analogical with native traditions of representation.[210] The constitutional division of the warring parties would consequently have a major transnational impact in Sweden towards the end of the war, as we shall see.

The constitutional debates of the 1910s nominally concerned interpretations of the Instrument of Government of 1809 and the extent of the royal prerogative. Social changes seemed to have undermined much of the basis of this constitution. However, republican views were mainly limited to the Social Democrats, who had made the abolition of the monarchy a party goal in 1911. Radicals such as Carl Lindhagen had put forward a motion for a republican constitution in 1912 and 1914, but the party leader Hjalmar Branting opposed such changes as long as the king did not openly violate the spirit of the constitution: the monarchy would die out anyway once universal suffrage was achieved.[211] The Social Democratic Party could not agree on the concept of democracy either: the majority considered universal suffrage, not a revolution, the best way to achieve democracy, which led in practice to the exclusion of the revolutionaries from the party. In spring 1917, leftist Social Democrats, inspired further by the ongoing Russian Revolution, broke away

---

209   von Sydow 1997, 113–15; Möller 2007, 67; Hadenius 2008, 38–9, 41.
210   von Sydow 1997, 114–15; Nilsson 2004, 144–5; Möller 2007, 69–70; Brandt 2008, 167–8. A liberal school of political scientists, exemplified by Fredrik Lagerroth, had since the mid-1910s tried to prove the existence of a development towards parliamentary democracy in Swedish history parallel to the British one. This led to tendentious readings of the history of the Diets of the Age of Liberty and Swedish parliamentary history in general. See Ihalainen 2010, Tikka & Karonen 2014 and Ihalainen 2015 on the related debates.
211   Möller 2007, 68; *Tvåkammarriksdagen* 1985–1996, vol. 5, 238.

from the mainstream Social Democrats,[212] an action that in hindsight can be seen as facilitating evolutionary political development in Sweden.

The Swedish constitution, though in principle still based on the Instrument of Government of 1809, had experienced major transformations during the two first decades of the twentieth-century. In principle, the monarch alone continued to make decisions on state affairs. In practice, however, monarchical influence had varied depending on the ruler. Developments towards parliamentarism had been consistently opposed by the monarchs, and hence Sweden was still neither a democracy nor a parliamentary government at the beginning of 1917. The government had nevertheless become more dependent on the parliament. It had been united by party political confrontations between the Liberals and The Right as well as by friction between the Liberals and the King. At the same time, the prevailing electoral and parliamentary system made reforms hard to carry out as this would have required the agreement of both chambers. In practice, the First Chamber, with its more united conservative opinion, continued to exert its dominance with regard to reform issues. But the growth of the working class was challenging the constitution as the number of voters grew as a result of the tax limits for suffrage remaining unchanged despite increases in incomes. In 1907–9, universal suffrage for men had been introduced in the election of the Second Chamber, while the election of the First Chamber had been reformed to the extent that no more than forty votes could henceforth be awarded to a single voter. Proportional representation had also been adopted in all elections. Despite such minor reforms, to contemporary leftists, the Swedish system appeared old-fashioned, resembling that of Prussia, and in need of an immediate revision.[213] The fate of such a reform would turn out to be very dependent on the course of international affairs – and events in at least Russia, Germany and Finland as well. In the sections on Sweden we shall explore the complexities of the reform debates in wartime comparative and transnational contexts.

2.4 Finland – a grand duchy of the Russian Empire with exceptionally broad suffrage but no parliamentary government

The Finnish transition to more democratic and parliamentary government is of particular interest in an international comparison in that the country pioneered universal suffrage for both men and women in Europe. In constitutional debates elsewhere, Finland consequently provided either encouraging or warning examples with regard to extended suffrage. However, in 1917 the country failed in the aftermath of the Russian Revolution, which offered it a chance for independence, to move peacefully over to parliamentary democracy and experienced instead the fiercest disputes on the meanings of democracy and parliamentarism. A parliamentary

---

212 Möller 2007, 68–70.
213 Nyman 1965, 8–10, 18–23; Nyman 1966, 71, 74–5; *Sveriges konstitutionella urkunder* 1999, 34–7; Rydén 2001; Möller 2007, 46, 70–3, 79.

democracy only emerged gradually after a civil war and a major turn in international affairs caused by the end of the First World War and the defeat of Germany.

In a radical parliamentary and electoral reform introduced in the context of the First Russian Revolution of 1905 – and dependent on the preceding Russian defeat in the Russo-Japanese War – the Finnish representative institution had suddenly turned from an archaic four-estate diet into a modern unicameral parliament, the Eduskunta. This new parliament was evidently inspired by the model of the Norwegian Stortinget.[214] It was also supported by a general endeavour, backed by Western intellectuals, to demonstrate the progressive potential of Finland to defend its special status within the Russian Empire. Universal suffrage including both men and women in elections for the Eduskunta (unlike those for the Imperial Duma, in which the Finnish representatives never sat) was introduced, one goal of female suffrage being simply to double the size of a small nation in the sea of peoples that made up the Russian Empire. After rapid political mobilisation, the first 19 female MPs in the history of the world were elected side by side with 181 men in the first election in 1907. The most surprising feature of the election was, however, the sudden rise of the Social Democrats to become the largest socialist group in any parliament with their 80 seats.

By 1917 the country already had 10 years of experience of the new unicameral parliament, which had been elected with great expectations for reform but had, under renewed Russian restrictions on Finnish autonomy, failed to deliver what many voters were hoping for. Many of the leading politicians in 1917 had been members of the Parliamentary Reform Committee in 1906. The conservative Swedish People's Party had been represented by Emil Schybergson and R. A. Wrede, the conservative but social reformist Finnish Party by J. K. Paasikivi, the liberal Young Finns by E. N. Setälä, K. J. Ståhlberg and Santeri Alkio (now the leader of the Agrarians) and the Social Democrats by Yrjö Sirola and Edvard Valpas. The Social Democrats took little part in the Reform Committee owing to their sceptical attitude towards the upper classes, who, they believed, just wanted to dilute democracy. They had spoken for a national constituent assembly and striven for a political system dominated by the parliament – both of these goals were central among the Social Democrats' demands in 1917 as well. Edvard Valpas had begun to build connections with the Russian Social Democrats, whose revolutionary ideas and potential takeover in Russia encouraged reformist demands and feelings of dependence on Russian developments in Finland, but whose anarchism was foreign to most Finnish socialists who were conscious of differences between Russian and Finnish circumstances. On the Finnish non-socialist side, the liberals had already been divided in connection with the parliamentary reform into advocates of far-reaching parliamentary democracy (Ståhlberg and Alkio), on the one hand, and supporters of the traditional dualism of government (Setälä) on the other.[215] In a sense, the constitutional confrontations of 1917–19

---

214 Mylly 2006, 124, 130–2; Jyränki 2006, 22, 24.
215 Kujala 1989, 325; Mylly 2006, 104, 106, 109–10, 117, 126.

had been present since at least 1906 and were only reactivated by the new Russian Revolution.

In connection with the first parliamentary election of 1907, both the Social Democrats and Agrarians (radically anti-elitist by international standards) had challenged the traditional elite by appealing to popular antagonism towards the upper classes. This strategy provoked an interest in politics among lower-class voters, and it radicalised expressions of discontent,[216] which would lead to the corresponding radicalisation of political discourse. The lower classes had entered the Finnish parliament to an extent not seen in the other countries of comparison: their spokesmen immediately won nearly half of the seats in the Eduskunta. While in the old Estates, only ten per cent of the members, mainly those of the Peasant Estate, had had little or no or education, this group was extended to nearly half of the new MPs. This would not be quite so significant as feared by the old elite given that the powers of the parliament remained strictly curtailed: the Russians never recognised any sovereignty of the Finnish parliament; new legislation could only be adopted if it was promulgated by the Tsar as the Grand Duke of Finland; the parliament could be dissolved by the Tsar at any time; strong provisions for minority protection in constitutional issues made postponements easy; no ministerial responsibility to the parliament was established; and much of the elite remained critical of a quarrelling and class-based parliament. As a result of its failure to implement reforms, the legitimacy of the Eduskunta deteriorated rapidly in the eyes of the public, and voting rates declined. The Eduskunta served rather as a forum for free debate on national affairs,[217] a lot like the Reichstag in Germany. Since no ministry could be formed by the parliamentarians, they did not see any reason for compromise, and this led to heated ideological confrontations in parliamentary debates, which in turn were one-sidedly reported and commented on in the different party newspapers.

The first sessions of the Eduskunta already saw verbally violent plenary debates, in which party conflicts were brought into the open. No working parliamentary majority could be formed. The political weakness of the parliament was embodied in the unlimited power of the tsar to dissolve it, and repeated elections diminished the initial trust in the parliament as an organ that represented the people. Major differences in understandings of the aims and methods of parliamentary work also remained evident. The Social Democrats rejected 'bourgeois' and elitist conventions of parliamentary speaking and behaviour as limiting their freedom of action. They continued to agitate using methods they liked and addressing the reading public rather than the chamber, many of the MPs being editors themselves. Edvard Valpas, for instance, pointed to August Bebel of the German Social Democrats as his model because of the latter's readiness to attack the values of bourgeois society.[218] Valpas, who was in principle in favour of parliamentary methods,

---

216   Mylly 2006, 259.
217   Haapala 1995, 231; Jyränki 2006, 21, 24; Tikka & Karonen 2014, 229–30.
218   Soikkanen 1975, 126, 128; Haapala 1995, 24; Kujala 1989, 325; Liikanen 2003, 299; Pekonen 2014, 109–10, 301. Valpas would also use the German Reichstag as a model in debates in 1917.

recommended the use of interjections during debates, something he discovered in the records of foreign parliaments.[219] Noteworthy here are this transnational adoption of procedural practices by social democratic parliamentarians and shared understandings of the parliament as a means of advancing reform or revolution rather than as a goal itself.

Finland remained part of the Russian Empire until the Bolshevik Revolution of late 1917. The eighteenth-century Swedish constitutional tradition in its authoritarian Gustavian form was still observed in Finland, and this, together with the measures of the Russian administration, kept the political influence of the parliament within strict bounds. The pre-war international tensions led to the reinforcement of Russian pan-imperial policies, including a suspension of the Swedish constitution of Finland, which from the Finnish point of view represented a form of Russification. Despite both passive and active opposition to Russian limitations on Finnish autonomy, only a few activists strove for full independence before late 1917. Finland had, after all, benefited from a long peace, had access to Russian markets, experienced rapid progress in the development of Finnish-language culture as a counterbalance to the Swedish heritage, was not required to send soldiers to the Russian army, and until 1917 actually profited from the First World War in economic terms.

Despite its seemingly democratic parliament, Finland remained an essentially monarchical polity, as it had been under Sweden since medieval times; it cannot really be said to have been 'the spearhead of state democracy in Europe' merely on the basis of women's suffrage.[220] It was only with the Russification measures imposed since 1899 that anti-monarchical and republican ideas had been awakened in some circles. More generally, republican and democratic ideals only became relevant as a consequence of the fall of the Romanovs,[221] and these could hence be regarded by the right as Russian or socialist imports. Among all the political groups, Finnish political discourse remained dependent on transnational influences, the monarchists finding a model in the Prussian and Swedish constitutional monarchies, the socialists in Russian and German Social Democrats and the liberals from different directions.

The Russification measures had strengthened previously established feelings of the separateness of Finland from Russia. The special status of the country was based on the inherited Swedish constitutional, legal, political and cultural tradition, actively defended by all political groups but most openly by Swedish-speaking constitutionalists, who were ready for passive resistance to Russification, and more cautiously by the conservative Finnish Party, which preferred appeasement.[222] While for the Svecomans (members of a nationalist movement of Swedish-speakers in Finland) connections with Sweden were important in order to maintain the Scandinavian cultural heritage as a counterweight to the Russian administrative practices, the Old

219   Pekonen 2014, 222–3.
220   Sulkunen, Nevala-Nurmi & Markkola 2009, 1.
221   Vares 1998, 38–46.
222   Pekonen 2014, 60.

Finns (the party of the Fennomans, a group that represented a corresponding Finnish nationalist ideology) tended to see the union with Russia as a means to advance Finnish-speaking culture in relation to Swedish language and culture.[223] Their ideological inspiration originated from German national romanticism rather than from Sweden. At the same time, the Fennomans were sceptical about the application of foreign models to Finland as they believed that the country should rather endeavour to reach a higher cultural level on its own. The liberal Young Finns, by contrast, preferred to look to other European countries (including France and Britain) to find instances of democratic reform.[224] What united the Old Finns and the Young Finns was an emphasis on procedure as an essential element of parliamentary politics, especially under universal suffrage.[225] The parliament should be seen as an honourable institution based on rules in the spirit of the Swedish tradition of constitutionalism and legalism. The Finnish-speaking bourgeoisie shared with the Swedish People's Party an understanding of the parliament as a forum where the common good and traditions of the nation could be discussed and defended[226] and where the observance of rules of procedure supported the legitimacy of policy-making. This legalistic attitude, together with the idealisation of Germany as an advanced nation, explains to a great extent the formation of a united bourgeois front in 1917 despite social differences and disagreements on language policies.

As for the Social Democrats, their ideological inspiration originated likewise from German-speaking countries. In principle, they prioritised parliamentary politics in the spirit of 'Western' social democracy, which distinguished them initially from the Russian revolutionaries.[227] Even though the party manifesto of 1903 emphasised the need of the proletariat to be aware of class contrasts, to avoid cooperation with bourgeois parties and to fight internationally against capitalism,[228] it was moderate in comparison with the programme of the Austrian Social Democrats, approved by Karl Kautsky, a leading German theorist of the socialist movement. According to Kautsky, the proletariat should try to take over political power by winning a parliamentary majority and then declare a socialist revolution aiming at democracy.[229] The manifesto of the Finnish Social Democrats made no mention of democracy and implied the sovereignty of the people only by emphasising popular representation through the parliament. It rather viewed the workers as the proper rulers.[230]

223 Pulkkinen 1989, 114–15.
224 Pekonen 2014, 60–1, 180.
225 Pekonen 2014, 110.
226 Pekonen 2014, 136, 177.
227 Kirby 1976, 100, 109–10; Kirby 1986a, 132; Haapala & Tikka 2013, 110; Borisova & Siro 2014, 89.
228 *Sosialidemokraattisen puolueen ohjelma*, 1903.
229 Kautsky 1907, 151–2; Gronow 1986, 232; Rinta-Tassi 1986, 19, 21; Kettunen 1986, 79–80, argues that Kautskyist socialism that just waited for a revolution was sometimes used to motivate the political activities of the Finnish labour movement after 1906; Häupel 1993, 158, 216–17.
230 Hyvärinen 2003, 86; Liikanen 2003, 298–9.

According to the Kautskyist deterministic conception of history, the transition to socialism would be unavoidable. While waiting for this transition, the Social Democrats could participate in parliamentary work – despite the obvious impotence of the Finnish representative institution – provided that they emphasised continuing the class struggle, used the parliament as a forum for agitation and maintained a distance from the bourgeois parties. At the same time, the party was creating a class-conscious mass movement, and the parliamentary election of 1916 was productive in this respect as the number of socialist MPs rose from 80 to 103 out of 200. Unlike most Social Democratic parties, Bernsteinian revisionism or 'minister-socialism' had no place in this party, which did not hesitate to proclaim militant class hatred to win votes. A willingness to engage in extra-parliamentary activities was also present: the Red Guards (a paramilitary force that later constituted the Red army in the Finnish Civil War) had already become active in some localities in the aftermath of the first Russian Revolution,[231] so it was nothing new in 1917.

At first, for Finnish socialists revolution was a concept that mainly concerned a new revolution in Russia, although after 1905 Otto Wille Kuusinen could already envision revolutionary developments in Finland, too, so that 'the rule by the people in the state' would be realised. In 1911, the party agreed on the goal of seizing political power from the bourgeoisie and, together with the workers of the other capitalist countries, realising 'the revolutionary goal of social democracy to end all class power and exploitation'.[232] This programme was to be applied in the constitutional confrontations of 1917, inspired by the radicalising revolutionary discourses of the time.

The reform demands of the party were radical, in response to grass-roots activism. Jari Ehrnrooth, who has analysed the discursive struggles within the pre-war Social Democratic movement, has challenged previous interpretations of the history of the Finnish labour movement which fail to explain why the Social Democrats rejected their parliamentary strategy in favour of violence against a parliamentary majority.[233] The Kautskyist concept of revolution as unavoidable when the time was ripe may have been dominant in printed texts and in agitator training, but Ehrnrooth has shown that at the micro-level such orthodox Marxism tended to be rejected, under the pressure of a people who wished to hear more radical talk. The grass-roots level was not so interested in the parliament as a medium of revolutionary reform, nor did it see anything procedurally or historically wrong in extra-parliamentary activism as a reaction to experienced or imagined injustices.[234] In the countryside, the revolution was expected to come from Russia and to be realised in Finland through a general strike.

---

231 Lindman 1968, 9; Upton 1970, 9; Soikkanen 1975, 160; Kirby 1976, 100; Kirby 1986, 139, 141; Soikkanen 1990, 84; Alapuro 2003, 537.
232 Ehrnrooth 1992, 84; Alapuro 2003, 536–8.
233 Also Liikanen 1993, 578, who criticises Ehrnrooth for emphasising 'archaic hate' and neglecting the organised nature of the Finnish labour movement.
234 Ehrnrooth 1992, 23–4, 40, 120–3, 486–8.

Such views may have been rejected by the party leaders and many members of the parliamentary group,[235] but they nevertheless influenced them in the revolutionary atmosphere of 1917. Discourses of class hatred and revenge arising from everyday experiences and the obvious inefficiency of the parliament as an institution of reform flourished.[236] They were supported by the notion of the Finnish bourgeoisie cooperating with the tsarist government to stop socialism, by wartime contacts to Russian revolutionary workers and soldiers[237] and also by the party press which (actually in the case of all parties) translated Russian revolutionary speeches word for word. The radicalisation of the Social Democratic parliamentary discourse in 1917 was evidently influenced by micro-level policy discourses that were familiar to the party elite and were shared and accelerated rather than confined by them in the revolutionary atmosphere of that year, with further inspiration coming from the Russian Bolshevik revolutionaries.[238] Revolutionary experiences made the MPs talk in ways that sounded to their non-socialist audiences as Bolshevism.

Confrontations with the bourgeois parties over constitutional issues also had a long history. Kautskyist ideas included parliamentary sovereignty, the principle of majority rule, the notion of the representatives being bound to the mass of the people and the party as delegates and an understanding of universal suffrage as the means to reform society. The primary duty of every Social Democratic MP was thus to advance the interests of the working class rather than some unspecific common good, and certainly not bourgeois interests. The parliament was a site in which the will of the majority of the people was realised by voting: it 'put power in the hands of the people'. When the pace of reform proved modest as a result of the lack of parliamentary government, the use of minority provisions and the upper-chamber-like Grand Committee as an 'organ of obstruction' employed by the non-socialist parties and the imperial veto, the Social Democrats became increasingly critical of parliament as an institution of betrayal. They tended to conclude that universal suffrage with its limitations and majority rule were insufficient in advancing the cause of the workers in comparison with the revolutionary activities of 1905–6. Revisionist and parliamentary ideas became overshadowed by those of the class struggle and class hatred, particularly as Kautsky had also provided a description of a crisis of parliamentarism that might lead to a revolution. Parliamentary deliberation was of value only insofar as it advanced the cause of the majority of the people, which for the Social Democrats was constituted by the workers or the proletariat.[239] Parliamentary procedure, too, was of secondary importance with regard to the realisation of reforms called for by the majority of the

---

235 Ehrnrooth 1992, 91–2.
236 Ehrnrooth 1992, 266, 468.
237 Upton 1970, 11–13.
238 Cf. Liikanen 1993, 579.
239 Kautsky 1906, 84; Kautsky 1918a; Upton 1970, 11; Soikkanen 1975, 157, 191; Pekonen 2014, 64, 136, 177, 180, 296.

people.²⁴⁰ According to Otto Wille Kuusinen, it had been formulated by the bourgeoisie in ways that violated democracy.²⁴¹ Indeed, one conclusion was that the entire Finnish government was undemocratic and it was hence questionable to participate in such a regime at all.²⁴²

In transnational socialist debates, the Finnish Social Democrats were relatively isolated,²⁴³ and they tended to become increasingly so during the First World War. The Finns openly rejected revisionism of the type represented by Hjalmar Branting as the underestimation of class boundaries and hence the creation of links with Scandinavian socialists. The German revisionist thinkers did not find much support in the Finnish party, either. On the other hand, nor were the anarchical methods used by the Russian revolutionaries to fight the 'backward' conditions in that country regarded as applicable to Finland, and after 1907 distance to the Russian party was maintained. The Russian socialists, for their part, had difficulties in understanding the parliamentary dimension of the Finnish party, while the notion of the separate statehood of Finland united the parties. Contacts with Russian socialists were based mainly on the activities of a few Finnish Bolsheviks and on personal encounters with revolutionaries in Petrograd and Finland. These activities included helping V. I. Lenin to hide in lodgings around Helsinki and to travel through Finland in disguise. Russian revolutionaries could meet and scheme freely in Finland – including the first meeting of Lenin and Stalin in Tampere in 1905 – which enabled the formation of links between individual socialists but did not necessarily increase the Finnish socialists' understanding of Bolshevik tenets and differences between Russian socialists: they took Lenin as a social democrat among others. They also had limited contacts with the international wartime activities of German and Scandinavian Social Democrats and remained badly informed about the divisions that the war had caused among socialists in various countries. They learned about the Zimmerwald movement – constituted by the pacifist and leftist minorities of socialist parties – via Swedish leftist Social Democrats who had contacts with Swedish-speaking socialists in Finland and through the Bolsheviks. Edvard Valpas (the editor-in-chief of the party organ *Työmies*, the largest socialist newspaper in the world with up to 88,000 subscribers) read German and French socialist papers, while K. H. Wiik visited German and Swedish Social Democrats in 1915 and together with Yrjö Sirola travelled in May 1917 to Stockholm, where they met Friedrich Ebert and Eduard David of the Swedish SPD in an attempt to win support for Finnish self-determination, albeit with little success. Only the far left seemed to understand them. Hjalmar Branting criticised the Finns for their indifference to the international revolution and the war and their excessive concentration on national issues. Karl Kautsky, Zimmerwald socialists and even the far left in Sweden were annoyed about

240 Pekonen 2014, 301, 322.
241 Pekonen 2014, 276.
242 Soikkanen 1975, 122–3, 158.
243 See Hentilä 1980, 138, however.

the Finnish Social Democrats prioritising the sovereignty of the Finnish parliament over the internationalist socialist cause.[244]

It has been suggested that the Finnish socialists became increasingly Kautskyist, emphasising the class struggle and revolution.[245] In the lack of support from the German or Swedish socialists, who were mostly revisionist, the Finnish socialists, supported by the native micro-level radical tradition and dominant revolutionary discourses of the Russian type, were rather approaching the Russian Bolsheviks in their stances.[246] Kautsky would in fact soon be criticising Lenin for deviating from the original teachings of Karl Marx and Friedrich Engels with his application of the dictatorship of the proletariat, while Lenin considered Kautsky a traitor. Kautsky defended non-militant methods, including democracy as a means of building socialism and parliament freely chosen by the people as a means of controlling the government.[247]

In Finland, the sudden transnational revolutionary tide of democracy and republicanism of spring 1917 had a major effect on the political debate. It was felt particularly strongly because of the absolute majority which the Social Democratic Party had won in the election of 1916, after an anti-revisionist campaign in which the bourgeoisie had been attacked both for their alleged anti-reformism and for economic speculation that had caused food shortages.[248] The rhetoric of class hatred had been heard previously and was being intensified *before* Finland actually experienced any serious shortages. Contrasts between the malicious rich and the oppressed poor had even been emphasised in a children's book,[249] and thus such agitation fell on fertile soil. The existence of a discourse of class hatred made it easy to exaggerate physical hardships and overinterpret the malicious intentions of the political enemy, which made a difference in comparison with other countries experiencing food shortages. The debates in the Eduskunta, too, had been characterised by one-sided declarations about the supposed good of the people, deep divisions between political parties and an unwillingness to compromise.[250] Each party could carry on preaching its own truth with little risk of being held responsible as a power-holder, since there was no parliamentary government. Once responsibility was given to the parties in spring 1917, the practices and rhetoric of the impotent parliament were

---

244 Upton 1970, 9–12; Kirby 1974, 65–6, 75, 77–9; Soikkanen 1975, 148, 152, 164–8, 191, 215–16; Kirby 1976, 99–100; Kirby 1986a, 149–50; Kirby 1986b, 142–3, 165; Polvinen 1987, vol. 1, 116; Ketola 1987, 13–14, 17, 26, 44, 82, 124–8; Kujala 1989, 316–17; Soikkanen 1990, 84–5; Heikkilä 1993, 386–7; Alapuro 2003, 537; Eskola 2011, 13, 16, 18; Haapala & Tikka 2013, 110.
245 Rinta-Tassi 1986, 497; Hentilä & Hentilä 2016, 100; cf. Ehnrooth 1992 as cited above.
246 Ketola 1987, 130.
247 Kautsky 1918b, chapters 3–5, repeating his statements from 1893 and 1900; Kautsky 1919, chapter 8; Winkler 1999, 3; Hentilä 2015, 152.
248 Lindman 1968, 9; Upton 1980, 38–9. The same accusations appeared in connection with the election of 1917. Rinta-Tassi 1986, 40.
249 Kirby 1986, 162.
250 Pekonen 2014, 320.

continued, leading to political tensions caused by hate speeches getting out of hand and parliamentary government being destroyed before it was even established. The sections on Finland aim at understanding this discursive process in the particular national and international circumstances of 1917 and to evaluate its impact on the process that led to a civil war.

After this review of constitutional tensions before 1917, it is time to move on to empirical analyses of the constitutional debates between spring 1917 and summer 1919. In 1916, the legitimacy of both the political and the military leadership and the functioning of the political systems had become increasingly questioned in all four countries. Leaders had been changed in Britain, France and Germany, whereas in Russia a clash between a stubborn tsar and a divided political elite began to seem unavoidable. The people in all countries were becoming increasingly impatient about the ongoing war with the constant demands for new resources and huge human losses.[251] Measures were expected that would strengthen the say of the people at large. In spring 1917, many of the dams of restrained discontent would break, both in the great powers and in connected smaller states, to the extent that some contemporaries talked about a flood or wave of democracy. The continuing and ever more total war, a revolution producing a system change unseen since the French Revolution and the entry of the United States into the war with promises to secure democracy seemed to be changing the course of world history. These transnational impulses gave rise to a wide variety of expectations and hopes among contemporaries, including both negative and positive visions of the future of democracy and parliamentarism. Especially in spring 1917, these visions would be transnationally linked to an unprecedented extent.

---

251 Leonhard 2014, 609–10, 614.

3. The spring of democracy in 1917: The new constitutional scene created by the prolonged war, the Russian Revolution and the American intervention

3.1 Britain: The wartime situation used to force through a postponed reform

3.1.1 A CONTINUING CONSTITUTIONAL CRISIS

In Britain, the unforeseen total war had cooled down the heated constitutional dispute caused by the establishment of lower house sovereignty with the Parliament Act of 1911 and by the Irish Home Rule Bill of 1914. The severity of the confrontation had even led the Conservative critics of the Liberal government to use expressions like 'a civil war' to describe it and to challenge the authority of Parliament.[252] The outbreak of the First World War and the consequent party truce had saved the country from a deepening constitutional crisis, but it had left certain underlying constitutional disagreements unsolved, including a long-running debate on women's suffrage.

During the war, parliamentary legislation had mainly served the purposes of the war effort. At the same time, the totality of the warfare increased awareness of the need to reform suffrage and perhaps Parliament more generally – either to strengthen popular representation and the legitimacy of Parliament or to restore the pre-reform political order. The extension of suffrage was increasingly used in patriotic speeches to engage the people in a common struggle. Universal male suffrage had come to be seen as undeniable as a result of the sacrifices of soldiers of all classes, while the contributions of women to ammunition manufacturing and other sectors of society decreased Conservative resistance to female suffrage.[253] However, Conservative political discourse continued to combine reactionary ideas with seemingly progressive ones,[254] for instance justifying women's suffrage by appealing to patriotic and Christian values rather than principles of equality. There was no full certainty about the sincerity of the Conservative conversion.

---

252 Saunders 2013b, 66, 78–9.
253 McCrillis 1998, 11; Machin 2001, 130–1, 139–42.
254 Webber 1986, 8.

The reform process had been launched by the War Cabinet in late 1916 – after a contentious parliamentary debate on the register of voters – with a call for an extraordinary inter-party Speaker's Conference. The Coalition wished for a consensual proposal on a moderate reform, and the task was given to James Lowther, the long-serving Conservative Speaker of the House of Commons. The alleged aim of Lowther's Conference, which consisted of five peers and 27 MPs representing all the major parties, was to seek an impartial solution.[255] The mandate and representativeness – and hence legitimacy – of the Conference continued to be questioned by the opponents of the reform, however. They were unhappy with the parliament that had been elected in 1910 and was responsible for destroying the position of the House of Lords in their quest for further reform. Nevertheless, the recommendations of this Conference for universal suffrage for men and the extension of franchise to married and over-30-year-old women and the redistribution of parliamentary seats, which were published on 27 January 1917, constituted a turning point in the British reform process.[256] On the other hand, schemes for proportional representation and the alternative vote system, also proposed by the Conference, were postponed and, in practice, abandoned.

This reform would seem to have made progress as a result of domestic pressures inherited from pre-war constitutional confrontations and increased by the unifying war experience. However, the British reform was also influenced by inter- and transnational developments. The decision to bring the bill to Parliament at the end of March 1917 rather than immediately or shortly after the proposals of the Conference was obviously influenced by the course of international affairs. The debate shows that British MPs, too, were transnationally connected, though more with America and the dominions than Europe. Their debates were affected by the state of war especially now that the United States – whose president Woodrow Wilson had raised 'making the world safe for democracy' into a war goal – was expected to finally join the war. Germany was increasingly criticised in Allied war propaganda for the militarism of the Prussian political system, and Russia was experiencing a supposedly democratic revolution. The first reading of the Representation of the People Bill took place in the context of these developments and recalled parallel constitutional debates in the German, Swedish and Finnish parliaments of the time, though this has gone unnoticed in British research. The debates in the Commons on 28 March and 22–23 May 1917 were in many ways parallel to suffrage debates in Sweden on 21 March, 14 and 27 April and early June 1917. On 29–30 March, the German Reichstag addressed the old question of reforming suffrage in Prussia. At the same time, Finland, which in principle already possessed a democratically elected parliament, began to debate the possibilities for a parliamentarised government.

255 McCrillis 1998, 12; White & Parker 2009, 3–4, 10. The Speaker's Conference consisted of 13 Conservative, 13 Liberal, four Irish Home Rule and four Labour MPs or peers.
256 McCrillis 1998, 13.

The Russian Revolution gave rise to some speculation in the British press, and a supportive internationalist Marxist mass meeting was held in London on 24 March.[257] However, more important for the British debates was the American entry into the war. Once the US joined in early April, democracy was increasingly claimed to be the common denominator and war goal of the Entente.[258] Pressures to democratise domestic policies in Britain increased: the country's major ally was a proclaimed democracy, and democracy was also expected to make progress in Russia, a previously autocratic ally. The British domestic political discourse on democracy was inevitably affected by these changes. The concept had been in use before, but a comparison between references to democracy in March and May 1917 on the one hand and in December 1917 and early February 1918 on the other demonstrates the effects of Wilson's propagandistic language of democracy on British conceptualisations of democracy in domestic politics. The first effects were felt in the debates in May. By the end of 1917, democracy was increasingly used in British parliamentary discourse on the reform, and the concept was politicised in domestic political battles, initially by the Irish nationalists. Ideological differences in usage would remain: the Conservatives talked about democracy mainly with a view to retaining the established order, the Liberals of the Coalition addressed the question of democracy more extensively only after ensuring their hold on power, and from 1918 onwards Labour increasingly challenged the government with calls for reform in the name of democracy.

The Representation of the People Bill was radical compared with the history of gradual cautious reform in the nineteenth century and in view of the controversies that the Parliament Act had already provoked. It was made possible by the exceptional wartime circumstances. The Liberal prime minister Lloyd George wanted to have a clear but suitably restricted and timed reform that would enable him to declare a new election at the right moment for the Coalition Liberals. On 26 March 1917, over two months

---

257 *The Herald*, 'Great Russian Rally in London', 31 March 1917. The meeting, which had been organised by George Lansbury, the editor of *The Herald*, (Cowden 1984, 11) attracted 7000 participants and adopted a resolution in which 'the true democratic forces in Russia, headed by the class-conscious proletariat struggling for its revolutionary class-aims [should] carry through the complete democratisation of the country'. *The Herald* published a call for 'the democracy of England' to demonstrate its sympathy for 'the democracy of Russia', monopolising democracy in a Marxist fashion to the proletarian cause. *The Herald* bypassed parliamentary debates on extended suffrage and rather speculated on 'a German Revolution' that would liberate the masses from 'the Prussian Junker class' ('After the Revolution', 31 March 1917). On 7 April 1917, it claimed that 'The Revolution at the Albert Hall' had been 'epoch-making: it marked a turning-point in the mood, the spirit, the activities of our country' towards 'a revolution in the political, social, and economic life of the British Commonwealth'.

258 The American military representative emphasised the view that 'the present war is one of democracy against [the] autocracy' of the Central Powers, which were seen as striking at 'the very existence of democracy and liberty'. *The Times*, 'Trotsky's Diplomacy' and 'War Aims of U.S.', 5 December 1917.

after the publication of the report and the ensuing hesitation,[259] and roughly two weeks after the outbreak of a revolution in Petrograd, the prime minister decided to proceed – at a time when other governments or parliaments were also engaged in constitutional issues. The bill was introduced by H. H. Asquith, a former prime minister who had previously opposed female suffrage and now led the Liberal opposition in Parliament, which suggests that the different Liberal factions and their Conservative allies considered the moment right and that the choice of the speaker was intended to reflect a more general change in political opinion. In press reports, Parliament was thanked for aiming to solve this old party-political controversy and a general approval of the bill was anticipated.[260] The government's proposal to introduce the bill was, after a substantial debate, approved with a clear majority (341–62). Many former opponents appeared to have become convinced by the united war effort about the necessity of universal suffrage (including women's suffrage). The party leaders had already committed themselves with the Speaker's Conference to carrying through the compromise,[261] but the debate nevertheless addressed the principles of the British constitution and deserves to be subjected to a comparative conceptual analysis.

While the proposal passed even more clearly through its second reading on 22–23 May, the debate reveals that the redefinition of parliamentary representation remained far from unproblematic. The context of the reform would change considerably during the long committee stage before the third reading, the debates of the Lords and the consideration of the Lords amendments between December 1917 and February 1918. Comparisons with the other three countries and the consideration of transnational links in what follows help us to see to what extent the British reform process and the attitudes of its participants were unique to Britain and in what respects they repeated general ideological models and were part of a broader constitutional transformation, even indeed of a transnational process of constitutional change. Let us first review the MPs' understandings of the impact of the war on the political system and then analyse the implications for democracy, popular participation and democracy.

3.1.2 Creating 'a new Britain' consensually in a time of war and revolution

The political implications of the war were strongly felt. In Britain – just as in Germany – a nation involved in total warfare was the context in which the reform was interpreted, though the interpretations differed in the former, an established parliamentary polity, from those in the latter, a constitutional monarchy where scepticism about parliamentarism prevailed. Several actively serving officers contributed to the British debates, and numerous civilians also emphasised the unique nature of the ongoing conflict and

---

259 Grigg 2003, 106.
260 *The Times*, 'Reform by Consent' and 'Electoral Reform', 29 March 1917; *The Manchester Guardian*, 'Government and Electoral Reform', 29 March 1917; 'The Coming Franchise Bill', 30 March 1917.
261 Machin 2001, 142–4.

its fundamental influences on the British polity. The war experience was generally represented as having united the national community, but the conclusions to be drawn from this varied: either the reform had been made necessary by the war, or it was considered undesirable to have a constitutional controversy at that time.[262]

The latter, opposing, view, supported by a Unionist minority, was that success in warfare should be prioritised and unrealistic aspirations for an immediate reform abandoned. Arthur Salter, an officer and a leading lawyer who had expected the backing of up to 140 Unionists but was disappointed with much more limited support, stated: 'We are standing upon the threshold of the greatest crisis of the greatest war in all history. We must win victory, if not peace, in the next few months.'[263] In his view, the survival of the nation called for a complete concentration on the war effort instead of debating for several months about a constitutional reform of secondary importance.[264] Salter recognised the redefinition of the relationship of 'the sailor and the soldier' to the state as a necessary compensation for their services,[265] and other Conservative opponents could also see enfranchising soldiers (not necessarily women) as timely in the relatively near future, but they considered the timing wrong.[266] Salter's further suggestion, which went back to the constitutional confrontations of the early 1910s, was that a crisis resembling a civil war might arise as a consequence of constitutional revisions: they might be taken by extra-parliamentary extremists (the far left rather than the ultra-Conservatives) as 'the trumpet of domestic war'.[267] Henry Craik (Scottish Unionist), the MP for Glasgow and Aberdeen Universities, saw it as 'not only a crime but criminal folly to plunge this House and the country and every constituency into an angry controversy which will turn their attention from the affairs of the War'.[268] These minority Unionist arguments were forcefully rejected by the majority of the Commons,[269] but their expression constituted an axiomatic part of the British parliamentary decision-making process.

During the May debates, Colonel Robert Sanders, a Conservative assistant whip who was leading the opposition of rural counties to the decrease in the number of their seats, ignored the compromise on the bill and put forward an amendment stating that the ministry, Parliament and

---

262 *The Times*, 'Reform by Consent', 29 March 1917.
263 Hansard, Arthur Salter, 28 March 1917, c. 479; *The Manchester Guardian*, 'Premier Rejects P.R.', 28 March 1917.
264 Hansard, Arthur Salter, 28 March 1917, c. 472–3.
265 Hansard, Arthur Salter, 28 March 1917, c. 472.
266 Hansard, Arnold Ward (Conservative), 28 March 1917, c. 496–7. Ward was son of Mary Augusta Ward, a founder of the National League for Opposing Women's Suffrage. Gullace 2002, 167–8.
267 Hansard, Arthur Salter, 28 March 1917, c. 479–80; also Lowe, 28 March 1917, c. 482.
268 Hansard, Sir Henry Craik, 28 March 1917, c. 550–1.
269 *The Times*, 'Electoral Reform', 29 March 1917.

the people should focus on the war instead.[270] Hugh Cecil (Conservative) – son of a former prime minister, MP for Oxford University and a militant opponent of Liberal constitutional policies and hence suspected of leading the opposition this time, too[271] – presented a pseudo-parliamentary view, claiming that the wartime prevented MPs from appropriately scrutinising the reform and that it was wrong of the executive power to press for it.[272] Henry Wilson-Fox (Conservative) added that Parliament and the nation had not been able to consider the proposed 'dangerous experiments' properly owing to restrictions to political meetings, while the Commons had demonstrated an unacceptably 'lethargic attitude' (not all MPs were in attendance that morning) towards such changes.[273]

However, the Unionist opponents were a declining minority,[274] and the majority of the party had decided to go for a reform that was expected to favour the Conservatives in elections after a ceasefire. Supporters of the reform consistently used the extraordinary momentum created by the war as an argument. However, Halford Mackinder (Scottish Unionist), the Director of the London School of Economics, who at the time was working on a book on the politics of reconstruction, saw the war as having unbalanced the constitution, increasing the power of Parliament in principle but that of the government in practice. The reform, he believed, would prevent to a post-war crisis:[275]

> We all admit that we are coming to a time without parallel. We have had to adopt very powerful, and perhaps arbitrary, rough, crude methods in order to render this country capable of dealing with this great crisis of war. We have to face the fact that the crisis after the War will be equally difficult, and that there will be equally crude methods of equipping us with machinery, unless we do what we did not do before the War.

Both the opposition and the Coalition liberals presented the reform as a way of preparing for peace. The current Parliament had been prolonged from 1915 onwards, and the current electoral register was outdated. According to H. H. Asquith, an election based on the pre-war register would lead to a Commons that would lack 'even the semblance of real representative authority';[276] what was needed was a reformed electorate 'which represents

---

270 Hansard, Robert Sanders, 22 May 1917, c. 2144–6; also Harry Hope, 23 May 1917, c. 2412; *The Manchester Guardian*, 'Electoral Reform', 23 May 1917; Turner 1992, 215–16.
271 *The Manchester Guardian*, 'Electoral Reform', 24 May 1917.
272 Hansard, Hugh Cecil, 22 May 1917, c. 2187–8; see also Arnold Ward, 23 May 1917, c. 2425–6.
273 Hansard, Henry Wilson-Fox, 23 May 1917, c. 2339–40; *The Times*, 'The Reform Bill', 24 May 1917. The point was played down in *The Manchester Guardian*, 'Electoral Reform', 24 May 1917.
274 *The Manchester Guardian*, 'Electoral Reform', 24 May 1917,
275 Hansard, Halford Mackinder, 28 March 1917, c. 512.
276 Hansard, H. H. Asquith, 28 March 1917, c. 463.

the considered opinion and will of the nation as a whole.'[277] Prime Minister David Lloyd George himself went in for crusading nationalistic rhetoric when he argued – in a speech in which he appeared as 'the prophet of a new political era' and was cheered by the MPs throughout its duration[278] – that Britain should be ready to show to the world the way forward after the war. The new parliament to be elected immediately after the ceasefire had a global mission:[279]

> [It will] have to settle questions which will practically determine the course of things, not merely in Great Britain and in the British Empire, but very largely throughout the world for generations to come.

The prime minister said – after an interruption criticising his gendered language – that it had become impossible to exclude from suffrage 'the men and the women that had made the new Britain possible.'[280] The real-political argument was carried further: the war had created unique circumstances for realising this reform; it was better to solve the controversial issue in time and not when it would be too late and potentially productive of civil strife resembling that of the early part of the decade:[281]

> You will not have time, but suppose you had, suppose you had nothing to do but pass a Franchise Bill after the peace, ... We can fight all these questions, not in an atmosphere of War, but in the freer atmosphere of peace, a more encouraging atmosphere for political controversy. All the regrets, and all the controversies of the past, which have been kept under with great difficulty during the three years of war, will then have a full and free play. What a prospect!

This meant that the exceptional wartime party truce was to be used to solve a constitutional question that had become over-politicised in peacetime. Edward Shortt, a lawyer, a Liberal and a member of Lloyd George's cabinet, was cynically realistic when he stated: 'We have a war, and we know therefore that we must accept in these times things which we should not be prepared to accept in normal times.'[282] Bonar Law, the Conservative leader and Chancellor of the Exchequer, supported his government partner by conceding: 'We are going to have a new world when this war is over.'[283] There was thus no going back to the pre-war world, even for Conservatives. A constitutional reform was needed as the entire polity – and the environment in which it found itself – had changed as a consequence of the war. This fact was recognised by the British Conservative leadership, although it remained in the interest of the War Coalition to ensure continuity in its hold on power.

---

277 Hansard, H. H. Asquith, 28 March 1917, c. 465–6; also Sir John Simon (Liberal), 22 May 1917, c. 2201; also George Wardle (Labour), 23 May 1917, c. 2366.
278 *The Manchester Guardian*, 'The Coming Franchise Bill', 29 March 1917.
279 Hansard, David Lloyd George, 28 March 1917, c. 488.
280 Hansard, David Lloyd George, 28 March 1917, c. 489.
281 Hansard, David Lloyd George, 28 March 1917, c. 494.
282 Hansard, Edward Shortt, 28 March 1917, c. 551.
283 Hansard, The Chancellor of the Exchequer, 28 March 1917, c. 557.

And they could count on such continuity in the patriotic atmosphere of wartime.

According to the leaders of the Labour Party, too, spring 1917 was 'a most opportune moment' for suffrage reform; as J. R. Clynes, a Labour MP and trade unionist, stated: 'The War period has been used, I think rightly used, in many quarters in order to try to compose and conclude differences which we found difficult to discuss and settle during times of peace.'[284] Despite its having been a major tragedy for the national community, the war was also seen as offering a dynamic moment for reform. For the British Labour Party, which was represented in the War Coalition by Arthur Henderson and was optimistic about electoral advances, the war even constituted, at least rhetorically, a chance to bridge rather than underscore class distinctions, a view that differs radically from contemporary Social Democratic discourse elsewhere (especially in Russia and Finland). According to Clynes, the war had increased the willingness to make compromises and offered Britain, unlike most countries engaged in the war, 'the best and not the worst time to face facts and try to come to a conclusion'.[285] The stance of this leading British Labour politician was an ostentatiously constructive one, though the party organisation had decided that the proposal made at the Speaker's Conference only met the party's minimum demands.[286] More radical claims would need to wait, despite any temporary enthusiasm inspired by of the Russian Revolution.

Conservative and Liberal ministers and the Liberal members of the opposition opposed postponements. Sir George Cave (Conservative), the Secretary of State for the Home Department, summarised the feeling that 'the spirit manifested in this War by all classes of our countrymen has brought us nearer together, has opened men's eyes, and removed misunderstandings on all sides'.[287] Discursively playing down class confrontations that complicated constitutional reforms in most countries, Cave maintained:[288]

> [I]t is only during a war that these questions are reduced to their true perspective. The consciousness of the existence of graver issues renders agreement on such matters as electoral reform not only possible but imperative. I confess that I contemplate with intense dislike the prospects of engaging after the War in a series of barren wrangles.... I would like to get these questions behind me, and to be free to deal with the bigger things with which we shall be faced.

In order that the political system would be ready to focus on the postwar reconstruction, the issue of reform just needed to be solved. Sir John Simon, a lawyer with ministerial experience and now an opposition Liberal, likewise argued that the war had an immense importance for 'the immediate and the more distant future of our own people and our country in the

---

284　Hansard, J. R. Clynes, 28 March 1917, c. 528.
285　Hansard, J. R. Clynes, 28 March 1917, c. 529.
286　Pugh 2010, 118.
287　Hansard, Sir George Cave, 22 May 1917, c. 2134–5.
288　Hansard, Sir George Cave, 22 May 1917, c. 2143–4.

domestic sphere . . . , questions which will require the most authoritative treatment from the most representative bodies'.[289] The war had created a unique possibility to settle the long-standing constitutional disputes in a spirit of good will and to design a political machinery by means of which future political problems could be solved. It would have been much more complicated to try and introduce a parliamentary reform after the war.[290] The war experience had changed the political system for good, and the representativeness of the decision-making bodies needed to be guaranteed. Legislating on suffrage in wartime was indeed 'a piece of national work not unconnected with the War' as it aimed at a 'fairer distribution of power' and was thereby supportive of the war effort.[291]

Opposition complaints about the wrong timing of the bill caused Herbert Samuel, a former Liberal home secretary, to point out that it always seemed to be the wrong time for those who did not dare to state aloud that they rejected the extension of suffrage. Samuel viewed the reform as a technical war legislative measure that would prepare the British Empire for victory and peace:[292]

> We shall never drive home the victory which I know we are going to obtain unless we are prepared for peace when it comes, . . . you must have a representative Parliament. A representative Parliament can only be represented if the electors are those who are really and truly qualified after a great war to return Members to this House. I agree that all those who have taken part in this War must be electors of the new Parliament which is destined to settle the foundations of our great Empire. Therefore, it is our absolute duty during this War, and part of what I conceive to be war legislation.

Walter Long – the Secretary of State for the Colonies, who had played a key role in converting other Unionist leaders over to the side of the reform by appealing to the future of the party[293] – pushed the argument further, implying that, once the bill was passed, the war would be won with power 'derived from the people'. This conceptualisation of a militaristic people's power offered a nationalistic substitute for the rather more American concept of democracy and one that was persuasive for ultra-Conservatives as well. Britain would prevail over Germany thanks to her unity, which would stem from up-to-date popular government:[294]

---

289 Hansard, Sir John Simon, 22 May 1917, c. 2199–2200.
290 Hansard, Sir John Simon, 22 May 1917, c. 2201–2; see also Sir Gordon Hewart, the Solicitor General, 22 May 1917, c. 2239.
291 Hansard, Sir John Simon, 22 May 1917, c. 2201; also George Thorne, 23 May 1917, c. 2414.
292 Hansard, Herbert Samuel, 22 May 1917, c. 2182–3, see also Sir William Bull, 22 May 1917, c. 2212; The *Times*, 'The Reform Bill', 24 May 1917; *The Manchester Guardian*, 'Electoral Reform', 24 May 1917.
293 McCrillis 1998, 12.
294 Hansard, Walter Long, 23 May 1917, c. 2438.

> We shall have to meet our enemies, and must be prepared with the power which we can only derive from the people. Let us be fortified by the strength which only a contented and satisfied people can give to the Government of the country. Let us realise that, blessed, as we have been, above all the nations of the world in our relief from internal dissensions, strife, and trouble, yet the world is full of anxiety and difficulty, and those people will be wise and prudent who take time by the forelock, and give their country those reforms which will make us strong and able to do our duty in the day of peace.

This was an argument on the strengths of a parliamentary democracy that was considered seriously by German debaters as well, as we shall see in section 3.2.

However, there was no denying that constitutional tensions still existed. A major opposition Conservative argument against reform was that the constitutional status of the Lords, which had been altered by the same parliament in 1911, should also be restored.[295] Arthur Salter complained 'our Constitution [has] been incomplete and in suspense' since 1911.[296] Only the restoration of the right of veto to the upper house and its reaffirmation would make democratic suffrage possible. Aneurin Williams (Liberal), a reformist member of the Speaker's Conference, also addressed the intensity of constitutional conflicts after the Parliament Act of 1911 and the Irish Home Rule Act of 1914:[297]

> I realised that there were before the country several matters of the greatest importance which had very nearly brought us to the verge of civil war before this war broke out, and at any rate relieved us from that terrible danger of civil war. I realised also that these great questions must either be settled on a national basis now or very soon, or that after the War is over they will again plunge us into violent and most disastrous controversy.

This characterisation of the atmosphere in the Speaker's Conference suggests the continuing impact of the constitutional crisis of the early 1910s. By 1917, the war had assuaged open confrontations, bringing most Liberals and Conservatives to the same side in the reform debates. However, it was their awareness of the continuing existence of tensions that made the political elite agree on the settlement. Williams's statement suggests that even in Britain constitutional compromises were, to some extent, seen as a means of avoiding civil war; this corresponded to some extent with a latent civil war in Germany in 1919, a feared civil war in Sweden in 1918 and in Finland the threat of a civil war in 1917, an actual one in 1918 and a repetition of this in 1919. Updated parliamentary representation of the people was prioritised and extra-parliamentary means for settling political disputes rejected. The adoption of this view parliamentarised Britain further and was expected to

---

295 This was also the view of the party leaders. McCrillis 1998, 14–15.
296 Hansard, Arthur Salter, 28 March 1917, c. 478; see also Francis Lowe, 28 March 1917, c. 484–5, Ernest Pollock, 28 March 1917, c. 501, and John Gretton, 23 May 1917, c. 2355.
297 Hansard, Aneurin Williams, 23 May 1917, c. 2330.

strengthen the people's trust in parliamentary democracy. The leaders of the Conservative, Liberal and Labour parties appeared to be exceptionally united about the timing and content of the reform, a consensus that marginalised the Unionist opposition within the Conservative Party. Britain differed from Germany, Sweden and Finland (and from its own parliamentary traditions) in the consensual advance of the constitutional reform. This smooth progress was mainly due to changes in Conservative attitudes (or expressions of them) produced by the war.

Unlike other parliaments, much of this debate was independent of any relationship with the rest of the world, building on shared assumptions about an exceptional British political tradition. The understanding of the British political system as a global 'progressive' model[298] and the relative ignorance of – or indifference to – developments in continental Europe contributed to selectiveness in British international references. Some familiarity with Continental constitutional debates are nevertheless obvious in the speeches of a number of representatives of the Labour Party and a few Liberals; Conservative thought, on the other hand, remained focused on the British Empire.

For the Labour Party, the ideology of which contained internationalist elements, the war had initially proved divisive, with some pacifists denouncing it while the majority supported the war effort. After May 1915, the party had participated in coalition governments; in other words, Labour had been integrated to the polity much more efficiently than Social Democrats in the other three countries – the Swedes and the Finns attempted integration in 1917 with very different results. Though moderate and barely socialist, the British Labour Party, too, was affected by the revolutionary spirit of spring 1917. Arthur Henderson, a Labour leader and a minister without portfolio until August 1917, visited Russia in June to demonstrate British Labour support for the government of Alexander Kerensky. He certainly did not turn into a revolutionary in Petrograd and indeed was rather disillusioned about the possibilities of Russia being able to carry on the war without undergoing another revolution – an assessment that led to tension within the Coalition, whose other members wanted to keep Russia as an ally. Labour representation in a peace conference in Stockholm in May-June 1917 was likewise viewed with suspicion by the other parties, as the meeting was attended by radical socialists from several countries (including Germany, Sweden and Finland). The suffrage reform, by contrast, was a commonly accepted project of the Coalition, and Labour expected the number of working-class voters to increase dramatically as a result of it.[299] When defending it, the British Labour Party, unlike the Continental Social Democrats, did not use internationalist arguments, obviously in order to avoid any association with the Russian Revolution and the radical Zimmerwald International and thereby create friction with its Coalition partners.

---

298   On the rise of this notion in Britain and Prussian counter-arguments to that national case in the late nineteenth century, see Pombeni 2005, 225–6.
299   Kirby 1986b, 152; Pugh 2002, 158–61; Pugh 2010, 119.

Most British MPs shared an understanding of the British political system as a universally valid global model, a view that strengthened a different kind of internationalism – one based on the protection of the interests of the British Empire. An opposition Conservative argument against the reform was that the imperial Parliament should have considered the implications of constitutional changes for the Empire and the wider world. For Arthur Salter, Britain was 'the keystone of the Alliance', the strength of which depended on the unity of the British as '[t]he trustees of interests which transcend even the Kingdom and the Empire'.[300] Salter was recalling traditional beliefs in the global historical mission of Britain: she defended liberty both in Europe and all over the world. The British constitution was, by implication, a universal property that could not be so lightly changed.

The counterargument was that, since the British constitution provided a model for the world, it needed to be updated. Walter Long (Conservative), who was in no way an advocate of progressive political views but saw the reform from the point view of the Empire, pointed to the pressures that the dominions imposed on Britain with regard to suffrage:[301]

> They are looking anxiously to the old land. They know that some part of our Constitution here is old, and as they think, worn out. They are asking us this: 'Are you going to put yourself on the same solid foundation on which we rest? Are you going to clear your decks so that the moment this War is over you can face and settle those great Imperial problems.

Such transnational – or rather imperial – references were always selective, vague and interpretable in various ways: they could be used to argue either against or for the introduction of universal suffrage. Mainly dominions with populations of British origin were seen as relevant in such arguments, though they, too, might appear as too different to provide conclusive evidence.[302] Leslie Scott (Conservative) pointed out: 'We are the Mother of Parliaments. We are here to set an example to the British Empire,' whereas the dominions could not make demands of the British Parliament.[303] William Burdett-Coutts (Conservative) contrasted 'this democracy of ours at home' with 'the great democracies of the Dominions', with the latter looking at 'the Mother of Parliaments as the model' and likely to be disappointed this time.[304]

Speakers might cite examples of technical electoral details taken from the dominions or the United States that they just happened to be familiar with in order to support their arguments. Joseph Walton (Liberal) admired the universal suffrage of the 'democratic communities' of Australia and New Zealand, which (like many parts of the Empire but not Continental

---

300   Hansard, Arthur Salter, 28 March 1917, c. 481.
301   Hansard, Walter Long, 28 March 1917, c. 521.
302   Hansard, Richard Chaloner, brother of Walter Long, 28 March 1917, c. 526
303   Hansard, Leslie Scott, 4 July 1917, c. 1153.
304   Hansard, William Burdett-Coutts, 22 November 1917, c. 1411.

Europe) he had visited.[305] Alfred Mond, a Liberal businessman, considered these dominions together with Canada and the United States to be relevant models of the successful introduction of women's suffrage,[306] whereas the Conservatives Arnold Ward and Sir Stuart Coats took the rejection of female suffrage and female passivity in elections in some US states as evidence against female suffrage.[307] George Reid (Unionist), the former prime minister of Australia and an archetypical political agent, who had travelled within the British Empire and whose mobility connected national political debates within it, presented Australia as 'an advanced democratic community' that was worthy of British emulation.[308] This caused other MPs to refer to Australia as well.

Continental examples were even more selective and controversial than those referring to the dominions. The smaller European states rarely appeared as relevant objects of comparison – or disappeared behind vague phrases like 'one or two European States'.[309] The Belgian model of proportional representation was for Ramsay MacDonald no more than an 'idea which is in the air, epidemic'.[310] According to the former Labour leader, it would be best to keep to British 'political methods, practices, machinery, and ideas' and to reject ideas that it was 'absolutely meaningless to apply to our particular system of Government'.[311] No social democratic internationalist accompaniment to the typical internationalism of the labour movement was to be heard in the British parliament; Labour's party-political interests lay in obtaining a majority through the existing system. A Liberal MP might likewise state that 'we need not go all round the world' for models,[312] a statement that illustrates the limits of British Liberal internationalism.

On the other hand, some Liberal supporters of proportional representation did look across the English Channel. John Bertrand Watson, a lawyer, argued that it had been successfully introduced in countries such as Belgium, Switzerland, Sweden and Finland.[313] Aneurin Williams, the Treasurer of the Proportional Representation Society, being a Welshman, listed small

---

305 Hansard, Sir Joseph Walton, 19 June 1917, c. 1707–8.
306 Hansard, Alfred Mond, 19 June 1917, c. 1714–15; also Minister of Blockade Robert Cecil (Conservative), 19 June 1917, c. 1731–2.
307 Hansard, Arnold Ward, 19 June 1917, c. 1746–7; Sir Stuart Coats, 19 June 1917, c. 1728–31.
308 Hansard, George Reid, 23 May 1917, c. 2368.
309 Hansard, Joseph Compton-Rickett. 19 June 1917, c. 1726.
310 Hansard, Ramsay MacDonald, 22 May 1917, c. 2229–30; also Leslie Scott (Conservative), 23 May 1917, c. 2364.
311 Hansard, Ramsay MacDonald, 22 May 1917, c. 2230, 2233.
312 Hansard, Thomas Palmer Whittaker (Liberal), Chairman of the Select Committee on Parliamentary Procedure, 4 July 1917, c. 1166.
313 Hansard, John Bertrand Watson, 22 May 1917, 2168. The Finnish example of proportional representation would not convince a Conservative such as Richard Barnett, who considered it as relevant for the British parliament as any from 'Nova Zembla or Lapland or some other country'. 22 November 1917, c. 1477. By 26 November 1917, Barnett simply replaced 'Finland' with 'Lapland' in order to reject any comparison. The persuasive force of Finland as a model for suffrage should clearly not be overinterpreted.

'democratic nations' such as Switzerland, Belgium, Finland, Sweden, Wurttemberg, (white) South Africa and Tasmania as examples. In the United States and the British colonies, too, proportional representation was making progress, and the Netherlands, Russia and Rumania had recently adopted the system.[314] These were for Williams 'the leading countries of the world' and demonstrated that proportional representation made governments strong by 'really representing the people'.[315] This was hardly an argument that was acceptable to most MPs, who regarded the British tradition and the Empire as sufficient sources of examples.[316] Some French and German parties, too, were known to be supportive of proportional representation,[317] but that did not really count.

Women's suffrage was another subject to which conflicting foreign examples were applied. One opponent referred to the USA and Australia as examples of 'hysterical' women disrupting military decisions, while Finland provided an example of a country where both sexes voted but where no national military force existed,[318] meaning that the polity was pitifully weak, even feminine. Reginald Blair (Conservative), who had seen active service in France and had entered Parliament as an opponent of women's suffrage, pointed out that patriotic Frenchwomen, who were just as supportive of the war effort as their British sisters, were not demanding the vote.[319] For Henry Craik (Scottish Unionist), too, Britain and France were established democracies that were in no need of such suffrage.[320] The Paymaster-General Joseph Compton-Rickett (Liberal), by contrast, speculated in June 1917 about the possibility that Germany would experience a revolution like the Russian one and introduce female suffrage.[321] This indicated that there was a real expectation of change in the enemy country. Generally speaking, examples taken from the dominions were more general among both reformists and anti-reformists than any European ones; imperial internationalism dominated over any European. Britain was seen to have her own tradition of popular government and democracy; it was not dependent on foreign examples.

3.1.3 Cautious Labour and Liberal democrats versus patently democratic Conservatives

Despite the proposed constitutional change, which could have been interpreted to mean a major step in the 'democratisation' of parliamentary government, 'democracy' was not the concept by which the Representation of the People Bill would be primarily described, even though the press

---

314 Hansard, Aneurin Williams, 22 May 1917, c. 2250. Proportional representation was a major goal of Irish Protestants.
315 Hansard, Aneurin Williams, 23 May 1917, c. 2331.
316 See the suggestion by Hansard, Leslie Scott, 23 May 1917, c. 2362.
317 Hansard, Aneurin Williams, 23 May 1917, c. 2325.
318 Hansard, Sir Frederick Banbury (Conservative), 19 June 1917, c. 1646-7.
319 Hansard, Reginald Blair, 22 May 1917, c. 2216. The same point was made by Mary A. Ward in *The Times*, 'Woman Suffrage', 23 May 1917.
320 Hansard, Sir Henry Craik, 22 May 1917, c. 2237.
321 Hansard, Joseph Compton-Rickett,19 June 1917, c. 1727.

had occasionally emphasised democracy as an ideal for which the war was being fought. The Western Allies were, after all, by proclamation fighting on the side of democracy. The 'democratisation' of suffrage and government, however, was something that concerned Germany only.[322] Democratisation did not yet possess the academic connotations given to it in Anglophone political science much later in the twentieth century.

At the same time, Conservative arguments against the reform were not infrequently based on rhetorical redescriptions[323] that presented the established system of representation as democratic. In the May debates, William Burdett-Coutts, a successful businessman familiar with American political discourse, opposed the reform selectively using the language of representative democracy. Conservatives had used this strategy in the early 1910s, suggesting that it was *they* who were defending true democracy against questionable constitutional changes. According to Burdett-Coutts, the War Coalition was acting in 'a spirit of dictatorship' with the result that the British system was moving towards 'autocracy'; this was hard talk as the war effort had increasingly been defined as a fight against Prussian autocracy. According to Burdett-Coutts, the claims of the government about the representative nature of the preparation of the bill demonstrated 'how far a War Government can get from the fundamentals of a democratic Constitution'. The 'unconstitutional' means of the executive struck 'at the foundations of a democratic Government based on the representative principle', and this endangered 'Parliamentary Government'.[324] Burdett-Coutts was the first to explicitly describe the British constitution and government as 'democratic' in the context of the reform debates. He was acting as an historical body connecting political debates across the ocean – though for argumentative purposes changing the Wilsonian rhetoric of democracy beyond recognition. Burdett-Coutts was doing what fellow Conservatives had done before the war when they presented themselves as defenders of democracy against a government that was about to destroy it.

This oppositional attempt to take over 'democracy' provoked a defender of the bill, too, to speak more explicitly about the meaning of democracy. For Herbert Samuel, democracy in Britain would remain one of a limited type. It connected Britain with other polities (now in particular with that of allied Russia) that were going through constitutional changes. However, the British reform distinguished itself from that in Russia in that Britain was seeking a regulated democracy within an evolutionary system and was hence in no need of a corresponding revolution:[325]

322 Müller 2002, 326–7. *The Manchester Guardian* wrote on 29 March 1917 about a necessary conflict between the Hohenzollerns and other Junkers on the one hand and democracy on the other. It did not refer to the British reform as 'democratisation' and would not do so in 1918 either.
323 A rhetorical redescription of a concept aims at a reinterpretation and is often based on renaming, changing its range of reference or re-evaluating its normative nuances. Palonen 2015. For related polemical techniques used by conservatives to oppose democratisation, see Hirschman 1991, 6.
324 Hansard, William Burdett-Coutts, 22 May 1917, c. 2173–6.
325 Hansard, Herbert Samuel, 22 May 1917, c. 2186.

> You do not have a revolution in Russia for nothing. You find that the democracies of the world are thinking, always thinking. A democracy is one of the finest things you can have if, for the moment, you can guide its thoughts.

As a Jewish activist concerned about the Russian refugee problem, Samuel had taken an interest in Russian affairs. In his case, as in the case of Burdett-Coutts, transnational connections with another great power played a role in the discursive constructions of democracy. However, Samuel was careful to point to the inherent instability and associated shortcomings of democracy and thus shared the scepticism of it that prevailed in the international theoretical debate. As we shall see, the German debate would make use of any such Western doubts about democracy.

This brief exchange on democracy was the only noteworthy one in the British Commons in spring 1917. Only a few Conservative critics of the reform occasionally referred to democracy; this should be contrasted with the central position occupied by the concept in the war propaganda. It also differs from the much more extensive debates on democracy in the other three parliaments during the first half of 1917. However, a political debate on democracy did emerge in Britain, too, in late autumn 1917, when the Irish problems were brought up and the Lords' amendments were made in early 1918, but an extended debate had to wait. Democracy was not yet regarded as a concept that could be used to describe the reform of the British parliamentary system in spring 1917, as one might have assumed. Rather, it remained a matter that was discussed in passing in international comparisons brought up by transnationally connected MPs; it did not, despite the occasional use of the term in pre-war reform debates, constitute any major normative political concept used in competing ways to define the future of the nation's own polity.

At least before Woodrow Wilson's speech to the Congress on 2 April 1917, which brought democracy forcefully onto the ideological agenda of the Entente, when he declared that '[t]he world must be made safe for democracy' through the cooperation of democratic nations, democracy was not a concept by means of which the British parliamentary elite would have conceptualised their constitution.[326] Still in May one of the few MPs to identify himself with the concept of democracy was the Liberal Willoughby Dickinson. Dickinson claimed to have been 'flying the flag of democracy' himself in calling for universal suffrage and set out to describe the universal political rights that democracy required: '[R]eal democracy cannot be established on a proper basis unless you recognise the principle that a vote is not a privilege that we choose to give to this man or that man, but is a right which he is entitled to claim, as much as the right of individual liberty.' For Dickinson, universal suffrage was a basic premise of all future democracy. He was also the only speaker to use the verb 'democratise' in this context.[327] Democratisation, as we have seen, was not yet a generally held *goal* of the British reform.

---

326 See Reimann 2000, 283, on democratic liberties, however.
327 Hansard, Willoughby Dickinson, 23 May 1917 c. 2397.

The impact of Wilsonian rhetoric was nevertheless felt in British wartime discourse[328] and in Parliament. This suggests that a transnational shift in political discourse towards an emphasis on democracy – which was essentially of American rather than Russian revolutionary or Continental European origin – did have an effect in Britain, albeit only very gradually. In his maiden speech on 22 May, John Bertrand Watson (Liberal), inspired by Wilson's words and wartime patriotism, flatteringly praised Prime Minister Lloyd George for 'waging a great fight for democracy.'[329] This phrase explicitly associated the British engagement in the war with the government's policy to extend suffrage. Aneurin Williams placed Britain in a larger group of 'democratic nations' in arguing for proportional representation.[330] On the following day, *The Manchester Guardian* wrote about a landmark in political history turning Britain 'towards the recognition of true democracy'[331] and argued for extended suffrage as 'part of the democratic ideal for which we are fighting.'[332] Herbert Samuel had already regarded democracy as such a self-evident defining feature of the British political system that he had characterised its major institutions as 'democratic' and stated that the reform concerned 'the problems of democracy and government'.[333] This is an example of the interaction that was typical between parliamentary debates, the press contributing to transnational Anglophone wartime discourse.

Even though democracy had been connected with aspects of the British political system in the eighteenth century[334] and increasingly from the 1880s on, and even though, as we saw, the Conservatives had presented themselves as champions of true democracy in the early 1910s, the discourse on domestic democracy had been dormant during the war. Wilson's speech inspired some British Liberals and later on other parliamentarians to conceptualise both the ongoing military conflict and the parliamentary reform at home as interconnected advancements of democracy. Such a conceptualisation linked the British constitutional change to the broader transnational development even though it primarily emphasised the war effort of the Entente.

Even so, few Labour or Liberal MPs used democracy as a programmatic concept to promote the reform, which left the Conservative opponents of the bill the chance to employ it themselves. Labour's continuing passivity in both Parliament and the press,[335] in comparison with Social Democratic

---

328 See Reimann 2000, 281, on the press and parliamentary discourses affecting private discourses in this respect.
329 Hansard, John Bertrand Watson, 22 May 1917 c. 2168. The suffragist leader Sylvia Pankhurst had praised Lloyd George as a 'democratic' man in March, after the proposal on women's suffrage. *The Manchester Guardian*, 'Premier and Women's Suffrage', 30 March 1917.
330 Hansard, Aneurin Williams, 22 May 1917, c. 2250–1.
331 *The Manchester Guardian*, 'The Electoral Reform Bill', 23 May 1917.
332 *The Manchester Guardian*, 'The Electoral Reform Bill', 23 May 1917.
333 Hansard, Herbert Samuel, 23 May 1917, c. 2343, 2346.
334 Ihalainen 2010.
335 Neither did *The Herald* of 31 March 1917 call for 'democracy' in the British context; democratic advances were rather expected in Russia and Germany. However, on 7 April the paper reported a meeting in which bureaucratic attempts

discourses in Germany, Sweden and Finland, arose from its desire to avoid association with the Russian Revolution as long as the direction of the revolt remained uncertain; the party prioritised governmental cooperation over expressions of ideological enthusiasm. Just days before the May debates, the French government had forbidden the attendance of French socialists at the Stockholm peace conference, in which Russian revolutionaries were known to be active, and the British government would soon follow suit.[336] The only Labour MP to talk about democracy was Ramsay MacDonald from the pacifist opposition. This party ideologist conspicuously despised the radicalism of the Russian Revolution and – in opposing proportional representation stated a preference for a democracy based on a political intelligentsia over majority democracy, for which the Social Democrat leaders in the other countries studied here were campaigning:[337]

> Democracy does not consist of counting noses; it consists of intelligence, activity, and enthusiasm, and upon the counting of that political vitality upon which progress depends. . . . I am very strongly in favour of a system of election which will give its due influence to the vitality of politics as apart from the mere counting of noses.

MacDonald seemed to be happy with 'the national representation of this House', which would allow 'the will of the nation' to be heard,[338] especially once universal suffrage was introduced. At the same time, Labour hoped that the majority vote would permit them to win seats from the Liberals, and the unpopularity of MacDonald's pacifism threatened his own seat (which he would lose in the general election in December 1918). Labour would adopt a more explicitly socialist programme only in summer 1918. Thus, for these party-political, personal and ideological reasons, the party's cautious rhetoric of democracy distinguished itself from Continental Social Democratic discourse in 1917.

The strongest arguments for Britain as an established democracy were heard from Conservative circles. Building on the argument of the early 1910s that they defended the cause of democracy, the Conservatives provided an alternative to potentially revolutionary definitions. The same strategy of rhetorical redescription would be used by the Swedish right up to 1918 to oppose universal suffrage and by the Finnish right in 1918–19 to obstruct the rise of a parliamentary republic; it was to some extent also used by the German right, which simply rejected democracy.

> 'to silence and cripple the democracy' would be stopped; *the* democracy standing in the Marxist sense for the working classes. The paper demanded that claims by British politicians to be 'the leaders in democracy in the world' be put into practice at home. The parliamentary debate and division of 28 March only came up indirectly in *The Herald*'s ironic descriptions of an indecisive and servile Commons, an expression of its deep lack of trust in Parliament.

336 Wade 2000, 172. Hjalmar Branting, too, denounced the Lenin's ventures in connection with the Stockholm conference. Kirby 1986b, 90.
337 Hansard, Ramsay MacDonald, 22 May 1917, c. 2227.
338 Hansard, Ramsay MacDonald, 22 May 1917, c. 2229–31.

British Unionist opponents of the reform used the positive senses of democracy against their allegedly democratic political rivals. Sir Henry Craik (Scottish Unionist) mentioned that Britain had already been making such progress towards democracy that no reform was needed. The gradual nature of democratic development should be maintained:[339]

> Does anyone think that the Reform Bill is really going largely to increase or affect the main stream of democratic movement that has asserted itself long since in this country far too strongly to be gainsaid? . . . Our stream of democratic feelings is passing on easily and safely without let or hindrance.

Given the constitutional opposition by the Conservatives in the early 1910s, many in the party had adopted the role of defenders of democracy in the sense of maintaining the established British political order and allowing 'democratic feelings' to be expressed but opposing sudden reforms – an attitude also known as 'Tory democracy'. Such an intention is visible in Craik's parallel between Britain and France as polities in no need of major reform: 'Let us look at the country where democracy rules as it does here. Let us look to that closest of our Allies, France. There, as here, democracy is safe, needs no guarantees, needs no defence.'[340] Democracy stood either for one of the undeniable elements of the traditional mixed constitution or for a 'democratic movement' consisting of the political groups of the lower classes advancing their interests; it did not stand for the political system as a whole. Craik was saying that Britain already had enough democracy, suggesting that democratic forces had already become dominant in society, and insisting that no further extension of the status of this democracy was needed. In opposition Conservative reasoning, if constitutional changes were introduced, they should restore the practices preceding 1911. Colonel John Gretton complained that, after the Parliament Act, the Lords lacked the political power that belonged to the second chamber 'in the principal democratic countries of the world.'[341] Similar arguments for bicameralism as a condition for proper democracy were often heard in the Swedish First Chamber, which was dominated by the right.

The Unionist opponents' employment of the rhetoric of democracy certainly did not mean that they were giving up their struggle against extended suffrage. Rhetorically, they presented themselves as defenders of democracy while nevertheless opposing what they considered excessive changes in the political system. Their rhetoric probably indicated a willingness to adapt themselves to an expected increase in the use of the language of democracy rather than the advocacy of the political reforms that it might imply: traditional and novel ways of thinking continued to appear side by side in conservative discourse. The British discursive turn, nevertheless, represented a significant shift in that mainstream Conservatives no longer opposed reform, while the minority, too, articulated their opposition

---

339 Hansard, Sir Henry Craik, 22 May 1917, c. 2237.
340 Hansard, Sir Henry Craik, 22 May 1917, c. 2237.
341 Hansard, John Gretton, 23 May 1917, c. 2355–6.

through the language of democracy. This turn took place earlier than in the other studied countries and can be contrasted with German rightist outright rejections of all democracy, Swedish rightist scepticism of democracy and the Finnish monarchists' opportunistic redefinitions of a monarchical constitution as democracy.

The British Conservatives, too, continued to have doubts about democracy and even representative government. John Gretton's comment is revealing of the party's enduring cynicism; representative government was acceptable mainly as a means of legitimating government with popular consent in the lack of a better system:[342]

> Representative government is not a logical institution. It cannot be argued or justified on logic. It is merely a convenient and useful method of carrying on government, claiming the assent of the people to the proceedings of the government of the day and exercising control upon the proceedings of the Government which the people disapprove of. The whole thing is convenient and has been generally accepted, but it is not logical.

Gretton's concepts of representative government and democracy did not stand for a representative mass or majority democracy; he remained an advocate of the traditional representative government of the elite.

The deliberate use of 'democracy' to oppose reforms is even more visible in the proposal of the National League for Opposing Women's Suffrage for 'a democratic settlement of the controversy' by subjecting female suffrage to a referendum after the war.[343] The proposal was quoted by Arnold Ward, whose mother, a major anti-suffragist, published a letter in The *Times* on the very same day rejecting the handing over of 'political sovereignty' to the other sex as undemocratic and unconstitutional.[344] Just as amongst the Swedish right, the Conservative opponents of the reform abused appeals to a referendum or a new election to stop or postpone reform. The same tactic had been used by the British Conservatives during the disputes around the Parliament Act. Ward further suggested that if such a referendum were not held, the opponents of women's suffrage would use 'every legitimate Parliamentary means' to torpedo the reform.[345] Such readiness to appropriate not only the concept of democracy but also that of parliamentarism in order to oppose reforms was something that the Secretary of State for the Colonies, Walter Long, a leading Conservative who had recognised the Parliament Act of 1911 and accepted the new reform as well, rejected as 'violent obstruction'.[346] The Conservatives were thus divided over the extent and means by which the extended suffrage should be opposed, the mainline being ready to make concessions within a system that they believed, on the basis of their wartime experiences, would ensure continuous electoral support.

342   Hansard, John Gretton, 23 May 1917, c. 2356.
343   Quoted by Hansard, Arnold Ward, 23 May 1917, c. 2426–7.
344   Mary A. Ward, *The Times*, 'Woman Suffrage', 23 May 1917.
345   Hansard, Arnold Ward, 23 May 1917, c. 2426–8.
346   Hansard, Walter Long, 23 May 1917, c. 2429.

Nevertheless, genuine reconsiderations of the meaning of 'democracy' were also taking place among the Conservatives. Colonel Henry Cavendish-Bentinck advised the leaders of his party, after it had already made a strategic decision in that direction, to 'cultivate friendly relations with the great forces of democracy'. 'Democracy' was still used to refer to an element of the constitution or to the masses of the people rather than to any dominant form of government, but a readiness to welcome mass democracy in the spirit of 'Tory democracy' was nevertheless evident. Once the Conservative Party allied itself with 'the forces of democracy' and set out to promote the welfare of the people, this aristocrat argued, it would win 'a great and glorious future'.[347] The Conservative mainline turn to democracy was thus explicitly announced in May 1917 and would lead to success in the general election of late 1918. Wartime experiences of patriotism and cross-class cooperation and the feeling that the victory had been won together, contributed to this change of attitudes. This shift was earlier and more distinct than a similar change among the Swedish right, who remained unwilling to give up their dominant position until the fall of the German monarchy. The Finnish right, though reformist and viewing itself as the champion of the cause of the people, interpreted Social Democratic policies in 1917 and 1918 as arising from a wrong kind of mass democracy but were forced to rethink their stance after the fall of the Prussian system and the need for recognition from the Entente powers. The German right, by contrast, never voiced any readiness to approve democracy during the constitutional ferment of 1917–19.

3.1.4 Creating a 'Parliament of the people' while avoiding a 'constitutional revolution'

As we saw in subsection 3.1.2, the British debate remained relatively independent of that in other countries. However, the outbreak of the Russian Revolution had an effect on it, even if the timing of the Representation of the People Bill probably depended more on the preparatory process launched in late 1916 and the American entry into the war than on reactions to the upheaval going on in Britain's ally in the east. Owing to the considerable geographical distance and differences in the political cultures, the British were interested in the implications of the Revolution for the British war effort, not in its effects on the political order at home, the far left being the only exception. No revolutionary party of notable significance existed, so it was hard for most to see how the Russian Revolution could change Britain; in Berlin, Stockholm and Helsinki, the Russian transformation next door was observed with greater enthusiasm or concern. Nevertheless, after the Bolshevik Revolution, the potential implications for domestic politics were seen more distinctly in Britain as well.

When the opposition leader Arthur Salter claimed that the Representation of the People Bill would disrupt relations with the Allied nations, someone

---

347 Hansard, Henry Cavendish-Bentinck, 23 May 1917, c. 2409. In his *Tory Democracy* (1918), Bentinck would complain about the decline in nationalism and paternalism. McCrillis 1998, 29.

interrupted him by shouting: 'What about the Russian Revolution?'[348] The interpellator's implication was that constitutions were changing internationally and that the political role of the people was changing transnationally. In the March debates, the MPs were wary of drawing conclusions about the meaning of the Russian Revolution for the world – and for Britain – as so little was yet known about it. The concept of 'revolution' was nevertheless in the air. A Conservative opposed to any revolutionary change applied the term to what the British government was doing, basing his argument on the initial decision of the Conservative party organs to question the mandate of the current parliament to introduce such a change:[349] According to Arnold Ward, the War Cabinet was attempting to impose a revolution on Britain by unfair means, after first changing its mind. Ward quoted Lloyd George's speech from 1915, in which he had stated: 'I cannot conceive of a *revolution* of this character being introduced into our Constitution without the opinion of the country being asked upon it definitely.'[350] This intertextual reference, a device always available to parliamentary debaters seeking a line of argument that could be revived, made the Prime Minister contradict himself. Ward's seemingly democratic Conservative conclusion was that the revolution should be halted and the proposal subjected to a referendum *after* the war, or at least made an issue in a new election.[351]

After Ward's rhetorical redescription of revolution, other Conservative anti-reformists made use of the concept to describe in derogatory terms what was happening or might occur in Britain. If revolution in Britain was to be avoided, why did the government intend to introduce 'the most disastrous and revolutionary measure that could be conceived' by proposing the extension of franchise to women? For the nobleman Richard Chaloner, this was 'the greatest revolution which has ever happened in any country of the world' as it meant that the female majority would take over power from men many of whom had died in the war.[352] Sir Henry Craik suggested that the British government had understood the recent events in Russia wrongly, there being no need for a revolution like the Russian one as Britain was not an autocracy:[353]

> If there were great changes necessary in this country, if we were curbed under a military or bureaucratic autocracy or an aristocratic or Imperial autocracy, it might be necessary to do what our great Ally in Russia has done – out those chains by revolution. But does anyone think at this moment that this country has its political instincts curbed or its liberties checked? . . . Do we think that this country's democratic interests are being set aside?

---

348   Hansard, Arthur Salter, 28 March 1917, c. 473.
349   McCrillis 1998, 14–15; Evans 2000, 87.
350   Hansard, Arnold Ward, 28 March 1917, c. 499–500; see also P. Magnus, 28 March 1917, c. 538; see Saunders 2013b, 78, for similar pre-war claims.
351   Hansard, Arnold Ward, 28 March 1917, c. 500.
352   Hansard, Richard Chaloner, 28 March 1917, c. 526.
353   Hansard, Sir Henry Craik, 28 March 1917, c. 549–50.

The juxtaposition of the Russian Revolution and women's suffrage in Britain was a rhetorical ploy, suggesting that the War Cabinet was bringing about a revolution for the wrong reasons.

The Russian Revolution was present in Walter Long's reformist Conservative contribution in March in a more implicit way – connected with the impact of the war in general. For Long, Britain was a fortunate country which had experienced no revolution since 1688 but had developed its political system evolutionarily through moderate reforms. The reform at hand concerned the involvement of *all the people* in the political process in order to strengthen the legitimacy of Parliament:[354]

> Great events have happened. If we are wise, we shall retain all the blessings that we have got, and we shall, I believe, get many new ones. But if we are going to face these great problems, Imperial and domestic, it will only be possible if we make this House, so far as it is possible, really representative of the people of this country. Let them feel that they have a grievance, let them feel that you have refused a reform of a moderate character when the reform was possible, and you will have a discontented House of Commons and, what is worse, a highly discontented people, who will refuse to recognise your right to act in their name or decide these great issues for them.

The reform, if supported by the opposition Conservatives, would remove political discontent among the people, who were in principle capable of turning the balanced system from the path of evolutionary development onto that of revolution. While the Conservatives were holding this internal debate on revolution in March, the Labour MPs made no explicit reference to the Russian Revolution even though (or perhaps precisely because) their supporters were enthusiastic about it.[355] The Liberals were not excited by the event at all.

In May, a couple of Conservative opponents continued to criticise the government proposal as revolutionary. According to Sir Frederick Banbury, Member for the City, the government was proposing 'a greater revolution' than any previous suffrage reform at a questionable time.[356] Ramsay MacDonald from the Labour opposition was now ready to insinuate that a real revolution of the Russian kind, 'the doctrinaire illusions' of which were constantly in the news,[357] might reach Britain if this reform failed. According to MacDonald, 'the people outside' were concerned about concrete problems which they expected Parliament to solve effectively. If this did not happen, an actual revolution might come about:[358]

---

354 Hansard, Secretary of State for the Colonies, 28 March 1917, c. 521.
355 Thorpe 2001, 37; Wrigley 2009, 91.
356 Hansard, Sir Frederick Banbury, 23 May 1917, c. 2387, 2392; also Lord Hugh Cecil, 22 May 1917, c. 2187.
357 See *The Manchester Guardian*, 'Russian Democracy's Peace Aim', 22 May 1917.
358 Hansard, Ramsay MacDonald, 22 May 1917, c. 2222. *The Herald* had written about an incipient revolution on 7 April, and on 26 May it would complain about 'an effete Parliament' that had 'abdicated its functions'.

> Is this House of Commons going to waste month after month ... with the sorry spectacle of wrangling over questions of franchise when these tremendous vital problems are being fought outside. As a matter of fact, you will have a revolution if you try that game.... [Y]ou are going to have the country rising up and telling you to be gone.

In the exceptional consensual atmosphere of spring 1917, when only a few Conservatives were critical of the proposed reform, this was a provocative use of language, particularly as even moderate socialists tended to be suspected of revolutionary endeavours. MacDonald was making use of the same tactic that such reformers had in their possession everywhere: the extreme left might attempt a revolution if the proposals of the moderates were not accepted. The Finnish Social Democrats were making this point throughout 1917 in order to force the non-socialist parties into concessions; the Swedish Social Democrats did so in 1917 and 1918 in order to push through the suffrage reform; and the German Social Democrats emphasised the undesirable alternative of the far left in spring 1919. MacDonald argued that in comparison with the possibility of a real revolution, the bill on the table was not going to 'bring about very revolutionary results.'[359] Some Conservatives, he claimed, were exaggerating the degree of constitutional transformation and were increasing the risk of a real revolution with their unyielding opposition.

This hint of revolution gave rise to Conservative condemnations. Sir Henry Craik explained again that no need for a revolution of the Russian kind existed in Britain, which, unlike other countries, had long traditions of liberty and democracy making evolutionary, peaceful progress.[360] The accelerating dynamics of the parliamentary debate led to the clarification of the arguments on both sides: other speakers continued to imply that the lack of a reform reconstructing the relationship between the people, Parliament and the government could lead to more revolutionary developments, or alternatively to oppose such a reform as revolutionary. Britain might not be that different from other nations in the post-war situation: possible upheavals might destabilise the established political order and institutions like Parliament. Without indulging in any openly Marxist or anti-parliamentary argumentation, George Wardle (Labour), Parliamentary Secretary of the Board of Trade, considered the changes brought about by the war so fundamental that 'a real constitutional reform' had become timely to restore the legitimacy of Parliament:[361]

> The War has thrown institutions, ideas, and opinions all into the melting-pot, and we want to get the people of the country absolutely associated with this House in all its proceedings, and unless we can get the people with us there will be changes of another and worse character effected. I believe in constitutional reform. I believe that you can associate the people and the House of Commons

---

359 Hansard, Ramsay MacDonald, 22 May 1917, c. 2224.
360 Hansard, Sir Henry Craik, 22 May 1917, c. 2237.
361 Hansard, George Wardle, 23 May 1917, c. 2367.

and the Government together, and that the more closely you associate the people with this House the more certain will it be that the Government and the people will tend more and more to become one.

Provocations from both sides were leading to clearer arguments, albeit still reasonably moderate and constructive ones, explaining leftist revisionism in a way that remained acceptable to the Conservative allies in the War Cabinet. In Wardle's vision, Britain would strengthen legitimacy and avoid revolution by carrying out an immediate suffrage reform and creating a stronger association between Parliament, the government and the people. Wardle, who had earned the respect of the right with his full support for the war effort, justified his argument with conventional references to historical examples of parliamentary reforms rather than with any socialist ideology, but still pointing out that revolution and violence could be expected from the people if a proper reform was not carried out. Labour pressure was formulated using the constitutional history of the nation in a way that was challenging and persuasive at the same time:[362]

> [I]f this franchise reform is not to meet with, as has so often happened in the past, a dead wall of opposition, which has provoked strong feeling to such an extent in the country on all these occasions hitherto we have had the burning spirit of revolution spread among the people and there has actually had to be bloodshed before franchise reform was carried; if we do not want to provoke that result we must face things in a calm atmosphere with a desire to have these things settled. The people will demand it.

Wardle, like revisionist Social Democrats elsewhere, represented the people as a potentially active agent in the process of constitutional change. The proposed reform, would give the House of Commons 'a new glory and a new position in the minds of the people'[363] provided that the people did not need to engage in revolutionary activities. Parliamentary government would just be made more popular.

Wardle's point contributed to a cross-party spirit among the defenders of the bill: it was followed by a call from William Hayes Fisher (Conservative), Parliamentary Secretary for the Local Government Board, for the creation of 'a Parliament of the people' (as opposed to the current parliament) that would be able to deal with future problems without a danger of confrontation with the people.[364] This provides an illustrative example of the dynamics of the parliamentary debate, in which a discursive attack was answered with a counter-attack that led to more radical joint definitions across party lines of what the entire constitutional change was about. The process of parliamentary debate in Britain allowed the majorities of the left and the right – both sitting in the War Coalition – to construct a compromise. A decisive background factor was that the Labour leaders had been

---

362 Hansard, George Wardle, 23 May 1917, c. 2367–8.
363 Hansard, George Wardle, 23 May 1917, c. 2368.
364 Hansard, William Hayes Fisher, 23 May 1917, c. 2380.

effectively integrated into the wartime government – unlike in Germany or in Finland, where the parliamentary reform process failed fatally in 1917. Cooperation in a coalition removed extreme ideological arguments from the debate and supported attempts to find common denominators. Even leading Conservatives might call for the creation of 'a Parliament of the people', recalling Lloyd George's controversial People's Budget in 1909. This was something that no representative of the German, Swedish or Finnish right, who on principle did not cooperate with socialists, would do. The attitudinal transition of the British right into an era of mass democracy had proceeded further than in the other three countries, and this was built on experiences of compromise with the Labour Party, which had collaborated in government from 1915 on.

3.1.5 A new Parliament – 'a mirror of the nation' engaging the citizens and placing its trust in the masses

A 'Parliament of the people' had become the goal of the British War Coalition. All the parties participating in the Speaker's Conference had in principle agreed on the creation of a parliament that would be both trusted by the people and able to carry out the massive legislative tasks that were expected after the war. As H. H. Asquith (Liberal) put it when introducing the bill, 'the nation' should be given 'a truly representative House of Commons, capable of dealing, and dealing effectively, with the many gigantic problems which it will have to face and solve'.[365] The proposal would lead to the creation of 'an authentic and authoritative exponent of the national will' in solving the post-war crisis.[366] Such deliberate wartime usage of the collective concept 'national will' differed from the conventional British understanding of parliamentary politics as confrontational resulting from the plurality of interests and views that were involved in it. The emphasis on 'the nation' rather than 'the people', too, underlined this impression of an unanimity of opinion. Even though the British concept never reached the inclusiveness of the Swedish or Finnish or especially the German concepts of the will of the people, the war also strengthened British ways of thinking about a uniform national community with one will – although such a community did not, of course, necessarily support parliamentary democracy.

The ideals of parliamentarism were not to be questioned in Britain. At the opening of the May debates, George Cave (Conservative), the Secretary of State for the Home Department, introduced the bill as a move towards 'the ideal of representative Government', in which Parliament was 'a mirror of the nation'.[367] The government emphasised the stability of the British system in comparison with Europe since 1832: it had been reformed through gradual evolution rather than revolutions of the Continental type. The suggested extension of suffrage would, again, free 'this country from the

---

365 Quoted by Hansard, H. H. Asquith, 28 March 1917, c. 465–6.
366 Hansard, H. H. Asquith, 28 March 1917, c. 471.
367 Hansard, Sir George Cave, 22 May 1917, c. 2134; the notion of 'a faithful mirror of the whole nation' was repeated by John Bertrand Watson, 22 May 1917, c. 2167.

civil turmoil which we have seen during that period in almost every country in Europe'.[368] All Conservatives were expected to be proud of a unique parliamentary polity which had grown gradually and consensually towards greater perfection. The reform at hand suited this view, distancing Britain from unwanted revolutionary anarchy and reinforcing its model status in the world.[369]

Conservative lawyers defined the bill as aimed at realising a more proper representation of the people in Parliament. Ernest Pollock considered it necessary to establish 'a fair mirror of what the thoughts and feelings of the people are'.[370] For party leader Bonar Law, whose business background had helped to modify the aristocratic image of the party, the reform was about developing 'constitutional and Parliamentary government' so that it could 'represent the feeling of the people as a whole.'[371] Law had lost two sons in the war, which had made him highly aware of the sacrifices of all classes of the people and of their expectations of representation. The same wish for a more representative Commons was put in even stronger terms by a Conservative who had fought in the war himself: Major E. F. L. Wood declared: 'This House ought to regain the leadership of the nation, which, in my opinion, it is in danger of losing.' The Coalition's 'bold scheme of reform' would constitute 'the foundation stone of your post-war policy.'[372] The restoration of the power of the Commons was to take place not only in the eyes of the people but also in relation to the government, the power of which had grown during the war.

Henry Cavendish-Bentinck went furthest in emphasising the urgency of strengthening the political engagement of the people. This aristocratic but reformist Conservative was convinced that 'never in the history of this country was it more important that the Government of the country should be broad-based upon the people's will' and Parliament 'thoroughly representative of the people'.[373] Building on what he had read in the papers and experienced in the field, Cavendish-Bentinck sketched a pessimistic scenario in which 'the power and the sovereignty of this House' were being questioned and a further concentration of power in the person of the prime minister and the bureaucracy without their being constantly answerable to Parliament was being planned.[374] Cavendish-Bentinck, who also talked about an alliance between the Conservatives and democracy, was the only MP to explicitly take up parliamentary sovereignty and governmental responsibility.

There was total disagreement among some opposition Unionists in their interpretations of the popular will. According to Arthur Salter, a suffrage reform carried out by the parliamentary elite at a time of war would give

---

368 Hansard, Sir George Cave, 22 May 1917, c. 2134.
369 See Seaward & Ihalainen 2016.
370 Hansard, Ernest Pollock, 28 March 1917, c. 505–506.
371 Hansard, The Chancellor of the Exchequer, 28 March 1917, c. 559.
372 Hansard, Edward Frederick Lindley Wood, 28 March 1917, c. 547.
373 Hansard, Henry Cavendish-Bentinck, 23 May 1917, c. 2408–9.
374 Hansard, Henry Cavendish-Bentinck, 23 May 1917, c. 2408–9.

rise to deep 'popular exasperation'. In Salter's traditional 'country' rhetoric, the parliamentary politicians and parties appeared to be in opposition to the people and the soldiers. He also questioned the representativeness of the views of the local political elites, with whom the parliamentarians communicated, regarding the people, suggesting that the opposition knew better what the people wanted.[375] This constructed contrast between a parliamentary majority supporting the bill and the supposed views of the people at large recalled images from the early 1910s, when the Liberal government had been accused of preventing the Lords from acting as a truer representatives of the people than the Commons could be.

Ernest Pollock (Conservative) responded by insisting that ordinary soldiers viewed the reform as a more useful piece of legislation than many other laws passed during the war. Whereas some soldiers might consider the closure of Parliament best for the nation, the parliamentary elite needed to explain to them that 'while they are fighting we are engaged in giving them something which will be useful to them when they return home'.[376] Despite the divide between the people and Parliament, 'the people at large' wanted Parliament to solve the old disputes on suffrage. A crisis concerning the legitimacy of the entire parliamentary form of government might arise if the Commons was not sensitive to interpreting this will of the people; there was the risk that 'the impatience will be extreme' and 'the people will turn from us in disgust.'[377] The nation could not afford to let the people reject Parliament. This had become the conviction of the majority of the parliamentary Conservative Party by spring 1917, despite some remaining bitterness over the Parliament Act.

Halford Mackinder (Scottish Unionist) likewise viewed the reform as an opportunity for 'a more general compromise affecting the whole political machinery' so that the political system would be capable of focusing on solving more concrete problems affecting the lives of the people. This had to be done as 'it is an entire mistake to imagine that they [the people] have lost interest in politics'; they were just 'taking quite a different interest in politics' than the parliamentarians themselves.[378] A failure to reform the constitution would endanger not only the political future of individual parliamentarians but, much more grievously, that of the British political system as a whole, including Parliament and the monarchy. According to Mackinder, the atmosphere was favourable for compromise between the politicians and should be used to solve constitutional disputes. Such a compromise was, indeed, 'important to us far more than it is to the masses of the people of this country.' It was to duty of the politicians 'to adapt our Constitution to the new time'.[379] One implication of this was that the Lords also needed to be

375   Hansard, Arthur Salter, 28 March 1917, c. 476, 481.
376   Hansard, Ernest Pollock, 28 March 1917, c. 503.
377   Hansard, Ernest Pollock, 28 March 1917, c. 504.
378   Hansard, Halford Mackinder, 28 March 1917, c. 508; for a related argument on the uniqueness of the moment for overcoming party feeling, see Edward Frederick Lindley Wood (Conservative), 28 March 1917, c. 547, and William Hayes Fisher (Conservative), 23 May 1917, c. 2384.
379   Hansard, Halford Mackinder, 28 March 1917, c. 511, 509.

reformed.³⁸⁰ Commander Josiah Wedgwood, an independent Liberal radical, made a related point when he suggested that 'representative government' demanded the reform; otherwise the people would lose interest and be deprived of 'effective action in politics', which might lead to 'Parliamentary institutions' being challenged by 'the direct action . . . of a minority'.³⁸¹ This reflects a rising concern about the direction that the Russian Revolution might take. Reform was needed to prevent a revolution or – as Caradoc Rees (Liberal), Parliamentary Secretary for Home Office, put it – to make every citizen 'take a keen interest in politics'.³⁸²

A further noteworthy feature in the debate is the recognition of the essentiality of publicity for parliamentary government. The relationship between parliamentary debates and publicity had changed profoundly since the late eighteenth century. After prolonged defences of the parliamentary privilege to deliberate in secret, most of the British parliamentary elite had recognised the role of public debate as a necessary part of the parliamentary decision-making process, an element that constituted much of the legitimacy of parliamentary politics.³⁸³ The war had naturally changed the implementation of this principle: official censorship, despite the free reporting of parliamentary proceedings and the liberation of editorials from control, did not allow the normal functioning of the public debate; much of the press, in supporting the war effort, also tended to defend the domestic policies of the government.³⁸⁴ The British parliamentarians continued to recognise the significance of public opinion in wartime to a greater extent than their colleagues elsewhere. However, they drew their own political conclusions as to what the current trend of public opinion was. According to the Prime Minister, David Lloyd George, the opinion of the public on women's suffrage had changed as a consequence of the war and so had that of the majority of parliamentarians.³⁸⁵ Two years previously, he had still said that the ordinary methods of democracy were not applicable to publicity in wartime.³⁸⁶ At the same time, opposition Conservatives were not so certain about this change in public opinion and maintained that any necessary public debate on the reform was likely to lead to controversies that should be avoided in wartime.³⁸⁷ Hugh Cecil, who had already fought against the Parliament Bill, complained that the circumstances of the war had marginalised public opinion as a necessary extra-parliamentary element of the decision-making process:³⁸⁸

380 Halford Mackinder, 'The Reform of Parliament' and 'Reform by Consent', *The Times*, 22 May 1917.
381 Hansard, Josiah Wedgwood, 26 June 1917, c. 339.
382 Hansard, Caradoc Rees, 4 July 1917, c. 1181.
383 Ihalainen 2010; Ihalainen 2013.
384 Rose 1995, 1, 26; *The Times* commented on 5 December 1917 on the inadequacies of the British system. While the press was required to 'respect the privacy' of the Commons, government speakers could openly express their views in the House.
385 Hansard, David Lloyd George, 28 March 1917, c. 492–3; see also J. R. Clynes, 28 March 1917, c. 528.
386 Rose 1995, 101.
387 Hansard, Francis Lowe, 28 March 1917, c. 482, 485.
388 Hansard, Hugh Cecil, 22 May 1917, c. 2186–7.

> Under normal circumstances you have the Cabinet preparing a Bill. You have Parliament discussing it at length. You have a vigilant public opinion outside noting what Parliament is doing and assisting in criticising it, and the like. We have no public opinion at present. Then how are you going to get this Bill properly criticised by all those various sorts of people interested in it in different parts of the country? . . . Now at present nobody will pay the slightest attention to it. They are inevitably concerned with the War.

Cecil, though opposed to extended suffrage, was touching on the very point of the legitimacy of representative parliamentary government: it included the participation of the press in the legislative process and through the press the public at large. The public could assist in developing a bill through an interactive discussion, but such a debate was impossible in the circumstances of a total war. Frederick Banbury likewise argued that there was no excitement in the press about the reform as everybody was concerned with the war and remained unfamiliar with the content of the debate – particularly as the press did not dare to challenge the government on such a key issue during the war.[389] This was certainly true, and it was used by the opposition as argument to obstruct the reform.

Claims about the lack of a public debate caused some supporters to offer evidence of the extra-parliamentary popularity of the bill,[390] and some asserted that there was indeed 'an intelligent discussion of these great problems in the Press' going on.[391] Herbert Samuel (Liberal), a spokesman for women's suffrage, asked whether 'any expression of public opinion of any moment in any portion of the nation' which would oppose the parliamentary attempt to solve the constitutional issues could be shown. Should Parliament fail to find a solution, 'the opinion of the nation at large' would take it as a demonstration of the incompetence of Parliament, and 'Parliamentary institutions themselves would be brought into contempt.'[392] To put it another way, public opinion was present despite the war, and it put pressure on Parliament to introduce the reform and thereby earn its legitimacy. Harry Hope (Conservative) concluded with a related point that the House of Commons needed to bring 'the public opinion of the country . . . more into direct contact with this House'. This meant taking 'the people into our confidence . . . [and] establish[ing] the Constitution on a sound basis.'[393] The majorities of both leading parties thus interpreted public opinion as being in favour of the agreed policy of reform.

Parliament should be truly representative of the people, and public opinion should be in contact with Parliament, but what exactly would the political role of the citizens be? While any debate on citizenship was meagre and focused on the need to extend the concept to include women, there were several Conservative assurances of the competence of British citizens

---

389 Hansard, Sir Frederick Banbury, 23 May 1917, c. 2386.
390 Hansard, Cecil Cochrane, 22 May 1917, c. 2208.
391 Hansard, George Reid, 23 May 1917, c. 2369.
392 Hansard, Herbert Samuel, 23 May 1917, c. 2345; cf. Samuel's complaint about the lack of interest in the bill in the press. *The Times*, 'House of Commons', 24 May 1917.
393 Hansard, Harry Hope, 23 May 1917, c. 2416.

to exercise the right to vote (the essence of citizenship) since the basic education of the people had been much improved.[394] Henry Wilson-Fox (Conservative) was positive that the people in Britain constituted a thinking electorate 'competent to consider and take an interest as citizens in the great public questions of the day, and who will give you a Legislature which will be worthy of the country and the people'.[395] Henry Cavendish-Bentinck recommended with elevated rhetoric that Parliament should 'throw open widely the gates of liberty' as 'liberty will be justified of its children, and we may look forward to the future with confidence and hope'.[396] Opening the gates of liberty stood for the introduction of universal suffrage, including women, and trust in its positive effects on the political system. Such confidence in the people at large in building a better future was rarely expressed by the members of the right in any of the other studied countries. That the British Liberals had come to share this view by 1917 is not so surprising, even though many among them had only recently changed their views on women's suffrage. George Thorne, an old campaigner for women's suffrage, asserted that both sexes had 'exhibited . . . citizenship in the highest possible form' during the war and were now, with the bill, enabled 'to carry on their citizenship in time of peace'. He insisted that 'our future and our destiny depend upon our broadening the base of the people's confidence in this House of Commons'.[397] Herbert Samuel accused the opponents of the bill of being ready to 'deny the rights which ordinary citizens should have',[398] while Aneurin Williams declared that the parliamentarians wanted to 'represent all our citizens'.[399] Samuel's optimistic message to the political elite was that they should 'take the mass – the good and bad – and trust to them, and, in the long run, they will prove trustworthy'.[400] His practical advice was that the reform could be supported not only by speeches but also with 'opportune silence' during the committee stage.[401] This represented a rhetorical attempt to curb parliamentary deliberation.

The prospects for the reformed parliamentary polity were depicted in overwhelmingly positive terms. It was part of the official line of the War Cabinet that a major change in political life was unavoidable as a consequence of the war. H. H. Asquith, a former opponent of female suffrage, recognised that women would play a more considerable role 'in the new order of things – for, do not doubt it, the old order will be changed'.[402] Prime Minister David Lloyd George went beyond the gender issue in drawing conclusions about the fundamental change that the war had already brought about in British

---

394 Hansard, George Welsh Currie (Scottish Unionist), 28 March 1917, c. 534. Currie would later move to the Labour Party.
395 Hansard, Henry Wilson-Fox, 23 May 1917, c. 2336.
396 Hansard, Henry Cavendish-Bentinck, 23 May 1917, c. 2409.
397 Hansard, George Thorne, 23 May 1917, c. 2415–16.
398 Hansard, Herbert Samuel, 22 May 1917, c. 2181.
399 Hansard, Aneurin Williams, 23 May 1917, c. 2329.
400 Hansard, Herbert Samuel, 23 May 1917, c. 2346.
401 *The Manchester Guardian*, 'Electoral Reform', 24 May 1917.
402 Hansard, H. H. Asquith, 28 March 1917, c. 469–70.

politics, arguing (over)optimistically not only that 'there has been a new temper created in this country' but also that:[403]

> there will be a new temper created by the peace, a new determination, a new spirit, not the spirit of party-wrangling and conflict, but the unity which you have had during the War will be transposed to, will be infused into the efforts of peace.

Though it was a rhetorical manoeuvre, the Prime Minister's argument illustrates how fundamental were the political changes that the war was seen to have brought about. The political parties were a commonplace object of criticism; party politics would, in Lloyd George's propagandistic vision, be avoided after the restoration of peace. The people might even take over from the parties:[404]

> [T]hey do not mean that the tremendous question of the reconstruction of this country and this Empire shall be entrusted to the control of any party machine. They mean to take it into their own hands.

The Prime Minister, although very much a party politician aiming at re-election, was challenging the political elite and especially the opposition in populistic terms. This speech act aimed at constructing consensual support for the current government. Such an anti-party attack did not go totally unopposed: Leslie Scott (Conservative) set out to defend 'the party system as essential to the good working of all democratic institutions'.[405]

The Unionist opponents did not share the optimism of the government. Arthur Salter spoke ironically about 'an augury for the future of the happiest kind. We are witnessing the dissolution of the old order, and as soon as the War has ended we shall look about us in a new world'.[406] Henry Craik, too, conceded that 'we know that after the War things will be changed, and nothing will be as before'.[407] Bonar Law, the Conservative leader, responded by emphasising the immense possibilities which would be opened to Britain once the war was over, if only the reconstruction could start under a settled constitution. The momentum created by the war was to be used because 'Conferences of this kind would be condemned for the future'.[408] Leslie Scott believed in the nation being able to build 'national prosperity, happiness, and well-being in the future' given that the reform would provide adequate representation for all 'in the process of moulding the new life of the nation that we call reconstruction'.[409] Henry Cavendish-Bentinck went furthest in forecasting a major turn in the British political culture: people all around the country had started to realise 'newer and wider sympathies

---

403   Hansard, David Lloyd George, 28 March 1917, c. 495.
404   Hansard, David Lloyd George, 28 March 1917, c. 496.
405   Hansard, Leslie Scott, 23 May 1917, c. 2362.
406   Hansard, Arthur Salter, 28 March 1917, c. 471.
407   Hansard, Sir Henry Craik, 28 March 1917, c. 550.
408   Hansard, The Chancellor of the Exchequer, 28 March 1917, c. 558.
409   Hansard, Leslie Scott, 23 May 1917, c. 2359, 2361.

and possibilities of a community of aim which is utterly beyond the ideas of the old oligarchy'.[410] Cooperation with such new forces would affect politics and social life positively.[411] The other parties did not need to get engaged in a debate with the Conservative sceptics since most of the Conservative speakers, having selected extended suffrage as their party strategy, were arguing so consistently for the reform of parliamentary government.

3.1.6 THE COMMITTEE STAGE DURING A CAMPAIGN FOR AMENDMENTS

In early June, extensive debates in a committee of the entire Commons started. Conservative opposition had by no means withered away, and the Unionists now focused actively on amending the bill.[412] Much discussion concerned technicalities, such as the qualifications for citizenship, the redistribution of seats or the realisation of representation in constituencies. In the public debate, the lack of which had been lamented, all this was overshadowed by news from the battlefields,[413] which strengthened doubts about how necessary and popular the reform actually was. Under war censorship and a rising awareness of a potentially spreading transnational revolution, no extensive public debate for and against a constitutional reform ever emerged. As some speakers had insinuated, it was in the interest of the political elite, once they had reached a compromise on the extension of suffrage, to pass the bill among themselves, without too many appeals to extra-parliamentary publicity. And as Vernon Bogdanor has pointed out, the public had mainly been interested in the controversial question of female suffrage and had left the questions of male suffrage, proportional representation and the constitutional status of the Lords to the political elite to decide.[414] Hence the impression given by the parliamentary debates, too, was that the MPs considered it their duty to design a working political system for the people to employ after the war through the privilege of voting.

British political history has mainly focused on the stances of the parties on extended suffrage. As we also saw in the analysis above, the bill was a source of controversy particularly for the Conservatives. Many in the party, as in its sister parties elsewhere, had initially been opposed to suggestions to extend suffrage and continued to hold divergent views on the need to support the reform. Though some speakers had declared their trust in the masses in accordance with the line of the party leadership, they were not so sure about the possibilities of educating the newly enfranchised sections of the people politically (though some saw the existence of possibilities for this[415]) and thereby restraining democratic excesses that might include rising taxes, social

---

410 Hansard, Henry Cavendish-Bentinck, 23 May 1917, c. 2410.
411 Hansard, Henry Cavendish-Bentinck, 23 May 1917, c. 2410.
412 McCrillis 1998, 15–16, 19.
413 Machin 2001, 142–4.
414 Bogdanor 2003a, 27.
415 The Bolshevik Revolution gave rise to a discussion about the relationship between democracy and education. *The Times*, 'An Educated Democracy', 20 December 1917.

programmes, demagoguery, revolution and even dictatorship. However, many British Conservatives reconsidered their stands on democracy earlier than their ideological brethren on the Continent: in the end only 40 MPs, mainly from the countryside, voted against the bill. The majority believed in Conservative support among the soldiers, many were moving towards an acceptance of limited female suffrage, and several were genuinely touched by the patriotism exhibited by the workers during the war. It also seemed obvious that the reallocation of constituencies – agreed between Liberal and Conservative party officials in order to prevent competition within the Coalition – would affect Conservative seats in a positive way. During the committee debates, many wanted to bring up features of the old electoral system that had been favourable for them, including plural voting on economic grounds and university constituencies, rather than the principle of universal suffrage or the nature of the future parliamentary polity.[416] As some Liberal back-benchers wanted to do the same, there was a lot of intra-party debate in addition to the usual inter-party confrontations, a situation that tended to frustrate the government.[417] The press, for its part, mostly focused on the success of the parliamentary performances rather than on the substance of the arguments,[418] which certainly did not encourage a public debate on the principles of democracy and parliamentarism.

The British suffrage reform has understandably often been discussed from the perspective of gender. In this analysis, questions of gender have been viewed only insofar as the parliamentarians regarded them as directly affecting the nature of the future political community. The issue of female suffrage had been postponed by the war: it had, in fact, already received majority support in the Commons before the war but had divided the parties and hence remained unresolved.[419] For many Conservatives, the gender issue remained relevant in 1917: voting women continued to be – despite all the arguments of female contributions to the war effort and the growing support for female suffrage – a spectre to be opposed. The Liberals, by contrast, wanted to see a simultaneous extension of suffrage to both men and women. However, many Conservatives, too, were becoming increasingly confident in their stands in favour of suffrage reform, whereas the opponents were losing faith as a consequence of indications in the press, the party organisation and the army that public opinion was strongly in favour of women's suffrage. By late spring 1917, even many anti-suffragist peers began to consider that it was hopeless to oppose the majority of the Commons on this issue.[420] The conversions may not have been entirely sincere[421] but perhaps it would make more sense to try to win the women over to the Conservative side instead. Ian Machin suggests that women's suffrage was introduced in order to prevent

---

416 Close 1977, 895, 908, 917; Ball 1995, 63; Pugh 2002, 157, 172–3.
417 Turner 1992, 216.
418 *The Manchester Guardian*, 'Electoral Reform', 23–24 May 1917.
419 Machin 2001, 126.
420 Close 1977, 904–5; Machin 2001, 126.
421 Gullace 2002, 187.

the expected revival of this old and (in the circumstances of fighting for 'democracy', as the war propaganda claimed) internationally inconvenient problem after the war. An age limit of 30 on female suffrage was needed to ensure Conservative support as well.[422] We might also regard limited female suffrage as a measure designed to prevent revolutionary tendencies: women were expected to think about their male relatives at the front and vote Conservative, whereas among the combatant men there might be radicals who were sympathetic to revolutionary demagogy.

Nor was universal male suffrage an easy political right for the Conservatives to award. Even if they did not say so aloud, they were particularly concerned about indications since the start of the Russian Revolution that support for the Labour Party was rising as a reflection of the spreading revolutionary mood, and they assumed that any extension of the franchise would benefit the Socialists. It was thought that a Labour victory would lead to growing demands for social reforms that would jeopardise Conservative interests and should therefore be resisted with measures such as the introduction of proportional representation in large cities[423] or with selective female suffrage.

However, few Conservatives accepted being labelled as 'defenders of the old world' and openly opposed the reform; this was in contrast to the adoption of similar self-description by the German, Swedish and much of the Finnish right. David H. Close has suggested that it was their fear of Labour that made many Conservatives assent to the reforms of 1917.[424] In much the same way, the Finnish right had opposed further parliamentarisation out of a fear of a Socialist majority but finally agreed to a republican compromise in 1919; the Swedish right would reduce their resistance to universal suffrage in November 1918 when they saw reform as the only option for securing their remaining interests; and much of the German right would stay quiet in the Weimar Assembly, allowing the republican constitution to be passed without actively backing the project. The British Conservative strategy of confining socialism was successful and guaranteed a gentler transition to parliamentary democracy than continued opposition would have done.

As far as the views on revolution, democracy, the participation of the people and parliamentarism are concerned, the committee stage brought little that was new to the plenaries of the spring. Some points – mainly concerning the continued opposition of a minority within the Conservatives and summarising the main counterarguments – are nevertheless worth making. There was a clear tendency to obstruct the process by excessive repetition of the same arguments. These were:

(1) 'We do not want a revolution.' Some Conservatives continued to insist that the introduction of women's suffrage stood for a revolution (potentially of the Russian kind) and that the current Parliament, elected in 1910, had no mandate to introduce the bill, so it should be postponed

---

422 Machin 2001, 140.
423 Close 1977, 905–906.
424 Close 1977, 910.

till after the war.⁴²⁵ Joseph Compton-Rickett, a Liberal who supported the reform, on the contrary, considered it necessary for Britain to participate in the transnational 'revolutionary and complete' change of franchise that was taking place.⁴²⁶ A Conservative reformist like Robert Cecil answered the opponents with a further rhetorical redescription, suggesting that the anti-suffragist attitude against women's suffrage entailed 'a complete revolution in the institutions of our country'.⁴²⁷

(2) 'No majority- or female-dominated democracy.' John Rawlinson (Conservative), MP for Cambridge University, while viewing Britain as a 'democracy' among other democracies, called for the strengthening of the upper chamber in the fashion of the United States and France as a safeguard against the negative consequences of reform.⁴²⁸ In the British context, this stood for the repeal of the Parliament Act of 1911. Another repeated claim derived from the concept of 'democracy' was that a stable government demanded the concentration of political power in the hands of those who possessed physical force, i.e. men capable of military service. The opponents of women's suffrage, who included some individual Liberals, refused to give the supporters the sole right to call themselves 'true democrats' or to accuse the opponents of 'Prussianism'. One counter-argument was that the government's proposal was not democratic as it did not award suffrage to men and women on the same terms.⁴²⁹ After the reformists started to defend their cause with increasing appeals to the advancement of democracy, thereby politicising the concept, their opponents came up with further details which in their eyes failed to fulfil the demands of such a concept of democracy. At the same time, both Liberal and Conservative MPs spoke in an increasingly positive tone about 'democracy' as a political system.⁴³⁰ Parliamentary Under-Secretary Leo Amery summarised the majority Conservative view, one which was evidently shared by most Liberals as well: while this critic of Woodrow Wilson was not so sure whether the war was being fought 'for democracy against autocracy', he conceded that the war and post-war reconstruction would 'put democracy on its trial'. Amery's conclusion was that '[w]e have to be experimenting, we have to try to find ways and means of bringing democracy up to date with the immense needs of the time'. Without the suggested reform, Britain would 'either end in revolution or in the wholesale disgust of the people of this country with Parliament and democratic institutions'.⁴³¹ Democracy simply required an

---

425 Hansard, Sir Frederick Banbury, 19 June 1917, c. 1640–1.
426 Hansard, Joseph Compton-Rickett, 19 June 1917, c. 1726–7.
427 Hansard, Robert Cecil, 19 June 1917, c. 1736.
428 Hansard, John Rawlinson, 7 June 1917, c. 476; a group of democratic countries was cited by Charles Hobhouse (Liberal), who even characterised Germany as a democracy 'so far as the nominal franchise goes'. 25 June 1917, c. 97.
429 Hansard, Alexander MacCallum Scott (Liberal), 19 June 1917, c. 1690; see Ramsay MacDonald (Labour), 19 June 1917, c. 1691–9 questioning the logic of the argument.
430 See Joseph Compton-Rickett above and Robert Cecil (Conservative), 19 June 1917, c. 1734–6.
431 Hansard, Leo Amery, 4 July 1917, c. 1198.

update of the British form of parliamentary government; it was not so much an issue of imposing the British political system on Germany (which Amery had become acquainted with during his travels). Liberal reformists, in turn, might advise the opponents to universal suffrage to give up their unfounded appeals to the will of the people and suggestions that Britain already was a 'democracy'. Alfred Mond defined the concept: 'By democracy', he claimed, 'is meant that the people shall send to Parliament those whom they desire to represent them.'[432]

(3) 'This is not real parliamentarism.' Hugh Cecil, an old opponent of Liberal constitutional amendments, continued criticisms of the dire state of 'the self-respect of the House of Commons', claiming that '[u]nder the present Government there is no reality of Parliamentary government' as Parliament was expected to simply pass any decree issued by the government. For Cecil, the current British parliament appeared to be no better than that of the French under Napoleon III, a state of affairs that questioned much of the value of the institution: '[T]here is to be a pretence of discussion which despots have always liked to give to the sham Parliamentary institutions which have existed.'[433] Even though it was exaggerated for the sake of argument, Cecil's point demonstrates genuine concern over the development of parliamentarism in the circumstances of the world war. Such concerns were, however, much greater in the camp of the leading enemy, the German Reichstag, to which we shall now turn.

3.2 Wartime demands for the democratisation and parliamentarisation of Imperial Germany

3.2.1 THE GERMAN POLITY IN A PROFOUNDLY TRANSFORMED WORLD

The German political system was more fundamentally affected and changed by the First World War than that of any of the other three. In addition to internal pressures of previously unsolved constitutional tensions and the great sacrifices required by the total war from all classes of the people, external pressures challenging the German political order exerted by the enemy great powers played a role in the constitutional transformation; the process was forced to become transnational. Even though German scholars generally rejected the claims of the Entente about the need to liberate the Germans from their 'autocratic' political system, they had to admit that such propaganda successfully blackened the reputation of the Prussian order and might split the German home front as well.[434] In that sense, the German public and political elite tended to increasingly view the war as one about political systems, including democracy and parliamentarism, not only about 'culture' versus 'civilisation'.

---

432 Hansard, Alfred Mond, 4 July 1917, c. 1217.
433 Hansard, Hugh Cecil, 6 June 1917, c. 179–80; see Garrigues & Anceau 2016.
434 Bruendel 2003, 155.

Police reports on the mood of the people had revealed rising indifference and dissatisfaction among the population. On 28 March 1917, a day before the demands for reform were brought up at the Reichstag, Max Weber famously argued in *Frankfurter Zeitung* that the soldiers who had fought the war should also have a say in the reconstruction of the fatherland after the conflict, thus linking sacrifices in the war to political participation and making an exceptional theoretical intervention in favour of a reform. The standstill in the constitutional debate, which had followed the *Burgfrieden* of the German parliamentary parties in August 1914 and which had been wavering before, could no longer be maintained. The country was struggling under military and economic difficulties that called for the reconsideration of the decision-making structures, which were tending to degenerate further in wartime.[435] In previous German research, contemporary parliamentary debates on the political implications and connected press debates have received little attention, however, as Reichstag has not been regarded as the forum where political decisions were made.[436]

On 30 March, some papers reported that President Wilson would soon address the Congress about the necessity of declaring war on Germany.[437] The participation of the United State seemed to portend a change in the course of the war, though the Central Powers did not rate its military capability very high. The US involvement was a direct result of the total submarine warfare which Germany had been waging since January. German attempts to bring Mexico into the world war also played a role in provoking the American involvement. Even though the appropriateness of such strategic choices was not openly questioned in the German parliament, unhappiness with the consequences increased criticism of the executive and the very limited possibilities which parliamentarians had to scrutinise their actions. The running of the German economy, too, had led to constitutionally exceptional solutions that had started to provoke criticism: the parliamentarians felt that even the parliamentary power to decide on the budget had been to a great extent lost.

More constitutional challenges were emerging. The revolution in Russia, with Nicholas II abdicating on 15 March 1917, immediately gave rise to a constitutional debate in Germany as well. While the differences between the Russian and German polities were considerable and the two countries had been enemies for over two and a half years, there were parallels, especially in the case of Prussia: the imperial thrones had been held by second cousins; influential land-owning nobility had formed the backbone of the state bureaucracy in both countries; and, Germany, too, had a representative institution, during the elections for which promises of democracy and reform had been given but had produced few changes benefiting the citizens. In a similar way to the situation in Russia, the

---

435 Morrow 2004, 213; Leonhard 2014, 737–8.
436 Bollmeyer 2007 and Seils 2011 are exceptions but with a different analytical interest.
437 *Berliner Tageblatt*, 30 March 1917.

Reichstag had remained marginal in scrutinising the executive power. From spring 1917 on, however, after a hard winter, which had given rise to hunger demonstrations, the Reichstag became more actively involved in the political debate. At the same time, the German Social Democratic Party was split when the Independents, who had opposed the continuation of the war credits, left the party. The Majority Social Democrats responded in the party's central organ *Vorwärts* by calling for the extension of parliamentary influence and an electoral reform in Prussia.[438] The left was clearly becoming active in demanding reforms in Germany as well.

The involvement of the United States, as the largest republic of the combatant nations, in the battle against Germany, increased the constitutional character of the war further. The war, which had started as a result of great power tensions, was increasingly seen as a fight between democratically and autocratically governed states. German war propaganda had also contributed to this view ever since 1914 by emphasising the war as a fight against the West and democracy.[439] U.S. President Woodrow Wilson stated in a speech to the Congress on 2 April 1917 that it was a goal of the United States to defend peace and justice in the world against selfish and autocratic power. In Wilson's view, the war had begun as a result of dynasties and small elites serving their own interests and ambitions at the cost of those of the people. The battle against the Central Powers turned highly ideological when the US President described it as being fought for the universal values of democracy and the rights of the oppressed: the pronounced intention was to make the world 'safe for democracy'. After the Russian Revolution, such an emphasis on the advancement of democracy did appear as an increasingly credible argument in defining the objectives of the war.[440] The political systems of the Central Powers had been openly challenged with suggestions that they did not serve the interests of the people and worked against the supposedly universal values of democracy. What added to the seriousness of the challenge was that Wilson was not merely an American *Democratic* politician recycling the rhetoric of his party: in his academic work he had carefully studied German political theory[441] and knew his enemy well.

Andreas Schulz and Andreas Biefang have argued that the Reichstag had been increasingly developing into a forum of public debate even though its controlling powers had remained limited.[442] During the war, it had – despite its engagement in much legislation and budgetary matters – tended to become marginalised. In late March 1917, the National-Liberals and the Catholic Centre introduced an initiative to change the constitution and to create permanent committees for foreign affairs and constitutional issues. The motivation for this reconsideration of the role of the parliament was that the contribution of the entire German people to the war effort implied that

---

438 Dahlmann 2014, 46.
439 Bavaj & Steber 2015, 17–18; Llanque 2015, 70–1.
440 Llanque 2000, 107; Seils 2011, 213–14; Leonhard 2014, 671–2.
441 Leonhard 2014, 656.
442 Biefang & Schulz 2016.

their views should also be heard to a greater extent.[443] The Catholic Centre wished to see the German people educated politically so that they would be able to think for themselves in fields such as foreign policy; eventually they would also be able to participate in foreign policy through the parliament.[444] Such views, found in the writings of Arthur Ponsonby and in Swedish and Finnish leftist discourse as well, reflected a general desire, arising from the pre-war crisis, to extend the control of representative government to foreign affairs. This control might include the founding of foreign affairs committees and the democratisation of recruitment to foreign ministries, but its realisation in the late 1910s remained very limited.[445] In Germany, the demands led first to the establishment of a parliamentary constitutional committee on 30 March 1917, a couple of weeks after the outbreak of the Russian Revolution, two days after the introduction of the Representation of the People Bill in the British parliament and a week before the US declaration of war.

The decision of 30 March reflected the increasingly difficult situation on the home front and pressures to open a constitutional debate despite the war. As soon as the new Constitutional Committee convened, it adopted the abolition of the Prussian unequal and indirect franchise, which was based on a three-class division of taxpayers, as its main goal. Chancellor Theobald von Bethmann Hollweg responded by introducing a proposal for a change in the Prussian suffrage law, and on 7 April, a day after the US declaration of war, the Kaiser delivered an Easter message in which he promised to bring in direct and secret elections in Prussia *after the war*. This was a response both to the claims of the Allied war propaganda about Prussianism and to the alternative offered by the new revolutionary regime in Petrograd. In practice, the reform was prevented by resistance from the Kaiser, the Prussian representative institutions, leading executives and the military leaders, who despised the Chancellor for forcing the Kaiser to make such a promise.[446] The Prussian Landtag and Herrenhaus regarded electoral questions as being their prerogative, not that of the Reichstag or the executive powers of the Reich. The overwhelmingly dominant position of Prussia within the Reich made any progress in constitutional issues at the national level dependent on the decisions of these representative bodies. Despite such obstacles to constitutional reform and its actual postponement, serious suggestions were already made and preparatory measures taken in spring 1917. These debates took place almost simultaneously with suffrage reform debates in the British parliament, the reintroduction of the question of electoral reform in the Swedish parliament, and the reconvening of the Finnish parliament to discuss constitutional issues in a post-revolutionary situation. As I shall show, all these debates were highly intertwined as a result of the war and the transnational impacts of the Russian Revolution.

---

443   Especially Adolf Gröber of the Catholic Centre was active in the Reichstag in voicing this view. Cited in Seils 2011, 194–6.
444   Boden 2000, 40.
445   Götz 2005, 267.
446   Mommsen 2002, 77; Bollmeyer 2007, 143–4; Leonhard 2014, 651, 737.

The spring of 1917 was one of ferment in German party politics, especially on the left, which was divided at an early stage. While the conservative leaders of Germany were helping Lenin to return to Russia via Germany, Sweden and Finland (a very concrete transnational instance of mobility leading to meetings with far-left socialist politicians on the way), hoping that he would initiate a more radical revolution there, bring the new regime down and increase Russia's readiness for peace, socialist opposition at home in Germany was becoming increasingly active. The Social Democrats had been divided over cooperation with the bourgeois parties with regard to support for the war effort. At the end of March 1917, the Social Democratic organ *Vorwärts* called for cooperation that would produce 'the political rearrangement of the German Reich',[447] emphasising the capability of 'the large parties of the left' for joint action.[448] Disagreement over support for the war nevertheless led to a mixed group of anti-war, far-left and revisionist parliamentarians breaking away and founding the Independent Social Democratic Party of Germany (USPD) on 6–8 April 1917. The new party was loyal to Marxist traditions but did not set concrete revolutionary goals.[449] This division of the German Social Democrats was symptomatic of divisions among socialists elsewhere as well: a comparable split had taken place in Sweden in late February, before the Russian March Revolution, and was formalised in May 1917. In Finland, by contrast, there was no such split. In the meantime, the importation of Russian revolutionary discourses to the country radicalised the Social Democratic Party further.[450] In wartime circumstances, the party became discursively associated with the Russian Revolution to a degree that differed from its previous history – and especially with the Bolsheviks who were the only organised Marxist group that strove for a dictatorship of the proletariat.[451] In the meantime, links to Western Socialists remained weak and distance to German and Swedish Majority Social Democrats was growing.

The German Social Democrats had constituted a major model for Swedish and Finnish Social Democrats – as they had been for the Russian socialist revolutionaries until 1914.[452] In its Erfurt program of 1891, 'classical' Marxism had constituted the theoretical basis of the German SPD; this embodied a natural process of revolution between oppressed and oppressor leading finally to the creation of a democratic society. However, by the 1910s German revisionists, headed by Eduard Bernstein, no longer believed in such a general law and looked for more cooperative ways to introduce reforms. They became increasingly opposed by radicals who continued to hold to Marxist principles. The revisionists aimed at changing society by political and parliamentary means, preferably through a majority in the Reichstag and possibly together with other political parties. The radicals,

---

447   *Vorwärts*, 29 March 1917.
448   *Vorwärts*, 31 March 1917.
449   Krause 1975, 35, 91; Seils 2011, 181.
450   Soikkanen 1990, 87.
451   Liebich 1999, 21.
452   Liebich 1999, 20.

not only in Germany but also in Sweden, Finland and elsewhere, rejected the idea of parliamentary politics as a means to achieve social justice and rather counted on the extra-parliamentary class struggle as the agent of progress.[453] The concepts of revolution and democracy thus stood for very different things within the German left: the German Majority Social Democrats did not regard a violent revolution as essential for a transition to democracy, whereas for the Independents in Germany, the far left in Sweden and a considerable majority of Social Democrat speakers in the Finnish parliament, a revolution like the one launched in Russia offered a promise of a democratic society – 'democratic' in the sense of the rule by the proletariat or the working class generally.

From 1916 onwards, the majority of the German Social Democrats had demanded constitutional reforms as compensation for cooperating with the executive and the bourgeois parties. By spring 1917, they were publicly calling for the abolition of the unequal three-class franchise in Prussia. The vague reform promises with which the Chancellor and the Kaiser responded only caused disappointment within the labour movement, and demands for reform were intensified. In July, the Catholic Centre, the Progressivists and the Socialists called for a compromise peace, challenging the conservatives and nationalists, which brought the crisis of the legitimacy of the Prussian order into the open nationally and internationally. However, during this crisis it soon became clear that the executive power and army leaders would not allow major reforms to take place while the war lasted.[454] It would be only after the expected fall of the German army in September 1918 and the abolition of the monarchy in November 1918 that the realisation of these reforms became possible. Even if the debates of spring 1917 changed little in Germany, they reflect prevalent views among the political elites and they contributed significantly to the transnational constitutional debate especially in Sweden and Finland.

3.2.2 IMPLICATIONS OF THE WAR, THE RUSSIAN REVOLUTION AND THE BRITISH REFORM FOR THE GERMAN CONSTITUTION

In March 1917, after over two and a half years of total war, awareness of the profound influence of this particular struggle on all the engaged societies was high among German parliamentarians. The war had started in a spirit of national superiority, with the nation rallying around the monarchy and the well-ordered German state, one that was also admired by many in other countries, not least in Sweden and Finland. By 1917, an increasing number of politicians believed that the war, which affected everyone and altered the social dynamics of society, would inevitably change the German political system as well. Even Chancellor Bethmann Hollweg recognised that the war experience was likely to lead to a restructuring of domestic politics, though he did not specify its implications.

In practice, both foreign and domestic policy had been run under the imperial prerogative in wartime Germany. Yet the Reichstag had already

---

453 Seils 2011, 58–9; Jörke & Llanque 2016, 266–7.
454 Pohl 2002, 12–13; Becker 2014, 27–8; Dahlmann 2014, 46–8; Leonhard 2014, 738.

touched on constitutional questions when discussing new war legislation in November 1916. Eduard David, a Bernsteinian revisionist who was chairing the parliamentary group, pointed out that the Reichstag had given away most of its political powers since the outbreak of the war but now the time had come to demand them back.[455] David pointed to the enduring inequality of Prussian citizens in terms of voting rights and declared that the war had demonstrated that the workers should finally demand equality in representation. The opposition to such a demand was undeniable, he conceded: it came from those in Prussia who did not realise that a new era was dawning as a consequence of the war and that this new era required a new spirit in Germany, including the rethinking of the interrelations between citizens.[456] Ewald Vogtherr, representing the anti-war minority, presented a similar challenge by complaining about the tendency to exclude the Reichstag and thereby the German people from involvement in the political process.[457] No more extensive constitutional debate took place in the Reichstag in late 1916 as the parties of the centre continued to demonstrate their patriotism.[458] Friedrich von Payer, the chairman of the parliamentary group of the Progressive People's Party, who advocated strong parliamentarism on the basis of his experience in Wurttemberg, was the only one to recognise that the rights of the Reichstag had been bypassed without due consideration.[459]

Though such reformism achieved little, it is noteworthy that these calls for reform followed the launch of planning the suffrage reform in Britain in October 1916. The state of war brought into the open related domestic political problems in the two major warfaring nations, as *Vorwärts* observed.[460] The debates were also intertwined in that news from the enemy country was observed with keen interest, even if there was some delay in its delivery via the Netherlands.[461] Furthermore, legislative measures that might bring out comparisons with Germany were not reported in the rightist press. The readers would merely be told that the Commons had approved the proposal of an all-party conference 'concerning various questions of electoral reform and supporting female suffrage',[462] while Social Democrat readers learned that the British government had campaigned intensively for the reform, that this had increased respect for the Prime Minister, that opposition in Parliament had been smaller than expected, and that the majority of the Unionists were ready for a compromise.[463] The nature of the communicated news clearly depended on party positions.

455   Verhandlungen, Eduard David, 29 November 1916, 2168.
456   Verhandlungen, Eduard David, 29 November 1916, 2171.
457   Verhandlungen, Ewald Vogtherr, 29 November 1916, 2191.
458   See Verhandlungen, Ernst Bassermann, a military judge and chairman of the National Liberal Party, 29 November 1916, 2171; Johannes Giesberts, chairman of the parliamentary group of the Catholic Centre, 2 December 1916, 2288–9.
459   Verhandlungen, Friedrich von Payer, 29 November 1916, 2174.
460   *Vorwärts*, 31 March 1917.
461   *Berliner Tageblatt*, 29 March 1917.
462   *Freiburger Zeitung*, 29 March 1917.
463   *Vorwärts*, 31 March 1917.

The German constitutional debate became more intense in late February 1917, after the compromise of the British Speaker's Conference had been reached on 26 January but before it was introduced as a bill in Parliament, and also before the outbreak of the Russian Revolution. The British model as such was hardly germane since Anglophobia was common in German wartime discourse. Britain was seen as aiming at the destruction of Christian monarchical values,[464] and the British parliamentary system of government was generally rejected as the 'English malady' of liberalism.[465] Nevertheless, awareness of the British plans encouraged the German reformists to use it in justifying their cause: if the constitution could be revised in an enemy country despite the war, the Germans would certainly be able to do the same. In connection with a budgetary debate on 23 February 1917, the anti-war leftist Social Democrats pointed again to the existence of constitutional problems that called for an immediate solution. Georg Ledebour, a former London correspondent, reported about the developments in Britain, complaining that the German government continued to dismiss all claims for political rights by the people and that it responded to all criticism with mere empty promises. Urgently needed suffrage reforms at the level of both the Reich and the individual states (especially Prussia) were being constantly ruled out with appeals to the wartime situation. There was also a strange tendency among German MPs themselves to downplay the political role of the parliament.[466] The allied country of Austria provided Ledebour with a warning instance of how a parliament and thereby the rights of the people could be ignored in wartime decision-making. On behalf of the anti-war Social Democratic Labour Community, Ledebour declared that they would continue to fight 'for the rights of the people' against politicians possessed by a war psychosis.[467] This insinuation about the lack of true defenders of popular rights was evidently directed at the Social Democrats, too, as supporters of the war effort. The attack from the far left forced the SPD to respond: Friedrich Ebert, the leader of the party, promised that they would continue consistently to speak out for the political rights of the German people and especially the workers.[468] Pressures on the SPD to take more concrete measures to further reform as a compensation for its patriotic support for the war effort were growing as a result of the split in the left. But cooperation with the parties of the centre was needed before the reform could be advanced.

The executive were aware of the pressures for reform as a response to the war effort – and perhaps of the desire to show that Germany was no worse than Britain in considering the political rights of its citizens. The three major European powers against which Germany was fighting – Britain, France and Russia – were generally recognised as relevant objects

---

464 Stibbe 2001, 4–6. Stibbe has not considered the continuing admiration of German Anglophiles in his book.
465 Leonhard 2006, 211.
466 Verhandlungen, Georg Ledebour, 23 February 1917, 2368–9.
467 Verhandlungen, Georg Ledebour, 23 February 1917, 2369.
468 Verhandlungen, Friedrich Ebert, 23 February 1917, 2369.

of comparison in constitutional questions. The constitutional aspect could no longer be bypassed once even the Chancellor Bethmann Hollweg had recognised the challenge which the Western powers posed to Germany.[469] On 27 February, he joined the debate with the obvious aim of reintegrating the Social Democrats in the common front. The Chancellor defined the war as a battle for the life and future of the Reich. It would be decisive for later parliamentary debates that the progressive first minister – who had held vacillating views on Prussian suffrage reform, having first made a proposal for it in 1910 but later withdrawing it under political pressure – now conceded that the war had led to the emergence of 'a new era with a renewed people' and recognised that it was time to consider 'the right political way to express what this people constitutes' – even though such a redefinition of political rights was not intended to recompense the people for their sacrifices.[470] Bethmann Hollweg's ambiguous expressions of what might be understood as the representation of the people in the sense of either the monarchy or the parliament representing the people (recalling the doctrine of the duality of government) did not necessarily imply launching a constitutional reform. Bethmann Hollweg, who wished to be on good terms with all sides, evidently wanted to please the reformists. However, he proceeded to dampen down overly optimistic expectations of an immediate reform by emphasising the variety of political, economic and social problems that called for a solution after the war and that could only be solved by maintaining 'the internal strength of our state' that had been created by the war.[471] The unity of the political community remained the ultimate goal of all constitutional reconsiderations, and it was hoped that this argument would persuade even the right to make some concessions. Unity stood for nationalism centred on the Prussian monarchy rather than for any new democratic polity created through reform.[472]

Bethmann Hollweg's strategy of pleasing everyone found support: the chairman of the parliamentary group of the Catholic Centre and the chairman of the Main Committee, Peter Spahn, who held conservative values, responded by emphasizing the support of the entire German people for the monarchical constitution as the principle on which the relationship between the people and the government would be continue to be based in the future.[473] Otto Wiemer, chairman of the Progressivist group and a member of the Prussian lower chamber, went on to describe the political consequences of the war for the German people in words that at first sight were supportive of the established order. According to Wiemer, the awareness of the people concerning matters of state had increased as a result of their wartime experiences. The reformist argument was hidden in a sentence that claimed that the German people also possessed an increased desire to participate in affairs of state. This was to say that the possibilities for the people to

---

469 Verhandlungen, Theobald von Bethmann Hollweg, 27 February 1917, 2375.
470 Verhandlungen, Theobald von Bethmann Hollweg, 27 February 1917, 2375.
471 Verhandlungen, Theobald von Bethmann Hollweg, 27 February 1917, 2375.
472 Verhandlungen, Theobald von Bethmann Hollweg, 27 February 1917, 2375.
473 Verhandlungen, Peter Spahn, 27 February 1917, 2380.

express their political opinions should be increased. Wiemer concluded that a change to a democratic constitution had become inevitable in Germany.[474]

A month later, the debate on this issue would deal with the future prospects of the German polity more extensively. On 29 March 1917 – three weeks after the outbreak of the Russian Revolution, a day following a debate in the Prussian Herrenhaus, in which the Conservatives had rejected further democratisation and parliamentarisation[475] and, incidentally, one day after the first plenary reform debates in the British House of Commons – the Reichstag debated the issue of electoral reform in Prussia in connection with what was supposed to be a budget debate. Gustav Noske, a Social Democrat journalist who was known as a defender of the authority of the parliament, drew more challenging conclusions about the constitutional implications of the war experience, conclusions that were very similar to those drawn by British, Swedish and Finnish parliamentarians.

Vorwärts would characterise Noske's speech as reflective of the 'pulse of an onward-rushing time' that required 'the political rearrangement of the Reich'. It reported that the Chancellor was criticised for his inability to see clearly the signs of the era.[476] In Noske's description of the state of the world, the foundations of all the countries participating in the war were being shaken. The war portended a major upheaval in the fates of peoples and states, leading to 'a restructuring not only of Europe but of the world', which suggested that a global transformation (if not revolution) was at hand. For all the new things that would emerge out of the war, a horrible price was being paid in human lives and the sacrifices of ordinary citizens. Noske's conclusion was that a major constitutional restructuring of Germany, as a result of the war, could no longer be postponed.[477] Everyone understood that this meant the immediate introduction of an electoral reform in Prussia.

Noske drew a daring parallel between Germany and Russia, drawing far-reaching conclusions from the fall of 'the sinister absolutist system in Russia, the bulwark of all reactionary action', which its ruler had desperately attempted to revive through warfare.[478] The implication was that the German monarchy was trying to do the same. In Russia, 'the proletarian masses' no longer supported the war effort but stood firmly and clearly on the side of the Revolution.[479] Noske then proceeded to discuss the need to increase the speed of constitutional reform in Germany. This suggestion of an interconnection between the circumstances of the two hostile countries provoked express protests from the right.[480]

Noske quoted a previous promise by the Chancellor to legitimate the reform demands: the future of Germany required the recognition of

---

474 Verhandlungen, Otto Wiemer, 27 February 1917, 2399–400.
475 This was reported also in *The Times*, 'Prussian Electoral Reform', 30 March 1917. Bollmeyer 2007, 77.
476 *Vorwärts*, 30 March 1917. *Berliner Tageblatt*, 30 March 1917, reporting Gustav Stresemann's intertextual reference to the Chancellor's own words.
477 Verhandlungen, Gustav Noske, 29 March 1917, 2835, 2839, 2842.
478 Verhandlungen, Peter Spahn, 29 March 1917, 2833, 2837–8.
479 Verhandlungen, Peter Spahn, 29 March 1917, 2838.
480 Verhandlungen, Kuno von Westarp, 29 March 1917, 2859.

the political rights of the people as a whole, including the broad masses. Noske's conclusion was that it was in the interest of the Reich to finally start preparations for reform. Prussianism was a problem, however: many in the Herrenhaus wanted to get on with waging the war and opposed all constitutional changes at the level of both individual federal states and the Reich as a whole. As a consequence, economic progress in Germany had not been followed by the needed political reforms.[481] Noske challenged the Prussian Herrenhaus and the right in the Reichstag by declaring that it was in the Reichstag, elected by universal male suffrage, that 'the language of the German people and German life was to be heard'.[482] The Chancellor still seemed to be rejecting the call for a profound constitutional reform either during the war or immediately after it on the assumption that such a reform would cause unnecessary disputes and take attention away from practical political questions.[483] According to Noske, the Social Democrats were not ready to wait until the war was over for a new approach to constitutional reform, particularly as the reform in Britain had just got under way.[484] The reform needed to be realised immediately now that the enemy had launched its own. The constitutional histories of the two great powers became thereby intertwined – in the end in a fatal way for German democracy.

On the second day of the debate, Eduard David (SPD) interpreted the Chancellor's speeches more optimistically, seeing a readiness to proceed with reform despite the war. For David, the willingness of the government to appoint a new committee to discuss constitutional relations between the Reichstag and the government was a step forward.[485] He repeated the provocative suggestion that the Russian Revolution had direct implications for Prussia: the Prussian political elite could no longer appeal to the Russian model in postponing electoral reforms. David even drew an ironical parallel between the opposition of the Prussian parliament to suffrage reform and the failed parliamentary reform of 1905-6 in tsarist Russia: 'The Prussian Duma has now happily managed to isolate itself from all the world.'[486] This was an implicit suggestion that the isolated political culture of Prussia had led Germany to the state of affairs in which it currently found itself. The same day's issue of *Vorwärts*, for its part, reported on the rise of the Finnish Social Democrats to govern the country with a Social Democrat parliamentary majority. It likewise reported about the introduction of female suffrage in Britain, a further sign that the times were changing elsewhere in the world.[487]

On the Prussian and more generally conservative side, the timing of the Social Democrats' calls for reform was malevolently associated with noxious influences from abroad imported by treasonous countrymen. It was, after

---

481 Verhandlungen, Gustav Noske, 29 March 1917, 2839.
482 Verhandlungen, Gustav Noske, 29 March 1917, 2839.
483 Verhandlungen, Gustav Noske, 29 March 1917, 2840.
484 Verhandlungen, Gustav Noske, 29 March 1917, 2840.
485 Verhandlungen, Eduard David, 30 March 1917, 2908.
486 Verhandlungen, Eduard David, 30 March 1917, 2904. The alleged ideological alliance between Prussia and tsarist Russia was also criticised by MP Wolfgang Heine (SPD) in *Berliner Tageblatt*, 31 March 1917.
487 *Vorwärts*, 30 March 1917.

all, an old Bismarckian practice to regard the constitution as unchangeable and to view dissenting social groups as enemies of the Reich.[488] Associations with the intensification of the Allies' war propaganda on Western democracy, the concomitant reform in Britain and most seriously the outbreak of the Russian Revolution were difficult to avoid – if not yet in March 1917 then certainly by the time of the appearance of a rightist theory that the war had been lost as a result of a domestic conspiracy of the Social Democrats and their allies.

The awareness of what was going on British politics – resulting from the traditional German interest in the British polity as an alternative political system, the ties between the royal families and the fact that Britain was the leading enemy – remained high. German parliamentarians were well informed about what Prime Minister Lloyd George had said in the Commons on the Russian Revolution and its implications for the war effort as well as about links between British and Russian socialists.[489] British policies could also be presented as a model for what the *German* government should do. Noske did not hesitate to declare, on the day following the first reading of the Representation of the People Bill in the House of Commons, that Britain was planning to change its electoral system in the middle of a war and to extend suffrage so that most women would also be allowed to vote. The British example demonstrated that claims about the impossibility of an electoral reform during a war were unfounded. Noske's conclusion could not have been clearer: 'In this case the Chancellor might learn from the enemy.'[490] Such a provocative admonition would not be forgotten by the right.

Noske's arguments in support of immediate electoral reform resembled those presented by the British government: he justified an early electoral reform by the good impression it would make 'on the masses of the people in the country', raise the morale of the troops in the field and – once the soldiers returned home from the trenches – remove any feelings that they were third-class Prussians and citizens of the Reich. Discontent was already rising among the masses of the people, and the German government could no longer disregard this.[491] As in Britain, a central Social Democrat justification of the reform was recognition of the sacrifices which the soldiers and the people at large had made for the war effort. Another common feature was concern about a rising resentment of politicians among ordinary people. The Prussian political order was thus being challenged with appeals to both Russian and British examples and with suggestions that a development like that which had happened in Russia might happen in Germany as well – if the government did not choose the British line of reform. In Social Democratic circles, parliamentary discourse had clearly reached a high degree of transnationality.

The Social Democratic Party being already split, the supporters of the war no longer could (or wished to) prevent the leaders of the far left from

---

488   Ullrich 2010.
489   Verhandlungen, Peter Spahn, 29 March 1917, 2837–8.
490   Verhandlungen, Gustav Noske, 29 March 1917, 2841.
491   Verhandlungen, Gustav Noske, 29 March 1917, 2841–2.

speaking. The far left, whose supporters were unashamedly enthusiastic about the revolution in Russia, attacked by using the Chancellor's failure to fulfil his promises of reform. Even the new Constitutional Committee would only provide a chance to present various prospects for the future.[492] Hugo Haase, a Jewish lawyer from Königsberg who had defended workers in numerous court cases and exposed cooperation between the Prussian and Russian secret services, attacked the Chancellor for having failed to understand the significance of 'the great historical moment when the flames of the Russian Revolution lighten up every corner' and for maintaining the Prussian electoral system despite outspoken calls for reform in the Reichstag.[493] Haase insinuated that the Junkers had triumphed over the Chancellor in domestic politics just as they had in the country's imperialistic foreign policy; therefore, what the leading minister offered was no more than 'a slap in the face of the broad masses'.[494]

For a dedicated Marxist like Haase, who had actively participated in international Socialist congresses, there remained no doubt that the Russian Revolution was 'a tremendous event in world history', spreading its influence beyond Russia with the message of a victory over despotism that liberated all humankind.[495] A revolutionary change (or at least reform) was becoming possible in Germany as well – even if Haase did not claim that the circumstances in Russia and Germany were directly comparable and denied the existence of an immediate threat of a revolution at home.[496] The concept of revolution was of major ideological importance, nevertheless, and Haase went on to point out in a Kautskyist vein: 'Revolutions arise when the social, political and psychological preconditions pre-exist; if they are lacking, it is impossible to make a revolution.'[497] What could be learnt from the Russian example was that the revolutionary government there had set it as a goal to restructure the conditions of politics so that a future 'democratic republic', supported even by the Russian bourgeoisie, would be based on 'the will of the people' and thus on 'popular sovereignty'.[498] What must have sounded particularly unthinkable in Haase's application of the Russian model to the German situation was the abolition of the monarchy and the democratisation of the military. Demands for female suffrage and the abolition of the Herrenhaus, by contrast, found support from other political groups.[499] For Haase, the postponement of the introduction of equal suffrage in Prussia to an undefined time in the future entailed nothing less than the risk that 'the masses in Germany' would start to 'talk Russian',[500] which might include revolutionary action. Such a suggestion about a possible revolution – a suggestion that had been implicitly taken up by leading Social Democrats

492 Verhandlungen, Georg Ledebour, 30 March 1917, 2924.
493 Verhandlungen, Hugo Haase, 30 March 1917, 2887–8.
494 Verhandlungen, Hugo Haase, 30 March 1917, 2888.
495 Verhandlungen, Hugo Haase, 30 March 1917, 2888.
496 Verhandlungen, Hugo Haase, 30 March 1917, 2889.
497 Verhandlungen, Hugo Haase, 30 March 1917, 2889.
498 Verhandlungen, Hugo Haase, 30 March 1917, 2891.
499 Verhandlungen, Hugo Haase, 30 March 1917, 2891.
500 Verhandlungen, Hugo Haase, 30 March 1917, 2888.

as well – gave credit to suspicions of treason and strengthened opposition among the anti-reformists.

Peter Spahn (Catholic Centre) addressed the need for reform in Prussia but did not see the future constitutional solutions in Russia as having any implications for Germany. He rather congratulated the Germans on the stability of their political system.[501] An immediate reform of suffrage in elections for the Reichstag (meaning women's suffrage, which he opposed) was not a priority for any party and could hence wait until after the war. Nor did Spahn speak in favour of an immediate suffrage reform at the level of the German states. On the other hand, he spoke positively about a reform in Prussia at a later stage as it would strengthen the country politically both internally and externally so that 'the political rights of the entirety of the people in all of its layers, including its broad masses, would be fully recognised, and thereby a joyous contribution to the work of the state (*staatlichen*) would be made possible.'[502] The Catholic Centre would have liked to allow 'a powerful and young people to grow forth from its current calamity' and thus maintain Germany as 'a strong realm and a strong people' ready to fulfil its duties.[503] The nationalist goal of the suffrage reform appeared here in quite similar terms to those used by the majority of the Conservatives in Britain: an increase in the political rights of the people at large would mean the recognition of their contribution to the united war effort and strengthen the nation in military and political terms.

Gustav Stresemann, the reformist chairman of the National Liberals, who were supportive of the current war effort, nevertheless opposed the Chancellor on the state of the political system.[504] Stresemann made use of an historical analogy with the Napoleonic Wars, which had brought the Holy Roman Empire to an end, in suggesting that the ongoing war, too, concerned the future of the German constitution. Idealising the liberal principles of 1848, he described how the Prussian and German peoples had expected a renewal of their political life after 1815 but had been disappointed by the united reactionary policies of tsarist Russia and absolutist Prussia.[505] This suggested that parallel expectations of constitutional renewal were present now, particularly as tsarism no longer existed to support Prussian reactionary policies. Another war – that between Germany and France – had also given rise to constitutional changes in the founding of the current Reich, but Stresemann did not refer to it here. His conclusion was that 'the new era demanded new justice', that 'a reorganisation of things in the future' had become indispensable and that after the war experience the reform of the German system of government could no longer be postponed. In Stresemann's view, this concerned above all the strengthening of the responsibility of the executive to the Reichstag[506] – in other words the

---

501 Verhandlungen, Peter Spahn, 29 March 1917, 2833, 2835.
502 Verhandlungen, Peter Spahn, 29 March 1917, 2832.
503 Verhandlungen, Peter Spahn, 29 March 1917, 2832.
504 *Vorwärts*, 30 March 1917.
505 Verhandlungen, Gustav Stresemann, 29 March 1917, 2852.
506 Verhandlungen, Gustav Stresemann, 29 March 1917, 2853–4.

parliamentarisation of the constitutional monarchy. When Stresemann called for a rethinking of the relationship between the representative institution and the government, he, too, was openly recommending the introduction of a principle of ministerial responsibility resembling that pertaining in Britain.[507] The speedy reform of the Prussian three-class suffrage system and increased parliamentarisation of the Reich thus received support from the National Liberal leader in the aftermath of the Russian Revolution.

The Progressive People's Party likewise saw the war as having necessitated a rethinking of political structures. In Ernst Müller-Meiningen's nationalistic rhetoric, the trust of the German people in their army had made it possible for the parliamentarians to start planning for a new Germany.[508] This vague reference bypassed all open criticism of wartime policies: for Müller, any 'upgrading' remained dependent on the outcome of the war. For the German Progressivists, the renewal of the parliamentary system would obviously mean a more extensive engagement of the parliament in building legitimacy for the use of power, while the will of the people could still also be channelled through other institutions such as the army. Their expressed enthusiasm for parliamentarism was rather subservient to the Prussian order and modest by comparison with that of liberals in Britain, Sweden or Finland. However, they, too, were ready to challenge the Chancellor, the upholders of Prussianism and the Herrenhaus on the issue of suffrage.[509] Müller contrasted the readiness of the British higher nobility to make concessions to the lower classes when that was necessary (as in the Parliament Act of 1911) and their ability to maintain 'the political leadership of the people' with the failed strategy of the Prussian nobility. According to Müller, the majority of the Prussian aristocracy remained incapable of making the political concessions that the sacrifices of the people in the war required and were concentrating instead on safeguarding their privileges.[510] This implied that the Prussian nobility should learn from their British peers, who were ready to accept universal suffrage. Both the German liberal parties thus used Britain as a model to challenge the Prussian elite. This was not done so explicitly in Sweden, and such comparisons were rare in Finland as well.

Not even the National Conservatives denied that the moment when major decisions were to be made on the future of the German people as well as on the future of the world was at hand, though their understanding of the measures that this required differed fundamentally. As far as 'questions concerning the internal political future' of Germany were concerned, they thought that they should be bypassed in a time of war. Count Kuno von Westarp, a Councillor of the Prussian High Administrative Court, saw a considerable risk of constitutional debates splitting those forces that had been united for the war effort.[511] The German constitution was not to be

507 Verhandlungen, Gustav Stresemann, 29 March 1917, 2824.
508 Verhandlungen, Ernst Müller-Meiningen, 29 March 1917, 2843.
509 Paul Michaelis, *Berliner Tageblatt*, 30 March 1917.
510 Verhandlungen, Ernst Müller-Meiningen, 29 March 1917, 2852.
511 Verhandlungen, Kuno von Westarp, 29 March 1917, 2857, 2857.

touched; the emphasis should be on solving the conflict by winning the war. Von Westarp's argument was not so different from those of conservative anti-reformists in Britain or Sweden, though in Britain the holders of such strictly militarist views were a small minority. As far as suffrage in Prussia was concerned, according to the National Conservatives, it was an internal Prussian affair which the Reichstag had no mandate to even discuss. The standpoint of the Conservatives on the suggested constitutional reform was clear: even if post-war reconstruction entailed huge challenges and the rise of new views, they would stand firm and defend their unchanged principles.[512] As a concession, however, they could accept the nomination of a constitutional committee, as long as no major reform was to be planned by it.[513] The creation of a committee appeared for them as a way to remove the reform debates from the parliamentary agenda.

Erich Mertin of the German Reichspartei, a lawyer who also was a member of the Prussian House of Representatives, put this point even more outspokenly: the war had provided no reason to rethink suffrage.[514] The Reichspartei, a party consisting of members of the higher nobility and top civil servants that had traditionally supported the chancellors, had no desire to parliamentarise the constitution of the Reich or to reform Prussian suffrage. It, too, used comparisons with Britain – but to play down the claims of the reformists: the calls for an electoral reform were totally unfounded in that German suffrage was already 'the freest in the world, freer than that in England, the mother of all parliaments' and was thus in no need of extension.[515] If some changes in suffrage were being planned by the enemy, that had no relevance for the German constitution, which the conservatives could rhetorically describe as already free. The dominance of Britain as the object of international comparisons for all parties is interesting, Russia being the only other mentioned polity while France and the USA – not to mention irrelevant minor powers – were completely ignored.

Only the left and a few liberals in the Reichstag drew the conclusion that the electoral reform and parliamentarisation should be advanced during the war. The left-liberal *Berliner Tageblatt* nevertheless celebrated the bravery of the Reichstag in the face of 'the icy silence of official figures', i.e. the government, in arguing and voting for the creation of a constitutional committee in accordance with 'the popular will'.[516] But what would a German democracy based on the popular will look like? That is the subject of the next subsection.

512 Verhandlungen, Kuno von Westarp, 29 March 1917, 2857, 2859.
513 Verhandlungen, Kuno von Westarp, 29 March 1917, 2857, 2863.
514 Verhandlungen, Erich Mertin, 30 March 1917, 2921.
515 Verhandlungen, Erich Mertin, 30 March 1917, 2921.
516 *Berliner Tageblatt*, 31 March 1917.

3.2.3 THE WESTERN DEMOCRACIES AND A NEW DEMOCRATIC ORDER IN GERMANY[517]

Spring 1917 was when the notion of 'Western democracy' became conceptualised to a higher degree than ever before – in British parliamentary discourse rather modestly as a consequence of American influences through Allied war propaganda; in Germany as a reaction to the vague Allied concept of 'Western' democracy and its counter-concept Prussianism; and in third countries such as Sweden and Finland when the elites needed to choose whether they wanted to have democracy of a national, Anglo-American, German or Russian type – or no democracy at all. The concept of democracy divided Europe by including some political cultures and excluding others, the dividing line running primarily between the Western allies and Germany.

In German discourse on the so-called 'democracy' of Britain, France, the United States and other Western powers, much criticism had arisen from the classical notion that democratic systems are prone to being taken over by demagogy and public opinion.[518] This discourse reached a new phase as British and French war propaganda and that of the US President Woodrow Wilson increasingly emphasised opposition to Prussianism as the war goal of the Allied powers. In the propaganda – and consequently also in constitutional debates and domestic policy discourse – the war tended to turn into a battle for democracy. Democracy appeared as a universally valid form of government with implications for political practice rather than as a mere element of representative government. The Allies increasingly viewed themselves as fighting under the banner of democracy. This political concept would become a uniting and normative concept affecting the self-understandings of the political elites of the Allied powers. The concept of Western democracy, which had been rarely used before, came to unite the powers – despite obvious residual differences in how it was understood.

Marcus Llanque has pointed out that, seen from a sceptical German perspective, Allied war propaganda attacks on the German polity as being the opposite to democracy, at a time when the Russian Revolution and the planned suffrage reform in Britain were taking place, could be viewed merely as an enemy attempt to alienate the German government and people from each other.[519] One way to respond was to emphasise the German political system as 'true' democracy as opposed to the pseudo-democratic systems of the West.[520] The German left, and to a more limited extent the centre, however, seemed to the right to have adopted this enemy propaganda and were alienating the government and the people from each other. This tended

---

517 An earlier shorter version of this subsection will appear in Kurunmäki, Nevers & te Velde (eds) 2018.
518 Llanque 2000, 102; cf. interpretations proposing a longer-term democratisation within the German Reich, summarised in Müller 2014, 47–8, who accepts contemporary interpretations of Germany as being ahead of its time in many fields. Müller even suggests that 'the civil service already worked during the war for a democratic Germany'.
519 Llanque 2000, 214.
520 Stibbe 2001, 171.

to be the interpretation even though the message of the reformists was that the relationship between the German state and the people should rather be reconstructed and strengthened through the democratisation of suffrage and the parliamentarisation of government.

As a consequence of this external and internal challenge to the Prussian political order, democracy became more extensively debated in the German Reichstag in February and spring 1917 than in the British House of Commons. Before the war, at least the German Social Democrats had been interested in discussing the need to democratise the Reich, in view of the fact that, although universal male suffrage had existed since 1867, the real influence of the Reichstag had remained limited. There was no ministerial responsibility to it; it could not supervise the executive power, which generally loathed parliamentarism and turned to extra-parliamentary means as support for the socialists increased. The Reichstag was made weaker by the extensive powers of the Bundesrat, divisions within the parties, the inability of the Social Democrats and the liberals to agree on cooperation and the lacking esteem of parliamentary work among both the public and the parliamentarians themselves. At the same time, the increasing variety of state activities and the growth of public spending had made cooperation between the civil service and the Reichstag indispensable. Before the war, the politicisation of the people had already turned the Reichstag into a forum of public discussion where competing interests could be debated, and this had increased the expectations projected on it. In the circumstances of spring 1917, the non-conservative parties found common interests, which to some extent concerned the democratisation and parliamentarisation of the constitution,[521] though their goals remained contradictory.

The debate on democracy started to come into the open when on 27 February 1917 the Chancellor himself pointed out that the British and French prime ministers were declaring to the world that their goal was to liberate Germany from Prussian militarism and 'to endow the German people ... with democratic liberties'.[522] The Chancellor rejected the suggestion that Germany needed to be liberated but could not deny the existence of an external ideological challenge to which the German parliamentary elite needed to respond. Bethmann Hollweg's response was to emphasise the specifically monarchical character of the German polity: the German monarchy was not an autocracy; it had its roots 'in the people and its different classes' and was based 'on the love of free men'.[523]

Individual MPs who were ready to challenge the Chancellor's view of the German polity soon emerged: Otto Wiemer of the Progressivists asked on behalf of the soldiers returning from the trenches to what extent the shortcomings of the prevailing system of government were responsible for failing to prevent the military catastrophe in which Germany was involved. Making use of the authoritative voice of the soldiers, Wiemer declared that 'the development of the state in a democratic direction' was the only solution

---

521 Ullrich 2010, 161–5; Biefang & Schulz 2016.
522 Verhandlungen, Theobald von Bethmann Hollweg, 27 February 1917, 2375.
523 Verhandlungen, Theobald von Bethmann Hollweg, 27 February 1917, 2375.

for the future.[524] Just as in Britain, the soldiers in the trenches were presented as the most magisterial source of public opinion in determining the proper constitutional settlement for the future. As Richard Bessel has pointed out, soldiers on leave did effectively influence public opinion with their despondent reports from the front,[525] so Wiemer's argument corresponded well with the wartime reality. The Progressivist leader had them speak for a future democracy. Wiemer's vision of the democratic future of German political life after such reforms was optimistic,[526] recalling that of reformist liberals in the other countries studied here, though otherwise German liberals were cautious in their reformism.

Such liberal calls for democratisation were harshly rejected by the Prussian elite. Kuno von Westarp (National Conservatives) totally denounced 'the democratisation of all of our constitution' in line with enemy models as a violation of the monarchical order and the rights of the Prussian parliament.[527] Such misleading notions had been propagated since autumn 1916, and now they threatened to find their way into the minds of the troops as well, thereby endangering the battle for the fatherland. An antidote to democratisation could be found in 'the strong monarchical power', which had survived the war and should be maintained.[528]

Marcus Llanque has shown how the First World War and Allied war propaganda created circumstances in which the critics of the traditional authoritarian state (*Obrigkeitsstaat*) began increasingly to refer to democracy as an alternative political system that challenged established German and more particularly Prussian notions of a constitutional state. As a consequence of the experiences of the war, democracy became an unavoidable concept in political discourse for the first time. The war gave rise to the concept of 'Western democracy' in German discourse as well: by 1917 it was increasingly clear that for the debaters it referred to the political systems of Britain, France and the United States *as opposed to* the German – and more particularly Prussian – political order. While 'Western democracy' was rarely defined, it was nevertheless seen as an alternative to the Bismarckian and Williamite order.[529] The question for German MPs was whether democracy should in the future continue to be rejected as degenerate, whether a more developed German version of democracy existed, or whether the Germans should reform their polity to better correspond with the supposed ideals of 'Western democracy'.

The very same question was acute for the parliamentary elites in Sweden and Finland, too. The rise of this new concept also forced these German cultural 'hinterlands' to take a clearer stand on what 'Western democracy'

---

524 Verhandlungen, Otto Wiemer, 27 February 1917, 2400.
525 Bessel 2014, 130–1.
526 Verhandlungen, Otto Wiemer, 27 February 1917, 2400.
527 Verhandlungen, Kuno von Westarp, 27 February 1917, 2404.
528 Verhandlungen, Kuno von Westarp, 27 February 1917, 2404.
529 Llanque 2000, 12–13. Llanque questions the existence of a proper debate on democracy in wartime Germany but nevertheless concedes that there was a rise in the use of the concept from 1917 on; cf. Bruendel 2003, 19, 109, 241. In the Reichstag we can certainly find some interesting debate.

might imply for their political systems. A conservative reaction might be that the concept stood for political systems that were in no way applicable to the Nordic states, which traditionally looked to the German constitutional monarchy as a model for an economically and culturally strong and well organised polity. A shared nationalist one was that the countries possessed an immemorial democratic tradition of their own.[530] The Swedish and Finnish political elites as a whole would soon be forced to rethink their relation to the concept, however, as a result of the obvious outcome of the war and domestic demands for reform.

Llanque has emphasised how rapidly the context of the discourse on democracy changed in Germany, starting in March 1917. The outbreak of the Russian Revolution provoked an international interest in developments in Russia and the meaning of democracy there and elsewhere. The British government, too, introduced its proposal for an electoral reform, which gave rise to expectations for the complete democratisation of the oldest of parliamentary governments. Once the United States, as the world's self-declared leading democracy, joined the war and presented the democratisation of Germany as a major war goal, the German debate could no longer bypass democracy as a mere 'Western' phenomenon; the Germans had to discuss it in relation to their established political order, which was being openly challenged by their enemies. On the side of the Entente, democracy could be understood as a uniting ideological concept for the Americans, British, French and now also the Russians, distinguishing the Allies from the Central powers. It was repeatedly used in declarations that the war was about the defence of liberty and democracy. However, the concept remained a contested one: while 'democracy' was a favoured term in American war literature, the French rather viewed themselves as fighting for civilisation. As preceding subsections have shown, it also took time before the British political elite began to talk about democracy more extensively and politicise the concept in the domestic context; that could be done freely only after the war was over. It is, therefore, no wonder that German critics of the Prussian political order, too, continued to have problems in relating themselves to the rarely defined and patently propagandistic concept of 'Western democracy'. Democracy had certainly not been a dominant defining characteristic of Western popular governments before the war, and there had never existed a single Western model of parliamentary democracy that could be exported to non-democratic states: Britain and France represented different varieties of parliamentarism, while in the course of the nineteenth century the United States had adopted an understanding of itself as the world's leading democracy. The British parliamentary system, which had historically been much discussed in Germany, had usually been regarded as unique to that country and as being vitiated by a number of shortcomings. The concept of democracy, for its part, had been used in Germany mainly by its critics, who wished to show what was to be feared from the proposed democratisation.[531] German writers might also react by arguing that democratic ideals had

530 Ihalainen 2015; Jakobsen & Kurunmäki 2016.
531 Llanque 2000, 102–104, 106, 111–12; Ihalainen 2016a.

already been realised in particularly German ways that were suited to the national context, while the Western politicians who criticised Germany were merely defending their own pseudo-democratic systems, the viable functioning of which even their own theorists might question.[532] The same point was often heard from the academic right in other northern European countries as well.

In the Reichstag, the discourse on democracy was actualised in Gustav Noske's famous speech of 29 March 1917 and in Eduard Bernstein's references to 'the distrust of democracy in the German Reich all over the world'.[533] According to Noske, the Western enemies were justifying the war as a battle against 'the non-liberty and hostility to freedom of the German system of government'.[534] German 'non-liberty' (*Unfreiheit*) and 'hostility to freedom' (*Freiheitsfeindlichkeit*) were contrasted with the vague but overwhelmingly positive Anglo-American and French concepts of democracy and liberty.[535] German academia would respond by emphasizing 'German liberty' as the counter-concept to Western plutocracy and imperialism, though some self-critical remarks also emerged.[536] Noske did not deny the significance of the Western contempt for German political institutions but pointed out that 'institutions in the Western democracies' also had their deficiencies.[537] The use of the concept 'Western democracies' recognised differences between the political systems of the Entente and Germany. Noske's speech implied that a constitutional reform in Germany was timely, but it patriotically challenged the political systems of the enemies. His proposal was by no means to copy the democratic institutions of the Entente but to democratise existing German institutions.

More daring than his proposal for a national kind of democratisation was Noske's use of the major Western counter-concept to democracy, 'Prussianism'. While criticism within Germany was nothing new, the highly pejorative content which the concept had been given in the war propaganda of the Entente was thus expressed in Germany too, albeit indirectly. Noske's estimate was that the British and French interpreted the Russian Revolution as constituting 'a blow against reactionary Prussianism' since they viewed the fallen autocratic regime of the tsars and the German polity as similar.[538] Noske rejected such a parallel as unfounded, in view of the fact that the Germans enjoyed universal male suffrage while in Russia suffrage was unequal and indirect and in some ways parallel to the Prussian taxation-based three-class voting system or the Swedish system of forty tax and vote grades. However, Noske pointed out, in line with a warning in *Vorwärts* about Germany fighting against an alliance of democratic peoples, that reactionary policies of the Prussian type, including unequal suffrage, were

532 Llanque 2000, 114; Llanque 2015, 7475.
533 Reported in *Vorwärts*, 30 March 1917.
534 Verhandlungen, Gustav Noske, 29 March 1917, 2839.
535 This is exemplified by Frederic Harrison, 'No Terms with Hohenzollerns', *The Times*, 27 March 1917, which contrasted 'Kaiserism' and 'freedom'.
536 Stibbe 2001, 169; Bruendel 2003, 156–7.
537 Verhandlungen, Gustav Noske, 29 March 1917, 2839.
538 Verhandlungen, Gustav Noske, 29 March 1917, 2839.

becoming difficult to maintain now that the country was 'surrounded by democracies not only in the west, north and south but hopefully now also in the east, where it will always and evermore have a democracy as a neighbour'.[539] While Noske was unable to view Germany, despite its universal suffrage in the Reichstag elections, as a full democracy, he saw the German constitutional development as bound to an ongoing transnational transition towards democracy. He recognised the democratic nature not only of Britain and France but also of the Scandinavian constitutional monarchies and Switzerland and hoped – like many other optimists in March 1917 – that Russia, too, would become a democratic republic after its revolution. Germany, and Prussia in particular, was now practically alone in Europe with its limitations to democracy, and it needed to join the trend of democratisation.

Some members of the German Social Democratic Party were thus very optimistic about the international constitutional trends of the spring of 1917, and this had an influence on how the prospects for reform were seen among the Swedish and Finnish Social Democrats: in spring 1917 both believed that the time for suffrage and parliamentary reforms was at hand. The high degree of transnational thinking among the German Social Democrats can be seen in Noske's conclusion that the ongoing democratisation was forcing the most resistant political forces into concessions everywhere, the question being only which form the inevitable reform would finally take. While any Western hopes of the Social Democrats launching a revolution in Germany were unfounded, there was no denying the rising pressures for reform in Germany.[540]

Eduard David likewise defended a timely transition to 'a constitutional democratic body politic' within which the constitutional rights of the monarch would be limited even though the monarchy as an institution might be allowed to remain;[541] this was an important qualification in the aftermath of the fall of the Russian imperial throne. For David, the transition meant, first of all, the introduction of 'democratic suffrage' in all German states.[542] David, too, made use of the concept of Prussianism as a counter-concept to the necessary democratisation. Whereas the suggestion of the Entente was that Prussianism was completely contrary to democracy, David raised the problem of the dominant position of Prussia within the German federation, which meant that the executive powers of Prussia and the Reich were the same; it was not possible to simultaneously serve the Prussian Herrenhaus and Abgeordnetenhaus, which was elected on the basis of the unequal Prussian system of suffrage, and the Reichstag as

539 Verhandlungen, Gustav Noske, 29 March 1917, 2839; *Vorwärts* was quoted in *The Times*, '"Vorwärts" on New Russia', 27 March 1917. The German Social Democratic organ saw the emergence of a democratic alliance as foreshadowing the Chancellor's expected speech to the Reichstag. *The Herald* cited *Vorwärts* and other German socialist papers on 31 March calling for democracy lest Germany remain an isolated reactionary state in a democratic world.
540 Verhandlungen, Gustav Noske, 29 March 1917, 2839–40.
541 Verhandlungen, Eduard David, 30 March 1917, 2902.
542 Verhandlungen, Eduard David, 30 March 1917, 2902.

the parliament of the entire Reich elected by universal suffrage. A major problem in the German constitution thus continued to be the amalgamation of what David characterised as the 'modern' constitution of the Reich with 'the old Prussian system'. The latter had now been dealt a heavy blow by the war.[543] In the context of March 1917, from the Majority Social Democrat point of view, the kind of democratisation required in Germany was limited to the democratisation of suffrage in Prussia; that would remove much of the influence of Prussianism, increase Social Democratic influence and enable wider democratisation. The voting system for the Reichstag in itself appeared to be democratic – even without female suffrage. The problems of parliamentarism were another matter, and we shall return to them below. Although limitations to the monarchical prerogative were demanded, the institution as such was not attacked. What was revived in the name of democracy in the aftermath of the Russian Revolution and the opening of the British reform debate was the old battle about the Prussian three-class suffrage system.

At the same time, the Majority Social Democrats emphasised their patriotism and respect for the established order. David did not accept the simplifying representations of Germany as a non-democratic country that implied that it was 'the land of barbarity and backwardness'. David's suggestion was rather that Germany was highly developed but in a particular way: the country surpassed the other European great powers in the fields of economy, technology, art, science, education and social security. The country was, admittedly, lagging behind in its political institutions, which were now in need of rapid reform.[544] David's indirect argument was that with the democratisation of suffrage and adjustments to the parliamentary control of the executive power Germany would easily remove this backwardness and thereby all grounds for Western aspersions and appear as an advanced democratic country among the other European nations. His view of the advanced nature of German society was widely shared in northern Europe.

Despite the moderate nature of their demands and more widely expressed Centrist wishes for an electoral reform, the Social Democrats did not receive much support for their calls for further democratisation; democracy thus remained a party-political concept. Outside the left, it was felt to be problematic as a concept to define the German polity. The National Liberals were not too enthusiastic about adopting political models from the West, though their spokesman Gustav Stresemann, a major champion of ruthless warfare but also a constitutional reformist, denounced the tendency of some members of Reichstag and especially the Prussian Herrenhaus to dismiss 'the democratically governed [federal] states' as being unable to fulfil their tasks as states.[545] This statement suggested that Germany was not to be defined as a democratically governed country in the Western sense but one which could nevertheless learn something from the Western democracies. Democratic government created an involvement of the people that evidently

---

543 Verhandlungen, Eduard David, 30 March 1917, 2904.
544 Verhandlungen, Eduard David, 30 March 1917, 2009–10.
545 Verhandlungen, Gustav Stresemann, 29 March 1917, 2854.

made the states strong opponents in war; democracy and parliamentarism were thus not simply to be rejected.

For the right, no need for any democratisation of the suggested kind existed. According to Kuno von Westarp of the National Conservatives, there was no reason for Germans to change their established monarchical constitution merely because Russia had joined the so-called 'democratically governed, liberally administered countries'. From the rightist point of view, there were political forces within Germany – both in the press and among the Social Democratic and liberal groups in the Reichstag – who talked about constitutional reforms, but the right was determined to fight such attempts.[546] Albrecht von Graefe, a lawyer and army officer, likewise challenged the Social Democrat claim that the fall of the tsarist regime would mean that Germany was surrounded by democracies and would hence be forced to 'fully democratise' its government. Von Graefe suspected that the reformists aimed at creating a republic, in other words were questioning the monarchical political order, which for him constituted outright treason.[547] This determined attitude was familiar abroad as well, including countries such as Sweden and Finland, where the right was equally resolute not to allow democratisation to go too far – though usually not quite so condemnatory of the concept as such. The German right demonstrated no sign of compromise in its defence of the established order. In the Western press, by contrast, the confrontation of late March 1917 led to predictions that 'the democratisation of Germany will come quickly . . . sooner than the German authorities wish and more speedily than England expects';[548] to distinctions being made between German democracy and Prussian monarchy; and to beliefs in the possibilities of 'a democratic opposition within Germany' but also, on the other hand, to questions about 'whether the German people really aspire to be democratic or not'.[549] Both foreign observers and the left in Germany were overly optimistic about a discursive turn towards democracy, which, however, for the time being remained only a Social Democratic intervention.

3.2.4 The role of a 'free' German people and the masses in a new era

Appeals to the people had been typical of German political culture since the early nineteenth century: the representatives of the Frankfurt Parliament in 1848 and 1849 understood themselves as representatives of the people, and universal male suffrage in the Reichstag elections since 1867 supported the idea of the parliamentary representation of the people – despite the limited powers of the parliament.[550] A long tradition of seeing the people as the ultimate authority existed, but as a result of the First World War appeals

---

546 Verhandlungen, Kuno von Westarp, 29 March 1917, 2859.
547 Verhandlungen, Albrecht von Graefe, 30 March 1917, 2919.
548 *The Manchester Guardian*, 'Democracy in Germany'. 30 March 1917.
549 *The Manchester Guardian*, 'The Socialist Revolt', 30 March 1917; 'The German Government and the European Peoples', 31 March 1917.
550 Biefang & Schulz 2016.

to the people were rising in an unprecedented manner. They increased particularly in war propaganda, as military leaders tried to mobilise all possible resources necessary for a victory through the collective will of the nation.[551] The concept of the community of the people was gaining ground.

The ideological influences of the Russian Revolution were also immediately felt in German political discourse. Georg Ledebour of the Social Democratic Labour Association (the far left) was inspired by the outbreak of the Revolution and spoke for the rise of the people to the leadership of the state, demanding the replacement of the monarchy with a democratic republic. The republic would be founded on the will of the people, a political proposition that challenged the established political order of imperial Germany, which was based on a hereditary monarchy. Ledebour's argument was extreme, but the notion of the will of the people was to be increasingly used by parliamentarians to legitimate their political demands or, alternatively, to reject ideas presented by their political opponents.[552]

Gustav Noske (SPD) also took up the growing discontent of the masses of the people as a justification for demands for immediate electoral reform. For Noske – in a deterministic Marxist manner – it was the people and not the monarchy, the leading ministers or the Prussian elite who constituted the force that would determine the pace of constitutional reform: 'The speed at which Germany will be modernised does not depend on the will of individual persons; it will depend on the will and energy of the masses of the people.'[553] In British reform discourse, few speakers had so explicitly threatened the ruling elite with the possibility of the people taking the political process into their own hands if reform was not enacted. In Sweden and Finland, the left did not hesitate to suggest that the time for a popular initiative of the Russian kind was at hand.

Gustav Noske suggested that, should the government and the bourgeois majority to fail to introduce 'a democratic reorganisation' of the German political system, a most brutal campaign to determine the issue would follow after the war (not during the war as in Russia). Instead of such a struggle over the constitution, 'the German people' would need to dedicate all its power to healing the wounds of the war. A reform during the war, by contrast, would create 'free paths for a free people in a new era' and save Germany from unnecessary post-war confrontations.[554] *Vorwärts* also cited Gustav Stresemann, who had contrasted 'the spirit of popular defence' with the realities of the Prussian system.[555] The Social Democrat argument in favour of a suffrage reform was in many ways analogous to that in Britain: the war – and in the case of Germany also the ongoing democratisation in surrounding countries – offered a unique chance for introducing a reform that would be much more awkward to realise in peacetime. Confrontations during the time of post-war reconstruction should be prevented in advance.

---

551   Stibbe 2001, 6; Smith 2007, 9.
552   Verhandlungen, Georg Ledebour, 30 March 1917, 2924; Bollmeyer 2007, 87.
553   Verhandlungen, Gustav Noske, 29 March 1917, 2842.
554   Verhandlungen, Gustav Noske, 29 March 1917, 2842.
555   *Vorwärts*, 30 March 1917.

The principal actor in reforming the current system appeared to be the people rather than the parliament as their representative, which reflects a limited degree of trust in parliamentarism even among Social Democrats. However, in Germany only a minority consisting of the left and some members of the centre parties were convinced of the necessity of an immediate reform in 1917. Among the Social Democrats, a constitutional reform was generally presented as necessary for the future of the German body politic, as can be seen in Eduard David's attempt to persuade the centre parties to join the reform front. He defined the electoral reform as a starting point for further progress by legal means: it would enable 'a healthy development' leading to the peaceful 'transformation of our body politic in a more appropriate direction'.[556] The reform, he asserted, would maintain the Germans as the leading civilised nation.[557]

Appeals to the will of the people were useful for the German Conservatives as well, though for quite different reasons: while the Conservatives avoided the use of the term 'popular sovereignty', they were happy to speak about 'the will of the people' in senses that resembled the concept of a community of the people (*Volksgemeinschaft*, see also section 7.2 for an extended discussion). The explanation for this conceptual choice is obvious: popular sovereignty would stand in direct opposition to the principle of the sovereignty of the princes, which the Conservatives by no means wanted to give up. The Conservative view was that the will of the people might very well correspond with monarchical sovereignty. The emerging USPD on the far left, by contrast, used the term 'popular sovereignty' to associate themselves with the Russian revolutionaries. Nonetheless, in the wartime discourse of 1917, the use of popular sovereignty remained rare in German debates. The connections between the *Volk* and the Reichstag were drawn conventionally and not in any revolutionary sense.[558]

In reality, the Reichstag remained constitutionally too weak vis-à-vis the Kaiser, the Prussian bureaucracy and the commanders of the army to force though the reforms that some of its leftist members envisioned. In wartime Germany, much of political power was vested in the army leaders, who in the middle of a total war wanted to hear no mention of political reorganisation. Indeed, they were unhappy that the Chancellor had not been able to prevent the creation of the new Constitutional Committee. When the crisis following the increased activity of the Reichstag in constitutional and foreign policy issues escalated in July 1917, Chancellor Bethmann Hollweg proved unable to mediate between the two sides and was forced to resign.[559] With his resignation, promises of a future constitutional reform went by the

---

556 Verhandlungen, Eduard David, 30 March 1917, 2907, 2909.
557 Verhandlungen, Eduard David, 30 March 1917, 2910. Here he was referring to the German concepts of '*Kultur*' and '*Kulturnation*' that emphasised the primacy of tradition and community over individual rather than the British or French notion of 'civilisation' and its progress and individualism. On the war as one of national cultures, see Muschick 2001, 180–1, 214; Pyta 2011, 32; Rasmussen 2014, 395–6.
558 Bollmeyer 2007, 91, see also 88–90.
559 Gusy 1997, 5.

board: there would be no reform or even any major discussion on it before the end of the war in autumn 1918.

3.2.5 What would the co-sovereignty of parliaments mean?

The German right was infamous for its contempt of parliamentarism, but such views were not unknown among the other German political groups either. Despite the ferment caused by the state of warfare, the global impact of the Russian Revolution and the entry of the United States into the war, constitutional views remained unchanged in this respect among the right and even the centre. To some extent the left, too, continued to express reservations about *Western* parliamentarism. *The Manchester Guardian* interpreted the German confrontation of March 1917 as having actually arisen from the outspoken denunciation of 'Parliamentarism, a disease which from the beginning of the war had been making insidious progress', the defence of militarism by the Conservative leader Count Heinrich Yorck von Wartenburg in the Prussian Herrenhaus and the reaction of the Chancellor to it with a promise of reform after the war.[560]

In the Reichstag, the Conservative deputy Albrecht von Graefe advocated the traditional duality of the German political system, in which parliamentarism might have a balancing but by no means a ruling role: the constitution consisted of two independent and equal powers, the crown and the representation of the people. This German tradition, which had been reinforced by Bismarck, was superior to any form of parliamentarism as practised in the West: in this model, the power of the monarch was suitably curtailed by the parliament.[561] This Conservative constitutional assumption was shared by many members of the political elites in Northern Europe; we shall encounter it especially among the Swedish and Finnish right, and it continued to influence constitutional thought in these three countries after the constitutional upheaval was over.

The Social Democrats' spokesmen, among whom doubts about parliamentary work as the proper strategy had existed until the split in the party,[562] now emphasised the political role of the parliament. As Eduard David – who had hoped that the Social Democrats' support for the war effort would open the way to parliamentarisation – put it, 'the bold step to a parliamentary system' had become necessary, and no one should doubt its inevitability any longer. He maintained that 'the majority of the people' as well as that of the representatives of the people in the Reichstag supported the reorganisation of the political system.[563] Georg Ledebour, a proponent of idealised classical parliamentarism allied with mass action in the Marxist sense, complained that the established system did not enable 'the search for communication through argument and counter-argument in the

---

560 *The Manchester Guardian*, 'Germany and the Russian Revolution', 29 March 1917.
561 Verhandlungen, Albrecht von Graefe, 30 March 1917, 2919–20; Bollmeyer 2007, 107.
562 Jörke & Llanque 2016.
563 Verhandlungen, Eduard David, 30 March 1917, 2908, 2910.

parliament';[564] such esteem for *pro et contra* argumentation was rare among leftist parliamentarians of the time. It is worth considering to what extent the German leftist calls for parliamentarisation in spring inspired Social Democratic and Liberal demands in countries like Sweden and Finland, where German developments were traditionally followed with great interest. As we shall see, the awareness of what was going on in Germany was also acute in 1917: the German example was frequently cited as a major argument for immediate further parliamentarisation in both countries.

The Catholic Centre, too, was ready to defend the standing of the Reichstag even though far-reaching parliamentarism was not one of its goals. Peter Spahn was unhappy about how the Prussian Herrenhaus had transgressed its constitutional competence in rejecting the engagement of the Reichstag in constitutional questions. The Prussians had viewed the aspirations of the Reichstag to intrude on the use of executive power (especially in foreign policy) as downright 'revolutionary', a label that associated it with the subversion that had caused the fall of the Russian imperial throne. The view of the old Prussian elite had been that 'the German people deserved a better parliament than the current Reichstag could provide'.[565] Spahn tried to clarify the situation by denying the existence of any tendency among the parliamentarians to get involved in the use of executive power but defended the rights of the Reichstag.[566] Despite this principled defence of parliamentary rights, the Catholic Centre, with its conservative values, did not actively pursue reform, a fact that was lamented by the Social Democrats, who had already received some support from the two liberal parties.[567]

Gustav Stresemann of the National Liberals, although aware of divisions within his party on the issue of parliamentarism, spoke warmly in favour of a 'parliamentary system' in which ministers and undersecretaries would be responsible to the Reichstag. Stresemann was no uncritical advocate of British or French parliamentarism but could not accept the contempt of the members of the Prussian Herrenhaus for strengthening the rights of the parliament. They seemed to mistakenly believe that these would violate the rights of the monarchy and lead to the implementation of a republic. They accused parliamentarism of creating a system of levelling down, with government by lawyers, internal corruption and causing the fall of the entire political system. The current war had demonstrated to Stresemann that this was not the case, as the conservative *Neue Preußische-Zeitung* maintained.[568] Britain and France, two great powers with parliamentary systems, had proved their strength in the war. The war had indeed demonstrated that 'the parliamentary system does offer a strong glue cementing the connection between the people, the government and the state'.[569] Stresemann supported

564 Verhandlungen, Georg Ledebour, 30 March 1917, 2923; Grosser 1970, 142.
565 Verhandlungen, Peter Spahn, 29 March 1917, 2831.
566 Verhandlungen, Peter Spahn, 29 March 1917, 2832.
567 See Verhandlungen, Eduard David, 30 March 1917, 2907.
568 *Vorwärts*, 29 March 1917.
569 Verhandlungen, Gustav Stresemann, 29 March 1917, 2854–5; *Vorwärts*, 30 March 1917; see Roussellier 1997, 21, on the success of and challenges to French parliamentarism.

stronger parliamentarism as a link between the people and government: parliamentarism made states stronger in warfare, and even Germany should make use of this potential weapon. The point was surprisingly similar to those presented by all parties in the British House of Commons in March and May. Stresemann himself would recall his argument after the fall of the Prussian order.

Stresemann thus spoke in favour of a closer connection between the people and the government via the parliament, though this would remain a qualified form of parliamentarism. The chancellor should at least consult the party leaders on planned legislative reforms. Such an increase in the role of the parliament in the political process would, according to Stresemann, in no way violate the rights of the executive power. On the contrary, it was likely to strengthen the position of the monarch by showing how his government enjoyed the support of the majority of the people – thus providing the kind of legitimacy that the British government enjoyed – and liberate political energy to benefit the state and the war effort. All claims about Germany not being ready for increased parliamentarism were, in Stresemann's view, unfounded: he insisted that the war had provided such political training for the German people that they were ready to take further steps towards parliamentarisation.[570] Stresemann thus presented the war as a political force that made the introduction of parliamentarism necessary. He presented a positive interpretation of parliamentarism that had been rare in Continental political discourse; indeed not even all National Liberals shared it. Some Finnish liberals may have been encouraged by Stresemann's views on parliamentarisation, while Swedish Liberals were already pro-parliamentary.

Other expressions of trust in the potential of parliamentary means of proceeding include the left-liberal Ernst Müller's proposal that the international connections of parliaments should be employed more efficiently to serve the war aims of the nations. The proposal challenged the views of Count Yorck, who had questioned the interparliamentary connections of national parliaments and complained about their intrusion into the field of royal sovereignty. From the point of view of a Junker with a hereditary parliamentary seat (but also a doctor of law), interparliamentary connections violated the established constitutional order in that the parliaments used them to attempt to become 'joint sovereigns'. In Müller's view, the Germans should rather make a more efficient use of 'the parliamentary instrument of public opinion' so that the parliaments would communicate more closely with each other and thereby contribute to bringing the combatant peoples politically closer to each other. The Germans would do better to learn from the Allied powers here: the members of their parliaments had met each other in wartime and brought the political views of the representative bodies closer to each other,[571] with the result that their transnational activities had united the Western peoples. A corresponding form of parliamentary transnational

---

570 Verhandlungen, Gustav Stresemann, 29 March 1917, 2855–6.
571 Verhandlungen, Ernst Müller-Meiningen, 29 March 1917, 2843–4.

interaction among the Central Powers was needed to counter the Western powers. This proposal again suggests that parliamentarism was being re-evaluated among the German liberals and that the internationalism created by the need to overcome the enemy could be productive of reform.

For Müller, the basic function of the parliament was *not* to criticise or challenge the executive power but to support it by constructing supportive *national* and *international* public opinion:[572] the parliament could be an instrument for the construction of a stronger state and an alliance. However, Müller did share some of the ideals of parliamentarism as understood in Britain or France: he recognised the role of the parliament as the defender of the rights of the citizens against the military; it was a duty of parliaments to protect 'the Magna Charta of the individual freedom of the citizens',[573] using an expression that linked his reasoning not only to the British tradition of parliamentarism but also to pre-war military violations of civil rights in Germany. However, Müller was calling for a more extensive use of the Reichstag to serve the purposes of the German Reich rather than demanding any profound parliamentarisation of government: these were only 'small reforms towards parliamentarisation', his aim being to revive the parliamentary debate. Müller emphasised that the Reichstag possessed an understanding of the political situation that made it worthwhile to employ it more efficiently in serving the military goals of the Reich.[574] Over-interpretations could not be avoided, however: Wolfgang Heine (SPD) wrote in *Berliner Tageblatt* that the German liberals and the Social Democrats were united in their recognition of British parliamentarism as capable of strengthening the state.[575] The newspaper itself also wrote about the introduction of 'real parliamentarism in the Reich'.[576] The right was certainly provoked by such openly pronounced Anglophilia even if it was limited to the admiration of only some aspects of British parliamentarism.

The Social Democrats, the leaders of both liberal parties and to a limited extent the Catholic Centre were thus speaking positively about the potential of some aspects of parliamentarism to support rather than weaken the German war effort. The Conservatives, by contrast, rejected all calls for the extension of the political influence of the Reichstag as incompatible with true monarchy. For them, the monarch alone was the proper leader to decide the fate of his people. They did not want a 'parliamentary regime' in which the monarch would nominate his ministers in accordance with the will of the majority of the parliament. Count Kuno von Westarp, a Prussian civil servant, considered that it was essential to maintain a clear distinction between legislative and executive responsibilities so that the Reichstag should continue to be involved in the legislative process and the budget but refrain from extending its power to issues belonging to the executive.[577]

572 On international public opinion and parliaments, see Harvard 2016.
573 Verhandlungen, Ernst Müller-Meinigen, 29 March 1917, 2844.
574 Verhandlungen, Ernst Müller-Meinigen, 29 March 1917, 2845.
575 *Berliner Tageblatt*, 31 March 1917.
576 *Berliner Tageblatt*, 31 March 1917.
577 Verhandlungen, Kuno von Westarp, 29 March 1917, 2860.

Similar views were echoed by Albrecht von Graefe, who questioned parliamentarism altogether, insisting that the ministers were the representatives of the opinion of the monarch. According to this Prussian civil servant and former soldier, if the monarch were forced to choose his ministers according to the will of the majority in the parliament, he would totally lose his relevance as a political agent. The German constitutional system meant that the crown and the representative institution had equal, independent powers in forming their opinions. This system would be destroyed if the monarch was made no more than an executive dependent on the parliament as then the parliament would exercise absolute rule.[578] Such a rejection of 'the absolutism of the parliament' had been the predominant pre-war argument against parliamentarisation and would reappear in the Weimar debates on a Reichspräsident and the referendum: an institution with authoritarian powers was considered necessary to balance the parliamentary system[579] and to maintain the traditional duality of government. A similar argument would be heard from the Swedish right throughout this period and from the Finnish right still in spring 1919, when a republican constitution combining parliamentarism and a strong presidency was planned.

Erich Mertin of the German Reichspartei put forward an empirical point against parliamentary government that was typical of conservative politicians elsewhere: parliamentarism was a form of government that belonged to the past and was declining; it was not a progressive form of government of the future. Its unavoidable decline had been demonstrated by the experiences of the war: parliamentarism had also decreased in significance in countries that had previously claimed to have practised it. Coalition administrations of those who were considered politically 'capable' and growing bureaucracies governed in Britain and France, too, so that the era of parliamentarism was over in Western Europe as well.[580] This weakening status of parliaments among the Western powers had been discussed in German political literature during the war.[581] A general assumption among the right was that the Prussian political culture offered a more lasting alternative.

Despite the profoundly antiparliamentary statements of the establishment, the German Social Democrats interpreted the attempts of March 1917 as a demonstration of the growing influence of the Reichstag. On 31 March 1917, *Vorwärts* declared that 'the German representation of the people' in the Reichstag had demonstrated its political potential to the entire world by determinedly bringing up the necessity of the political reorganisation of the Reich.[582]

The German constitutional reform would come to a complete stop in just a few months' time, however. Opposition to any far-going reform was heard

---

578 Verhandlungen, Albrecht von Graefe, 30 March 1917, 2920. The absolutism of the parliament was also rejected by the leading constitutional lawyers of the day, including Robert Redslob. Mergel 2002, 40.
579 Mergel 2002, 40.
580 Verhandlungen, Erich Mertin, 30 March 1917, 2921.
581 Llanque 2000, 222.
582 Bollmeyer 2007, 171.

most outspokenly at the end of May 1917, when the commander of a major warship denounced Social Democrat calls for the parliamentarisation of the German monarchy along Western lines, suggesting that such reform demands stood for collaboration with the enemy and urging his sailors to stop such plots against the imperial dynasty.[583] We shall return to this strong underlying opposition to reform in much of the German and especially Prussian polity in section 4.2, after an excursion into Swedish and Finnish parliamentary debates on constitutional questions. The German debates of late March and promises of reform from the executive constituted a primary point of reference for the Swedish and Finnish MPs when they debated their reform needs in the spring and summer of 1917. Conclusions about future transnational developments were frequently drawn on the basis of the German case: the expected German changes were understood as having immediate relevance for the Swedes and Finns as well.

3.3 Sweden: Renewed reform demands under the threat of revolution

3.3.1 The situation created by a repeatedly postponed suffrage reform

Many Swedes had feared a Russian invasion during the First World War, but no such intervention ever materialised. The Swedish wartime government of Hjalmar Hammarskjöld consisted of civil servants and, prioritising the interests of Swedish exports, favoured Germany in its foreign policy. Relations with Britain were poor and tended to become worse in the course of 1917. Nevertheless, Sweden remained neutral despite attempts by the Germanophile court, the Swedish Ambassador in Berlin and several activists to bring Sweden into an open alliance with Germany. The pro-German line began to gradually weaken when no German victory was achieved and the rather more Anglophile left started to confront the government over its policies. The left was evidently turning from Germany to Britain as the primary political model to follow. Although no open alliance with Germany emerged, Sweden had remained a 'Prussia of the North' in terms of its political culture: the Swedish parliament was accused of being a copy of the Prussian representative institution, with its upper chamber (the First Chamber) elected on the basis of a taxation-based scale of forty grades. Much of the national academy, army, administration and political elite – including leading Social Democrats inspired by the German SPD – had traditionally had closer connections with Germany than with Britain and were hence inclined to sympathise with the war effort of that 'cultured' nation. The alliance with Germany was indeed primarily cultural rather than military or even ideological; just as in the case of Finland, it was based on the intertwining histories of the countries. Swedes and Germans (just like Finns and Germans) were viewed as natural allies in most areas of life; they were defenders of shared 'Germanic' values as opposed to those of the

---

583   Leonhard 2014, 649.

barbarians of the east, i.e. the Russians.[584] Ethnic notions of belonging to the same race were not foreign either, although the Finns were not included in them.

This condition of cultural and international relations influenced the postponement of constitutional reforms in Sweden, particularly since all fields of Swedish scholarship remained predominantly connected with the German debates. The sudden change in the state of international affairs created by the Russian Revolution in spring 1917 had an immediate transnational impact on Swedish domestic debates as well. A period of intense constitutional discussion began after its outbreak, bringing to a sudden end the so-called *borgfred* (cf. the synonymous German *Burgfrieden*) – an agreement that the various political groups should refrain from domestic political confrontations such as calls for electoral reform.[585] This activation of the discussion carried on pre-war reform debates but also saw the importation of new discourses created by the transnational events of the Russian Revolution, the British reform and the German Reichstag debates.

A particular national dynamic had been created by the split in the Social Democrat parliamentary group in February, before the outbreak of the Russian Revolution, when 15 MPs joined a separate leftist group.[586] While this split allowed the far left to express their radical views openly, the revisionist stand of the Social Democratic Labour Party was further strengthened under the leadership of Hjalmar Branting. The demands of this party remained moderate, focusing on universal suffrage and parliamentarism rather than revolution as starting points for reform. The party resembled the German SPD in that it was ready for parliamentary cooperation with reformist bourgeois forces. In the opening debates of the parliamentary session, Social Democrat and Liberal members jointly challenged the Prime Minister over food supply questions and trade policies. Even before the outbreak of the Revolution in Russia, the ministry was losing credibility,[587] and on 27 March 1917 King Gustavus V was forced to accept the resignation of the government.[588]

The Russian Revolution was reported extensively in the Swedish press from 16 to 20 March and received with sympathy not only by Socialists but also by many Liberals.[589] The rightist press suggested – revealingly – that the Revolution was a mere plot planned by the Entente and by the British in particular.[590] The Right also linked the strengthening of the Swedish opposition with this kind of sinister Western plotting aimed at subverting ordered government everywhere. The Liberals and Social Democrats had slightly different visions of the future at this time, the Liberals focusing

---

584   Hadenius 2008, 39–41.
585   Olsson 2000, 57.
586   Olsson 2000, 90.
587   Gerdner 1946, 8.
588   Brusewitz 1964, 79.
589   *Social-Demokraten*, 'Självhärskardömets fall', 17 March 1917.
590   *Aftonbladet*, 'Hård tid', 16 March 1917.

on a change in the domestic government. While their activities were not directly linked with the events in Russia, the spread of a revolutionary atmosphere in Europe encouraged them to challenge the ministry over its tendency to ignore the parliament and the press. The Social Democrats, for their part, had difficulties in finding a common policy in the aftermath of their split. While a revolution in an autocratic eastern neighbour was much welcomed – with Hjalmar Branting, the internationally exceptionally well connected Social Democratic leader,[591] heading for a visit to Petrograd in a spirit of socialist internationalism – an excessively radical revolution in either Russia or Sweden was not the wish of moderate mainstream Social Democrats. Despite their diverse interests, the Liberals and Social Democrats joined forces to vote against the ministry, an act that contributed to its disintegration.[592] Cooperation ran more smoothly between these parties than between corresponding sister parties in Britain, Germany and Finland.

The Swedish governmental crisis, which because of its timing was observed with real interest abroad, was resolved with the establishment of a rightist ministry led by Carl Swartz (prime minister) and Arvid Lindman (foreign minister). The parties of the left (which in Swedish political parlance included the Liberals) were unwilling to take the risk of a defeat in the expected election of the Second Chamber.[593] They wanted the government to conclude a trade agreement with Britain and thereby relieve the food situation.[594] They considered that electoral reform could be achieved through a future election victory. Both the Liberals and the Social Democrats were also inspired by transnational encouragement from reformists in Britain, Russia and Germany. In the Prussian conservative press, the Swedish Social Democrats were seen as aiming at as radical a government as possible, and hence the continuation of a non-parliamentary rightist government was welcomed;[595] this illustrates the reciprocity of the transnational connection.

The initial reception of the Russian Revolution among the Swedish left was enthusiastic, but doubts and divisions soon began to emerge: the organ of the Majority Social Democrats cut the amount of news from Russia, while the leftists aimed at augmenting the 'Russian' revolutionary atmosphere through extra-parliamentary demonstrations.[596] The gradually radicalising progress of the Russian Revolution contributed to three domestic crises in Sweden. The first, which began beginning on 11 April and involved inflation and food shortages, gave rise to spontaneous demonstrations around the country which were associated in press reports with the revolution in Petrograd. Radical socialist papers viewed these protests as a similar form of 'direct action against the government of starvation'. A revolutionary moment of transnational mobility, encounters between political agents and

591 Kirby 1986b, 83–92; Wavrinsky 1917, 206.
592 von Sydow 1997, 115; Andræ 1998, 12–13, 22.
593 von Sydow 1997, 116.
594 Olsson 2000, 59.
595 *Neue Pressißische Zeitung*, 29 March 1917. Swartz's studies at the University of Bonn were mentioned to emphasise his links with Germany.
596 Kan 1999b, 103, 107–8.

transnational transfers followed: Vladimir Lenin and his comrades, who had left in Basel Switzerland on 9 April and travelled through Germany to Sassnitz and Trelleborg crossed Sweden on their way back to Russia via Finland on 13 and 14 April.[597]

Hjalmar Branting was simultaneously returning from his visit to Petrograd – straight into a parliamentary debate on suffrage in local elections. The debate took place at the same time as the appearance of open extra-parliamentary agitation including hints of a revolution. Erik Palmstierna, a leading Social Democrat with an aristocratic background, recorded in his diary how people entertained ideas of revolution, which caused great concern among the conservatives.[598] In an interview given during his return journey, Branting stated that the Russian Revolution had started 'an entirely new era'.[599] In the parliament, he addressed the members using the French revolutionary term 'citizens', which made The Right laugh at his ostentatious revolutionary enthusiasm.[600] At the same time, regional newspapers were calling for the defence of 'Swedish democracy'. Reports of hunger demonstrations and the imperial promises of reform in Berlin were published, which supported interpretations claiming the existence of a transnational moment of transformation: the extension of suffrage and the parliamentarisation of government might soon involve the Prussian system, which the Swedish right had regarded as its model. A revolutionary atmosphere was spreading at the local level, in the press and in the parliament. On 21 April, demonstrators in Stockholm were reported to have cheered for a 'Sweden of the people' and sung the International in the front of the Riksdag. The crowd demanded both a solution to the food shortage and 'universal and equal suffrage in local and national elections for both men and women'. Decisively at this stage, the Social Democratic Party leaders emphasised parliamentary cooperation with the other parties of the left in order to achieve political and economic reform; they rejected such direct action. The same policy was reflected in the Social Democrat interpellation on suffrage on 27 April, which was accompanied by a joint call for calm from Branting and the bourgeois party leaders[601]. The party thus reacted to radicalisation at the local level very differently from the Finnish Social Democrats. As a consequence, confrontations between leftist Socialist and Social Democrats increased in Sweden, the former demanding a unicameral parliament and a republic. Shouts such as 'Down with the King' and 'Long live the Revolution' were heard in demonstrations organised by the far left,[602] but the Social Democratic Party leadership consistently followed a moderate line, keeping radical forces in check or out of the party. The leftists

597 Kirby 1986b, 98.
598 Palmstierna 1953, 4 April 1917, 45.
599 *Social-Demokraten*, 'Branting berättar om sin Petrogradresa', 13 April 1917.
600 Palmstierna 1953, 14 April 1917, 46; *Social-Demokraten*, 'En varning och en paroll', 16 April 1917.
601 *Aftonbladet*, 18 April 1917.
602 Palmstierna 1953, 27 April 1917, 52; Andræ 1998, 13, 23, 30, 34–5, 38–9, 50, 100, 108–109, 112; Olsson 2000, 60–1, 64.

combined parliamentary interventions with extra-parliamentary action as demonstrations of the popular will. In a parliamentary interpellation, they challenged the government over the hunger demonstrations and the delaying of constitutional reforms. They did not explicitly demand unicameralism or a republic, but their language was nevertheless revolutionary.[603]

When the conservative government responded to the interpellation, there were some direct anti-parliamentary reactions from the far left. Even though the leftists constituted only a small minority, it was far from evident that Branting's parliamentary line would automatically prevail against the radicals and the demonstrating crowds.[604] At the same time, news from Russia and Finland gave rise to concerns about the spread of revolution. The supporters of council (soviet) government came into the open, and the founding of workers' guards to counter the bourgeois civil guards was proposed.[605] This could well have led to a radicalisation of the type that took place in Finland, and indeed some syndicalists did reject universal suffrage and parliamentarism in favour of direct action.[606] For Finnish socialists, such radicalisation suggested that not only Russia and Germany but potentially Sweden, too, was heading for a revolution. This did not happen, however, as the majority of the Swedish Social Democrats chose a parliamentary strategy, won considerable electoral support and joined the Liberals in a coalition government in the autumn.[607]

The campaign of the left for universal suffrage in local elections, originally launched by the Liberals, did not yet lead to reform. The government wanted to postpone the issue rather than take measures at a time when the direction of the Russian Revolution or the possible reform in Prussia was not yet known. Prime Minister Carl Swartz responded to the interpellations by ignoring the principle of parliamentarism[608] and the international trends of democratisation that the left had emphasised. With its sixty-per-cent majority in the First Chamber, The Right could easily prevent all constitutional reform,[609] a situation similar to that prevailing in contemporary Germany through Prussian influence. The constitutional standstill continued in Sweden while awareness of the changing world around was increasing especially among members of the left. The ideological tensions and prevalent transnational ways of thinking can be reconstructed on the basis of parliamentary debates, something that has not been done systematically in previous Swedish research.

3.3.2 BUILDING 'DAMS OF ICE' OR WELCOMING THE SPRING IN THE MIDST OF TRANSNATIONAL CHANGE

Though not directly involved in the war, Sweden was experiencing its consequences, both economically and in the form of a mounting debate on

---

603   Andræ 1998, 51, 97.
604   Andræ 1998, 81.
605   Andræ 1998, 100.
606   Andræ 1998, 103–104.
607   Andræ 1998, 13.
608   Andræ 1998, 137–8, 142–3.
609   von Sydow 1997, 116.

the constitution. The degree of internationalism and transnational ways of thinking in the Swedish debate was exceptional among the four countries studied here: both the socialist groups and the Liberals were inspired by the transnational transformative and revolutionary spirit of the times, while the conservatives were known to be intellectually connected with German and especially Prussian traditions of thought.

The far left was most possessed by internationalism. As Carl Lindhagen of the leftists, mayor of Stockholm, put it six days after the abdication of Nicholas II and a week before the British and German parliaments would discuss constitutional change, 'the new time which must come' after the war required a revision of the constitution.[610] Drawing a parallel with the German wartime polity, Lindhagen insisted that the 'General Staff' should no longer rule Swedish domestic politics and foreign policy[611] and that exploratory commissions should be sent to Germany, Britain or France to study constitutional issues which had become the 'great question of the future'.[612] The totality of the war forced Sweden, too, to change and to choose between various constitutional models, and the debate focused on whether these models were relevant and which one of them was most suitable.

Among the Social Democrats, Harald Hallén, a radical clergyman, agreed with Lindhagen's rejection of the current political order in Europe, using war metaphors that emphasised the transnational nature of the war experience: 'The work for this new era demands an offensive on the great front, and that we on our little northern front also do what we can to participate in this work.'[613] Such militant socialism provoked the pro-German right to wonder who 'we' were and what the 'offensive' stood for: Did it perhaps imply extra-parliamentary action? Hjalmar Branting, too, described how 'development takes great leaps in backward countries', associating Russia with 'our backward country' and thereby hinting indirectly at a revolutionary moment.[614] Nils Edén, the Liberal leader, joined the call for a faster tempo of reform at a moment which he interpreted as portending a pan-European transition towards the direct participation of the citizens in public affairs.[615] The left thus immediately interpreted the Russian Revolution as a moment for a transnational constitutional change in Sweden as well.

Unlike in Germany or Finland but a little as in Britain, the expected American entry into the war was interpreted by the Swedish left as having constitutional implications. Carl Lindhagen presented American instruments of 'popular government' – including in his view the popular initiative, the referendum and the cancellation of the mandate – as models that deserved attention. This was exceptional in Northern European political discourse, in which doubts about the American system were

610 AK, Carl Lindhagen, 21 March 1917, 34:3.
611 AK, Carl Lindhagen, 21 March 1917, 34:15.
612 AK, Carl Lindhagen, 21 March 1917, 33:38.
613 AK, Harald Hallén, 21 March 1917, 34:11.
614 AK, Hjalmar Branting, 21 March 1917, 33:46. *Social-Demokraten* had reported on the preceding day about the introduction of female suffrage in Russia. 'Allmän kvinnorösträtt i Ryssland', 20 March 1917.
615 AK, Nils Edén, 21 March 1917, 33:48, 50.

commonly voiced. Lindhagen, who had links with Lenin[616] and other leftist socialists in exile in Switzerland, also idealised the Swiss system, according to which the government was formed by a committee of equal ministers elected by the parliament.[617] The same model was familiar at least to Finnish radical socialists and was used by them to challenge 'bourgeois' democracy and parliamentarism as they were applied in Western Europe. Among the Social Democrats, Viktor Larsson doubted the applicability of the American system but welcomed the idea of studying it together with the Swiss model when Swedish reforms were planned.[618]

The Right rejected the Anglo-American models altogether. The historian Karl Hildebrand, the former editor of *Stockholms Dagblad*, was unwilling to import American practices but nevertheless conceded that the war had given rise to a new constitutional situation so that the Swedes, even if not in acute need of constitutional amendments, should watch foreign developments.[619] The Right, on the other hand, emphasised the native tradition of peasant liberty in the form of representation in the diets and popular self-government at the local level and questioned the applicability of foreign versions of democracy and parliamentarism to Sweden.[620] Professor Carl Hallendorff, Rector of the Stockholm School of Economics, who had argued in 1911 that 'English' parliamentarism based as it was on a particular political culture could not be transferred to other countries, considered it pointless to explore foreign experiences as the native ones were so comprehensive. Switzerland was not comparable geographically, and experiences of the referendum in America were not promising.[621] As far as popular liberty, democracy and parliament were concerned, the Swedish tradition was to be followed.

The opposition challenged the government to extend suffrage in local elections in mid-April, after the British and German debates on constitutional reform, the US declaration of war on Germany and the Kaiser's vague promises of rearrangements. The parliamentary debate was preceded by suggestions in the press that Swedish right belonged to a conservative 'international' not unlike that of the socialists, backing the German ideal of the state and supporting such wrong kind of internationalism.[622] The Liberal paper *Dagens Nyheter* had reported that a new era had begun when 'Prussianism as a whole' or, provocatively, 'Kjellén's Prussia' (Professor Kjellén had been recognised by German academia for his criticism of democracy) – was falling apart 'in this strange spring'.[623] The debate was full of international comparisons used by the opposition to pressurise the government. Nils Edén emphasised the fact that Finland had extended suffrage in 1906 under the Russian tsar, that the Prussian monarch was contemplating removing

616 Pipes 1992, 392.
617 AK, Carl Lindhagen, 21 March 1917, 33:29, 64.
618 AK, Viktor Larsson, 21 March 1917, 33:33.
619 AK, Karl Hildebrand, 21 March 1917, 33:34.
620 Nilsson 2004, 79–80; Ihalainen 2015.
621 AK, Carl Hallendorff, 21 March 1917, 33:38–9; Kurunmäki 2014, 172–3.
622 *Dagens Nyheter*, 'Den starkaste känslan', 13 April 1917.
623 *Dagens Nyheter*, 'En ny tid', 10 April 1917; Llanque 2015, 74.

the classification of voters and that the British parliament would adopt a reform completing cumulative extensions of suffrage. Indeed, *all* the other European peoples but Sweden were taking major steps forward.[624] Since Norway and Denmark had already reformed their suffrage systems, Sweden was an island of backwardness that should finally change now that even Russia and Prussia were changing. Swedish conservatives should listen to 'the thunderous voices that can now be heard from Russia'. Sweden did not need a similar revolution, but the Russian Revolution nevertheless demonstrated the impossibility of retaining a regulated suffrage in an age when the principles of liberty and equality were making unprecedented progress.[625] Both Erik Palmstierna of the Social Democrats and Nils Edén of the Liberals referred to the Danish right as an example of realising from 'the voices of the time' that the moment to rearrange the polity had come and that anti-reformist policies had to be given up if a revolution was to be avoided.[626]

After the March debates in the British Commons, *Social-Demokraten* had written about a 'democratic development' that would in the near future lead to a 'growing, victorious advance of democratisation among people in all countries'.[627] The war had rendered the forces of democracy so strong that no country would be able to stop them.[628] The Prussian reactionary system could no longer be sustained; the Chancellor and the Kaiser were considering the abolition of 'the Prussian parody of suffrage' and democratising the Herrenhaus; and calls for parliamentarisation were rising in the new Constitutional Committee in Berlin, while in Sweden, at the same time, a new conservative government had been appointed.[629] In the Riksdag, Gunnar Löwegren saw a reform of suffrage in local elections as unavoidable since democratic breakthroughs were taking place 'everywhere in the outside world', and the examples of Norway, Denmark, Britain and France demonstrated that such a reform led to no radical changes.[630] Harald Hallén lamented the fact that the Swedish system of representation was regarded by foreigners as analogous to the Prussian,[631] which *Social-Demokraten* characterised as 'the old Prussian Junker rule [that was] under increasing pressure from the triumph of democracy throughout the world'.[632] The Swedish right, associated with Prussianism by its political opponents, was thus urged to understand that the world was changing: the revolution in Russia had arisen out of the sufferings of the masses during the war,

---

624 AK, Nils Edén, 14 April 1917, 41:14–15, 21.
625 AK, Nils Edén, 14 April 1917, 41:20–1.
626 AK, Erik Palmstierna & Nils Edén, 14 April 1917, 41:54, 56, 58, 70.
627 *Social-Demokraten*, 30 March 1917.
628 *Social-Demokraten*, 'Kejsar Wilhelms påsklöften', 10 April 1917.
629 *Social-Demokraten*, 'Tyska riksdagen inför den ryska revolutionen', 30 March 1917; 'Svenska högerns regering', 31 March 1917; 'Kejsar Wilhelms påsklöften', 10 April 1917; *Dagens Nyheter*, 'Branting har gjort starkt intryck i Petrograd', 13 April 1917.
630 AK, Gustaf Löwegren, 14 April 1917, 41:22, 25, 27.
631 AK, Harald Hallén, 14 April 1917, 41:32.
632 *Social-Demokraten*, 'Självhärskardömets fall', 17 March 1917.

and a similar rising seemed possible in Germany. Quoting intertextually (and 'trans-parliamentarily') the records of the German Reichstag and his ideological allies to make a transnational point, Hallén related that the pacifist Hugo Haase had already in 1915 complained about the masses of the people suffering both from the economic hardships caused by the war and the consequent loss of their voting rights as a result of the system of class suffrage. Philipp Scheidemann, an internationally well-known German Social Democrat, had similarly pointed out the contradiction between the men fighting in the trenches and their lack of the right to vote.[633] Now that even the Kaiser seemed ready for concessions, now that there was 'springtime in the outside world' and 'rolling waves of freedom' (in rather Wilsonian terms) were felt everywhere, the Swedish right should demonstrate farsightedness.[634] This was 'a memorable time in Swedish political history as far as the influence of the world war is concerned', but unfortunately little was to be expected from the Swedish right.[635] The clergyman went further, asking whether The Right did not at all 'fear a rebelling spirit among the people even in our country', referring to the food demonstrations and suggesting that the Social Democrats were aware of the rising readiness of the masses to revolt. Most provocative was his suggestion that 'Swedish democracy' – an exclusive concept that implied the reformist left as united political actors and also embraced the lower classes in a social sense – would receive foreign moral and material support if it decided to force through a turn to democracy.[636] This was a revolutionary suggestion: without an immediate reform following the German example, a revolution of the Russian kind, supported by foreign socialists, might break out. As we shall see in subsection 7.3.3, this threat constituted a revolutionary act that The Right would take up again intertextually over two years later.

The revolutionary atmosphere of the debate of 14 April 1917 intensified further when Hjalmar Branting, returning from a visit to Petrograd to congratulate the revolutionaries on the victory of the socialist proletariat and the birth of a new Russia,[637] after meeting the Finnish Social Democrats in Helsinki and writing his speech during the long train journey home, painted images of an ongoing global revolution. Here we have a political agent, an historical body, whose mobility and experiences in cross-national space contributed to transnational transfers, albeit of a selected kind. Branting bemoaned the fact that Sweden was 'a museum of relics with regard to its constitution […] in the new era which is banging on the door'.[638] He further asserted that the world had recently seen 'the greatest events since the time of the French Revolution': Russia was turning into a democratic republic. The expected reforms in Prussia were even more relevant for Sweden:

633 AK, Harald Hallén, 14 April 1917, 41:32.
634 AK, Harald Hallén, 14 April 1917, 41:34–5.
635 AK, Harald Hallén, 14 April 1917, 41:35.
636 AK, Harald Hallén, 14 April 1917, 41:35–6.
637 *Dagens Nyheter*, 20 March 1917.
638 AK, Hjalmar Branting, 14 April 1917, 41:67.

'[E]ven in the old solidly built state of the Junkers in the south, they have begun to feel that the time has arrived when democracy cannot be directly rejected or postponed to the future.'[639] Sweden, which had sometimes been characterised as the 'Mecklenburg of the North' owing to the strong political position of its landowners,[640] also needed to change. Branting considered that the signs of the age compelled the Swedish people to look for more forceful methods to make suffrage reform a reality and overcome the constant opposition.[641] This was a moderate suggestion in comparison with Hallén's, but it was nevertheless a challenge presented in a transnational context. Swedish Social Democrats, even more strongly than those in other countries, pointed to the revolutionary changes taking place everywhere in the surrounding world, which simply forced Sweden to change. Even if it was aimed at converting The Right, this discourse was based on the genuine beliefs of a moderate internationalist socialist (which was what Branting was), especially after his experiences in revolutionary Petrograd. The points were reinforced in the upper chamber: Ola Waldén saw 'the rule of the Junkers', the alleged ideological allies of The Right, coming to an end and the people liberating themselves from tsarism and receiving full civil rights, including equal and universal suffrage in Russia. Such upheavals made a reform in Sweden timely, particularly as the Swedes knew how to make their voices heard by legal means (i.e. in the German way) so that no revolutionary (i.e. Russian) methods were needed.[642] This view moderated the threat of revolution.

The transnational experiences of mobility by politically active historical persons were also noticeable in the contributions of the far left. Carl Lindhagen, who had on the preceding day hosted Lenin on his way via Sweden and on to Finland,[643] was enthusiastic about the current revolution remoulding the world. He congratulated the revisionist Branting and the Swedish people – somewhat ironically – for having brought revolutionary 'breezes' from Petrograd.[644] Fredrik Ström, who had arranged accommodation for Lenin in Stockholm,[645] repeated the point in the upper chamber, lamenting the constitutional deadlock in Sweden in comparison with developments in all of its neighbours and thanking Branting for having brought 'very strong eastern winds' from 'the country of revolution'. He urged *all* parties of the left (including the Liberals) to prepare for a more concrete 'constitutional battle' instead of a mere battle of words;[646] this implied that parliamentary debate was a somewhat ineffective way to achieve reform

---

639 AK, Hjalmar Branting, 14 April 1917, 41:66. Branting's comparison with the French Revolution was also cited by *The Herald* on 31 March 1917, using a report in *Social-Demokraten*.
640 Brandt 2009, 166.
641 AK, Hjalmar Branting, 14 April 1917, 41:66.
642 FK, Ola Waldén, 14 April 1917, 32:27.
643 Pipes 1992, 392.
644 AK, 14 April 1917, 41:71.
645 *Dagens Nyheter*, 'Trettio ryska revolutionärer på hemväg via Stockholm', 13 April 1917; 'De ryska socialisterna i Stockholm', 14 April 1917.
646 FK, Fredrik Ström, 14 April 1917, 32:17.

and suggested that the manipulation of parliamentary procedure or extra-parliamentary means might be used instead. Ivar Vennerström, for his part, stated: 'The Revolution is casting its shadow over Sweden, too.'[647] As few would accept the unpredictable Russian situation as a model, he emphasised the Prussian readiness for reform. Now that Norway and Denmark had modernised their constitutions, Sweden remained 'a little museum in Europe exhibiting all sorts of bureaucracy'.[648] In Carl Lindhagen's vision, Sweden should prepare for 'an outbreak of spring in all politics' and 'a breaking-up of the ice', with the people 'breaking their old fetters' and 'plunging into something new'.[649] This was not a mere application of vernal metaphors to describe the transnational revolutionary experience; it was also alluding to the Marxist revolutionary agitation linked to the hunger demonstrations in Stockholm on the preceding days, to discussions between international radical socialists staying in Stockholm and to the passage of Lenin, the most radical of Socialist leaders, via Sweden to Russia to prepare an even more far-reaching revolution. The revolution that the Kautskyists had been expecting had arrived, and it might turn into a more radical change than had ever been expected.

Lindhagen's vernal metaphors were characteristic of the Swedish constitutional debate more generally and especially in the spring of democracy in 1917. In addition to being a classical figure of speech symbolising revival and transformation, they reflected powerful Nordic experiences of spring more generally and implied the obvious need for a constitutional change in Sweden and the current revolutionary process, which the reformist left understood as transnational and unavoidable. The use of the spring metaphors made the revolutionary experience concrete by building on the climatic realities of March and April 1917: the north of Europe (Petrograd above all) had experienced an exceptionally cold winter accompanied by famine until temperatures had suddenly risen to spring-like figures in early March. People had come out in the sunshine in the Russian capital – first demonstrating, then rioting and finally joining in the revolutionary activity.[650] A promise of spring after a difficult winter was likewise experienced both physically and politically in Stockholm and Helsinki.[651] In the minds of the reformists, both left and centre, the change turned into a unique experience of an irresistible spring of democracy, and this was reflected in the use of vernal metaphors. For radical Marxists, the passage of Lenin via Stockholm constituted another physical demonstration of the arrival of their expected ideological spring. The Russian Revolution was experienced and internalised very concretely and the experience was expressed with metaphors of spring. The Liberals also used natural

---

647 AK, Ivar Vennerström, 14 April 1917, 41:75.
648 AK, Ivar Vennerström, 14 April 1917, 41:46.
649 AK, Carl Lindhagen, 14 April 1917, 41:47.
650 Pipes 1992, 274; Dahlmann 2014, 39; Bessel 2014, 129–30.
651 In Helsinki, the weather remained variable as usual. Although 17 March, when the news of a revolution in Petrograd was confirmed, began with a snowstorm, the cold winter was coming to an end there, too. Nyström 2013, 120, 157.

metaphors to describe the irresistibility of democratisation, referring to spring, waves and dams of ice.

Among the Liberals, Mauritz Hellberg, the radical editor-in-chief of *Karlstads-Tidningen*, and Otto von Zweigbergk, the editor-in-chief of *Dagens Nyheter*, challenged the historiography of The Right with the liberal alternative, suggesting that true Gothic liberty was still lacking and that the legacy of the national myth of popular representation since times immemorial[652] was still being violated in Sweden after the fall of the *ancien régime* in Russia. The semi-autocratic state of imperial Germany – and especially Prussianism – was idealised in both political theory and practice by the monarchy and The Right, who dominated the First Chamber just as the Junkers ruled the Herrenhaus, neither of which institutions truly represented the people. In a comparison of parliamentary systems, Sweden appeared as 'a kind of miniature Germany up here in the north, a solid reactionary bastion against our neighbours' albeit now facing a reform thanks to the expected changes in Prussia.[653] The progress of this season of reform was as irresistible as the coming spring was, and The Right should hence study the model of the German reform and stop 'building dams of ice in springtime'.[654] The Swedish left was encouraged in their argumentation for reform by news of a turn in German politics even more than by the Russian Revolution.

The Right conceptualised this spring quite differently. Karl Hildebrand, a leading Germanophile in Sweden, denied the validity of parallels between the political reconsiderations of the Kaiser and Swedish demands to reform regulated suffrage. Such 'democratic' circumstances prevailed in Swedish municipalities that Sweden was already more advanced in democracy and equality than, say, Britain, France or the United States, and Prussia would hardly catch up it as a result of its reform.[655] In Hildebrand's view, the more radical the events of the surrounding world got, the greater was the risk that their achievements would not endure and a backlash of the type witnessed after the French Revolution would ensue.[656] According to Erik Räf, the demands of the left for 'a political revolution everywhere in our country' should be simply turned down.[657] Ernst Lindblad complained about the abuse of the threat of a revolution by leftist leaders (i.e. Branting) who ran as envoys between Petrograd and Stockholm. Their attempts to persuade the Swedish people to believe in the necessity of a revolution of the Russian kind were useless as no grounds for deeper discontent existed. He claimed that Finnish and Russian workers were just aiming to gain what the

---

652   Nilsson 2002b, 88–9; Ihalainen 2015.
653   FK, Mauritz Hellberg & Otto von Zweigbergk, 14 April 1917, 32:22–3, 30–1.
654   FK, Otto von Zweigbergk, 14 April 1917, 32:31–2. Noteworthy is that similar metaphors of waves, flood and dams had been used by the Social Democratic Philipp Scheidemann to characterise the unavoidability of the reform in the German Reichstag in late February. Müller 2002, 294.
655   AK, Karl Hildebrand, 14 April 1917, 41:38, 68.
656   AK, Karl Hildebrand, 14 April 1917, 41:69.
657   AK, Erik Räf, 14 April 1917, 41:63.

Swedish already possessed.⁶⁵⁸ Samuel Clason emphasised the fact that the Swedish reform had already brought 'equal suffrage to the Second Chamber' and the Prussian case was hence not comparable.⁶⁵⁹ This overlooked both the remaining limitations on Swedish suffrage and universal male suffrage in Reichstag elections from 1867 on. For The Right, the Swedish system remained more advanced than any other and therefore in no need of reform.

A new confrontation followed as the interpellations of the Social Democrats and the far left that were presented in the parliament in a spirit of socialist internationalism interpreted foreign developments as directly relevant to Sweden. Hjalmar Branting depicted how '[g]lobal events of extraordinary extent and scope are revealing themselves before our eyes this spring of 1917',⁶⁶⁰ thereby emphasising the existence of a universal moment of revolution and associating it with the outbreak of spring, both of which were concretely visible and also audible in a simultaneous demonstration for women's suffrage outside the parliament building.⁶⁶¹ After hearing the government's response, Branting expressed his disappointment that 'the international movement for political equality which is making progress all over the world' and 'tremors that are greater than anything that Europe has experienced for several centuries' still had not made The Right rethink their position.⁶⁶² Natural metaphors of revolution of an almost Kautskyist deterministic type were being used here.⁶⁶³ Branting's interpretation of the state of reform in the European great powers was nevertheless optimistic: a stronghold of reactionary politics had fallen in Russia; in Germany there was no going back to a country ruled by the Junkers; belief in a democratic future had risen in Austria; and female suffrage had been approved by an overwhelming majority in the British House of Commons. Denmark had already received a democratised constitution, and the Dutch right had conceded the necessity of reform. What the Swedish Social Democrats wanted was not 'Russian methods or Russian solutions' but a national reform⁶⁶⁴ realised in line with German Social Democracy. Harald Hallén pointed out, however, that such strong calls for reform would not have been

658 FK, Ernst Lindblad, 14 April 1917, 32:24.
659 FK, Samuel Clason, 14 April 1917, 32:35.
660 AK, Hjalmar Branting, 27 April 1917, 50:21; see also Ivar Vennerström, 50:24.
661 *Social-Demokraten*, 'Ett imponerande kvinnotåg i Stockholm', 28 April 1917.
662 AK, Hjalmar Branting, 5 June 1917, 72:5–6.
663 The influence of Karl Kautsky as a leading Social Democratic theoretician may have been felt in the Swedish socialist use of vernal metaphors: reform, if not revolution, was unavoidable as a result of natural forces influencing societies globally. On the other hand, some Swedish Liberals, too, liked to use metaphors of spring burgeoning (*blomstertiden*).
664 AK, Hjalmar Branting, 5 June 1917, 72:5–7. Finland did not appear as a relevant point of comparison to Branting despite the simultaneous (perhaps excessively) radicalising aims of the Finnish Social Democrats for parliamentary sovereignty. Finland might have made an inconvenient comparison given that the country had a Social Democratic parliamentary majority after the introduction of universal suffrage and was nevertheless in a state of crisis. Since the country was still part of the Russian Empire, Finnish solutions might also be associated with Russian ones.

presented in Sweden without the Russian Revolution; the old calls for liberty had been revived because the Revolution had 'shaken the world' and caused 'liberation movements to sweep through societies'.[665] The Swedish electoral system was simply backward in comparison with the other Nordic countries and Europe more generally now that even the Hohenzollerns and Habsburgs had recognised the need to take the will of the people into consideration.[666]

The far left would not exclude the possibility of the Revolution reaching Sweden. According to Ivar Vennerström, the international situation demonstrated that a revolutionary wave originating from Russia was touching every country and would eventually prevail over the reactionary Swedes as well – if not otherwise then through a real revolution.[667] Zeth Höglund, a leftist activist recently liberated from Långholmen prison, quoted the historian Erik Gustaf Geijer in suggesting that Sweden was like Russia in allowing a revolution to come about and being surprised once it finally broke out.[668] Informed by the Finnish socialists K. H. Wiik and Yrjö Sirola, who had recently visited Stockholm, the far leftists also pointed to the socialist majority in the Finnish parliament striving for the further democratisation and parliamentarisation of the political system.[669] Carl Lindhagen criticised the Swedes for not following 'the daughter country Finland' in the introduction of a radical parliamentary reform with a unicameral parliament and universal suffrage for men and women.[670] Continuing the use of metaphors, Lindhagen foresaw the current *Ragnarök* (in Norse mythology the final great battle and rebirth of the world, known in German as *Götterdammerung*) of the world war turning into 'a terrible breakthrough' in the West, too, with consequences identical to those of the Russian Revolution.[671] Fredrik Ström, the party secretary of the far leftists, went further still, urging the democrats to crush the First Chamber[672] – a revolutionary declaration to which The Right would later return in intertextual references. The far left were quite daring in their predictions of a coming revolution; this distinguished them from the Majority Social Democrats and their more cautious ideological brethren in Germany, but they did not go quite so far as the revolutionary rhetoric of the Finnish Social Democrats. This radicalisation of the Swedish far-left nevertheless

---

665 AK, Harald Hallén, 5 June 1917, 72:21; quotes from AK, Erik Palmstierna, 5 June 1917, 72:44.
666 AK, Axel Sterne, 5 June 1917, 72:41–2; Ernst Hage, 7 June 1917, 76:25.
667 AK, Ivar Vennerström, 5 June 1917, 72:12, 14.
668 AK, Zeth Höglund, 5 June 1917, 72:72.
669 AK, Ivar Vennerström, 5 June 1917, 72:13.
670 AK, Carl Lindhagen, 5 June 1917, 72:59. Among the Social Democrats, too, Värner Rydén looked to both Norway and Finland as examples of how unicameralism could be limited with minority provisions or with organs like the Grand Committee in Finland, which functioned like an upper house. His contacts with Finland suggested to him that such a restriction on majority rule actually enabled the conservatives to halt a lot of reform legislation; this led him to speak for the preservation of the bicameral system. AK, 7 June 1917, 76:32–3.
671 AK, Carl Lindhagen, 9 June 1917, 78:71.
672 FK, Fredrik Ström, 9 June 1917, 56:48.

supported a similar trend in Finland as revolutionary forces seemed to be active both in Russia and in Sweden, and potentially in Germany, too.

The Liberals remained rhetorically more dedicated to transnational 'waves' of reform than their brethren elsewhere. Their leader Nils Edén viewed Sweden as a participant in the ongoing upheaval, 'the tremendous world events which involve us', and condemned opposition to reform as being against the 'spirit of the times'.[673] Mauritz Hellberg saw the war as having brought about 'a mighty democratic current in different countries, and even we have been touched by the waves of this current'; historical forces were involved so that 'times of destitution tend to become times of popular liberation'.[674] British, Danish, Dutch, Finnish and Norwegian examples spoke for an immediate introduction of female suffrage, and so did the contribution of Swedish women in wartime.[675] The Netherlands should be considered a particularly encouraging example as 'the country has an old culture' unlike the American one and certainly did not have an excessively radical constitution;[676] female suffrage was thus not merely an American, Finnish or Norwegian peculiarity. Though not threatening a revolution, Vice-Speaker Daniel Persson suggested that revolutions were more likely to occur in countries in which reforms were opposed.[677] This was a leading Liberal politician saying that the Swedish right was to blame should Sweden experience a revolution.

The Right would not give in to claims of backwardness[678] and rather denied transnational trends and the relevance of international comparisons. Karl Hildebrand again lauded the advanced status of the Swedish polity, denying any resemblance between the Swedish and Prussian electoral systems because Prussia lagged so far behind. Peripheral countries like Rumania would not surpass Sweden with their reforms, he claimed, and no one knew what the Russian reforms would lead to.[679] On the same day, *Aftonbladet* reported that the socialists were taking over in Russia and that total chaos was to be expected.[680] As for female suffrage in Britain, the model could not be applied to Sweden as Swedish women lacked any political education.[681] Restrictions on female suffrage remained in Britain, too, whereas 'none of the great civilised nations [countries with *Kultur*]' other than Britain had given women the vote. Finland was a smaller country (and obviously not so civilised) and found itself 'constitutionally in a less normal situation'; it did not provide an example that was 'encouraging or worthy of imitation',[682] particularly as the extension of suffrage had led to

673 AK, Nils Edén, 5 June 1917, 72:18, 20.
674 FK, Mauritz Hellberg, 9 June 1917, 56:19.
675 AK, Theodor Zetterstrand, 9 June 1917, 78:80; FK, Gerhard Halfred von Koch, 9 June 1917, 56:29.
676 AK, 9 June 1917, 78:62.
677 AK, Daniel Persson, 5 June 1917, 72:36.
678 AK, Conrad Vahlquist, 5 June 1917, 72:40.
679 AK, Karl Hildebrand, 5 June 1917, 72:51.
680 *Aftonbladet*, 'Upplösning i Ryssland närmar sig fullständig kaos', 5 June 1917.
681 FK, Rudolf Kjellén, 9 June 1917, 56:43.
682 FK, August Bellinder, 9 June 1917, 56:55.

a socialist parliamentary majority. Rudolf Kjellén rejected the unpatriotic internationalism of the left in borrowing ideas from sister parties abroad and presenting foreign achievements as their own,[683] the allusions being to the Social Democrats in Germany (and possibly Finland) and to the Liberals in Britain, the Netherlands, Denmark and Norway. Dedicated to German political theory, he warned about the rise of unreasonable mass power and party conflicts if 'Western' parliamentarism of the French type were to be introduced.[684] David Norman criticised attempts to persuade the masses to believe that Sweden was a leading reactionary country in Europe since the current problems were temporary, arising out of the war.[685] Erik Räf even insinuated that the left aimed at 'the old time of decadence in Israel' where 'women would prevail over the people',[686] women obviously not belonging to the people. Ultra-conservatism evidently had a stronghold in both houses of the parliament. Denying transnational change, its supporters succeeded in postponing democratisation for the time being.

3.3.3 A GLOBAL BREAKING-UP OF THE ICE FOR THE FORCES OF DEMOCRACY?

The conceptualisations and metaphors of democracy were highly divided in Sweden in spring 1917. It is noteworthy how dominant the concept of democracy and its derivations were in the Swedish debate, not only in the reform demands of the left but also in the counter-arguments from The Right. Reflections of the Wilsonian rhetoric of democracy were heard on the same day, 16 March, that the newspapers reported about the fall of tsarism. The old debate on suffrage reform was immediately activated by the Russian Revolution with its internationalist impulses. Carl Lindhagen, the Marxist Mayor of Stockholm, asked the foreign minister about Swedish plans for what he saw as an approaching era of 'true democracy' in a new world order.[687] He called for a constitutional reform that would create space 'for democratic people in democratic regimes' and for informed public participation in self-government. This would be achieved through universal suffrage, the popular initiative and the referendum, all projects of the international socialist movement.[688] However, Lindhagen viewed 'democracy' in its Western form with a critical eye: the United States also showed that not everything was democratic that was called so. For this active socialist internationalist inspired by the events in Petrograd, the goal should be 'direct popular rule' (*omedelbar folkstyre*) organised in such a way as to prevent demagogy from taking over and to secure the political education of the people.[689] Instead of Western models, the leftists argued for the Swiss 'democratic order'. Here they were motivated by Marxist discussions

683 FK, Rudolf Kjellén, 9 June 1917, 56:43.
684 Brandt 2009, 167; Kurunmäki 2014, 174.
685 AK, David Norman, 5 June 1917, 72:68–9.
686 AK, Erik Räf, 9 June 1917, 78:76, 78.
687 AK, Carl Lindhagen, 16 March 1917, 32:4.
688 AK, Carl Lindhagen, 21 March 1917, 33:28–9; 34:3. These ideas were discussed by Karl Kautsky. Kautsky 1907, 58–60; Häupel 1993, 217.
689 AK, Carl Lindhagen, 21 March 1917, 33:37.

about that system, Lenin's exile in Switzerland and the radical Zimmerwald movement, which had organised its meetings there and used Stockholm as an alternative venue for international activities.[690] Ministers were to be directly elected by the parliament, a system that differed from 'the so-called parliamentary formation of government', which was 'the opposite of democracy'.[691] Finnish radical Social Democrats would argue along similar lines later in 1917 to justify their constitutional radicalism.

This far-left view needs to be contrasted with Majority Social Democrat visions of a more process-like 'future democracy', in which parliamentarism provided the key mechanism. Hjalmar Branting set it as the goal of democratic development that 'free and enlightened peoples would decide on their fates as far as possible'. The 'democratic line of development' would gradually lead, thanks to universal suffrage and majority rule, towards 'an implemented democracy'.[692] Branting's would-be Liberal ally Nils Edén also called for a faster pace in 'the democratic development'.[693]

A typically rightist response came from Carl Hallendorf, who redescribed the established political order as democracy, speaking about 'the democracy which we have' and which, he thought, should be developed to create an increased political maturity and capability among the masses,[694] the implication being that much was still lacking in the understanding of the nation at large. The inherited Swedish system of representative government was presented as a ready-made democracy and hence in no need of radical reforms, just minor adjustments.[695]

British observers thought (wishfully) that the Swedes would move to the side of democracy as a consequence of the Russian Revolution and the increasing isolation of Germany.[696] In mid-April, the internationalists of the Majority Social Democrats were openly flying the flag of democracy. Gunnar Löwegren, who had studied in Germany, Britain and France, lamented how the Swedes had been left out while 'today, everywhere outside in the world one can see great and powerful democratic trends which have made the autocracy of the east fall and have penetrated even a country like Prussia'; this made the Swedish situation intolerable.[697] The breakthrough of 'democratism' (*demokratismen*)[698] was visible in every neighbouring country. The Swedish right, by contrast, rejected democratic control of the French and British type and wanted to maintain the 'non-democratic' governmental control of 'democratic institutions'. What was needed was a parliamentarisation of the constitution and a democratisation of government to end 'a parody of

---

690   Pipes 1992, 382.
691   AK, Carl Lindhagen, 21 March 1917, 33:64.
692   AK, Hjalmar Branting, 21 March 1917, 33: 44.
693   AK, Nils Edén, 21 March 1917, 33:50.
694   AK, Carl Hallendorf, 21 March 1917, 33:60.
695   See Ihalainen 2015 for a more extensive discussion.
696   *The Manchester Guardian*, 'Sweden', 30 March 1917.
697   AK, Gustaf Löwegren, 14 April 1917, 41:22.
698   AK, Gustaf Löwegren, 14 April 1917, 41:27. 'Democratism' had also appeared in the American *Webster's Revised Unabridged Dictionary* (1913), where it was defined as '[t]he principles or spirit of a democracy.'

popular government'.[699] For this transnationally connected Social Democrat, models of Western democracy and parliamentarism were directly applicable to Sweden irrespective of the result of the war. Löwegren believed in political progress achieved through parliamentarisation and democratisation as political processes: the establishment of democratic institutions at all levels would create opportunities for the talents of the people to develop and lead to the increase of reason among the masses; it would not produce upheavals as The Right claimed.[700] These evolutionary rather than revolutionary views differed dramatically from those of most Finnish Social Democrats, who emphasised immediate reforms as opposed to advancing democracy through education and discussion and who did not view Western European parliamentary systems as models for the Finnish constitution.

Hjalmar Branting's role as a political agent crossing frontiers with his mobility and contributing to transnational discursive transfers, becomes particularly clear in his contribution to the debate on democracy in the Swedish parliament on 14 April 1917. The chairman of the Social Democrats had just returned from a visit to Petrograd where he had met his old radical socialist contacts from the days of student activism and created new links. Branting had encountered a radical but diverse debate on democracy in Petrograd and also in Helsinki where he had met Finnish Social Democrats.[701] During the long train journey, he had authored a parliamentary speech and given interviews to Swedish journalists. Soon after the arrival of the train from Haparanda, where he crossed the frontier from Finland, he was in the parliament, declaring that the long postponed suffrage reform was 'a vital issue for the democratisation of Sweden', 'democratisation' standing for 'democratic equality with respect to the public affairs of state and community',[702] i.e. universal suffrage for men and women. Equal voting rights constituted 'simple democracy'.[703] While those calling for 'a democratic order' had looked to 'Western democracies' (Branting was constantly accused by The Right of being a supporter of the Entente[704]), Sweden's neighbours were taking steps towards democracy: Russia would overtake Sweden as 'a democratic republic', and Prussia was also preparing for reform. Even if enthused to some extent by his revolutionary experiences in Petrograd, the revisionist Branting had written a conspicuously moderate speech, in which the definition of democracy did not go beyond universal suffrage, the assumption being that the necessary reforms would follow later. Quite clearly, he did not regard the Russian Revolution (and perhaps also the plans of the Finnish sister party) as models for the Swedish socialists to follow.

---

699 AK, Gustaf Löwegren, 14 April 1917, 41:24, 27.
700 AK, Gustaf Löwegren, 14 April 1917, 41:26-7.
701 See also Ihalainen 2015, 4-5, on Branting's abuse of the spatial context during the debate.
702 AK, 14 April 1917, 41:63-4.
703 AK, 14 April 1917, 41:66-7.
704 *Aftonbladet*, 'Hr Branting som krigsaktivist', 13 April 1917.

Internationalist revisionism was Branting's line, but his party also kept open the possibility of a more revolutionary strategy to please those attracted by radical socialist revolutionary understandings of democracy. In terms recalling Marxist discourse, Harald Hallén accused The Right of 'class egoism amongst the ruling clique'[705] and indirectly threatened a potentially violent insurrection: their opposition would fall in the face of international pressures for democracy from the united masses (which could also be called a 'democracy' in Marxist parlance, as the contemporary British and Finnish examples demonstrate). The Russian example showed that this 'democracy (*demokratien*) can become the complete possessor of its own house'; 'The Swedish democracy' (*demokratien*) in the sense of the reformist masses would get moral and material support from the international democracy if they should decide to force through democracy as a form of government in Sweden.[706] Hallén's radical Marxist democracy was based on political and social forces, groups of people (the workers) who were prepared to take over and, with transnational support, create a democracy (as a system of government) to their liking. The socialist revolutionary understanding of the rule of the masses as democracy and the rather more Kautskyist or revisionist understanding of democracy as a process were combined here; what was radical was that the reform or revolution leading to democracy might also be effected with support from abroad. Under pressure from the far left, there were impulses among the Majority Social Democrats to retain some of the threat of possible revolution – and to simultaneously pressurise The Right: if you do not accept the moderate reform suggested by us, you will get a revolution by the radicals instead.

At the same time, the leftists, too, spoke for reform rather than revolution – despite Carl Lindhagen's discussion with Lenin on the days preceding the debate. Lindhagen presented the suggested reform as the start of a long (peaceful) process of building 'democratic forms' for Sweden, the goal of cooperation between 'the democratic parties' (excluding only The Right) being 'democratic life' in 'true democracy'.[707] Ivar Vennerström attacked the 'anti-democratism' (*anti-demokratismen*) of The Right, introducing a tactical counter-concept to 'democratisation'.[708] Fredrik Ström described the transnational reform: 'People around us are marching towards increased democracy,' whereas nothing was happening in Sweden.[709] Rightist anti-reformism does not seem to have led to any extreme radicalisation of the Swedish far left. A sociological explanation might be that many of the MPs of the Swedish left were highly educated professionals, some like Branting even from upper-class backgrounds,[710] arguing against the professionals of other parties. This decreased the inspiration for, and the influence of, socialist agitation, especially in comparison to Finland.

705   AK, Harald Hallén, 14 April 1917, 41:32.
706   AK, Harald Hallén, 14 April 1917, 41:36.
707   AK, Carl Lindhagen, 14 April 1917, 41:45.
708   AK, Ivar Vennestöm, 14 April 1917, 41.
709   FK, Fredrik Ström, 14 April 1917, 32:17.
710   Eskola 2011, 16.

The Right responded with further rhetorical redescriptions. The historian and newspaper editor Karl Hildebrand, who had travelled in Germany during the war, presented Sweden as a sufficiently democratic society, building on a conservative version of the Swedish historical narrative of the rise of liberty and democracy: both its constitution and 'the spirit of society' were already 'far more democratic than in most other countries'; also 'the development in Sweden is much more democratic' than in republics. Foreign constitutions might have 'democratic intentions', but they were overshadowed by what Hildebrand called 'democratic spirit' of Swedish society,[711] which referred to the traditions of peasant representation and to the extensions of suffrage carried out in the 1900s. Sweden was democratic by definition and was experiencing a process of further democratisation as the rising salaries of the workers were increasing the number of voters with the result that 'the whole suffrage system is about to be immensely democratised'.[712] 'A strong democratising development' existed, and 'democratic influence' had been extensive. Once this ongoing transformation towards democracy proceeded far enough, the formal constitution could also be changed, but that time had not yet arrived, Hildebrand declared.[713] While The Right rejected immediate further reforms as unnecessary, there was a promise of evolution towards more democratic forms in the future, which went some way to recognising the inevitability of change at least as far as the lower chamber was concerned. The upper chamber should not be 'democratised' as it was already one of the most democratically elected ones in the world.[714] Though this may have been true in relative terms, such a counterfactual claim shows that the Swedish right really believed in the power of redescription.

For the Liberals, democracy was a concept that called for immediate reform measures. In Mauritz Hellberg's view, many conservatives had been mistaken in assuming that the war would save European polities from democracy; on the contrary, it had made democracy inevitable everywhere. If Europe was to see 'a great democratic wave' after the war, the Swedish system would need to be changed anyway.[715] Otto von Zweigbergk had published an editorial in *Dagens Nyheter* complaining about a plutocratic minority denying 'the "reorientation" in a democratic direction that takes place out there in large countries' and trying to stop 'the entire democratic development'.[716] Democratic forces would inevitably overcome the rule of the Junkers in Germany as well.[717] Speaking in the parliament, he saw 'democratic development' as self-evident, pointing out that even the rightist leader Ernst Trygger had recognised the twentieth century as 'the century of democracy'. There was no way to halt 'the democratic development' and no sense in 'assaulting democracy'. What the political theorists of The

---

711   AK, Karl Hildebrand, 14 April 1917, 41:38.
712   AK, Karl Hildebrand, 14 April 1917, 41:40.
713   AK, Karl Hildebrand, 14 April 1917, 41:69.
714   FK, Knut von Geijer and Samuel Clason, 14 April 1917, 32:12, 35.
715   FK, Mauritz Hellberg, 14 April 1917, 32:22–3.
716   *Dagens Nyheter*, 'Situationsbilder', 14 April 1917.
717   *Dagens Nyheter*, 'Situationsbilder', 14 April 1917.

Right should understand was that the deconstruction of Prussianism by democratic forces offered the only way to end the war (as President Wilson had recently been suggesting).[718] A clear Social Democratic and Liberal ideological and discursive front on the side of democratisation had been formed, and it used transnational references to both Germany and the West as its rhetorical weapons.

In a Social Democratic interpellation, no revolution against the established order was declared but the rhetoric of democracy was used extensively to describe an ongoing transnational process of political change and its implications for reform in Sweden. The war had unexpectedly led to 'democratic demands' by 'all peoples' for 'a radical break with the old system', so that the few would no longer decide for the many.[719] The Russian Revolution had initiated this 'democratic wave' and 'the breaking-up of the ice for the forces of democracy all over the world' – the processes of change appearing as irresistible natural phenomena. This wave had first hit Germany and was influencing Austria (where the internal political crisis would lead to the recall of the Reichsrat in late May) and Hungary (where the prime minister would soon resign as a result of the crisis).[720] For Sweden, these political changes that were expected in the Central Powers were more significant than the Russian Revolution. This 'general advancement of democracy', added to the fact that Sweden's Scandinavian neighbours had already achieved the full democratisation of suffrage, meant that 'a truly democratic constitutional revision' had become unavoidable in Sweden as well.[721] 'Democracy' as an exigent transnational process was brought to the centre of Social Democratic policy and the expected reforms in the Central Powers (rather than those in Russia or Britain) were used to put pressure on The Right for immediate reform. Exploiting the teleological national narrative of immemorial democracy, Hjalmar Branting urged The Right to participate in a common policy for 'continued development in our country based on democracy as the only alternative'.[722] Like conservatives in other countries, they should see that '[t]he era of democracy has begun and does not allow itself to be suppressed'[723] and that 'a constitutional *revision* [a suitable word for a revisionist!] ... in accordance with the claims of democracy', that is general and equal suffrage, had become necessary.[724] Axel Sterne, a journalist writing in *Folkbladet*, accused The Right of denying 'democracy what belongs to democracy' – making use of the double meaning of the term – whereas 'nothing may reign over or alongside the sovereignty of the will of the people'.[725] Erik Palmstierna, known as 'the Red Baron', accused

718 FK, Otto von Zweigbergk, 14 April 1917, 32:29–30.
719 AK, 27 April 1917, 50:21.
720 AK, 27 April 1917, 50:22.
721 AK, 27 April 1917, 50:22–3.
722 AK, Hjalmar Branting, 5 June 1917, 72:5.
723 AK, Hjalmar Branting, 5 June 1917, 72:6–7.
724 AK, Hjalmar Branting, 5 June 1917, 72:63.
725 AK, Axel Sterne, 5 June 1917, 72:41, 43.

The Right of 'class rule',⁷²⁶ a rather rare usage in Swedish Social Democrat discourse in comparison with the Finnish, and interestingly employed here by an aristocrat.

The parallel leftist interpellation was more in tune with radical Marxist understandings of democracy, containing as it did descriptions of 'the voices of myriad crowds' crying out their longing for 'a profound democratic constitutional reform',⁷²⁷ a turn of phrase that had a physical counterpart in the extra-parliamentary suffragist demonstrations of the day. The Social Democrats, more focused on parliamentary work and cooperation with Liberals than revolution as a road to universal suffrage, the parliamentarisation of government and reforms,⁷²⁸ avoided so open an association with crowd action in order to dispel associations with rightist stereotypes; nor, for the same reason, did they take Finland as a model for 'a unicameral system and complete democracy' as the leftists did. The latter also referred to the 'democratic constitutional reform' in Denmark and to German preparations for 'the democratisation of the constitution' while talking more vaguely about the 'democratic reorientation' planned in Russia. The point was that only in Sweden were the holders of power hostile to 'the irresistible democratic demands of the time'.⁷²⁹ Their conclusion was that every country of any relevance for Sweden was more advanced in the democratisation of the constitution.

By the time of the government response, the far leftists had founded a party of their own. Though division at home and between the revolutionaries in Russia tended to make 'democracy' a disputed concept among the socialists, Ivar Vennerström paved the way for cooperation in future elections by dividing the Swedish parties into a 'democratic' bloc, which would agree on the direction of 'the democratic development' on one side, and The Right, who loathed 'the democracy of Sweden' on the other, 'democracy' here referring to the people at large.⁷³⁰ Carl Lindhagen complained of The Right wanting to prevent 'the possibilities of democracy and the people of the left from making progress',⁷³¹ which likewise implied the identity of 'democracy' and the left (the Liberals included).⁷³² This implicitly recognised the possibility of a *bourgeois* democracy – something that Lenin⁷³³ and many

---

726 AK, Erik Palmstierna, 5 June 1917, 72:44. The Finnish or German Social Democratic movement had not recruited similar prominent representatives of the nobility. This reflects differences in the social backgrounds and consequently ideologies of the two Nordic Social Democratic Parties. In Britain, too, there were some Labour lords who were able to smooth the party's path to power in the eyes of the old elite.
727 AK, 27 April 1917, 50: 24.
728 Eley 2002, 67, 88, 242.
729 AK, 27 April 1917, 50: 24.
730 AK, Ivar Vennerström, 5 June 1917, 72:11–12.
731 AK, Carl Lindhagen, 7 June 1917, 75:5.
732 See, however, Fabian Månsson's point that 'democratic parties' and 'democracy' were two separate things. AK, 7 June 1917, 75:16.
733 Pipes 1992, 393; Müller 2011, 36.

Finnish Social Democrats, among others, could not accept.[734] The Liberal and socialist discourses on democracy would seem to merge in Nils Edén's claim that it was imperative to direct Sweden towards 'democratic ways', which were 'the only ways that in the twentieth century can lead to real happiness and strength for Sweden and other peoples'.[735] What far leftists wanted to see, however, was 'a complete constitutional *reform*, complete democracy', and this included the abolition of the monarchy as this endangered 'the democratic order' and was potentially 'antidemocratic'.[736] This was an openly revolutionary demand. However, the will of the people was interpreted as calling for *both* democracy *and* parliamentarism.[737] Even Zeth Höglund, an old revolutionary and a friend of Lenin, who had been elected the chairman of the party after being released from prison, built his argument on the leftist theory of an ancient Swedish democratic tradition, recognising the existing parliamentary representation as 'the old democracy'.[738] Thus the Swedish far left, too, was calling for the restoration of an existing democracy rather than a total change of the Swedish political system.[739]

The Right turned down all the demands of the left by consistently claiming that democracy already prevailed in Sweden and warned about going any further, the Russian Revolution providing the best example of the consequences. Conrad Vahlquist emphasised the fact that there was 'a democratic outlook' in the Swedish parliament, arguing that 'this democratic development' had taken place under the current constitution and without interventions by extra-parliamentary forces.[740] Karl Hildebrand, too, insisted that 'plenty of space for a progressive democratic development' existed under the prevailing constitution.[741] Professor Carl Hallendorff warned that there was 'a much wider democratic dominance among us than in most parts of the world', which it would only produce a plutocracy.[742] Suggestions that the time for 'a full democratic breakthrough' had come[743] were refuted by Rudolf Kjellén, a professor of political science who had denounced the liberal concept of the state and democracy in his academic work, using the term 'democratism' pejoratively to describe the policy of the left, the contrast with the conservative organic understanding of the state and the people being evident.[744]

Noteworthy in the debate on unicameralism on 7 June 1917 is an open dispute between the Social Democrats and the far left on what should be seen as the protection of 'the democratic heritage of the Swedish constitution',[745]

734 Cf. Ketola 1987 for a contrary view.
735 AK, Nils Edén, 5 June 1917, 72:20.
736 AK, 5 June 1917, 72:11–12.
737 AK, Ivar Vennerström, 5 June 1917, 72:67.
738 AK, Zeth Höglund, 5 June 1917, 72:50.
739 On the alleged thousand-year-old tradition, see Ihalainen 2015.
740 AK, Conrad Vahlquist, 5 June 1917, 72:40.
741 AK, Karl Hildebrand, 5 June 1917, 72:52.
742 AK, Carl Hallendorff, 5 June 1917, 72:65.
743 FK, 9 June 1917, 56:18.
744 FK, Rudolf Kjellén, 9 June 1917, 56:45–6.
745 AK, Carl Lindhagen, 7 June 1917, 75:30; AK, Ernst Hage, 7 June 1917, 76:24.

a history-political notion much emphasised in Swedish constitutional discourse.[746] There was clearly, in the words of Harald Hallén, disagreement 'over the order of the democratic process of upheaval'.[747] Zeth Höglund accused 'the rightist Social Democrats' of being ready to retain the upper chamber as 'a check on democracy'.[748] This accusation offended Harald Hallén, who insisted that the Social Democrats only wanted to ensure a constitution that would allow 'a free and unlimited democracy' to prevail after 'this democratic breakthrough'.[749] These disputes between socialists reflect a deepening ideological division and show how the Majority Social Democrats had come to hold a revisionist concept of democracy that enabled cooperation with the Liberals and were willing to leave further reform for the future. The far left retained a more radically socialist understanding of democracy although even they did not call for the introduction of the dictatorship of the working classes.

3.3.4 The role of the Swedish people in the reformed polity

The parties of the Swedish left campaigned for universal suffrage while the right simply opposed extensions. A scrutiny of the relationship which different parties constructed between the people, the state and politics indicates general ideological differences as well as some ways of thinking that were peculiar to Sweden. A particular context for the debates on the political role of the people was provided by a widely held understanding of Sweden as a country in which the Peasants (as an estate) enjoyed a unique degree of liberty; all four estates had participated in politics from time immemorial – a circumstance that affected the Finnish debates as well. While the members of the political elite shared this construction of the national historiography, the right and the left drew opposite conclusions for its policy implications: The Right maintained that no further reform was needed thanks to the continuation of this exceptional freedom, whereas the left argued that a reform was needed to restore the popular participation that had existed in the distant past and then destroyed by the interest groups that were represented by The Right.[750]

After news of the outbreak of the Russian Revolution and the Wilsonian programmatic manifesto to defend democracy, the Swedish far left was especially eager to define what the Swedish people wanted. Carl Lindhagen contrasted the work of politicians and parties with the passive role of the people, emphasising the contrast between politics as discussed by the masses in popular meetings and politics as practised in the parliament. Disappointed with the Social Democratic Labour Party, from which the far left had recently been expelled, and for the sake of argument idealising the American model, Lindhagen spoke for the political education of the

---

746 Ihalainen 2015.
747 AK, Harald Hallén, 7 June 1917, 76:27.
748 AK, Zeth Höglund, 7 June 1917, 76:30.
749 AK, Harald Hallén, 7 June 1917, 76:35.
750 Ihalainen & Sundin 2011; Ihalainen 2015.

people and their involvement in legislative processes through referenda as an antidote to the corruption of Swedish political life.[751] Without mass education and activation to work for a better future, the people would never emerge from their 'current state of political degradation' and the world from its state of misery. Political parties were from this perspective 'the most dangerous of all associations' in that they manipulated the political information that the people received. Politically educated people respecting the ideological liberty of individuals, by contrast, would be able to restore reason to politics.[752] This was a far left challenge to both the established political system and to the Social Democratic Labour Party, contrasting theory with the realisation of the will of the people.[753]

The Social Democrats were also unhappy with the situation, but in a slightly different way: the current Swedish parliament was violating the interests of the majority of the people by preventing a suffrage reform.[754] Nor was the traditional Swedish right of the people to express their opinion on matters observed since their representatives bypassed their wishes.[755] Hjalmar Branting recalled the tradition of popular self-government and expressed his concern about a growing gap between the parliament and the people. Parliamentary representation was to be prioritised over the referendum, but the masses were to be kept politically informed and given the means to turn the course of politics should the First Chamber continue to block reform.[756] Otherwise, the Swedish people, too, might be forced to seek more forceful means of overcoming the continuous resistance of the upper chamber,[757] including the possibility of revolutionary action. When no progress was made in mid-April, *Social-Demokraten* interpreted this as 'a slap in the face of the Swedish people' and suggested that 'the battle must now be fought using other means'.[758] The paper believed that the masses, as a result of the pressures of the war, were readier than ever to demand their rights as citizens, but expected the consequent change to take place in Sweden by legal means.[759]

According to the Liberals, too, Sweden together with several European states would need to enable more direct involvement of the citizens in politics, possibly by building a direct connection between the people and government if the connection between the parliament and the government

---

751 AK, Carl Lindhagen, 21 March 1917, 33:36–7; 34:13–14.
752 AK, Carl Lindhagen, 21 March 1917, 33:58–60, 67; 34:12, 15.
753 AK, Fabian Månsson, 14 April 1917, 41:77; FK, Fredrik Ström, 14 April 1917, 32:17.
754 AK, Viktor Larsson, 21 March 1917, 33:41.
755 FK, Olof Olsson, 21 March 1917, 24:11.
756 AK, Hjalmar Branting, 21 March 1917, 33:45–7.
757 AK, Hjalmar Branting, 14 April 1917, 41:66. Carl Lindhagen ironically congratulated the Swedish people on the entry of such revolutionary thinking into the country. AK, 14 April 1917, 41:71.
758 *Social-Demokraten*, 'Ett slag i ansiktet på det svenska folket', 16 April 1917.
759 FK, Ola Waldén, 14 April 1917, 32:27–8.

did not function.[760] Eliel Löfgren challenged German and associated Swedish political theory that emphasised 'the sovereignty of the state' and 'the benefit of the state' at the cost of 'the sovereignty of the people',[761] according priority to the last-mentioned concept. Mauritz Hellberg regarded the Swedes as having all too long been excessively obedient to their rulers,[762] and Otto von Zweigbergk saw the current parliament as not providing 'a sympathetic representation ... of the Swedish people'.[763]

In their interpellation, the Social Democrats demanded 'the full right for the people to decide on their fates' and referred in passing to extra-parliamentary 'popular demonstrations' reflecting such demands,[764] while the far leftists saw 'the spontaneous rising of the people' as being caused not only by the failed economic policy of the government but also by 'politically short-sighted wielders of power' having 'denied the Swedish people their full rights as citizens'.[765] For the far left, the strong popular call for reform made an immediate constitutional change necessary.[766] Nor did the Majority Social Democrats shun references to a revolution of the people, even though Hjalmar Branting preferred to speak of an international wave of political reform and counted on 'the nation ... as an arbitrator' in the ensuing elections.[767] Harald Hallén seized on the Prime Minister's concession that in elections the people constituted 'the decisive factor' for Swedish politics, taking it as recognition of 'the will of the people as the highest norm for the government of the state'.[768] A constitutional reform was thus needed to maintain the unity of the people and to encourage the masses to carry the burden of the prevailing hard times. On the other hand, Hallén challenged the rightist supremacy, declaring that the Social Democrats aimed at 'seizing political power'[769] and thereby realising 'the happiness of the people'.[770] According to Erik Palmstierna, the maintenance of national unity called for 'the right of the entire people to decide together'.[771] The Social Democrats were clearly encouraged by the atmosphere of a transnational revolution and the challenge of the break-away far left to apply a double strategy to enforce the parliamentarisation and democratisation of government: moderation dominated most of the speeches, but at times threats of radicalisation among the people were also voiced, a strategy that was used in revisionist discourse in all four countries.

760 AK, Nils Edén, 21 March 1917, 33:47–8, 50.
761 AK, Eliel Löfgren, 14 April 1917, 41:25–6.
762 FK, Mauritz Hellberg, 14 April 1917, 32:23.
763 FK, Otto von Zweigbergk, 14 April 1917, 32:31.
764 AK, Hjalmar Branting, 27 April 1917, 50:23.
765 AK, Ivar Vennerström, 27 April 1917, 50:23.
766 AK, Ivar Vennerström, 27 April 1917, 50:25.
767 AK, Hjalmar Branting, 5 June 1917, 72:8.
768 AK, Harald Hallén, 5 June 1917, 72:21; also AK, Axel Sterne, 5 June 1917, 72:43; 7 June 1917, 75:18.
769 AK, Harald Hallén, 5 June 1917, 72:24–5.
770 AK, Harald Hallén, 5 June 1917, 72:27.
771 AK, Erik Palmstierna, 5 June 1917, 72:46.

The far-left challenge not only to The Right but also to the Social Democrats became increasingly obvious. Ivar Vennerström depicted the Swedish people as being present in the parliamentary debate (through parliamentary reports in the press at least), by observing the answer of the rightist government: '[Y]ou cannot prevent the Swedish people from listening anyway, and they listen and at this moment are waiting with excitement for what the answer of the Swedish government will be.'[772] The people were ready to show with 'mass action' that the dominance of a few rightists had come to an end.[773] Zeth Höglund rejected the use of force against demonstrators by the police on the same day (reported in *Social-Demokraten* as excess violence by 'the Stockholm Cossacks'[774]) and, regarding a revolution against the monarchy and the upper chamber as an increasingly likely option, simplified the political situation into antithetical processes: 'The rebirth of the monarchical power in our country has been the death of the people. The rebirth of the people will one day become the death of the monarchy.'[775] For the far left, the demonstrations of 'the people on the move' served as a major political argument and implied the possibility of a popular uprising. Even the Liberals joined in depicting a nationwide movement aimed at 'reforming and deepening the civic right to full self-government'.[776] Vice-Speaker Daniel Persson wanted to restore respect for the parliament by taking the will of the people more clearly into account.[777]

The Right defended its position by depicting the people as passive victims of political abuse rather than active agents in the ongoing political ferment. Hans Andersson accused the left of trying to divide the Swedish people and agitating for a revolution at a time of international danger.[778] Erik Räf rejected leftist understandings of 'the Swedish people' by recalling the estate-bound concept of 'the Swedish common people' or 'peasantry' (*allmogen*) as an organic and inclusive concept and suggesting that this people actually wanted to cut the influence of the parties for the benefit of the state.[779] Using the same logic, Karl Hildebrand and David Norman questioned the relevance of the demonstrations: they were manifestations of 'the so-called popular will' of one class only.[780]

Female suffrage in particular was opposed by The Right. Samuel Clason would exclude women from 'political battles' as they lacked 'an interest in politics' and had more important duties for the state and humanity to fulfil in

---

772 AK, Ivar Vennerström, 5 June 1917, 72:10, 15.
773 AK, Ivar Vennerström, 5 June 1917, 72:15–16.
774 *Social-Demokraten*, 'Stockholmskosackernas vilda framfart', 6 June 1917.
775 AK, Zeth Höglund, 5 June 1917, 72:49; also FK, Fredrik Ström, 9 June 1917, 56:48.
776 AK, Nils Edén, 5 June 1917, 72:18.
777 AK, Daniel Persson, 5 June 1917, 72:36.
778 AK, Hans Andersson, 5 June 1917, 72:28.
779 AK, Erik Räf, 5 June 1917, 72:30–1.
780 AK, Karl Hildebrand, 5 June 1917, 72:54; AK, David Norman, 5 June 1917, 72:68. Ivar Vennerström challenged what he saw as the tendentious rightist use of the concept of popular will in AK, 5 June 1917, 72:67.

other, higher spheres.[781] Rudolf Kjellén, a leading political theorist, likewise rejected what he saw as the illogical mixture of the political and private spheres if women, who lacking any political education, were allowed to vote. He proceeded to discuss the state of the Swedish polity in highly gendered terms: the problem was that Sweden as a state appeared as '*neutrum*' among other states and would even become '*femininum*' if female suffrage were adopted, whereas the goal, according to this professor, should have been to strengthen its nature as '*masculinum*'.[782] However, Kjellén demonstrated some readiness to rethink the matter: concerned about 'the realm' as the first priority rather than about 'the people', he conceded (not unlike Chancellor Bethmann Hollweg had previously done in Germany) that 'the state and the people must be reconciled' by involving the people in the state to a higher degree than before. This could be accomplished by making the Swedish state 'a private limited company' (*andelsbolag*) in which the shareholders felt themselves to be more directly involved – albeit obviously still possessing different amounts of shares depending on how much they owned. Like some British Conservatives, Kjellén concluded that 'the people are fundamentally good', which meant that one must be ready to make concessions to meet their demands, including possibly even women's suffrage. Otherwise the people would 'run wild', and the realm would be destroyed.[783] Kjellén's conservative analysis, despite its highly traditionalist tones and even abuse of academic authority to the degree of nonsense, opened up possibilities for The Right to rethink its position, as in the similar case of the British Conservatives' ultimate capitulation, and thus allowed for a gradual accommodation to reform. After the election of autumn 1917, there would be a real transition to parliamentarism in Sweden, but The Right would rethink its conception of the people only later.

3.3.5 SHOULD PARLIAMENTARISM BE SEEN AS THE ESTABLISHED SYSTEM, AN INSTRUMENT FOR CREATING A BETTER SOCIETY THROUGH DEBATE, OR A SYSTEM TO BE TAKEN OVER BY THE PEOPLE?

Unlike Norway and Denmark, Sweden did not have a parliamentary government when the First World War broke out. Even in March 1917, British observers noted that this was not 'a country governed on purely Parliamentary principles',[784] and a Prussian conservative paper hoped that it never would be. As long as parliamentarism was lacking, calls for the extension of democratic suffrage often addressed this question as well. The debates of spring 1917 preceded the actual introduction of parliamentarism after the election of the Second Chamber in September, when the first Liberal-Social Democratic coalition founded on a parliamentary majority

---

781   FK, Samuel Clason, 9 June 1917, 56:34–5, 37. Such views were challenged by Olof Olsson (Social Democrat), who suggested that The Right tended to either see themselves as the state or as governing over the state, and as thus being qualified to define what the interests of the state were. FK, 9 June 1917, 56:41.
782   FK, Rudolf Kjellén, 9 June 1917, 56:42–4.
783   FK, Rudolf Kjellén, 9 June 1917, 56:45–7.
784   *The Manchester Guardian*, 'Ministerial Crisis in Sweden', 30 March 1917.

was nominated, against the wishes of the monarch and The Right. The left had expected a change in that direction already in the spring, given the rise of domestic pressures and the progress of what, on the basis of news about the extension of the political say of the German Reichstag, was imagined to be a transnational revolution. But the decades-long debate on parliamentarism had changed little thus far; and the old arguments from conservative and liberal political scientists and historians continued to be recycled, the alternative interpretations being that Sweden already possessed a native parliamentarism that could and should not be replaced with any Western alternatives (the rightist view), or that Sweden had a thousand-year-old native parliamentary tradition that had been destroyed by the higher estates in the early modern period and now needed to be revived (the leftist view). The same historical arguments were also adopted by the two sides in the Finnish constitutional confrontation as a result of the continuing application of the Swedish legal tradition in that country.[785]

The Right – opposed to violating what they saw as the Swedish constitutional tradition through the introduction of majority parliamentarism – expressed their conservative doubts about human nature and society, appealing to German and Swedish political theory and historical experience. With professor's authority Carl Hallendorff[786] concluded that parliamentary institutions provided 'a concentrated display of human infirmities with simultaneous elements of the good that dwells in us after all'.[787] This was not an anti-parliamentary view as such. Hallendorff, who had published on parliamentarism, regarded the international 'criticism of the not insignificant mistakes and failures that were to be found in parliamentarism' as justified by the historical experiences of several countries. A major problem was that the people tended to 'overestimate the entire parliamentary apparatus so that everything possible is expected to be improved by this apparatus' and to be disappointed with its actual achievements.[788] The Third Republic was the implicit example here. Hallendorff also criticised the shortcomings of Danish and Norwegian parliamentarism.[789] And even if the British House of Commons had since 1867 been an object of considerable interest for politicians around Europe and members of European parliaments had taken the great parliamentarians of the British type as models, that era was over: the power of the representatives that had been lost during the war would not be easy to restore in Britain. Hence it was unthinkable that the Swedish parliament should now be made the sole possessor of political power.[790] Nothing radical was to be done in the midst of a global ferment; the aim should rather be to reinstate the pre-war political order 'to restore our health as much as possible so that we will really be able to function properly in such future trials as may come'.[791] In Hallendorff's organic understanding of the

---

785 Kurunmäki 2014, 177–8; Ihalainen 2015.
786 *Dagens Nyheter*, 'Hr Lindhagens dag', 22 March 1917.
787 AK, Carl Hallendorff, 21 March 1917, 33:53.
788 AK, Carl Hallendorff, 21 March 1917, 33:55.
789 Garrigues & Anceau 2016; Kurunmäki 2014, 173.
790 AK, 21 March 1917, 33:55; see also Kurunmäki 2014, 172–3.
791 AK, 21 March 1917, 33:60.

Swedish 'living body politic', the Riksdag remained one powerful institution among others, but by no means the sole forum in which decisions should be made,[792] a view that was shared by many German academics and much of the Finnish intellectual elite as well.

Among non-academic rural conservatives, the doubts about parliamentarism were even more unyielding, recalling the Junker attitude of which the Swedish right was constantly accused by the left. As Erik Räf, a landowner, put it, favourable weather conditions for the harvest would do more to improve the state of Sweden than useless vindications of parliamentarism. Parliamentarism in the sense of mere *bavardage* was counter-productive, weakening the joy of work and undermining the foundations of the national economy.[793] David Norman, a farmer and chairman of the antisocialist *Svenska folkförbundet,* who regarded the free land-owning peasantry as the true Swedish common people, denounced the workers' demonstrations for suffrage reform for putting 'improper pressure on the parliament'.[794] Both of these views question simple trajectories between early modern diets and modern parliamentarism; the connection was rather constructed by leftist academics, most famously by Fredrik Lagerroth, and has been maintained in Swedish historiography on the eighteenth century.[795] Conrad Vahlquist, a more moderate conservative, appealed to the commonplace argument that rising incomes were leading to the enfranchisement of the workers, which meant that a suffrage reform was already taking place and that any 'extra-parliamentary' measures suggested by the left were hence unnecessary.[796] Reflective of the tensions of early June 1917 is that Baron Erik Palmstierna of the Social Democrats responded by accusing The Right of an equal readiness to prosecute 'extra-parliamentary measures', as had been seen in the pre-war peasant demonstrations and the royal pressure used against a Liberal government. Moreover, the present rightist government had not demonstrated its claimed 'parliamentarism' by subjecting its programme to parliamentary scrutiny.[797]

The Right held to its view of the established system as healthy parliamentarism of a native kind and rejected extra-parliamentary challenges to it. Karl Hildebrand repeated the view that the two chambers were 'organically embedded in our social structure' and in no need of renovation. The agitation by the leftist press that misguided the workers into lawlessness, disorder, political strikes and other forms of mass action as extra-parliamentary means of putting pressure on the parliament was in his view totally irresponsible.[798] Ernst Trygger attacked the Liberals, too, for their readiness to break with the conventions of Swedish parliamentarism: the Liberals might not run riot in the streets like the socialists or adopt 'the

---

792   AK, Carl Hallendorff, 21 March 1917, 33:55.
793   AK, Erik Räf, 5 June 1917, 72:30.
794   AK, David Norman, 5 June 1917, 72:71.
795   Ihalainen 2015.
796   AK, Conrad Vahlquist, 5 June 1917, 72:40.
797   AK, Erik Palmstierna, 5 June 1917, 72:44–5.
798   AK, Karl Hildebrand, 5 June 1917, 72:51, 53–4.

extra-parliamentary path' and 'violence' to reach their political goals but seemed nevertheless ready to use unparliamentary means that were nothing short of a violent attempt to overthrow our constitution'. This exaggeration was based on the idea that the left might force the First Chamber into constitutional concessions by blocking the budget,[799] a suggestion that the leftists had made and one which recalled the measures employed by British Liberals to force through the Parliament Act in 1911. The Swedish right thus associated the proposed violations of parliamentary rules with open violence of the type used in the Russian Revolution, an association, which despite its rhetorical character reflects the depth of the constitutional confrontation – especially at a time when the Russian Revolution was in the process of becoming radicalised, political changes were expected in Germany and the constitutional direction of the socialist parliamentary majority in Finland was causing increasing concern. This rhetorical strategy was the common property of the conservatives: the established order represented true native parliamentarism but was threatened by the un- and extra-parliamentary and hence illegitimate methods employed by the left. At the same time, the leaders of the Swedish right clearly maintained deep-rooted doubts about parliamentarism in its 'Western' British and French varieties. Within a few months, however, they would face a 'parliamentary government' in the leftist sense.

Nor were the far left and the Social Democrats agreed on the nature of parliamentarism. On the one hand, there was a joint willingness to extend the political say of the parliament into areas such as foreign policy – an international Marxist goal reinforced in Sweden by the pro-German policy of the government and the Wilsonian interpretation of the causes of the First World War.[800] On the other hand, there was a division in attitudes concerning direct democracy as opposed to representative democracy: while the far left welcomed mass action and saw the referendum as an act of 'popular legislative work side by side with parliamentary legislative work',[801] the Majority Social Democrats defended parliamentarism as a political process. Harald Hallén denounced critical attitudes to parliamentarism and viewed 'parliamentary battles' as more than a mere campaign for power between parties: parliamentary debate was rather a battle through which a better society was sought;[802] this was a revisionist pro-parliamentary view that differed not only from that of radical socialists but also from those of some foreign Social Democratic parties, including the Finnish one, especially after its radicalisation.[803] There was a tendency among these groups to question

799 FK, Ernst Trygger, 9 June 1917, 56:49.
800 AK, Carl Lindhagen, 21 March 1917, 33:29.
801 AK, Carl Lindhagen, 21 March 1917, 33:36–7, 58.
802 AK, Harald Hallén, 21 March 1917, 34:9, 11.
803 No similar division into the supporters of parliamentary procedures and the critics of existing parliaments as institutions, with the latter being inclined to favour direct democracy and potentially ready for revolutionary measures, emerged within the Finnish Social Democratic Party in 1917. This led to attempts by the moderates in Finland to satisfy the radicals through the use of anti-parliamentary rhetoric. Kettunen 1986, 9–10, 24.

'bourgeois' parliamentarism, to doubt the efficacy of mere talking and to prioritise methods of direct popular rule. The readiness of the Swedish Social Democrats to distinguish between 'politics in popular assemblies' and 'politics in the parliament' annoyed Carl Lindhagen, who accused them of surrendering to 'parliamentary politics' of the bourgeois type.[804] Lindhagen saw nothing to idealise in the mere parliamentarisation of government in the British or French sense since 'the so-called parliamentary formation of government' was anyway 'the opposite of democracy'.[805] In transnational far-left thought on parliamentarism, government should be no more than a committee of the parliament, and the parliament could be overruled by the people. In the Swedish case, The Right appeared as a particular source of problems with its deliberate obstruction to reforms preventing the will of the people from being realised. This corrupted the system, increasing the power of party functionaries and adding to 'parliamentary corruption' even among the left.[806] Surrendering to bourgeois parliamentarism was not an option for the far left, who viewed the Majority Social Democrats as ready to give up parliamentarism proper, i.e. 'the idea based on the self-government of the people in the form of a parliament meeting to discuss the affairs of the entire country'.[807] In these circumstances, extra-parliamentary methods appeared as a viable option. Fredrik Ström hence called for the forced extension of parliamentary government through budgetary power instead of mere discussion 'to enforce the demands and wishes of the people'; this would be 'an open constitutional battle' to crush opposition from The Right.[808]

There was a connection between 'democracy and parliamentarism' for most far leftists,[809] for whom these concepts went together and were the goal of the popular demonstrations, but more revolutionary language was also heard when Zeth Höglund, an old revolutionary and a comrade of Lenin, re-occupied his seat. Höglund accused the government of having employed 'unparliamentary' means against the people by allowing violence to be used against demonstrators on the streets of Stockholm instead of dealing with their complaints in the parliament.[810] Such an alleged rejection of the 'parliamentary' process would justify the use of violence by the left as well, which shows that the radical arguments in Sweden in June were not so completely different from those in Finland in November 1917. Höglund lamented what he saw as the failure of the left to use the parliamentary power in its possession and concluded that 'the merely parliamentary way is not enough to carry through the demands of the people but really large-scale mass action is needed instead'.[811] Rejecting the parliament as the forum of reform to a previously unheard-of extent, Höglund maintained that the

---

804   AK, Carl Lindhagen, 21 March 1917, 34:13.
805   AK, Carl Lindhagen, 21 March 1917, 33:64.
806   AK, Carl Lindhagen, 7 June 1917, 75:5–6, 8.
807   AK, Fabian Månsson, 7 June 1917, 75:15.
808   FK, Fredrik Ström, 14 April 1917, 32:17.
809   AK, Ivar Vennerström, 5 June 1917, 72:12, 67.
810   AK, Zeth Höglund, 5 June 1917, 72:47.
811   AK, Zeth Höglund, 5 June 1917, 72:49–50.

masses no longer trusted their leaders either within or outside the parliament and should hence themselves take the initiative. Such revolutionary rhetoric strongly recalls that heard in the Finnish parliament five months later, though in the Swedish case it found no great acceptance. Höglund nevertheless saw the inability of the government and the parliament to introduce the necessary reforms as justification for a take-over by 'the parliament of the streets', crying out together with a simultaneous demonstration that was taking place outside the parliament building: '[L]ong live the mass movement, long live the parliament of the street!'[812] This speech act, challenging both the rightist and Social Democrat-Liberal understandings of parliamentarism and rejected by the rightist press as totally inappropriate for its references to the chaotic demonstrations of the day,[813] constituted the most radical moment of the 'Swedish Revolution' of 1917. At the level of parliamentary rhetoric at least, a few radical socialist leaders seemed ready for a revolution a week before the Finnish parliament would begin to debate parliamentary sovereignty, a stance that provided a further encouraging model for radical Finns. But Zeth Höglund remained a solitary revolutionary; most other leftist leaders suggested no more than politicking through parliamentary procedure to force The Right into concessions. The extent and militancy of the revolutionary rhetoric would be quite different in the differing circumstances of Finland.

Despite the far left's accusations that they had accepted the existing order, there was deep unhappiness amongst the Majority Social Democrats about the prevailing political system failing to produce the reform that the people wanted.[814] However, they were ready to work within it provided that suffrage was reformed and government parliamentarised. The party leaders were hopeful that the party would soon come into power and observed moderation in its rhetoric when calling for parliamentarism and indeed employed perennial arguments that were downright traditionalist: Hjalmar Branting liked to speak about an ancient Swedish tradition of popular assemblies that had in the course of social development experienced evolution from *tings* to twentieth-century parliamentarism.[815] The powers of the parliament originated from the Swedish people, and this demanded the maintenance of links between the parliament and the people so that no crucial gaps might emerge. The most serious failure of the current political system was the lack of 'an entirely clear parliamentary order', which allowed the government to function without responsibility to the parliament. The equal powers of the two chambers also weakened the possibilities for the parliament to introduce reforms. What must be done to accomplish 'Swedish parliamentarism' was to assert the power of the parliament and especially that of the Second Chamber, which was elected by the people. Branting's forecast was that proper parliamentarism of this kind would be achieved in Sweden in the course of 1917. As for the increased direct popular participation

812   AK, Zeth Höglund, 5 June 1917, 72:50.
813   *Aftonbladet*, 'Svaret från regeringsbänken' and 'Gatans parlament', 6 June 1917.
814   AK, Viktor Larsson, 21 March 1917, 33:41.
815   See also Jakobsen & Kurunmäki 2016.

demanded by the far left, the Majority Social Democrats might welcome the principle but rejected the proposal in practice, considering that it called for further deliberation.[816] An argument voiced by Gunnar Löwegren in April indicates that the party leadership – unlike the Finnish socialists and the far left in Sweden and Germany – had set Western parliamentarism as its goal. Löwegren viewed the Swedish system in its current form as not comparable with the parliamentary systems of France and Britain: in France both houses were elected through universal suffrage and no counterbalance to parliamentary power existed; in Britain, parliament had a decisive influence over the government. These features needed to be introduced before the Swedish system could be characterised as parliamentary.[817] In June, Harald Hallén provocatively interpreted the rightist ministry as being ready – despite continuous opposition from its own ranks – to recognise that parliamentarism concentrated in the lower chamber, as practised abroad, was the only political way that was available for Sweden to take.[818] This was still wishful thinking, but eventually The Right would have to adapt itself to parliamentarism after the election of September 1917.

While The Right remained reluctant, the far left critical and the Social Democrats defensive, the Swedish Liberals spoke at this stage for a parliamentarism of the Western European type with an intensity that cannot be found among the German or Finnish Liberals. Their papers constantly criticised the 'anti-parliamentary temperament', 'anti-parliamentary plans' and the 'anti-parliamentary building of opinion' of conservative governments and the 'sensational extra-parliamentary events' that these organised. The Liberals recalled how the rightist leader Arvid Lindman had compared parliamentarism with 'the Trojan horse' and been unwilling to cooperate with the parliament. By March 1917 the Liberal papers were already positive that 'parliamentarism has won'.[819] The British parliamentary tradition provided them with evidence that the trajectory of the Swedish constitutional tradition would inevitably lead to parliamentarism. The British system was also accepted as 'democratic' even if, up to then, it had been based on a small political class and had tended to exclude the masses from politics.[820] According to Nils Edén, himself a parliamentary historian, Britain possessed an 'ancient parliamentary culture and ... strong reverence for parliamentary power and sovereignty', and he recommended that Sweden, too, adopt a similar kind of ministerial responsibility.[821] Coming from a leading historian, this shows how the notion of the automatic long-term comparability of the British and Swedish political systems emerged.[822]

816   AK, Hjalmar Branting, 21 March 1917, 33:45–6; see, however, FK, Olof Olsson, 21 March 1917, 24:11.
817   AK, Gustaf Löwegren, 14 April 1917, 41:24.
818   AK, 5 June 1917, 72:21, 27; *Aftonbladet*, 'Svaret från regeringsbänken', 6 June 1917; *Dagens Nyheter*, 'Svaret', 6 June 1917.
819   *Dagens Nyheter*, 'Kontraparlamentariska akter', 22 March 1917; 'Hr Swarzs uppdrag' and 'Systemet Hammarskjölds fall', 30 March 1917.
820   Kurunmäki 2014, 177–8, on Karl Staaff; Ihalainen 2015, 73.
821   AK, Nils Edén, 21 March 1917, 33:48.
822   See also Ihalainen 2015 on the use of history in politics.

Liberal Anglophilia remained strong in Sweden despite the fact that the press reports on the reform debates in the British parliament were very brief in comparison with reports from Finland and Germany.[823] By summer 1917, both the Social Democrats and the Liberals in Sweden had made a clear choice in favour Western parliamentarism. This was not the so clearly the case in Germany or Finland.

3.4 Finland: The legitimacy of the parliament deteriorates at the moment of democratisation and parliamentarisation

3.4.1 SOVEREIGNTY IN THE FORMER GRAND DUCHY: IN THE PARLIAMENT, THE GOVERNMENT OR A RUSSIAN-STYLE 'DEMOCRACY'?

Finnish political culture combined a long tradition of monarchical government with conventions of the representation of the estates and – from the parliamentary reform of 1906 onwards – of the people in a unicameral parliament elected on the basis of universal suffrage (including women). Since 1809, Finland had been an autonomous grand duchy in the Russian Empire, while still observing applicable regulations of the Swedish constitutions of 1772 and 1789 and the Diet Act of 1617 (revised in 1869 and 1906). In the eighteenth century, these constitutions had reintroduced an almost absolute monarchy after the so-called Age of Liberty (1719–72), when the four-estate Diet (including the free Peasant Estate) had played a prominent role in Swedish-Finnish politics.[824] Much of the Finnish polity of the late 1910s was based on inherited eighteenth-century Swedish practices, though parliamentary life and public debate had been activated since the revival of the Diet in 1863 and the parliamentary reform of 1906. Within the Russian Empire, Finnish political culture was exceptional in its 'Westerness', which was admired by the Russian liberals and loathed by the conservatives; on the other hand, numerous physical links with Russia gave rise to transnational transfers from Russia that were unthinkable in the other three polities examined in this study.

For the Finnish polity, which combined the conservation of the Swedish early-modern legal and political inheritance with radically modern forms of representation that had been made possible by external stimuli from transnational European debates on parliamentarism and the Russian Revolution of 1905, the new Russian Revolution again opened up opportunities for alternative constitutional solutions. Once Nicholas II, the Grand Duke of Finland, had abdicated, the Romanov monarchy had come to an end and the Russian Provisional Government had started to draft a republican constitution for Russia, the foundations of the old political order could be interpreted as having disintegrated in Finland as well. The introduction of parliamentary responsibility of the government, the democratisation of local government, the transition to a republican constitution and even

---

823   *Dagens Nyheter*, 'Underhuset för kvinnorösträtten', 30 March 1917.
824   Ihalainen & Sundin 2011.

independence from Russia so that sovereign power would be transferred to the Finnish parliament or at least to a domestic government – all of these now seemed to be within reach. The revolutionary impact of events in Russia on a country which had lacked a revolutionary atmosphere (apart from the class hatred agitated by the Social Democrats or the engagement in military training in the German army by rightist activists) produced an unforeseen struggle for power at all levels. In a radically reinvigorated public discourse, democracy – or rather its vernacular translation *kansanvalta* (the rule by the people) which had specifically Finnish connotations[825] – was generally seen as an option that was available for Finland, as indeed it was for many other European countries,[826] although Finland remained isolated from some of the transnational debates in which the parties of countries participating in the First World War and even Swedish politicians were engaged. As will be shown below, this again had consequences for the dynamics of Finnish political discourse. In the Finnish context, it was particularly disputable what giving power to the people would mean: a democratically elected parliament existed but there was no parliamentary government or local democratic administration. Different parties had radically different conceptions of democracy, especially when rule by parliamentary majority – the Social Democrats holding 103 out of 200 seats in the parliament after the elections of 1916 – meant rule by a socialist party.

There were many different understandings of democracy and sources of ideological inspiration: revolutionary Petrograd became the most obvious source for the socialists, bypassing Berlin, whereas the non-socialist parties,

---

[825] The word *kansanvalta* had become a conventional vernacular translation of 'democracy' in Finnish. Owing to its linguistic derivation, it took on a slightly different tone from the terms for 'democracy' in the Germanic languages (though it resembled the Swedish *folkestyre*). *Kansanvalta* carried connotations of 'power' or 'rule' and 'the people' in an ethnic or social sense that were not fully identical with democracy in English, German or Swedish. It could refer to the unified power of or rule by the *Finnish* people as opposed to the *Swedish* people (and was hence not a concept that Swedish-speaking Finns would use); to the rule by the *common* people as opposed to that by the higher classes (thus recalling the opposition between the people and the intelligentsia emphasised also by the Russian concept of democracy); to the rule by *citizens* as opposed to the estates (as the Finnish word for citizen *kansalainen* is derived from the word for an ethnic community *kansa*); or to the fairness of political and administrative processes. The use of the non-vernacular word *demokratia* tended to carry the last, more formal, process-like connotation. Hyvärinen 2003, 83. The Finnish-speaking debaters had favoured the vernacular translation of democracy as 'the rule by the people' already in the parliamentary reform debates of 1905–6. *Kansanvalta* did not necessarily stand for the sovereignty of the people: it could also stand alternatively for the sovereignty of the nation as a whole (thus approaching the anti-parliamentary German concept *Volksgemeinschaft*), of parliament as the representative institution, of the Finnish-speaking majority of the population, of the common people or, in the Marxist sense, of the proletariat only. Kurunmäki 2008, 364–5. The connotations of the concept were thus very varied and contestable.

[826] Vares 1998, 50; Nyström 2013, 124–5.

while observing developments in Russia, looked mainly to Germany and Sweden and to a much lesser extent the Entente. In Finnish parlance, the non-socialist parties were generally called 'bourgeois parties', which reinforced the division into two blocs, particularly as the bourgeoisie formed a joint body that issued proclamations to the public calling for law and order.[827] In the other countries of comparison, no similar association combining the right and the centre against the Social Democrats existed, nor was such a strongly legalistic discourse generally employed. This bourgeois insistence on obedience to the law was a reaction to the Russification measures of the preceding years, and it was reinforced by violations of the law by Social Democrat supporters.[828] The confrontational discourses of class hatred and legalism are among the peculiarities of Finland that deserve more attention in the analysis of the political process.

On 20 March 1917, the Russian Provisional Government – following the wishes of a delegation of the Finnish parties – reconfirmed the validity of the Swedish-Finnish constitution, rescinded imperial degrees that had since 1890 limited the autonomy of the grand duchy and abolished censorship. The Finnish parties, however, were polarised by ten years of heated parliamentary debate. They had traditionally followed different policies towards Russia and, holding radically differing conceptions of the proper organisation of the polity and maintaining aforementioned competing discourses, disagreed on whether or not promises about a democratic constitution and social reforms should have been included in the decree. From the Russian perspective, its primary aim was to assuage a strategically important border country next to the capital and to ensure Finnish support for the ongoing war effort and revolution; no separatism or cooperation with the Germans would be allowed, and the state of war remained in force. The meeting of the delegations was nevertheless characterised as a 'new spring' in Fenno-Russian relations, reflecting the optimistic revolutionary atmosphere of spring 1917. From the Finnish perspective, most promising was the reconvening of the national parliament to prepare a proposal for a new constitution.[829] Enthusiasm in the contemporary press was considerable.

However, instead of the expected period of constitutional and social reform, one of constitutional confusion and power struggles followed. The course of events has been covered in detail in previous research, though not so thoroughly from the point of view of the discursive process in the parliament. As Pertti Haapala, among others, has shown, political order began to rapidly deteriorate – first from above in connection with the parliament but then increasingly from below among the people, which in turn had repercussions on the parliament. From the socialist perspective, the Revolution was coming to Finland and opening up chances to achieve

---

827 *Helsingin Sanomat*, 'Eduskuntaryhmäin waltuuskunta toimimassa', 18 March 1917, and 'Tiedonanto kansalaisille porwarillisten eduskuntaryhmäin waltuuskunnalta', 19 March 1917.
828 *Helsingin Sanomat*, 'Senaatin warapuheenjohtajan uusin lausunto', 14 June 1917.
829 Polvinen 1967, vol. 1, 16, 23, 27; Lindman 1968, 22; Upton 1980, 54–5; Sihvonen 1997, 19; Haapala 2010a, 60–2.

the postponed reforms through direct action should formal parliamentary politics fail to produce them. The need for reforms in many areas was obvious and delays in realising them politicised this need further: the relationship with Russia should be rethought, the constitution reformed and the circumstances of workers and tenant farmers improved. A major problem was the gross discrepancy between a democratically elected parliament and the lack of parliamentary sovereignty and responsibility. Disappointment with the results of voting and parliamentary reform work was deep, especially among the Social Democrats, who expressed this as soon as censorship was eased in March. They contrasted the Social Democratic pro-parliamentary ten-year struggle in- and outside the parliament for 'democratic progress and national liberty' with the reactionary, anti-reformist and downright antiparliamentary opposition of the *herraspuolueet* (parties of the masters).[830] Among the latter parties, the shortcomings of the parliament were explained by Russian policies on the one hand and the excessively radical demands of the incompetent representatives of the Social Democrats on the other.[831] The Social Democrats now called for the parliamentarisation of the political system so that the postponed reforms could be carried through with their majority in the parliament. They also called for a reform of local government that would enable universal suffrage to be introduced there, too. At the same time, Finnish towns saw the rise of two sets of authorities, recalling the situation in Petrograd: the imperial police force was being replaced by workers' guards. Furthermore, a *Parliament* ('eduskunta') of the Workers' Associations of Helsinki representing 96 associations was formed and openly challenged the established city administration,[832] both with its name and its resolutions.

The exceptional naming of a local revolutionary body in Helsinki as a 'parliament' deserves attention, as it reflected and tended to add to the workers' scepticism of the national parliament. Since no other institution was called by such a name, 'the workers' *Eduskunta*' implicitly challenged the sole authority of the 'bourgeois' national parliament, suggesting that a local assembly of the representatives of the workers as an interest group stood for an authority comparable to that of the national parliament (which did have a socialist majority after all). This alternative 'parliament' would play a key role once the revolutionary process escalated in late 1917. Even though the term 'soviet' in the Russian sense was not used, the name of the workers' parliament reinforced the notion of double authorities and could be used effectively to question the legitimacy of the national parliament. Comparable 'parliaments' of interest groups are not known to have played any role in Britain, Germany or Sweden in 1917.

Furthermore, a parliament of the streets was rising: Samu Nyström has argued that the streets and squares of Helsinki rather than the press (or the parliament) were becoming a dominant political stage, with the city space being used by political groups seeking common stands, propagating their

---

830 *Työmies*, 'Eduskunta. Työwäki ja porvarit', 17 March 1917.
831 *Hufvudstadsbladet*, 'Vår landtdag', 16 March 1917.
832 Ketola 1987, 32; Tuomisto 1990, 38; Haapala 2010c, 15; Nyström 2013, 125–6, 131.

views and exhibiting demonstrations of strength aimed at putting pressure on the decision-makers. The national parliament, which was located in Heimola House in the middle of this turbulent city space, experienced what practically amounted to states of siege at times: for instance on 12 and 14 July 1917, when the new local government laws were discussed just days before an act on parliamentary sovereignty was passed. The confrontational relationship between the national parliament and the parliament of the streets turned very real when a crowd consisting of Finnish workers and Russian soldiers shouted 'Down with the bourgeoisie' outside the assembly hall, and their chanting could be heard inside.[833] The MPs also took up these tensions in their speeches. The political initiative was in danger of moving from the national parliament to the parliament of the streets[834] or to the workers' parliament, particularly as the Social Democratic Speaker Kullervo Manner supported the use of the Russian soldiers to pressurise his parliament.[835] Parliamentary and extra-parliamentary politics confronted each other in Helsinki in ways that were familiar from contemporary Stockholm but which even more so resembled those used in revolutionary Petrograd. There was also a readiness to employ extra-parliamentary measures within the national parliament itself – by its president.

Up to March 1917, Finland had been relatively peaceful during the war despite Russian rule under military law, the growing number of Russian troops in the country, censorship, a long hiatus in parliamentary work and economic difficulties resulting from the closure of the Western markets. The last had to some extent been compensated for by the economic benefits resulting from the demands of the Russian market. The calm had also been supported by the fact that any political problem could be explained as arising from the tsarist Russian rule and not from any Finnish policies. Once the imperial power fell and a new Finnish government and parliament began to work, expectations for solutions to acute problems rose, and a crisis concerning the legitimacy of the state resembling that of the war-faring countries and Sweden emerged; this was caused particularly by the fact that, as Pertti Haapala has put it, instead of solving problems, the Finnish political institutions appeared to be creating new ones. These faltering institutions included the democratically elected but previously nearly powerless and discordant parliament, from which quick decisions had been expected. Political struggles among the Finns themselves in- and outside the parliament tended to politicise the problems of wartime daily life and consequently weakened confidence in the capability of the political institutions to solve the crisis, which further diminished their legitimacy. The parliament failed, and equally significantly, law and order, which had been maintained by regular police forces, was replaced by anarchical activities and armed guards, who were generally regarded as the defenders of rival interests and hence lacked legitimacy with the opposite side. By the end of

---

833 Tuomisto 1990, 40; Nyström 2013, 135, 139, 151.
834 Haapala 1995, 12, 220.
835 Soikkanen 1975, 227.

the year, there would be no power in Finland that was recognised by the majority of the citizens, be it the police force or the national parliament.[836]

In this section and in section 4.4, we shall focus on the gradual discursive deterioration of the Finnish polity at the parliamentary level as it became evident in constitutional debates, particularly when compared to parallel debates elsewhere. The rise of a confrontational revolutionary atmosphere was increased by concrete transnational links between Petrograd and Helsinki: there were regular train services that enabled visits both ways, and radicalised revolutionary Russian troops eager to demonstrate, commit illegalities and intervene in Finnish domestic matters were present in Helsinki.[837]

The crisis of parliamentary legitimacy in Finland was further complicated by the unclear constitutional relationship between Finland and Russia. The revolutionary Duma and the Provisional Government viewed themselves as having replaced the Grand Duke (the Tsar) as the sovereign authority in Finland. The Provisional Government would have given the Finnish parliament the right to initiate legislation, vote on the budget and control ministers, but it was not ready to recognise it as the representative body of an entirely sovereign state; at least foreign and military affairs would remain for Petrograd to decide. From the generally held Finnish point of view, by contrast, the union between Finland and Russia had been based on the Romanov dynasty only, and once that house had fallen, the relationship needed to be rethought and the power vacuum created by it in Finland filled in. The Finns interpreted the situation to mean either that, since the unlimited power of the tsars had ended, Finland should be recognised as an internally independent state – even if the Provisional Government continued to hold sovereign power – or that, after the abolition of the monarchy in Russia, the Provisional Government no longer had any supreme power over Finland, sovereignty belonged to the Finns and it was they who should freely decide on how to use it. This did not necessarily stand for full independence: during the first half of 1917, most Finns continued to recognise the authority of the Russian government in foreign and military affairs,[838] but these views became divided and changeable.[839] The degree of readiness to proceed to full independence varied: fears of the radicalism of the socialist majority in the parliament made the bourgeois parties hesitant, while the Social Democrats wanted to distance the country from the Provisional Government. By November, with a bourgeois parliamentary majority in power in Finland and a Bolshevik government in Russia, the parties' respective views would be the exact opposite, with the bourgeois parties supporting full independence and the Social Democrats seeking cooperation with the Russian Bolsheviks.

As we have seen, radical rhetoric had been increasing within the Finnish labour movement for years and culminated in the election campaign of 1916, which produced a Social Democratic parliamentary majority. The fact

---

836 Kettunen 1986, 85; Haapala 2010b, 58–60; Nyström 2013, 144.
837 Polvinen 1967, vol. 1, 21, 45–6, 48; Eskola 2011, 15.
838 Lindman 1968, 45; Sihvonen 1997, 1–2; Jussila, Hentilä & Nevakivi 1999, 92–6.
839 See Ketola 1987, 56–7.

that it was supported by revolutionary influences from Petrograd, explains much of the confrontational nature of Finnish constitutional debates during 1917. Until the Russian Revolution, in the circumstances of war, the socialist majority had been of minor political significance, but first the March Revolution and then the rise of Bolshevik opposition to the Provisional Government opened up prospects for the realisation of the postponed reforms through this majority; a revolution through the parliament in either a Kautskyist or a more radical Marxist sense seemed possible. Kautsky had suggested that a socialist parliamentary majority would automatically know the right policy to follow. The Bolsheviks, too, were interested in having a radical socialist party that already possessed a parliamentary majority in a 'Western' country within the Russian Empire.[840] The Finnish socialists could support the revolution in Russia and help to export it to the West – to Sweden, Germany and even Britain. Many of them had concrete contacts with Russian revolutionaries at this time, and some of them helped Lenin to hide in apartments around Helsinki between August and October 1917. Vyacheslav Molotov gave instructions to the Finnish-speaking Bolshevik Adolf Taimi on how to work as an emissary of the Revolution in Helsinki. It was easy for the Bolsheviks to find admiration and concrete support for their version of the Revolution among Finnish workers, who were used to revolutionary discourse – though many Finnish socialists did not speak Russian and were still uncertain about the sustainability of the Revolution.[841] The inherent internationalism of the socialist movement was supported by a transnational revolutionary spirit which was much more concretely present in Finland than in any of the countries of comparison.

When Finnish political life suddenly became active in late March 1917, the constitutional debates recalled those in Britain, Germany and Sweden, even though universal suffrage was no longer an issue and even more complex questions concerning sovereignty remained unsolved. On 26 March 1917, the Provisional Government nominated the first ever Finnish government supported by the majority of the parliament and with a nominal socialist majority; this had been agreed on by the Finnish parties. The Social Democrats became, in the words of the sociologist Risto Alapuro, 'a member of the polity' but remained unable to realise their policies because of the 'solidly bourgeois' character of the bureaucracy.[842] The all-party government was led by the Social Democrat Oskari Tokoi, a workers' union leader who had returned from emigration to America – as had many other Finnish Social Democratic activists, which is a further transnational context

840 Lenin assumed on 24 March that the majority of the Finns were already on the side of socialism and should be allowed to develop democracy on their own and thereby support the Bolshevik cause in Russia. Polvinen 1967, vol. 1, 56; Ketola 1987, 72; Palonen 2012, 256.
841 Polvinen 1967, vol. 1, 41–2, 46, 49, 69–70; Kirby 1976, 101; Rinta-Tassi 1986, 32; Ketola 1987, 70–1; Soikkanen 1990, 90. On 24 March, Lenin's sister Maria Ulyanova visited Helsinki to make a financial collection on behalf of the Bolsheviks.
842 Alapuro 1988, 151. Haapala 1995, 220, also notes their unwillingness to make compromises with the bourgeoisie.

to be considered. Tokoi became the first socialist head of government and acted in ways that revealed to many supporters of the 'bourgeois' parties the potential consequences of socialist rule. As we have seen, the German Social Democratic organ *Vorwärts* celebrated the creation of a socialist-dominated government in Finland. The leading newspaper in Helsinki, for its part, reported both about the British suffrage reform and about Social Democratic and Liberal expressions of the popular will for an immediate parliamentarisation of the German government as a reaction to the Russian Revolution.[843] *Hufvudstadsbladet*, the organ of the Swedish People's Party, also reviewed the main arguments of the various political groups in 'a strange debate' at the German Reichstag.[844]

The nomination of a government consisting of Finnish politicians, mostly parliamentarians, could from a judicial point of view be interpreted as a breakthrough of democracy and parliamentarism in Finland.[845] It might even be seen as a joint bourgeois and Social Democratic attempt to make use of the representative system to achieve social reforms,[846] particularly as the ministers' speeches suggested that they were aiming at a parliamentary government that would separate Finland from Russia. In reality, however, Tokoi's ministry had been nominated by the Russians; according to the constitution, it was not responsible to the parliament; and it lacked the full support of the Social Democratic Party[847]. The government was formed because neither the Social Democrats nor the bourgeois parties would allow the other side to rule alone; most Social Democrats rejected such a coalition with 'parties that had been deposed by the Revolution in Russia' as irreconcilable with the principle of class struggle and revolution; the Social Democrat ministers did not coordinate their actions among themselves or with their party; the parties were not committed to the government's programme, each wishing to be in government and in opposition at the same time; none of the leading politicians was ready to serve as a minister; and Social Democrat ministers were accused of neglecting their political responsibilities. The public and especially the supporters of the socialists expected rapid social and economic reforms from the government, which they considered should reflect the views of the parliamentary majority. There were Russian troops in the country whose actions were unpredictable, and there was no longer a police force. The expectations failed to materialise – owing to food shortages and outbreaks of violence according to the usual explanation,[848] but also as a result of the exceptionally confrontational nature of the political debate in Finland in comparison with that in the other countries studied here. A working parliamentary government might well

---

843 *Helsingin Sanomat*, 'Mieliala Saksassa', 30 March 1917; *Työmies*, 'Englannin parlamentti' and 'Saksan sisäiset uudistukset', 31 March 1917.
844 *Hufvudstadsbladet*, 'Tyskland. En märklig debatt i riksdagen', 1 April 1917.
845 Lindman 1935, 14; Jyränki 2006, 33.
846 Kettunen 1986, 85; Ketola 1987, 41.
847 *Työmies*, 'Nykyinen valtiollinen asema Suomessa. Uuden hallituksen muodostaminen', 29 March 1917.
848 Lindman 1968, 26, 28, 30, 39; Upton 1980, 60, 68; Haapala 2010a, 62.

have been able to solve the issue of maintaining order by discussion if there had been a readiness for compromise. While in Britain and Sweden, and later in Germany, Social Democrat minorities were capable of cooperating in government at least with the centre parties, the uncompromising discourse of the Finnish Social Democrat majority – strengthened by the importation of Russian revolutionary discourse – made this very difficult and tended to diminish the legitimacy of all parliamentary government.

According to Risto Alapuro, the spontaneous reorganisation of the police at the local level in spring 1917 obscured differences between the public and private maintenance of order. The mobilisation of the workers at the local level led to a growing distance from the parliamentary Social Democratic Party and favoured extra-parliamentary action. The parliamentary party was not fully supportive of the government, but the workers at the local level would not necessarily remain supportive of the party if it failed to achieve the promised reforms, as Pauli Kettunen and Osmo Rinta-Tassi have pointed out.[849] Consequently, according to Samu Nyström, the Social Democrat parliamentarians tended to reflect changes in volatile public opinion in their reform demands.[850] A working parliament fully integrating the Social Democrats with other political groups (as in Britain or Sweden or even Germany by this time) might have provided a forum in which various problems could have been constructively deliberated and then removed from the agenda after a vote; however, Finnish parliamentary discourse was confrontational and became increasingly so under the influence of revolutionary discursive models adopted from Petrograd.

When the Finnish parliament elected in 1916 convened for its first session in April, Social Democrats were elected to the positions of Speaker, Vice-Speaker and Chairman of the Constitutional Committee, which led *Pravda* to express hope for support from Finland for the Russian working class[851] as the first socialist takeover of a Western parliament seemed to have taken place. In speeches made in the opening sessions, optimism and expectations of a free, revolutionary and democratic Russia giving freedom (if not yet independence) to Finland prevailed.[852] Calls for full internal independence (still excluding foreign and military policy) based on Professor Rafael Erich's interpretation of the eighteenth-century Swedish constitution, which from the Finnish legal perspective remained in force, were increasing. The transition of the royal prerogative to the Finnish government was supported by all parties, but they disagreed on whether this transfer should be made in cooperation with the Provisional Government in Russia. Only some bourgeois activists called for full independence, while the bourgeois moderates wanted to wait and see. The Social Democrats increasingly counted on Bolshevik promises of independence – first given

---

849 Kettunen 1986, 86; Rinta-Tassi 1986, 41; Alapuro 1988, 152, 154.
850 Nyström 2013, 137–8.
851 Polvinen 1987, vol. 1, 43.
852 Evert Huttunen (Social Democrat), who was of Ingrian origin, quoted by Vares 2006, 55.

by Lenin in 1905[853] – and followed his advice not to cooperate with the Provisional Government.

A democratically elected parliament had organised itself and seemed ready to proceed towards the democratisation and parliamentarisation of government but on the conditions of the majority party: sovereignty would be vested unambiguously in the parliament and not in any Russian government or Finnish government independent of the parliament, and the duality of government of the German and Swedish type was to be abolished. This duality still appeared as desirable to the so-called bourgeois parties, who were concerned about the intentions of the socialist majority. In May, when relations with the Provisional Government were already deteriorating, the Social Democrats together with the republican and pro-parliamentary Agrarian League began to demand that all political power should be transferred to the Finnish parliament as the only legitimate representative of 'the power of the people'. In addition to legislative power, this would include considerable executive power as well. This uncompromising constitutional stand was supported by the Russian Congress of Soviets, representing leftist parties in Russia, in a resolution on 3 July – its stand having been influenced by transnationally linked Finnish Social Democrats (Evert Huttunen and K. H. Wiik), who assured the Congress that the Finnish socialists aimed at crushing the Finnish bourgeoisie and advancing the 'politics of socialist democracy'.[854] This demonstrates the tendency of the Russian revolutionaries to define how democracy was to be understood in Finland: it was the democracy of the Russian socialist revolution.

The Finnish socialists drew overly optimistic conclusions about the intentions of the Congress and ignored the lack of support among other Russian socialists than the Bolsheviks (let alone the Russian bourgeoisie); indeed, 'democratic associations in Russia' were surprised by the plan of the Finnish parliament to declare itself sovereign.[855] The Finnish socialists were not very familiar with the Russian socialist parties and regarded them as relevant only insofar as they took a stand on Finnish autonomy, an attitude that annoyed both the Russian revolutionaries and the Socialist International. The Finnish socialists turned to the Bolsheviks since these seemed ready to support Finnish independence; however, the Bolshevik aim was to weaken the Provisional Government rather than to advance the rise of an independent Finland. In the Finnish parliament, the Social Democrats were ready to make use of their parliamentary majority to force through an act of parliamentary sovereignty with the supposed support of the Congress of Soviets. They contemplated the possibility of bypassing the parliamentary procedure for legislating constitutional issues, which included strict

---

853 Polvinen 1967, vol. 1, 60; Haapala 2010b, 63. Prime Minister Oskari Tokoi's speech on independence on 20 April 1917 was inspired by a speech given by Alexandra Kollontai and freely interpreted by Jonas Laherma in the Finnish National Theatre on 9 April. Polvinen 1987, vol. 1, 60; Ketola 1987, 58, 73; Soikkanen 1990, 86.
854 Irakli Tsereneli, cited in Ketola 1987, 153.
855 *Työmies*, 'Pietarin toimiston lewittämä tiedonanto', 12 July 1917.

minority provisions. In the end, the leading party members rejected this kind of manipulation,[856] but even the contemplation of such measures made bourgeois MPs question the legitimacy of the procedure with regard to the consideration of minority views, especially as the Social Democrats had received fewer votes than the bourgeois parties in the previous election.[857] The so-called Power Act on the exercise of supreme power by the Finnish parliament was approved on 18 and 19 July – at a time when the Russian soldiers in Helsinki were supporting a Bolshevik policy and the Russian government was believed to have been taken over by the Bolsheviks. Furthermore, the German Social Democrats were known to be calling for peace and constitutional reforms, which also supported the impression of a transnational revolutionary moment, even if the news from Berlin was meagre in the Finnish papers.[858]

The bill on parliamentary sovereignty had changed considerably in the course of the legislative process: in the original proposal of 11 June, the Provisional Government would convene the Finnish parliament, while in the approved act the parliament itself would decide on its sessions and new elections, initiate legislation and nominate the government. The Social Democrats were convinced that a strong status of the parliament of this kind would prevent the postponement of social reforms; that the realisation of a revolution via the parliament had become possible; and that the Finnish workers would now be liberated from the rule of both the Russian and the Finnish bourgeoisie. Since they did not wish to put the opportunities for majority rule at risk, the Social Democrats did not want to send the Act to Petrograd for promulgation.[859]

Many bourgeois MPs disagreed, criticising the act as poorly prepared, judicially questionable, politically unrealistic and enabling political dominance by a socialist majority. A committee led by K. J. Ståhlberg, a leading constitutional lawyer and a Liberal politician, had recommended a republic based on the classical division of power, with a strong executive balancing parliamentary power. From the perspective of the Provisional Government, which consisted of Mensheviks and moderate socialists, both

---

856 The Social Democrats disagreed on whether or not the constitutional procedure (supported by Edvard Hänninen-Walpas, Speaker Kullervo Manner, Evert Huttunen, K. H. Wiik and Chairman of the Constitutional Committee Yrjö Mäkelin) as opposed to a revolutionary simple majority (advocated by Otto Wille Kuusinen) should be used. The majority decided to follow the constitutional procedure but concluded that the party would quit the government and demand new elections and the convening of a national constituent assembly should the bill not pass. Lindman 1968, 82; Soikkanen 1975, 218–19; Ketola 1987, 175, 196–8. According to Alapuro, the Power Act was adopted 'in accordance with regular procedures' and hence the elections of October and the decisions of the new bourgeois majority were regarded as illegal by the Social Democrats. Alapuro 1988, 159–60. Concerns about the legality of the procedure, even if exaggerated, were decisive from the point of view of the legitimacy of parliamentary work.
857 *Hufvudstadsbladet*, 'Rätten att lämna lagförslag hvilande', 13 June 1917.
858 *Työmies*, 'Saksan waltiopäivät ja rauhankysymys', 17 July 1917.
859 Polvinen 1987, vol. 1, 67–8; Kirby 1976, 101–3; Ketola 1987, 151–2, 189; Haapala 2010b, 63–4; Haapala & Tikka 2013, 110.

alternatives remained out of the question. They saw the enactment of the Power Act simultaneously with a Bolshevik rebellion in Petrograd as an open challenge to the supreme authority of Russia in Finland. Hence the Provisional Government, encouraged by non-socialist Finns who wished to get rid of the Social Democrat parliamentary majority, dissolved the Finnish parliament on 31 July 1917 and ordered a new election. The legality of this measure was questioned by the Social Democrats, to whom it appeared as a violation of the will of the Finnish people as represented by the Social Democrat parliamentary majority. It was also a threat to the realisation of revolution through the parliament and seemed to end the prospect of reforms enacted through the representative system. The Menshevik stand, on the other hand, caused the Finnish Social Democrats to turn increasingly towards the Bolsheviks. They summoned the dissolved parliament to further sessions until they were forced to concede that a new election would take place. The bourgeois parties accused the Social Democrats of using the Power Act to carry out a coup, while the Social Democrats presented the new election as a coup that called independence and parliamentary rule in question.[860] As a result, the Finnish parliament was divided into two hostile sides questioning the legitimacy of each other's policy and even of the legislative institution.

The bourgeois opposition to the Power Act was seen by the Social Democrats as challenging their position within the Finnish polity and seeking to expel them from power, which, according to Risto Alapuro, led to the rise of two rival polities[861] and in the long run, in the absence of an organised police force, to a civil war. However, I argue that it is also necessary to take into account the radicalisation of Social Democratic parliamentary discourse, questions of the legitimacy of the parliamentary procedure and the transnational aspects and dynamics of the discursive confrontation to fully understand the development. When the Social Democrats were disappointed with their failure to bring about a revolution through the parliament, many, encouraged by the Bolsheviks in Petrograd and Helsinki and news on revolutionary developments elsewhere, began to move from constitutional and parliamentary to extra-parliamentary and downright revolutionary linguistic and physical action. According to Eino Ketola, too, the party moved from constitutionalism to 'revolutionary democracy', evidently accepting to a great extent a Bolshevik understanding of democracy, within one month after the adoption of the Power Act.[862] At this time, Lenin himself was hiding in Helsinki and in contact with Social Democrat leaders.

For many among the bourgeois parliamentary minority, which turned into a majority in the election of September, the Power Act appeared as an utterly radical socialist enterprise that had been introduced using constitutionally

---

860 Kirby 1976, 102; Kettunen 1986, 87; Rinta-Tassi 1986, 22; Ketola 1987, 233; Sihvonen 1997, 2–3; Vares 1998, 50–1; Jussila, Hentilä & Nevakivi 1999, 94, 96–7; Vares 2006, 48; Jyränki 2006, 33; Haapala 2010b, 64–5; Kekkonen 2016, 51.
861 Alapuro 1988, 158–60, 189; Alapuro 1990, 21.
862 Ketola 1987, 262.

questionable and downright treasonous language and procedural means; it appeared as a means to import revolution and excessive or perverted parliamentarism to Finland. The Finnish Power Act was the most radical of the attempts to create a parliamentary government in wartime Europe. It was clearly a partisan attempt, even though it won support from the centre parties, which made the Finnish right – falling back on Swedish and German traditions of political practice and theory – determined to maintain limitations to majority parliamentarism. But how exactly did conceptions of the war, revolution, democracy and parliamentarism evolve in these connected constitutional debates?

3.4.2 THE INTERNATIONAL, IMPERIAL AND NATIONAL POLITICAL ORDER CHANGED BY THE WAR AND REVOLUTION

The Finns had, despite economic hardships, escaped from the direct impacts of the war until spring 1917. However, owing to the constitutional, political, physical and – in the case of many persons – transnational links with Petrograd, they could not escape from the consequences of the Revolution there. Finnish constitutional debates were transnationally linked to those in other countries, too: to Sweden through the two countries' common constitutional tradition and cultural affinity and the contacts of Swedish-speaking Finns; to Germany through cultural and ideological contacts and the possibility of an alliance in the fight for independence; and to Britain as an alternative model of parliamentary government and a leading power of the Entente, although this link was far less obvious. In this subsection, we shall analyse how, in debating the proposed parliamentary sovereignty, the Finns saw the implications of the war, the Russian Revolution, the revolutionary language of the class struggle and the different international models for the Finnish constitution.

Owing to the geographical distance of the battlefields, the First World War had touched Finland only indirectly, so that it was not so generally seen as such a decisive factor as in the countries of comparison. Yrjö Mäkelin, the Social Democrat Chairman of the Constitutional Committee, nevertheless addressed the matter from a Marxist perspective – in a situation when up to 50,000 Russian soldiers, Finnish workers and workers' guards had demonstrated in Helsinki against the war and counter-revolution and the revolutionary initiative in Petrograd was generally believed to be shifting to the Bolsheviks.[863] Mäkelin described how the Finnish people, too, had been forced to work without proper compensation to support the 'imperialistic' war, and the poorest had paid a high price both materially and physically. The time for the proletariat to pay imperialism back had arrived, thanks to the Russian Revolution.[864] Such formulations resembled Russian revolutionary discourse especially in its Bolshevist form, which sought to turn the war into a civil war and an international class struggle rather than that of the

---

863 *Työmies*, 'Suuri mielenosoituskulkue eilen' and 'Mielenosoituspäiwä Pietarissa', 2 July 1917; Nyström 2013, 137, 139.
864 VP, Yrjö Mäkelin, 10 July 1917, 878.

more patriotic Mensheviks[865] or the cooperative views of the Labour Party in Britain and the Majority Social Democrats in Germany or Sweden. The Bolsheviks had made a strong impression in a recent party convention of the Social Democrats, and the joint demonstrations had reinforced discursive transfers. The physical reality of the effects of the wartime inflation reinforced Mäkelin's interpretation, and protests resulting from the shortages were emerging.[866] The pattern of protest was not so different from the situation in Sweden, but there was no regular police force in Finland, and the majority party in the parliament was employing an openly Marxist discourse.

The right rejected Mäkelin's revolutionary language in clear terms. According to Emil Schybergson (Swedish People's Party) – a leading banker and Germanophile – the fate of the Finnish people would be determined by the result of the war and the following peace treaty and not by some revolution.[867] Eirik Hornborg, who had undergone military training in Germany as one of the so-called 'Jägers', fought on the eastern front and served as the head of the press section of the Finnish office in Berlin, rejected revolution and counted likewise on the goodwill that the Finns would encounter among the negotiators after the war.[868] Such comments reflected a belief in a German victory that would open the way to Finnish (internal) independence. Many members in the conservative Finnish Party, too, wanted to wait and see.

By contrast, Santeri Alkio, the leader of the Agrarian League, emphasised the unique possibility for Finns to determine their future and realise independence and hence urged the parliament to pass the act. Referring implicitly to Woodrow Wilson's policy of self-determination, Alkio foresaw the rise of national ideologies among most small European nations after the war; in his view, the Finns should express theirs early, while the war was still continuing.[869] Alkio did not view the war as a fight over democracy: Finland already had universal suffrage, and it was unclear whether Germany or the Entente would best advance the cause of Finnish democracy. Only Social Democrat speakers took up the ideological aspect of the war, identifying with the understanding of radical Marxists, if not Bolsheviks, that the war should be turned into a revolution in which the proletariat would crush imperialism. Most Finnish MPs actually viewed the war as a chance for the Finns to liberate themselves – as a nation and perhaps socially as well.

The Finnish discussion focused on the ideologically charged concept of revolution rather than on the war and its political implications. The geographical vicinity of Petrograd and the presence of Russian troops brought a revolutionary atmosphere to Helsinki more immediately than to any capital outside the Russian Empire. Most non-socialist Finns still viewed

---

865   Pipes 1992, 382; Zetterberg 2000, 331, 337; Rasmussen 2014, 394.
866   Haapala 2010a, 24–5.
867   VP, Emil Schybergson, 10 July 1917, 886.
868   VP, Eirik Hornborg, 10 July 1917, 887; Such trust in the Western powers was questioned by Karl Harald Wiik in view of the fate of Belgium in the war. VP, 10 July 1917, 894–5.
869   VP, Santeri Alkio, 10 July 1917, 890–1.

the Revolution as a Russian rather than a Finnish event, but its influence was nevertheless felt, and suspicions of an attempted revolution at home were increasing.[870] Mäkelin's language suggests that the notion of an ongoing international revolution had been adopted in socialist circles. However, the developments in Petrograd were difficult to interpret owing to the linguistic gap and the dual nature of the Russian revolutionary government, with both a committee of the Duma and a soviet of workers and soldiers claiming executive power. Tension between the two holders of power caused confusion, particularly as the dualism was extended to the local level,[871] including the representatives of the Russian power in Helsinki.[872] The Finnish Social Democrats tended to duplicate this duality. Lenin's return to Petrograd in April 1917 increased the tension further: Lenin refused to support the Provisional Government and called for the introduction of a soviet republic as soon as the Bolsheviks won majorities in the soviets. A propaganda campaign emphasising the need for immediate reforms, class antagonism, the prospect of a civil war and the vision of the Russian Revolution as the forerunner of a pan-European revolution was launched. All the socialists in Russia accused 'the bourgeoisie' of counterrevolutionary intentions – no matter what the non-socialist parties were doing – and contrasted 'democracy' with 'the bourgeoisie'. Such revolutionary categorisations into true revolutionaries and the bourgeoisie had found their way into the Finnish parliament as well, reinforcing similar expressions of class hatred in Finnish Social Democratic agitation. The Bolsheviks may have held only a small minority in the Congress of Soviets,[873] but they dominated the Russian contacts of the Finnish socialists and provided the clearest revolutionary message. This was reinforced by general Russian socialist discourse and the traditions of Finnish socialist parlance.

By July 1917 some Finnish Social Democrats believed that a revolution could be expected soon in Britain, Germany and Sweden,[874] and many thought that the Bolsheviks would take over power in Petrograd, when the demonstrations turned into an uprising. Communication between Petrograd and Helsinki was not without its problems, however, and misleading information, some of it purposely disseminated, was rife owing to the chaos. During the final debate on parliamentary sovereignty, many Finnish socialists believed in a Bolshevik victory as their organ had just published 'a piece of secure information' that the Provisional Government had fallen, though details were still lacking.[875] The Provisional Government nevertheless soon crushed the uprising, and Lenin and other Bolshevik leaders were forced to

---

870 Alapuro 2003, 540.
871 Zetterberg 2000, 335, 337.
872 Upton 1980, 52–3.
873 Soikkanen 1961; Polvinen 1987, vol. 1, 8; Pipes 1992, 407; Wade 2000, 74–5, 80; Zetterberg 2000, 339–40.
874 Soikkanen 1975, 208.
875 *Työmies*, 'Wenäjän wäliaikainen hallitus kukistunut', 17 July 1917; on the following day, the news was that capitalist ministers had resigned in Russia. *Työmies*, 'Taistelu hallituswallasta Wenäjällä', 18 July 1917.

go into hiding to Finland,[876] which led to the intensification of transnational contacts with some Finnish socialists.[877] Contacts between Finland and Russia were numerous, with activists travelling between the capitals, and they led to reinforced transfers of revolutionary language from Petrograd to Helsinki, even though these did not necessarily make for common interests or even a proper understanding of the state of affairs in the other country. Such transfers of revolutionary language have received fairly little attention in Finnish historical research, in which the Social Democrats have rather been presented as acting out of patriotic motives and any discussion of the multiple reasons for the Civil War has tended to be overshadowed by the treatment of its violence and victims.

The German connection also mattered, despite the war. The concept of revolution as used in the programme of the Finnish Social Democratic Party had been borrowed from the manifestos of German Marxists. The Finnish socialists tended to adopt the interpretations of the more radical of these leftist groups, who were ready to use the parliament mainly as a forum for socialist agitation provided that the class struggle was also fought simultaneously on the streets. However, such a theory did not help to determine whether the time of a socialist revolution was at hand and the party should actively participate in it or just go on waiting. Yrjö Mäkelin – the Chairman of the Constitutional Committee – was in favour of active revolutionary action,[878] which influenced his parliamentary oratory when the future of the Finnish polity was being defined.

By July, for the majority of the Finnish Social Democrats, the Provisional Government no longer represented a true revolution, and they believed that the initiative was moving to the Bolsheviks, who seemed prepared to allow the socialist parliament in Finland to extend its powers.[879] According to Mäkelin, the Finns, unable to trust the leaders of the Russian Revolution, needed extensive independence to ensure that 'the achievements of the revolution could at least partly be made permanent'. Independence and parliamentary sovereignty would enable an intensified class struggle and the establishment of reasonable conditions for the working class.[880] Alexandra Kollontai and Jukka Rahja – the former a constant advocate of 'civil war' as the proper form of class struggle, an opponent of ministerial socialism and a critic of all cooperation with the bourgeoisie, the latter a Finn who

---

876   Kirby 1976, 104–105; Ketola 1987, 233; Ketola 1990, 98; Pipes 1992, 421; Zetterberg 2000, 340–1; Wade 2000, 183. In August 1917, Lenin was back in Finland in hiding and working on his manuscript on *State and Revolution*, which recommended the destruction of 'bourgeois' and 'bureaucratic' institutions. Pipes 1992, 468–9.
877   See Ketola 1987, 286, on K. H. Wiik's contacts with Lenin in late summer 1917, and 327 on party contacts with the Bolsheviks in Helsinki and Petrograd.
878   Upton 1980, 16–17; see Jörke & Llanque 2016, 266–8, on Karl Kautsky's instrumental ideas on parliament, Eduard Bernstein on limitations to the majority principle and calls for a separation of powers and Rosa Luxemburg on the multi-sited class struggle and the rejection of bourgeois parliamentarism.
879   Ketola 1987, 147.
880   VP, Yrjö Mäkelin, 2 July 1917, 689.

had been agitating to promote Bolshevism since 1903 – had made the same points in their meetings with Finnish socialists. They had agitated for revolution in accordance with Lenin's instructions, dazzling many Finnish Social Democrats and actively influencing the decisions of the party. In a party convention in June, Kollontai had successfully pressurised the left of the party into joining the Zimmerwald International (which represented socialist internationalism as the Bolsheviks understood it) and thereby supporting the dissemination of the Bolshevik version of the Revolution in the hope of continued Bolshevik support for Finnish independence. Kollontai's personality and knowledge of Finnish evidently had an effect here. The Social Democrats' political discourse tended to be taken over by this revolutionary alternative, even though they continued to have difficulties in understanding the dynamics of the Russian revolutionary debate and the limited extent of support for the Lenin and his circle in Petrograd.[881]

In the same convention, the party also defined its stand on constitutional issues and ordered the majority in the Constitutional Committee to follow it.[882] Lenin supported this development as he expected a Finnish revolution, when realised by the socialist parliament, to lead to a voluntary reunion with Russia. The Finnish Social Democratic Party, on the other hand, found itself emphasizing the class struggle to a degree unknown in its British, German and Swedish sister parties. Rejecting cooperation with the bourgeois groups, the party was ready to employ the entire arsenal of the Marxist discourse of the class struggle to give expression to popular discontent, as Anthony D. Upton has also concluded.[883]

On 3 July, the Congress of Soviets, 'in accordance with the stand of the Finnish Social Democratic Party', concluded that the Finnish question depended on 'the victory of the Revolution' in Russia. Alexandra Kollontai attended the meeting, describing an impending revolution in Finland and the strong ties between the Finnish and Russian proletariat.[884] Here she was functioning as a political agent mediating discursive transfers in both directions. In the second reading of the act on parliamentary sovereignty, Yrjö Mäkelin accordingly described the current Finnish situation in revolutionary terms, presenting the Finnish dispute as a part of the Russian Revolution, which was about to turn into a global one. He saw counterrevolutionary tendencies emerging – from the Provisional Government[885] and implicitly from the Finnish bourgeoisie – that might endanger the prospects that were being opened up by the Revolution. Hence the Finnish people should support 'the Revolution and the liberty of Russia' by allowing 'the people themselves' to decide as stipulated in the Power Act,[886] which meant the Social Democratic majority of the parliament or the representatives of the

---

881   Polvinen 1987, vol. 1, 71–2; Soikkanen 1975, 208–209; Rinta-Tassi 1986, 21, 49; Kirby 1986b, 114; Ketola 1987, 72–3, 80, 136–9, 146; Soikkanen 1990, 87.
882   Soikkanen 1975, 216.
883   Upton 1980, 17; Wade 2000, 193.
884   Polvinen 1987, vol. 1, 79; Ketola 1987, 158–9, 162.
885   On Soviet attitudes to the Provisional Government in Petrograd, see Pipes 1992, 324.
886   VP, Yrjö Mäkelin, 10 July 1917, 879.

proletariat. The Chairman of the Constitutional Committee of the Finnish parliament thus presented parliamentary sovereignty in Finland as a means to support the transnational revolutionary cause; this stand differing from Labour goals in Britain and Social Democratic ones in Germany and Sweden, where direct associations between domestic constitutional reforms and the Russian Revolution were avoided, with some far-left exceptions. Concepts in line with Bolshevik policies were taking over in the discourse of the Finnish Social Democratic Party.

In the meantime, a constitutional compromise with the bourgeoisie remained out of the question. Mäkelin used the revolutionary situation in Russia and its extension to Finland to put pressure on the bourgeois parties, implying that revolutionary times meant standing next to a barrel of gunpowder which might explode as a result of a seemingly harmless spark. The Social Democratic 'youth' of the country (excluded from voting by the 24-year age limit) should prepare to defend the cause of the people together with the party in the spirit of popular socialism:[887]

> Freedom! Let the long-lasting slavery come to an end. Let the chains so long carried by our people loose their hold. Let the era of free work and action, longed for from generation to generation, begin. Let there be a Finland free in her own affairs to emerge side by side with a Russia aiming at freedom.

Mäkelin's revolutionary declaration, which was primarily addressed to audiences outside the parliament,[888] produced a parliamentary debate on a reformulated bill in the aftermath of the decision of the Congress of Soviets to support the extension of Finnish autonomy. The Social Democrats were evidently aiming at ensuring the implementation of reforms by joining the Russian Revolution.

The Social Democrat prime minister Oskari Tokoi, too, viewed the Russian Revolution as the creator of 'a new free Russia' and as a factor that would transform Finland.[889] 'The great revolution' was expanding and the Finns should participate in this 'revolutionary age'. Some news already suggested that the Bolshevik uprising in Petrograd might fail, but Tokoi wanted to get the bill on parliamentary sovereignty through anyway,[890] recognising the Petrograd Soviet as 'the real representatives of the revolutionary Russian people', defining the Power Act in revolutionary terms and declaring his all-party government, too, to be a revolutionary one, though one that acted within the Swedish-Finnish constitutionalist framework without manipulating parliamentary procedure as had been proposed by some Social Democrat leaders:[891]

887   VP, Yrjö Mäkelin, 10 July 1917, 880. On similar ideas expressed in the party, see Ketola 1987, 197 and the discussion of Ehrnrooth 1992 in section 2.4.
888   A version of the speech was printed in *Työmies*, 'Suomen korkeimman hallintowallan siirtäminen eduskunnalle', 12 July 1917.
889   VP, Oskari Tokoi, 12 June 1917, 505.
890   Cf. the determination of the Rump Parliament to elect a king despite the fall of Germany in October 1918, discussed in section 6.4.
891   VP, Oskari Tokoi, 17 July 1917, 1033. On Petrograd, see Ketola 1987, 194, 203, 212, and Ketola 1990, 98; Wade 2000, 182–3.

This decision, [...], is a part of the revolution, one part of the great revolution which is now taking place, part of a revolution which, it has been proposed, should be carried out, so to speak, according to the constitution. I, as a representative of the revolutionary government, have no right to become an obstacle in the way of the revolution.

The Finnish constitutional debate of 1917 differed fundamentally from those in Britain, Germany and Sweden in that the Prime Minister was associating himself with the radicalising Russian Revolution though still asserting – in accordance with the decisions of the Social Democratic parliamentary group – that his government was carrying out the revolution constitutionally through the parliament. In the party organ, which printed Tokoi's speech and only reviewed opposing views very selectively, a socialist MP called Eetu Salin declared that the vote involved the last fight between the capitalist class – the internal enemy – and the unprivileged proletariat and the transfer of legislative power to the people.[892] Subsequently, the paper declared in its editorial that 'the big bourgeoisie' had lost the battle.[893] While winning support from their radical supporters and the pro-parliamentary Agrarians, the Social Democratic policy alienated the legalistically constitutionalist right, who opposed the extension of the Revolution to Finland and preferred a cautious policy aimed at maintaining the established political order in the country.

More revolutionary discourse followed from the Swedish-speaking Social Democrat K. H. Wiik, who had attended a meeting of the Executive Committee of the Congress of Soviets in Petrograd and did not hesitate to announce this in the Finnish parliament.[894] This importer of revolutionary discourse, with his contacts with Lenin and Kollontai and experience in negotiating with various Russian revolutionary groups,[895] spoke for cooperation with the representatives of 'Russian democracy'[896] and 'the revolutionary Russian people' on the streets of Petrograd, i.e. the Bolsheviks rather than the Provisional Government.[897] Wiik bypassed the fact that there were many on the Russian left, too, who did not support the sovereignty of the Finnish parliament in the proposed form.[898] Instead, he criticised the parliament for its ineffective resistance to Russian imperialism and reluctance to advance social reforms.

In Social Democratic discourse, the Russians were carrying out 'the most glorious revolution in the world'.[899] Edvard Hänninen-Walpas – whom

---

892 *Työmies*, 'Mistä kysymys', 18 July 1917.
893 *Työmies*, 'Eduskunta julistautunut Suomen waltiowallan omistajaksi', 20 July 1917.
894 Ketola 1987, 192–3.
895 Polvinen 1987, vol. 1, 22; Upton 1980, 81; Ketola 1987, 79.
896 It is worth noting the association between the Bolsheviks and democracy, which Wiik had adopted in Petrograd.
897 VP, Karl Harald Wiik, 17 July 1917, 1021.
898 Ketola 1987, 183–4, 212.
899 VP, Konrad Lehtimäki, 17 July 1917, 1031.

Alexandra Kollontai considered the leader of the Finnish leftist socialists[900] – accused the Finnish 'bourgeois classes' and 'exploiting classes' of fearing that the Social Democratic majority was aiming at a socialist revolution through the extension of the powers of the parliament. His interpretation was that the bourgeoisie aimed at preventing the reform and the revolution by ignoring the parliament, which had been elected by the Finnish people.[901] In other words, they would be acting as counter-revolutionaries. As the editor-in-chief of *Työmies*, the organ of the Social Democratic Party, Hänninen-Walpas had long been propagating an uncompromising doctrine of class struggle[902] while nevertheless also recognising the parliamentary way as a strategy for the advancement of reform.[903] Disappointment with the results of the seemingly radical parliamentary reform of 1906 and universal suffrage, the Social Democrat parliamentary majority of 1917, Bolshevik influence, support for the Social Democratic policy received from the Bolsheviks and the ongoing Bolshevik uprising in Petrograd caused Hänninen-Walpas to adopt increasingly revolutionary rhetoric in which he contrasted the socialist revolution with the counter-revolutionary bourgeoisie.

The class struggle played a considerably stronger role in the discourse of the Finnish Social Democrats than it did in the countries of comparison; this was a result of a combination of a tradition of violent class struggle rhetoric and contacts with the Russian revolutionary discourse. The language of class was not the sole province of the Social Democrats, however: it was used by all parliamentary groups, which to some extent reflects the fact that class differences had been acerbated by the socio-economic circumstances. However, it was essentially manifested in a *discourse* of class confrontations that had been radicalised as a reaction on both sides of the ideological divide in Finland. Similar class differences, reinforced by the everyday realities of the war, existed elsewhere, but they did not lead to such a fierce discursive confrontation in the parliaments. The Finnish radical socialists were tempted to adopt Lenin's ideas of the class war as a civil war and distance themselves from parliamentary cooperation in the expectation of a revolution.[904] Finnish society was discursively divided into two opposite groups: the socialists presenting themselves as a party of the working class (the people proper), and the 'bourgeois' parties manifesting a developed class consciousness as property-owners. The use of the language of class by both sides deepened the realities of the social divisions at the local level, emphasised by Pertti Haapala,[905] and certainly in the parliament, too.

The legitimacy of the political system was also wavering as a result of questions about the fairness of the observation of law and parliamentary rules. In the introduction of the bill, Prime Minister Tokoi had already argued that 'the classes holding power have followed the forms and literal

---

900   Ketola 1987, 142.
901   VP, Edvard Hänninen-Walpas, 17 July 1917, 1055.
902   Upton 1980, 17.
903   Ehrnrooth 1992, 185.
904   See Winkler 1999, 4; cf. Hentilä & Hentilä 2016, 100.
905   Haapala 2010a, 30.

letter of the law' and held to the established order in ways that had aggravated the workers.[906] Such an attitude caused the right and the centre to conclude that Tokoi did not respect law and order and was unwilling to take measures to stop violence at the local level and the exertion of extra-parliamentary pressure on bourgeois MPs. As a consequence, any possibilities for consensus and compromise between the government parties were fast disappearing.[907] The first minister's parlance produced on one side a more radical class discourse and on the other legalistic defensive arguments as a reaction. The Social Democrat contemplations of bypassing the Parliament Act in order to get their will through clearly weakened trust in the system.

The debate also exhibited a transnational discursive construction of opponents (a phenomenon familiar from Sweden). Yrjö Mäkelin, the Chairman of the Constitutional Committee, with his background as an agitator and journalist, pointed to representatives of 'the international reactionary class' among 'the upper-class groups' in the Finnish parliament.[908] In the opinion of the futurist writer Konrad Lehtimäki and also of a farmer called Antti Juutilainen, who was a representative of the Agrarians, the opposition to parliamentary sovereignty demonstrated that the Finnish upper class was 'antiquated', unable to learn from experience, having lost their previous intellectual leadership and failing to understand the interests of the lower classes and to thereby fulfil their responsibilities to the people. The Finnish right was advocating 'ultra-traditionalist reactionary views' and 'notions that will be removed from the stage' since 'new notions will definitely replace them'.[909] All this reflected a Russian revolutionary concept of the people proper as opposed to the educated classes. By July, the divisions in the Finnish parliament were interpreted as constituting a social (socialist) revolution, with the prospects for future equality and liberty being opposed by reactionary stagnation. The confrontation over parliamentary sovereignty was explained as being a result of 'class differences',[910] with the bourgeoisie appearing as the enemy of the workers.[911] The speaker, Evert Huttunen, who was a journalist, had participated in Bolshevik meetings and led a delegation to the Congress of Soviets only a week earlier, thus acting concretely as an historical body importing discourse from Petrograd. Edvard Hänninen-Walpas likewise repeated the accusations against 'the reactionary leaders of the bourgeois classes'.[912]

The 'class interests' of bureaucrats who were in danger of losing their power were also criticised by the anti-elitist and anti-capitalist but non-socialist Agrarian League which aimed at the abolition of class boundaries.[913]

906 VP, Oskari Tokoi, 12 June 1917, 508.
907 *Hufvudstadsbladet*, 'Den nuvarande senaten och laglösheten', 14 June 1917; *Helsingin Sanomat*, 'Senaatin warapuheenjohtajan uusin lausunto', 14 June 1917.
908 VP, Yrjö Mäkelin, 10 July 1917, 880.
909 VP, Antti Juutilainen, 10 July 1917, 907–9; Konrad Lehtimäki, 10 July 1917, 909.
910 VP, Evert Huttunen, 10 July 1917, 904; Rinta-Tassi 1986, 31.
911 This is what Evert Huttunen had said to the Congress of Soviets on 3 July. Huttunen's newspaper *Työ* [Work] agitated Bolshevik ideas. Ketola 1987, 162.
912 VP, Edvard Hänninen-Walpas, 17 July 1917, 1055.
913 *Maalaisliiton ohjelma*, 1914.

Santeri Alkio rejected both capitalist exploitation and socialist doctrines of a class struggle, being concerned about the rise of 'class feeling' and 'class power' among the socialist parliamentary majority.[914] MPs from the right responded, likewise using the language of class antagonism, something that rarely happened in the other parliaments, though visible in the argumentation of the Swedish Right. Emil Schybergson (Swedish People's Party) criticised the Social Democrats for denying the sacrifices made by the upper classes on behalf of the Finnish nation.[915] Georg Rosenqvist (Swedish People's Party), a Professor of Dogmatics, complained about Finland being ruled at a decisive moment in history by 'a senate of one class'.[916] This reflected the deteriorating legitimacy of parliamentary government among reform-minded bourgeois circles as well, Rosenqvist having previously sympathised with the reform demands of the workers. Such feelings added to a readiness to turn from parliamentary to extra-parliamentary methods on both sides. When Kaarle Rantakari (Finnish Party, a defector from the Social Democrats) lamented the fact that 'class hatred' had been effectively propagated in Finland for several years, the Social Democrats responded by accusing the propertied classes of precisely such agitation.[917] Earlier Marxist discourse was reinforced by revolutionary discursive models imported from Petrograd, which removed any chances of compromise. The concrete context of these expressions of class hatred was the gradually worsening food crisis. Radical Social Democrats, who had previously warned about bourgeois conspiracies, had been propagating class hatred constantly. Their imaginary accusations of conspiracies had been countered in equally hard terms by 'the bourgeoisie'.[918] A revolutionary class division had become discursively established.

Bourgeois MPs still remained uncertain about the implications of the Russian Revolution for Finland. Santeri Alkio of the Agrarians saw it as having removed not only 'the former bureaucratic government of Russia but also its henchmen in this country'.[919] Constitutionally it had brought about a revolution in Finland as well.[920] However, Alkio later emphasised the fact that there was no revolution going on in Finland: the Finns were simply making use of the revolutionary situation in Russia to reform their constitution in a revolutionary direction.[921] The right deprecated the Revolution: Minister of Justice Antti Tulenheimo (Finnish Party) accused the Social Democrats of adopting a concept of revolution according to which 'power and not law' tended to become dominant in the parliament.[922] Kaarle Rantakari (Finnish Party), having rejected the socialist internationalism of his youth, said that the socialists mistakenly believed that the course of world

914 VP, Santeri Alkio, 12 June 1917, 511.
915 VP, Emil Schybergson, 10 July 1917, 909.
916 VP, Gustaf Rosenqvist, 12 June 1917, 514.
917 Vares 2000.
918 Upton 1980, 96, 98.
919 VP, Santeri Alkio, 12 June 1917, 511.
920 VP, Santeri Alkio, 2 July 1917, 696–7.
921 VP, Santeri Alkio, 17 July 1917, 1036–7.
922 VP, Antti Tulenheimo, 2 July 1917, 680; 17 July 1917, 1006.

history had changed as a consequence of a single revolution and that there was a revolution going on in Finland rising from local circumstances.[923] They had been possessed by the spirit of revolution, interpreting acts of violence around the country as reflections of their supposed revolution.[924] Onni Talas (Young Finns), a Professor of Administrative Law, pointed out that such a belittling of violence made it impossible for the bourgeois parties to accept Social Democratic policies.[925] Eirik Hornborg (Swedish People's Party) accused the Social Democrats of having combined the question of independence with their ideological goals of social and domestic political revolution, forcing the other political groups either to oppose or to support both. This linkage was unfair given that many Finnish members of the right held views that 'in a European parliament' (obviously the Prussian Landtag, which had recently questioned parliamentarisation) would have been regarded as leftish.[926]

In addition to Russia, political ferment in the established political models of other countries was also referred to, albeit selectively. References to contemporary Sweden, as opposed to the eighteenth-century Swedish constitutions, were rare in the Finnish constitutional debates. This reflects the intellectual distance between the countries in the late 1910s,[927] though there had been reports of a 'revolutionary movement in Sweden'[928] and the threat of a general strike[929] during the hunger and reform demonstrations of the spring there. Nor did the other Scandinavian countries or the Anglo-American world appear as objects of comparison when a major step in parliamentarisation was debated in the Finnish parliament. The conventional view remained that parliamentarism was only suited to the specific circumstances of Britain.[930] Wilsonian ideas of national self-determination were not taken up either, though Santeri Alkio justified the Finns' demands for liberty as 'a civilised people' (a highly Fennoman concept) by emphasising the Finnish struggle for freedom against both Swedish and Russian suppression.[931]

The Finnish constitutional debaters rather looked to Germany, an old exemplar for the right, which seemed to be doing well in the war. The German model appealed to most educated MPs who, independently of their party affiliation, viewed German culture as closely related to Finnish, whereas few regarded the Entente in a positive light.[932] The success of the German war effort against Russia and the links of Finnish activists striving

923 VP, Kaarle Rantakari, 10 July 1917, 897; 17 July 1917, 1022–3.
924 VP, Ernst Nevanlinna, 12 June 1917, 515.
925 VP, Onni Talas, 12 June 1917, 516.
926 VP, Eirik Hornborg, 10 July 1917, 887–8.
927 Ihalainen 2015.
928 *Työmies*, 'Wallankumousliike Ruotsissa', 28 April 1917.
929 *Hufvudstadsbladet*, 'Socialdemokratiska demonstrationer i Stockholm', 8 June 1917.
930 Professor of Roman Law Rabbe Axel Wrede (Swedish People's Party) in the Constitutional Committee. Lindman 1968, 91.
931 VP, Santeri Alkio, 12 June 1917, 510.
932 Upton 1980, 33.

for independence with Germany supported the prevailing positive image of its being a well-ordered state. Finnish juridical discourse was traditionally closely connected with that of Germany,[933] as was discourse in most academic fields. Kaarle Rantakari, the leading agitator of the Finnish Party, presented the German model as an ideal one: it had been created by 'the most organised' and 'the bravest people in Europe and at present in all the world' and was therefore admired even by the enemies of Germany.[934] Prussian nineteenth-century history provided a working model for building a new state, being based on discipline and order, austerity and the strong and centralised power of the state. Since German unification, the Reich and the German people had followed the Prussian model at all levels (the rising criticism of Prussianism in the Reichstag being ignored). The Finns, too, should adopt a similar constitution that would overcome party government, promote industry, austerity and the right kind of discipline and lead to success, as was being demonstrated by the Germans in the war.[935] This German model was to be contrasted essentially with the Russian order, which had already been regrettably influential in Finland.[936] Rantakari's comparison with Germany went further, turning into a defence of strong executive power and a criticism of parliamentarism based the experiences of *das tolle Jahr* of 1848 and referring ironically to the 'bustle' and 'elegant parliamentary speeches' in the Paulskirche Parliament: when the parliament failed to unify Germany, the Prussian government had done so with methods that earned the respect of the German people.[937] The German model was explicitly used to speak for the maintenance of the established Gustavian constitution in Finland with its emphasis on the government over the parliament. Such openly ideological interpretations of the German constitution were not made by the Swedish right, who were constantly accused by the left of defending the established order in alliance with Prussianism. The Finnish right, by contrast, did not hide its admiration of Prussianism.

The Finnish left was provoked by such talk.[938] Frans Rantanen presented the German militarism of the day as being equally as tragic as that witnessed in the Thirty Years' War – the historical analogy referred to the alliance between Sweden and the German Protestants. In both situations, the Germans mistakenly believed that social and economic development could be determined through the use of violence.[939] The news from Berlin, though even more fragmented than that from Petrograd, suggested that the Social Democrats and the centrist parties were challenging the war policies, calling for an electoral reform in Prussia and winning concessions from the Kaiser; even Prussian militarists were thus showing a willingness to allow democratisation. The Finnish right, by contrast, admired Frederick William

---

933   Pulkkinen 2003, 243.
934   VP, Kaarle Rantakari,17 July 1917, 1022–3.
935   VP, Kaarle Rantakari, 17 July 1917, 1023.
936   VP, Kaarle Rantakari, 17 July 1917, 1023.
937   VP, Kaarle Rantakari, 17 July 1917, 1024–5.
938   VP, Helenius-Seppälä, 17 July 1917, 1028.
939   VP, Frans Rantanen, 17 July 1917, 1029.

IV, a Prussian king who had rejected the imperial throne when it was offered to him by the revolutionary Frankfurt Parliament. But he, too, had in the end been forced to recognise constitutional monarchy. According to Rantanen, 'in Germany, too, the social rule by the people' (*yhteiskunnallinen kansanvalta, die Soziale Demokratie*, which can also be translated simply as 'social democracy', implying the rule by the workers) would be realised in the near future.[940] This reflected a strong transnational awareness among the Finnish socialists of the German situation and can be characterised as an 'adapting translation'.[941] The German Social Democratic example mattered, particularly as it supported the view that the world revolution was also making progress in more developed countries; that the Kautskyist moment had arrived; and that the Finnish socialists were bound to participate in this transnational revolution. Rantanen's choice of words reinforced the assumption of the synonymity of 'social democracy' and 'parliamentary democracy', the ideological goals of the socialist party appearing as universal and exclusive of other forms of parliamentarism and democracy. No sister party in Britain, Germany or Sweden defined its ideology as identical with parliamentary democracy in the sense of the rule by the workers, which reflected the influence of the party's unique majority position, the developments in confrontational rhetoric and the transnational transfers of Russian revolutionary discourse on Finnish Social Democracy. Both the concept of class and that of democracy had become defined along Russian revolutionary lines that sounded in non-socialist ears as Bolshevism.

Rantakari's and Rantanen's parallels between Germany and Finland are illustrative of the use of international comparisons in parliamentary constitutional debates in this and indeed any historical period: foreign examples are interpreted highly selectively in order to support particular goals in current domestic political struggles. They by no means imply direct transfers between political cultures, but they do illustrate the relative importance of various foreign political cultures and offer ways to redefine the prospective future of one's own political community. The case of the Agrarian leader Santeri Alkio is illustrative of this context-bound nature of international comparisons. In summer 1917, Alkio joined the left in viewing the German model critically by speaking out for parliamentarisation and doubted the future of the Prussian system after the war.[942] In 1918, Alkio would, despite his republicanism, be sharing in the cultural admiration of Germany, while in 1919 he would look at the Western powers as models for organising a parliamentary democracy.

3.4.3 INTERNATIONAL DEMOCRACY OR THE VERNACULAR 'RULE BY THE PEOPLE'?

'Democracy' had been discussed in Finland to some extent during the parliamentary reform of 1906,[943] but the debate now became active when

---

940 VP, Frans Rantanen, 17 July 1917, 1030.
941 Leonhard 2011, 256.
942 VP, Santeri Alkio, 17 July 1917, 1036.
943 Kurunmäki 2008, 364–5.

the democratisation of government seemed a real possibility. When the parliament convened, Jaakko Mäki of the Social Democrats, a socialist agitator who had remigrated from the USA, called for 'a new, more democratic form of government' also for Finland.[944] Here, as everywhere in the contemporary press, the vernacular term *kansanvalta* (the rule by the people) was used. When parliamentary sovereignty was first discussed, Prime Minister Oskari Tokoi talked about 'the new democratic Russia' and its 'democratic intentions'.[945] The Finnish concept had slightly different connotations from those of the international concept of 'democracy', combining as it did notions of ethnicity, Finnishness and class.

For the Social Democrats, the connotation of the rule by the common people or the workers as opposed to the upper classes was central; hence the above-mentioned attack by Yrjö Mäkelin, the Chairman of the Constitutional Committee on 'a fear of the rule by the people' among the bourgeoisie.[946] For him, parliamentary sovereignty in the proposed form stood for the creation of a 'Finland based on the rule by the people', in which the working classes would rule in ways that would find acceptance in revolutionary Russia. This explicitly defined democracy as the rule of the workers and more particularly the proletariat in the sense in which the term was used in Russian revolutionary and especially Bolshevik discourse. The uncompromising contrast between bourgeois rule as 'exploitation' and proletarian rule as 'democracy' was expressed in orthodox Marxist language:[947]

> Where the bourgeoisie is in power, there are constant attempts to exercise exploitation and slavery as much as possible. But wherever the proletariat gains power, there not only one's own freedom but the happiness and freedom of all peoples will be unceasingly advanced.

In the constantly mounting revolutionary fervour of July 1917, the cause of democracy was defined in Finnish Social Democratic discourse as being identical with that of the Social Democratic Party and its majority rule. This excluded the bourgeois parties (including the Agrarian League, which actually supported the Power Act) from cooperation in establishing democracy: only the socialist majority of the Finnish parliament were democrats. In a report in the Social Democratic organ, *Työmies*, Mäkelin was said to have emphasised the fact that 'the Russian democracy' and the Finnish Social Democrats were united in their goal to establish 'global rule by the people' (*yleismaailmallinen kansanvalta*), whereas on the other side they had a reactionary international[948] – two internationalisms being typically set against each other.

944 VP, Jaakko Mäki, 10 April 1917, 12.
945 VP, Oskari Tokoi, 12 June 1917, 506.
946 VP, Yrjö Mäkelin, 2 July 1917, 687.
947 VP, Yrjö Mäkelin, 2 July 1917, 689.
948 *Työmies*, 'Suomen korkeimman hallintowallan siirtäminen eduskunnalle', 12 July 1917.

The resolution accepted by the Congress of Soviets in Petrograd, to which the Finnish Social Democrats referred, also addressed the question of 'the Finnish democracy and especially Finnish Social Democracy'.[949] Alexandra Kollontai, the most influential intermediary between Bolshevist discourse and the Finnish socialists, had indeed urged 'a distancing of the democracy of the workers from the domestic bourgeoisie both in Russia and Finland and the observance of the line of the class politics of the proletariat'.[950] This definition of democracy as the rule of the proletariat, borrowed from Russian revolutionary discourse, removed any possibilities of finding a common or even compromise-seeking Finnish national discourse on democracy. The adoption of this discourse by the Finnish Social Democrats differs radically from the vague British concept of democracy, which Labour had not yet politicised, and from the Majority Social Democratic concepts of democracy in Germany and Sweden, which invited the Liberal Parties in these countries at least to participate in the construction of democracy. Even the Swedish far left was willing to join a common cross-party campaign for democracy, whereas the Finnish socialists now found themselves by international standards on the far left of revolutionary socialist discourse.

Mäkelin's notions of revolution and democracy might have been derived from Karl Kautsky, who has customarily been presented as the theorist who inspired the Finnish Social Democrats. In 1903 Mäkelin had employed Kautskyist thinking in emphasising the contrast between the rulers advancing their own interests and the lower orders who rejected institutions and laws.[951] However, by 1917 Mäkelin's views were more strongly influenced by contemporary Russian revolutionary discourse than the works of remote German theorists, and in that discourse parliaments played a minor role. The Russian debate had long entertained a more radical concept of democracy than that of Social Democratic discourse in western and central Europe and had turned increasingly leftist since the outbreak of the Revolution.[952]

Ever since 1905 the Russian socialist parties had been struggling to control key concepts such as *revolutsiia*, *demokratiia* and *proletarii*, trying to monopolise their own understandings of them and ignoring alternative liberal and populist interpretations. The contrast between the workers and the peasants as the real 'common people' (*narod*), the 'toilers', the 'mob', the 'have-nots' or 'democracy' with the 'the bourgeoisie' or the privileged classes had become evident well before 1917. All these words for the people were used interchangeably in Russian revolutionary discourse, and the flexible concept of *narod* (comparable in some respects with the Finnish word *kansa*) was used to propagate a wide variety of visions for the future of society. By July 1917, even the boundaries of the working class had been more narrowly defined by the revolutionary Social Democrats in Petrograd, the rhetoric of a militant struggle between 'us' and 'them' was increasing, and the language of an irreconcilable class conflict took over. Democracy no longer included all

---

949 Polvinen 1987, vol. 1, 79.
950 Ketola 1987, 162.
951 Kettunen 2003, 189.
952 Gorham 2003, 7–9; Beuerle 2018.

the people in a democratic republic but turned into an exclusive social term dividing the working population from the bourgeoisie. The implication was that democracy stood for the rule of the workers and essentially for the rule of the proletariat. Such a concept of democracy now defined the objectives of the revolution: Democracy stood for 'democratic organisation' as realised in soviets and for the 'democratic forms' of government provided by socialism. 'Revolutionary democracy' in this sense meant the complete rejection of the 'bourgeois' state and all 'bourgeois' parties, which by definition could not be 'democratic'. As a consequence, the alternative liberal understandings of democracy used within the Russian educated classes came to be totally excluded.[953] The consequences of these exclusive definitions of the people and democracy for the revolutionary process not only in Russia but also in Finland were decisive, both before and during the Finnish Civil War.[954]

As we have seen, this radically revolutionary and essentially Bolshevik understanding of democracy was transferred to Finnish discourse by transnationally linked socialists, with Finnish MPs attending revolutionary assemblies in Petrograd and Bolshevik leaders visiting Helsinki. Furthermore, Finnish papers tended to translate Russian revolutionary speeches word for word. Mäkelin, too, excluded the bourgeois parties from cooperation in the construction of democracy: only the socialist majority represented true democrats. Long-lasting domestic agitation along the lines of orthodox Marxism,[955] close transnational connections with Bolshevist discourse and a parliamentary majority made the Finnish Social Democrats' concept of democracy exceptionally exclusive and divisive. Through uncompromising and universalist definitions and accusations that the Finnish bourgeoisie were counter-revolutionaries, the policy line of the Social Democrats became associated by the Finnish bourgeois parties with that of the Bolshevik revolutionaries.

Such discursive transfers from Petrograd to Helsinki and the historical contestability of concepts have received marginal attention in previous research on developments leading to the Finnish Civil War, in which structural explanations[956] have been favoured and the influence of Kautskyist

---

953 Figes & Kolonickij 1999, 121–5, 188–9; Gorham 2003, 9, 25, 60.
954 For terminology referring to the people and to soviets borrowed from Russia during the period of Soviet rule, see Rinta-Tassi 1986, 275–81; Borisova & Siro 2014, 93. See also Haapala 1995, 235.
955 See, however, Kettunen 1986, 82, on the limits of the radicality of the Finnish labour movement.
956 Liikanen 1993. See Haapala 1995, 14, 223, 242, Haapala & Tikka 2013, 112–14 and Haapala 2014 on structural explanations. According to Haapala, social confrontations contributed to the political crisis. The politicians themselves caused a political stalemate as a result of 'political thought' favouring party interests. Political attempts to solve questions of subsistence only led to the politicisation of these issues and to attempts to create a new order. In the parliament, the politicians quarrelled over interpretations of the constitution and accused each other of plans to stage a coup. Haapala 1992. Instead of merely blaming the parliament, it would be important to problematize the dynamics of political discourse by analysing language use empirically, particularly as Haapala suggests that it was political divisions rather than the economic situation that

theory on Finnish socialism emphasised. The sociologist Risto Alapuro – who prefers to compare Finland with the countries of Eastern Europe rather than with states that shared legal and representative traditions of the Swedish-Finnish kind – suggests that the impact of the Russian Revolution on the attempted class-based revolution in Finland happened through 'the state'. According to Alapuro, the revolutionary situation followed from the crisis in Russia, which suddenly changed 'the conditions of the contests for state power' and, together with the character of the polity and the class structure, led the reluctant 'non-revolutionary working-class movement into a revolution'.[957] On the other hand, some within the movement had been expecting a Finnish revolution since 1905. The consideration of ideological discourses demonstrates the centrality, even if the ambiguity, of the concept of the revolution.[958] Alapuro's understanding of the reformist nature of the Finnish labour movement is not shared by Pauli Kettunen, though he, too, considers that the Finnish workers were not preparing a revolution.[959] According to Alapuro, the Social Democratic Party saw itself as the leading advocate of the extension of democracy but its conception of revolution remained indefinite and was not focussed on the class struggle in a revolutionary sense[960] – a conclusion not supported by an analysis of parliamentary discourse in 1917. Alapuro concedes, nevertheless, that the proletarian nature of the Finnish Revolution may have followed from political events related to Russian history, allowing the Finnish socialists first to enter the polity in 1907 and then allowing them to attempt a takeover without liberal support in 1917.[961]

Seppo Zetterberg, on the other hand, has pointed to news from Russia suggesting that the political influence of the Bolsheviks was rising and that they might soon seize power and continue to support the Finnish socialists.[962] Pauli Kettunen and Osmo Rinta-Tassi have discussed the tendency of both Communists and Social Democrats to emphasise – after the Civil War – the weakness of the links between the Finnish and Russian labour movements before the war, though actually the strengthening status of the Bolsheviks had played an important role, as had the tendency of some Social Democratic leaders to propagandistically instigate class hatred in

---

explain the Civil War. Haapala & Tikka 2013, 121, also recognise the influence of the ideological and political goals of the political leaders. Kekkonen 2016, 50, 56, 332–4, recognises the debate on the extent of democracy and references to a possible civil war in 1917 but does not analyse them, emphasising structural explanations instead. On the neglect of the contemporary use of language and conceptualisations of democracy in political scientific structural analyses of political culture, see Kurunmäki 2012, 121–30.

957 Alapuro 1988, 3–12, 16 (quote), 143 (quote); Alapuro 1990, 12, 20–1.
958 Alapuro 2003, 537–41.
959 Kettunen 1986, 84, 89.
960 Alapuro 1988, 150, 191; also Kettunen 1986, 80. On different approaches that have considered the effects of divisive class discourse on political action, see Soikkanen 1961.
961 Alapuro 1988, 196.
962 Zetterberg 1992, 29.

a Bolshevistic manner. This does not, of course, mean that Lenin's ideas would have been understood and absorbed in full.[963] An analysis of parliamentary discourse strongly supports the interpretation that Bolshevik-like parlance was already taking over the Finnish party in summer 1917.

Mäkelin continued using revolutionary definitions of democracy during the second reading of the Power Act bill on 10 July, calling the Representative Assembly of the Workers' and Soldiers' Soviets 'the plenipotentiary representative' of 'Russian democracy' and presenting the constitutional views of the Finnish Social Democrats as identical with its definitions. Mäkelin transnationalised the goals of both institutions by talking about 'endeavours to create a universal rule by the people'.[964] Evert Huttunen – born in Ingria close to Petrograd, fluent in Russian and hence a transnational link between Bolshevik revolutionary and Finnish political discourses[965] – made the Social Democratic exclusive definition of democracy even more explicit by insisting that 'the revolutionary democracy of Russia' (or the Congress of Soviets) had always supported 'the campaign for Finnish democracy (in this case *Suomen demokratia*, which underscored the identical nature of democracy and Social Democracy) against tsarism and the Russification policies of the Russian bourgeois imperialistic groups'.[966] The soviets famously associated 'revolutionary democracy' with the lower classes preparing for a socialist revolution, which would become inevitable after 'the bourgeoisie' had betrayed the Revolution.[967] According to Huttunen, the Congress had invited 'the Finnish democracy and especially the Social Democracy to join forces with the Russian democracy to ensure the victory of the Russian Revolution'.[968] Frans Rantanen insisted that a turn towards social democracy was to be expected in Germany as well.[969] It is revealing of the expectations of a more radical revolution taking over in Russia that Matti Helenius-Seppälä (Christian Labour Party) and August Hyöki (Finnish Party) also saw 'this same democracy' as forming the core of the future constituent national assembly in Russia.[970] The Petrograd soviets showed the way forward and were used by the Finnish Social Democratic parliamentary group to define what democracy in Russia and in Finland was. The Bolsheviks of Petrograd had managed to take over the language of the Finnish Social Democratic parliamentary majority, describing it as 'the

---

963 Kettunen 1986, 80, note 40, 87, 90, 97; Rinta-Tassi 1986, 30–1, 33, 41.
964 VP, Yrjö Mäkelin, 10 July 1917, 878–9.
965 Polvinen 1987, vol 1, 62–3, 74; Rinta-Tassi 1986, 31; Ketola 1987, 79–80. Thanks to the fact that over 20,000 Finns were living in Petrograd, there were over 600 Finnish members in the Bolshevik Party there. This group connected the Bolsheviks and the Finnish socialists, who might otherwise have been separated by cultural and linguistic differences. Upton 1980, 85; Haapala 1995, 56.
966 VP, Evert Huttunen, 10 July 1917, 900; Polvinen 1987, vol. 1, 76.
967 Wade 2000, 66, 84.
968 VP, Evert Huttunen, 10 July 1917, 900. Notice a slight conceptual distinction here.
969 VP, Frans Rantanen, 17 July 1917, 1030.
970 VP, Matti Helenius-Seppälä, 10 July 1917, 905; August Hyöki, 10 July 1917, 907.

legal representative of the workers of the Finnish people' in a revolutionary sense.[971] This implied that only they represented the people proper and that only they could constitute a democracy.

This exclusive concept of democracy was used by the Finnish Social Democrats to draw conclusions about their political opponents. Kalle Suosalo questioned the intentions of the Finnish Party to advance the cause of the rule by the people and suggested that the Finnish right and centre did not recognise the Russian Revolution but had allied themselves with the counter-revolution.[972] Only the Revolution (meaning the Bolshevik opponents of the Provisional Government in Russia) and that of the Social Democrats in Finland were true revolutions; their rivals were counter-revolutionaries, 'the Swedes of this parliament', while the Finnish (often Swedish-speaking) civil servants were presented as the most blatant defenders of class privileges and opponents of democracy.[973] K. H. Wiik, responsible for the international relations of the Social Democrats, a friend Lenin and a publisher of his ideas, spoke about the common interests of 'the Russian democracy' (the Soviets) and 'the Finnish democracy', suggesting that 'enemies of democracy' were to be found in Finland as well.[974] The Finnish bourgeoisie opposed the leadership of the people (as represented by the Social Democrats) instead of uniting with the people. As for 'the international democracy' that supported Finnish independence, it, too, was above all 'the international Social Democracy' that opposed imperialistic endeavours.[975]

This Social Democratic domination of the discourse on democracy left little space for alternative centrist or rightist definitions. As a result of its universalist and exclusive understanding of democracy, the policy of the Finnish Social Democratic Party became linked with that of the Bolshevik revolutionaries, which provoked opposition among the Finnish bourgeois parties, some of which had already been speaking in favour of the rule by the people for some time, though willing to retain the duality of government. The Social Democratic monopolisation of the concept also made them cautious about offering alternative bourgeois definitions of democracy. The language of democracy had been hijacked by the socialist majority of the Finnish parliament, in line with a common rhetorical practice among socialists,[976] and this majority was giving it exclusive connotations inspired by the Bolshevik version of the Russian Revolution. This hijack had serious consequences as it prevented all compromise between the Social Democrats and the bourgeois parties until well after the Civil War.

971   VP, Evert Huttunen, 10 July 1917, 901; cf. Ketola 1987, 81, for the situation in April.
972   VP, Kalle Suosalo, 2 July 1917, 700.
973   VP, Frans Rantanen, 17 July 1917, 1030; Edvard Hänninen-Walpas, 17 July 1917, 1058. The same message was included in a declaration of the Reds at the beginning of the Civil War. Borisova & Siro 2014, 91, 94–5.
974   VP, Karl Harald Wiik, 10 July 1917, 894–5; Rinta-Tassi 1986, 31.
975   VP, Karl Harald Wiik, 10 July 1917, 895; 17 July 1917, 1021.
976   Previous examples are discussed in Pekonen 2014, 276–7 and 301–304.

Among the leading non-socialist politicians, Santeri Alkio (Agrarians) had been the most consistent spokesman for democracy (in the vernacular form of 'the rule by the people') in the days of the parliamentary reform of 1906. He still envisioned the future as one of democracy and considered that the right moment for constructing democracy was at hand: [977]

> The future belongs to the rule by the people. But if that future is destroyed before the rule by the people has taken a stronger lead in this country than what we have at the moment, it is possible that the dreams of the realisation of the rule by the people in this country will not be fulfilled.

What threatened the cause of democracy was not only opposition from the former ruling classes but also the class-based policies of the Social Democrats. Alkio opposed the Social Democrats' amendments to the constitution as likely to lead to the nomination of (Socialist) ministers who were ready to 'bow before the apparent rule by the people'; in his view, excessive subservience to a parliamentary majority might fail to serve the proper cause of the rule by the people.[978] The interests of parliamentarism and democracy were not identical but needed to be reconciled so that an ideal balance might be attained. During the second reading, Alkio stated his belief that the soviets would take over in Petrograd, seeing them as representatives of 'Russian revolutionary democracy' and as showing the way that the Finnish people should follow as opposed to other political forces in Russia.[979] Alkio also referred to 'international democracy (*kansainvälinen demokratia*), the influence of which in the future settlement of European issues will be considerable' and which would recognise Finnish independence,[980] obviously having Wilsonian principles in mind. Even Russian Liberals such as Prince Lvov had recognised Russian democracy as the proper leader of 'world democracy',[981] and the expected parliamentarisation in Germany could also be seen as part of the trend. Generally speaking, however, the concept of 'world democracy' received little attention in the Finnish parliament in comparison with the German and Swedish ones. Finnish politicians tended to view developments predominantly from a Finnish point of view.

The liberal Young Finns did not refer to the rule by the people in this context even though their platform had long presented democracy as its goal.[982] *Hufvudstadsbladet*, the organ of the Swedish People's Party, had recognised the representativeness of the parliament thanks to the realisation of democratic suffrage,[983] but the party did not discuss democracy in these debates. Antti Tulenheimo of the Finnish Party, the minister responsible for juridical affairs, set out to define proper democracy. Tulenheimo, well aware of German constitutional discourse, argued consistently for limiting the

977 VP, Santeri Alkio, 12 June 1917, 511.
978 VP, Santeri Alkio, 2 July 1917, 698; also Hyvärinen 2003, 86.
979 VP, Santeri Alkio, 10 July 1917, 890.
980 VP, Santeri Alkio, 10 July 1917, 891.
981 Wade 2000, 60–1.
982 Liikanen 2003, 298.
983 *Hufvudstadsbladet*, 'Ställningen och vårt folks plikt', 18 March 1917.

power of the parliament in relation to the ministry. It would be more in line with 'the real rule by the people' that the government should be able 'to appeal to the people' through new elections when it believed that the will of the majority of the parliament no longer corresponded with that of the people. In his view the Social Democrats were abusing the concept of democracy by describing any measures that were not to their liking as *epäkansanvaltaista* (opposed to the rule by the people or anti-democratic).[984] The constitutional confrontations within the all-party government evidently concerned the very concept of democracy, with radical socialist and bourgeois conceptions countering each other and the Social Democrats trying to monopolise the discourse.

3.4.4 Defining the position of the people within the Finnish polity

The Social Democrats thus presented themselves as the sole advocates of the will of the Finnish people, while the bourgeois parties were sceptical of the (Social Democratic) parliamentary majority being capable of expressing the true will of the people: a re-elected parliament might communicate a popular will of another kind. This kind of debate on the popular will had long historical trajectories: early modern Sweden, then including Finland, had already seen the rise of a native tradition of appealing to the people by rival parties and even by monarchs.[985] Appeals to the people had never been successfully monopolised by a single ideological grouping; rather they had been increasingly employed by numerous different political actors for a wide variety of purposes along with the rise of the notion of the sovereignty of the people, the emergence of the nation-state, the extension of popular representation and the popularity of constitutionalist political strategies.[986]

The Finnish adult population had been given the vote in 1907, and the people had been activated by various parties to use that right, but the concrete involvement of the people in politics, especially in local government, had otherwise remained limited. The Social Democrats had nevertheless done their share to encourage their involvement. Oskari Tokoi, the prime minister, gave a highly positive and nationalistic characterisation of the political potential of the Finnish people, pointing out:[987]

> [T]he intention of the Finnish people and the Finnish parliament is the achievement of Finnish independence and freedom – an independence that corresponds with the esteem of the Finnish people among nations; that corresponds with the position which we as a civilised[988] people must undoubtedly have in current society.

---

984 VP, Antti Tulenheimo, 2 July 1917, 682; This argument may have arisen out of the fact that the Social Democrats had received their parliamentary majority with only 47.3 per cent of the votes. This had been recognized by the Social Democrats themselves, too. Lindman 1968, 11, 26.
985 Liikanen 2003, 266, 295; Ihalainen 2011; Ihalainen 2015.
986 Liikanen 203, 257–8, 302.
987 VP, Oskari Tokoi, 12 June 1917, 506.
988 Again in the Germanic sense of possessing *Kultur*.

By the time of the final debate on the Power Act, he had identified the will of the people with that expressed by the Social Democratic Speaker Kullervo Manner and by himself.[989] The will of the people appeared as the highest authority, albeit one that was correctly interpreted by the socialist majority of the current parliament only.

Popular, even nationalistic, rhetoric was heard also from Yrjö Mäkelin in a way that served the Social Democratic cause. Mäkelin admired a people who had – 'despite long-standing oppression and persecution' – been able to maintain 'a clear understanding of the state' and 'built a state, developed it and created an original civilisation'.[990] Within this people, however, 'the lower classes constitute the core',[991] the Finnish people being defined as constituted essentially by the proletariat, not by all the inhabitants of the country, and as being represented by the Social Democrats. This corresponded with the Russian revolutionary concept of the people. Matti Airola spoke about 'a demand from among the deep ranks of the people forcefully supporting the Social Democratic group', calling for the introduction of reforms without further postponement.[992] Edvard Hänninen-Walpas greeted what he saw as the people having – despite bourgeois disinformation – obtained a proper understanding of their rights, which could now be realised through the parliament[993] with its Social Democrat majority.

While the Social Democrats combined socialist and nationalist discourses, non-socialist MPs focused on the discourse of national self-determination and optimistically viewed the Finnish experience of democracy as a justification for independence. Ernst Nevanlinna of the Finnish Party appealed to 'the maturity of the people with regard to liberty' given that 'our people have been one of the freest in the world in domestic issues'.[994] The generally held but particularly rightist notion of a long native tradition of (peasant) liberty was central: Nevanlinna called for the preservation of 'the dearest national property that we possess, inherited from our fathers and preserved through the centuries'.[995] His conclusion was that the Finnish people were mature in the affairs of the state and worthy of considerable self-determination'.[996] Gustaf Arokallio of the Young Finns echoed this view, concluding that 'our naturally slow people has received sufficient time to define their opinions on the future activities of the state'.[997] Several speakers from the Agrarian League, the party manifesto of which made extensive use of the concept 'citizen' in order both to emphasise the activeness of the citizens and to build a political community,[998] likewise agreed about the political maturity of the

---

989   VP, Oskari Tokoi, 17 July 1917, 1033.
990   VP, Yrjö Mäkelin, 2 July 1917, 689.
991   VP, Yrjö Mäkelin, 2 July 1917, 699.
992   VP, Matti Airola, 12 June 1917, 516.
993   VP, Edvard Hänninen-Walpas, 17 July 1917, 1056.
994   VP, Ernst Nevanlinna, 17 July 1917, 1012.
995   VP, Ernst Nevanlinna, 17 July 1917, 1012; Ihalainen 2015.
996   VP, Ernst Nevanlinna, 17 July 1917, 1012.
997   VP, Gustaf Arokallio, 17 July 1917, 1013.
998   Stenius 2003, 351.

Finnish nation. According to Juho Kokko, the Finns had been preparing for independence for centuries. Thanks to improved levels of education, the Finns were 'a people that goes its own way, with an educated parliamentary institution'.[999]

Confidence in the people was high among both the Social Democrats and the Finnish-speaking bourgeoisie in the Finnish parliament in summer 1917; the extension of the political independence of the country was a common goal, and the dispute concerned the means of achieving it. Disagreement about the role of the parliament in the expression of popular will was at the centre of this constitutional controversy.

3.4.5 Prospects for a parliamentary Finland: opposing Social Democratic and bourgeois views

There were also those who felt that they could not count on the maturity of the people and especially on the parliament as the way to determine the will of that people. The introduction of parliamentarism in the sense of the legally regulated political responsibility of the government to the parliament had already been demanded before and proposed by the Social Democrats in the inter-party discussions following the abdication of Nicholas II. The idea was then received with some caution among the bourgeois parties as no legislation guaranteeing such parliamentarism was, in their view, in force in any other country, but the majority of a committee on constitutional issues supported the introduction of parliamentary responsibility. In practical terms, the nomination of an all-party government implied that parliamentarism was recognised as the norm on the basis of which the relationship between of the parliament and the government should be regulated; at least the era of the bureaucratic governments of the tsarist regime was over. Oskari Tokoi emphasised the responsibility of his government to the parliament:[1000]

> [W]e do not have any other policy than the policy which the parliament has approved, and it is that policy that we will pursue. . . . And I put it very clearly that we do not have any other intentions than the fulfilment of the decisions and will of the parliament. . . . the government is . . . committed to be accountable and responsible to the parliament on all questions and actions. . . . And we are also always ready to resign our positions for the parliament to fill [i.e. appoint new ministers].

According to Tokoi, parliamentarism was already being practised. The majority of an extraordinary committee also agreed on the introduction of parliamentarism in the draft constitution in the sense of governmental responsibility, and the government agreed on the principle of parliamentarism in May, a step that has been seen as being ahead of its time. Recent experiences of Russian-nominated ministers lacking the confidence of the Finnish parliament facilitated the agreement on governmental responsibility despite the remaining existence of theoretical and party-political doubts. The

---

999 VP, Juho Kokko, 17 July 1917, 1048.
1000 VP, Oskari Tokoi, 20 April 1919, 48–9; Lindman 1968, 20, 37–8, 63, 91.

adopted formulation was close to that of the French Third Republic, which is a measure of the considerable extent of the planned parliamentarism.[1001]

These agreements did not remove doubts about how the Social Democrats, reluctant to cooperate with the bourgeois parties, understood parliamentarism. Experiences from negotiations in the all-party government raised suspicions about their dedication to parliamentary government. Their view of the parliament as merely instrumental in the class struggle was reinforced in the party convention of June 1917: participation in the government of a capitalist country (which had previously been rejected for good) was presented as part of the *current* tactics, but the party reserved the right to either support or reject the government as best served the interests of the workers. The simultaneous commitment for the government and opposition to it, together with the violent acts committed by Social Democrat supporters at the local level, made it difficult for moderates to pursue cooperation across the ideological division.[1002] Finnish parliamentarism had run into a deep crisis before it had even been properly established.

The Power Act was a one-sided attempt by the Social Democrats to legislate on parliamentary sovereignty on their terms. Although the Agrarian League decided to support the proposal, its leader Santeri Alkio was concerned about the rise of extra-parliamentary pressure groups among the Social Democrats trying to determine what the parliament should decide. He complained how a labour association in Helsinki (which had founded a workers' assembly bearing the name of 'parliament') was ready to threaten the national parliament and to limit its freedom of action and force it to do what the crowds surrounding the parliament building were demanding with the support of the rifles of Russian soldiers.[1003] Instead of such extra-parliamentary and potentially unpatriotic measures by the right and the left, Alkio urged the Finnish people and their parliament to cooperate and arrange the political order so that the Russian Revolution would not lead to the loss of national liberty.[1004] When the Social Democrats accused the Agrarian League of denying the right of 'the parliament of the people' to nominate ministers,[1005] Alkio did his best to explain what he viewed as its proper limits. Alkio, like most non-socialists in northern Europe, was highly critical of complete parliamentarism, rejecting Social Democrat attempts to make the government no more than 'a slave or lackey of the parliament' as detrimental to the people. A government could not be built simply on the basis of the will of a parliamentary majority so that the government 'would only obediently take care of the office duties given to it by the parliament'.[1006] Alkio did advocate the principle of the responsibility of the government to the parliament but did not want to see a government constituted by mere parliamentarians, as suggested by the Social Democrats:[1007]

1001 Lindman 1968, 90–2; Garrigues & Anceau 2016.
1002 Lindman 1968, 38–9.
1003 The rise of this parliament of the streets was described in subsection 3.4.1.
1004 VP, Santeri Alkio, 12 June 1917, 511.
1005 VP, Yrjö Mäkelin, 2 July 1917, 688.
1006 VP, Santeri Alkio, 2 July 1917, 698.
1007 VP, Santeri Alkio, 2 July 1917, 698.

> If an attempt is made to realise the rule by the people through a weak government, that will lead to the destruction of the state. It is entirely mistaken to assume that a government which would consist of persons enjoying the confidence of the parliament, being constituted in accordance with purely parliamentary principles ... it is wrong to assume that this would not be in line with the rule by the people. We have all been ready to pass a law according to which the Finnish government will be responsible to the parliament for all of its measures.

Alkio was here summarising much of the understanding that prevailed among the non-socialist parties. At the same time, some Social Democratic MPs also brought up the contempt for the parliament among their supporters. Evert Eloranta presented the anti-reform policies of the bourgeoisie as having created among the lower classes the unhappy conception that the use of legal and parliamentary means did not bring the necessary reforms.[1008] The inability of the reformed parliament to agree on reforms, and the vetoes of the Grand Duke on such reforms, had indeed demonstrated to many radical socialists that the parliamentary way of proceeding was ineffective, which led to further radicalisation and calls for direct action.[1009]

In the divisive Social Democratic discourse, all the blame for this was to be placed on the bourgeoisie. The Power Act was seen as a last chance to make the representative institution with its Socialist majority responsive to reform demands and to hence restore its legitimacy in the eyes of leftist supporters. At the same time, however, the concept of the parliament was intentionally obscured: the Congress of Soviets was presented as a provisional parliament in Russia comparable to the Finnish parliament;[1010] this was done by Evert Huttunen, who had attended an irregular meeting in Petrograd as a Finnish representative and interpreter and who was hence better informed about the nature of the soviets than any other Finnish MP.[1011] Huttunen drew a misleading parallel between the two very different institutions, legitimating the Russian soviets and implying that the Finnish parliament, too, was revolutionary. As in the choice of the name of the workers' parliament in Helsinki, the Social Democrats were redefining 'parliament' to better serve their potentially revolutionary goals.

Among liberals and conservatives, who tended to find common ground in this debate (unlike in contemporary Sweden or Germany), the extension of parliamentary sovereignty along the lines of the Social Democrat majority caused rising concern. K. J. Ståhlberg (Young Finn) was the leader of the extraordinary committee which had prepared the original proposal and spoke for an update of the inherited eighteenth-century constitution with a degree of parliamentarism (which he basically supported) but with the maintenance of the duality of government. The submission of certain issues to the Russian government as well as regulations on the nomination and dismissal of government had in his view no precedents in other

1008 VP, Evert Eloranta, 12 June 1917, 518.
1009 Tuomisto 1990, 41.
1010 VP, Evert Huttunen, 10 July 1917, 901, 903; Rinta-Tassi 1986, 31; Ketola 1987, 168–9.
1011 Lindman 1968, 127; Upton 1980, 81, 155.

countries.[1012] Tekla Hultin, the first female academic doctor in Finland and possessing a good knowledge of the Third Republic, expressed her trust in parliamentary procedures being integrated in the Finnish political system through practice. She wished nevertheless to reserve the right for the government to dissolve the parliament and to ask the opinion of the people in case severe disagreements between the government and the parliament emerged.[1013]

In the meantime, the 'Prussian' right in Finland rejected what they saw as extreme parliamentarism in harsher terms, fearing that the division of power would be bypassed, the problems of the Age of Liberty reintroduced and in the end all power be given into the hands of the socialist majority.[1014] Gustaf Rosenqvist (Swedish People's Party) complained about the removal of boundaries between the parliament and the government and about nearly all power being handed over to the representative assembly.[1015] According to Karl Söderholm (Swedish People's Party), 'an autocratic popular representation just like an autocratic monarch can abuse its power to the detriment of the country and the people'.[1016] The suspicions of parliamentarism among the right were partly motivated by experiences from the eighteenth century, and parallels drawn between the Swedish Diet of the Age of Liberty and the proposed system of extended parliamentary sovereignty are particularly revealing. This analogy was also supported by the classical conception of the cycle of polities with republics and autocracies, oligarchies and ochlocracies following each other.[1017] According to Kaarle Rantakari (Finnish Party), the proposal would reintroduce 'the state in which our country was when it was joined to Sweden during the so-called Age of Liberty: the tyranny of the parliament' (*eduskunta-mielivalta*).[1018] In his conservative understanding, the Age of Liberty demonstrated how difficult it would be for the parliament to act satisfactorily in the absence of a true representative of executive power.[1019] When the Social Democrats criticised the comparison as reflecting a bourgeois 'fear of the entry of democracy into force' and rather saw the eighteenth-century crisis as a conflict of class interests,[1020] Rantakari nevertheless repeated warnings about 'parliamentary absolutism' (*eduskuntayksinvaltius*). Such warnings were also typical of German political discourse.[1021]

According to Frans Rantanen of the Social Democrats, the suggested

1012 VP, Kaarlo Juho Ståhlberg, 2 July 1917, 994.
1013 VP, Tekla Hultin, 2 July 1917, 695–6.
1014 Rabbe Axel Wrede, 'Lagförslaget ang. styrelseledamöternas juridiska ansvarighet', an editorial in *Hufvudstadsbladet*, 9 June 1917; Upton 1980, 170, written on the basis of a memorandum by Lauri Ingman.
1015 VP, Georg Rosenqvist, 10 July 1917, 883.
1016 VP, Karl Söderholm, 10 July 1917, 904.
1017 VP, Kaarle Rantakari, 10 July 1917, 896.
1018 VP, Kaarle Rantakari, 10 July 1917, 896.
1019 VP, Kaarle Rantakari, 10 July 1917, 896; more extensively in Ihalainen 2015.
1020 VP, Konrad Lehtimäki, 10 July 1917, 909; 17 July 1917, 1032; Frans Rantanen, 17 July 1917, 1029.
1021 VP, Kaarle Rantakari, 17 July 1917, 1021; Biefang & Schulz 2016, 71.

'parliamentary democracy or the democracy of the Social Democratic workers' (by implication one and the same thing) would create a completely different system.[1022] This radicalised Finnish Social Democratic conception of Social Democratic democracy being synonymous with parliamentary democracy was exclusive and should be contrasted with Eduard Bernstein's revisionist view of democracy standing not for the mere rule of the masses or for any type of class power but for self-government by the people.[1023] The Finnish Social Democrats advocated a party-political instrumental concept of parliamentarism, whereas the Finnish right, like the Swedish conservatives, took the national past as evidence for the rejection of unregulated parliamentarism.

The right typically turned to filibustering through rhetorical redescriptions. Ernst Nevanlinna (Finnish Party), with his reformist background, pointed to the far-reaching parliamentarisation of government that would *de facto* take place in Finland as a result of the original proposal and which removed any need for strict rules concerning the formation of the ministry. According to this professor of finance, the budgetary power of the parliament had already been extended, and it had become difficult to nominate a government that did not enjoy the confidence of the parliament. The Social Democratic policy meant 'the unlimited sovereignty of the current majority of each parliament' and indeed implied, that 'our people would in reality also gain the decisive power to nominate and dismiss the executive power, i.e. the government'.[1024] His forecast was that the introduction of such a parliamentary sovereignty would lead to the 'healthy majority of the people' soon regretting their election of a parliament that had rejected, without proper deliberation, the ideally functioning eighteenth-century constitution in favour of parliamentary absolutism. Or, as Nevanlinna put it in a reference to a propagandistic phrase 'law-bound liberty' that Gustavus III used in 1772 when limiting the powers of the Diet, it would be to 'exchange the law-bound civic liberty enjoyed by our people for centuries, the most beautiful and invaluable heritage of Swedish rule, for the tyranny of the parliamentary majority.'[1025]

Finnish political history had throughout the Russian period concentrated on conserving this Gustavian monarchical constitution, which combined elements of constitutionalism with the Diet as a forum for royal representation. Now the pernicious order of the Age of Liberty with a ruling diet, from which the current constitution had saved the country, was in danger of being restored. Karl Söderholm (Swedish People's Party) feared that such an excessive concentration of power in the parliament would lead to 'political considerations' becoming dominant in purely administrative matters. This could not be right as, according to the Finnish constitution, 'the supreme

---

1022 VP, Frans Rantanen, 17 July 1917, 1029.
1023 Müller 2014, 45.
1024 VP, Ernst Nevanlinna, 17 July 1917, 1011–12.
1025 VP, Ernst Nevanlinna, 17 July 1917, 1012; for eighteenth-century parlance, see Ihalainen 2010, and for further conservative history politics, see Ihalainen 2015.

power in the country belongs to the monarch'.[1026] The rightist discourse on parliamentarism was clearly built on eighteenth-century constitutionalist developments and German principles of constitutional monarchy.

The conceptual confrontation was escalated by different understandings of parliamentary procedure (discussed in section 2.4). Since the Social Democrats were known to have considered passing the Power Act with a simple majority should an attempt to use minority provisions to prevent this be made, Minister of Justice Antti Tulenheimo (Finnish Party) warned about the risks of disregarding parliamentary principles. Furthermore, parliamentarising all legislative and administrative power would mean the annulment of the older constitutional laws, and, under unlimited parliamentary power, the only way for the people to change the parliament would be through a revolution.[1027] This statement implied that resistance and outright revolution on the part of the people against such a (potentially socialist) parliament appeared as an option for some bourgeois leaders as well. Edvard Hänninen-Walpas, the editor-in-chief of *Työmies*, the largest socialist organ in the world, implied that more concrete violence against their rightist opponents might occur, if not by fellow members of the party, at least by the people,[1028] which shows how the notion of an unavoidable violent civil war against a stubborn bourgeoisie instead of parliamentary discussion was creeping into Social Democratic discourse. In the debate of the day, too, an interjection from the left would suggest that a civil war had become possible.[1029] An instance of such violence replacing parliamentary procedure had been seen only three days previously when Russian troops had entered the parliament building to put pressure on the MPs.[1030] More explicit talk about the possibility of a civil war replacing parliamentary procedures would be heard from November 1917 onwards.

According to Ernst Estlander (Swedish People's Party), a professor of the legal history who was dedicated to constitutionalism and extreme formal legalism and had campaigned for the rights of the Finnish parliament under Russian rule but opposed the inclusion of parliamentarism in the Finnish constitution,[1031] the measures of the socialist majority demonstrated the questionability of 'the frequently advertised parliamentarism of the left'.[1032] Parliamentarism was turning into a mere hoax, and the Finnish parliament had 'a lower political culture' than this critic could ever have imagined.[1033] In the deepening crisis of parliamentary legitimacy, the Social Democrats implicitly threatened to use violence should their radicalised concept of parliamentary sovereignty as the rule of a Social Democratic majority not be accepted. On the other hand, neither did the legalists of

---

1026 VP, Karl Söderholm, 17 July 1917, 1018.
1027 VP, Antti Tulenheimo, 17 July 1917, 1007.
1028 VP, Edvard Hänninen-Walpas, 17 July 1917, 1056–7.
1029 Lindman 1968, 85.
1030 Polvinen 1987, vol. 1, 70.
1031 Lindman 1968, 92.
1032 VP, Ernst Estlander, 17 July 1917, 1054.
1033 VP, Ernst Estlander, 17 July 1917, 1054.

the non-socialist side exclude the replacement of parliamentary means with outright violence if the established system were infringed. The crisis of the legitimacy of parliamentary government, provoked by exclusive Social Democratic definitions of the war, revolution, democracy, the people and parliamentarism, was being acerbated by the exceptional strength and inflexibility of the legalistic and constitutionalist ideology of their opponents.[1034] This way of thinking was particularly important for many members of the centre and the right, but it was abhorred by the left as obstructing reform.

1034 Brandt 2009, 172, also suggests that these traditions were stronger in Finland than in Sweden.

4. The autumn of 1917: A completed, a suspended and a partial reform – and a failed reform leading to a civil war

4.1 Britain: The rising politisation of democracy

4.1.1 A final confrontation on extended suffrage between the two chambers

Despite the consensual reform proposal made by the Speaker's Conference and limited opposition to it during the first readings in the Commons, further points of disagreement arose during deliberations on the technical details of the Representation of the People Bill. The members shared the view that the pressures of the war had changed the nature of the polity in such fundamental ways that constitutional modifications were needed, but they continued to disagree on the timing and the extent of the revisions. No one denied the need to update the registers of voters or the principle that at least all men who had served in the army deserved the right to vote. While some Unionist opponents remained concerned about the consequences of extending suffrage, especially to women, the defenders of the bill held optimistic views on what a reformed Parliament with the strengthened support of the people would be able to accomplish once the time of post-war reconstruction came.

Procedural arguments for preventing the extension of suffrage or at least postponing the reform had been made during the spring. The Unionist opposition had questioned the mandate of an extra-parliamentary body to prepare such an unusual constitutional change and also the mandate of a parliament elected in 1910 to decide on one. They would have preferred to see the pre-1911 rights of the Lords restored rather than extending suffrage. However, the reformists had managed to persuade the majority of the Conservatives to come over to their side. They argued for an entirely new, stronger political community, in which the interests of the people and Parliament would be better united. In practice, the majority of the Conservatives were expecting extensive electoral support from both the fighting men and the women on the home front. The Unionist opposition now also concentrated on modifying rather than opposing the reform.

Foreign examples had been used selectively in the British debates, the focus being on the dominions; other great powers were referred to only to support particular points, not in search of any applicable models. While some anti-reformists had suggested that the bill was a deliberate attempt to introduce a revolution to Britain, several reformists presented it rather as the means to prevent revolutionary developments of the Russian or some other type. A division in references to democracy had been visible, though by spring 1917 the concept had in no way been dominant in descriptions of the goals of the reform or the British political system more generally. This suggests that the idea of fighting for democracy was a construct of war propaganda rather than a universalist goal to change the world; it was, furthermore, introduced more distinctly by President Wilson after the introductory debates of late March and hence its influence on the British reform debates was a delayed one. Unionists opposing the reform had argued that Britain already possessed such a degree of democracy that the extent of the proposed changes was excessive, or they had called for the restoration of the good old system instead. While the opponents had deliberately sought to define democracy in a way that supported their anti-reformist arguments, few reformists used democracy as a dynamic concept to describe the desirable future. The Wilsonian and revisionist concepts of democracy as a universal goal, a norm for good government and a starting point for further reforms at home were only gradually creeping into British political discourse.

By November 1917, the Commons had debated the details of the bill extensively in committee sessions of the entire House. The committee stage still produced only a few exchanges of opinion presenting the prospective future of the British parliamentary polity as a new type of democracy – not to say any serious problematisation of the political significance of the suffrage reform as 'democratisation'. One explanation might be that the British system was viewed as democratic by definition. A more plausible explanation is, however, that democracy was still not considered the proper concept to define the British polity – especially in wartime, when there were so many restrictions on ideal democracy and perhaps an awareness that demanding Prussia to democratise itself might backfire at home. The War Cabinet had not expressly defined the bill as a democratic reform, which reflects the reservations that some Liberals and Conservatives continued to have about this contested concept, which evidently meant different things to different ideological groups, including the representatives of Labour in the cabinet. For the ministry, the bill was therefore first and foremost a technical measure needed to boost morale for the war effort (though it did serve party-political purposes as well), and the opponents mainly seem to have accepted this interpretation. Democratisation or parliamentarisation did not concern Britain; they concerned Germany, just as Wilson had declared.

The MPs who attended the sessions, typically more hostile to the government than those who were absent,[1035] focused on controversial details such as proportional representation, the redistribution of seats and disqualification. With reference to the last-mentioned issue, the government was again accused of 'Prussianism', of being 'infected by German doctrines'

1035 Turner 1992, 227.

in the sense of seeing the state as superior to the individual conscience of conscientious objectors.[1036] This was a rhetorical trick making use of propaganda discourses, and it shows why the cabinet was wise not to highlight democracy and similar concepts too much. Many reformist arguments were equally context-bound, building on war experiences and news of revolutionary movements abroad. Josiah Wedgwood (independent liberal, later Labour) repeated in the aftermath of the Bolshevik Revolution the argument about the reform being necessary to save representative government: if 'a man's citizenship' were taken away by denying him the right to vote, he might well feel like 'a pariah so far as politics are concerned' and become a 'martyr', who would then be ready to take 'direct action' under the instigation of trade and syndicalist unions,[1037] or even Bolsheviks. Halford Mackinder (Scottish Unionist) was concerned about that the cooperating parties as 'two schools of a ruling class' might be replaced in Britain, too, with a confrontation between the proletariat and the bourgeoisie and that such a class divide might lead first to random parliamentary majorities and then to tyranny.[1038] This was to be countered, as the Liberal reformist Aneurin Williams argued, by basing 'government for the people and by the people' on 'the common sense and honesty of the great mass of the people' rather than on any prevailing 'undemocratic' voting practices.[1039] Generally speaking, however, 'democracy' (like 'parliamentarism') remained strangely absent as a concept from discussions on the details of the reform in autumn 1917. The press, for its part, tended to characterise these debates as unconstructive,[1040] which tended to diminish the trust in Parliament in wartime. Its limited enthusiasm for the reform in spring was now tending to turn into cynicism.

The next plenary debates in the Commons took place between 4 and 7 December 1917. As the principles of the constitutional change had already been discussed during previous readings, specific technical electoral issues or the treatment of special groups (such as conscientious objectors) now figured as objects of dispute. Most of this reading was taken over by arguments on Irish affairs in general and the Irish representation in the Westminster Parliament in particular. This was provoked by an attempted extension of the redistribution of seats to Ireland.[1041] Irish MPs used the opportunity to voice a number of grievances specific to Ireland and to defend the relative overrepresentation of Ireland in the Imperial Parliament. The December debates again brought to light what Herbert Samuel called 'anomalies' in the 'political situation in regard to the constitutional relations between Great Britain and Ireland'[1042] unsolved by Home Rule and deepened by the experiences of the Easter Rising of 1916. For many non-Irish members, the

---

1036 Interjection by an anonymous MP, Hansard, 20 November 1917, c. 1150; Edgar Jones (Liberal), 21 November 1917, c. 1253–5.
1037 Hansard, Josiah Wedgwood, 21 November 1917, c. 1270.
1038 Hansard, Halford Mackinder, 22 November 1917, c. 1444–5.
1039 Hansard, Aneurin Williams, 21 November 1917, c. 1311–12.
1040 *The Manchester Guardian*, 'Amendments to the Franchise Bill', 5 December 1917.
1041 *The Manchester Guardisan*, 'Amendments to the Franchise Bill', 5 December 1917.
1042 Hansard, Herbert Samuel, 4 December 1917, c. 366.

continuous debate on these anomalies appeared a waste of parliamentary time, reminding of earlier Irish obstructions, and hence the members of the cabinet hardly attended the debates.[1043] Proportional representation, included in the original proposal of the government, did not pass the vote, and the notion of the alternative vote was also later omitted. All the same, the bill led to major changes in addition to the inclusion of women over 30 in universal suffrage: constituencies would be radically redistributed, a deposit required to eliminate freak candidates, limits to expenditure set, and all voting ordered to take place on the same day.[1044]

Extensive debates in the Lords followed, providing an opportunity to go back to the principles of the reform. The bill was introduced on 11 December 1917, and the debates took place between 17 and 19 December 1917, again on 8–10 January 1918 and further on until 6 February 1918. There was not so much principled opposition any longer, with the Unionist peers also ready to compromise in the extraordinary circumstances of wartime, counting on electoral support for the Conservatives and seeing a chance to appease repeated reform demands without the threat of having a radical leftist parliament, especially in the aftermath of the Bolshevik Revolution. The bill passed the second reading, but some further dispute followed in early 1918. Illustrative of the marginality of the Lords after the Parliament Act (particularly from the point of view of the Liberals) is how selectively and without commentary *The Manchester Guardian* reported their proceedings: only the Lords' views on women's suffrage and their submission to the will of the Commons on proportional representation were considered worth commenting on. In the latter case, the paper focused on the point of view of the Commons and had nothing to say with regard to 'democracy' about the significance of the Lords' submissions for the constitution or the suffrage reform.[1045] Not even the British Liberals regarded the reform as a transition to democracy. This differs sharply from German, Swedish and Finnish Liberal ways of viewing the constitutional changes of the period.

The relatively early timing and the seemingly indigenous origin of the British reform meant that it was viewed by contemporaries as much less dependent on the state of international affairs and transnational influences than was the case with the other constitutional reforms of the time. The British parliament remained a self-esteeming, even self-satisfied, representative institution with no need to relate its decision-making to past, current or future constitutional developments abroad. Transnational contacts were weaker than those of Continental MPs, particularly among the rather more imperially oriented Conservatives. By December 1917, nevertheless, the American involvement in the war, which had intensified discourse on democracy among all the Allied Powers and particularly trans-Atlantic

---

1043 Hansard, William Hayes Fisher, 5 December 1917, c. 492.
1044 Machin 2001, 144–5.
1045 *The Manchester Guardian*, 'Electoral Reform Bill', 18–19 December 1917, 10 January 1918; 'Peers and Votes for Women', 11 January 1918; 'Reform Bill Passed', 7 February 1918.

Anglophone discourse,[1046] and the outbreak of the Bolshevik Revolution in early November, did influence the views of the British parliamentary elite somewhat. There was a growing tendency to view the Bolshevik regime as expansionist and a feeling that its spread could be limited best with a well-managed parliamentary reform at home.[1047] However, Russian influences or the fear of Bolshevism were in no way dominant in Britain in late 1917. Owing to the peripheral geographical position of Russia from a British point of view, its internal turmoil had mainly been considered from the perspective of the war – at least until the Bolsheviks took over and declared a world revolution. Even the October Revolution caused no immediate concern among the Western Allies.[1048]

The impact of the war had been felt in Britain much more concretely as a result of the intensified submarine war depleting the food markets. While this did not lead to any widespread questioning of the political and military leadership or to the rise of a widespread peace movement in Britain, the atmosphere suffered, with creeping doubts about the likelihood of winning the war. London was bombed by the Germans in late 1917, which created entirely new fears among the civil population.[1049] An obvious consequence was a weakened interest in the debate on political rights in Parliament, the thoughts of the population being rather occupied by every-day problems. As in the other studied countries, the public at large was not really involved in the reform debates; the democratic process was in this sense restricted.

The Revolutions in Russia most clearly affected the ideological stand of the Labour Party even though its MPs had been very careful not to side with the March Revolution during the debates of the spring. A positive interpretation of the revolution had been, especially among the more patriotic MPs, that Russia was about to turn into a democracy fighting against autocracy. In March, Russia had been cited a few times as an encouraging example, but by May such assumptions had evaporated and more was heard about the chaotic state of the revolutionary regime. The Bolshevik Revolution, by contrast, offered a warning vision of a global revolution that might encourage the workers to revolt, remove bourgeois parliamentary democracy and install the soviets as holders of power or some feared direct action of the masses. This became a matter of concern not only for the 'bourgeois' parties but also for the moderate Labour leaders, particularly as there had been considerable industrial action in Britain, too, although reactions among the population at large remained overwhelmingly anti-Bolshevik. Most Labour leaders concluded soon after the October Revolution that Bolshevism represented an undesirable kind of undemocratic socialism. Their goals remained fairly

---

1046 See *The Times*, 'The End and the Means', 6 December 1917, thanking Wilson for contributing to the understanding of the war by combining an ideal with concrete means of achieving it: the democracies should destroy Prussian militarism. This was supported by 'Mr. Wilson's Triumph', which reported 'the democracies of the world' welcoming Wilson's recent address.
1047 Rose 1995, 68.
1048 Pipes 1992, 607.
1049 Leonhard 2014, 729–30.

moderate, albeit undergoing a slight radicalisation from summer 1918 on, which immediately gave rise to accusations of Bolshevism from the centre and the right. For some British socialists, direct action also remained a possibility,[1050] which provoked debate for and against representative parliamentary government among the public. In Parliament such radicalism was reduced by the modest number of Labour MPs and their ideological moderation. Revolution was debated, but one of the Russian type was regarded as impossible.

4.1.2 'This Bill is a revolution': The reform in relation to British constitutional history and foreign examples

Given the long history of debates on representation, going back to at least the seventeenth century,[1051] Stanley Buckmaster, a Liberal peer and former Lord Chancellor, wanted to move on from 'the old tiresome arguments as to what is the system of government' and to modify 'Parliamentary institutions' to meet the challenges of the future.[1052] No doubt remained as to the importance of the bill in British constitutional history. Towards the end of the committee stage and soon after the Bolshevik Revolution, the Attorney General, Frederick Smith (Conservative), pointed out that no one really knew what politics after the conclusion of peace would be like, the Revolution having further strengthened the sense of the inception of an entirely new era. Smith foresaw the economic losses of the war as potentially leading in Britain, too, to 'revolutionary demands' that should be obviated with a Commons that represented 'the nation and community as a whole'.[1053] This again reflects the Conservative adaptation to universal suffrage in the circumstances of the late 1910s. Andrew Anderson (Liberal) was likewise concerned about 'flood or spate politics' (a current international metaphor) arising from revolutionary fervour or opposite reactionary stands after the war. The only way to prevent this in Britain was to make the Commons 'a real reflex of the people outside' in accordance with 'democratic' or 'representative' government'.[1054] Edward Hemmerde (Liberal, later Labour) echoed the view that only a proper reform providing for adult suffrage and a free electoral system would prevent 'labour trouble' and even 'revolution' after the war.[1055] The reform was a preparation for the post-war situation, justified by each party from its own particular perspectives, though a distinctly Social Democratic perspective of the kind that existed in Germany, Sweden and Finland was still lacking.

Voices critical of the reform were also heard. James Bryce (Liberal), 1st Viscount Bryce, who had made a distinguished career both as an academic in law and history (he had written a book on US institutions and was

---

1050 Pugh 2002, 172; Leonhard 2014, 730–1.
1051 Seaward & Ihalainen 2016.
1052 Lords, Stanley Buckmaster, 19 December 1917, c. 267–8.
1053 Hansard, Frederick Smith, 22 November 1917, c. 1427.
1054 Hansard, Andrew Anderson, 22 November 1917, c. 1465–6.
1055 Hansard, Arthur Hemmerde, 22 November 1917, c. 1488.

President of the British Academy) and as a top civil servant (among other things holding the post of Ambassador to the United States) saw the bill as one which 'revolutionises the Constitution of this country more than any measure since the great Reform Act of 1832'. In Bryce's view, its adoption in wartime, when 'the people' could not give it the attention it deserved, was a mistake.[1056] Bryce would elaborate his criticism of the reform in *Modern Democracy* (1921), joining an international group of leading academics who had difficulties in accepting what they saw as mass democracy. He was one of the Western authorities to whom Germans would refer in countering Western calls for democratisation.

Nor was women's suffrage yet unanimously accepted among the British political elite. In Sir Charles Bathurst's (Conservative) sexist reasoning, the combination of 'the more level-headed male opinion on political matters' and 'the more emotional opinion of the other sex' could well lead to 'a revolution' should no buffer (such as proportional representation) be adopted.[1057] Many peers also believed that proportional representation would keep radicalism under control in future elections, whether women were allowed to vote or not.

As in spring, 'revolution' was used on both sides and with a variety of connotations: the Home Secretary, Sir George Cave (Conservative), wondered whether 'everybody in the House thoroughly realises the tremendous revolution which we are asked to make in our electoral system'.[1058] Britain was here viewed as introducing a revolution (in both a good and a bad sense) through parliament. Among the reformist aristocracy, Victor Bulwer-Lytton (Conservative), the 2nd Earl of Lytton, who had supported the Parliament Act and was a long-standing advocate of female suffrage, saw the bill as unique in that it was no longer a 'Representation of Some People Bill' like previous parliamentary reforms. It was a bill made necessary by the war and hence a piece of 'strictly war legislation',[1059] rather than being a revolution as suggested. Harry Levy-Lawson (Liberal Unionist), 2nd Lord Burnham, the owner of *The Daily Telegraph*, by contrast, was positive that 'this Bill is a revolution', but he was optimistic that this parliamentary revolution would be 'a pacific and, as we all hope, a peaceful revolution'.[1060] The notion of 'revolution' via parliamentary reform thus received at times a highly positive connotation. The British political elite was actively redefining the feared concept of 'revolution' here, giving it a parliamentary reformist sense that was opposed that attached to the Bolshevik Revolution in Russia: the argument that Parliament was able to revolutionise itself was even stronger than in spring. And many (for good reasons) were confident about the continuity of the political order thanks to the wartime patriotic atmosphere once Bolshevism had been prevented from entering the country by means of this reform.

1056 Lords, Viscount Bryce, 17 December 1917, c. 176; also Richard Chaloner, 1st Baron Gisborough, 10 January 1918, c. 488–90.
1057 Hansard, Sir Charles Bathurst, 30 January 1918, c. 1631.
1058 Hansard, Sir George Cave, 30 January 1918, c. 1694.
1059 Lords, The Earl of Lytton, 19 December 1917, c. 277–8.
1060 Lords, Lord Burnham, Lords, 17 December 1917, c. 201.

No such understanding of 'revolution' was shared by George Clarke, Baron Sydenham of Combe, an expert on defence and imperial affairs, who had become highly critical of universal suffrage after his experiences as Governor of Victoria in Australia. He wanted to retain a strong hereditary upper house. This constant denouncer of socialist and Jewish conspiracy plots responded pessimistically to Burnham, viewing the bill as 'a revolutionary change of the most controversial character' as it contained 'the germs of a disease which may bring about the destruction of our Empire'.[1061] Sydenham, who had argued for a written constitution and feared the destruction of the established order, saw the entire procedure as 'a flagrant breach of constitutional practice', 'revolutionary', as lacking 'any sanction from the people of this country' and as creating a dangerous precedent for the future.[1062] This was legalistic conservative anti-reformism at its strongest, resembling that of the right in Germany, Sweden and Finland. Such an attitude was also reinforced by concern about the future of the Empire.

Frank Russell, 2nd Earl Russell, who was the first peer to join the Labour Party, responded by conceding that the bill was indeed revolutionary, but he provoked Sydenham further by declaring: '[Y]our Lordships, if you are afraid of revolution, have some reason to fear it.'[1063] Thus leading advocates of the reform recognised its revolutionary character. However, in their view, revolution in any Russian sense was not to be feared as the British government and Parliament had taken the initiative to introduce their own restricted revolution. George Curzon, Earl Curzon of Kedleston, even viewed the year 1917 as marking a transition to a permanent revolutionary era, into which the new act would safely transfer the British parliamentary system:[1064]

> If we are at the end of one epoch we are also at the beginning of another, and if the epoch which we are closing has been darkened by all the horrors and tragedies of warfare, the epoch that is coming will be disturbed by convulsions and agitations, not less remarkable and very likely destined to shake even more profoundly the whole machinery of State.

According to this widely travelled former Viceroy of India, the Leader of the House of Lords and a member of the War Cabinet, the bill prepared the British parliament to play the role which the British state would have 'in the future regulation of the life of its citizens'. It also gave 'the great masses of the people in this country' the share of political power they had been striving for.[1065] From his distinguished position, Curzon argued strongly for the bill and abstained from voting against it despite his continued opposition to female suffrage as the former president of the National League for Opposing Woman

1061 Lords, Lord Sydenham, 17 December 1917, c. 210–11.
1062 Lords, Lord Sydenham, 17 December 1917, c. 214; also Philip Stanhope, 1st Baron Weardale (Liberal), president of an anti-suffrage organisation, 8 January 1918, c. 354–6.
1063 Lords, Earl Russell, 17 December 1917, c. 220.
1064 Lords, Earl Curzon, 19 December 1917, c. 300.
1065 Lords, Earl Curzon, 19 December 1917, c. 300, 303.

Suffrage.[1066] His speech act reflects the Conservatives' wartime adaptation to an interventionist state, constitutional evolution and universal suffrage.

The Lords finally approved the suffrage bill with an amendment which reintroduced the principle of proportional representation in it, motivated by the above-mentioned belief that it would hinder radicalisation.[1067] This constitutional intervention by the upper house provoked bitter comments in the Commons. According to Austen Chamberlain, a Liberal Unionist whose opinion in favour of the reform had been influential within the party, the bill had been skilfully formulated by the Commons and should not have been amended by the Lords, an act which now tested the principle established by the Parliament Act:[1068]

> This Bill, as it left our House, . . . was going to produce a revolution in our electoral system, a peaceful revolution, a revolution on the lines on which we have proceeded hitherto, and therefore the best kind of revolution, but still a revolution.

By the end of January 1918, the idea of a parliamentary revolution had been fully accepted by Chamberlain. His argument that the bill was revolutionary enough was intended to express support for the retention of the old majority election system and to thereby prevent the revolution from going too far. He wanted to maintain traditions that were 'the really broad and solid foundations on which our political system rests'. Proportional representation would not produce 'an effective representation of the national will' and thus should be opposed as a mistaken kind of revolution. Exaggerating the degree of potential change, Chamberlain called for a further reform of the Lords, since that house, which should have been a defender of traditions that checked 'revolutionary change', was now proposing a wrong kind of revolution itself.[1069] By emphasising the already revolutionary nature of the bill, Chamberlain played down any suggestions for a more extensive reform of the Commons and addressed the incomplete reform of the upper house instead – all issues that were connected with party politics.

Thus the concept of revolution touched Britain metaphorically, but the British reform was still, despite the constitutional ferment in other countries in 1917, viewed as so exceptional that examples from elsewhere did not apply. European countries were not seen to be going through comparable processes – despite the fact that constitutional debates about suffrage had started in Germany, the Netherlands, Sweden and Finland, at least by spring 1917, and the new Swedish parliamentary government was also expected to make a proposal for reform soon. In comparison with spring 1917, the sense of transnational interaction would even seem to have diminished now that Britain was being defended against anything resembling Bolshevism.

1066 McCrillis 1998, 13; Gullace 2002, 168; *The Manchester Guardian*, 'Peers and Votes for Women', 11 January 1918.
1067 Evans 2000, 88.
1068 Hansard, Austen Chamberlain, 30 January 1918, c. 1610; see also William Burdett-Coutts, 30 January 1918, c. 1605; Grigg 2003, 106.
1069 Hansard, Austen Chamberlain, 30 January 1918, c. 1617.

The peers used examples from abroad somewhat more readily, but still very selectively, than the MPs, which is reflective of their more cosmopolitan attitudes. Anti-reformists were always eager to point out warning instances. James Bryce emphasised the experiences observed in countries that already had women's suffrage when arguing against it.[1070] For him, anarchical Bolshevik Russia constituted a particularly deterring example of claims about 'the abstract natural rights' of anyone to actively participate in government. In countries with female suffrage, women tended to vote as their male relatives or the party organisations advised. Great nations such as France had not experimented with female suffrage, and there was hence no reason for Britain to do so either. The Finnish and Norwegian cases did not count as their experience of the practice was so short (in Finland 11 years and in Norway four). In Australia and New Zealand and some states of the United States, a tiny group of women appealing to democratic principles had managed to gain the vote, but women did not even seem desirous to use that right. A further anti-suffragist argument was that it was unfounded to expect that female suffrage would improve political life in any way: in New Zealand, women's votes had 'confused and perplexed politicians', while in Australia women voters had prevented general conscription and thereby damaged the interests of the British Empire. There had not even been any increase in female interest in politics; it was rather in Britain, where no female suffrage existed, that more women 'study politics, think about politics, talk about politics and take part in political work';[1071] consequently, the vote and political activity did not go together. George Curzon had similar opinions about the irrelevance of minor states as examples, pointing to the French and Italian exclusion of women from suffrage, bypassing Germany and condemning universal suffrage in the form in which it had been introduced in Russia. He was convinced that, wherever women had been allowed to vote, the result had been victories for socialism,[1072] though he did not refer explicitly to Finland, where the crisis resulting from socialist challenges to parliamentary government was acute and would soon turn into a civil war.

Transnationally connected spokesmen for reform found some encouraging examples from abroad. Charles Cripps (Conservative, from 1923 Labour), 1st Baron Parmoor, an internationalist lawyer who opposed the war and campaigned for the creation of the League of Nations, contrasted the less fortunate examples of majority elections in the British dominions with ones based on proportional representation in Sweden. Most MPs had heard about the Swedish elections of September 1917, which had led to the introduction of parliamentary government with a Liberal and Social Democrat majority and to the preparation of universal suffrage in that country, and this evidently inspired British leftist reformists as a potential future vision. It was of particular interest to Parmoor, who had transnational

---

1070 Lord Sydenham later praised Viscount Bryce for being such 'an old and earnest student of practical politics in all lands'. Lords, 17 December 1917, c. 187-90.
1071 Lords, Viscount Bryce, 17 December 1917, c. 189; Lord Sydenham, 17 December 1917, c. 212-13.
1072 Lords, Earl Curzon, 10 January 1918, c. 510, 514, 521-2.

connections with Sweden via the administration of the Church of England: he was an acquaintance of the pacifist Archbishop of Uppsala, Nathan Söderblom, who had several times visited his estate and evidently informed him about the ongoing political changes there.[1073] According to Parmoor, the Swedish system, which was based on proportional representation, allowed both Hjalmar Branting, the leader of the Social Democrats, and Arvid Lindmann, a leading Conservative, to be elected by the Stockholm electorate to the national parliament. Archbishop Söderblom had recommended such a system as it enhanced cooperation between different parties. Leading Swedish politicians, too, claimed that the system was fair and decreased personal attacks during election campaigns.[1074] The description of the Swedish representative system and its consensual orientation offered by Söderblom and Parmoor was rather idealised in the light of the unsolved confrontation on suffrage reform there.

Parmoor added examples from Belgium and other countries where cooperation rather than confrontation between interest groups and classes was said to predominate.[1075] In the Lords, such an argument might count among those Conservatives who were seeking a consensual polity. Lord Burnham (Liberal Unionist), a lawyer with academic connections with the dominions and Belgium, likewise spoke for a comparative examination of contemporary politics.[1076] Roundell Palmer (Conservative), Viscount Wolmer, referred to half a dozen 'democratic countries' which had been happy with proportional representation,[1077] while Edward Hemmerde (Liberal) questioned the relevance of a system that 'has happened to have worked fairly well in Belgium and possibly better elsewhere' as the British voters were simply not asking for the abolition of the majority voting system.[1078] The divergent deliberative approaches of the two Houses made a difference: the Commons debates tended to be patriotic, even xenophobic, whereas the peers could afford to contemplate matters from more general, comparative, cosmopolitan and even universalist perspectives. However, in the Commons, too, Andrew Bonar Law (Conservative), the Chancellor of the Exchequer, favoured the use of international comparisons to promote proportional representation, claiming that it was an insult to the British electors to suggest that a system that worked well 'in countries less well-educated than ours' would not be applicable in Britain.[1079] International comparisons and transnational links thus had a role in the British parliament even though they remained a minor phenomenon and were considerably fewer than in the countries of comparison. Britain was making this revolution on its own terms.

1073 Anon. 1970. Nathan Söderblom, a speaker of English, had been the Archbishop of Uppsala since 1914 and campaigned internationally for peace.
1074 Lords, Lord Parmoor, 17 December 1917, c. 195.
1075 Lords, Lord Parmoor, 17 December 1917, c. 195.
1076 Lords, Lord Burnham, 17 December 1917, c. 206.
1077 Hansard, Roundell Palmer, 30 January 1918, c. 1663.
1078 Hansard, Arthur Hemmerde, 30 January 1918, c. 1629.
1079 Hansard, Andrew Bonar Law, 30 January 1918, c. 1672.

4.1.3 The increasingly contested definition of 'democracy'

While democracy had not really been a defining concept in debates on the Representation of the People Bill in spring 1917, it was used slightly more frequently and in a greater range of senses in the autumn, which reflected a tendency especially in opposition circles to politicise the suffrage reform by interpreting it as an act that concerned democracy. The committee phase had given the politicians time to reflect on the political implications of the reform; Wilson's discursive intervention declaring democracy as a war goal had gained support; and the calls for democratisation in other European countries (especially Germany) had been recognised by some MPs. The definition of the Western Allies as 'democratic States' was becoming commonplace,[1080] but 'democracy' as a normative designation of the British political system or 'democrat' as a self-definition by an MP were still rare. John David Rees's (Unionist, formerly Liberal), a former imperial civil servant, nevertheless defined the imperial Parliament as 'democracy' since it consisted of great democrats and was based on majority rule,[1081] and thereby fulfilled the Conservative criteria of democracy.

In spring, some Unionist anti-reformists had redescribed democracy for oppositional purposes. These men were now underrepresented in the debates, and, uninterested in pursuing an issue that the majority considered already resolved, had since June focused on amendments rather than open opposition. Unionist critics were either absent or followed the proceedings in silence. The rightist opposition recognised that they had lost and did not regard it worth continuing with their expressions of dissent; they adopted a pragmatic approach, attempting to mould the act to their liking so that it would serve their party interests.[1082] This differs from the more inflexible strategy of the Swedish right in late 1918 and that of the Swedish People's Party in Finland in 1919, not to mention the stance of the German right.

It was rather the Irish Nationalists who adopted democracy as a concept that embodied a variety of positive senses, thereby enabling them to engage in politicking. Joseph Devlin, for instance, criticised the Northern Ireland Unionists for turning to 'anti-parliamentary' measures in supporting the redistribution of seats in Ireland at a time when electoral reforms were supposed to turn Parliament into 'a constitutional and progressive machine'. According to Devlin's ironical remark, self-nominated Conservative 'democrats' were ready for 'revolution',[1083] and consequently any Conservative arguments based on 'democracy' were to be regarded with suspicion. The redistribution of Irish seats did not pass the Commons,[1084] but it contributed to the attempted politicisation of democracy in the House.

1080 Hansard, Ronald McNeill, 4 December 1917, c. 288.
1081 Hansard, Sir John David Rees, 4 December 1917, c. 295.
1082 McCrillis 1998, 16.
1083 Hansard, Joseph Devlin, 4 December 1917, c. 347; John Dillon added that the British government was contributing to the rise of 'the revolutionary party' in Ireland with its policies and leading the Irish to turn to 'revolutionary methods'. 4 December 1917, c. 381; 5 December 1917, c. 458–9, 462; see also F. Meehan, 5 December 1917, c. 484.
1084 McCrillis 1998, 14, 17; Evans 2000, 88.

The Irish Parliamentary Party together with some Labour and Liberal MPs also identified themselves with democracy more openly than in the spring. Charles O'Neill called John Dillon, an old Irish Nationalist reformer, 'a democrat of the deepest dye'.[1085] The Wilsonian emphasis on democracy and the sovereignty of small nations suited the Irish Nationalists and was reinforced by trans-Atlantic connections between Ireland and American political discourse. Devlin's suggestion was that Britain, unlike its democratic allies, was not acting like a democracy in Ireland.[1086] William Field presented himself as 'a democrat' and challenged the Conservative redescriptions of the concept: 'It is very difficult to know who is a democrat these days, because in this House we have Gentlemen of red-hot Tory principles declaring themselves democrats.' The motivation for this was that 'democracy is fashionable now, and of course it has a large following'.[1087] Among the Labour MPs, William Tyson Wilson, a trade union activist and party whip, promised the support of 'organised labour and democrats' for the bill.[1088] This was an expression of a Marxist association between democracy and the working classes even though no attempts to monopolise the concept of democracy were made. A similar Marxist association is evident in the emphatic assertion of Philip Snowden (Labour), a radical utopian socialist and a critic of capitalism, that he represented 'certain democratic principles'.[1089] In the far left press, a discourse using terms like 'the new democracy', 'the future democracy' and 'the coming of true democracy' had been activated, as had calls for new elections after which the people would govern themselves.[1090] On the other hand, the Labour leaders continued to avoid openly programmatic declarations of democracy. Democrats appeared in all parties, but it was patently clear that the word had a wide variety of meanings.

In comparison with the spring, 'democracy' had become a positively charged but still relatively sparsely used concept: it could be used to characterise the fairness of parliamentary procedures, to evaluate the domestic policies of the government and to define one's identity or that of some party fellow. Having one's support for democracy questioned by a political opponent was taken as an insult, and argumentative confrontations followed about who was more clearly on the side of democracy. When Sir John Lonsdale (Irish Unionist), a whip of his group, attacked the Irish Nationalist Party for opposing 'a thoroughly democratic proposal' on the redistribution of seats in Ireland and thereby challenging the principles of justice and fair play,[1091] Devlin responded by emphasising what his party had done to support the representation of the working classes and hence

---

1085 Hansard, Healy, 4 December 1917, c. 329; Charles O'Neill, 5 December 1917, c. 470.
1086 Hansard, Joseph Devlin, 5 December 1917, c. 548.
1087 Hansard, William Field, 5 December 1917, c. 531.
1088 Hansard, William Tyson Wilson, 6 December 1917, c. 792.
1089 Hansard, Philip Snowden, 30 January 1918, c. 1687.
1090 *The Herald*, 'A Plea for the Use of Brains' and 'Labour's Supreme Duty', 8 December 1917; 'Quo vadis?', 15 December 1917.
1091 Hansard, Sir John Lonsdale, 4 December 1917, c. 319–20.

'the story of continued progress along every line of Radical and democratic advance'.[1092]

The Irish Nationalist Party, in particular, set out to ask whether the War Cabinet represented 'the democracy of this country',[1093] the definite article suggesting that this was now a class issue. William Redmond received cheers from both sides of the House[1094] when he questioned the democratic character of current constitutional policies by characterising the reform proposal as 'Prussianism' – making use of the strongest counter-concept to democracy thinkable in the circumstances of 1917. Woodrow Wilson's speeches and the consequent rise of 'democracy' into a war goal and 'Prussianism' into a phenomenon against which the war was being fought now inspired a domestic constitutional dispute about what democracy was. Rather than concerning the political system in general, this debate was about imperial policies in Ireland and hence about the degree of democracy within the British Empire from a class perspective. The Irish Nationalists also made use of the authority that soldiers (including Irish volunteers like Captain Redmond himself and his brother, who had been killed in June 1917) enjoyed in contemporary debates everywhere:[1095]

> I have come from a portion of the world where we are fighting what we call Prussianism. I have come from a place where I have been in company with Englishmen, Irishmen, Scotsmen, men from all quarters of the British Empire, who are all combined in a common object, action, as well as desire, in combating the system known now in the stereotyped phrase as Prussianism. I have fought Prussianism face to face, but it is very hard indeed when one comes back to one's own country to find oneself stabbed with Prussianism in the back. Was there ever a more flagrant instance of patent Prussianism perpetrated by any combination of men calling themselves up-to-date and democratic rulers of a great democratic Empire than the spectacle of this coalition Government in its treatment of Ireland to-day?

Redmond was constructing a 'stab-in-the-back' theory (cf. the German *Dolchstoß* myth) of his own, insinuating that the current rulers of Britain were destroying what had been achieved in the war with the attempted redistribution of seats in Ireland. The War Cabinet had not presented themselves as champions of 'democracy', although they had made it clear that the intention was to take the will of the people better into account, and in radical public discourse 'democracy' was increasingly referred to as having implications not only for Germany but also for Britain. Being accused of anti-democratic measures at home despite contrary claims was grave particularly as the accusations came from an army officer. According to this Irish Nationalist, 'The present British Government have acted the part of Germany in regard to Ireland and torn up once more treaties with Ireland just as Germany tore up treaties of Belgium.' There was 'a system

---

1092 Hansard, Joseph Devlin, 4 December 1917, c. 349.
1093 Hansard, Thomas Scanlan, 4 December 1917, c. 354.
1094 *The Times*, 'Electoral Reform', 6 December 1917.
1095 Hansard, William Redmond, 5 December 1917, c. 559.

of pure Prussianism practised by the Government which is supposed to be doing all it can to destroy Prussianism elsewhere'.[1096] This may well have been excessively virulent parliamentary rhetoric (which it undoubtedly was given the differences in the electoral systems of Britain and Prussia) but it nevertheless challenged the government to state its stand on democracy. The ministry, however, chose to ignore the Irish provocation as irrelevant opposition polemics and to avoid a more awkward debate on the issue.

There would be no such extensive attempts to politicise the issue in the Lords' debates, which lacked Irish Nationalist and Labour members and were attended only by Conservatives and several recently nominated Liberal peers. Not unlike the Herrenhaus in Prussia and the First Chamber in Sweden, the Lords could have turned into a bastion of conservatism, its members not needing to worry about the electoral consequences of expressing traditionalist views. However, British Conservative peers talked rather positively about democracy in the wartime situation, redescribing it creatively into a democracy to their liking. James Gascoyne-Cecil, the Marquess of Salisbury, an opponent of the Parliament Act, wondered:[1097]

> Why should the Government . . . wish to avoid controversy except through the weakness of the flesh? After all this is a democratic country which prides itself on the fact that it governs itself, and to smuggle a Bill through when people are thinking of something else does not seem to me the right way to be loyal to the democratic institutions of our country.

Lord Sydenham, a defender of a stronger hereditary House of Lords and an opponent of democracy, likewise used the pre-war Conservative understanding of democracy to justify the anti-reformist line. In insisting that 'no revolutionary change' should be carried out before 'the will of the people' had been consulted through a new election, Sydenham urged the Lords to 'vindicate the principles of the Constitution and incidentally the theory of democracy'.[1098] Henry Petty-Fitzmaurice, 5th Marquess of Lansdowne, who had made a career as an imperial administrator and key minister, shared these aristocratic views and declared: 'We live in a democracy. We are fulsome in our professions of faith in the democratic system. Surely the essence of a democratic system is that the ascertained will of the people should prevail.'[1099] Opposition to the bill was rhetorically redefined by Lansdowne as the defence of constitutional 'democracy' against 'revolution'. In leftist public discourse, Lansdowne's sincerity in calling for democracy had been questioned on both sides of the Atlantic as an attempt to save the aristocracy.[1100] Definitions of 'Tory democracy' familiar from pre-war opposition to Liberal reforms continued to be used

1096 Hansard, William Redmond, 5 December 1917, c. 560, 562.
1097 Lords, The Marquess of Salisbury, 17 December 1917, c. 164.
1098 Lords, Lord Sydenham, 17 December 1917, c. 210; also Alexander Bruce, 6th Lord Balfour of Burleigh (Unionist), 9 January 1918, c. 214.
1099 Lords, Marquess of Lansdowne, 9 January 1918, c. 442.
1100 *The Times*, 'More Criticism of the Lansdowne Letter', 4 December 1917; *The Herald*, 'A Republican's Fears', 15 December 1917.

by the Conservative opposition: Britain was already a democratic country based on parliamentary government. The War Coalition was abusing the democratic institution by introducing a radical reform in wartime when neither Parliament nor the public could concentrate on such changes. Whether such rhetoric would convince many outside the Lords in late 1917 was another matter. On the far left, *The Herald*, for instance, declared that the rulers of Britain had shamefully 'not fought democracy in the open, but have used its own sacred name to destroy itself',[1101] an indication that the awareness of political language games was high.

At the same time, Lord Haldane, a leading Liberal, ironically pointed to how the Conservative Party was becoming more democratic, being 'infected with the spirit, and [claiming] to represent democracy'. For Haldane himself, democracy stood for 'government by the whole of the people of the nation with the exception and exclusion of those who are unfit' (but not excluding women). Democracy was as impossible to resist as the tide of the Atlantic (a very Wilsonian metaphor referring to trans-Atlantic discourses), and the extension of the representation of the nation was a way to keep potentially revolutionary movements in check.[1102] Some British Liberals evidently used democracy as a normative concept for setting criteria for the constitution.

The debate on democracy was participated in from quite a different perspective by Baron Parmoor, a pacifist peer who sympathised with Labour and was inclined to international leftism. Parmoor recognised that the proposed reform was a way to allow the expression of 'the democracy of the time',[1103] with democracy appearing as an irresistible transnational trend. Parmoor defined the concept in arguing for proportional representation as the way to proper democracy:[1104]

> I have no fear of democracy. I welcome it, but with this proviso – that the democracy must be, a true and not a false one. It must be a democracy that is really representative. . . . We want the co-operation of all classes of this country. . . . We want to get rid as far as possible of friction and antagonism.

Parmoor held a leftist understanding of democracy, in which the proposed parliamentary reform would increase political and social cohesion by removing party and class confrontations and lead to further later reforms. The Lords should use their constitutional rights to advance 'a democratic cooperation between classes' rather than 'a democracy which may lead to friction and trouble'.[1105] Parmoor's reasoning was supported by his transnational acquaintance with Swedish Liberal and revisionist Social Democratic ideals on democracy, not by the concept of class struggle.

Baron Burnham (Liberal Unionist), also held an optimistic conception of democracy as a means to unite a class society, but his conclusion differed

---

1101 *The Herald*, 'A Clean Sweep, a Clean Peace', 15 December 1917.
1102 Lords, Lord Haldane, 9 January 1918, c. 428.
1103 Lords, Lord Parmoor, 17 December 1917, c. 194.
1104 Lords, Lord Parmoor, 17 December 1917, c. 194.
1105 Lords, Lord Parmoor, 17 December 1917, c. 195, 200.

from that of Parmoor. For Burnham, British democracy had already brought the classes closer to each other so that 'to talk of the governing classes now is almost a contradiction in terms' when 'all the classes are governing classes'.[1106] This was an overstatement used to counter leftist discourse, but it also reflects a belief in democracy as a way to build national unity. Burnham, like Parmoor, was arguing for proportional representation as a check on majority rule:

> Democracy, . . . is often unjust and often cruel, but its worst vice is its tendency on all occasions, if it can, to suppress minority opinion; and you cannot guard against the danger by any system of representation I know . . . unless you follow the sure rule which gives minorities their proper weight in the affairs of the State, and carries out Burke's maxim that—'the virtue, the spirit, the essence of the House of Commons consists in its being the express image of the nation.'

It would be through proportional representation that the best possible democracy would be achieved. Any 'tyranny of the mob' would be avoided by 'giving democracy a fair chance' through proportional representation.[1107] Burnham's optimism is also reflected by his questioning of previous predictions of the levelling consequences of the introduction of democracy. Instead, he offered a positive forecast of the evolutionary potential of a democratic constitution reformulated by the people:[1108]

> I do not believe that the form of Government makes the character of the people. On the contrary, I believe that the character of the people moulds and forms the Government. If our character is sound, so I believe, under all the conditions of the wide and popular franchise we are now creating, the institutions will be sound and stable too.

Britain, as the pioneer of parliamentary government, had provided precedents for the entire civilised world and continued to have a particular mission in the advancement of democracy of this kind.[1109]

Some other Liberals in the meantime rejected democracy as a normative concept: even the 85-year-old Leonard Courtney, 1st Baron Courtney of Penwith, a former professor of political economy and a peer with progressive views on parliamentary reform, expressed doubts concerning 'the enthronement of a democracy' and was worried about the socialist revolutionaries taking over the concept, and mutilating democracy into the rule of one class. Some other term might hence be more appropriate to describe the goals of the new British legislature:[1110]

> That word 'democracy' is one that I am not very fond of using. It seems to me that we are in great danger of employing it, as I think it I often see it employed,

1106 Lords, Lord Burnham, 17 December 1917, c. 203.
1107 Lords, Lord Burnham, 17 December 1917, c. 209.
1108 Lords, Lord Burnham, 17 December 1917, c. 209.
1109 Lords, Lord Burnham, 17 December 1917, c. 209.
1110 Lords, Lord Courtney, 18 December 1917, c. 248.

as a mere word of cant, not covering what is properly understood by democracy, but what in a confused way is limited to one class, often the most numerous class of the community. There is a spirit abroad which suggests that democracy and proletariat are identical, the same thing. I venture to suggest that history, experience, and clear thought demand that there shall be no confusion between these terms.

This conceptual problematisation of democracy arose from the increasingly ideologically contested nature of democracy in the aftermath of the Bolshevik Revolution. Courtney wanted to reform the British parliament but not to have it associated with a concept that could be interpreted as referring to the power of the proletariat. Courtney's Parliament would express 'the whole mind of the nation' and constitute 'the People's House'; it would be inclusive of all classes. He was, furthermore, still unsure whether the current bill would create a Parliament that would reflect 'the exact image of the outer nation which it professes to represent' – as had been proposed by Edmund Burke. Proportional representation, by contrast, would 'make the Parliament of the future a true representative of the whole mind of the nation and the exhaustive collection of the opinions of the kingdom'.[1111]

Several Liberal lords had visions of a democracy based on a new kind of (proportional) representation and contemplated the alternatives more freely than the party politicians of the Commons. However, their views counted little in the legislative process. Even less significant was the ultra-conservative opinion: William Hugh Clifford, 10th Baron of Clifford of Chudleigh, could well suggest that it was impossible to govern by the will of the people as 'the people is a herd', that the rise of democracy inevitably led to civil wars and that a civil war was to be expected in Britain unless the aristocracy was allowed to lead 'the mass of society . . . to success'.[1112] No other speaker echoed such traditionalist views, although in the Lords there was no restriction on their free expression.

The Lords made a controversial decision in adopting an amendment in favour of proportional representation, which had already been rejected by the Commons no matter what its 'democratic' justification might be. Such an independent use of constitutional power by the upper house provoked claims that the Lords was being revolutionary in a way that endangered democracy. William Burdett-Coutts (Conservative) expressed his unhappiness about the amendment, although he considered that the former influence of the Lords had provided a counterweight to radical political changes such as the French Revolution. Thanks to the Lords, 'the freest and most democratic Constitution in the world' had been secured in the past, but now, Burdett-Coutts claimed, the peers had adopted a purely academic notion of proportional representation.[1113] He presented the British constitution as the most democratic one existing. British democracy had grown in an evolutionary manner and lacked the revolutionary fervour of the Continental kind. What the Lords were doing was, in Burdett-Coutts'

1111 Lords, Lord Courtney, 18 December 1917, c. 249–51.
1112 Lords, Baron Clifford, 8 January 1918, c. 369.
1113 Hansard, William Burdett-Couts, 30 January 1918, c. 1605.

partisan rhetoric, participating in a 'great revolution' that would destroy the delicate balance of that excellent constitution. The Commons should thus throw out the amendment and retain the bill in a form which would ensure 'the future welfare of democratic government in this country'.[1114] Even more than in other parliaments, the dynamics of British parliamentary discourse led to argumentative and rhetorical uses of 'democracy' determined by the political interests of the moment and building creatively on the linguistic resources of the time.

The Commons rejected the amendment, which gave rise to some disappointed protests in the upper house about its traditional constitutional status being ignored.[1115] Most peers conceded, however, that the reform would take place anyway. The supporters just wanted to see that 'this great change in democratic government' would be a decent one,[1116] and they argued for 'giving a fair chance to this tremendous experiment in democracy'.[1117] By 1918, the majority of the British peers had recognised the inevitability of the transformation, and many were already defining the political system as essentially democratic. At the other end of the ideological spectrum, *The Herald*, in which the reality of British democracy and parliamentarism had been questioned in comparison with 'that very process of democratisation … in Germany', was now also ready to declare that 'the hour of democracy comes'.[1118] This was an instance of an interpretation according to which Britain was about to become a democracy that was spreading in a variety of political circles in spring 1918.

4.1.4 'Women in Parliament, in Governments': The widening involvement of the people in politics

The feeling that the political character of the British people and hence the relationship between the people and politicians was changing also found expression in both Houses. Appeals to the people were generally regarded as authoritative arguments in endeavours to legitimate policies and Parliament as an institution. Yet the legitimacy of the procedure of constitutional reform was questioned by Hardinge Giffard (Conservative), the 1st Earl of Halsbury, a former Lord Chancellor, complier of an encyclopaedia on *The Laws of England* and old opponent of the Parliament Act, who argued that it constituted a needless reinvigoration of unsolved conflicts, created disturbances in a war-faring polity and was vitiated by the impossibility of critical debate in wartime.[1119] This was an example of even an arch-aristocrat rhetorically turning to the people as the source of legitimacy. According to Lord Curzon, the Leader of the House, the bill was by no means based on any plot that bypassed the constitution but was instead 'a Parliament Bill,

---

1114 Hansard, William Burdett-Couts, 30 January 1918, c. 1609.
1115 Lords, Earl Curzon, 6 February 1918, c. 403–404.
1116 Lords, Burnham, 6 February 1918, c. 412.
1117 Lords, William Palmer (Liberal), The Earl of Selborne, 6 February 1918, c. 412.
1118 *The Herald*, 'The Prussian Reform Bill', 15 December 1917; 'Appeal to the Congress', 29 December 1917; cf. 'For Peace or Revolution?' and 'At Home & Abroad' by *The Herald*, 9 February 1918.
1119 Lords, The Earl of Halsbury, 18 December 1917, c. 227.

a People's Bill, a Nation's Bill, in which the Government have given such assistance as they can to enable Parliament and the people at large to carry into effect the views which at any rate a very large number of them are believed to hold'.[1120] The Conservative elite did not hesitate to use a combination of parliamentary and popular rhetoric to get this bill through – especially in this case as it was Curzon's parliamentary duty to ensure its smooth passage.

The relationship between parliamentary and public discourse was a recurrent theme in the British reform process, which is reflective of the fact that the sophisticated relationship between Parliament and the press was felt to be out of balance. While Conservative opponents of the bill suggested that the lack of a proper public debate made it questionable to decide on such a major constitutional amendment in wartime, John Dillon, an Irish extreme reformist, put forward an opposite argument, suggesting that the press had obtained disproportionate influence over the government in the question of the suffrage of conscientious objectors, for instance.[1121] Lord Weardale, a leading anti-suffragist, likewise lamented the replacement of 'a Parliamentary régime' with 'a Press régime, where the Press practically governs the country, and not always the best part of the Press, to the detriment of popular and constitutional government'. Governments had been changed as a consequence of press campaigns, which had replaced 'Parliamentary action'.[1122] An alternative way of thinking was presented by Colin Coyote (Liberal), who assumed that 'the deliberations of this House, and of the nation' had taken place side by side despite the war.[1123] There was also the traditionalist virtual representation kind of argument that extending voting rights was unnecessary as 'public opinion' took care of the advancement of women's rights.[1124] Lord Burnham, the owner of *The Daily Telegraph*, who supported proportional representation, depicted the potential influence of the newspaper press in relation to the parliamentary system: if the reform was not realised, only the press would be available for minorities to express their views.[1125]

More serious from the point of view of the parliamentary elite was a suggestion of Roundell Palmer (Conservative) that strong anti-party and anti-politician feelings existed throughout the country and that these decreased confidence in Parliament as well.[1126] Politics appeared to the common man and woman as a sinister game played by the parties in Parliament. There was a shared understanding among the parliamentary elite that measures had to be taken to restore the legitimacy of Parliament by allowing a larger segment of the population to vote. It was particularly important to activate the soldiers: they were 'our own people at large' and 'the most loyal and the most public-spirited of our people', as Conservative lords

1120 Lords, Earl Curzon, 19 December 1917, c. 288–9.
1121 Hansard, John Dillon, 4 December 1917, c. 299, 303.
1122 Lords, 8 January 1918, c. 346–7.
1123 Hansard, Colin Coyote, 4 December 1917, c. 360; cf. Seaward & Ihalainen 2016.
1124 Lords, Viscount Bryce, 17 December 1917, c. 181–2, 186; cf. Ihalainen 2010.
1125 Lords, Lord Burnham, 17 December 1917, c. 205–207.
1126 Hansard, Roundell Palmer, 30 January 1918, c. 1655–6; cf. the reports on the mood in Germany discussed in subsection 3.2.1.

put it,[1127] recycling the stereotype of an armed male citizen. Robert Crewe-Milnes (Liberal), 1st Marquess of Crewe and former Secretary of State for the Colonies, leader of the House and Lord President of the Council, spoke about a 'great citizen army'.[1128] In the Marquess of Salisbury, a Conservative Privy Councillor, this widening of the concept of the people as a consequence of the war led to the important conclusion that it was necessary to extend suffrage to cover all men and women. After the joint national experiences of the Great War, democratic suffrage could be justified on race- rather than gender-bound grounds as the political virtues of the entire population independently of their social rank had been demonstrated:[1129]

> I have great confidence in my countrymen. I believe that they all share the public spirit, the political instinct, the administrative capacity, which are characteristic of the race to which they belong. They do not differ diametrically from the classes above them. . . . They have the same instinct and the same high quality. I am willing to trust them. . . . I ventured to urge . . . that it was necessary and in the highest interest of the State that we should trust the working classes, and that the old attitude of suspicion and want of confidence should be swept away. . . . We are not afraid of them; we are prepared to trust them; . . . . There is no reason why we should not trust the women. They belong to the same race and have no doubt the same instincts.

Among some Conservatives, such justifications of the extension of suffrage were connected to concerns about the consequences for both the old elites and the political community at large.[1130] Hence, despite his principally positive argumentation, Salisbury spoke *against* immediate women's suffrage.[1131] He categorised citizens, furthermore, into 'the most loyal citizens the soldiers' and 'the less loyal citizens of the Empire', who could be found particularly in Ireland.[1132] He was opposed to 'introducing politics amongst the troops' by holding elections before the end of the war.[1133] Thus an opponent of immediate reform was – reflective of the pressures of the wartime – speaking reformist language.

Some peers still maintained that women were not ready to receive the political right to vote. According to James Bryce (Liberal), the majority of women lacked the knowledge and interest in public affairs that would advance the cause of the nation:

> They do not meet and talk about politics; they do not attend meetings; they do not read political news, as we all know, in the way in which men do . . . [H]ow many women whom we know . . . read the political news or know anything of what is passing in the political sphere?[1134]

1127 Lords, Marquess of Salisbury, 17 December 1917, c. 165–6, 175.
1128 Lords, The Marquess of Crewe, 18 December 1917, c. 256.
1129 Lords, The Marquess of Salisbury, 17 December 1917, c. 167–8.
1130 Lords, The Marquess of Salisbury, 11 December 1917, c. 169–70.
1131 Lords, The Marquess of Salisbury, 11 December 1917, c. 168–9.
1132 Lords, The Marquess of Salisbury, 11 December 1917, c. 173.
1133 Lords, The Marquess of Salisbury, 11 December 1917, c. 174.
1134 Lords, Viscount Bryce, 17 December 1917, c. 183.

Their assumed lack of interest thus excluded women from the privilege of being involved in politics.[1135] For Bryce, politics remained a gendered sphere of activity in which men sitting in Parliament were the qualified agents although at times of election this sphere could be extended to include other males as well. Women had other roles in politics and public life and would do better wait until they were properly qualified to receive suffrage. Bryce could not see any 'brighter and better era' following the entrance of women into Parliament either: it was doubtful whether 'we shall have politically a new heaven and a new earth' or whether 'women will bring a purer and nobler spirit into politics'.[1136] Lord Sydenham – a developer of conspiracy theories who was afraid of 'a triumph of feminism' of the type witnessed in Australia – did not hesitate to accuse British suffragists of encouraging Germany to wage war against a weakened British polity in which even women could disturb the established order. Women should not be allowed to govern the British Empire as they might support socialism and thereby ruin the entire state.[1137] Henry Chaplin (Conservative) was utterly opposed to the idea of having 'women in Parliament, in Governments'.[1138] The gendered character of politics was strongly defended by a handful of peers, some of them of considerable academic standing, even though the party as a whole had decided to embrace female suffrage.

The claim about women's lack of interest in politics and their failure to attend political meetings or read newspapers was disputed by several other peers.[1139] Earl Russell (inclined towards Labour) argued that women should be given a vote as human beings, not in the expectation of better politics. It was unjustified to deny women suffrage by claiming that male voters understood 'all the political considerations' linked to voting: indeed, many a male who had 'never bothered his head about politics' would now be allowed to vote. Women may have lacked 'political education', but they had demonstrated their capability of political action and should hence be allowed to vote.[1140] The Church of England had also become convinced of the necessity of the extension: Arthur Winnington-Ingram, the Bishop of London, pointed out that women would be needed in the post-war reconstruction of the country and should hence be represented.[1141] Randall Davidson, Archbishop of Canterbury, interpreted the division of the Commons to indicate that the time for women's suffrage had come and that any other decision by the Lords would just split the nation.[1142] The war experience had evidently united much of the nation behind the decision. The justification for the reform came from outside Parliament.

1135 Lords, Viscount Bryce, 17 December 1917, c. 183–5.
1136 Lords, Viscount Bryce, 17 December 1917, c. 185.
1137 Lords, Lord Sydenham, 17 December 1917, c. 212–13.
1138 Lords, Viscount Chaplin, 18 December 1917, c. 235–6.
1139 Lords, Lord Burnham, 17 December 1917, c. 201–202; The Marquess of Crewe, 18 December 1917, c. 258; Lord Buckmaster, 19 December 1917, c. 269–74.
1140 Lords, Earl Russell, 17 December 1917, c. 216–18.
1141 Lords, Arthur Winnington-Ingram, 9 January 1918, c. 458.
1142 Lords, Randall Davidson, 10 January 1918, c. 481–3.

Some peers might doubt the political qualifications of women, but few questioned the political potential of the people during the final stages of the bill, as for instance some members of the upper house in Sweden did. Speakers from all political groups referred to 'the people' or 'the nation', whose representation in Parliament should be extended. Lord Haldane (Liberal) insisted that 'Parliament is entitled to take cognisance of the changes which are going on outside its own walls' – to interpret public opinion.[1143] Reflective of the patriotic and nationalistic wartime spirit is Baron Parmore's description of Parliament as 'a reflex of national life' and 'representative of all the forces and ideas which in the aggregate we connote by the term "nationality"'.[1144] The concepts of the people and nation had traditionally been nearly synonymous in British parliamentary discourse, but Parmoor's persuasive rhetoric reflects an emphasis on the national community as being strengthened by the war rather than on popular sovereignty only. His message was addressed especially to Conservative peers. The people as a nation were entering British politics as a consequence of the war, a nationalist interpretation that overshadowed some of the potentially more radical implications of democracy.

4.1.5 The future of a democratic parliamentary polity after the war

Just as the British parliamentary elite generally agreed about the experience of the war uniting the nation and the need to engage the people in politics, most of them shared a feeling that the parliamentary system was about to change as a consequence of the entry of the masses into politics in ways from which there was no going back. The constitution and the functioning of the political system simply needed to be updated. As Roundell Palmer who had warned about popular discontent with Parliament, put it: 'You have to face a new England, a new party situation, and a new set of problems, and those cannot be dealt with by the old methods.'[1145] Parliament, too, had to adapt itself to new the political circumstances created by the war.

Many described Parliament as being easily adaptable. Herbert Samuel (Liberal) set out to define the lengthy process of debating on the constitutional reform as one that would save Britain from revolutionary fervour in the future:[1146]

> [W]e shall undoubtedly have to pass through times of stress and of difficulty, and there may be a revolutionary feeling in the air; but the great safeguard against revolution always has been, and is now, wise constitutional reform, and it is only when the masses of our people see that our political institutions are broad-based and a real expression of the popular will, and that there is full and free access to Parliament for all sections and classes of the community, that the spirit of revolution can be exorcised.

1143 Lords, Lord Haldane, 9 January 1918, c. 422.
1144 Lords, Lord Parmoor, 17 December 1917, c. 193.
1145 Hansard, Roundell Palmer, 30 January 1918, c. 1162.
1146 Hansard, Herbert Samuel, 7 December 1917, c. 824.

This description of the political process demonstrates an understanding of the constitution as an evolutionary instrument for defining the functioning of a political community. The goal of the reform had been to demonstrate to an extended British people the genuinely popular base of Parliament and to thereby restore the legitimacy of the institution, which was under pressure as a result of the war. The reform showed how the British state was able to 'perfect our constitutional and electoral system' even in time of war.[1147]

William Peel, Viscount Peel, introduced the bill to the Lords using related though differently formulated ideas about 'enormous changes' being vital in order to prepare the country for solving a variety of post-war problems that were likely to give rise to 'clamorous voices outside the gates of Parliament'.[1148] Potential revolutionary tendencies after the war, the threat of which had become acute after the Bolshevik Revolution, would be dampened with a wartime parliamentary reform. A similar argument on the electoral reform passed by Parliament being an efficient antidote to revolution was made by Earl Russell, a peer close to Labour:[1149]

> [W]e grant the vote for ... the protection of the State, in order that through the ballot-box the State may learn, from the organised opinion of those who have grievances and who desire their remedy, what those grievances are. I suggest that the vote is granted nowadays ... as a substitute for riot, revolution, and the rifle. We grant the suffrage in order that we may learn in an orderly and civilised manner what the people who are governed want.

The strengthening of the connection between popular opinion and Parliament would make the British polity stronger by removing the causes for direct action, which seemed to be on the rise internationally and which had been experienced in British history so many times before. William Adamson (Labour) concluded in line with Samuel and Peel that constitutional reform 'as a safety valve is one of the greatest assets that any country could possess'.[1150] The momentum for transition was considered unique by the majority of the Conservatives as well. As the Chancellor Bonar Law put it, the degree of party confrontation around the proposal had been considerably reduced by the war from what it had previously been.[1151]

Some peers saw the global future and world order beyond the British Empire as matters for deliberation. Courtney (Liberal) referred to Wilsonian ideas about the founding of an international organisation that would use diplomacy to prevent further wars and coordinate economic cooperation between the member countries. The name of an organisation based on a fundamental rethinking of the world order had not yet been established – it might be 'the Family of Nations', 'the Society of Nations' or 'the League

---

1147 Hansard, Herbert Samuel, 7 December 1917, c. 824.
1148 Lords, Viscount Peel, 11 December 1917, c. 102. Such voices were not heard in Westminster – unlike Stockholm and Helsinki – owing to the continuation of the wartime party truce and the distance of the assembly halls from the streets.
1149 Lords, Earl Russell, 17 December 1917, c. 216–17.
1150 Hansard, William Adamson, 7 December 1917, c. 826.
1151 Hansard, Andrew Bonar Law, 7 December 1917, c. 825–6.

of Nations'[1152] and reminded 'the Parliament of Man' which had sometimes been envisioned by nineteenth-century British internationalists. Given the internationally discussed plans and the serious domestic problems awaiting a solution after the war, the British people should design their representative institution already during the war since the extent of the challenges justified 'abnormal' legislative measures. Britain needed a 'Legislature of the future competent for the discussions of the future'.[1153]

A particularly vivid description of the renewal of parliamentary suffrage initiated by the joint war effort was put forward by Lord Lytton, a Conservative reformist, who suggested that a parliamentary polity based on a broad popular legitimacy would be better prepared to meet the future challenges. Lytton's thinking combined Conservative pessimism with trust in the potential of popular government:[1154]

> The future is certainly dark, impenetrably dark and uncertain, and the only light by which we can be guided is that which we carry in our own hands, . . . the light which comes from faith in our cause and confidence in our people. . . . the Bill is a trumpet call blown in the midst of the battle to the democracy of this country. It is at the same moment an expression of confidence and an appeal for help.

By 'democracy' Lytton was referring within the traditional framework of a mixed government to the people at large, whose support legitimated the work of Parliament, an institution separate from the people. His thinking was patriarchal, even patronising: the bill demonstrated to the people: 'We trust you with the destinies of this country; and as for the future, though we cannot see, we need not fear what it may bring, because we shall face it as one people with united efforts and with a single purpose.'[1155] The people, in turn, would have a stronger trust in parliamentary government once Parliament had demonstrated its readiness for compromise, as Charles Stuart-Wortley (Conservative), 1st Baron Stuart of Wortley, pointed out. This experienced Conservative politician viewed the reform as a demonstration of the continuing status of the British polity as a model:[1156]

> [I]t has provided for the whole civilised world the most splendid evidence of our national strength; evidence, too, that this country is still devoted to those political ideals which have placed it in the lead of all free peoples in the world, and is determined that even in the great discussions that are before us there shall

---

1152 Andrew Bonar Law also referred to the future League of Nations, which might already have been created by the Inter-Parliamentary Union had there been time for it before the war. Hansard, 30 January 1918, c. 1676. An interesting point is the unrealised possibility of constructing the organisation on the basis of inter- and transnational parliamentarism. The League of Nations, too, would have a parliamentary assembly. On this change in international relations produced by the war, see Götz 2005, 267.
1153 Lords, Lord Courtney, 18 December 1917, c. 247–8.
1154 Lords, Earl of Lytton, 19 December 1917, c. 281.
1155 Lords, Earl of Lytton, 19 December 1917, c. 281.
1156 Lords, Lord Stuart of Wortley, 19 December 1917, c. 286.

be the fewest possible number of unenfranchised citizens taking part in those discussions . . .

Britain was thus demonstrating to the observing world that it was a true democracy – or, at least, the leader of the 'free peoples'.

When the bill was returned to the Commons after amendments by the Lords, the arguments defending it in its original form were mostly repeated in a spirit of lower-house parliamentarism, though some supporters of the amendments also emerged. Robert Cecil (Conservative), from the perspective of a former parliamentary civil servant, wanted to prepare Parliament for further constitutional challenges and develop it as part of the democratic system:[1157]

> It seems to me to be wilfully shutting our eyes to suppose that the House of Commons occupies the same position of influence and authority as it used to occupy or that it is in a position to stand the very serious test which I am convinced the next few years will impose upon all our constitutional machinery. I believe we must go back to the first principles of democracy. I am not saying that a good deal might not be said for and against democracy as a general principle. I am quite certain that a democratic form of government is the only possible form of government for this country, and that it ought to be made the very best form of democracy that we can make it. I am perfectly convinced of that.

By January 1918, the Representation of the People Bill could thus be interpreted, at least by an MP who contributed actively to the planning of the League of Nations, as touching on the very principles of representative democracy as the future political system. Democracy, despite its obvious shortcomings, provided the best available basis for political order, building as it did on the tradition of 'representative institutions'.[1158] Once such pro-democracy statements began to appear among the Conservatives in the British parliament, the British act, too, could be seen as a major step towards building a democratic political system. Proportional representation, for instance, would help to realise 'the true principle of democracy', the accurate representation of the electorate.[1159] It was the Bolshevik Revolution that persuaded Cecil to declare the strengthening of representative democracy by strengthening parliamentary institutions as the only way forward:[1160]

> [I]n the course of the next few years we in this country, and, I believe, the people of every country in Europe, are going to have great tests applied to the solidity and the reasonableness of our institutions and to many of our most cherished

---

1157 Hansard, Robert Cecil, 30 January 1918, c. 1647–8.
1158 Hansard, Robert Cecil, 30 January 1918, c. 1649–50.
1159 Hansard, Robert Cecil, 30 January 1918, c. 1649.
1160 Hansard, Robert Cecil, 30 January 1918, c. 1650; see Ihalainen 2010. *The Times* had published a letter by Kerensky in which he questioned the democratic character of Bolshevik rule. 'The Voice of M. Kerensky', 7 December 1917. Trotsky was reported to have said that it was the right of a 'democracy' to crush another class. 'Trotsky Against the Cadets', 18 December 1917.

beliefs. I wish to see our Constitution made as strong, as vigorous, and as well-founded as possible, in order to resist the shock of the times that are coming upon us.

Cecil, who was a visionary in seeing the future pan-European challenges to democracy and parliamentarism, regarded parliamentarism as an antidote to radicalism. In Britain, the constitutional reform for which he spoke would be successful, winning the support of a great majority of the old elite, maintaining the essence of the old constitution while democratising it to a degree sufficient to absorb the pressures of the time. With its reform Britain would avoid 'the paralysis of Parliaments' and related revolutionary developments.[1161] The story of the transition to democracy and parliamentarism would not be quite such a fortunate one in the leading enemy country. It would also be more confrontational in Sweden and Finland.

4.2 Germany: Democratisation and parliamentarisation come to a halt

Constitutional debates had been intensified in Germany during spring 1917 by difficulties encountered in the war and on the home front, the tendency of the Entente war propaganda to present a change in the German political system as a war goal, the Russian Revolution and the US declaration of war. In practice, pressures for constitutional changes which had been expressed forcefully by several leftists and a few centrists in March were buried in the committees of the Reichstag and did not lead – despite a further parliamentary attempt in July 1917 – to any governmental initiative on reform. The German 'inter-party conference', if one is permitted to draw an imperfect parallel with the British extraordinary body, was limited to the activities of the parliamentary committees and failed in the end both in forcing through a constitutional reform and in restoring peace.

On 27 June 1917 – simultaneously with the Finnish debate on parliamentary sovereignty – the parliamentary representatives of the Social Democrats were again calling for an electoral reform in Prussia, which had been vaguely promised by the Chancellor and the Kaiser in spring. The committees were still discussing constitutional questions in early July 1917, when the Social Democrats, the liberals and the Catholic Centre formed a new Inter-Party Committee.[1162] This led to a confrontation between the General Staff and the Reichstag majority, which reached a climax in connection with debates on further war loans when the Majority Social Democrats, breaking the wartime party truce, promised to approve further funding only if a peace resolution were accepted at the same time.[1163] These expectations for reform, which intensified in July, also had a transnational significance: promises by

1161 Taken up in *The Herald*, 'For Peace or Revolution?' 9 February 1918.
1162 Leonhard 2014, 738.
1163 Gusy 1997, 5.

the Chancellor and the Kaiser in April to amend the Prussian suffrage system affected discourses on democratisation and parliamentarisation in Sweden and Finland. The timing and content of the German debates of late March and July 1917 mattered for Finnish parliamentarians, for instance, since they gave the impression of a transnational revolution. If both Russia and Germany, the geographically proximate great powers became democracies, then why not Sweden and Finland?

As we saw in section 3.2, the adoption of the defence of 'democracy' against 'Prussianism' as a major ideological war goal of the Entente provoked a new kind of debate on the significance and implications of democracy in Germany. The frequent use of the term 'democracy' in calls for the reconsideration of the German constitution increased polarisation between the Social Democrats and the right. Scholars have dated this polarisation to the summer of 1917, but we found it already in the reform debates of late autumn 1916 and early spring 1917. A new cycle of discourse followed in July. Hugo Haase – the leader of the far-left Independent Social Democrats and a friend of the Marxist theoretician Karl Kautsky – demanded the full democratisation of the German constitution and the administration of the Reich and the federal states.[1164] The current leader of the Social Democrats, Friedrich Ebert, repeating the Social Democratic arguments of late March, likewise stated on 3 July 1917 that the democratic reform of the German political order was essential for both the internal and the external strength of the country.[1165] These interventions provided support for the simultaneous calls for full parliamentary sovereignty by the Social Democratic parliamentary majority in Finland, although the inspiration for the rhetoric of the Finns came from the Bolsheviks in Petrograd.

When suggestions for reform by the majority of the Constitutional Committee were introduced on 6 July 1917, it was emphasised by Dr. Ernst Müller (Progressivists) that the extensions of suffrage had been agreed on in principle by the large parties before the war and that only the war had led to their postponement. In his view, the moderate proposal of the Constitutional Committee consisted mainly of an increase in the number of constituencies and the introduction of proportional representation and could hence be passed.[1166] Matthias Erzberger of the Catholic Centre took a major risk when speaking in the Main Committee about the need to solve the constitutional crisis of the Reich, thus deviating from the stances of several leading members of his party, although the centrist leaders generally were confident about the potential of the Reichstag to achieve reforms.[1167]

For the Social Democrats, the compromise proposal was insufficient. According to Georg Gradnauer, a journalist with *Vorwärts*, the proposal constituted no real political reorganisation and watered down the suffrage reform. *Vorwärts* had been critical of the 'oligarchical' or 'dictatorial' features of existing parliamentary systems, too, which in its view made

1164 Bollmeyer 2007, 136.
1165 Llanque 2000, 200.
1166 Verhandlungen, Ernst Müller-Meiningen, 6 July 1917, 3507.
1167 Grosser 1970, 122, 134.

them far from ideal for the self-government of the people. The Social Democrats would begin to rethink their attitudes to parliamentarism more generally after the July crisis, beginning to see parliamentary elections as a way to engage the people in the affairs of the state and also accepting the idea of participating in a parliamentary government. Even so, theoretical criticism of parliamentarism as a plutocratic system of representation and warnings about its degenerating effects on the workers' parties continued to appear in German Social Democratic circles, which still prioritised the democratisation of suffrage over parliamentarisation.[1168] Thus the parliamentary model provided by the German Social Democrats for the Swedes and Finns was certainly not an uncritical one, although it could also be used to support the idea of the Social Democratic takeover of parliaments through universal suffrage.

During the July crisis, the German Social Democrats thus focused on the extension of suffrage. A proposal for women's suffrage was missing from the compromise proposal. According to Gradnauer, in this respect Germany lagged behind countries such as Australia, Britain, the United States, Norway and Denmark. Gradnauer pointed out that in Finland, which he probably knew little about but which provided him with a peripheral example to underscore the backwardness of the German Reich, 'An entire row of highly capable women sit in Parliament.' In Revolutionary Russia, too, women's suffrage was being planned. Particularly bitter was the fact that Britain was preparing to introduce women's suffrage in elections for the House of Commons, whereas Germany did not intend to do anything about the matter.[1169] Here Britain appeared again as the standard, which annoyed the right. Thus it was possible for a Social Democrat to make constitutional comparisons not only between Germany and the Allied powers, which were presenting themselves as defenders of democracy, and those Scandinavian countries that had introduced female suffrage but also, in the revolutionary atmosphere of 1917, even with Russia, where the direction that political development would take remained highly uncertain.

The Social Democrats, both the Majority and the Independents of the far left, viewed democracy as their future goal. At the same time, criticism of both democratisation and parliamentarisation remained commonplace among non-socialists. Even the left-liberals were uncertain and disunited as to what the suggested reforms might mean in practice. Friedrich von Payer, a lawyer from Wurttemberg and a former speaker of the regional parliament who defended parliamentary powers, complained about the multiple meanings assigned to the concept of parliamentarism, while liberal papers

---

1168 Grosser 1970, 137, 153–5. This more positive interpretation of parliamentarism and cooperation with bourgeois parties would seem to have arisen in Germany *after* the Finnish Social Democrats had attempted a more radical introduction of parliament-dominated democracy in the sense of Social Democratic majority rule. In autumn 1917, they would be unwilling to look to their German comrades, who had failed in their reform, since more radical and obviously more successful models could be found in the east.

1169 Verhandlungen, Georg Gradnauer, 6 July 1917, 3508–10; Leonhard 2014, 782.

sometimes also published arguments claiming that parliamentarism was the way to respond to the needs of the masses.[1170] Marcus Llanque explains such ambivalence among the liberals by their lack of experience in parliamentary government. The German parties had difficulties in defining what they expected from the proposed reform, particularly when it was demanded in wartime, a situation that set evident limits to radicalism:[1171] no party wished to be seen as unpatriotic. Subsequently, the German liberals have also been presented as being to blame for the failure of German democracy – as not being consistently supportive of it, like members of Liberal Parties in most countries.

When the Inter-Party Committee, formed from the Social Democrats, the Catholic Centre and left-liberals and for some time also the National Liberals but with no members from the right, started to meet on 6 July, parliamentary reform was very much on its agenda. Some, though not all, the leaders of the centrist parties had been rethinking their stands on parliamentarisation, and Gustav Stresemann of the National Liberals welcomed it as well.[1172] The work of this committee was based on collaboration between the reformist parties on constitutional matters; it was not considered representative of all major political groups and was hence ignored by the conservative *Neue Preußische Zeitung*, for instance. *Vorwärts*, the source which foreign papers most actively followed and whose news sometimes created wrong impressions outside Germany, wrote boldly about the chances for a government supported by the masses of the people that would realise democratisation, at the same time criticising the Chancellor for attempting to reconcile nationalism and internationalism, conservatism and social democracy, uncompromising fighters and peace-seekers, opponents and supporters of democracy and reform, in other words, of trying to please everyone. The expectations of cooperation from the parties of the centre tended to turn into criticism of their vacillation. At the same time, reports from the debates of the Constitutional Committee confirmed to Social Democrat readers the fact that the Conservatives were not willing to agree to equal suffrage in Prussia or to other reforms during the war.[1173]

The Constitutional Committee nevertheless challenged the wartime government and the General Staff to a degree that some scholars have interpreted as having contributed significantly to the transformation towards a parliamentary system in Germany. This interpretation probably goes too far given the wartime circumstances of the government, the unrepresentative nature of the committee, the wavering stands of the parties and the reservations about parliamentarisation that still persisted in 1918 and 1919. Even so, several changes in the political system were demanded by this committee in line with suggestions made in the debates of the spring, including the appointment of secretaries of state by the Reichstag and the formation of advisory boards to supervise the executive. Chancellor

---

1170 Julius Lissner, *Berliner Tageblatt*, 6 July 1917.
1171 Llanque 2000, 203, 206.
1172 Grosser 1970, 121, 132.
1173 *Vorwärts*, 7 July 1917.

Bethmann Hollweg reacted by repeating promises for a suffrage reform in Prussia on 11 July 1917 and invited leading parliamentarians to advise the government, but by this time his authority in the leadership of the Reich had become contested not only by reformist parliamentarians but above all by the army chiefs of staff, who were unhappy with the course of the reform debates. Bethmann Hollweg consequently lost his position on 13 July with the adoption of a peace resolution by the Reichstag.[1174]

On 19 July, the Reichstag nevertheless accepted, despite many dissenting voices, a proposal to be presented to the Entente on the restoration of peace without changes of borders or indemnities and formed one more committee to prepare a constitutional revision.[1175] *Vorwärts* described this as the first 'act of will of the German representation of the people' intervening in foreign policy: the Social Democratic organ claimed that even if opposed by influential power-holders, this would force the government to act according to the will of the Reichstag majority.[1176] The paper continued to publish overly optimistic descriptions of the successes of the party, as a result of which, it even claimed, 'Germany is democratising itself!'[1177] The left-liberal *Berliner Tageblatt* also declared that it had consistently prioritised the introduction of 'the parliamentary system', referring to the restructuring of the Reich and a new division of power and responsibility (which was again a rather ambiguous demand). The paper saw such a reform as inevitable in the current era of mistrust of Germany abroad. Conrad Haußmann described the formation of the parliamentary majority and the consequent rise of parliamentary powers overoptimistically as a turning point in the history of the Reich and of Europe.[1178] An interesting detail from a transnational perspective (though of minor significance) is that the *Berliner Tageblatt* on 21 July reported about a decision of the Finnish parliament on 'independence'; this, it claimed, reflected a parallel decisiveness in a parliamentary body and 'a virile people', to whom the paper wished all the best.[1179]

The German situation was constitutionally confusing, both for Germans and outsiders, and consequently for later historians as well. Marcus Llanque has concluded that the constitution was not even the key issue for the parliamentary parties in July 1917: instead of concentrating on the democratisation and parliamentarisation of the constitution, they prioritised a joint peace proposal (somewhat in line with the aims of the Stockholm peace conference in June). The initiative was immediately turned down by the Western powers,[1180] which regarded the proposal as mere propaganda – even if the majority of the German political leaders were aware of the difficult strategic position of Germany and evidently ready for peace at this

---

1174 Grosser 1970, 127; Pohl 2002, 7–8; Seils 2011, 342, 351; Leonhard 2014, 739.
1175 Leonhard 2014, 738, 740.
1176 *Vorwärts*, 20 July 1917.
1177 *Vorwärts*, 21 July 1917.
1178 *Berliner Tageblatt*, 19 July 1917, 20 July 1917.
1179 *Berliner Tageblatt*, 21 July 1917.
1180 Llanque 2000, 203; Wade 2000, 172.

stage and on these terms.[1181] This reaction further diminished the credibility of the reformists in Germany: democratisation and parliamentarisation were associated with giving up fighting the war, while even the West did not take the proposals seriously. According to Dieter Grosser, no German party attempted to introduce a parliamentary system at this stage, at least as far as the choice of the chancellor was concerned. The left-liberals and Social Democrats, also criticised Western models rather than defined what the right type of democracy should be. This added to the confusion in constitutional thinking and to a delay in the transition to parliamentary government.[1182] All this speaks against a silent parliamentarisation thesis and explains the mixed interpretations that socialists outside Germany could make about what was expected to happen in Germany. The Prussian conservative press made effective use of this confusion by publishing declarations that rejected 'Reichstag democracy', 'parliamentary dominance' and mere political talk as ways to bring about peace.[1183] As far as the conservatives were concerned, the war must be won with 'blood and iron', quoting Bismarck's famous speech.

Whether the cooperation of the parties of the left and the centre in July 1917, which aimed both at the restoration of peace and a rather indefinite constitutional reform in Germany, should be characterised as an early or gradual parliamentarisation of the German monarchy is a question that has divided German historians for nearly sixty years. In both older and more recent research, a link has been drawn between the attempts of summer 1917 and the actual reforms of autumn 1918.[1184] The fact that there was a parliamentary intervention in foreign policy and calls for a suffrage reform continued is beyond question, but it is an overstatement to characterise the majority of the German political elite (or even of the future Weimar Coalition) as ready for the full parliamentarisation of the constitution of the Reich in summer 1917. As Llanque argues, peace was considered more urgent than an immediate constitutional transition. And as an analysis of debates of summer 1917, autumn 1918 and spring 1919 suggests, there were evident limits to how far the German parties envisioned democratisation

---

1181 Soutou 2014, 513.
1182 Grosser 1970, 129, 139.
1183 *Neue Preußische Zeitung*, 18 July 1917.
1184 For early theses on creeping parliamentarisation, see Epstein 1960, 562–84, Rauh 1977, 379, and Gusy 1994, 753. The later debate has been summarised in Schönberger 2001, 624–5, 665, Kühne 2005, 293, 316, and Bollmeyer 2007, 35–9, who all consider speculation about a gradual structural transition to parliamentarism to have been wishful thinking. See also Retallack 1996, 38, and Retallack 2006, 12, who challenges interpretations that claim that early twentieth-century Germany was in a state of transition to democracy. Seils 2011, 395, who has studied the wartime history of the Reichstag in detail, cannot see any reason to talk about parliamentarisation before the autumn of 1918. Jörn Leonhard, building on Udo Bermbach's argument of 1967 and emphasising the emergence of networks, repeats the interpretation that claims that the constitutional debates of summer 1917 were a reflection of an early parliamentarisation of Germany anticipating the rise of the Weimar Republic. Leonhard 2002, 33, and Leonhard 2014, 739, 763. This thesis is also repeated by Müller 2014, 45, so that the debate goes on.

and parliamentarisation proceeding, the lines of the Social Democratic and liberal parties being far less clear than those of their sister parties in Sweden and Finland, for instance. The preparation of the peace resolution itself certainly increased the political determination of the Reichstag parties, allowing the parliamentarians to think that they possessed unprecedented influence over the affairs of the Reich. This interpretation was especially strong in the Social Democratic and liberal press.[1185] However, such beliefs in the parliamentarisation of foreign policy would soon turn out to be completely premature, and the same is true of the constitutional reform. Expectations were nevertheless high among the Social Democrats not only in Germany but also in countries such as Sweden and Finland, where German developments were observed with great interest and overt optimism.

In Germany, constitutional questions remained intertwined with the war – even more concretely than in Britain, Sweden or Finland – in that the Social Democrats had presented the continuation of their support for the war effort as dependent on the advancement of domestic reforms. They had also received a degree of support from the left-liberals and the Catholic Centre for these demands,[1186] which made all the reformist parties appear to be an unpatriotic home front in the eyes of the right. Expectations for the further parliamentarisation of German politics or even for the promised democratisation of suffrage in Prussia were nevertheless overoptimistic. The decision of the reformist parties to put forward foreign political initiatives before their previous calls for constitutional reforms had led to any concrete concessions from the executive left the constitutional reform, too, at a complete standstill when the foreign policy initiatives failed. The intervention in foreign policy issues, which were traditionally regarded as the prerogative of the executive, diminished the credibility of the parliamentary groups in question with regard to the preparation of the proposed constitutional reforms as well.

A breakthrough in the reform issue had been expected by German and Northern European reformists in July 1917, but all came to nothing with the nomination of a new chancellor. Both the peace resolution and calls for parliamentarisation had little worth in the eyes of those who would now lead the German war effort. Chancellor Georg Michaelis, nominated by the Kaiser without consulting the Reichstag, had not committed himself to the proposed changes in the established political system. As an ally of Paul von Hindenburg and Erich Ludendorff of the General Staff, Michaelis rejected the peace resolution and opposed all calls for further parliamentarisation and democratisation of the government.[1187] In his speech to the Reichstag on 19 July 1917, the new chancellor turned down all proposals for constitutional reform. While recognising the need of the government and the parliamentary parties to communicate more intensively, Michaelis insisted that all such cooperation should take place 'without harming the constitutional and federal foundations of the realm'. In principle, the government of the Reich

---

1185 Bollmeyer 2007, 173.
1186 Gusy 1997, 5.
1187 Llanque 2000, 205; Becker 2014, 28; Leonhard 2014, 741.

would aim at strengthening 'the relation of trust between the parliament and the government' so that ministers could count on enjoying the backing of the large parties 'in the great representation of the people'. This formulation might seemingly recognise a degree of the kind of parliamentarism favoured by the left (who cheered in the chamber), but it by no means stood for the concrete parliamentarisation of the government, only for the involvement of the parties in policy planning. To the delight of the rightist parties in the chamber, Michaelis asserted: 'The constitutional rights of the head of the realm in the leadership of politics may not be diminished.'[1188] That was to say that the Reichstag could only be engaged in projects that served the interests of the imperial government. Its old limited role within the duality of government would be maintained. Even some members of the centre shared these views: the Catholic Centre remained far from enthusiastic about the parliamentarisation of the government and continued to defend the established system.[1189]

Neue Preußische Zeitung concluded decidedly on 20 July that there would be no 'parliamentary joint government' for which the leftist bloc, with its criticisms of the Prussian system, had been campaigning.[1190] In the debates, Social Democrat spokesmen still tended to insist that full democratisation and parliamentarisation had become the goals of the German people – the term did not matter so much for them as long as 'democratic development' was secured.[1191] At the same time, their leader Friedrich Ebert, too, advised the party not to be obsessed in the quest for parliamentary government in the prevailing circumstances.[1192] Hugo Haase of the far left optimistically insisted that the democratisation of the German constitution would lead to an early peace – partly because the Western powers would be more willing to conclude a peace with a democratic Germany.[1193] Among the Progressivists, too, Friedrich von Payer, on the basis of the discussions of the preceding weeks, was optimistic about the democratisation and parliamentarisation of the constitution in the sense of the government and parliament being brought into closer cooperation with each other. He maintained: 'Democratic thinking has proceeded apace in Germany during the last few weeks'[1194] – a statement that has been used to support those interpretations that regard parliamentarisation as having progressed in Germany in summer 1917. The left-liberal Bernhard Dernburg, a Prussian businessman and civil servant in the colonial administration who had served in the United States as well, also argued in these days for the necessity of democratising Germany by strengthening the political role of the Reichstag.[1195]

However, such reformers remained a minority; the executive power would stay in the hands of the supporters of the established Prussian political order.

1188 Verhandlungen, Georg Michaelis, 19 July 1917, 3570–3.
1189 Verhandlungen, Constantin Fehrenbach, 19 July 1917, 3574–5.
1190 *Neue Preußische Zeitung*, 20 July 1917.
1191 Verhandlungen, Philipp Scheidemann, 19 July 1917, 3576–8.
1192 Grosser 1970, 131.
1193 Verhandlungen, Hugo Haase, 19 July 1917, 3587.
1194 Verhandlungen, Friedrich von Payer, 19 July 1917, 3581–2.
1195 Llanque 2000, 196.

The government continued to be responsible to the Kaiser alone. The centrist press soon concluded with disappointment that the parliamentarians lacked the will to enforce a truly parliamentary system. The plausibility of the entire idea of parliamentarisation by the current parties consequently tended to be questioned: left-liberals and centrist commentators regarded the Reichstag itself as responsible for its own weak position.[1196] Businessmen, for their part, warned the politicians against democratising and parliamentarising the country.[1197] The far right soon formed the German Fatherland Party (Deutsche Vaterlandspartei), bringing together nationalist forces in defence of the established Prussian order and the much advertised 'German freedom'. In its founding manifesto, this rapidly growing party defined itself as an alternative to Western democracies, which it represented as hypocritical and materialistic advocates of 'false democracy', whose only aim was crush Germany militarily. The first versions of the 'stab-in-the-back' (*Dolchstoß*) myth also began to circulate in autumn 1917, suggesting that the soldiers were being betrayed by internal enemies who had been persuaded by Western propaganda about democracy.[1198] Conservative forces in Germany – and potentially also in Lutheran countries such as Finland and Sweden – made effective use of the fourth centenary of the Lutheran Reformation in October 1917 to emphasise German national virtues and the historical tradition of fighting against surrounding ideological enemies to the very end.[1199]

Doubts about the parliamentary parties and their motives were strengthened by the episodes of summer 1917 and contributed to the diminution of the credibility of parliamentary government even before the system had been established in Germany. These attitudes did not disappear when the Weimar National Assembly was established in spring 1919; they were indeed reinforced by the even more serious '*Dolchstoß*' of autumn 1918, when the political system collapsed although there was no visible evidence to the general public of the war having been lost. This matter will be analysed in section 6.2.

We can hence argue with Jörn Leonhard that the problematic role of parliaments not only in Germany but also in Russia and Austria had been demonstrated during 1917: in none of these great powers could a consensus be reached and domestic politics be stabilised on a constitutional and parliamentary basis. On the contrary, the parliaments turned into forums of deepening ideological polarisation within which the forces both of the right and the left were radicalised.[1200] In none of these national cases were the parliaments truly powerful, and hence, in the lack of any necessity to arrive at a consensus and to seek the compromises that would have been necessary in parliamentary governments based on coalitions of parties, they easily turned into forums of political polemic. A comparison with Finland

---

1196 Llanque 2000, 194–6, 198, 208.
1197 Stibbe 2001, 173.
1198 Grosser 1970, 179; Stibbe 2001, 184; Leonhard 2014, 741–3.
1199 Ihalainen 2009; Leonhard 2014, 745.
1200 Leonhard 2014, 763–4.

in 1917 is helpful here: there, too, expectations of the final democratisation and parliamentarisation of government were high after a 10-year experiment with universal suffrage and the development of parliament into a leading forum of societal debate, but the political parties failed to agree on the reform in the aftermath of the Russian Revolution, which led to the diminution of mutual societal trust and to a deepening crisis of parliamentary government not only among its traditional critics on the right but also among the liberals and socialists. Since the political power of the parliament had remained limited, it had developed into a site of polemic in which inflexibly ideological views could be expressed without any consequent need for compromises in a joint ministry. In Finland, the parliament failed even more seriously to reach a consensus on a constitutional political order. In Sweden, by contrast, the parliamentarisation of the government progressed early enough, during the second half of 1917, and there were also promises of further democratisation, which prevented a similar acerbation of the crisis. Otherwise the Swedish parliament might well have remained a forum of ideological polarisation for a longer time. In Britain, the majority of the parties possessed shared views on the principles of parliamentarism and had recognised the necessity of suffrage reform as a consequence of common war experiences. The early wartime reform supported belief in the capability of parliamentary government to implement revisions and prevented the potential for polarisation; thus the parliamentary process was able to handle ideological eruptions without turning into a cycle of mutual provocation.

Alternative ways to introduce reforms were proposed in Germany, too, including the idea that the political system could be democratised in a 'wise' and controlled way without parliamentarisation. Centrist writers, in particular, were sceptical about the sense of further parliamentarisation of the system.[1201] Distinctions between democracy and parliamentarism were typical of the German debates, though they could sometimes also be combined into an ambiguous reformist package. In the other three national debates, the two concepts were more commonly associated with one another; distinctions between them were drawn mainly by the far right and the far left. In the German Social Democratic press, too, the defenders of parliamentary democracy tended to increasingly suggest that democracy could be realised only through parliamentarism.[1202]

After the crisis of July 1917, which had further decreased the legitimacy of the Reichstag as capable of initiating a reform, German debates on the constitution came to a standstill that would last for over a year – until September 1918. Some further optimistic speculations on a possible new start for parliamentarisation in the sense of bringing the will of the people and that of the government closer together occurred in the aftermath of the nomination at the beginning of November 1917 of the new government of Count Georg von Hertling (Catholic Centre). Such speculations had no noteworthy consequences, however: the Chancellor was not in favour of the parliamentarisation of the government despite his dependence on the

1201 Llanque 2000, 208–9
1202 Llanque 2000, 284.

reformist parties and his willingness to negotiate about peace. The plans for suffrage reform in Prussia were in practice given up. The Chancellor was old and unable to influence war policies, which were dictatorially determined by the army commanders. In the meantime, the Reichstag proved incapable of asserting any influence on the policy of the government and unable to play the role of an active agent in promoting either democratisation or parliamentarisation.[1203]

At the same time, the debates on constitutional reform were proceeding in the countries of comparison, although the progress partly depended on German developments: the British House of Commons would complete the suffrage reform by February 1918. The Swedish Riksdag debated a similar reform proposed by its first parliamentary government in spring 1918, but its upper chamber, dominated by the German-oriented right, voted it out. The majority of the Finnish Eduskunta first set out to formulate a republican constitution in late 1917, and then in the course of 1918 it would make several attempts to force through a monarchical polity designed according to the German model. In Germany, the population tended to lose their confidence in the ability of the government (or the parliament in late 1917 and much of 1918) to introduce major reforms as long as the war continued.

Nevertheless, the transnational significance of the German development is evident. The rise of democratisation as a goal for constitutional reforms in the language of the German Social Democrats during the first half of 1917 had effects in Sweden and Finland, and so did the anti-reformist attitudes of the Prussian right, whether they were aristocrats, military men or academics. The German model encouraged the Swedish Social Democrats and Liberals to accept joint responsibility for forming the first parliamentary government and setting electoral reform as its major goal after their election victory in September 1917. This change of government simultaneously implied a turn in Swedish foreign policy, which had until autumn 1917 been directed by the King and the right, both of whom shared pro-German views, but which now aimed at building good relations with the Western Allies. This turn in Swedish foreign policy was noticed in the German Reichstag as well: Dr Ferdinand Werner, a member of the radically anti-Semitic German Ethnic Party (Deutschvölkische Partei), commented on the Swedish election result, the rise of the Social Democrats and Liberals to power and the expected change in foreign policy, implying that the peace resolution of the Reichstag had influenced the election result in Sweden in a negative way, weakening trust in the Prussian system. Werner had been informed by his rightist allies that while Sweden, as 'altogether a thoroughly Germanic country', had initially been 'almost completely pro-German' in 1914, the mood there had changed as a result of 'the agitation of Branting and the Entente' and by October 1917 Swedish opinion had become far less sympathetic towards the German war aims.[1204] This German rightist comment on Germano-Swedish relations can be seen as a further indication of a notable turn in Sweden towards the Anglo-American political model even if the shift continued

---

1203 Llanque 2000, 206–208; Becker 2014, 28; Bessel 2014, 130.
1204 Ferdinand Werner, 6 October 1917, 3749.

to be fiercely opposed by the Swedish right until the fall of the German monarchy – and indeed would be completed only after the Second World War.

The Finnish Social Democrats, who had won the first ever socialist parliamentary majority in 1916 and retained it until the elections of October 1917, were likewise encouraged by the German Social Democratic example to stay firm in their demands for full parliamentary sovereignty in the summer of 1917, particularly as they had been ideologically influenced by the German Marxists. The transition of supreme power to parliament was supported by the Social Democrats and most centrists. For the Finnish right, and especially for independence activists, including those who were receiving military education in Germany or serving on the Baltic front, Germany remained the model polity. This was also definitely true of those academics who were active in the Finnish- and Swedish-speaking conservative parties. The Anglo-American model, by contrast, appeared as politically relevant only in the eyes of a few Anglophile Finns.

4.3 Sweden: The introduction of parliamentary government as a safeguard against domestic upheaval

Despite some socialist hints and rightist fears, Sweden saw no revolution in spring 1917. Compared to the war-faring Central Powers and Finland, the danger of one breaking out may have been small but such a threat was unique in Swedish history. Without a doubt, there were tensions: demands for electoral reform remained unanswered and decisively affected the results of the parliamentary elections of autumn 1917. The voters were effectively informed by all parties that they were voting on a possible change in the parliamentary power balance and hence on a constitutional change[1205] – a lot like the Finns at about the same time.

Expectations of the extension of suffrage in other countries encouraged the parties of the left to speak out for female suffrage and equal voting rights. The Social Democratic election manifesto from July 1917 took up the Danish, Dutch, Finnish, British and Russian wartime transitions to 'clearly democratic forms of government' and presented 'the stormy democratic wave' as having reached Prussia, 'the old model country of anti-democracy', which was now on the way to democracy and parliamentarism (which was not true, as we just saw). These developments made 'the democratic breakthrough' and 'the democratisation of the constitution' unavoidable in Sweden as well, the goal of international Social Democracy being 'the power of the people' (*folkmakt*).[1206] The Liberals spoke for parliamentary government and 'the full self-government of the Swedish people' as a precondition for 'democratic progress' towards 'a democratic society'.[1207] The Right, by contrast, continued to defend the policies of the preceding

---

1205 Gerdner 1946, 9.
1206 *Till Sverges arbetande folk!*, 1917.
1207 *Frisinnade Landsföreningens valprogram*, 1917.

caretaker governments and regarded the existing electoral legislation as perfect for the country's national circumstances: the constitution guaranteed the continuity of lawbound liberty while previous reforms allowed 'continuous development to a democratic direction'; revolutionary agitation was thus unfounded.[1208]

External attempts to influence the Swedish elections were also evident: while the Germans backed the monarchy and The Right, Britain and the United States favoured the left, expecting them to distance the country from Germany at least in trade; increasing idealisations of Western models of parliamentarism prevalent among members of the left were also seen favourably by the Entente. Hjalmar Branting was generally known to have become sympathetic to the Western powers as the German war effort stagnated, and he expressed his sympathies during visits to the Allied Powers. He was consequently accused in rightist papers in Sweden of 'Entente activism' and being ready to renounce the policy of neutrality, which had been the official line of the country, although the policies pursued by Sweden during the war were actually pro-German. As could already be seen in the metaphors of democratisation in spring 1917, the Social Democrats tended increasingly to view the war – in line with Woodrow Wilson – as a struggle between democracy and autocracy, and in this division they felt that Sweden should take its place in the Western democratic camp and oppose the Prussian power of the Junkers. A diplomatic scandal revealing the German connections of the rightist minority government added to the increasingly suspect nature of links with Germany: the German Foreign Ministry had used Swedish channels to communicate information concerning submarine warfare – the controversial aspect of the war that finally brought the United States into it. The revelations undermined the Western powers' trust in Swedish neutrality, threatened vital trade connections for food and industry and made the open advocacy of Germanophile attitudes by the right increasingly difficult. Among other things, this explains the lack of comparisons with the German constitution in parliamentary debates after 1918. The left responded by calling for the democratic control of foreign policy to prevent such scandals in the future.[1209]

With the example of the pernicious consequences of the Prussian connections cherished by the monarchy and the landowning and academic elites, the left did well in the elections. The number of the seats received by The Right in the Second Chamber consequently sank to 57, the Liberals gained five more seats and had 62 representatives, the Social Democrats won 14 seats, becoming the largest group with 86 seats, and the two Agrarian parties (ideologically opposed to constitutional reforms and supportive of The Right[1210]) gained 12 seats. This would give the prospective Liberal-Social Democratic coalition an overwhelming majority but also called for close cooperation between these parties of the left. The leftist Social Democrats,

1208 *Allmänna Valmansförbundets valupprop*, 1917.
1209 Gerdner 1946, 10; von Sydow 1997, 116; Olsson 2000, 89–90; Hadenius 2008, 41–4, 48–9.
1210 *Bondeförbundets valprogram*, 1917.

by contrast, failed to win much support for their programme that associated socialism, democracy and revolution a lot like their Finnish comrades,[1211] being left with just 11 seats. In the election for the First Chamber, The Right continued to benefit from the inequitable suffrage system and received 88 seats against 45 for the Liberals and just 17 for the Social Democrats.[1212] This majority would be able to stop any constitutional reform endangering the influence of The Right, a situation that was often compared with that of the Prussian Herrenhaus. Although the diplomatic scandal did contribute to the victory of the left, the result was nevertheless mostly determined by the existing unsolved constitutional and acute economic issues.[1213]

The formation of the government after the elections has been regarded as a turning point, even a regime change, in Swedish political history:[1214] a ministry based on a parliamentary majority was formed for the first time within the apparent continuity of the Instrument of Government of 1809. This Liberal-Social Democratic coalition was expected to soon bring a proposal for a suffrage reform before the parliament – particularly as the British parliament, which had been increasingly viewed by the parties of the left as a model that surpassed the German type of constitutional monarchy, was about to implement a major extension of suffrage. Similar reforms had already been seen in Finland, Norway, Denmark and the Netherlands and were expected to take place in other countries too, although the German reform was unlikely to make progress under the new chancellor. The decision of the Finnish parliament on extensive parliamentary sovereignty in July, which had only deepened the constitutional crisis in the country, did not provide a model that the Swedish leftists wished to follow; rather it provided a warning example that called for caution in reformism. The radicalising Russian Revolution affected the Swedish debate as well, suggesting that it might be good to have a timeout before a reform proposal was brought before the parliament. This would happen in April 1918, after the Finnish Civil War was over. This section hence contains no detailed analysis of Swedish constitutional debates during autumn 1917.

Parliamentarism in the sense of governmental responsibility to a parliamentary majority – representing the Western European model of parliamentarism – was brought into the Swedish system in autumn 1917 without changing the letter of the constitution or debating extensively. However, this transition only took place after a constitutional confrontation between King Gustav V and The Right on the one hand and the Liberals and Social Democrats on the other concerning the implications of the election result. The monarch, and his wife Queen Victoria von Baden, who was a cousin of Kaiser Wilhelm, feared that the Entente was hatching a plot to incite a revolution in Sweden and intending to replace the monarchy with a republic.[1215] The royal couple and their rightist supporters were

1211 *Till Sverges valmän!*, 1917.
1212 Gerdner 1946, 10–11; von Sydow 1997, 116; Eskola 2011, 16.
1213 Carlsson 1985, 85–6.
1214 Olsson 2000, 88.
1215 Stibbe 2001, 176–7.

also concerned about traditional Swedish sympathies for Germany being replaced by open warfare against the country's natural cultural ally. They could not trust the left and preferred a more moderate coalition; even the Liberals were suspect as they had been supporting the cause of democracy and parliamentarism and rejecting 'Prussianism' (and by implication a constitutional monarchy of the German type). An alternative coalition was unrealistic, however: no parliamentary majority could be found as long as The Right remained unwilling to make any concessions over the suffrage question, and minority government continued to lose credibility. The royal attempts to nominate a coalition government that went against the election results consequently failed in a humiliating manner, and the King was forced to accept a Liberal-Social Democrat ministry. The Bolshevik Revolution in Russia made him increasingly concerned about the future of the monarchy and about the risks of parliamentary government, even leading him to consider abdication. This possibility of the fall of the monarchy together with the election losses forced The Right, too, to give in – even though their views on parliamentarism had by no means changed. The concession could also be understood as tactical and temporary in that The Right yielded the responsibility for running the country in hard times to the left, while retaining the ability to prevent radical reforms with their majority in the upper house. Anyway, the general assumption among The Right was that parliamentarism was on the retreat globally. The court retained its influence over foreign policy, and the conservative civil service, which prepared and implemented every law and decision, would not let through any radical break with the past. Bureaucracy was another feature that was common to Prussia, Sweden and Finland and an object of constant complaint by the left in all of these countries. All in all, this pragmatic Swedish-style introduction of parliamentary government without any change in the constitution was facilitated by the flexibility of the Instrument of Government of 1809: no changes in it were needed even though the actual functioning of the political system changed so dramatically.[1216] This flexibility enabled a peaceful transition to a parliamentary government that offered an alternative to the German and Finnish confrontations.

Decisive for the Swedish transition to parliamentarism was also the fact that the parties of the left had become ready to cooperate and govern the country together; the Social Democrats accepting the so-called 'minister socialism' and cooperation with the bourgeoisie, to a greater extent than their German comrades and a lot like the British Labour Party. The parliamentary discourse used by the government parties on questions of democracy and parliamentarisation had already become mutually supportive, as the analysis in section 3.3 has demonstrated. A coalition government of the Social Democrats and Liberals, led by Nils Edén, was nominated on 19 October 1917. The Social Democrat leader Hjalmar Branting and three of his party fellows were appointed as ministers, though Branting resigned

---

1216 Gerdner 1946, ix, 12–15; Nyman 1965, 159–62; von Sydow 1997, 116–17; Molin 1992, xxi–ii; Olsson 2000, 88, 99–100, 110, 114; Nilsson 2004, 145.

as Minister of Finance in January 1918. The rise of the Social Democrats to participate in a functioning majority government for the first time in Sweden (though not in the world, given the Russian and Finnish precedents in spring 1917 and the fact that the Labour Party had been represented in the British War Coalition) was a major political shift, and it led the party to view its chances of changing society by parliamentary means very optimistically and distanced the Swedish Social Democratic Labour Party further from the kind of direct action advocated by the far left.[1217] This was clearly a revisionist party cooperating with relatively a radical Liberal party, something that its German sister party had failed to do as effectively, and which its Finnish sister party did not even consider after failing to introduce a form of parliamentary rule that was to its liking.

Parliamentarisation, after a lengthy argument on parliamentary responsibility that had brought the coalition partners closer to each other, together with a clear election result, had a more promising start in Sweden than in Finland, where the coalition partners in the all-party government had not been fully committed to cooperation: the Social Democrats demurred for ideological reasons and strife within the government became overt in connection with the Power Act, with the result that the Social Democrats left the ministry in early September and began to adopt extra-parliamentary tactics. Parliamentarisation proceeded in Sweden also because most ministers were members of parliament and could defend the government's proposals in the debates. Further democratisation was promised: disregarding the expected opposition in the upper house, the ministry pledged itself to introduce a proposal granting equal suffrage to all tax-payers in local elections and hence universal suffrage in national elections as well. The King agreed to rely on his ministers and not use any extra-parliamentary measures to prevent the planned reform.[1218]

Despite these high expectations, the debates would continue to be heated in spring 1918, at a time when a German victory in the war still seemed possible and there were hence no guarantees for the expected dawn of an era of democracy and parliamentarism, which could be stigmatised as a mere leftist fantasies. A decisive turn in the course of the First World War would be needed before the reform would be realised in Sweden; even then the Swedish right would remain patently reluctant and need considerable time to rethink its suspicious attitudes to the democracy and parliamentarism that was being championed by the left.

At the same time, the Swedish debates on constitutional issues would seem to have become more internally oriented than had been the case in spring, when hopes for a global revolution had taken over. The German promises for a peaceful revolution through the parliamentarisation of government and the democratisation of the Prussian suffrage system, which had been discussed briefly in the rightist and extensively in the Social Democratic press, withered away after July, *Social-Demokraten* concluding

---

1217 Nyman 1965, 154–6, 164–7.
1218 von Sydow 1997, 116–17; Andræ 1998, 243; Olsson 2000, 88.

that 'bureaucracy' had prevailed in Germany.[1219] There was not much news about the British reform, either. The Bolshevik Revolution in early November 1917 tended to be overshadowed by the domestic upheaval caused by the nomination of a leftist government. Only the far left was openly enthusiastic about the Revolution, while the Majority Social Democrats distanced themselves further from developments in Russia. Most Swedes presumed that what had happened in Petrograd was no more than a temporary coup and rejected all revolutionary action of the Bolshevik kind. However, the rightist press became increasingly alarmed about the situation in Finland,[1220] where constitutional and ideological confrontations between the Social Democrats and the bourgeoisie were getting out of hand after parliament had 'proclaimed the independence of the country' in July and now a revolution imported from Russia appeared as a real possibility due to a socialist parliamentary majority that was seeking Bolshevik support.[1221] The common constitutional tradition of the two countries seemed to be under serious threat in Finland, and there was no full certainty that a similar deterioration of the established order might not spread into Sweden as well.

4.4 Finland: Discursive struggles over democracy and parliamentarism turn into an attempted revolution

4.4.1 THE BOLSHEVIK REVOLUTION AND THE QUESTIONED LEGITIMACY OF FINLAND'S DISPUTATIOUS NEW PARLIAMENT

The approval of a law on parliamentary sovereignty by the votes of the Social Democrats and the centre parties in the Finnish parliament on 18 July 1917 openly challenged the Russian Provisional Government. In response, the Provisional Government ordered new elections, something to which the Finnish bourgeois parties also contributed.

The crisis that followed has been summarised by Esko Ketola and Hannu Soikkanen: The Social Democrats consequently resigned from the all-party government in September, leaving a bourgeois minority government to run Finland in the midst of a deepening crisis of subsistence, order, trust and legitimacy. They started to openly oppose the Provisional Government and the Finnish bourgeois government and the application of the current Parliament Act at all levels. Kullervo Manner, the Speaker of the dissolved parliament (in which there had been a Social Democratic majority), convened this assembly a few times in early autumn. At first only a few and later no bourgeois MPs attended, and extra-parliamentary demonstrations reinforced this opposition, but the Social Democratic parliamentary group nevertheless decided on 28 September that this old 'parliament' would enact

---

1219 *Aftonbladet*, 7 July 1917, 11 July 1917, 12 July 1917 and 'Krisen i Tyskland avveklas i samförstånds tecken', 13 July 1917; *Social-Demokraten*, 12 July 1917, 13 July 1917.
1220 Andræ 1998, 13; Olsson 2000, 110.
1221 *Aftonbladet*, 20 July 1917.

the Power Act and the reform laws demanded by the Social Democratic Party. This was done in a meeting that was declared to be legal on the argument that the dissolution of the old parliament had, according to the Social Democratic interpretation, been illegal. Such procedural practices denied the authority of any other parliament than one with a Social Democratic majority. The party took a Social Democratic majority among the people as self-evident and expected a victory in the new election, declaring it to be 'the election of revolutionary democracy'. It showed no readiness to surrender its parliamentary majority to the non-socialists by boycotting the election; nor was it willing to fully reject parliament as a political forum and let the parliament of the streets take over the political process. Parliamentarism was rather depreciated through the above-mentioned practices and the compilation of a list of candidates with anti-parliamentary views.[1222]

In the meantime, Vladimir Lenin was hiding in Helsinki in the home of MP Evert Huttunen, who was later accused by the right of being a Bolshevik emissary,[1223] and there he met Otto Wille Kuusinen, Kullervo Manner and K. H. Wiik, among others – all opponents of bourgeois democracy and Western parliamentarism. Lenin himself was by this time about to abandon cooperation with the moderate socialists and to opt for a Bolshevik take-over. He viewed revolutions in Russia and Finland as inseparable and pointed this out to the Finnish socialists. The Finns knew that a Bolshevik coup was coming and were encouraged by Lenin and other revolutionary visitors from Petrograd to prepare for a takeover by a revolutionary democracy. Kuusinen became the most prominent of the revolutionaries dedicated to Lenin's goals, though he and his comrades remained hesitant about proceeding – until the Social Democrats lost their parliamentary majority in the election of 1–2 October. The message of the non-socialist parties, whose campaign had emphasised the risks of the Social Democrats usurping supreme power, had got through to the majority of the voters. A bourgeois government based on the new parliamentary majority was appointed, an action that accelerated the fall of parliamentary legitimacy in the eyes of the Social Democrats. While the party had previously considered parliamentary elections and work in the parliament to be a temporary means to advance the class struggle and revolution, its leaders now declared the elections and the new parliament illegal. The new parliament met on 1 November nevertheless, and the MPs, who disagreed on the legitimacy of the institution, set out to solve the deepening constitutional and socio-economic crisis[1224]. An emerging solution to the relationship between Finland and Russia was rejected by the

---

1222 Soikkanen 1975, 236; Ketola 1987, 333–4, 340.
1223 *Hufvudstadsbladet*, 'Från kammare och kuloar', 10 November 1917.
1224 The economic situation was rapidly deteriorating with increasing unemployment arising from the lack of Russian orders and construction work as well as a currency crisis and rising inflation. In this state of shortages and unemployment, the streets of Helsinki tended to become even more politicised than they had been in spring. The situation was particularly acerbated by cases of hoarding foodstuffs. Nyström 2013, 153, 164–6, 181.

Finnish Social Democrats, and the agreement was not ratified in Petrograd by the Bolsheviks, who assumed power on 7 November.[1225]

The Bolshevik Revolution upset the constitutional situation in Finland completely, making the supporters of various parties change their views on independence. While the Social Democrats had been willing to proceed to the full sovereignty of the Finnish parliament under the Provisional Government, after the Bolshevik takeover in Petrograd it was now the bourgeois parties that sought immediate full independence. The latter found a formal justification in paragraph 38 of the Gustavian Instrument of Government of 1772, according to which the Riksdag was legally authorised to elect a new holder of supreme power in case the royal family should cease to exist. The Social Democrats – unable to accept the election result as reflective of public opinion – insisted on recalling the previous parliament in which they had held a majority. They also called for the election of a national constituent assembly (an idea that emphasised the Russian-like revolutionary nature of the situation) and aimed at independence on the basis of a declaration issued by the Bolshevik government. The bourgeois parties rejected such contacts with Lenin and looked rather to Germany to provide possible support for a unilateral declaration of independence, an independent Finland being a desirable option for Germany with regard to the ongoing war in the east. On 15 November, the bourgeois majority of the Finnish parliament declared itself the holder of supreme power, and on 27 November a bourgeois senate aiming at international recognition of the country's independence was nominated. On 4 December, a proposal for a republican constitution was put before the parliament simultaneously with the publication of a declaration of independence. In a vote on 6 December (which was later chosen as Independence Day), on the declaration, the parliament was divided between the bourgeois parties, who were ready for a unilateral declaration, and the Social Democrats, who proposed the establishment of a Fenno-Russian committee to negotiate about independence. Before Sweden or Germany or any of the Entente powers recognised Finnish independence, however, recognition from the Bolshevik government was needed. This was received on 31 December 1917 from Lenin, who assumed that the Finnish workers, who had insisted on their desire for independence and their dedication to the class struggle, would make a revolution, provide the Swedish socialists with a model and finally reunite with Bolshevik Russia. French, Swedish and German recognitions were consequently received, but Britain and the United States refrained from recognising Finland owing to its pro-German line and their expectations of the rise of a new non-Bolshevist Russian government, whose stand on Finnish independence might be negative.[1226]

1225 Lindman 1935, 14; Soikkanen 1975, 235; Kirby 1976, 105–6; Rinta-Tassi 1986, 31; Polvinen 1987, vol. 1, 106; Ketola 1987, 335–8, 340, 344; Haapala 1995, 240; Sihvonen 1997, 3; Jussila, Hentilä & Nevakivi 1999, 98; Wade 2000, 222, 225; Vares 2006, 71, 74; Nyström 2013, 140.
1226 Polvinen 1987, vol. 1, 192–5; Ketola 1987, 351, 368; Sihvonen 1997, 4–6; Jussila, Hentilä & Nevakivi 1999, 101–106.

Researchers have generally agreed on this course of events but have had difficulties to explain why the widely shared goal of Finnish independence ended up with the deterioration of mutual trust and an internal confrontation by November 1917. There is no simple explanation. Turning to the dynamics of parliamentary debate and related discourses in the press we see the impact of the complex international situation on definitions of democracy, the political role of the people and parliamentarism in late autumn of 1917. With several alternative models and allies available the debate tended to become transnational to an exceptional degree. The MPs understood that the Finns were not deciding about their future constitution in a vacuum but in a context in which the choices that were made would have concrete implications for the immediate future of the country, including its foreign policy.

4.4.2 Reforms to be implemented by a national parliament or by an international revolution?

The preparations for independence were characterised on both sides by accusations of transnational connections of the worst kind. In Social Democratic discourse, the word 'revolution' appeared with increasing frequency and tended to be associated with the potential use of force for taking over power. This was especially true of the Red Guards, who were motivated by the example of, and contacts with, the Bolsheviks and by Lenin's exhortation to launch a revolution. The leaders of the party, however, worried about the consequences of such an attempt. Risto Alapuro has argued that the party leadership did not aim at a popular rising but called for a revolution only to intimidate the bourgeoisie into agreeing to the Power Act and invalidating the election of the autumn.[1227] However, its violent rhetoric inside and outside the parliament also opened possibilities for the use of violence in the deepening political confrontation.

Suggestions of an alliance between counterrevolutionary forces in Finland and Russia or in Finland and Germany (Prussia) against democracy became commonplace in Social Democratic parliamentary speeches.[1228] They found background support, for instance, from the fact that some professors of law in Berlin took a stand in favour of Finnish independence,[1229] and by 5 December it was known that Germany had decided to send troops to Finland.[1230] K. H. Wiik, who had visited Germany and met Finnish activists there, protested against this development by talking about Germany as 'an object of the admiration of our bourgeois class' and as a country in which 'the

---

1227 Rinta-Tassi 1986, 52–3; Alapuro 2003, 540–1.
1228 See VP, Jaakko Mäki, 8 November 1917, 15; Edvard Hänninen-Walpas, 10 November 1917, 64, 82; Jussi Kujala, 15 November 1917, 139; Eetu Salin, 24 November 1917, 187–9; Oskari Tokoi, 26 November 1917, 199; Jussi Vuoristo, 26 November 1917, 219; Jussi Kujala, 26 November 1917, 257; Yrjö Sirola, 9 January 1918, 824.
1229 *The Times*, 'Berlin Professors on Finland's Status', 6 December 1917.
1230 Ketola 1987, 395. This had been discussed by Finnish activists on 26 November. Hentilä & Hentilä 2016, 23.

state power and militarism have enchained civil liberty and free thinking'.[1231] In response, bourgeois MPs pointed at cooperation between the Finnish socialists and the Bolsheviks.[1232] Such accusations on both sides of the ideological divide added to the deteriorating legitimacy of parliamentary government: parliamentary deliberation at the national level appeared to have been replaced by transnational plotting with external forces. What made things worse was that competing transnational connections were indeed being actively maintained on both sides, and their influence in the constitutional debates was obvious.

In the immediate aftermath of the October Revolution, the Finnish Social Democratic Party published a parliamentary declaration uniting the party with 'the Social Democratic parties of various countries that were engaged in the class struggle and supported the international brotherhood of the workers'. The emphasis on the class struggle in the declaration alienated the party from the Western revisionists and their alternative internationalism. It implied joining a global revolution as 'the brotherhood' stood for 'the unwavering class struggle of comrades in Russia who are heroically advancing the cause of the Russian Revolution and thereby of all oppressed people and the cause of liberating the workers of all countries'.[1233] A telegram was sent to Petrograd stating that 'the Finnish democracy' was ready to fight with 'the Russian democracy' against 'the bourgeoisie'.[1234] When the line of the party was being discussed, K. H. Wiik, for one, had worried about the Bolsheviks forcing the Finnish Social Democrats into a revolution against their will, regardless of their own success in Russia.[1235] However, despite such dissent, the party decided on 8 November (one day after the Bolshevik takeover and on the day of the following debate in the Finnish parliament) to opt for a revolution. The hesitation and reluctance of some members is reflected by a double strategy of working both inside and outside the parliament.[1236]

On 8 November, *Työmies* declared that 'the bells of the Revolution are ringing', summoning the workers to fight against repression, reaction and bourgeois plans for a coup;[1237] on the following day it accused the bourgeois parties of conspiring against the Power Act and the Finnish people and called for the removal of bourgeois politicians from power.[1238] Oskari Tokoi,

1231 VP, Karl Harald Wiik, 7 December 1917, 419. Such suggestions had already appeared in summer 1917. Ketola 1987, 164; Rudolf Nadolny of the German Foreign Ministry and Ernst von Hülsen of the German General Staff had negotiated with three Finns on possible German support for Finnish independence on 18 November 1917. Biewer 1994.
1232 VP, Oswald Kairamo (Finnish), 24 November 1917, 185; Annie Furuhjelm (Swedish), 24 November 1917, 192.
1233 VP, Jaakko Mäki, 8 November 1917, 17.
1234 *Hufvudstadbladet*, 'Finska socialdemokratin och den nya ryska revolutionen', 10 November 1917.
1235 Lindman 1968, 177; Upton 1980, 269–73; Rinta-Tassi 1986, 50; Kettunen 1986, 96; Haapala 1995, 240.
1236 Rinta-Tassi 1986, 53.
1237 *Työmies*, 'Suomen työwäelle! Walweille! Woimat kokoon!', 8 November 1917.
1238 *Työmies*, 'Riippumattomuus Suomen kansalle waiko riippumattomuus Suomen kansasta', 9 November 1917.

the former prime minister, described the state of the Russian Revolution in the plenary session, reporting that the Provisional Government had resigned 'as a response to the will of the revolutionary Russian people' and that the revolution was continuing and affecting Finland more concretely than before. Tokoi went on to claim that the Social Democrats alone represented the will of the people and to question the legitimacy and future of the bourgeois institutions:[1239]

> We are in the middle of a vortex of revolution and, therefore, in a revolutionary age, one needs to listen more closely than at other times to the voice of the people, more carefully than at another time take into account those opinions, the demands which the people impose on the parliament and more particularly on the government, as the future of the ruling institutions is nowadays very uncertain.

The Social Democrats were trying to force the bourgeois parliamentary majority into concessions with threats of extra-parliamentary action: in the new situation, the bourgeoisie could no longer count on the continued existence of their representative institution. The Social Democrats had already partly joined the Bolsheviks discursively during the previous Bolshevik attempted coup in July 1917; now they adopted revolutionary discourse with increasing confidence in the inevitability of the ongoing revolution. Tokoi's speech was generally interpreted as revolutionary and inspired by the events in Petrograd.[1240] It contained seemingly moderate calls for governmental and parliamentary observation of the will of the people. However, he also demanded the promulgation of the Power Act, which had been passed under his government and was emphasised in the Social Democratic election campaign,[1241] and he threatened revolution and civil war in case the current parliament should fail to do this. Within the party, he had already broached the possibility of extra-parliamentary measures in October.[1242] Now he asked whether 'we want it [the Russian Revolution] to roll in here, covering and possibly drowning us?' and answered 'No!', suggesting that a parliamentary majority would still be able to save the country from a revolution by adopting the reforms demanded by the Social Democrats.[1243]

Yrjö Sirola, who had taken part in the general strike of 1905, translated the writings of Karl Kautsky (but now had evidently renounced Western social democracy[1244]), been active in the radical labour movement of American Finns, admired the Bolshevik revolutionaries, belonged to the radical majority of the party committee, and had been elected secretary of the revolutionary committee on the same day, was even more explicit about

---

1239 VP, Oskari Tokoi, 8 November 1917, 19–20.
1240 *Hufvudstadbladet*, 'Från kammare och kuloar', 9 November 1917.
1241 Soikkanen 1975, 239; Alapuro 1988, 161.
1242 Rinta-Tassi 1986, 22; Ketola 1987, 343.
1243 VP, 8 November 1917, 20.
1244 *Hufvudstadbladet*, 'Från kammare och kuloar', 9 November 1917.

the consequences of this 'third revolution' affecting the Finns. According to Sirola, the revolutionary situation must have been 'a very unpleasant surprise' to the bourgeois majority in 'this meeting'[1245] – an expression that questioned the legitimacy of the Finnish parliament, especially when it came from a member of the committee that had prepared the parliamentary reform of 1906. The representatives of the bourgeois parties, by contrast, did not share the claim that the revolution had now reached Finland.[1246]

On 10 November 1917, three days after the Bolshevik Revolution and a week before the first decision on an active revolution was made by the Social Democratic Party, Finnish socialists celebrated the progress of an international revolution. Yrjö Mäkelin (a former chair of the Constitutional Committee) outspokenly put revolution above parliamentarism. Yrjö Sirola encouraged the Parliament of the Workers (another alternative parliament) to call for a revolution.[1247] Oskari Tokoi brought this radicalisation up in a plenary session, warning the parliament once again that the bourgeois parliament would be bypassed should it not immediately join the cause of the revolution. The bourgeoisie should[1248]

> listen to the bells of revolution which are currently ringing in large parts of Europe, those bells of revolution which ring in Russia and which will without a doubt be echoing throughout the known world and whose tolling will awaken the Finnish workers. And it is possible that it will not take a long time, if the parliament treats the opinions that inspire the Finnish people in this way before the people themselves take the lead and determine their own fate independently of what the parliament decides.

The Finnish Social Democratic Party continued to regard itself as the sole representative of the people (like in one-sided Russian revolutionary conceptualisations) and overtly adopted the revolutionary cause, demanding that the reluctant non-socialist parties do the same. Otherwise extra-parliamentary action challenging the representative institution would follow and would inevitably lead to a civil war. Such language in the circumstances of the day was denounced in the bourgeois papers.[1249]

According to David Kirby, Otto Wille Kuusinen who, like Yrjö Sirola, was familiar with Lenin's writings (and there were not many such men among the Finnish Social Democrats), had adopted a revolutionary attitude and accused the rest of the party of revisionism.[1250] Now he told the parliament that 'a European proletarian revolution' was likely to follow but depended on the progress 'in Russia, Germany, France, England'; without an international proletarian revolution of this kind no such revolution would

---

1245 VP, Yrjö Sirola, 8 November 1917, 24; Rinta-Tassi 1986, 56.
1246 Professors Rabbe Axel and Ernst Estlander of the Swedish Party, VP, 8 November 1917, 29, 33.
1247 Soikkanen 1975, 243, 246.
1248 VP, Oskari Tokoi, 9 November 1917, 54.
1249 *Helsingin Sanomat*, 'Hallituskysymyksen ratkaisu', 10 November 1917.
1250 Kirby 1976, 109.

follow in Finland either.¹²⁵¹ This reflected a certain (calculated) hesitation on his part. Lenin, who had left Finland two weeks previously and whom Sirola would meet again in two days' time, believed that Germany was now ripe for revolution.¹²⁵² Kuusinen said he hoped that 'the red flame' ignited by the Bolshevik Revolution would be extended to Germany and consequently become 'a general European fire', but he was not so certain about the British or French post-war revolutions turning proletarian. Nevertheless, the Finnish bourgeoisie should prepare for anarchy and the burning of estates as a reaction to their 'rule of terror' and not from any socialist agitation.¹²⁵³ This was, in the circumstances of November 1917, no less than a threat of civil war of the Bolshevist type presented in a parliamentary debate about supreme power – days before the Social Democrats' decision to start a revolution and two and half months before the actual Red uprising. For the Social Democrats, a revolution had become inevitable, but its timing remained linked to the progress of a pan-European, even global revolution. At the same time, a bourgeois reaction might be that similar threat-filled language had been heard so many times before that this was really nothing new.¹²⁵⁴ Uncompromising views on both sides deepened the confrontation.

An MP called Erkki Härmä made a Marxist point in universalist terms: The bourgeoisie had learned from previous revolutions how all victories by the working class could be overturned by introducing oligarchic forms of government; they had done so during the French Revolution and again after the victories of the Russian and Finnish workers in 1905. This tactic had also been used in 1917: the reforms in favour of the workers introduced by the majority of the Finnish parliament had been nullified by the Finnish bourgeoisie in cooperation with reactionary forces from Russia.¹²⁵⁵ This implied that the Finnish bourgeoisie was 'counterrevolutionary' in a universal sense, which caused Härmä to use references going all the way back to the French Revolution: they were trying to introduce 'a Directory' and making a coup just like the counterrevolutionaries in 1795 when nominating regents.¹²⁵⁶ The Marxist conclusion was that only a proletarian revolution would bring an end to these repeated bourgeois plots – that history demanded a revolution to stop the Finnish bourgeoisie. Such suggestions

---

1251 10 November 1917, 56; The Revolutionary Council in Helsinki, founded on 8–9 November 1917, though not aiming at an immediate revolution, had decided in favour of taking over power earlier on the same day under pressure from the Russian revolutionaries. Lindman 1968, 176–7; Ketola 1987, 356; cf. Kirby 1976, 110, and Rinta-Tassi 1986, 55, on Otto Wille Kuusinen's doubts in late October and throughout November; Upton 1980, 275; Ehrnrooth 1992, 185, 268. The council's readiness was encouraged by the ease with which the Bolshevik coup had been carried out in Petrograd three days earlier. Wade 2000, 233.
1252 Ketola 1987, 361; Wade 2000, 223.
1253 VP, Otto Wille Kuusinen, 10 November 1917, 56.
1254 *Hufvudstadsbladet*, 'Från kammare och kuloar', 20 November 1917 (dated 11 November).
1255 VP, Erkki Härmä, 10 November 1917, 73.
1256 VP, Erkki Härmä, 10 November 1917, 73; Herman Hurmevaara explicitly declared the government's proposal to be a 'counterrevolutionary attempt'. VP, 10 November 1917, 85.

of an unavoidable revolution at the beginning of the new parliament also corroded trust in parliamentary solutions among members of the centre and the right, and they began to prepare for the use of extra-parliamentary force themselves through the Civil Guards (White Guards).

More threats followed: according to Edvard Hänninen-Walpas, ever since 1905 the Finnish workers had hoped for a new revolution in Russia as a way to create a truly democratic parliament in Finland. This expectation had prevented them from themselves engaging in 'bloody revolutions, which have been seen in times of transition in almost all countries'.[1257] The implication was that if no democratic parliament in a Social Democratic sense were established, a domestic revolution was to be expected. This denied the democratic stature of the current parliament. Hänninen-Walpas interpreted the election of regents as proposed by the bourgeois government as a further demonstration by the bourgeoisie that[1258]

> it is possible to introduce reforms that are beneficial to deep layers [of the people] only through extra-parliamentary action, that they need to be realised through outright revolutionary action. In my view, the current proposal is such a declaration of war on the Finnish workers and the Finnish people; it is an oligarchic declaration of war against democracy.

In Social Democratic parliamentary discourse, in which revisionist supporters of parliamentary methods played no role (if indeed any had been elected since such candidates had been excluded from the lists), extra-parliamentary and revolutionary action on behalf of 'democracy' appeared not only as possible but as inevitable, and the full blame for a possible revolution was laid at the feet of the bourgeoisie: they themselves had already declared a revolution and a civil war through their actions. The radicalisation – indeed what appeared as the Leninisation[1259] – of Finnish Social Democratic discourse and its insistence on the impossibility of compromises left few options open other than turning from violent rhetoric to the actual use of violence. These discursive transfers have not been sufficiently considered in previous analyses of Finnish Social Democracy and the progress to a civil war in 1917.

The bourgeois parliamentary groups rejected Social Democratic claims that the war and the Russian Revolution should determine the course of Finnish politics. Some of the Agrarians recognised that the Russian Revolution affected Finland but warned the socialists against involving themselves in it. Santeri Alkio, who tried to resolve the dispute over the adoption of the Power Act but failed to receive Social Democratic support,[1260] emphasised the fact that the current Finnish parliament was the representative of the Finnish people, the mirror of its divisions and

---

1257 VP, Edvard Hänninen-Walpas, 10 November 1917, 62.
1258 VP, Edvard Hänninen-Walpas, 10 November 1917, 82–3.
1259 Winkler 1999, 4; Cf. especially Alapuro's claim that the Bolsheviks had little influence on the Finnish Social Democrats. Alapuro 1988, 167.
1260 Rinta-Tassi 1986, 51.

responsible for solving the problems of the country through reforms carried out in cooperation. The Social Democrats should therefore not proceed 'selfishly out of revolutionary principles' as that would not lead to a 'class victory' but to a 'national disaster'.[1261] Socialist demands for convening a constituent assembly, in particular, constituted an illegal and revolutionary challenge to the legitimate parliament.[1262] Mikko Luopajärvi urged the left and the right to cooperate in adopting reforms that would pacify class struggles and prevent 'revolutionary tempests'; otherwise the one-sided extra-parliamentary agitation of hatred between groups of people on the one hand and the obstruction of reforms on the other would result in anarchy and suffering for the whole nation.[1263] Artur Wuorimaa defended the current parliament against the Social Democrats' claims by arguing that it had been elected by the Finnish people 'in an atmosphere of revolution' to decide on a new constitution for the country.[1264] According to Antti Juutilainen, on the other hand, the looming threat of a revolution justified the establishment of the Civil Guards.[1265]

By mid-November, most bourgeois members shared Gustaf Arokallio's (Young Finns) conclusion that independence was the only way 'out of the chaos into which the world war in the form of Russian anarchy is about to cast us'.[1266] Santeri Alkio characterised the situation of Finland as revolutionary but in a way that facilitated a declaration of national independence:[1267]

> We are now in a new revolutionary situation. In connection with this revolution there has appeared a chance for Finland, too, to implement such a revolutionary measure as will enable it to take into its own hands that power which is currently free and available for us to take. . . . [T]his does not constitute any revolution against a legal government.

While giving supreme power to the Finnish parliament did not constitute any political or social revolution, the use of power by the new government would be 'revolutionary' in the sense that it would need to create something completely new in the history of the Finnish state.[1268] Alkio was redescribing revolution in order to legitimate non-socialist constitutional policies towards independence.

On the following day, 16 November, the party committee of the Social Democrats decided to initiate a revolution, only to immediately revoke that decision. However, a revolution increasingly appeared as the only option for Social Democrat MPs. As Kuusinen's speech indicated, there had been a lot of obscurity in the use of the concept 'revolution' in Social Democratic discourse: on the one hand, it had suggested that a 'revolutionary road' might

---

1261 VP, Santeri Alkio, 8 November 1917, 23.
1262 VP, 15 November 1917, 124–5.
1263 VP, Mikko Luopajärvi, 10 November 1917, 78.
1264 VP, Artur Wuorimaa, 10 November 1917, 60.
1265 VP, Antti Juutilainen, 8 November 1917, 36.
1266 VP, Gustaf Arokallio, 15 November 1917, 130.
1267 VP, Santeri Alkio, 15 November 1917, 135.
1268 VP, Santeri Alkio, 15 November 1917, 136.

be opened by a general strike declared by the Revolutionary Central Council of the Workers; on the other, it had claimed that a revolution in Finland alone was not possible and that the proposed general strike constituted no more than an ordered action of the masses.[1269] Some radicals supported joining the Russian Revolution when the moment seemed right in order that a dictatorship of the proletariat might be created.[1270]

One day after the start of the general strike, which led to a revolutionary situation with Workers' Guards taking control of several towns and trying to force the parliament to pass laws on an eight-hour day and universal communal suffrage, the bourgeois majority put forward a proposal that aimed at transferring sovereignty to the parliament.[1271] This caused the Social Democrats to adopt an increasingly radical revolutionary discourse. Jussi Kujala declared: 'Only the victory of the working class, which is an historical necessity and which will one day become a reality, will secure real liberty and happiness for Finland, too.'[1272] For this agitator, a revolution was coming no matter what the bourgeois parliamentary majority did. After the strike, Eetu Salin – another radical speaker, who had become a socialist in Germany and Sweden but had turned to militancy during the Revolution of 1905 and emigrated to the United States – interpreted the constitutional dispute in deterministic Marxist terms of the class struggle as being about to turn to a civil war: when 'the last social class comes to power and when there are now arms in the hands of this class, I will not wonder if it, too, uses them to achieve its goals – to achieve its constitutional goals – as all other historical classes have done and still do.'[1273] The Finnish bourgeoisie was to blame for the mounting support for a revolution, and the Social Democrats were unable to contain those forces.[1274] In Salin's thinking, which was expressed in nearly biblical terms, the world war had led capitalism to the day of final reckoning, and the Finnish battle had become an aspect of a struggle between awesome global forces – 'the last fight' between classes described in the words of *The International*. Since this class struggle had been taken to the extreme, it was no longer possible for Finns to agree in their parliament on how to reconstruct their polity, particularly as the representatives of the people on the two sides were, according to Salin, no longer allowed even to greet each other.[1275] The replacement of unproductive parliamentary methods with an openly revolutionary class struggle appeared as inevitable in this agitator's language, which was in no way modified

---

1269 Upton 1980, 276–7; Alapuro 2003, 541.
1270 Kirby 1986b, 200; Rinta-Tassi 1986, 50. Sirola, Kuusinen, Manner and Salin supported the revolution, while Mäkelin, Vuoristo and Airola preferred to continue the class struggle by putting pressure on the parliament.
1271 Kirby 1986, 150; Alapuro has argued that the Bolshevik Revolution had no big influence on the Finnish Social Democrats, whose leaders in mid-November 1917 wished to prevent the general strike from turning into a socialist revolution by emphasising political and social reforms. Alapuro 1988, 167–9; Alapuro 2003, 541.
1272 VP, Jussi Kujala, 15 November 1917, 140.
1273 VP, Eetu Salin, 24 November 1917, 188.
1274 VP, Eetu Salin, 24 November 1917, 189.
1275 VP, Eetu Salin, 24 November 1917, 190.

for the parliamentary audience; it was addressed to the audience outside. Radical Marxist discourse in the parliament and press had also begun to be implemented in extra-parliamentary action. This was the impression shared (and readily overinterpreted) by the bourgeois members of parliament.

From the point of view of rightist MPs, it was evident that the Social Democrats were under the influence of 'revolutionary intoxication' and ready to give up the ballot and parliament for methods that ignored the conventions of the Finnish polity. According to Oswald Kairamo (Finnish Party), the socialists wished to make Finnish politics dependent on 'the erratic upheavals of the political life of St Petersburg'.[1276] They had allied themselves with the Bolsheviks, opting for unbounded claims of class interest and the rejection of legal and parliamentary means of advancing their cause,[1277] the implication being that the bourgeoisie might be forced to do the same. Annie Furuhjelm (Swedish People's Party) could not understand how revolution could be propounded in a country that already had universal suffrage, freedom of association and liberty of the press and which provided full possibilities to achieve one's goals by parliamentary means. Why was the Finnish Social Democratic Party looking for support from the Bolsheviks, whom even the leftist socialists in Russia did not recognise? Social Democrat women at least should, according to this activist for women's rights, oppose violent methods and support the restoration of a constitutional and parliamentary line in the party.[1278] But this fight clearly was not a gender issue, and women MPs were not able to save the country from a civil war, as David Norman in Sweden would later ironically point out.

The centre was equally concerned about Social Democratic discourse and acts of violence initiated by 'the so-called revolutionary committee', in which Social Democrat parliamentarians were involved.[1279] The boundary between parliamentary debate and engagement in the initiation of extra-parliamentary violence had been crossed, which proved to many that the Social Democrats had abandoned democracy and parliamentarism in favour of violence. Antti Mikkola (Young Finns), a lawyer who was the founder of the Turku newspaper *Turun Sanomat* and Chairman of the Legal Affairs Committee, doubted whether the French revolutionary principles of liberty, equality and fraternity had any hope of being realised as a result of the violent acts of the Social Democratic Red Guards and proposed the creation of an organised military force as a response.[1280] While Agrarians such as Kalle Lohi saw the socialist agitation of class hatred as stemming from the real grievances of the people,[1281] Santeri Alkio concluded that the Finnish

1276 VP, Oswald Kairamo, 24 November 1917, 185.
1277 VP, Oswald Kairamo, 24 November 1917, 185. This was an old suggestion that had already appeared in the election platform of the Finnish Party in 1907.
1278 VP, Annie Furuhjelm, 24 November 1917, 192.
1279 VP, Antti Juutilainen, 24 November 1917, 192–3.
1280 VP, Antti Mikkola, 26 November 1917, 237. On bourgeois press debates about the deterioration of public order, see Nyström 2013, 173. Mikkola himself would be shot by the Reds Guards in Helsinki on 1 February 1918.
1281 VP, Kalle Lohi, 26 November 1917, 238.

socialists were imitating the worst aspects of Bolshevism.[1282] MPs from the bourgeois parties, including the most fervent defenders of democracy and parliamentarism, were already giving up any hope of solving the crisis by parliamentary means. As Hannu Soikkanen has pointed out, each of the two blocs believed in its one-sided and ideologically coloured interpretations of the situation. These interpretations, which were constantly reinforced in the parliament and in press discussions, supported the escalation of the crisis as new incidents occurred.[1283] However, the origin of the crisis can be found in the challenge to parliamentarism in the one-sided discourse that the parliamentary Finnish Social Democratic Party was fostering, sometimes openly, sometimes disguised under the rhetoric of democracy, and that sounded like Bolshevism, and not so much in its legalistic defences.

Despite the tendency of the Social Democratic parliamentary group to borrow the parlance of the radicalised Russian Revolution, views among them about the chances for an actual revolution continued to vary. In the party convention of 25–27 November 1917, the majority still voted in favour of parliamentary means,[1284] even though the example of the Petrograd Pre-Parliament suggested the futility of parliamentary debate as opposed to an armed take-over.[1285] According to David Kirby and Juha Siltala and others, this indecisive compromise, which was intended to keep the radicals within the party (and to avoid a division seen in Sweden and Germany), actually led to a situation in which the more Kautskyist moderates, who were sceptical of violent revolution, increasingly associated themselves with the views of the radicals. At the same time, the drift towards violence continued at the local level, with the Red Guards supplementing and even replacing what they regarded as unproductive parliamentary methods. This had led the rightist press[1286] to conclude that the party planned to use mass violence against the parliament. The moderates did not actively oppose plans for a violent coup in the name of defending the workers against a bourgeois 'counter-revolution', and this in practice opened the way for a decision to launch a revolution in January 1918 in the face of fears that rightist armed activists would make a coup. Many Social Democrats would be driven into a civil war in the belief that it was just another means of putting pressure on the bourgeoisie. The majority of the workers thus joined the revolution, and once the revolutionary process had started, it tended to become increasingly radical, turning into a proletarian revolution, as moderates either resigned or associated themselves with the increasingly violent measures.[1287]

1282 VP, Santeri Alkio, 9 January 1918, 827.
1283 Soikkanen (ed.) 1967.
1284 Upton 1980, 284, 330.
1285 Wade 2000, 234.
1286 *Hufvudstadsbladet*, 'Från kammare och kuloar', 11 November 1917.
1287 Kirby 1986, 151; cf. Kirby's previous interpretation of external pressures such as the economic crisis and political confrontations leading to a rising by reluctant socialist leaders. This interpretation bypasses the role of discourse in the political process. Kirby 1976, 100, 106–107; Rinta-Tassi 1986, 499, 501; Polvinen 1987, vol. 1, 129, 203; Siltala 2009, 525–7; Nyström 2013, 220.

The views of the supposedly moderate majority within the Social Democratic Party were not heard in the parliamentary plenaries. The extremist language used by the speakers of the party, even if intended only to intimidate the bourgeoisie, inevitably contributed to the development towards a civil war. The description of Oskari Tokoi, the former prime minister, of the state of affairs on 26 November provides an illustrative example. According to Tokoi, the different classes of the Finnish people had been agitated into a violent struggle against each other by bourgeois opposition to reforms. This radicalisation could no longer be stopped by Social Democratic attempts to placate the workers and persuade them to keep on waiting. A pan-European revolution was, after all, removing old institutions; in this situation, the Social Democrats were responsible to present the popular will, which was opposed to the bourgeois government.[1288] Tokoi here linked the pan-European war, the Russian Revolution and the Finnish constitutional confrontation in internationalist terms that were likely to further provoke the nationalist supporters of the bourgeois parties. In the words of Jussi Kujala, too, the Finnish Social Democrats 'were cooperating with international social democracy in order to raise and finally liberate the proletariat', and opposing 'the international class of employers, which internationally is using all means against both us and the proletariat of all countries'.[1289] Internationalism was being again used here in a Bolshevist fashion to argue for the inevitability of an armed conflict with the bourgeoisie. According to Erkki Härmä and Yrjö Sirola, too, membership in the Zimmerwald International obliged the Finnish Social Democrats to fight against the imperialistic propertied classes.[1290]

After the acts of violence committed during the general strike, the right and the centre concluded that a revolutionary coup was being attempted and that the established political order was in danger.[1291] Paavo Virkkunen (Finnish Party) said that the Social Democrats had rejected parliamentarism in favour of a violent revolution supported by foreign troops: they were serving the cause of a foreign revolution by importing it to Finland and introducing 'socialist tyranny aimed directly against this parliament'. This 'revolution' had in Virkkunen's view not been initiated by any oppressed majority of the people against an oppressing minority; in this 'revolution' a minority was rebelling against the majority, who had voted against continued revolution and socialist government. Virkkunen foresaw the revolutionary road of the socialists leading an open confrontation.[1292] Santeri Alkio (Agrarians) gave voice to the fears of the non-socialist political nation: the general strike with its incidents had entailed the arrival of the world war in Finland in the form of 'a civil war' (*kansalaissota*). This civil war

1288 VP, Oskari Tokoi, 26 November 1917, 197–201.
1289 VP, Jussi Kujala, 26 November 1917, 257. Cf. the obvious uncertainty about international developments. Upton 1980, 310.
1290 VP, Erkki Härmä, 7 December 1917, 409; 7 December 1917, 411; Rinta-Tassi 1986, 20–1.
1291 Haapala 1992, 126.
1292 VP, Paavo Virkkunen, 26 November 1917, 206, 208–209.

(used here two months before its actual outbreak) had certainly escalated as a result of famine, but it had also been escalated especially by agitation for a 'class struggle' by the uncompromising and unparliamentary left.[1293] Alkio lamented the way in which Finland was being dragged into this war at a time when 'the first spring birds of peace have started to sing' in Europe, this vernal metaphor being highly ironical. The current policies of the Social Democrats threatened the achievement of 'the earthly, social paradise which they currently are trying to create in midst of a global tempest'.[1294] According to Alkio, the Socialists were to blame for the crisis which threatened to destroy the nation.

Such expressions of concern from the right and the centre had little effect; the Social Democrats, encouraged by their current party convention, which Stalin himself attended, carried on with their revolutionary discourse. Matti Airola, a solicitor, who was an activist in the Red Guards, presented the use of violence as justified as long as capitalist society existed, since such a society inevitably led to the deepening of class confrontations and to the desperation of the oppressed. Besides, both sides had already turned to violence at all levels of Finnish society.[1295] Jussi Vuoristo presented the societal power structures of bourgeois society as a further reason for the readiness to turn to violence: the bourgeois press glorified battles and atrocities, and school history was 'entirely constructed in a spirit of admiration for human slaughter and wars, and [it continues] to educate people in that spirit'.[1296] The ongoing revolution was a consequence of the Finnish bourgeoisie having used Russian power to dissolve the preceding parliament, in which 'the workers' had held a majority, and having chosen revolution by taking over supreme power in the current parliament; this had made the Finnish workers themselves launch a revolution, 'the first class war in Finland'.[1297] The perverted structures of bourgeois society, the selfish party tactics of the bourgeois parties and conspiracy theories (a claim typical of Russian revolutionary discourse[1298]) thus explained the outbreak of a justified class war of the type recommended by the Bolsheviks. This deterministic Social Democratic interpretation offered no alternative but violence, revolution and civil war.

Yrjö Sirola, a supporter of a Bolshevist-type of revolutionary movement, presented revolution in Finland as part of an international popular movement and a general pattern of revolutions as seen in the French Revolution; this interpretation included the conclusion that the legitimate cruelty of the revolutionaries arose from the unjust acts of their masters. The internationalist Sirola willingly reported to the Finnish parliament about his

---

1293 VP, Santeri Alkio, 26 November 1917, 223–4. *Hufvudstadsbladet*, 'Från kammare och kuloar', had already mentioned the possibility of a 'feud between brethren' (*brödrafejd*) and a 'civil war' on 20 November 1917 (dated 11 November 1917).
1294 VP, Santeri Alkio, 26 November 1917, 226.
1295 VP, Matti Airola, 26 November 1917, 214.
1296 VP, Jussi Vuoristo, 26 November 1917, 217.
1297 VP, Jussi Vuoristo, 26 November 1917, 219.
1298 Wade 2000, 192.

recent visit to Petrograd.[1299] During the visit, Lenin had advised the Finnish socialists to initiate a political general strike – a suggestion that the party followed.[1300] He had condemned the suspension of the general strike, which, according to Sirola, was no more than a temporary 'armistice in a class war' since a revolution might still break out against the armed propertied classes.[1301] Again, following what sounded like Lenin's logic, Sirola's rhetoric presented civil war as inescapable. According to Santeri Mäkelä, too, a 'national war' (*kansallissota*) had already come about as a result of the wartime economy and the militarism of the bourgeoisie; it was part of the current universal revolution, in which monarchies, parliaments (!) and the press – all institutions of the old world – were being crushed, and individuals just had to adapt themselves to the forces of history:[1302]

> The revolution does not care about what is thought in throne rooms, in parliaments or editorial desks. When history creates itself, when the labour pains of the new world shake the body politic, the learned may freely argue about whether the people are the law and whether the events that take place before their eyes are a revolution, hooliganism or hunger riots. The revolution does not care about this. It sings a song of its own. It breaks and creates, it destroys and builds with speed. It does not understand us. We need to understand it. If we cannot, it will remove us from the stage.

This was openly revolutionary, deterministic and militant thinking that rejected all traditional political order – including parliamentary institutions defended by Kautsky[1303] – in favour of a newly created society. It had evolved in the mind of an immigrant miner, editor and orator during his stay in the United States and been developed by a popular author and socialist agitator. Mäkelä would carry out his mission as an administrator of the Red Guards during the Finnish Civil War and later as a teacher of military history and a *politruk* in the Soviet Union – until his death in a Stalinist prison camp.

Hilja Pärssinen, the editorial secretary of the socialist women's paper *Työläisnainen*, asserted that a proper revolution should have been a mental phenomenon, but that the revolution had now been turned into a concrete one by the wrong policies of the bourgeoisie:[1304]

> We have always preached that the revolution needs to take place in the mind, that it needs to originate from the mind. We have carried out enlightenment work, enlightenment work that prepares for the revolution, prepares for a new system, a humane system. We have always rejected anarchy.

1299 VP, Yrjö Sirola, 26 November 1917, 221.
1300 Rinta-Tassi 1986, 31, 54; Polvinen 1987, vol. 1, 124–5; Haapala 1995, 221.
1301 VP, Yrjö Sirola, 26 November 1917, 223; Rinta-Tassi 1986, 54; Polvinen 1987, vol. 1, 126–7.
1302 VP, Santeri Mäkelä, 26 November 1917, 232–4; cf. Winkler 1999, 4.
1303 Kautsky 1919, chapter 8.
1304 VP, Hilja Pärssinen, 26 November 1917, 245.

Thus this leading female labour activist, too, accepted the prevalent conspiracy theory, claiming that the propagators of anarchy within the labour movement had been sent by the bourgeoisie, who wished to tarnish the reputation of the movement, and that the revolution had actually been provoked by the bourgeoisie. The Finnish Social Democrats could not help it if Marxist ideology turned to violence as the workers were merely[1305]

> resorting to the struggle of class against class; they have believed in it and today still believe that the fight of the working class against another class will one day bring class oppression to an end. Through a fight against the system we can one day create a new humane system.

Uncompromising fundamentalist Marxism had progressed so far within the Finnish Social Democratic Party that a class war appeared as the only available solution. In this version of Marxist ideology, which recalls Bolshevist goals rather than anything found among revisionist Social Democrats or even among the parliamentary far left in Germany or Sweden, parliamentary discourse was no longer one of the means by which political change would be achieved: the old system simply needed to be destroyed. Or, as Nestori Aronen put it, bourgeois violence had caused revolution to 'rise out of the stomachs of the workers', and this had led to 'the regrettable but necessary consequences of the giant waves of revolution'.[1306] The time of complying with laws passed by bourgeois parliamentary majorities was over; the laws passed 'by your parliament of the estates' had been observed by the working people, and though 'we Social Democrat speakers . . . have always tried to explain to our numbers that laws must be respected until they have been changed by legal means',[1307] this no longer sufficed: revolutionary means had replaced parliamentary ones for changing society, and the Social Democrats were not to blame for this change, he claimed.

The Social Democrats were selective in their use of international constitutional comparisons. While Russia did not yet provide authoritative examples, Switzerland did. However, instead of expressing any genuine interest in the Swiss model, these socialist hardliners used it, indeed misrepresented it, in making their claims for parliamentary sovereignty (in the form of the Power Act of July 1917). The Marxists knew about the Swiss socialist demands for direct popular rule as opposed to parliamentary social democracy, and Karl Kautsky had discussed the Swiss constitution,[1308] which according to him removed the boundaries of executive, legislative and judicial power and had in the course of the late nineteenth century incorporated the referendum and the citizens' initiative. Western European models of parliamentary representative government could be challenged with this established alternative. Otto Wille Kuusinen referred to the Swiss case when arguing

---

1305 VP, Hilja Pärssinen, 26 November 1917, 246.
1306 VP, Nestori Aronen, 26 November 1917, 247.
1307 VP, Nestori Aronen, 26 November 1917, 247.
1308 Kautsky 1907, 5, 58–9; Lindman 1968, 352–3.

for democratic reforms and against the division of power.[1309] He attacked 'so-called parliamentary governments' in France, Britain and Italy for their weakness and constant 'parliamentary cockfighting' and opposed the French and US presidencies to democracy, contrasting them with Switzerland.[1310] The Swiss model, as perfected in the Finnish Power Act, entailed the direct election of the government by the parliament and the rotating post of head of state. Unlike governmental responsibility to parliament, the system was based on a government consisting of persons who enjoyed the confidence of the parliament.[1311] On 6 December 1917, K. J. Ståhlberg of the Young Finns rejected Kuusinen's 'Swiss' model of 'parliamentary democracy' as being based on a tendentious interpretation and illustrated by the actions of the Red Guards during the recent general strike.[1312] The bourgeois MPs felt that the Social Democrats were questioning democracy, popular rule and parliamentarism in the senses in which they understood those concepts. The conceptual strife on the revolution in the Finnish parliament was approaching an impasse, and the transition to violence – as explicitly pointed out by many Social Democrats – had become only a matter of time.

4.4.3 The Finnish 'rule by the people' in the shadow of Bolshevism

Democracy or 'rule by the people' was at the centre of this conceptual strife in the Finnish parliament in the immediate aftermath of the October Revolution. As already in the summer, the discourse on democracy tended to be one-sidedly dominated by the Social Democrat parliamentary group, even though the bourgeois parties also defended their alternative interpretation of democracy with growing intensity. Introducing the demands of the party to the parliament on the day following the Bolshevik Revolution, the chairman of the Social Democrat parliamentary group Jaakko Mäki (described in the rightist press as an uneducated demagogue from America[1313]) accused the bourgeoisie of being 'hungry for violence and illegality in their fear of the rule by the people' and of having thus prevented from coming to force 'a constitution passed to protect the democratic liberty of Finland', i.e. the Power Act of July 1917.[1314] *Työmies*, the organ of the party, defined it as 'the constitution of the rule by the people', which 'the Finnish democracy' would never abandon.[1315] Mäki's speech, according to Osmo Rinta-Tassi authored by Otto Wille Kuusinen before the new revolution

---

1309 VP, Otto Wille Kuusinen, 10 November 1917, 55; Kuusinen had already cited the Swiss example in the debates of June 1917. It was favoured by other Social Democrats as well. Lindman 1968, 92, 349.
1310 VP, Otto Wille Kuusinen, 5 December 1917, 350–1.
1311 VP, Otto Wille Kuusinen, 5 December 1917, 351–2.
1312 VP, Kaarlo Juho Ståhlberg, 6 December 1917, 370.
1313 *Hufvudstadsbladet*, 'Från kammare och kuloar', 20 November 1917.
1314 VP, Jaakko Mäki, 8 November 1917, 15.
1315 *Työmies*, 'Porwariston wallankaappaushanke', 8 November 1917; 'Riippumattomuus Suomen kansalle waiko riippumattomuus Suomen kansasta', 9 November 1917.

in Russia, was employed to put pressure on the parliament, its ambiguous formulations leaving space for the interpretation of both parliamentary and revolutionary means. The declaration was designed to placate the radicals in the party; some of these demands were naturally impossible to fulfil without the parliament resigning in favour of its predecessor. In the ears of the non-socialists, Mäki's speech sounded like a declaration of revolution.[1316]

Marxist definitions of democracy followed, reinforced by *Työmies*, which claimed that 'our modest rule by the people' was being destroyed by the bourgeoisie at a moment when revolution was about to enter the country.[1317] Yrjö Sirola, who admired the organisation of the Russian Bolsheviks, and Otto Wille Kuusinen, another Marxist theorist, pointed out that Finland lacked democracy at the local level (which was true) and demanded that 'democracy, the rule by the people' (*demokratia, kansanvalta*) should be rapidly created with 'a thorough democratisation of society' (*kansanvaltaistuttaminen*) and of the administration at all levels. Such a demand might still have been accepted by the Agrarians, whose manifesto contained an occasional reference to *kansanvaltainen* (democratic),[1318] and the parliament would actually pass a law on universal suffrage in local elections on 15 November. Sirola (who on 21 November would propose to the parliamentary group that a revolution be instigated) nevertheless went on to describe the Bolshevik power in Russia as 'genuine democracy',[1319] which alienated any bourgeois members who might have supported it. Given the central role that Sirola played in the ideological training of the party, this definition of the Bolshevik system, which was still an unknown quantity, as the standard illustrates how far Finnish Social Democratic ideology had moved towards that kind of radicalism.

Kullervo Manner (the former Speaker of the parliament) and Edvard Hänninen-Walpas (the current editor of *Työmies*), next proposed that the Social Democrats were advocating democracy against the oligarchic goals of the bourgeoisie, the simple choice being between 'the rule by the people' and 'the rule by the masters',[1320] which reproduced the simplistic dichotomies of Russian socialist discourse (and would appear in the draft constitution

---

1316 See *Hufvudstadsbladet*, 'Landtdagens maktfråga och socialdemokraterna', 11 November 1917; Rinta-Tassi 1986, 47–52. Not every Social Democrat member had approved the declaration but the group decided to adopt it and demonstrate its radical aims to the masses.
1317 *Työmies*, 'Eduskunta eilen', 9 November 1917.
1318 *Maalaisliiton ohjelma*, 1914.
1319 VP, Yrjö Sirola, 8 November 1917, 25–6; Otto Wille Kuusinen, 10 November 1917, 55; Yrjö Sirola, 26 November 1917, 221–3; 7 December 1917, 411; Rinta-Tassi 1986, 56. In Petrograd Lenin asserted in the meantime that the Bolsheviks would observe 'genuine democracy' during the future Constituent Assembly as formulated by him before the Revolution. Pipes 1992, 545; Müller 2011, 35. To the Finnish workers he promised support against the Finnish bourgeoisie. Kirby 1976, 108. Sirola himself argued for a union with this 'true' revolutionary democracy in an article published on 17 November. Kirby 1974, 81.
1320 VP, Kullervo Manner, 8 November 1917, 38; Edvard Hänninen-Walpas, 8 November 1917, 45; Kullervo Manner, 10 November 1917, 71.

of Red Finland as well). Indeed, according to Hänninen-Walpas, the Finnish workers had hoped for this revolution in Russia as it would allow 'the democratic parliament' of Finland (the dissolved first parliament of 1917 with its socialist majority) to gain 'democratic power'. The new revolution in Russia meant democracy for Finland, whereas the Finnish bourgeoisie lacked 'a democratic conscience' and had been ready to use the Russian counter-revolutionaries (the Provisional Government) 'against the democratic parliament of Finland, against Finnish democracy',[1321] a Social Democratic majority being again identified with democracy as opposed to the bourgeoisie as abusers of procedure. With their proposal to elect three regents, the Finnish bourgeoisie would now create another body aimed at destroying the decisions of 'a democratic parliament' and 'Finnish democracy'.[1322] They were, according to Hänninen-Walpas, thereby associating themselves with German militarism, which hated democracy, and their ultimate intention was to prevent all 'democratic reforms' planned by 'the democratic parliament'.[1323] Oskari Tokoi, the former prime minister, likewise argued that the Finnish bourgeoisie was opposing the 'democratic winds' that were blowing across the world.[1324] Socialism was democracy by definition, while the bourgeoisie represented counterforces to revolution and democracy in alliance with imperial Germany.

When the transfer of the supreme power to the parliament and the general strike took place in mid-November, Jussi Kujala considered the Finnish right to be fighting 'a political and economic class struggle against the democracy of the proletariat', here reasserting the identification of the proletariat with democracy and the notion of democracy being about the class struggle. Furthermore, he accused the right of stigmatising the proletarian form of democracy as pernicious and irrational while they themselves had throughout history abused the idea of democracy with fallacious appeals to the rule by the people in order to advance their class interests.[1325] When the agenda of the new bourgeois government was introduced, Eetu Salin, a socialist agitator who had connections with Lenin, declared that the class war which the bourgeoisie was fighting would never be able to 'bury democratic activities and communal suffrage'.[1326] During these days, Sirola, Manner, Kuusinen, Wiik and Hänninen-Walpas received a letter from Lenin calling for a socialist revolution in Finland.[1327] In the parliament Sirola pointed out again that Finland had never been a genuine democracy. While suggesting that far-reaching democratisation might still help to solve the

1321 VP, Edvard Hänninen-Walpas, 10 November 1917, 62–3.
1322 VP, Edvard Hänninen-Walpas, 10 November 1917, 63, 65. The speech was greeted with applause from the left and the galleries; see also Vilho Lehokas, 10 November 1917, 86.
1323 VP, Edvard Hänninen-Walpas, 10 November 1917, 82–3.
1324 VP, Oskari Tokoi, 10 November 1917, 54.
1325 VP, Jussi Kujala, 15 November 1917, 138–9.
1326 VP, Eetu Salin, 24 November 1917, 188–9; Rinta-Tassi 1986, 31; Polvinen 1987, vol. 1, 128.
1327 Polvinen 1987, vol. 1, 130; Ketola 1987, 378. The letter was dated 24 November 1917.

problems, he concluded that 'our numbers are very afraid that there will be compromise'.[1328] The deliberation between further parliamentary attempts and outright revolution continued, but the chances for compromise were consistently diminished in discourse.

Among the non-socialists, democracy (or the rule by the people) raised mixed feelings. There were statements by members of the right describing the Finnish polity as democratic, aimed at defending the established order. Eirik Hornborg (Swedish People's Party) recalled that the Finnish parliament was, on the basis of universal suffrage, already 'one of the most democratic assemblies of representatives in the world'.[1329] Emil Schybergson insisted that the parliament had already received 'as democratic a proposal for a constitution as such a proposal can be, and which can of course be made even more democratic';[1330] this illustrates the desire of some Swedish-speaking conservatives, too, to hold on to a positively charged concept of democracy despite their doubts about excessive parliamentarisation and to even negotiate about it. At the same time, *Hufvudstadbladet*, the organ of the Swedish People's Party, presented the Social Democrats as the least democratic of all parties because of their opposition to the parliamentary majority[1331] and wrote ironically about Bolshevik 'democrats'. It welcomed help from monarchical Sweden to save Western civilisation in Finland from the Russian Revolution.[1332] At this stage it also defended the republican constitutional proposal as the most 'democratic' possible.[1333] Lauri Ingman, a professor of theology and the leader of the Finnish Party, likewise talked about 'a far-reaching proposal for a new democratic constitution',[1334] which illustrates a rightist defence of democracy, albeit a form of democracy defined by a bourgeois republican compromise which would retain the duality of government.

The new bourgeois coalition, led by P. E. Svinhufvud, explicitly aimed at a constitution based on the principles of democracy,[1335] which shows that the centre and the right were unwilling to leave the definition of the concept to the radicalised Social Democrats. In that respect, the Finnish bourgeois coalition, although it wished to set limits to both democracy and parliamentarism, stood more clearly for representative democracy and parliamentary government than the right in Germany or Sweden. Rather than defining what bourgeois democracy stood for, the coalition was united by a common enemy: they defined themselves as democrats in opposition to Social Democratic policies. Their extreme conclusion was that the Social Democrats, in demanding a socialist government, had in reality rejected the principles of both democracy and parliamentarism in favour of the

---

1328 VP, Yrjö Sirola, 26 November 1917, 220.
1329 VP, Eirik Hornborg, 8 November 1917, 28.
1330 VP, Emil Schybergson, 10 November 1917, 54.
1331 *Hufvudstadbladet*, 'Landtdagen och dess rätt', 10 November 1917.
1332 *Hufvudstadbladet*, 'Den ryska demokratin och Finland', 1 December 1917.
1333 *Hufvudstadbladet*, 'Grunderna för regeringsformen', 6 December 1917.
1334 VP, Lauri Ingman, 15 November 1917, 121.
1335 VP, 24 November 1917, 182.

rule of terror.¹³³⁶ Pekka Ahmavaara (Young Finns) lamented the fact that democracy had not made a breakthrough in Finland as a result of so many socialists being ready to 'trample all democracy and proceed to terrorism and fratricide'.¹³³⁷ Awareness of the discursive process having got out of hand was widespread.

While centrist members consistently emphasised the democratic endeavours of the reformists in the parliament, Social Democrats such as Yrjö Sirola questioned the willingness of the Finnish farmers to understand genuine democracy,¹³³⁸ thereby excluding the peasantry from political cooperation in the building of democracy. This confrontation alienated the Agrarians further, provoking them to call explicitly for the rule by the people. Mikko Luopajärvi asserted that the Agrarians wanted to do everything possible to get democratic reforms passed, while the Social Democrats were playing opportunistic procedural games that were inconsistent with their calls for 'extreme democracy'.¹³³⁹ Artur Vuorimaa also pointed out ideological divergences between the centre and the right: according to him, there was also a battle between present-day ideas about the rule by the people and past notions of monarchy and bureaucracy that was being fought.¹³⁴⁰ Minister of Agriculture Kyösti Kallio declared the Eduskunta to be 'the most democratic parliament in the world' and thereby a powerful tool for leftist endeavours to realise their goals despite reactionary opposition from the right.¹³⁴¹ Kalle Lohi pointed out that there were also 'democratic, radical elements' among the bourgeois parties outside the Agrarian League and that the bourgeois coalition was ready to take the democratic measures required by the times.¹³⁴² The Finnish centre parties declared themselves on a broad front to be democrats who opposed both extremes and to be ready to accept democratic reforms – indeed to an even greater extent than centrists in Britain or Germany, in this respect resembling the Swedish Liberals.

Bourgeois democracy found defenders among the Finnish liberals, many of whom were radical by international standards. Among the clerical representatives of the Young Finns, Gustaf Arokallio still welcomed the principle of the rule by the people on which the Power Act of July 1917 had been based, pointing to its ongoing breakthrough in a number of countries.¹³⁴³ Antti Rentola was critical of the Social Democrats for not respecting the principles of parliamentary democracy and for rejecting the possibility of socialists and bourgeois radicals fighting together for democracy,¹³⁴⁴ as had happened in many other countries. There was an explicit willingness among

1336 VP, Paavo Virkkunen (Finnish), 26 November 1917, 206, 244.
1337 VP, Ahmavaara, 26 November 1917, 210.
1338 VP, Yrjö Sirola, 10 November 1917, 74.
1339 VP, Mikko Luopajärvi, 10 November 1917, 76.
1340 VP, Artur Vuorimaa, 15 November 1917, 133.
1341 VP, Kyösti Kallio, 26 November 1917, 201.
1342 VP, Kalle Lohi, 26 November 1917, 238-9.
1343 VP, Gustaf Arokallio, 15 November 1917, 129-30. Ernst Estlander immediately questioned the truly democratic nature of the Power Act. 15 November 1917, 130.
1344 VP, Antti Rentola, 24 November 1917, 190-1.

both parties of the centre to cooperate with the Social Democrats in a way that had recently been carried out in Sweden and had been attempted in Germany. However, positive responses from the Social Democratic side were lacking, and cooperation with even reformist bourgeoisie continued to be excluded.

By the time of the declaration of independence, both the Social Democrats and the bourgeois coalition claimed to be striving for democracy: the former agitated for an understanding of democracy that sounded in the ears of contemporary non-socialists practically inseparable from the ways in which the Bolsheviks used the concept. The non-socialists, on the other hand, were united more by reactions to one-sided Social Democratic definitions than by any shared concept of the rule by the people. All political groups had nevertheless adopted a discourse based on the concept of democracy, and most claimed that they stood for democracy. The Finnish parliamentary debate on democracy was, owing to this ideological confrontation, and to the positive and widely held ethnic and/or social connotations of the coinage 'rule by the people' (*kansanvalta*), more extensive in 1917 than corresponding debates in Britain, Germany or Sweden. The confrontation was about the kind of democracy that a nation aiming at independence would build. Democracy became defined by the socialists on the one hand and the bourgeois parties on the other in ways that made it practically impossible to find a common discourse that would enable compromises on the constitution, since the Social Democratic understanding of proletarian democracy was so categorical. On the bourgeois side, there existed some readiness for concessions but, on the other hand, the legalistic stand of the lawyers and other academics of the right, who remained devoted to the eighteenth-century Swedish constitutional tradition[1345] in ways that recalled the Prussian and Swedish right, tended to limit the concept of democracy to the representation of the people in legislative measures and not to extend it to include the responsibility of the government to the parliament. By the end of November, the right saw the formation of armed guards as the only way to maintain law and order against those whom *Hufvudstadsbladet* called 'the hooligans of the left'.[1346]

When the new republican constitutional proposal was debated on 5 December 1917, Otto Wille Kuusinen, encouraged by a letter from Lenin,[1347] rejected it for its 'undemocratic character' (*epäkansanvaltaisuus*). As Yrjö Sirola put it, it would not make Finland 'a democratic republic' in the sense that the Social Democrats wanted. What Kuusinen offered instead sounded in principle acceptable to many: it was a system of 'sovereign parliamentary democracy' (*suvereeninen eduskunnallinen kansanvalta*), albeit one defined in the Social Democratic Power Act.[1348] However, it had become clear that the Social Democratic parliamentary democracy was far removed from

---

1345 See *Hufvudstadsbladet*, 'Landtdagens maktfråga och socialdemokraterna', 11 November 1917
1346 *Hufvudstadsbladet*, 'Det politiska perspektivet', 25 November 1917.
1347 Polvinen 1987, vol. 1, 130.
1348 VP, Otto Wille Kuusinen, 5 December 1917, 348–9, 352; Yrjö Sirola, 6 December 1917, 371.

what the bourgeois coalition was aiming at. Kuusinen now denounced the coalition's 'democracy' as mere 'bourgeois democracy', which, although based on a ruling government enjoying the confidence of parliament, did not represent genuine democracy at all.[1349] Kuusinen was making a point recalling not only the conventional Marxist historical narrative but also the one made by Lenin on his arrival in Petrograd[1350]: bourgeois democracy was incompatible with the democracy of the Bolshevik Revolution. Kuusinen repeated the definition of the Social Democrats as the only true Finnish democrats, accusing the Agrarians of letting their democratic voters down by helping the right to transform 'the present democratic system into a more undemocratic one'.[1351] Kullervo Manner provocatively echoed the insinuation that the centre could not choose between democracy and reactionary politics.[1352] The conclusion of the Social Democratic leaders was that this parliament was unlikely to adopt 'a progressive democratic' line that would demonstrate to the workers that parliamentary means would relieve their suffering.[1353] According to Alma Jokinen, both the right and the centre had rejected the Power Act as 'too democratic' since they feared democracy and the reforms that a socialist parliamentary majority would introduce.[1354] The abnegation of non-socialist democracy was unwavering.

The Social Democrats also challenged the government about a proposal to create a parliamentary committee for foreign affairs.[1355] Sirola called for 'a democratic foreign policy' based on cooperation with 'the democracy of the peoples of the world', which his audience probably understood as Bolshevik internationalism rather than Wilsonianism. Sirola and the Social Democrats, consistently identifying true revolutionary democracy with Bolshevism, argued that democracy would prevail in Russia only with the victory of the Bolsheviks. Joseph Stalin, the People's Commissar responsible for national questions, had during the Social Democratic party convention in Helsinki on 25–27 November promised a way to 'the democratic self-determination of Finland'.[1356] Evidently, Stalin and Alexandra Kollontai,

1349 VP, Otto Wille Kuusinen, 5 December 1917, 350.
1350 Pipes 1992, 393.
1351 VP, Otto Wille Kuusinen, 5 December 1917, 354; cf. Otto Wille Kuusinen, 5 December 1917, 361.
1352 VP, Kullervo Manner, 5 December 1917, 360.
1353 VP, Otto Wille Kuusinen, 5 December 1917, 355.
1354 VP, Alma Jokinen, 5 December 1917, 363–4.
1355 Ketola 1987, 396.
1356 VP, Yrjö Sirola, 7 December 1917, 412, 416. Stalin had recognised the right of the Finns to independence on 7 May 1917 (Polvinen 1987, vol. 1, 64) and on 27 November 1917 but expected there to be a union between the Finns and the Russians. His views caused concern to Evert Huttunen in December, and they were also reported with suspicion in the rightist press. *Hufvudstadsbladet*, 'Den ryska demokratin och Finland', 1 December 1917. On 4 January 1918 Stalin rejected Lenin's recognition of the Finnish bourgeois government but expected the Finnish socialists to now finally make a revolution. Kirby 1974, 81, 83; Kirby 1976, 108; Rinta-Tassi 1986, 59; Polvinen 1987, vol. 1, 188. As for the Marxist monopolisation of the concept of democracy, it should be noted that *The Herald* also wrote about 'the democracy' and 'the democracies of the world' on 22 December 1917 and preferred 'democratic diplomacy'.

presenting themselves as 'democrats', had used the meeting to propagate the Bolshevik conception of an international socialist revolution as opposed to the use of parliamentary tactics. Even if the policy of continuing parliamentary work had still won out in the convention, the ambiguously worded resolution had left the possibility of a revolution open.[1357] Finnish independence was in any case presented as dependent on cooperation with the Bolsheviks and the world revolution. In early January 1918, after the Bolshevik government had recognised Finnish independence, the Social Democrats accused the Finnish bourgeoisie of fighting against democracy in Finland and being unwilling to maintain relations with 'the purely democratic elements in Russia'.[1358] The Bolsheviks as representing the Russian democracy were to be thanked for recognising Finnish independence.[1359] Quite clearly, cooperation with the Bolsheviks seemed to be the form of democracy that the parliamentary speakers of the Finnish Social Democrats endorsed, which made the reformist bourgeoisie defend their democracy by all possible means.

Space and time for constructive non-socialist definitions of democracy were running out, however. The Agrarians insisted that the parliament had the full liberty to adopt a sufficiently democratic constitution.[1360] Onni Talas (Young Finns), the minister responsible for introducing the proposed constitutional reform, also took it as self-evident that the future Finnish constitution should be based on 'the most democratic principles' because 'the Finnish people are in their entire essence democratic' and hence 'only a completely democratic constitution can be adopted by the Finnish people'.[1361] This spokesman of the bourgeois coalition argued for democracy, defining all aspects of the constitutional proposal (rhetorically) as democratic, concluding that the proposal was entirely based on 'democratic principles' and hoping that this 'step towards full democracy' would prevent further power struggles. The new Finland would be a democracy in name, but in line with most liberals and conservatives in Northern Europe, Talas defended limitations to the power of the parliament, maintaining that unlimited parliamentary power would produce an oligarchy.[1362] K. J. Ståhlberg, the chairman of the preparatory committee, also insisted on the highly democratic nature of the proposal despite its emphasis on maintaining the power of the executive side by side with that of the parliament.[1363] The leading lawyers of the centre parties, too, distinguished between representative democracy and far-reaching parliamentarism, echoing transnational liberal thinking of the time. For them, the maintenance of the dualism of government within representative government constituted a desirable type of democracy. This bourgeois compromise on democracy remained irreconcilable with the

1357 Soikkanen 1975, 248; Rinta-Tassi 1986, 56–7; Polvinen 1987, vol. 1, 130–1; Ketola 1987, 379–80; Tuomisto 1990, 44.
1358 VP, Karl Harald Wiik, 9 January 1918, 819. Wiik had met Lenin on 27 December 1917.
1359 VP, Yrjö Sirola, 9 January 1918, 827.
1360 VP, Artur Wuorimaa, 5 December 1917, 362.
1361 VP, Onni Talas, 6 December 1917, 368.
1362 VP, Onni Talas, 6 December 1917, 369–70.
1363 VP, Kaarlo Juho Ståhlberg, 6 December 1917, 370–1.

revolutionary concept which the Finnish Social Democratic Party was agitating for, and an open conflict on the nature of democracy followed.

4.4.4 A PEOPLE DIVIDED BY CLASS AND PARLIAMENTARY DISCOURSE

The clash of the socialist and bourgeois concepts of democracy was based on and reinforced by equally confrontational ideological understandings of 'the people'. The Social Democrats aimed at monopolising the concept in line with the polarised Russian definition, which was countered in parliamentary debate by alternative centrist and rightist discourses. Oskari Tokoi maintained at the opening of the new parliament that, it had lost any connection with the will of the people within the period of a single month and that the people were ready to take revolutionary measures to bypass it, should it not assent to the Social Democrats' reform demands. The centrists found it impossible to agree with this claim: in their view, the current parliament was the best possible representative of the Finnish people: its democratic nature and legitimacy was strengthened by the fact that the people had voted more actively in October than in previous elections.[1364]

The contemporaries were highly aware of these ideological and conceptual confrontations and their potential risks. They made Wäinö Valkama of the Finnish Party pessimistic over the political outlook for the Finns as a people: if they really were as divided and inclined to quarrel at a decisive moment as the parliamentary debates suggested, it was questionable whether they were ready for independence. Parliamentary discourse had been turned by the socialists into mere agitation of the class war while the real duty of the representatives should have been to advance the cause of the nation.[1365] The left was undermining the relationship of trust between the people and the parliament, or rather the relationship between the people and themselves, with the constant agitation that was being reiterated in the workers' press.[1366] In the Social Democratic press, speeches by the party's own MPs were indeed published in detail, whereas those of the other parliamentarians were only selectively summarised. Valkama's conservative statement, for its part, still reflects a high degree of trust in the observance of the law by the majority of the people and in parliamentary government: the Finnish people followed the parliament through the press, respected it and could distinguish between proper and improper parliamentary discourse. Pekka Ahmavaara (Young Finns) also counted on the workers not to follow the Social Democratic policy once they had seen it put into practice during the violent general strike.[1367] Many representatives of the Finnish-speaking right (Fennomans) and liberals were clearly on the side of democracy as far as counting on the

---

1364 VP, Eero Pehkonen and Mikko Luopajärvi (Agrarians) and Gustaf Arokallio (Young Finns), 10 November 1917, 69, 76; 15 November 1917, 129; also *Hufvudstadsbladet*, 'Landtdagens maktfråga och socialdemokraterna', 11 November 1917.
1365 VP, Wäinö Valkama, 8 November 1917, 39; also *Hufvudstadsbladet*, 'Landtdagens maktfråga och socialdemokraterna', 11 November 1917.
1366 VP, Wäinö Valkama, 8 November 1917, 39.
1367 VP, 26 November 1917, 210.

people as a political force was concerned. The Civil War would certainly disabuse some of them of such optimism, albeit only temporarily.[1368]

The revolutionary concept of 'the people' agitated by the Social Democrats supported opposite conclusions. According to Tokoi, the ongoing revolutionary and democratising international trends called for the concentration of political power in the hands of the people,[1369] i.e. the workers. Otto Wille Kuusinen contrasted the bourgeois proposal to nominate three regents for the realm with the socialist demands that political power belonged to 'the parliament of the Finnish people' (the dissolved parliament) as defined by the unpromulgated Power Act.[1370] Vilho Lehokas declared that the Finnish people were tired of hollow reform promises[1371] and hence tired of the parliament as an institution. According to Nestori Aronen, the bourgeoisie stubbornly opposed the Power Act because of their fear of a takeover of political power by the Finnish people and of the (preceding) parliament.[1372] Claims about the will of the people and the proper realisation of the power of the people remained confrontational and irreconcilable, and the parliamentary discourse referring to the people reinforced ideological divisions – and indeed the concrete division between Finns at the local level. All this contributed to the diminution of trust in parliament.

4.4.5 Diminishing trust in parliamentary government escalates the crisis

A repeated claim of the Social Democrats was that the will of the parliamentary majority of November 1917 did not correspond with the will of the people. Ever since September, their leaders had lost what was left of their faith in parliamentary cooperation with the bourgeois parties as a way to achieve reforms. In the new parliament the critical attitude towards the efficacy of parliamentary work turned into the official party line, as the parliamentary group put it with reference to social reforms: 'We do not have great hopes that even these ... can be happily solved through the recently elected parliament.'[1373] One claim was that the parliament lacked legitimacy since the electoral law did not allow the youth to vote (the age limit being 24) and made it impossible to achieve 'the massive democratic majority' needed for reforms, instead allowing a bourgeois minority to obstruct them.[1374] Disappointed with the rules of the parliamentary system and the bourgeois majority that the October election had produced, the Social Democratic group, inspired by the Russian example, demanded the election of a national constituent assembly that would legislate on a new constitution. Such an assembly would possess unlimited supreme power and would make decisions on the basis of simple majorities;[1375] the principle

---

1368 See Virtanen 2015.
1369 VP, Oskari Tokoi, 10 November 1917, 54.
1370 VP, Otto Wille Kuusinen, 10 November 1917, 55.
1371 VP, Vilho Lehokas, 10 November 1917, 86.
1372 VP, Nestori Aronen, 26 November 1917, 253.
1373 VP, Jaakko Mäki, 8 November 1917, 16.
1374 VP, Jaakko Mäki, 8 November 1917, 17.
1375 VP, Jaakko Mäki, 8 November 1917, 17.

of the unpromulgated Power Act would apply and the majority quotas of the Parliamentary Act of 1906 would be annulled. Instead of seeing this simply as an anti-parliamentary declaration, it can also be interpreted as an attempt to give one more chance to parliamentary government – admittedly along the lines set by the Social Democrats. However, the proposed solution violated the Swedish-Finnish constitutional and parliamentary tradition that was so prized by the bourgeois parties and was also counter to the results of the recent elections.

Yrjö Sirola already set a revolution and the parliament as alternatives to each other, suggesting that a failure to comply with the Social Democrats' demands would unavoidably lead to a Russian-style revolution by direct action: 'the parliament of the streets will speak its language with thousands of voices' – or 'is starting to speak', as an interjection from another Social Democratic member had it.[1376] The Finnish parliament had in fact had to make decisions under the threat of crowd violence on several occasions.[1377] Street demonstrations had been heard in the chamber in July, when a Bolshevik coup in Petrograd was under way. Now that this revolution had taken place, the masses having entered the Duma and forced it to take action,[1378] the Social Democratic suggestion that extra-parliamentary revolutionary fervour might take over and circumvent the parliament in Helsinki, too, sounded all the more threatening. For Sirola, moreover, the current parliament was no more than a mere 'meeting, not a legitimate parliament.[1379] The problems of the country should be solved by new political institutions formulated by a constituent national assembly.[1380] For Sirola, the time for bourgeois parliamentarism had come to an end. Kautsky believed in the ability of parliaments to reflect political and social power relations.[1381] Lenin, who considered parliaments to be seemingly democratic institutions that the bourgeoisie merely abused to bolster their class rule, saw no value in them other than for propagating the challenge to the bourgeois polity from within.[1382] This seemed to have become the dominant attitude in Finnish Social Democratic parliamentary discourse as well.

Bolshevik-like discourse could also be heard in a revolutionary challenge to parliamentary government by Kullervo Manner, the Speaker of the previous parliament, which was interpreted by the rightist press as reflecting 'anti-parliamentary views'.[1383] According to Manner, 'this society'

1376 VP, Yrjö Sirola, 8 November 1917, 26.
1377 Nyström 2013, 154.
1378 Wade 2000, 43.
1379 VP, Yrjö Sirola, 8 November 1917, 24; Matti Airola, 9 November 1917, 44. Jaakko Mäki, the chair of the parliamentary group, talked about 'this meeting or parliament, whatever this is', which reflects the existence of doubt among the Social Democrats, too, as whether to recognise the current parliament or not. 8 November 1917, 34.
1380 VP, Yrjö Sirola, 8 November 1917, 26.
1381 Kautsky 1918b; Kettunen 1986, 93; Häupel 1993, 166.
1382 Gronow 1986, 233; Kettunen 1986, 90–3; Müller 2011, 36.
1383 *Hufvudstadbladet*, 'Från kammare och kuloar', 9 November 1917; 'Landtdagen och dess rätt', 10 November 1917.

or 'meeting is not the legal Finnish parliament', and no decisions that might bring comfort to the working people could be expected from it. It followed that the Social Democrats had no reason to respect and support such a parliament. Instead, the previous parliament, nicknamed 'Manner's parliament', could in his view still be reconvened.[1384] He did not hesitate to present himself as the Speaker of the legal parliament and to suggest that he remained entitled to decide when that parliament would meet.[1385] His fellow MPs even implied a readiness to use personal violence against the actual Speaker (the Oldest Member) in protest against his procedural decisions in this context. This represented an extraordinary denial of the legitimacy of a democratically elected parliament by the Speaker of its predecessor, and it is an example of how the crisis of parliamentarism was further aggravated by the contemptuous way in which the Social Democrat leaders spoke about the representative institution. Parliamentary government had little chance to flourish under a former Speaker and an opposition leader who had no respect for parliamentary government in any other sense than as a forum for agitation and a takeover by a socialist majority.

The representatives of the right and the centre disagreed strongly over the claims concerning the illegality of the current parliament. Eirik Hornborg (Swedish People's Party) considered it, thanks to the extensive suffrage, more legitimate as a 'national assembly' than any other representative institution on earth.[1386] Juhani Arajärvi (Finnish Party) required the Social Democrats to say whether they really wanted to invalidate the current parliament, from which the people outside expected decisions. For the majority of the members of parliament, there was no questioning the legality of the present institution, Arajärvi emphasised.[1387] Mikko Luopajärvi and Artur Wuorimaa (Agrarians) likewise condemned the unwillingness of the party that had lost the election to recognise the present parliament.[1388]

The Social Democrats did make an effort to explain why they thought parliamentary government had failed. According to Edvard Hänninen-Walpas, the reform had only gone half-way following the Russian Revolution of 1905: the parliament was based on universal suffrage but lacked any real political power. When the opportunity to democratise the parliament had come, only seeming and temporary 'so-called parliamentarism' had followed. In his opinion the bourgeoisie admired British parliamentarism only because oppression of the workers was easiest in that system and had allied themselves with the Russian administration whenever their class interests had been in jeopardy. Consequently, only a revolution in Russia was capable of creating a 'serious democratic parliament' in Finland.[1389] Hänninen-Walpas already opted for extra-parliamentary means, a revolution, to force the reforms through.[1390]

1384 VP, Kullervo Manner, 8 November 1917, 37–8.
1385 VP, 10 November 1917, 70.
1386 VP, Eirik Hornborg, 8 November 1917, 28.
1387 VP, Juhani, Arajärvi, 8 November 1917, 30, 41.
1388 VP, Mikko Luopajärvi, 8 November 1917, 32; 10 November 1917, 60.
1389 VP, Edvard Hänninen-Walpas, 10 November 1917, 61–2, 82.
1390 Kirby 1986, 163.

According to Jussi Vuoristo[1391], too, the workers no longer trusted parliamentary activity. The Social Democrats had used all possible means to try to prevent the workers from turning to extra-parliamentary measures, but it was doubtful whether they would still be able to do so and, indeed, 'it is hardly our duty to prevent it', which statement can be related to various explanations for the Civil War presented in previous Finnish research.[1392] This was, after all, yet another way of suggesting that the time of parliamentary reform efforts was over and that the supporters of the Social Democrats, who were calling for participation in local government, demanding guarantees of employment and food supplies and were outraged by alleged bourgeois plots,[1393] were likely to turn to extra-parliamentary measures. The claim that the masses were disappointed with parliamentary activities had been reiterated by Otto Wille Kuusinen, Kullervo Manner and other party leaders for some time.[1394] Quite clearly the workers' leaders had – in the aftermath of the lost election, with local struggles for power and in expectation of a Bolshevik Revolution – been reconsidering the need to use force. On 22 October, the local association in Helsinki had already called for

---

1391 He was himself an opponent of revolution. Rinta-Tassi 1986, 48.
1392 VP, Jussi Vuoristo, 10 November 1917, 84. Risto Alapuro has emphasised the fact that the party was no longer able to prevent the ongoing revolutionary radicalisation in the Red Guards at the local level, which arose mainly from discontent over the distribution of food by local government authorities (there had been no reform of local government) and over the organisation of the White Guards. The authority of the party over the masses was declining, but it was able to postpone the outbreak of the revolution. Pauli Kettunen, too, argues that the 'Kautskyist' party leadership tried to prevent this radicalisation. Kettunen 1986, 87–8; Rinta-Tassi 1986, 39, 41; Alapuro 1988, 162–70, 190–4; Alapuro 1990, 20. The shortages were not always real, as Alapuro states, and it was rather feelings of injustice concerning the political system that accelerated radicalisation, as Haapala & Tikka 2013, 109, point out. The harvest of 1917 was not exceptionally bad (Nyström 2013, 187, 218), and social and economic difficulties by no means automatically led to a violent confrontation (Haapala 1992, 126; Haapala 1995, 218). Since much worse shortages did not lead to a revolution in many other countries, the impact of discursive trends and weaknesses in parliamentary work arising from violations of its rules should also be considered as additional factors in the progress towards a civil war. Even if the Social Democratic discourse of class antagonism hardly created the confrontations alone, it contributed to their exacerbation by repeating the chimera of the greedy bourgeoisie and promises of a proletarian takeover. Siltala 2009, 524; cf. Kirby 1986, 162–3; The role of parliamentary procedure has previously been recognised by Rinta-Tassi 1986, 57, 65, who concludes that the inconsistent 'Kautskyist' strategies adopted by the SDP led to the weakening of its legitimacy in the eyes of the bourgeois parties, its own parliamentary group, the Russian Bolsheviks, the Red Guards and the trade unions, and hence the party became unable to control the situation. An alternative interpretation is offered by Borisova and Siro 2014, 88, who argue – in a rather simplistic manner – that 'the Finnish Revolution' followed from the disintegration of the Russian Empire and a declaration of independence that led to a power vacuum.
1393 Kirby 1986, 153.
1394 Rinta-Tassi 1986, 49.

a revolution, distancing itself from Kautskyist notions and ready to move from radical words to radical acts. Typical of the time were insinuations about the evil-intentioned plans of the rival side at every level of society: all the problems were presented as being produced by their political opponents. Local labour associations might warn the workers against participating in activities organised by the bourgeoisie. The Social Democratic organ *Työmies* tried to keep the masses under the direction of the party by openly accusing the employers and the bourgeoisie of intentionally crushing the workers and failing to help the economically distressed.[1395]

The Social Democrats declared a general strike, while in parliament they continued to challenge the bourgeois side, which, according to Jussi Kujala, was afraid of 'those powers which are now active elsewhere, outside the parliament, those powers whose members demand more'.[1396] The 'powers outside the parliament' stood for the proletariat, 'the lower layers of the people, its deep lines excited to the highest degree' as a result of the failed food supply policies of the government.[1397] Kujala emphasised the progress of extra-parliamentary and revolutionary action as an alternative to the current parliament. Nor did Edvard Hänninen-Walpas believe in parliamentary government as long as the bourgeois parties held the majority. Even if 'revolutionary workers strangled this parliament and forced it to make a decision favourable to them' (again a reference to the use of violence), the bourgeois government would still annul the parliament's decisions. With its tactics of obstruction and the help of 'the butcher guards of the bourgeoisie' the government could rule alone and in the end extinguish all parliamentary activity from the country,[1398] the current government being represented as a violent destroyer of parliamentarism. The uncompromising demand of the Social Democrats for the reintroduction of the Power Act *and* for the necessary majority power of the workers (as their Marxist ideology had it) led to the conclusion that no concessions whatsoever from the centre and right could save the parliamentary system. The bourgeois parties were defined in a radical Marxist, Russian revolutionary and Bolshevik manner as a class enemy that lacked any honest intentions of advancing democracy or parliamentarism and aimed instead at violent suppression of the demands of the working class. The militant revolutionary rhetoric of Finnish Social Democracy was leading Finnish parliamentary government into an impasse in which either an armed rising against the current parliament or its armed defence appeared as the only alternatives. The Civil War was already being fought discursively.

The bourgeois majority was shocked by the openness of the Social Democratic revolutionary challenges to parliamentary government. The

---

1395 Kirby 1986, 147; Tuomisto 1990, 42; Haapala 1992, 126; Nyström 2013, 175, 178, 185.
1396 VP, Jussi Kujala, 15 November 1917, 140.
1397 VP, Jussi Kujala, 15 November 1917, 140.
1398 VP, Edvard Hänninen-Walpas, 15 November 1917, 144. On similar discussions in the Social Democratic press concerning the Civil Guards, see Nyström 2013, 175.

general strike was explained by the workers' leaders as an attempt to prevent the escalation of direct action, but it undoubtedly exacerbated the revolutionary atmosphere. As the national parliament was due to take over sovereignty on 15 November, members of the Parliament of the Workers' Associations of Helsinki called for a coup by the workers, and the Revolutionary Workers' Central Soviet decided to start a revolution.[1399] In the national parliament, Lauri Ingman, the leader of the Finnish Party, forcefully denounced this soviet, in which many leading Social Democratic parliamentarians were participating, and its insistence that 'Manner's parliament' remained the only legitimate representative institution. Ingman rejected calls for the adoption of the Power Act, describing it as utterly pernicious since such a constitution would make 'party strife' a permanent feature of Finnish politics.[1400] The right was determined to maintain the duality of government despite the transfer of the supreme power to parliament: there had to be limits to parliamentarism. It did not question the need to strengthen the parliament provided that the government retained a certain independence of it, and an increase in the powers of the parliament was hence mentioned in the programme of the new bourgeois government.[1401]

The Agrarians called more clearly than the other bourgeois parties for the introduction of full parliamentarism; this would include the parliamentary nomination of the government and the responsibility of the ministers to the parliament, which was to be seen as representative of the power invested in the Finnish people.[1402] Santeri Alkio questioned the rightist criticism of the increase of the power of parliament on the one hand while on the other making it clear that the Agrarians would never recognise 'Manner's parliament'; the current parliament should just assume supreme power. There was, according to Alkio, a threat that the country would fall into total anarchy should parliamentarians themselves or the people outside not submit to parliamentary decisions.[1403] This was indeed happening.

The government's promises of extended parliamentarism had no effect on the Social Democrats' views on parliamentarism. Eetu Salin continued to emphasise the diminution of trust in parliamentarism among the Finnish working class, threatening that if the bourgeoisie did not 'assent to the justified demands of the proletariat, the Finnish workers may abandon parliamentary means of struggle and move on to the ways of anarchy'.[1404] Salin, although he was generally regarded as an advocate of parliamentary means, said that the bourgeoisie were to blame for the rising number of people who considered voting useless and opted for 'extraordinary measures, unparliamentary measures': bourgeois opposition to reforms had

1399 Nyström 2013, 205–206.
1400 VP, Lauri Ingman, 15 November 1917, 122; see also Paavo Virkkunen, 26 November 1917, 244.
1401 VP, Lauri Ingman, 24 November 1917, 182.
1402 VP, Kalle Lohi, 15 November 1917, 137; see also Mikko Luopajärvi, 15 November 1917, 141.
1403 VP, Santeri Alkio, 15 November 1917, 123–5.
1404 VP, Eetu Salin, 24 November 1917, 188.

made the masses 'unparliamentary' and ready to participate in 'anarchical phenomena'; it had 'goaded these unparliamentary masses into this fight against parliament itself'.[1405] At the level of parliamentary discourse, a revolutionary and increasingly anti-parliamentary struggle had begun, and it found physical counterparts in violent incidents at the local level. Anti-parliamentary discourse among the Social Democrats had reached such a degree that hardly anything but the total surrender of power to the Social Democrat minority could have prevented a civil war. Disappointment with the results of the parliamentary system, which had not corresponded with the high expectations created by the parliamentary reform of 1906, and above all the Social Democratic agitation of uncompromisingly Marxist views about parliament were leading to the collapse of parliamentary government before one had even been properly implemented. Matti Paasivuori was the only Social Democrat MP to reject demands for a government dominated by his party as unparliamentary – only to be countered with an interjection from fellow party members inveighing against the 'parliamentarism of the masters' (*herrojen parlamentarismia*).[1406] The Social Democrat parliamentary group denounced parliamentarism as a failed strategy that served only the interests of their class enemies.

Some bourgeois MPs continued their defence of parliamentarism. Chaplain Antti Rentola of the Agrarians declared that in a 'democratic parliamentary government' the minority in the parliament, as the Social Democrats were, could not form the government and determine its policies.[1407] Paavo Virkkunen (Finnish Party), too, explicitly defended parliamentarism, which illustrates the devotion of some Finnish conservatives to parliamentarism in ways that resemble the attitudes of British Conservatives rather than those of the German and Swedish right. The Finnish right was ready to cooperate with the centre to stop Social Democratic anti-parliamentarism and to make concessions to that end, the feared alternative of a Bolshevik-minded socialist government in the aftermath of the October Revolution forcing them to opt for majority parliamentarism. According to Virkkunen, who would turn to questionable rhetorical redescriptions of democracy after the Civil War, parliamentarism was realised in Finland for the first time as the members of parliament were[1408]

> representatives of the people raising their voices in support of parliamentary demands for the appointment of the government of the country, in support of an appointed government that really enjoyed the confidence of the majority of parliament and concomitantly the confidence of the majority of the people.

This was a positive description of the current policy of the bourgeois majority being based on 'healthy parliamentarism'. But it was more than mere rhetoric: some in the Finnish Party felt that parliamentary principles

---

1405 VP, Eetu Salin, 24 November 1917, 189.
1406 VP, Matti Paasivuori and interjections, 26 November 1917, 231.
1407 VP, Antti Rentola, 24 November 1917, 190.
1408 VP, Paavo Virkkunen, 26 November 1917, 205.

were being threatened by the violent revolutionary actions of the Social Democrats, who did not 'care about parliamentarism' in calling for a socialist minority government. The preceding prime minister had, indeed, 'cast the principles of parliamentarism and democracy far behind his back'.[1409]

To be sure, there were influential bourgeois MPs who already felt that parliamentary work had proved to be useless. Professor of Finnish E. N. Setälä (Young Finns), the acting prime minister, called for *actions* instead of parliamentary *debate* in its radicalised form,[1410] which is a noteworthy statement coming as it did from a linguist who had participated in formulating the draft constitution and now served as the head of the executive. Oswald Kairamo (Finnish Party), the owner of a country estate, was shocked by violations of his parliamentary immunity outside parliament, which arose from his previous statements on the relationship between estate owners and tenants, but which he considered concerned all MPs as such illegalities had hindered the work of parliamentary committees. Parliamentary activity was impossible when 'men with bayonets disturb its work and when no one protects it against the violence and arbitrary power of the public in the streets'.[1411]

Most bourgeois speakers however, agreed on the value of parliamentarism. Pekka Ahmavaara of the constitutionalist Young Finns said that the Finns had taken power into their own hands once the parliament had unanimously declared itself the possessor of supreme power.[1412] Santeri Alkio (Agrarians) emphasised the parliamentary way of thinking among the bourgeoisie, who had allowed the nomination of a government with a socialist majority in the previous spring. The Social Democrats, by contrast, had chosen an unparliamentary line in demanding a majority in government despite their minority in parliament. Such demands made parliament anarchical and unable to carry out its responsibilities to the people.[1413]

The strengthening view of the right and the centre about the need to defend the cause of parliamentarism and democracy against a Bolshevik revolutionary minority brought together what came to be the White side in the Finnish Civil War – despite their remaining disagreements on how democratic, parliamentary and republican the future polity should be. Rhetorically at least, the Finnish-speaking right was from the end of November 1917 on united on the side of parliamentarism, whereas the Swedish People's Party remained doubtful about majority parliamentarism: its organ wrote about 'ultra-democratic parliamentary circumstances' and about 'horse-trading' in a unicameral parliament. It described the ranting of the socialists and the applause from the 'mob' in the galleries, it compared the crisis to a degenerating illness and it concluded that the only solution was to replace the 'completely impossible' unicameral system with a proper

---

1409 VP, Paavo Virkkunen, 26 November 1917, 205–206, 244.
1410 VP, Emil Nestor Setälä, 26 November 1917, 256.
1411 VP, Oswald Kairamo, 26 November 1917, 256; Nyström 2013, 206–207.
1412 VP, Pekka Ahmavaara, 26 November 1917, 213.
1413 VP, Santeri Alkio, 26 November 1917, 224–6.

bicameral one.[1414] Nevertheless, the threat of the Bolshevik Revolution spreading to Finland forced many of the Finnish right to move to the side of democracy and parliamentarism, although this support might still be wavering, as was demonstrated by the constitutional debates of 1918.

All political groups were disappointed in the aftermath of the general strike, being either horrified at the violence or frustrated about a further delay in the revolution. The Parliament of the Workers' Associations of Helsinki – the name of which continued to cause confusion about what 'parliament' stood for, especially as it was established to decide on revolutionary measures[1415] and openly challenged 'the dominant bourgeois class'[1416] – considered launching a revolution but chose instead to challenge the city council.[1417] The contrast between the non-socialists' and the Social Democrats' views on parliament expressed in November and December 1917 is striking, as is illustrated by a final example from the Social Democratic side. In the words of Otto Wille Kuusinen on 5 December 1917, the Social Democrats refused to recognise any 'parliamentary democracy' in the constitutional proposal for a presidential republic by the bourgeois government as it would only mean a 'bourgeois parliamentarism' based on the power of the parties and the kind of 'parliamentary cock-fights' that were familiar in Western Europe. Democracy and parliamentarism stood for two different things and were defined by the Marxists in ways that made all bourgeois proposals unacceptable. At the same time, Kuusinen accused the constitutional proposal of constituting a coup against the power of parliament.[1418] The major question in Kuusinen's view was whether the Finnish system would award supreme power to the parliament without retaining an executive body capable of opposing the will of parliament, or whether the dual system would be retained with some power being placed in the parliament and some in the government so that the latter would regulate the parliament. In other words, 'whether the people are to be allowed to rule themselves via the parliament or whether the people shall remain under oligarchic power?'[1419] Kuusinen's suggested 'parliamentary democracy'[1420] of the Social Democratic kind would include an imperative mandate: 'When the supreme power is invested in the parliament, then the people must also have a democratic right to control the dealings and failures of every representative in the parliament. . . . The parliament can fulfil its duties properly only under the healthy control of democracy.'[1421] Kuusinen's speech left the impression that the Social Democrats were, despite their anti-parliamentary rhetoric, aiming at a truer parliamentary democracy than the

1414 *Hufvudstadsbladet*, 'Från kammare och kuloar', 20 November 1917.
1415 *Työmies*, 'Tiedonanto työwäelle', 9 November 1917.
1416 *Työmies*, 'Porwariston likaista syytöstulvaa wastaan', 24 November 1917.
1417 Nyström 2013, 208, 220.
1418 VP, Otto Wille Kuusinen, 5 December 1917, 348, 350–1, 355; see also Matti Airola, 5 December 1917, 358.
1419 VP, Otto Wille Kuusinen, 5 December 1917, 349; also Alma Jokinen, 5 December 1917, 364.
1420 VP, Otto Wille Kuusinen, 5 December 1917, 355.
1421 VP, Otto Wille Kuusinen, 5 December 1917, 353.

bourgeois parties. There is no doubt, however, that many Social Democratic MPs were inspired by Lenin's idea of destroying the structures of the class state such as parliaments rather than aiming to take them over.[1422] The Parliament of the Workers' Associations soon called for the renunciation of parliamentary activity, but the struggle within the party would continue until late January.[1423]

There were now fewer bourgeois responses to Kuusinen; an increasing number of representatives were giving up arguing with the Social Democrats as unproductive. Onni Talas (Young Finns), responding on behalf of the government, argued that even under the most democratic suffrage system the parliament did not always express the true will of the people, as 'the parliament is by no means the same thing as the people';[1424] this would have represented an average liberal view in Germany or Sweden as well. Talas also presented British parliamentarism as exemplary, which was exceptional in the Finnish debates of 1917 or 1918. However, he stated that the discrepancy between the broad suffrage and the limited power of parliament should be resolved. Instead of making parliament an omnipotent user of potentially 'oligarchic' power, however, Talas preferred – in the name of democracy – that the people be allowed in certain cases, after a presidential intervention, decide whether the parliament had interpreted their wishes correctly.[1425] Parliamentarism and presidential power would thus be combined in ways that resembled the later formulation in the Weimar Constitution. Here, his proposal was influenced by the transnational theoretical debate on the deficiencies of parliamentarism. The Finnish debate would, however, be interrupted by a civil war, and after it the constitutional debate would take on a very different tone.

1422 Pipes 1992, 396.
1423 Soikkanen 1975, 258.
1424 VP, Onni Talas, 6 December 1917, 368.
1425 VP, Onni Talas, 6 December 1917, 368–9.

5. The spring of 1918: Western and Prussian versions of 'parliamentarism' clash in the Swedish and Finnish parliaments

5.1 Britain after of the Representation of the People Act

The year 1918 opened with an international debate following Woodrow Wilson's Fourteen Points, presented to the U.S. Congress on 8 January and calling for the reorganization of the international order after the war. The general principles concerning the future world order put forward by Wilson shaped the course of transnational discourse during the year once again. During the spring, Wilson added explicit demands for the democratization of Germany as a precondition for peace as he interpreted the terms of the Treaty of Brest-Litovsk as an expression of German imperialism that needed to be countered with heavier demands. He spoke in particular about the rejection of *European* traditions of secret diplomacy and about making the world safe with the universal adoption of liberal democracy (in its American form) everywhere. David Lloyd George, the British prime minister, also took a stand on the war aims in January, albeit a still rather speculative one; he did not call for a regime change in Germany since, in the aftermath of the Bolshevik Revolution, his concerns were focused on the rise of the working class both at home and abroad. When the German spring offensive of 1918 started, however, he joined Wilson's definition of the war as an act of self-defence of the democracies of the world. In his foreign policy, Lloyd George used references to democracy more to divide the Germans than to really campaign for democratisation there; even less did he aim at any radical democratisation at home. Generally, the discursive turn of spring 1917 was reinforced in spring 1918, and the war between the imperialist great powers was even more clearly transformed into a war for the defence of Western democracy worldwide. This Wilsonian discourse included notions of a free economy and the right of self-determination (relevant for smaller nations like the Finns), and it proposed that the administration of future international relations should be given to an intergovernmental organisation of democratic nations that would solve conflicts peacefully while respecting the territories of the member states.[1426]

1426 Soutou 2014, 522–3; Leonhard 2014, 807–808, 810; Müller 2014, 32; cf. Newton 1997, 416, Cunningham 2001, 238, and Fry 2011, 144–5, on Lloyd George's changing tactics being motivated by domestic political interests.

In the meantime, Britain had concluded a suffrage reform but kept public discussion on the country's future form of government to the minimum. In the final debates on the Representation of the People Bill in the Lords, criticisms of female suffrage and technical aspects of the reform were still heard, but the opposition peers mainly abstained from voting against the reform in order to avoid a further confrontation with the Commons. Universal suffrage was recognised by the great majority of the Conservatives – even including many of the opposing minority – as unavoidable. Proportional representation was advocated by the Lords but was voted down by the Commons. A plan for further reform, too, was rejected in May.[1427] Some matters concerning related practicalities such as the costs of the Act, were taken up in several parliamentary questions in the following session, but there were no extensive debates on them. The suffrage reform seemed to have been completed, and constitutional discussion now turned to other matters.

Owing to the continuing war and the reservations of the government in referring to democracy, the British act was not really celebrated as a measure of democratisation. In practice, however, it would – when it was implemented after the ceasefire – change the political system in the direction of a representative parliamentary democracy based on nearly universal suffrage in a more radical way than any of the numerous previous reforms.[1428] Britain was about to become a representative democracy, at least to the extent to which William Hurrell Mallock had defined the concept in November 1917, and one with nearly universal suffrage to boot:[1429]

> *Democracy* is a word which may be conveniently and correctly employed to designate the constitution of any complex State, if by all parties concerned it is understood to mean simply a state in which the democratic principle is powerful within certain limits; in which it is provided with legal means of expressing itself; and which is thus contrasted with States in which no such means exist.

The democratic principle within certain limits did not mean for the anti-socialist Mallock or the conservatives in general that 'in political government . . . merely popular power . . . can be supreme in any great State whatever'. Oligarchy would still be needed side by side with democracy.[1430]

Universal male suffrage had been introduced in many European states (including France and Germany) before that, and women's suffrage in some (including Finland and Norway). Britain was nevertheless a pioneer in the transnational wave of democratising and parliamentarising constitutions in 1918 and 1919, and the British reform added to the pressures for reform in other countries, Germany and Sweden included. The British constitutional reform was not to the same extent a result of outside pressures as in Germany, Sweden and Finland, although the exceptional wartime

---

1427 Machin 2001, 144–6; Curtice 2003, 505.
1428 Machin 2001, 146.
1429 Mallock 1918, 389.
1430 Mallock 1918, 390–2.

circumstances made it possible with the joint war experience changing the attitudes of the Conservatives and to a lesser extent those of the Liberals. The suffragette violence had also ceased during the war, and there was a general determination to avoid its re-emergence during or after the war. Both of these factors supported a wartime revision of the political system.[1431]

For many of the British political elite, the Representation of the People Bill had not really been about democracy; it was about motivating the nation to support the war effort and to prepare for post-war reconstruction. Democratic ideals continued to be emphasised during the first half of 1918 mostly in the international context with reference to Wilson's Fourteen Points.[1432] Nor did the War Cabinet hesitate to suggest that the war was being fought for 'democratic government' and that, as a consequence of the war, 'the whole community has received an education in the problems of practical democracy'.[1433] The continuing rarity of comments in both Conservative and Liberal papers on the constitutional change as a further democratisation or parliamentarisation of the British government is noteworthy. *The Manchester Guardian* consistently used these terms for the Prussian reform only, reporting on 27 February how the Prussian government, with its proposal to 'the Prussian Diet' (not recognised as a parliament), was attempting to turn the Herrenhaus into an even stronger bulwark against the democratisation of Germany. The conclusion was that any Prussian franchise reform (much expected during the first half of 1917), should it be realised, 'will be as far as ever from what Western Europe calls democracy'.[1434] If someone suggested the democratisation of the German government in the Reichstag, or if 'the Junker press' wrote against such democratisation, this was readily reported in *The Manchester Guardian*.[1435] Such news only deepened the divide between the (still vague) Western conception of democracy and Prussianism as defined in Allied war propaganda.

Within the British Labour Party, the rhetoric of democracy in an international Wilsonian or socialist sense was favoured in referring to a democratic peace, for instance, and the domestic political implications of the concept also appeared in phrases like 'the democratic control of society'.[1436] In the eyes of radical reformists, by contrast, the constitutional reform remained deplorably incomplete after the Representation of the People Act,[1437] as the wartime realities of the concentration of power had not changed. *The Herald* complained with irony how '[w]e are all kept slaves toiling and suffering and groping in the dark of this "war for democracy"' and saw as the only solution the Commons replacing 'the

1431 Machin 2001, 154.
1432 *The Times*, '"Hard, Practical Necessity"', 12 January 1918, for instance.
1433 *The Times*, 'The War Cabinet Report', 19 March 1918.
1434 *The Manchester Guardian*, 'Franchise Reform in Prussia', 27 February 1918.
1435 *The Manchester Guardian*, 'Economic Policy', 14 May 1918; 'As the Germans See It', 14 June 1918.
1436 *The Times*, 'President Wilson's Message', 10 January 1918, 'Labour's Election Plans', 6 March 1918, 'New Social Order', 9 May 1918, 'Labour Policy', 24 June 1918.
1437 Close 1977, 907.

present self-constituted and bungling bureaucracy' – an accusation familiar in Germany, Sweden and Finland as well – with 'a Government that the people can trust'. The new government of the people should adopt 'a new policy of publicity, democracy, and peace by negotiation', ending a war that was 'the very negation of democracy'. *The Herald*, while recognising the merits of Woodrow Wilson, questioned the sincerity of his calls for democracy given the concentration of power in his own hands.[1438] As for Britain, the Commons had 'abrogated all authority as well as all decency, and become a laughing-stock even to itself'. Parliamentarism did not work, and the will of the people did not count despite the calls for democracy in war propaganda. The organ of the pacifist far left opposition was also unhappy with the unwillingness of the War Cabinet to get Britain out of the war, suggesting that secret diplomacy and military rule did not allow even the prime minister to govern, the implication being that Britain was not any better than Prussia, despite claims to the contrary:[1439]

> The nation acquiesces, it is true, in a sense. But if this sort of depressed and embittered acquiescence is democracy, then militarist Prussia is a democracy, and Tsarist Russia was a democracy. Have our brothers died to make the world 'safe' for *this* sort of democracy?

The Herald insisted that it was neither the army nor the press but the people who should rule in a genuine democracy.[1440] H. N. Brailsford, in particular, questioned whether Britain was 'a civilian democracy' and implied that the country was ruled by Lord Northcliffe's press, not Parliament – just as Germany was ruled by Ludendorff and not the Reichstag;[1441] this analogy with Prussia was extremely provocative. Evidence of 'Prussian' measures were also found in the field of foreign policy: the British government was accused of planning to recognise the 'anti-Socialist, anti-democratic, oligarchical and militarist' Finnish White government in summer 1918 after the civil war in that country while refraining from recognising the Bolshevik government.[1442] The far left was marginal in Britain, to be sure, but it kept the debate on democracy going.

Nor were the Conservatives all that satisfied with the reformed polity, despite the optimistic expectations of the majority. Many of those who had opposed the reform still considered a reform of the upper house essential to counterbalance the extensions of suffrage: according to them, the constitutional circumstances preceding the Parliament Act of 1911 should be restored. If such a reform were introduced, perhaps full universal suffrage could also be awarded as the Lords would again be able to hold up the measures of a potential Labour government until a general election or

---

1438 *The Herald*, 'Then go, Lloyd George!', 14 February 1918.
1439 *The Herald*, 'Who rules Britain now?', 18 March 1918.
1440 *The Herald*, 'Who rules Britain now?', 18 March 1918.
1441 *The Herald*, H. N. Brailsford, 'Nationality, Party, and Class', 29 June 1918, and 'The Fall of von Kühlmann', 20 July 1918.
1442 *The Herald*, 'Bourgeois and Bolshevik', 1 June 1918.

a referendum.¹⁴⁴³ This reasoning of the opposition Conservatives resembles that of the Swedish right in their opposition to universal suffrage as long as the continued existence of an upper house as a counterweight was not guaranteed – and the desire of the Swedish People's Party to establish a second chamber in Finland.

The Speaker's Conference had also taken up the possibility of reforming the Lords and restoring some of its influence, but the proposals were not taken any further.¹⁴⁴⁴ Another commission – nominated in 1917 and chaired by Viscount Bryce (Liberal), a sceptic of modern democracy – reached a compromise on the future tasks of the upper chamber but not on its membership. The Lords would not regain power over financial matters, and disagreements would be solved by a joint committee. But even this proposal was not brought before the Commons by the government.¹⁴⁴⁵ The War Cabinet rejected the reform, and the House of Lords remained very much what it had been since 1911.¹⁴⁴⁶ As we have seen, Britain had become a parliamentary democracy in a twentieth-century sense as far as the lower chamber was concerned, but it retained the House of Lords as an advisory deliberative body.

Jörn Leonhard has shown how the degree of parliamentary government in Britain faced a major test in spring 1918 simultaneously with some of the worst battles on the Western Front. In Britain, too, the relations between military and political leaders tended to become confrontational under the pressures of the war. A serious parliamentary crisis seemed to be at hand when the War Cabinet wished to cut recruitment numbers to save the work force for coal and food production, as a result of which a top military officer publicly accused the government of failing to supply sufficient troops and of hiding this failure from Parliament, and some of the Liberal opposition joined the criticism. Prime Minister Lloyd George, by attacking officers for leaking military secrets, managed to turn the debate in Parliament and win support for the political control of the military. A vote of no-confidence on the war policies of the cabinet followed, and the government emerged from the division a clear winner. This was a demonstration of the residual strength of parliamentary government, for even though Parliament had been marginalised from significant decision making in the wartime, the principles of parliamentary government had survived. This differs distinctly from the German case, where the military had practically taken over political power both from the representative institution and from the monarchy, which was supposed to supervise all executive power. The Prussian model, as applied during the First World War, forced the politicians to blindly count on their military leaders – to the extent that the legitimacy of the monarchy became dependent on the achievements of the military.¹⁴⁴⁷

1443 Close 1977, 909–10.
1444 Pugh 2002, 157.
1445 Walters 2003, 229.
1446 Rush 2001, 74; Lyon 2003, 390.
1447 Leonhard 2014, 866, 932–3.

5.2 Germany: All quiet on the reform front

Spring 1917 had seen rising demands and expectations for a suffrage reform in Prussia and for the parliamentarisation of government in Germany. During the summer of 1917, the overly optimistic prospects of the reformists had been effectively quashed by the new chancellor and the stubborn General Staff, and a conservative reaction against reform followed in the autumn. By spring 1918, it had become evident that any future political reform depended on when and how the war would end. The Reich would not be parliamentarised nor the Prussian suffrage democratised before the restoration of peace. Indeed, it had become increasingly unclear whether these would change even after the war, especially as the Central Powers were still expected to win it. The German army launched a new operation in the west in spring 1918 with the aim of ending the war. The parliamentary majority might be complaining about its lack of influence in deciding about peace terms and military strategy, but that changed little in the actual policy that was pursued.[1448]

In the prevailing circumstances, reforms had little chance of making any progress. Indeed, setbacks followed: we have already mentioned the news in British papers about the Herrenhaus opposing reform. In the Preußisches Abgeordnetenhaus (the Prussian House of Representatives), the leading conservative parties, half of the National Liberals and some of the Catholic Centre used their majority and threw out a government proposal on a Prussian suffrage reform on 2 May 1918. As the spring offensive seemed to make good progress, political stability was prioritised to equal political rights. The Kaiser, for his part, continued to vituperate Western plutocracy in his speeches. For him, political reform in Germany meant vindicating German freedom,[1449] that is, retaining as much of the established order as possible. This Prussian stubbornness and proclivity for conservative rhetorical redescriptions also strengthened the inflexible line of the Swedish right in its opposition to a parallel reform, and it was even more decisive for the determination of the Finnish right to replace the republican constitutional proposal of December 1917 with a monarchical one in summer 1918. The stagnant state of constitutional affairs in Germany thus made the future of political reform uncertain in other countries, too. In the eyes of the Swedish and Finnish right, the Treaty of Brest-Litowsk in the east and the new German offensive in the west appeared as further demonstrations of the unbending strength of the Prussian political system which spoke against extended democratisation or the extension of the powers of their own national parliaments. Spring 1918 consequently saw the reinforcement of Prussianism as a political model in both countries.

Such optimistic and downright opportunistic interpretations inside and outside Germany overlooked the evident weaknesses of the German polity. The earlier political truce between the parties, for instance, no longer existed. In January 1918, there were hunger demonstrations and extensive strikes in

---

1448 Grosser 1970, 152; Dahlmann 2014, 49.
1449 Stibbe 2001, 190–1; Müller 2002, 308.

several German towns accompanied by calls for for peace and a suffrage reform in Prussia and expressing sympathy with the Russian workers. When the spring offensive failed to bring the war to the expected victorious end, German public opinion turned increasingly sceptical about its outcome,[1450] and the legitimacy of the prevailing political order began to wither away. In Sweden and Finland, it took longer for public opinion, and especially rightist views, to rethink and to re-orientate themselves. In both countries, developments not only in Germany but also in their neighbouring countries tended to reinforce the conservative reactions that dominated their political scenes in the spring and summer of 1918.

5.3 Sweden: A parliamentarised ministry introduces its first reform proposal

5.3.1 Anti-reformism bolstered by a civil war next door

By autumn 1917, it had become obvious that revolutionaries of the Russian type would find only marginal support in Sweden: the far left did very badly in the elections, and the Social Democrats had prioritised parliamentary work and cooperation with the reformist bourgeoisie over direct action. They only even hinted very selectively at the possibility of a popular uprising. Soon after the October Revolution, the Swedish Social Democratic Labour Party officially denounced the revolutionary methods used by the Bolsheviks as hostile to democracy and set out to help Lenin's political rivals instead. The party consequently also condemned the revolutionary attempt to overthrow a parliamentary majority and parliamentary government by the radicalised Finnish Social Democrats in late January 1918. Social Democratic papers waged a fiercely anti-Bolshevist campaign, and the revisionist party leaders spoke for reforms that aimed at strengthening parliamentary democracy in Sweden. This had become their first priority; the longer-term goals of building socialism would need to wait. At the same time, only the marginal leftist press in Sweden sympathised with the Bolsheviks in Russia and the Reds in Finland.[1451] They were the only group to express understanding for the Finnish revolution in the Riksdag as well.

Swedish politics, and especially the constitutional reform, were in this period intimately entangled with developments in Finland, as well as with those in Germany and Russia, even though that has not been generally recognised in Swedish research. Even if the Civil War in Finland of January–April 1918 did not concern the Swedish constitution as such, its influence on Swedish reform discussions was inevitable: a class-based ideological and highly emotional debate for and against an intervention in the Finnish war and on the possible exportation of weapons to the army of the Finnish government ensued. Even if a revolution in Sweden seemed increasingly unlikely, the Red rebels rising in arms against a legal non-socialist government in a sister country caused concern among the Swedish right as well.

1450 Dahlmann 2014, 49; Bessel 2014, 131; Leonhard 2014, 873.
1451 Kan 1999a, 146; Olsson 2000, 122.

Indeed, a Finnish revolution was much more alarming for them than the tumults in the culturally and geographically much more remote Russia; the cause of Finland was at this critical moment easily interpreted as the cause of Sweden. Some rightist activists had been considering an intervention in Finland earlier during the First World War, but by January 1918 all Swedish parliamentary parties had already rejected an open intervention. Much of the press and bourgeois public opinion together with many Liberal ministers nevertheless wished to support the Finnish White government, justifying this (in rather racial if not downright racist terms) by the cultural connections between Swedish-speaking Finns and Sweden. The labour movement, by contrast, opposed and organised an extensive counter-campaign to condemn alleged bourgeois plans to intervene or sell weapons to the Whites in Finland.[1452]

Since the Liberals did not wish to endanger their new-born coalition with the Social Democrats, in view of the agreed plans for extensive reforms, they refrained from suggesting open support for the Finnish Whites. The Majority Social Democrats, on the other hand, also prioritised reformist cooperation at home and hence made a concession to the Liberals by in practice allowing the smuggling of weapons to Finland.[1453] This was not even against their principles in the sense that they had denounced the Finnish rising. At the same time, revolution in Sweden had become an all the more unrealistic option once the Social Democrats saw what was happening east of the Gulf of Bothnia. Cooperation with the Liberals at home to advance reforms was for them a much better option than support for the ideologically dubious revolutionary struggle of the Finnish working class; associations with that isolated and over-radicalised – even Bolshevik – movement were rather to be avoided. The domestic political situation thus led to the Liberal-Social Democratic ministry not taking any official stand on the Finnish conflict while allowing private Swedish activists to support the White government there.[1454] The Finnish cause was important for the Swedish parties but secondary to domestic and foreign policy concerns.

All the same, the divisions caused in Swedish society by the Finnish Civil War were deep. Many rightists saw the White Finns as fighting a war of independence that official Sweden should support. The historian Olof Palme (a Swedish-speaking Finn in origin) asserted that the struggle of the Finns was 'to save that social order and culture which the Swedes have founded in past times and which have ever since been maintained and cherished'.[1455] It was 'the struggle of the Swedes themselves that is going on in Finland', condescendingly implying that the Swedes should also take care of the semi-barbarous Finns.[1456] Stopping the Reds in Finland was viewed

---

1452 *Aftonbladet*, 'Dödsfaran för svensk kultur i Finland', 20 February 1918; *Social-Demokraten*, 'Mot Finlandsaktivismen', 20 February 1918; Andræ 1998, 13–14, 158, 165–6, 170, 174.
1453 Andræ 1998, 174.
1454 Olsson 2000, 122–3.
1455 Quoted in Nilsson 2002a, 22.
1456 Nilsson 2002a, 26.

as a way to discourage revolutionary socialists in Sweden, but not even the rightist leaders called for an intervention. Moderate Social Democrats were critical of the Red rebellion but repudiated support for the White government, whereas more radical Social Democrats and leftists viewed the Finnish war in Marxist lines as a concrete class struggle between the workers and the upper classes; what made the struggle even worse for them was the fact that the Finnish bourgeoisie had turned to the Prussians for help: the Finnish Civil War was a truly fundamental ideological conflict that reflected the ideological and international confrontations of the time. The Social Democratic press was doubtful about sending volunteers, and leftists denounced all such one-sided involvement in the class struggle. The Liberal-Social Democratic ministry looked for a middle way, determined to avoid engagement in the war on the German side, rejecting intervention and refraining from giving direct help. In the meantime, rightist volunteers were able to leave for Finland, Swedish companies sold arms to the Whites and German troops were allowed to travel through Swedish maritime waters to Finland, the last a concession that might compromise Swedish neutrality in the eyes of the Entente. There was one interventionary measure on which the Swedes did agree, however: Swedish troops were sent to the Åland Islands to support a local separatist movement that aimed at a union with Sweden and to take over an important strategic area. This was a measure that violated the interests of White Finland[1457] and caused tension between the two countries for years to come. Together with the perceived unwillingness of the Swedish government to openly support the legal Finnish government, this intervention led to contemporary Sweden being marginalised to an exceptional degree in Finnish constitutional debates, which differed from the usual Finnish cultural practice of comparing Finland with Sweden.

There was rightist sympathy for Finland, and particularly for Swedish-speaking Finns, whereas transnational contacts between Swedish and Finnish socialists remained few. The Swedish Social Democratic Party – unlike the Finnish one – had been divided before the Russian Revolution, and its majority focused on obtaining governmental power through elections; in this the Finnish example was uncomfortable rather than encouraging. Some contacts had been created with K. H. Wiik and Yrjö Sirola from the Finnish sister party during spring 1917, but the Swedish Social Democrats still continued to read reports of events in Finland from bourgeois newspapers, in particular the ultra-conservative *Hufvudstadsbladet*. The party wanted to avoid all association with Bolshevism, and this included the radical Marxism that had taken over the Finnish party in 1917. Once the Finnish party sought to launch an armed struggle, the Swedish Social Democrats denounced the uprising as 'a denial of the founding principle of democracy, a declaration of violence of a minority over the majority of the people'. The leftists, in the meantime, retained direct contacts with their Finnish comrades, reported on their campaign positively, attacked the bourgeois and Social Democratic papers for disparaging the Finnish working class, criticised rightist activism

---

1457 Nyman 1965, 19–20; Carlsson 1985, 91; Hadenius, Nilsson & Åselius 1996, 374; Nilsson 2002a, 24–8.

and shared many of the ideological premises cherished by the Finnish Reds. For instance, both were ready to engage in extra-parliamentary violence if parliamentary methods failed to produce the necessary reforms. Such conflicting attitudes to the Finnish Civil War deepened confrontations between the two socialist parties in Sweden, especially when, in the leftists' view, the governing Social Democrats consistently prioritised the coalition with the Liberals and seemed to have capitulated to 'bourgeois' democracy and 'Western' parliamentarism for power-political reasons. The Majority Social Democrats condemned the attack against 'a democratic constitution' by the Finnish Social Democrats and presented themselves as fighting 'for a more democratic constitution' in Sweden.[1458] The reactions to the Finnish situation helped to clarify the ideology of the party further: revolutionary means were rejected and democracy obtained through parliamentary means was firmly set as the goal. The Right might view their calls for parliamentarisation and further democratisation with concern, but fears about demonstrations and uprisings never materialised as the majority of Swedish workers believed that the Liberal-Social Democratic ministry was capable of bringing in a constitutional reform. The Swedish workers were discouraged by news about the failed strikes in Germany and the internecine revolt in Finland, so the Social Democratic leaders had no problem in keeping their supporters placated. The far leftists in Sweden hence never managed to form councils that would have radicalised the workers in the way they did in Finland and Germany.[1459]

The much expected proposal on suffrage reform was introduced to the Swedish parliament once it had become clear that the Finnish Civil War would end with the defeat of the Red rebels. It was introduced despite the enduring belief in a German victory in the war and knowledge of the postponement of reforms in Germany. Both international factors were likely to strengthen the rightist opposition, which, having retained a majority in the First Chamber, could vote the proposal down in any case.[1460] At the same time, the state of international affairs was also changing in some respects: Britain was demonstrating increasing diplomatic interest in Scandinavia in order to prevent the expansion of the Bolshevik Revolution and perhaps engage Sweden in pacifying the situation in the Baltic states (if not in the war against Germany). Sweden was increasingly dependent on British supplies as opposed to those from Germany, which was in deepening economic trouble. The Swedish media paid increasing attention to the Entente, no longer prioritising the German point of view, and willingly published news on Bolshevik acts of terror in Russia and Finland.[1461] A turn from a pro-German to a pro-British foreign policy had begun, although it would be completed only after the defeat of Germany was beyond doubt.

1458 Andræ 1998, 175–82.
1459 Andræ 1998, 13–14, 186, 191–2, 194, 196.
1460 Andræ 1998, 244, 269.
1461 Andræ 1998, 214–15.

5.3.2 SURROUNDING WARS AND REVOLUTIONS AS TRANSNATIONAL AGENTS OF POLITICAL CHANGE

The Finnish Civil War was intensively debated in the Swedish parliament and the press in February 1918: members of the upper chamber crowded the galleries of the lower house, where representatives shouted interjections in a way rarely heard in the Swedish representative institution.[1462] The debate was initiated by a far left interpellation that urged the government not to intervene in the Finnish conflict. The Liberal prime minister Nils Edén, who had just met a delegation of Finnish bourgeois parliamentarians asking for help,[1463] talked about a 'brother country' whose internal strife touched all Swedes, presented the acts of the Reds as 'anarchical delusions' and was determined to prevent possible 'contagions' in Sweden.[1464] Hjalmar Branting emphasised the condemnatory stand of the Social Democrats with regard to the Red rebellion and questioned the necessity of 'the revolutionary measures' which the far left at home appeared to be supporting. According to Branting, a revolution should be made peacefully through parliament; it was a mistake by the Bolsheviks (and by implication the Finnish Reds and the Swedish far left) to view universal suffrage as an outdated institution.[1465] Arvid Lindman, the leader of The Right could side with the ministry on this issue, condemning the leaders of the Reds (in Finland and by implication in Sweden as well) as 'commissars of the people'.[1466] Anti-Bolshevism united the great majority in the lower chamber.

Even Ivar Vennerström of the leftist Social Democrats recognised that 'from the point of view of Western European democracy the attempt of the Finnish revolutionaries appears rather dubious'.[1467] However, whether this Western bourgeois democracy constituted an ideal to follow was another matter. The desperate situation of the Finnish comrades actually legitimised their actions: in parallel circumstances, Vennerström suggested, the Swedish workers would also have found themselves 'on the side of the revolutionaries now that the revolution must come and could no longer be stopped';[1468] this was an expression of transnational far leftist beliefs that the time for an unavoidable revolution had arrived. The Swedish leftists shared the Red interpretation of the causes of the Finnish Civil War: the Finnish bourgeoisie had malevolently allied itself with the Russian bourgeoisie and German militarism, made an illegal coup against the Social Democratic majority of the Finnish parliament and acted as counter-revolutionaries against the constitution in advocating a monarchical republic of the American type as opposed to a democratic republic of the Swiss type (as suggested by Otto Wille Kuusinen in December 1917). A further factor behind 'the Finnish

---

1462 *Aftonbladet*, 'Regeringen och Finland', 20 February 1918; *Dagens Nyheter*, 'Regeringens ställning till Finland', 21 February 1918.
1463 *Aftonbladet*, 'Den finländska deputationens första framträdande', 19 February 1918.
1464 AK, Nils Edén, 20 February 1918, 16:6.
1465 AK, Hjalmar Branting, 20 February 1918, 16:39.
1466 AK, Arvid Lindman, 20 February 1918, 16:29.
1467 AK, Ivar Vennerström, 20 February 1918, 16:11.
1468 AK, Ivar Vennerström, 20 February 1918, 16:11.

revolution' was the existence of famine there,[1469] a matter that concerned Sweden as well. If 'Swedish revolutionaries' did emerge, however, they would not opt for the violence used by the Finns. Internationalism among the socialists existed, to be sure, but the Swedish rightists belonged to a different international network, one that was guilty of instigating both the world war and, as a consequence, the rise of revolutions.[1470] According to this transnational Marxist conspiracy theory, they must now be prevented from joining their cronies in fighting 'a so-called anti-revolutionary preventive war' on Finnish soil.[1471] The constructions of two rival internationalisms, familiar from the Finnish context, were present in the Swedish parliamentary discourse as well.

Further international comparisons and interpretations of the position of Sweden in a war-faring and revolutionary Europe were heard in debates on the proposal for suffrage reform in April. The Liberals now set out to define Sweden as a Western democracy, thereby challenging both the right and the far left: Minister of Justice Eliel Löfgren, Prime Minister Edén and Vice-Speaker Raoul Hamilton justified equal suffrage for men and women by comparisons with Norway, Denmark,[1472] Finland, Britain, the Netherlands, the United States and Australia; the experiences of these countries, as well as the conduct of Swedish women, showed that neither riots nor revolutions would follow from women's suffrage. The case for female suffrage had made considerable progress internationally after the war had removed the plausibility of counterarguments, constituting, in the words of the feminist activist and socialist intellectual Ellen Key, a decisive 'moment in world history'.[1473] This moment made it necessary to reject older political conceptions, to communicate an activating message to the people at large and to thereby demonstrate willingness by the political elite to take 'a major step towards a new age'.[1474] The Swedish Liberals had no explicit reservations at all about the reform being necessitated by the war, which differs from the stance of many liberals in Britain and Germany.

The Social Democrats linked the war experiences and the essential need for a global reform in similar terms.[1475] According to Harald Hallén, the front lines of the war had now reached Sweden, where the battle was being fought between democratic and anti-democratic ideals,[1476] the suggestion being that Sweden should clearly change sides from Prussianism to democracy and introduce a constitutional reform. The continuous insinuations about

---

1469 AK, 20 February 1918, 16:12–13, 16.
1470 AK, 20 February 1918, 16:17, 21.
1471 AK, 20 February 1918, 16:23.
1472 Erik Röing, a businessman from Gothenburg, pointed to the elections in Denmark a few days earlier with women participating peacefully in the voting. AK, 27 April 1918, 44:51.
1473 AK, Eliel Löfgren, 27 April 1918, 44:15, 20; FK, Nils Edén, 27 April 1918, 27:26, 30–1, 89; AK, Raoul Hamilton, 27 April 1918, 44:60; *Dagens Nyheter*, 'Kvinnornas rösträtt fallen ännu en gång', 28 April 1918.
1474 FK, Nils Edén, 27 April 1918, 27:77, 79.
1475 FK, Olof Olsson, 27 April 1918, 27:48.
1476 AK, 27 April 1918, 44:37.

ideological links between the Swedish and German right were plausible as the transnational contacts between them had indeed been intimate and news expressing admiration of Germany constantly appeared in rightist papers.[1477] Various transnational arguments were used to persuade The Right to rethink such links. Arthur Engberg (who had himself studied in Germany) suggested that the rightists had overlooked Friedrich Meinecke's recommendation to award political rights to the people at large after 'the globally historic teachings of the world war'.[1478] Engberg contrasted – in a counterfactual manner given the prevailing conservative reaction in Germany since summer 1917[1479] and Meinecke's rejections of the popular state and parliamentarism in favour of a militaristic monarchy[1480] – 'the Prussian right with its modern trends of thought' with the outdated notions of the Swedish right.[1481] Hjalmar Branting emphasised the unavoidable impact of 'external' political trends on Swedish politics, presenting the uncompromising rightist opposition to female suffrage as belying news of developments in Germany and the rest of the world.[1482]

The Right had a different conception. Claims about a progressing transnational wave of democracy in the sense of extended voting rights were hardly supported by events in contemporary Germany (apart, at least, from the Social Democratic *Vorwärts*). On the contrary, a transnational anti-democratic counter-reaction was visible: The victory of the reactionary forces in Germany had made the Swedish right unwilling to make any further concessions, particularly as the already awarded parliamentarisation needed to be kept in check and there was no evidence of Germany losing the war. The Finnish case, for its part, demonstrated that a hard line by the bourgeoisie worked best: the Civil War had ended two days previously with the victory of the Whites over the socialist revolutionaries. In these circumstances, Swedish Social Democrats avoided all analogies between Sweden and Finland as counterproductive to their reformist cause. Axel Sterne rather emphasised that there was no evidence of female suffrage having contributed to the Finnish Civil War, as some rightists had insinuated, whereas the current world war had been started by male leaders.[1483] For Swedish MPs, the Finnish crisis remained a disaster the potential relevance of which was known but played down by the reformists to counter rightist use of Finland as a demonstration of what democratisation might entail.

1477 Erik Palmstierna reported in his diary that the leaders of The Right were visiting Berlin every year. Palmstierna 1953, 23 March 1918, 154; Aftonbladet. 'De politiska nybildningarna vid Östersjön', 27 April 1918.
1478 AK, Arthur Engberg, 27 April 1918, 44:58.
1479 However, there had also been news about the continuation of reform plans in Prussia. *Aftonbladet*, 19 February 1918. *Social-Demokraten* wrote on the preceding day about a turning point in the democratisation of Germany. 'Inför en vändpunkt?', 26 April 1918.
1480 Stibbe 2001, 169; Bruendel 2003, 187–8; Leonhard 2006, 218; Meinecke would only give in to 'wahre und gute Demokratie' [true and good democracy] in late October 1918. Bruendel 2003, 240, 249.
1481 AK, Arthur Engberg, 27 April 1918, 44:59.
1482 AK, Hjalmar Branting, 27 April 1918, 44:74–5.
1483 AK, Axel Sterne, 27 April 1918, 44:67.

Reforms abroad warranted no reform in Sweden as far as the rightist academics was concerned.[1484] Harald Hjärne, a professor of history and the grand old man of The Right, pointed out that authoritative figures (both political and academic) in Britain and Germany continued to warn against extensions of suffrage,[1485] Viscount Bryce being a British case in point. Ernst Trygger took the higher age limit for women as a demonstration of well-founded British doubts.[1486] Women remained 'politically all too immature' to vote, and 'cultured countries' such as France – 'particularly advanced in questions of social understanding and social development' – had no intention of extending the franchise to women.[1487] No advances in social policy, increased justice or peace would follow anyway,[1488] as could be seen in Norway and Finland: women voters may not have caused the Finnish Civil War, but they had not been able to prevent it either.[1489] While some rightists played down all need for reform, others turned to a crisis discourse that viewed reform as impossible in the current circumstances, and all accused the left of abusing the manipulative power of the press to create a sense of urgency in the need for reform.[1490] In Sweden, there was, in fact, too much public debate, they claimed.

A further confrontation was seen when the government's proposal was put before a plenary session again in June 1918. The consequences of the victory of the Finnish Whites had become clear. A monarchical, reactionary constitutional proposal was expected to be introduced to the Finnish Rump Parliament. The eastern neighbour now provided warning examples for both sides of the Swedish dispute, though the Social Democrats denied any comparability, looking to the West or back in history rather than appealing to any openly Marxist principles. Axel Sterne, building on an assumed historical comparability of the British and Swedish polities,[1491] went back to what he interpreted as the declaration of the sovereignty of the people through the abolition of the House of Lords by the English Commons in the aftermath of the Civil War in the 1640s, the implication being that the Swedes were deplorably late in abolishing the dominance of the First Chamber.[1492] Gustav Möller, the party secretary, conceded that reactionary views on reform dominated the international scene but nevertheless believed in the rapid recovery of the democratic cause.[1493] Harald Hallén redescribed the situation by quoting the German chancellor Count Georg von Hertling, who had conceded in the Prussian House of Representatives (which had recently rejected a reform) that universal suffrage was the only way to avoid ferment among the people. The German right seemed to understand the

1484 AK, Arvid Lindman, 27 April 1918, 44:40.
1485 FK, Harald Hjärne, 27 April 1918, 27:44–5.
1486 FK, Ernst Trygger, 27 April 1918, 27:90.
1487 AK, Axel Sundberg, 27 April 1918, 44:69–71.
1488 FK, Samuel Clason, 27 April 1918, 27:57.
1489 FK, Carl Boberg, 27 April 1918, 27:42.
1490 FK, Knut von Geijer, 27 April 1918, 27:67.
1491 See Ihalainen 2010 and Ihalainen 2015 on this.
1492 AK, Axel Sterne, 8 June 1918, 72:4.
1493 AK, Gustav Möller, 8 June 1918, 72:24.

necessity of a reform while the Swedish did not.¹⁴⁹⁴ The transnational quotes here reinforced the image of the Swedish right as uncritical sympathisers of Prussia by over-interpreting the news from Berlin, where all reform efforts, as we have seen, remained at a standstill.

The Right was not persuaded by accusations that Sweden was a retarded Prussia. Sweden was doing much better than Finland, which had universal suffrage; clearly, such practices did not protect states against illegal outbreaks of violence challenging the established order.¹⁴⁹⁵ Karl Hildebrand referred to a supposed turn in philosophy, suggesting that 'the syndicalists and members of the Red Guard in Finland' were 'the leading individualists of our time' who stood close to 'pure anarchy'.¹⁴⁹⁶ Universal suffrage would cause similar forces to rise up in Sweden. Hallén, who had attended the party convention of the Finnish Social Democrats in June 1917,¹⁴⁹⁷ questioned such comparisons between Sweden and Finland as unfair because of the different 'cultural conditions' in the two countries. The Finns followed 'zigzag-politics in an extreme form' anyway, and were now proceeding in an undemocratic direction. The Swedes should rather look to Germany, Denmark and Norway to perceive that the time was ripe for democratisation.¹⁴⁹⁸ Hjalmar Branting ignored Finland and saw the history of constitutional reform in nineteenth-century Sweden as being inspired by the Norwegian model of a unicameral parliament.¹⁴⁹⁹ As Wilhelm Gullberg of the Liberals put it, once the Swedes had seen the terrifying scenes of civil strife in Finland, they would never opt for revolutionary methods.¹⁵⁰⁰ Even the far left now referred to revolutionary examples from ancient Rome and modern France rather than to contemporary Marxist examples, especially the Finnish Reds.¹⁵⁰¹ The discredited Finns had been removed for the time being from the list of model polities by all the Swedish parties. Their failed revolution had made a revolution in Sweden a practical impossibility and encouraged a search for other ways to achieve democracy.

5.3.3 An attempted democratic breakthrough

In hindsight, the timing of the government reform proposal of April 1918 was unfortunate: given the circumstances, with reform obstructed in Germany and Finland and the progress of Bolshevism in Russia, there was little incentive for The Right to reconsider. The Finnish crisis had nevertheless helped the various parties to clarify their stands on democracy. All parties had spoken positively about Finnish democracy as such during the Civil War, albeit using this 'democracy' in senses that supported their goals in the incomplete reform process in Sweden.

1494 AK, 8 June 1918, 71: 50; 8 June 1918, 72:25–6.
1495 AK, David Norman, 8 June 1918, 72:9.
1496 AK, Karl Hildebrand, 8 June 1918, 72:17.
1497 Ketola 1987, 140; Eskola 2011, 14–15.
1498 AK, 8 June 1918, 72:26–7, 29.
1499 AK, Hjalmar Branting, 8 June 1918, 72:35.
1500 FK, Wilhelm Gullberg, 8 June 1918, 48:23.
1501 FK, Fredrik Ström, 8 June 1918, 48:15.

Only the leftists had a degree of understanding for the Finnish radical Marxist concept of democracy, which, they admitted, differed from that of 'Swedish and Western European democracy'. The Finnish socialists were not to be condemned for having scorned 'the most democratic society in Europe' or accused of 'dragging the ideal of democracy into the dirt', as Ellen Key and the entire Swedish Social Democratic Labour Party had claimed. The Finnish constitution remained 'the most democratic in the world or at least in Europe' provided that it was observed[1502] – which may have been true of the Finnish Parliament Act or the Power Act but certainly not of the Gustavian constitution, which was still in force. Understanding of the Finnish system was limited and selective. Sympathy with the Finnish Reds was expressed by the leftists but direct associations with them avoided: the Swedish far left did not advocate the sort of extreme 'democracy' that the Finnish Red government aimed at imposing.

Interestingly, the Swedish right also expressed esteem for democracy in Finland during the Civil War, defining the existing political system there (and implicitly in Sweden) as sufficiently democratic, in the Finnish case 'the most democratic that exists in Europe'.[1503] The Swedish Social Democrats were thanked for their condemnation of 'an armed uprising against a parliament elected by the broadest popular vote', which had been against 'the basic principle of democracy';[1504] This brought the Swedish opposition and government onto the same side in support of democracy, at least discursively with regard to a foreign policy issue. Democracy was not, however, the main motivation for The Right to help the White government: the shared constitutional tradition and political values of the two countries counted for more. David Norman, certainly not a democrat himself, made intertextual references to Social Democratic views on the Finnish constitution as 'the most democratic in the entire world', emphasising this recognition of the democratic nature of the Finnish (and implicitly Swedish) societal order as being based on majority parliamentarism and the rejection of rebellion. Norman wondered rhetorically about the Swedish government's reluctance to support the Finnish government on 'the broadest democratic basis' and quoted Harald Hallén's controversial speech of 14 April 1917, in which he had predicted international support for 'Swedish democracy' in its attempts to ensure a democratic development.[1505] Norman turned Hallén's challenge to the Swedish established order rhetorically into an argument for support for the established order in Finland. The Right was making use of the opportunity to put pressure on the Social Democrats, who had presented themselves as transnational advocates of democracy but were now unwilling to give international support for a system they recognised as democratic. While the Finnish Civil War forced the Social Democrats to distance themselves from notions of direct democracy, the Swedish right propagated an interpretation of the established Swedish-Finnish order as inherently

---

1502 AK, Ivar Vennerström, 20 February 1918, 16:10–11.
1503 AK, Arvid Lindman, 20 February 1918, 16:29.
1504 AK, 20 February 1918, 16:32.
1505 AK, David Norman, 20 February 1918, 16:51–3.

'democratic'; this was a conservative argument, but paradoxically it brought The Right over to the side of democracy, at least as they envisioned it.

The Social Democrats indeed saw no justified reason for the Finnish Socialists to make a revolution 'against an entirely democratic social order, against a democratic order which was not endangered' and 'against a democratic parliament elected on the basis of universal suffrage'.[1506] Hjalmar Branting thus defined the political order represented by the Finnish bourgeois government as democratic. He declared further that 'every democracy universally requires that certain basic principles must be observed so that it can be called a democracy', the most important being the power of the majority as opposed to that of a minority. Such a notion of democracy made it impossible to defend any violent seizure of power away from a parliamentary majority.[1507] Democracy and majority parliamentarism became identified with each other, and Bolshevik methods, including those of the Finnish Reds and Swedish leftists, were denounced. According to Per Albin Hansson, the editor-in-chief of *Social-Demokraten*, the Finnish Social Democrats had held such a strong parliamentary position that they could have stuck to parliamentary means to safeguard democracy. By using violence against a parliament elected with universal suffrage they had jeopardised both democracy and the interests of the working class.[1508] A major problem with the Finnish Civil War was that any result might endanger democracy: a victory for the Reds would lead to 'Bolshevist anti-democracy', while a victory for the Whites would produce an extreme reaction; it was best to bring this war to a quick end and to rebuild the democratic foundation of Finland. Hansson, himself regarded as a radical, also pointed ironically to the surprising interest of the Swedish right in democracy outside Sweden;[1509] this illustrates the contemporary awareness of the contingent nature of the rhetoric of democracy opening up possibilities for reconceptualisations.

As soon as the Finnish Civil War was over, the Swedish government set out to increase democracy by extending suffrage. Whereas progress in constitutional reform had stagnated in Germany and Finland, the British parliament had approved a reform in February, the majority of the Conservatives in both houses conceding the necessity of universal suffrage. The Liberals and Social Democrats perhaps hoped that the Swedish right, wishing to avoid the fate of Finland and understanding that the German polity was also bound to be reformed after the war, would be ready for similar concessions. However, scepticism about the possibilities of getting the proposal through existed even in the government ranks despite supportive popular meetings in which Social Democratic leaders reiterated the arguments put forward in parliament. Hjalmar Branting gave an extra-parliamentary speech in which he viewed democracy as the very heart of political life and the means by which society could be changed: 'To work for and to believe in democracy means the recognition of belief

---

1506 AK, Hjalmar Branting, 20 February 1918, 16:37, 39.
1507 AK, Hjalmar Branting, 20 February 1918, 16:39–40.
1508 AK, Per Albin Hansson, 20 February 1918, 16:58.
1509 AK, Per Albin Hansson, 20 February 1918, 16:63.

in humankind.'¹⁵¹⁰ At the same time, the party organ *Social-Demokraten* anticipated that this would be only the beginning in the battle for democracy both inside and outside parliament. The paper conceived of a common front by talking about the left (including the Liberals) as 'democracy', which was opposed to The Right.¹⁵¹¹

In parliament, the coalition contrasted its 'democratic demands' with the policies of The Right.¹⁵¹² The left was moving towards a process-like concept of democracy. Minister of Justice Eliel Löfgren (Liberal) defined the goal of democracy as 'ensuring the undisturbed development of society by giving the privilege of responsibility and a share in it to the many, not only to the few.'¹⁵¹³ Axel von Sneidern (Liberal) suggested that The Right were relying on the uncertainty that the democratic countries would win the war and the possibility of autocracies being restored and were hence unwilling to promise any reform in Sweden.¹⁵¹⁴ Harald Hallén (Social Democratic Party) openly accused The Right of having sided with the 'anti-democratic ideals' of the old regime, which had caused the world war, and of standing against 'the democratic ranks of the people'. This still remained the rightist attitude despite the ever more widely accepted fact that 'only the politically liberated, informed democratic will of the people' was capable of restoring world peace. The Right did not regard democracy and popular sovereignty as capable of rational development, and this increased the pressures for democratisation among 'the masses of the democracy'.¹⁵¹⁵ According to Axel Sterne, Sweden was nevertheless involved in a global 'process of democratic development' and 'a battle of the democracy for political equality' so that The Right would need to adapt themselves to 'the democratic demands of the people, the inevitable demands of the people'.¹⁵¹⁶ Hjalmar Branting, too, viewed democratisation as an ongoing process: Sweden should build on 'democratic ideals' despite transnational signs of a weakening of 'the forces of democracy' in 'the great global battle between democracy and its antithesis'.¹⁵¹⁷ Delays and setbacks in Germany and Finland, the battles on the Western Front and uncertainty about the outcome of the war would not prevent reform in Sweden.

The Right did not share this view that 'a democratic era' had begun. Samuel Clason disliked the way in which *Social-Demokraten* had envisioned democratisation as leading to the takeover of the upper chamber by the left¹⁵¹⁸ and to the consequent removal of a 'counterbalance' to Social Democratic

---

1510 *Social-Demokraten*, 'Nej:et', 29 April 1917; 'Opinionsmötet för en demokratisk författning', 8 June 1918; 10 June 1918; *Aftonbladet* reported that 'the people' were weakly represented in the meeting. 9 June 1918.
1511 *Social-Demokraten*, 'Ett välde på vacklande grund', 8 June 1918; 10 June 1918. *Dagens Nyheter*, 'Den 40-gradiga skalan', 7 June 1918.
1512 FK, Nils Edén, 27 April 1918, 27:74; also Axel Sterne, 27 April 1918, 44:67.
1513 AK, Eliel Löfgren, 27 April 1918, 44:21–2; FK, 27 April 1918, 27:32.
1514 AK, Axel von Sneidern, 27 April 1918, 44:31.
1515 AK, 27 April 1918, 44:37; also Arthur Engberg, 27 April 1918, 44:56–7.
1516 AK, Axel Sterne, 27 April 1918, 44:64–5, 68.
1517 AK, Hjalmar Branting, 27 April 1918, 44:72–5.
1518 FK, Samuel Clason, 19 April 1918, 25:6.

class interests. The Right had reason to doubt any pan-European victory of democracy: the Russian and German attempts of 1917 had failed; the Finnish Civil War had let loose the worst traits of democracy. The British Act, as all things British, was exceptional and peculiar to that system, and was not a relevant model for Sweden. In these circumstances, rightist politicians were reluctant to engage in a debate for and against democracy. Arvid Lindman just complained about the politicisation of the concept: the Liberals uncritically regarded 'the mere word "democracy" as satisfactory', assuming that every reform *they* declared to be 'democratic' was positive and in no need of further consideration.[1519] Samuel Clason insisted that pure democracy had never produced a happy society.[1520] Unlike in spring 1917 and implicitly during the Finnish Civil War, the rightists did not insist that Sweden was already a democracy, which reflects the inflexibility of their stance in the atmosphere of spring 1918. No real debate on democracy emerged, nor was there any explicit rethinking of the concept.

The Liberal and Social Democratic speakers were right in claiming that the obstinate attitude of the Swedish right was inspired by the slow progress of the German reform: The Right counted on Germany winning the war, the reform being postponed and the need for it being removed. Caution was recommended by the result of the Finnish Civil War as well: democratisation there had ended up with a civil conflict, which the bourgeois parties had won, and the winning side was reformulating a reactionary constitution based on the Swedish constitutional tradition and theory with concrete support from Germany.[1521] Democracy seemed to be retreating transnationally. As its position in the upper house remained untouched, the Swedish right considered it best to just wait and see. The conservative paper *Aftonbladet* could not help rejoicing over Bolshevism turning into a fiasco, which had nullified Branting's advocacy of democracy in the name of the Entente and against Germany.[1522] The Finnish Civil War had not launched a series of risings as the Bolsheviks had planned.[1523] Both Bolshevism and democracy seemed to be on the retreat, so why not counter both by postponing the constitutional reform? A leftist counter-argument was that the Swedish people wanted this reform. The Right, on the other hand, claimed that this was not the case and asked who represented the people anyway.

5.3.4 Bypassing the political rights of the Swedish people

Few Swedish MPs sympathised with what seemed like the Bolshevik concept of 'the people' adopted by the Finnish Red government, which had attempted to replace parliamentary democracy with violence or the dictatorship of the proletariat. The Swedish Social Democrats could not accept 'putting

---

1519 AK, Arvid Lindman, 27 April 1918, 44:42–3.
1520 FK, Samuel Clason, 8 June 1918, 47:56.
1521 See *Aftonbladet*, 'När tyskarna erövrade Hälsingfors', 26 April 1918, and 'Preussiska valrättsreformen', 28 April 1918.
1522 *Aftonbladet*, 9 June 1918.
1523 *Aftonbladet*, 9 June 1918.

violence in place of the majority of the people'.¹⁵²⁴ Rightist speakers intimated that Swedish socialists would do better to give up any plans to challenge a parliamentary majority elected by the people¹⁵²⁵ – the people for them being constituted by the unreformed electorate and parliament being elected according to the existing law.

When the Liberal-Social Democratic coalition attempted to extend suffrage to women, Harald Hjärne regarded such an idea in wartime as a demonstration of a lack of political maturity since all the forces of the people should be united in striving to bring the country out of the crisis.¹⁵²⁶ Samuel Clason insisted that suffrage was not a universal human right; it was a political duty reserved for those who were qualified to fulfil it, women having other natural duties.¹⁵²⁷ According to Ernst Trygger, women lacked political maturity and their influence in political parties would consequently endanger the common good and the interests of the state.¹⁵²⁸ Arvid Lindman recognised that the people were entitled to criticise the political views and actions of MPs but saw the activation of women as detrimental both to the state and to women themselves.¹⁵²⁹ The rightist concept of the people clearly remained traditional, male and property-dominated.

Various strategies of persuasion were applied to counter the conservative concept. Perhaps a reference to Otto von Bismarck himself, who had recognised the value of suffrage motivating the people, might help? Gerhard Halfred von Koch (Liberal), an expert in social policy, tried one, emphasising that the war had extended politics to affect all areas of human life¹⁵³⁰ and that popular involvement hence needed to be broadened. Prime Minister Edén pointed out that the Swedes were like other European peoples, unable to depend solely on male power in seeking a better future; women, too, needed to be involved.¹⁵³¹

The Social Democrats were positive that political power should be awarded to all people as only 'the informed democratic will of the people' could advance peace, reason and justice in the world.'¹⁵³² Arthur Engberg challenged the way in which The Right used the traditionalist concept of 'reason of state' (*statsnyttan*) to claim that some objective definition of the interests of the state existed, ignoring the tendency of every class to associate its own interests with that pretext. From a Social Democratic point of view, the polity should be strengthened by connecting the mass of the people and the state¹⁵³³ through 'the political citizenship of women'.¹⁵³⁴ Gender equality

---

1524 AK, Hjalmar Branting, 20 February 1918, 16:39–40.
1525 AK, David Norman, 20 February 1918, 16:52.
1526 FK, Harald Hjärne, 27 April 1918, 27:45.
1527 FK, Samuel Clason, 27 April 1918, 27:57.
1528 FK, Ernst Trygger, 27 April 1918, 27:83, 86.
1529 AK, Arvid Lindman, 27 April 1918, 44:39.
1530 FK, Gerhard Halfred von Koch, 27 April 1918, 27:70.
1531 FK, Nils Edén, 27 April 1918, 27:79.
1532 AK, Harald Hallén, 27 April 1918, 44:37.
1533 AK, Arthur Engberg, 27 April 1918, 44:57, 59; also Axel Sterne, 27 April 1918, 44:67 and Hjalmar Branting, 27 April 1918, 44:76.
1534 AK, Axel Sterne, 27 April 1918, 44:64.

and democracy were thereby implicitly linked, though such a connection was not explicitly drawn even by woman activists.[1535] Women's suffrage was in the contemporary understanding more about citizenship than about democracy.

The entire left spoke for the sovereignty of the people in spring 1918, countering the rightist argument appealing to 'reason of state' and arguing for the inclusion of female voters in 'the people'. Axel Sterne of the Social Democrats advocated popular sovereignty as the principle on which the polity should be based.[1536] Also in the language of the far left, 'the will of the people' was the first authority to be obeyed,[1537] which differed from the Bolshevik claim that universal suffrage was outdated.[1538] But in spring 1918, the Swedish people would still need to wait for the extension of their political rights. Parliamentarism alone did not bring about democracy.

5.3.5 All parties on the side of parliamentarism – but different kinds of parliamentarism

Sweden is generally regarded as having moved to parliamentary government as a result of the elections of 1917 and the nomination of the Liberal-Social Democrat coalition. This change does not mean that parliamentarism was generally accepted, given the remaining doubts among The Right that were manifested in their opposition to the extension of suffrage. For the Liberals and Social Democrats, the Finnish Civil War made it all the more necessary to demonstrate that Swedish parliamentarism – as introduced a few months previously – was working and involved no risk of a similar degradation of ordered government.

Debates on the Finnish crisis nevertheless reflected the diverse understandings of parliamentarism that existed. According to the leftist Ivar Vennerström, the Finnish crisis of parliamentarism had emerged out of an alliance between the bourgeoisie and the tsarist regime aimed at annulling the reforms demanded by the Social Democratic parliamentary majority; this repeated the Finnish socialists' interpretation. As a consequence of the obstruction of the reforms supported by the Social Democrats and the nullification of their work, 'the anti-parliamentary and extra-parliamentary mood was growing, and Social Democracy was gradually being forced from the solid ground of parliamentary ways of thinking'. This suggested that Social Democracy was inherently parliamentary and that the rise of anti-parliamentarism among its ranks arose out of bourgeois abuses. Developments since the Russian Revolution had restored 'the parliamentary beliefs of the Social Democrats' but the Finnish bourgeoisie had made a coup against the Social Democratic parliament in ignoring the law on parliamentary sovereignty. From a radical Marxist point of view shared by the Swedish far left, it was a natural consequence of the actions of the bourgeoisie that the Finnish Social Democrats had been alienated from

---

1535 *Social-Demokraten*, 'Kvinnornas protestmöte', 29 April 1918.
1536 AK, Axel Sterne, 8 June 1918, 72:4.
1537 FK, Fredrik Ström, 8 June 1918, 48:15.
1538 *Dagens Nyheter*, 'Regeringens ställning till Finland', 21 February 1918.

parliamentary measures and forced to engage in anti-parliamentary activities.[1539] Parliamentarism had failed in Finland as a consequence of the deeds of the bourgeoisie and not because of any anti-parliamentary sentiments among the socialists who, Vennerström repeated, had previously stood for parliamentary principles.[1540] The Finnish bourgeoisie had, furthermore, rejected the genuinely parliamentary republic of the Swiss type proposed by the socialists and advocated a 'masked monarchy'.[1541] This standpoint, which was critical of parliamentarism in its Western European form, constituted a further justification for the radical measures of the Red Finns, who were to be viewed as inherently parliamentarian in a Marxist sense.

The other groups did not share such an understanding of radical Marxist parliamentarism. The rightists did not speak for parliamentarism as such, but their leader Arvid Lindman nevertheless welcomed the Social Democratic rejection of a violent uprising against a parliament elected by the broadest possible popular vote.[1542] The Social Democrat leader Hjalmar Branting reasserted the stand of his party by denouncing violent opposition to a parliamentary majority[1543] – a stance that was valid in Sweden as well. Even Per Albin Hansson from the left of the party said that it would have been the responsibility of the Finnish Social Democrats to employ parliamentary means to achieve their goals. They were unlikely to gain with violence against the parliamentary majority what they failed to achieve through parliament.[1544] Such consistent defence of parliamentary strategies by the more radical of the Swedish Social Democrats – recognised by The Right with a certain irony – demonstrated their dedication to parliamentary government and perhaps convinced some among The Right that the social order in Sweden might not be threatened under this parliamentary ministry. As even the Swedish far left refrained from openly defending the armed rising in Finland, the Finnish crisis helped the Swedish parties to view parliamentarism in the form it had taken on in autumn 1917 in predominantly positive terms: Swedish parliamentarism was, and should remain, something different from the Finnish version.

The Right had no particular reason to question parliamentarism in the upper house given the majority with which they were able to vote down any constitutional reconfiguration. In the lower chamber, a leading rightist nevertheless continued to attack parliamentarism: Karl Hildebrand challenged the extension of suffrage by referring to anti-parliamentary sentiments among the public arising from the actions of the members elected to the parliament after previous reforms: 'It has above all not heightened the quality of the Second Chamber of the Riksdag, and it contributes decisively to the increase of that disgust with the parliament (*parlamentsleda*), the

1539 AK, Ivar Vennerström, 20 February 1918, 16:12.
1540 AK, Ivar Vennerström, 20 February 1918, 16:12.
1541 AK, Ivar Vennerström, 20 February 1918, 16:13.
1542 AK, Arvid Lindman, 20 February 1918, 16:32.
1543 AK, Hjalmar Branting, 20 February 1918, 16:40.
1544 AK, Per Albin Hansson, 20 February 1918, 16:58.

contempt for the national assembly, which continues to spread in our country as in other countries.'[1545] This speech deplored the fact that popular representative bodies had replaced parliaments whose members were gentlemen, a reflection of the conservatives' elitist view of the parliament as a kind of gentlemen's club. Hildebrand was convinced that a new extension would reduce the quality of parliamentary representation further: doubling the number of voters and including women would increase 'that great and formidable section of voters who are uninterested and ignorant and who act erratically'.[1546] The ministry ignored this anti-parliamentary criticism; The Right were free to recycle their old-fashioned views on parliamentarism.

Hjalmar Branting, frustrated at the delayed progress in the democratisation of suffrage, brought up the possibility of aggravated confrontations and extra-parliamentary action if there was any further postponement. Branting had indirectly referred to the threat of extra-parliamentary forces being used in spring 1917 and had consistently emphasised the parliamentary stance of his party during the Finnish Civil War. Now he opted for a tactic used by Social Democrats in all parliaments: if the conservatives blocked a moderate reform, they should be ready to face a more revolutionary attempt by the radicals or the Social Democratic voters. Branting suggested that the longer the justified reform demands were ignored 'the more compelled the masses are to consider such extra-parliamentary measures as something they nevertheless need [to resort to] to counter the unreasonable'.[1547] This was a two-edged argument from a moderate socialist leader: instead of merely trying to persuade The Right to give up their resistance, it referred to the possibility of an outbreak of the irregular power of the masses. Hildebrand protested immediately against 'the once again repeated threat presented by Mr Branting – it comes up in this form a few times a year – concerning the use of outright extra-parliamentary means'.[1548] *Social-Demokraten* again rejected rightist appeals to the constitution, dismissing the alleged 'threat of democracy' as pathetic.[1549] This debate certainly did not bring the two sides closer to a compromise. Frustration had led a government party to hint at extra-parliamentary measures, which hardly advanced conciliation. Further accusations about the readiness of the rival bloc to turn to 'extra-parliamentary' or 'illegal' means followed. The Social Democrats then assured the Riksdag that extra-parliamentary means would not be used by the supporters of the Swedish democracy provided a reform was passed. However, *parliamentary* means might be employed to force the reform through.[1550] In other words, an extraordinary joint vote of the two chambers might follow.[1551]

1545 AK, Karl Hildebrand, 27 April 1918, 44:26.
1546 AK, Karl Hildebrand, 27 April 1918, 44:26.
1547 AK, Hjalmar Branting, 27 April 1918, 44:75; *Aftonbladet*, 28 April 1918 and 9 June 1918; *Social-Demokraten*, 10 June 1918.
1548 AK, Karl Hildebrand, 27 April 1918, 44:76.
1549 *Social-Demokraten*, 10 June 1918.
1550 AK, Axel Sterne, 8 June 1918, 72:4; Arthur Engberg, 8 June 1918, 72:18.
1551 *Social-Demokraten*, 10 June 1918.

The Right did not use threats of extra-parliamentary measures but rather criticised the Social Democrats for their alleged readiness to employ them.[1552] Ernst Trygger still maintained that parliamentarism had not brought about any positive effects in countries which had adopted it.[1553] He problematised the distinction between 'parliamentary and extra-parliamentary means of coercion', concluding that Branting's suggested 'parliamentary means of coercion' by procedural means were illegal.[1554] The rightist press also expressed concern about the challenges to the established parliamentary order: *Aftonbladet* predicted a risk of 'the triumph of demagogy', but concluded that the interest of 'the parliament of the street' was modest in comparison with 'the breakthrough of the spring of liberty', i.e. spring 1917.[1555] The debate thus illustrates the possibility of parliamentary procedure being manipulated in the atmosphere of an obstructed reform. Had the left violated what The Right saw as established parliamentary procedure, a deeper crisis of parliamentary legitimacy of the type experienced in Finland in 1917 might have emerged even though the discursive and ideological confrontation had not reached comparable tensions. In Finland, a very different kind of constitutional confrontation ensued when the Civil War was followed by a revived parliamentary debate.

5.4 Finland reconstructed to resemble a little Prussia

5.4.1 THE ATTEMPT TO RESTRICT REFORM BY RESTORING THE MONARCHY

At the moment of declaring independence in December 1917, the Finnish parliament had been deeply divided over the nature and degree of democracy and parliamentarism and over the right policies to pursue in solving the multiple problems that the country faced. Confrontations of class, ideology and party, accelerated by Bolshevik intrusions, had led to an armed conflict that had raged from late January to April 1918. No fewer than 37,000 Finns (including both those who perished in the wartime terror and those who died in post-war prison camps) lost their lives as a consequence of the Civil War. The war caused implacable bitterness for generations on both sides and had many international implications as well.

The leaders of the Finnish Social Democrats had been unable or unwilling to stop the process of radicalisation within the party in 1917. In the parliamentary debates, many of them entertained the possibility of extra-parliamentary, even violent, action once parliamentary means did not seem to be producing reforms to their liking. The rejection of their Power Act of July 1917, which would have concentrated political power in the hands of the Social Democratic majority of that parliament, by the

---

1552 See AK, David Norman, 8 June 1918, 72:33, 49.
1553 FK, Ernst Trygger, 8 June 1918, 47:54.
1554 FK, Ernst Trygger, 8 June 1918, 48:35.
1555 *Aftonbladet*, 'Författningsfrågan inför riksdagen', 7 June 1918; 'Enfaldens rösträtt', 9 June 1918. Also *Dagens Nyheter*, 9 June 1918.

Russian Provisional Government after encouragement from the Finnish bourgeois parties together with the loss of their majority in the new election of October 1917 added to the disappointments that had accumulated from previous obstructions of reform. In addition to a long tradition of agitating bitter class antagonism of a kind not traceable to the same extent in the countries of comparison, the situation induced Social Democratic voters to engage in extra-parliamentary action. The model and active support of the Bolsheviks, in particular, made several Social Democratic leaders ready for a revolution.[1556] Ideologically, it appeared to them to be their world-historical duty to make a revolution; they had a unique chance – a kind of second 1905–6 – to force reforms through.

Unlike the British Labour Party or the German or Swedish Social Democratic Parties, the majority of the leaders of the Finnish Social Democrats in the end chose revolution rather than parliamentary measures. It has been often emphasised that the Finnish revolutionaries were not Bolsheviks, and that it was White wartime propaganda that presented them as such.[1557] Sociological explanations for the Civil War and descriptions of the suffering of the losers of the war have been favoured, especially since the 1960s. As for the proposed constitution of Red Finland, it has been seen as not aiming at a system of soviets but rather resembling a Swiss or French type of republic so that the principle of the sovereignty of the people would have executed by 'a parliament of the people' (described to some extent by Otto Wille Kuusinen in the parliament on 5 December 1917, as was analysed in subsection 4.4.5). The people themselves would make legislative initiatives, participate in referenda and dissolve the parliament should its majority violate the constitution – the last formulation implying a continuous revolution by the workers. The definition of 'the people' in the proposal stood for the workers only, which was in line with radical Marxist and Bolshevik discourse and made contemporary observers regard the proposal as class-based. The proposal was formulated by Kuusinen, debated in unclear circumstances during the Civil War in February 1918 but never enacted after a referendum.[1558] In the wartime propaganda of the Red government, the people as a united wielder of power was defined in such a way that any bourgeois government appeared as an illegitimate representative of property-owners and was to be replaced with the 'democratic' revolutionary bodies of the workers. These, in turn, were identical with 'the people's own trustworthy hands'.[1559] All of this echoed conceptualisations of the people and democracy typical of Russian revolutionary and especially Bolshevik discourse. The actions of the Red government, furthermore, were presented as the defence of 'the democratic achievements of the revolution' of the previous year[1560] without distinguishing between the Bolshevik and Finnish

1556 Jussila, Hentilä & Nevakivi 1999, 107.
1557 Haapala & Tikka 2013, 109.
1558 *Suomen kansanvaltuuskunnan ehdotus*, 1918, 5, 7, 9, 14–15; Rinta-Tassi 1986, 322–6, 330; Alapuro 1988, 174–5; Jussila, Hentilä & Nevakivi 1999, 109; Haapala & Tikka 2013, 111.
1559 Hyvärinen 2003, 81–2.
1560 Alapuro 2003, 541.

revolutions. These wartime examples call for a serious consideration of the discursive process that led to the Civil War, as analysed in sections 3.4 and 4.4 above.

The analysis showed that the Social Democratic discourse consistently constructed concepts of democracy and parliamentarism that were in conflict with what was usually understood by 'Western' democracy and 'bourgeois' parliamentarism and which allowed for no negotiation on alternative concepts. The way in which the Reds continued to talk about 'the rule by the people' during the Civil War made some bourgeois parties increasingly cautious about the concept; they rather contrasted the 'arbitrary power' of the Reds with the sovereignty of the parliament (with few references to the sovereignty of the people, though the concept 'the people' remained in use).[1561] In the battle between the supporters of parliamentary and revolutionary means within the ranks of Finnish socialists, the latter had clearly prevailed with the inspiration of the Bolsheviks to support them; this was the conclusion drawn not only by the Finnish bourgeois parties but also much of the left in Sweden. The relationship of the Finnish labour movement to both democracy and parliamentarism would need to be fundamentally rethought in the aftermath of the failed revolution. After the Civil War, two entirely new socialist parties would emerge.

The attempt of the revolutionaries to introduce what appeared as no less than a dictatorship of the proletariat, and their rejection of the parliament as a forum for societal reform, led to a gradually growing monarchical reaction among the parties of the right aptly analysed by Vesa Vares among others. In some cases, this reaction progressed during spring 1918 to embrace outright anti-democratic and anti-parliamentary ideas, and some bourgeois politicians who had spoken for democracy and parliamentarism in autumn 1917 began to reconsider their stance. The monarchical reaction was inspired especially by military help from imperial Germany, which, in the circumstances of spring and summer 1918, appeared to most non-socialist Finns as the only foreign power from which security guarantees against the Russian and domestic Bolsheviks were available. The possibility of asking for military assistance from Germany had already been discussed at the time of the declaration of independence, since the Germans clearly sympathised with Finnish aspirations for independence. In mid-January, the Finnish government asked Germany to return activist Finnish volunteers who were receiving military training in Germany during the war. However, on 14 February, Edvard Hjelt and Rafael Erich – representatives of the Finnish government in Berlin – contacted the German General Staff, without the permission of the Finnish government, asking for troops. Germany did send troops but only in early April, after the conclusion of the Treaty of Brest-Litovsk, when the intervention served German interests by turning Finland into a German military bridgehead. Such a direct involvement in the Finnish Civil War was uncomfortable for the White government and especially for the anglophile Commander-in-Chief of the White Army C. G. E. Mannerheim. The intervention may not have been decisive for the result of the war, but

---

1561 Hyvärinen 2003, 82.

it shortened the conflict,[1562] and it affected the course of the constitutional debate in Finland after the war. The fact that the German troops appeared as the liberators of Helsinki was psychologically decisive in that it turned the non-socialist inhabitants of the city into uncritical admirers of Germany as being the only possible guarantor of Finnish independence.[1563]

The White Finnish government would have preferred military assistance from Sweden, but that was not available for the domestic political reasons discussed in the subsection 5.3.1: the Liberal-Social Democratic coalition prioritised suffrage reform at home over getting involved in a war that was ideologically divisive in Sweden as well. Instead, Sweden did try to occupy the Åland Islands, an intervention that was condemned by White and Red Finland, Germany and Bolshevik Russia alike,[1564] and which led to an exceptional exclusion of references to Sweden from Finnish constitutional debates for years to come.

Thus there followed a radical turn in the constitutional views of Finnish centre-right parliamentarians, who had mostly been republican in autumn 1917: a growing number of conservatives and liberals turned monarchist, emphasising the Swedish monarchical Instrument of Government of 1772 as the proper basis for a new constitution. The apparent strength of the German monarchy in spring 1918 induced some to refer to paragraph 38 of this constitution (already applied during 1917), according to which the Diet was entitled to elect a new king after the demise of a dynasty. This view gained ground in the new government and in the Rump Parliament (consisting of no more than 111 members) that convened between 15 May 1918 and 28 February 1919. The socialists had been practically excluded from participation as a result of their rebellion against the parliamentary majority; only a single Social Democrat, who had outspokenly opposed the revolution, was allowed to attend. The logic of this rising monarchism derived from the assured belief that Germany would win the war and that a Fenno-German military alliance confirmed with the election of a German prince to the Finnish throne constituted the wisest foreign and constitutional policy in the prevailing circumstances by creating a link with 'the large politico-economic bloc of the Central Powers' that was believed to be taking shape[1565]. It was believed that a monarchical link would persuade Germany to support the national romantic dream of the annexation of Russian Karelia as well.[1566] Given the long-term cultural connections with Germany, the Entente's recent support for Russia and the suspension of recognition of Finnish independence by the West, few Finnish parliamentarians regarded Western democracies and parliamentary governments either as helpful sources of security or as models for making a constitution in spring and summer 1918.[1567]

1562 Jussila, Hentilä & Nevakivi 1999, 116–17, 119; Vares 2006, 91–2, 99.
1563 *Hufvudstadsbladet*, 'Förslaget till regeringsformen', 12 June 1918; Kolbe 2008, 112, 114, 116; Nyström 2013, 303.
1564 Jussila, Hentilä & Nevakivi 1999, 117.
1565 *Hufvudstadsbladet*, 'Förslaget till regeringsformen', 12 June 1918.
1566 Sihvonen 1997, 11; Jussila, Hentilä & Nevakivi 1999, 121–3; Vares 2006, 101.
1567 Ikonen 1995, 343.

The monarchical and pro-German reaction thus emerged out of the fact that the bourgeois parties had experienced an attempted socialist revolution partly imported from Russia and overcome with German military help. In the new constitution, monarchical prerogatives would surpass those proposed for the president of the republic in 1917 and include an absolute veto on constitutional changes.[1568] They resembled those of the seemingly stable German polity, and it was believed that they would keep excessive reformism and possible reincarnations of Bolshevism in check. Many Swedish-speakers, supporters of the Finnish Party and nationalist activists were deeply disappointed with the lack of maturity of the Finnish people, as they put it, feeling that the radical parliamentary reform and universal suffrage of 1906 had failed and had consequently persuaded some to oppose the very principles of democracy. The 10-year experience of parliamentary life suggested that parliamentarism, too, needed to be strictly restricted if not rejected, universal suffrage reconsidered and parliament perhaps divided into two chambers as in more 'advanced' countries with a representative institution such as Sweden, Germany and Britain. Many parliamentarians were frustrated about the constant parliamentary elections and unproductive sessions that had often ended with an Imperial dissolution of the parliament. The class-based, radical and anti-elitist attitudes of fellow parliamentarians, embodied in the Social Democratic Party but also visible in the Agrarian League – not to mention the rebellion that the socialists had finally made – had antagonised conservatives. Most rightist MPs consequently saw monarchy as the only stabilising option, while most centrists continued to favour a republic, democracy and parliamentarism.[1569] A new discursive confrontation on the form of government, democracy, the political role of the people and parliamentarism followed. The divide permeated the civil society, with popular meetings in the countryside and the liberal press being at first nearly unanimously in favour of a republic,[1570] while the old elites of the capital argued for a monarchy.

After the defeat of the Reds in May, the right saw a unique opportunity to restore the traditional political order and to set the politically immature Finns back on the correct path after a failed experiment with extreme democracy. The course of the world war, as they understood it, seemed to support this goal: the successful war effort of Prussia against superior numbers demonstrated the strength of that monarchical polity. Many Finnish liberals, unlike their brethren in Sweden, considered German support essential for safeguarding the country's fragile independence in circumstances in which no help was to be expected from the West or Sweden. This might involve constitutional imitation of Germany as well. They tended to view Finland

---

1568 *Helsingin Sanomat*, 'Kaksi hallitusmuotoesitystä', 12 June 1918.
1569 Lindman 1937, 13; Sihvonen 1997, 10; Vares 1998, 56, 64–6; Jussila, Hentilä & Nevakivi 1999, 123; Vares 2006, 109.
1570 *Helsingin Sanomat*, 'Hallitusmuotokysymyksemme kansalaiskokousten pohdittawana' and 'Mitä merkitsee "monarkia"?', 12 June 1918; note, however, the low number of deputies who attended the constitutional debate, *Helsingin Sanomat*, 'Eduskunnan lehtereillä', 13 June 1918.

as a Western outpost against Bolshevik Russia, an attitude that reflects the Finnish view of *Germany* as the strongest representative of Western values vis-à-vis Russia at a time when the West generally understood the war as a battle for Western democracy and against the Prussian political order.[1571]

The campaign for a monarchy, which was launched in April by activists of the Swedish People's Party and extended in May and June to the Finnish Party, produced a monarchist majority in the Rump Parliament, which passed a proposal aiming at an updated monarchical constitution. According to the tendentious monarchist argument, the republican formulations of the Declaration of Independence had been merely a temporary break from the Swedish-Finnish constitutional tradition inspired by the Russian Revolution[1572] and they had not changed the eighteenth-century Gustavian constitution, which, in comparison with a republic, would save the state from the political ferment associated with presidential elections, ensure continuity in foreign policy, protect the rights of the Swedish-speaking minority and restrict the powers of the parliament as 'an institution of agitation' (*yllytyslaitos*) abused by political amateurs and revolutionaries.[1573] The argument was built on respect for the Swedish constitutional tradition among the bourgeoisie – a respect that had been strengthened by the legalistic defence of Swedish law during the period of Russification after 1899.[1574] This questioning of the existence of the Republic of Finland caused the republicans to assert that the Declaration of Independence had indeed founded a republic, the constitution of which just needed to be finalised. In their view, the Red rebellion had not been a justified revolution, and it was hence unfair to associate republicanism with such a violent outbreak.[1575] Many conservatives who had spoken for a republic, democracy and limited parliamentarism in autumn 1917 now responded by representing monarchy as compatible with democracy and progress, as they were unable to completely reject the republic or the principle of the rule by the people even though they currently painted both in dark colours.[1576] Others declared republicanism to be no more than 'the product of the revolution and bloody rebellions',[1577] imported from Russia and without roots in the Swedish-Finnish tradition.

In the new monarchical constitution, a *German* rather than a Scandinavian monarchy would be implemented. The principle of parliamentarism would remain, but there would be no explicit reference to the responsibility of the ministers to parliament.[1578] The republicans opposed this, using minority provisions to prevent the passed motions from coming into force before a new election. The republican counter-proposals were correspondingly

1571 Vares 1998, 69–72; Ihalainen 2016b.
1572 *Hufvudstadsbladet*, 'Förslaget till regeringsformen', 12 June 1918; 'Statsformen och vår utrikespolitiska ställning', 13 June 1918.
1573 Vares 1998, 74–5, 152, 157; Vares 2006, 108.
1574 Ihalainen 2015.
1575 VP, Juho Kokko, 13 June 1918, 1309.
1576 Vares 1998, 80–1, 104, 160–1.
1577 VP, Bror Hannes Päivänsalo, 13 June 1918, 1304.
1578 Vares 1998, 171–2, 174.

voted down by the majority.¹⁵⁷⁹ When the attempts to pass a monarchical constitution failed and the monarchists knew that the next parliament, which the Social Democrats would again be attending, would not accept one anyway, they launched the election of a king in accordance with the Gustavian constitution. This took place on 8 August 1918 – the very day on which the German Western Front began to waver.¹⁵⁸⁰ However, no news from the front or Berlin would change the conviction of the monarchical majority of the Rump Parliament: Finland was now proceeding towards the accession of a German prince.

5.4.2 A COUNTER-REVOLUTION BUILT ON AN ASSUMED GERMAN VICTORY

In the circumstances of late spring 1918, after a rebellion associated with Bolshevism and at a time of a pro-German monarchical reaction, constitutional debates in the Finnish parliament were transnational in a very biased way – even to the extent that German representatives in Helsinki sought to influence the course of decision-making or were asked by Finnish politicians to do so: General Rüdiger von der Goltz, the leader of the German troops in Finland, pressurised leading republicans. The German Ambassador August von Brück let Finnish politicians know that the establishment of a strong monarchy would serve the interests of both countries. This pressure may in fact have been initiated by the Finnish government to support their monarchical cause – a case of international contacts being exploited in domestic disputes – and this was effective in that a few republicans did indeed change sides. The Finnish press, which one-sidedly emphasized German successes and ignored any problems on the Western Front, also attempted to sway public opinion.¹⁵⁸¹ The United States, in particular, was presented as a warning case of a degenerate plutocratic republic, whereas Germany, Britain, Japan and the Scandinavian countries were viewed as examples of highly developed societies with *monarchical* constitutions that Finland should imitate.¹⁵⁸²

Foreign policy and the future constitution were inseparably intertwined in this monarchist discourse. As we have seen, imperial Germany was viewed in Finland as a European, 'Western', force counterbalancing Russia. This conception built on the one hand on nineteenth-century discursive practices of understanding Germany *culturally* as part of the West in contradistinction to Russia. On the other hand, it accepted wartime German propaganda that contrasted German *culture* with Western *civilization* and condemned Western democracies and republics.¹⁵⁸³ Consequently, according

---

1579 Vares 1998, 84, 177; Jussila, Hentilä & Nevakivi 1999, 124.
1580 Sihvonen 1997, 11; Vares 1998, 204–209.
1581 Huldén 1989, 97–104. Germany had recognised the *Republic* of Finland on 4 January 1918. Georg Schauman saw the intervention as initiated by the Finns, and this is also the conclusion of Anders Huldén, who presents evidence demonstrating such activity; Vares 1998, 178–80, 192; Vares 2006, 118; Nyström 2013, 320; Hentilä & Hentilä 2016, 294.
1582 Vares 1998, 188–9.
1583 Bavaj & Steber 2015, 1, 4, 8–20; Llanque 2015, 70–1.

to Prime Minister J. K. Paasikivi, Finland should not move over to the side of the Entente by introducing a republic; it needed to build on German support by keeping the monarchy instead.[1584] After the Treaty of Brest-Litovsk, a German victory in the east was taken as inevitable even by Finnish republicans when they studied the map of Europe. Germany appeared as source of support against the Bolsheviks, vengeful Reds and enthusiasts of democracy and parliamentarism. Foodstuffs were available only via the Baltic Sea, which was controlled by the Germans. The Germans themselves continued to believe in victory, at least officially. Not even the joining of the United States in the war had changed the monarchists' confidence in Germany; the US was, after all, considered to be a materialistic upstart state that lacked a culture comparable to that of Germany. The Western Allies were, besides, excessively cosmopolitan and liberal and had recently allied themselves with Russia. It would be useless to turn to them as they lacked any genuine interest in supporting Finland against a potential Russian invasion. Germany, by contrast, was treated uncritically in Finnish discourse owing to feelings of gratitude for concrete German help in crushing the Red rebellion. Old cultural ties were emphasised, and the Finnish identity was defined as being derived from Germanic cultural roots, despite the very different languages of the two countries. The organ of Paasikivi's party, for instance, connected the Finnish Civil War with the participation of Finns in the Swedish troops in the Thirty Years' War: 'Luther's Germany had […] paid its old debt to the people who had participated in liberating it from Catholic servitude.' Germany was linguistically, culturally and academically a much more familiar country to the Finns than Britain, France or the United States. For many conservatives, as for the Swedish right, Germany constituted the model of a civilised and well organised society, the people of which were ready to sacrifice themselves for the fatherland. Swedish-speaking Finns emphasized their ethnic ties with the Germans, and many Finnish-speaking activists (Jägers) had been socialised in the Prussian system through military training. Even cultural liberals like the author Juhani Aho admired 'Prussian discipline and education'.[1585] The alliance of White Finland with Germany was a strong one, as Allied press reports also suggest.

The British or other Western models of parliamentary democracy did not appear attractive, also for foreign policy reasons. From early July onwards, there was even a risk of military conflict between Britain and Finland, Finland having condemned British military activity in Petsamo, which the Finnish government regarded as part of Finnish territory. This confrontation made the Germans propose a military alliance – provided that Finland confirmed its monarchical constitution and elected a Hohenzollern prince to the throne. The Finnish government persuaded the majority of the Rump Parliament to support the alliance, the monarchists being assured that a German king served Finnish interests and disregarding news of German setbacks on the Western Front, but the republicans continued to

---

1584 Huldén 1989, 105.
1585 Vares 1998, 106–10, 114–15; Nyström 2013, 320–1; Soutou 2014, 520. On the continuity of the Lutheran national identity, see Ihalainen 2005b.

oppose such a dynastic link. In early October, after news about the German peace proposal and constitutional changes had been read, the monarchists continued to reject all suggestions about contacting the Entente, claiming that German support against Russia would be lost as a result, an English prince installed or a republic restored, the rule of the Reds introduced, territories lost and the entire nation disgraced. When the monarchical constitution made no progress in parliament, provisions from the constitution of 1772 were used to elect a king.[1586]

The international comparisons and transnational references in these discussions differed clearly from those of 1917. In the Rump Parliament, Russia was consistently viewed as 'the other', if not the enemy. Bolshevism was associated with eastern barbarism imported to Finland through cross-border contacts. According to R. A. Wrede (Swedish People's Party), a former professor of Roman law and vice-chairman of the Judicial Department of the Finnish Senate, the Civil War followed from 'Russian anarchy ... of the most barbaric, primitive and socially disintegrating kind, a real oriental pestilent infection' imported by Russian soldiers and Russian Social Democracy.[1587] Annie Furuhjelm (Swedish People's Party) recalled how Lenin had intended to reconquer Finland by permeating Finnish society with Bolshevism.[1588]

At the same time, Sweden was removed from the objects of comparison as a result of its limited help during the Civil War and the Åland crisis; only early-modern Sweden, from which the Finnish constitution was inherited, was used as a source of reference.[1589] The Norwegian example of holding a referendum on the monarchy provided a precedent that the republicans used to try to postpone the decision to establish a monarchy, counting on a republican majority among the population at large, but the monarchists responded by emphasising the compatibility of monarchy and democracy in Norway.[1590]

For the monarchists, the Western Powers were suspect because of their inapplicable republicanism and parliamentarism and their alleged plotting against Finland with plans for an intervention in favour of a republican constitution.[1591] Britain provided a suitable example only in arguing for a constitutional monarchy, not with regard to parliamentarism.[1592] Wäinö Valkama (Finnish Party) questioned the democratic character of the United States, seeing it as a polity run by trusts, money and oligarchies in contradistinction to the 'democratic' features of the cooperative movement

---

1586 Vares 1998, 122–3, 127–8, 199; Nyström 2013, 321.
1587 VP, Rabbe Axel Wrede, 12 June 1918, 1251. Even Santeri Alkio, a moderate centrist leader, also used the metaphor of 'an international plague' to describe the Bolshevik rebellion in Finland. 12 June 1918, 1254. See also Emil Schybergson, 12 June 1918, 1261; Alapuro 1988, 200.
1588 VP, 13 June 1918, 1308.
1589 Ihalainen 2015.
1590 VP, Antti Rentola, 13 June 1918, 1291; Artur Wuorimaa, 13 July 1918, 1691–2; 13 July 1918, 1679–80; *Helsingin Sanomat*, 'Parantumatomain estelyjä', 12 July 1918.
1591 See VP, Gustaf Arokallio, 12 July 1918, 1656; Lauri Ingman, 13 July 1918, 1677.
1592 VP, 13 June 1918, 1303.

of German origin. As Bismarck had stated, republics such as France were not comparable with constitutional monarchies like Germany in military terms.[1593] Also for Annie Furuhjelm, the daughter of a former governor of Russian America (Alaska), the United States was no wonderland of democracy but a country of oligarchies, plutocracy and political corruption, followed on the road of degeneration by republics like France. The German monarchy, by contrast, had introduced social reforms and education to transform an initially revolutionary Social Democratic Party into a benevolent radical social reformist party.[1594] Such military strength and attenuation of socialism through reforms offered a model that White Finland could follow. British parliamentarism would be re-evaluated and the United States introduced as a source of positive examples only in summer 1919 after the Western Allies had won the war and recognised Finnish independence, which is illustrative of the contingent nature of international references in the constitutional debates of a newly independent state.

Germany had become a nonpareil model polity. As Prime Minister Paasikivi put it, Finnish independence was a result of Germany's victorious war and had been maintained with diplomatic and military help from Germany. Consequently, in formulating the Finnish constitution, the parliament 'should not disregard' the fact that the German political system was based on monarchy.[1595] Gustaf Arokallio, a supposedly liberal Young Finn, thanked Providence for the help sent by the Kaiser and called for a monarchical constitution with a German king.[1596] Even some who remained republicans praised the Kaiser for being a friend to the (German) people and argued that Germany did not wish to intervene in the construction of the Finnish constitution like the Entente.[1597] In the midst of a world war, in a small new state dependent on foreign powers, applications of international models tended to be opportunistic. The reference to the Kaiser as a people's monarch could hence even be used to defend a republican constitution for Finland.

K. J. Ståhlberg (Young Finn), a leading spokesman for the republican minority, challenged the monarchical constitutional proposal – convincingly for the republican audience[1598] but as mere a repetition of the polemic published in *Helsingin Sanomat* for the monarchists.[1599] Ståhlberg questioned the assumption of a monarchy being a pre-condition for cooperation with Germany, pointing out that even Bismarck had conceded that there were

---

1593 VP, Wäinö Valkama, 13 June 1918, 1287–8.
1594 VP, Annie Furuhjelm, 13 June 1918, 1307.
1595 VP, Juho Kusti Paasikivi, 12 June 1918, 1242, 1244.
1596 VP, Gustaf Arokallio, 12 July 1918, 1656; cf. Pekka Pennanen (Young Finn), 12 July 1918, 1659.
1597 VP, Artur Wuorimaa (Agrarian), 13 July 1918, 1691. Some members of the Red government had tried to persuade Britain and the United States to come over to their side but in vain. Rinta-Tassi 1986, 504.
1598 *Helsingin Sanomat*, 'Eduskunnan lehtereillä', 13 June 1918, advised every republican family to read Ståhlberg's speech aloud and then send it to their neighbours; 'Ewästyskeskustelu hallitusmuotoasiasta', 14 June 1918.
1599 *Hufvudstadsbladet*, 'Remissdebatten', 12 June 1918.

republican elements in the German constitution.[1600] Santeri Alkio (Agrarians) claimed that the strength of the German polity lay in its educational system rather than its constitution.[1601] Kusti Arffman added that it was nationalism rather than its constitution that had made Germany a leading power.[1602] Alkio anticipated that Germany would not lag behind in democratic development for long but would soon lead the way. Spring 1917 had demonstrated that Prussia was preparing for a democratic parliamentary reform: 'The mighty ruler of Prussia aims at a closer relation with the German people so that the influence of the Prussian people on the composition of parliament would be more extensive than it has ever been there.'[1603] This tendentious representation of the constitutional reform in Germany – of which there was no evidence in Germany in summer 1918 – was intended to persuade the Finnish monarchists to reconsider their anti-republican stands. The leading republicans still remained German-oriented for much of 1918, trying to demonstrate that a republican and parliamentary Finland would remain a loyal ally of imperial Germany. The republican press, too, supported an alliance with Germany against British aims for global supremacy.[1604] Unlike Sweden, there was no active Anglophile minority in the Finnish parliament in 1918.

Academic authorities encountered each other in this debate. R. A. Wrede referred to Aristotle and Cicero, who had evaluated different types of constitution. According to Wrede, the Swiss and American models were inapplicable owing to the special circumstances of the countries involved, while the fruitfulness of the French republican constitution was doubtful. For Germanic countries, to which Finland culturally belonged, only a constitutional monarchy was thinkable, the Norwegian 'republican' exception deserving to be disregarded in this respect.[1605] K. J. Ståhlberg responded by defending the French republican constitution and questioning parallels between the Germanic countries and Finland.[1606] Some MPs were already beginning to doubt a German victory and hence the sense of establishing a Germanic monarchy: Matts Björk, a court of appeal judge and a representative of the Swedish People's Party, differed from the party line in questioning the prevailing predictions for a future Europe,[1607] a contribution that was welcomed by the republicans but censured by the monarchists.[1608] All the same, the future Finnish constitution seemed to depend on international trends rather than on the will of the Finnish people or the suitability of a particular system for the country. The constitutional debate remained inter- and transnational albeit in a very unbalanced way.

1600 VP, Kaarlo Juho Ståhlberg, 12 June 1918, 1247.
1601 VP, Santeri Alkio, 12 June 1918, 1256.
1602 VP, Kusti Arffman, 13 June 1918, 1314.
1603 VP, Santeri Alkio, 12 July 1918, 1661–2.
1604 Vares 1998, 138–46, 149–50.
1605 VP, Rabbe Axel Wrede, 12 July 1918, 1648–9, 1653.
1606 VP, Kaarlo Juho Ståhlberg, 12 July 1918, 1666.
1607 VP, Matts Björk, 13 July 1918, 1698.
1608 *Helsingin Sanomat*, 'Eduskunnassa', 14 July 1918.

5.4.3 REDESCRIBED RIGHTIST OR PRINCIPLED CENTRIST DEMOCRACY – OR NO DEMOCRACY AT ALL?

Even if the Finnish Civil War had been preceded by a discursive and ideological confrontation on the meaning of democracy in which the bourgeois parties had seen themselves as defending the established constitutional order, which included representative government, against socialist radicalism, the construction of a democratic polity did not appear to be a primary goal for the victors after the war. The militant socialist rhetoric of democracy used in parliament before the war had associated the Finnish vocabulary of democracy with socialist extremism. The constitutional proposal of the Reds formulated by Otto Wille Kuusinen had echoed demands for 'true rule by the people' as opposed to 'the rule of the masters', emphasising the power of the people over the parliament, democracy, the executive power and the courts of law.[1609] Such socialist forms of democracy were definitely rejected by the bourgeois parties.

Even in autumn 1917, all bourgeois groups had still recognised the need for at least a degree of democracy based on universal suffrage in the future republican constitution. The majority of them had already conceded in 1906 that universal suffrage served the interests of the Finnish nation as part of the Russian Empire, but they had been seriously disappointed with its results. Extremes were hence to be avoided; on the one hand, reactionary views risked one being associated with conservative aspects of Prussianism while, on the other, calls for extended democracy might provoke accusations of defending the notorious Power Act, i.e. of being a crypto-Bolshevik. A suitable degree of popular power was sought, but the victors of the war were deeply divided over what the right amount was: some held principled views in favour of extended democracy, others redefined the monarchical order as democracy.

The rule by the people was most consistently defended by centrist politicians who had been involved in the planning of the republican constitution in 1917. K. J. Ståhlberg (Young Finns) insisted that 'the Finnish people are inclined [to favour] the rule by the people'.[1610] Augusta Laine also believed in 'democratic progress', which would not be achieved under a monarchy.[1611] Even Gustaf Arokallio, who considered that the Finns currently lacked the prerequisites for a democratic republic, nevertheless counted on the democratic spirit of the Finnish people and on their support for 'a purely democratic constitution', provided that Bolshevism were prevented from again confounding conceptions of democracy.[1612]

The strongest arguments for the rule by the people originated from the Agrarian League, whose leader Santeri Alkio insisted that it was 'a natural law' that 'the development of all humankind proceeds towards rule by the people' and that, in 1918 too, despite the standstill in the German reform process and the Bolshevik Revolution, he stated: 'The rule by the people is rising

---

1609 *Suomen kansanvaltuuskunnan ehdotus* 1918, 3, 17, 20.
1610 VP, Kaarlo Juho Ståhlberg, 12 June 1918, 1246.
1611 VP, Augusta Laine, 7 August 1918, 1839.
1612 VP, Gustaf Arokallio, 12 July 1918, 1653, 1655–6.

everywhere in the world, while oligarchies and monarchical authorities are declining.'[1613] Alkio was convinced that humankind was at a 'turning point' and that any future constitution must be based on popular participation in government. In an era of advancing democracy, the Finns could not possibly build on outdated models of government but needed to have trust in 'the development of the people, the inner power of the people, the education of the people and a constitution that enables the realisation of the rule by the people.'[1614] Building on Fennoman idealism, which emphasised the potential of education, Alkio insisted that the Finns should keep their hold on 'the sceptre of the rule by the people, which has already been admired here for a number of years', and not let the Civil War change that.[1615] Alkio was saying that Finnish political culture had already become so democratic that there was no turning back to a political order that had existed before universal suffrage and the introduction of parliamentary government. Alkio saw democracy and parliamentarism as inseparable: democracy would guarantee parliamentarism, whereas reactionary autocracy, which the right seemed to be campaigning for, would destroy both.[1616] The only way to restore domestic peace was to support 'democratic progress' within the nation. Democracy had not caused the Red rebellion; that had been a purely Bolshevik uprising that had been a reflection of a Russian reaction to Russian ultra-monarchism,[1617] imported into Finland along with Bolshevik demands for a spurious form of democracy. Democracy proper had found a home in Finland, while Bolshevism was foreign to such a democracy.

The speeches made by Agrarians with a farming background reinforced this principled demand for democracy. In summer 1917, the farmers had supported the sovereignty of parliament, and in summer 1918 they were determined to prevent the restoration of the monarchy; this reflects the politically self-assured standing of Finnish farmers, an assurance that derived from the long tradition of the representation of a free peasantry.[1618] Bertta Pykälä, the mistress of a farmhouse, distinguished between the perverted socialist and the true peasant rule by the people, which many Finns had demonstrated during the Civil War: 'The peasant population of Finland had for long listened to the socialist clamour about the rule by the people and wanted to show them what the true rule by the people was.'[1619] Pykälä presented peasant democracy as realisable peacefully through parliament but as being currently threatened by the undemocratic rightist plans against both democracy and parliamentarism.[1620] Eetu Takkula deplored the way in which the so-called Social Democrats had betrayed the rule by the people in launching a rebellion against the parliament and the legal government

---

1613 VP, Santeri Alkio, 12 June 1918, 1254.
1614 VP, Santeri Alkio, 12 July 1918, 1659–60.
1615 VP, Santeri Alkio, 12 June 1918, 1256.
1616 VP, Santeri Alkio, 12 July 1918, 1664.
1617 VP, Santeri Alkio, 12 July 1918, 1662.
1618 Ihalainen 2015.
1619 VP, Bertta Pykälä, 13 June 1918, 1282.
1620 VP, Bertta Pykälä, 13 June 1918, 1282.

'to steal the rule by the people for themselves and to use it arbitrarily to advance their own ends.'[1621] Pekka Saarelainen called for the construction of a democratic polity that would follow the global democratic trend, while he saw monarchy as leading only to further socialism and anarchy.[1622] Juho Niukkanen, an independence activist, added that the suggested bureaucratic system without responsibility to the people would constitute a complete opposite to democracy. It would not work, as the Finnish people had demonstrated in the Civil War how much they valued a democratic and republican constitution.[1623] Artur Wuorimaa summarised this constitutional confrontation as one between the democracy of the people on the one hand and the aristocracy and the bureaucracy of the old elites on the other. According to the Agrarians, the people proper (that is, the peasantry) had saved the country in the Civil War and was now supporting democracy to the same end.[1624] Even though the Agrarian defence of democracy had its class aspects, idealising the role of the peasantry and challenging the old elites, it was nevertheless noteworthy in international comparative terms for its unreserved non-socialist advocacy of mass democracy, comparable in this respect with Swedish and some British and German liberals but different from Swedish rightist uses of peasant liberty as an argument.

What threatened democracy was, according to Alkio, the monarchical proposals, which did not so much arise out of foreign policy pressures but were rather aimed at crushing the rule by the people, the rightist talk about 'democratic' monarchy being mere humbug. The rightist attempt was doomed to fail as democracy was a force of nature that could not be prevented from breaking through and from redefining the order of society.[1625] Such natural metaphors of breakthrough brought Alkio's rhetoric again close to that of the Swedish left, reflecting the distinctly more leftist views of the Agrarian League in comparison with the conservative peasant parties in Sweden; in fact, Alkio's group constituted the republican left in the Rump Parliament. The Agrarians were also disappointed with those centrists who had changed their minds about democracy, Onni Talas (Young Finns) included. On 6 December 1917, as the minister responsible minister for constitutional issues, Talas had presented the Finnish people as essentially democratic.[1626] During the Civil War, he had welcomed the Germans into Helsinki as protectors against Bolshevism,[1627] and now he was insisting that a monarchical constitution as well as a republican one could be democratic.[1628] This speech was the first of a series of rightist rhetorical redescriptions of a monarchical constitution as democratic.

As a result of the unwavering determination of the Agrarians and the remaining liberal republicans to defend democracy as the only political

1621 VP, Eetu Takkula, 13 June 1918, 1284.
1622 VP, Pekka Saarelainen, 13 June 1918, 1316.
1623 VP, Juho Niukkanen, 13 July 1918, 1693.
1624 VP, Artur Wuorimaa, 13 July 1918, 1690–1.
1625 VP, Santeri Alkio, 7 August 1918, 1848–9.
1626 VP, Santeri Alkio, 12 June 1918, 1258.
1627 Kolbe 2008, 124–5.
1628 VP, Onni Talas, 12 June 1918, 1264.

system suitable for the Finnish people, the monarchists (the Finnish Party, the Swedish People's Party and some of the Young Finns) found it necessarily to show that their constitutional proposal was reconcilable with democracy. This meant an implicit recognition that without democracy in the sense of universal suffrage a modern constitution was unthinkable. Especially Young Finns like Pekka Ahmavaara who opted for monarchy to counter-balance extreme forms of democracy pointed to the fact that the experiences of Britain and the Scandinavian countries demonstrated that limited monarchy was in no way undemocratic.[1629] Tekla Hultin, a liberal activist famous for her earlier campaigns for constitutionalism and women's rights, asserted that both the Finnish national character and international trends spoke for a democratic constitution but that democracy was also achievable under a monarchical constitution – as in Norway.[1630] What was to be avoided was a 'wrong democracy' of the Bolshevik kind based on the unpredictable will of popular assemblies.[1631] Annie Furuhjelm (Swedish People's Party), a women's suffrage activist with international connections, presented both Britain and Germany as examples of successful combinations of democratic reforms and monarchy, especially when contrasted with the republican United States.[1632]

The Finnish Party, known for its previous social reformism, likewise set out to sell monarchy to the republicans by redescribing it as a democratic institution; this stemmed from the necessity to define any future political system as 'democratic' – even in a purely bourgeois parliament. Prime Minister Paasikivi, who had studied law in Germany as a doctoral student, described the German constitutional monarchy both as the best option with regard to security policy and as entirely reconcilable with the rule by the people,[1633] even though this Fennoman conservative would never be quite happy about democracy. Paavo Virkkunen, the Speaker of the Rump Parliament and a clergyman who had had a public role in the ceremonies that welcomed the German liberators to Helsinki,[1634] carried the rhetorical redescription of democracy as reconcilable with constitutional monarchy to the extreme, insisting: 'Demands for a king represent at the present moment the most mature expression of democratic notions. The people know and acknowledge that they need a royal head of their democratic constitution. Therefore they want to establish a royal democracy.'[1635] Wilhelmi Malmivaara, an influential Pietist leader, likewise declared that the proposed monarchical constitution was 'entirely democratic' in the correct sense of the word, and Ernst Nevanlinna, the Chairman of the Finnish Party, insisted that the proposal would lead to one of 'the most democratic constitutions in the

1629 VP, Pekka Ahmavaara, 12 June 1918, 1249.
1630 VP, Tekla Hultin, 13 July 1918, 1678, 1680.
1631 VP, Tekla Hultin, 7 August 1918, 1833.
1632 VP, Annie Furuhjelm, 13 June 1918, 1308.
1633 VP, Juho Kusti Paasikivi, 7 August 1918, 1816.
1634 Kolbe 2008, 131.
1635 VP, Paavo Virkkunen, 7 August 1918, 1824. See Bruendel 2003, 242–3 on 'Demokratie und Kaisertum' and 'Volkskönigtum' in German debates.

world'.[1636] A similar definition of the Prussian monarchy would have been unthinkable among the German right in summer 1918, although some attempts to describe it in such a way would follow in spring 1919; in Swedish rightist or British opposition Unionist discourse, on the other hand, such redescriptions of the established order were commonplace. Iisa Räsänen has pointed out that the Finnish-speaking monarchists were redefining the concept of 'true' democracy as being realisable through monarchical power as an expression of the rule by the people.[1637] The same point was used in Swedish and Finnish political arguments based on the common past[1638] and appeared in German political theory, which was well known in Finland.

Another strategy that was used was to quibble about what real democracy in its classical sense meant. This was done by E. N. Setälä, a professor of the Finnish language, who had participated in the formulation of the constitutional proposal of 1917. He claimed in very orthodox terms that the Finnish system could never be democratic in the proper sense of the word as the people simply could not come together to make decisions.[1639] In 1919 Setälä would also criticise the choice of certain words, in a draft constitution which he feared tended to lead to extreme forms of democracy. Finally, the Finnish Party contained a conservative segment of peasant opinion that was shocked by the catastrophic economic consequences of the people wielding supreme power through parliament in 1917 and saw the associated decline in respect for the government as an argument against a democratic polity.[1640] Nevertheless the avoidance of openly anti-democratic argumentation by the Finnish Party, which basically favoured the people, albeit somewhat patronisingly, is noteworthy.

Many MPs from the ultraconservative Swedish People's Party were openly sceptical about democracy after the Civil War, which, they claimed, had endangered law and order, property and minority rights. R. A. Wrede, who was a devoted adherent of German academic scholarship, and a participant in the constitutional proposal of 1917, argued that the development towards increasing democracy and parliamentarism since the French Revolution had already culminated and that both were in decline as a result of party strife and political corruption. What had taken place in the unicameral Finnish parliament, within which democratic and parliamentary principles had been uncritically admired by several political groups, was for Wrede exemplary of such a degeneration and threatened to destroy the entire society. The only solution was to combine representation with a constitutional monarchy[1641] if 'majority oppression' in parliamentary democracies – worse than any

1636 VP, Wilhelmi Malmivaara, 7 August 1918, 1837, 1856. Malmivaara's counter-concept *kansanvallattomuus* is difficult to translate into English, but it meant something like 'the unruliness of the people'; See also Juho Snellman (Young Finns), 7 August 1918, 1845; Ernst Nevanlinna (Finnish), 7 August 1918, 1852.
1637 Räsänen 1998 267–8.
1638 Ihalainen 2015.
1639 VP, Emil Nestor Setälä, 7 August 1918, 1829.
1640 VP, Juho Erkki Antila, 7 August 1918, 1835.
1641 VP, Rabbe Axel Wrede, 12 June 1918, 1253; reviewed in an abridged form in *Hufvudstadsbladet*, 'Remissdebatten', 13 June 1918.

seen under absolutist power – was to be avoided,[1642] the reference being to the Social Democratic attempts of 1917 and 1918 and to the experiences of the Swedish-speaking members of the old elite in general. Democracy and parliamentarism had been seriously misunderstood in Finland, and hence the future constitution should curb rather than support such principles. Wrede nevertheless joined in the rhetorical redescriptions of democracy with the authority of a former rector of the Imperial Alexander University, insisting that the proposal for a monarchical constitution was 'built entirely on a democratic basis';[1643] 'went further in democracy . . . than any other constitution';[1644] and was 'particularly liberal and democratic'.[1645] Even this authoritative figure with his anti-democratic views thought that in 1918 any constitution should be 'democratic' at least in name. The most openly anti-democratic views in the Finnish Rump Parliament thus came from a few academics of the Swedish People's Party. While concern about the rights of the Swedish-speaking minority explains much of this constitutional conservatism, there was no way of avoiding the impression that their aim was the continuation of restrictions on the political influence of the Finnish-speaking majority of the people.[1646]

5.4.4 Disappointment with the Finnish people or continuing confidence in it

The discursive confrontation over the rule by the people demonstrated that the Agrarians continued to hold an optimistic conception of the Finnish people, while many both in the Finnish Party and the Swedish People's Party could not hide their deep disappointment with the Finns as a people. This inability to trust the people at large after a civil war led to them to exclude what they considered to be excessively democratic and parliamentary constitutional solutions. The Finnish Party, with its Fennoman roots, had initially believed in the Finnish common people but now wavered in its optimism, while some MPs of the Swedish People's Party did not hesitate to express their doubts about the masses as they thought that the rights of the Swedish-speaking inhabitants would be in danger under any form of majority rule.

Disappointment with the Finnish people is reflected in the views of the historian Artturi Virkkunen, a civil servant in the National Schools Board and the editor-in-chief of *Uusi Suometar*, the organ of the Fennoman movement, which had traditionally believed in the importance of educating the people. According to Virkkunen, only the common efforts of 'the better

1642 VP, Rabbe Axel Wrede, 12 July 1918, 1651; *Hufvudstadsbladet*, 'Från kammare och kuloar', 13 July 1918, regarded this anti-parliamentary speech as one of the best heard in the unicameral parliament.
1643 VP, Rabbe Axel Wrede, 13 June 1918, 1313.
1644 VP, Rabbe Axel Wrede, 12 July 1918, 1652.
1645 VP, Rabbe Axel Wrede, 7 August 1918, 1847–8.
1646 Cf. a statement of Gustaf Rosenqvist claiming that 'the principles of the rule by the people and demagogy' had no role in his thinking although he defended a republic and new elections. VP, Gustaf Rosenqvist, 13 July 1918, 1675; this was welcomed in *Helsingin Sanomat*, 'Eduskunnassa', 14 July 1918.

elements of our people' had crushed the Red rebellion. His evaluation of both the Finnish elite and the masses was harsh, and it reinforced conservative scepticism about democracy in the aftermath of the Civil War:[1647]

> ... we have been too credulous in thinking the best of our people, also its lower strata, and accepted the fallacy that our people are both ethically and informatively on a high level. This conception has however shown itself to be a complete fallacy.

Such a negative re-evaluation of the Finns as a people by a leading Fennoman made any type of mass democracy impossible until the masses were re-educated for proper citizenship.

Bror Hannes Päivänsalo, the leader of a missionary organisation, pursued Virkkunen's argument, lamenting how the so-called representatives of the people did not really know 'the soul of our people' – as his collective concept had it. The Civil War had made this Lutheran clergyman entertain severe doubts about the spiritual and consequently the political state of the Finnish people. These doubts turned into a criticism of the optimistic republicans and their appeals to the will of the people:[1648]

> There is a lot of talk about the people here, about the people as if the people could be carried in one's pocket and as if some had a particular privilege to talk about the people, about the will and the soul of the people. Who of you has found the key with which the soul of the Finnish people can be opened? I at least am greatly amazed when I see phenomena in the life of our people that I could have never foreseen, and I must say that I find myself facing great, great problems. I would not dare to say at this moment that I know the people and its soul.

Few Finnish conservatives dared to be this sceptical about the possibilities of understanding the people. Lauri Ingman, a professor of theology and the leader of the Finnish Party, now also set out to challenge the suggestions of the republicans that a republican constitution would be based on the prevailing wishes of the people. A republic was not possible as it would 'take our people into such circumstances that the best elements of our people cannot want it'.[1649] The sceptical views of the Finnish-speaking right about democracy were often connected with Lutheran conceptions of a sinful people,[1650] a view that had been reinforced by the experiences of the Civil War. Some speakers of the German and Swedish right exhibited a similar level of scepticism and questioned the whole basis of mass democracy and extended parliamentarism, but they rarely employed religious arguments; the British Conservatives avoided such religiously oriented argumentation, having party-political reasons for being optimistic about the people.

Instead of merely emphasising the collective guilt of the people for their national tragedy, many externalised it, thereby opening up possibilities

---

1647 VP, Artturi Virkkunen, 13 June 1918, 1302.
1648 VP, Bror Hans Päivänsalo, 13 June 1918, 1305.
1649 VP, Lauri Ingman, 13 July 1918, 1677–8.
1650 Discussed in Ihalainen 2005a.

for the construction of a new unified nation state. This strategy united republicans and monarchists by making the previous and current *Russian* political systems scapegoats for the crisis of the Finnish polity. R. A. Wrede (Swedish People's Party), an old constitutionalist, regretted the influence on the Finnish people of Russian autocracy, the lawlessness inspired by the war and outright 'Russian anarchy' in the form of 'Russian Social Democracy'.[1651] It was the pernicious influence of Russia rather than the Finnish people as such that was to blame. The Russian Revolution had reduced the Finnish people into a state of 'nightmare' and 'induced an almost pathological condition in broad levels of the people', a malady that had at times (in July and November 1917) entered the parliament as well.[1652] Such a pathologisation of the rebellion, even if patronising towards the people at large as a political force, tended to exculpate the Finns from responsibility for their national tragedy. This was the easiest way to explain away the Civil War, forgetting the active participation of domestic political groups in the preceding political process.

Vesa Vares has suggested that the Finnish Party saw the people as basically good but misled before the Civil War, while the Swedish People's Party considered the fallen people to be in need of strict guidance;[1653] the above examples would suggest the contrary, but certainly many of these views were shared by the conservatives. The Finnish Party opposed a referendum on the constitution and emphasised the moral duty of the parliament to solve the constitutional issues.[1654] The members of the Swedish People's Party continued to employ legalistic argumentation, sometimes with conflicting results. Gustaf Rosenqvist, a retired professor of theology whose views had been ultra-conservative and legalistic in relation to the extension of parliamentary power and who had resigned from the parliament as a protest in 1917, spoke in 1918 in favour of new elections before constitutional changes could be made, insisting that 'we do not now represent the entire people of Finland, we do not represent the Finnish people in a way that our constitution expressly presupposes'.[1655] Rosenqvist asserted that he believed in 'the historical mission and role of the people, even of the little people [*småfolket*]'; the pre-conditions for their suffrage should, however, depend on the ethical standing of each person,[1656] which would exclude many Reds. Nevertheless, the people, including the workers, needed to be heard as the current parliament did not express the will of the people in any reliable way. This could not be measured mechanically by a majority vote; it was an organic phenomenon that could be expressed only by a legally

---

1651 VP, Rabbe Axel Wrede, 12 June 1918, 1251.
1652 VP, Rabbe Axel Wrede, 12 July 1918, 1650. For Gustav Rosenqvist's critical response from within the same party, see VP, 13 July 1918, 1674; also *Helsingin Sanomat*, 'Eduskunnassa', 14 July 1918.
1653 Vares 1998, 164.
1654 Vares 1998, 165.
1655 VP, Gustaf Rosenqvist, 13 June 1918, 1299.
1656 VP, Gustaf Rosenqvist, 13 July 1918, 1674.

assembled representative body of the people, i.e. a parliament.[1657] Rosenqvist declared:[1658]

> I am optimistic as far as our development and the development of all humanity is concerned. . . . [H]ence I cannot agree with the pessimistic, downright generalising and disparaging conception of our people and the representative institution of our people that is now being expressed in many quarters.

A man who can be assumed to have favoured conservative constitutional solutions wanted to have the Social Democrats back in parliament as a matter of principle instead of advocating the monarchist and Swedish-speaking interests of his party. Rosenqvist's optimism differs from the attitudes that prevailed among the Swedish right in the yet unresolved issue of suffrage reform and from the views of hard-liner conservatives within the Finnish Party and the Swedish People's Party in Finland. The Swedish parliamentary group remained polyphonic in its understanding of the political role of the people, even though the sceptics tended to dominate the discourse.

The liberal Young Finns were divided even more in their conceptions of the people. Pekka Ahmavaara, a former Speaker of the Peasant Estate, emphasised the great contribution of the peasantry during the Civil War, while lamenting the questionable characteristics of the people at large that had come out in it.[1659] Gustaf Arokallio saw the Bolshevik spirit as having extended itself even to non-socialist groups of the people; this was reflected in the appearance of delegations threatening a new rebellion if their demands were not met.[1660] These Young Finns would in autumn 1918 join the conservative National Coalition Party, which gathered together monarchists who were suspicious of an extended popular government.

Led by K. J. Ståhlberg, the republicans among the Young Finns rejected doubts about the political abilities of the Finns: after all, 'the healthy elements of our people rose up to defend our social order' and put the rebellion down.[1661] The new constitution should be based 'on trust and not distrust of our people and their internal and external vigour'.[1662] This was to say that the new polity should be based on the people themselves rather than on any foreign support,[1663] implying that the decision should not be influenced by German models and wishes. Ståhlberg's consistent defence of popular government and opposition to monarchism would earn him the first presidency of the republic in 1919 and large support in later presidential elections despite the limited size of the Progressivist Party, which the republican Young Finns formed in late 1918.

1657 VP, Gustaf Rosenqvist, 13 July 1918, 1675–6.
1658 VP, Gustaf Rosenqvist, 13 July 1918, 1676.
1659 VP, Pekka Ahmavaara, 12 June 1918, 1250.
1660 VP, Gustaf Arokallio, 12 July 1918, 1655.
1661 VP, Kaarlo Juho Ståhlberg, 12 June 1918, 1246.
1662 VP, Kaarlo Juho Ståhlberg, 12 June 1918, 1246.
1663 VP, Kaarlo Juho Ståhlberg, 12 June 1918, 1247.

The concept of the people remained central for the uncompromisingly republican Agrarians, who justified their rejection of the monarchy as being derived from 'the living and healthy force of the people'.[1664] Santeri Alkio did not deny the 'sin of the Finnish people' in allowing the Civil War to happen, but (like Wrede) saw the reason in an international epidemic that was initiated by Russian autocracy and manifested in the Bolshevik Russian Revolution and the connected Bolshevik rebellion in Finland. Among the Finns, the Social Democrats were to blame for misleading and provoking some credulous persons into revolutionary ideas and activities:[1665]

> Here the people, the people who hold Social Democratic beliefs, have been inculcated with the idea that a social revolution is inevitable. This belief hypnotised our Social Democrat leaders and their flocks to the extent that they believed that the time had come when the predicted social revolution must be implemented by violent means. We all know that they were mistaken. That moment has not arrived. Finland stands, and no social revolution has been implemented.

Alkio's analysis was not unfounded: as we saw in section 4.4, the revolutionary language of Finnish Social Democratic discourse in November and December 1917 suggests that the Bolshevik example together with previous Marxist agitation on the necessity of revolution had played a major role in the process of disintegration of parliamentary government and progress towards a civil war. Alkio's explanation of the rebellion as being caused by external influence and involving only misled Social Democrats allowed him to maintain his optimistic conclusions about the capability of the Finnish people – and the peoples of Europe in general – to develop politically. According to him, a great advance would take place as a consequence of increased democracy and the intensified political education of the people by nation-states after the war:[1666]

> [P]olitical life will be renewed and brightened as peoples grow. The political life which the deep ranks of the people currently live in Europe is not the kind of political life they would like to have. Our political life has taken on this form to a great extent as a result of the state not having taken sufficient care of the education of the people.

The Parliamentary Reform of 1906 had already politically educated the Finnish people to the extent that they were demanding political influence. In Alkio's populist description of the political situation of the country, it was 'the Finnish people' itself that was actively 'forming a state here' and not just parliamentarians arguing over constitutional alternatives. Alkio referred to this popular activism in representing the attempts by the monarchical parliamentary majority to ignore the people in the formulation of the constitution as doomed to fail: the Finnish people simply had to be awarded

---

1664 VP, Antti Juutilainen, 13 July 1918, 1685.
1665 VP, Santeri Alkio, 12 June 1918, 1254.
1666 VP, Santeri Alkio, 12 June 1918, 1256.

the democratic power that they had learned they had the right to possess. The same people needed to be educated in such a way that they would be able to recruit new political leaders who would 'have the courage to believe in and venture forth with this people'.[1667] This was the Agrarians' approach to realising the rule by the people and at the same time their way of challenging the conservative political elite.

Alkio went on to argue that Finland should base its political future on 'the development of its people, the inner power of the people, the education of the people and a constitution in which the rule by the people is implemented'.[1668] Elitist doubts about the trustworthiness of the Finns as a people to govern themselves were unfounded. Instead, 'in this momentous period, power should still be entrusted to the people themselves [in the form of a referendum or new elections], as 'this realm will not be created by any other might but by this people itself'.[1669] Finland should never become a military state of the Prussian type but 'a state which lives primarily for itself, for the happiness of its people'.[1670] Such an unwavering belief in the potential of the people to grow politically through education brought Alkio's thinking close to that of the Swedish left.

Alkio further extended his criticism of a monarchical constitution into an analysis of what he saw as an ongoing Europe-wide transformation of political systems brought about by the war and Wilsonian ideas, a phenomenon that should be understood by the Finnish parliamentary majority. Alkio was positive that 'future foreign policy between peoples will not be the policy of kings, but rather a policy of peoples' since, after the 'education' provided by the war, 'the power and influence of peoples will rise everywhere' and progress towards an eternal peace would follow. Finland currently seemed unable to follow 'a policy of the people' (*kansanpolitiikka*) vis-à-vis foreign nations (Russia and Germany) and to be fundamentally divided on foreign policy, but this would need to change. Finnish foreign policy, too, would need to follow guidelines set by the parliament; it should be consistent and public, just as domestic governance should be based 'on the principles of a modern democratically governed state'. Even the Germans were – Alkio claimed – willing to accept in Finland a constitution 'dependent on the people and supported by the people', including the currently excluded workers.[1671] Alkio went back to the attempts for reform in Germany in 1917, which in his view (despite the fact that they had been halted) reflected the willingness of the Kaiser to have a closer interaction with his people via parliament.[1672] Alkio used his entire rhetorical arsenal with references to both national and international recent history in his endeavour to stop the monarchists by appealing to the political will and potential of the people.

1667 VP, Santeri Alkio, 12 June 1918, 1256.
1668 VP, Santeri Alkio, 13 July 1918, 1660.
1669 VP, Santeri Alkio, 13 July 1918, 1660.
1670 VP, Santeri Alkio, 13 July 1918, 1660.
1671 VP, Santeri Alkio, 13 July 1918, 1660–1.
1672 VP, Santeri Alkio, 13 July 1918, 1662.

In the Rump Parliament, republicanism was a characteristically Agrarian phenomenon derived from deep-rooted conceptions of peasant democracy. Alkio's party fellow Kyösti Kallio highlighted the bravery and glory of the people that had been demonstrated in the Civil War and emphasised the disappointment of the people over the distrust in them implied by the government's proposal.[1673] Kallio would resign from his ministerial post a month later as a result of a disagreement over the constitution. Santeri Haapanen provocatively implied that the reintroduction of a monarchical constitution entailed the risk of a new revolution.[1674] Some Agrarians, such as Juho Kokko, a teacher himself, recommended the re-education of the people to republicanism and parliamentarism as the way forward. Kokko put his argument in organic terms that were downright early modern in spirit: the people should learn to know 'what type of plague Tokoi-Mannerism is in our political body'; learn to 'abhor the Russian Red danger' and 'wrong socialism'; and grow into becoming 'elements of a Finnish people striving for healthy principles'.[1675] By contrast, Kusti Arffman held a more optimistic conception of the current state of the Finns' political conscience and capabilities: the past decades of resistance to foreign autocracy and the suppression of the Red rebellion had demonstrated the strength of the Finnish culture and national identity and the potential of the Finns to govern themselves under a republican constitution.[1676] Arffman had obtained a broader perspective from the long period he had spent as an emigrant in the United States.

Among the right, who supported monarchical notions and were suspicious of extended democracy and parliamentarism, the overall conception of the people was coloured by pessimism and scepticism. The centrists, on the other hand, although they also sometimes expressed their disappointment with some sections of the people, consistently emphasised the political health of the core of the people and the possibilities to improve the situation through a republican constitution and suitable political education. This would allow a proper parliamentary democracy to emerge.

5.4.5 Limited debates on parliamentarism in the Rump Parliament

The debates on the political role of the people in the future Finnish polity – monarchical or republican – lead us to more limited discussions on the nature of parliamentarism. Parliamentarism had been esteemed, though in the case of the non-socialist parties with clear limitations, by all sides in the parliamentary debates of summer and autumn 1917. It was viewed in much more negative terms and often ignored by many in the aftermath of the Civil War. The parliamentary process had not been able to solve the problems of Finnish society or to prevent the escalation of the conflict in 1917; instead, the violent parliamentary debates and the uncompromising views expressed in them had contributed to this escalation. Some representatives of the right blamed universal suffrage and the unicameral parliament for

---

1673 VP, Kyösti Kallio, 12 June 1918, 1257.
1674 VP, Santeri Haapanen, 12 June 1918, 1261.
1675 VP, Juho Kokko, 13 June 1918, 1311.
1676 VP, Kusti Arffman, 13 June 1918, 1314.

the crisis. The MPs disagreed about whether the parliament should remain a body that merely ratified legislation and a forum for public debate of the pre-war Finnish, Swedish and German types or whether it should be given an independent supervisory role by the introduction of full ministerial responsibility.

Republicans continued to advocate parliamentarism, *Helsingin Sanomat* as the largest newspaper in the country insisting that either form of government (monarchic or republican) should be first and foremost parliamentary.[1677] But the republicans found themselves in a weakened position in post-Civil War Finland: the critics of parliamentarism could argue that its worst consequences had already been seen in Finland. The defenders of parliamentarism could rely on the republican sympathies of the majority of the Finnish electorate once they were allowed to vote again. But in summer 1918 they could not yet count on countries with parliamentary governments winning the war. Furthermore, republicanism had no strong ideological roots in Finland – unless we take into account some eighteenth-century republican proclivities among the Swedish nobility[1678] – and the rule of the estates in the Swedish Age of Liberty could not be taken as parliamentarism in any modern or positive sense; on the contrary, in the circumstances of 1918, it rather served as a warning example.[1679] What was more, the parliamentary ministries of 1917 had not functioned properly as the crisis deteriorated.

Vesa Vares has shown that the republicans, often younger and less highly educated and despised for their inexperience by the monarchists,[1680] were nevertheless convinced of the progressive character of their ideals and hence unwilling to compromise: for them, a parliamentary republic remained the only democratic form of government which the majority of the people supported. Republicanism stood for the conviction that a republican form of government would produce a better future in a national democracy. Monarchism, by contrast, appeared to the republicans as a downright criminal reactionary plot of the Swedish-speakers,[1681] or at least the defence of an outdated aristocratic and bureaucratic system that lacked responsibility to the parliament and the people. Santeri Alkio had serious doubts as to whether the proposed monarchical constitution would lead to the king ruling in accordance with the will of the parliament.[1682]

To counter republican doubts about a monarchical constitution, the ministry emphasised the stability and continuity it would bring. The government also referred to limitations to monarchical power that would guarantee 'the rights of parliament and the people'.[1683] Even the most fervent advocates of monarchy were ready to recognise the current and future

---

1677 *Helsingin Sanomat*, 'Ewästyskeskustelu hallitusmuotoasiasta', 14 June 1918.
1678 Wolff 2009.
1679 Ihalainen 2015.
1680 *Hufvudstadsbladet*, 'Vår stora fråga', 13 July 1918.
1681 *Helsingin Sanomat*, 'Kenelle lankeaa edeswastuu?', 14 July 1918; Vares 1998, 131–3.
1682 VP, Santeri Alkio, 12 June 1918, 1255.
1683 VP, Juho Kusti Paasikivi, 12 June 1918, 1244.

constitution as 'parliamentary'[1684] – using a rhetorical redescription familiar from the uses of 'democracy'. *Hufvudstadsbladet*, for instance, asserted that ministerial responsibility and the influence of the representative institution would be maintained despite extensive monarchical prerogatives.[1685] This definition of what 'proper' parliamentarism meant differed radically from the conceptions of the republicans. The monarchists mentioned parliamentarism mainly to appease the republicans although they nevertheless implicitly recognised its value.

Despite continuing uncertainty about the outcome of the war, from July 1918 onwards the republicans were increasingly confident in their defence of parliamentarism, bringing up the possibility that Germany might not win. In this sense, the Finnish republicans were preparing the kind of turn away from Germany towards Western parliamentary democracies that was taking place in Sweden, though more cautiously. Santeri Alkio argued against monarchy, identifying parliamentarism with republicanism, and described a Europe-wide development that Finland should follow[1686]:

> In all countries the conclusion has been that absolute monarchy needs to be limited by parliamentary power. This has led to parliamentarism, which is nothing else but development towards a republic. In the future, beyond parliamentarism, republicanism is imminent everywhere, whatever else may be claimed.

The implication was that not only did the Entente consist of parliamentary governments but that Germany, too, was ready to parliamentarise its government as soon as the war was over. The future of the reigning monarchs was not certain, either. It hence made no sense to create a new throne at a time when parliamentarism, followed by increasing democracy, was making historical progress at the cost of monarchies.[1687] This was still in mid-July 1918 an overly optimistic claim, yet one that would soon turn into a reality. *Hufvudstadsbladet* took it as mere prophecy.[1688]

The monarchists ignored the claim. Gustaf Rosenqvist – an independent thinker who was critical of what he considered excessive parliamentarism but supportive of popular participation in politics and contemptuous of the idealisation of monarchy – responded by expressing his disrespect for such admirers of 'a power-seeking, autocratic representation of the people'.[1689] Many intellectuals like this retired professor of theology remained doubtful about a ruling parliament but wished to see the established conventions of the polity observed. There was no proper *pro et contra* debate on parliamentarism in the Finnish parliament in connection with the question of whether or not to have a German king. The Finns would find themselves in an entirely new position once the parliamentarisation of the German government got under way in autumn 1918, although even then the monarchists would remain unwilling to change their minds.

1684 VP, Ernst Estlander, 13 July 1918, 1703.
1685 *Hufvudstadsbladet*, 'Förslaget till regeringsformen', 12 June 1918.
1686 VP, Santeri Alkio, 12 July 1918, 1663.
1687 VK, 12 July 1918, 1663–4.
1688 *Hufvudstadsbladet*, 'Från kammare och kuloar', 13 July 1918.
1689 VP, Gustaf Rosenqvist, 13 July 1918, 1675.

6. The autumn of 1918: German, Swedish and Finnish constitutional debates in the face of a democratic turn

6.1 Democratic suffrage applied in Britain for the first time

The British Representation of the People Act had passed Parliament in February 1918, waiting for immediate implementation as soon as the war was over. The general election was held accordingly on 14 December 1918, only about a month after the conclusion of the armistice. The War Cabinet had reformed electoral legislation and planned this election during the war, but the voters were far from ready for such political mobilisation, and this resulted in low participation levels. With hindsight, the elections appealing to 'the new democracy' of 21 million voters, may appear to have been a decisive turning point in British political history, but contemporaries did not generally see them that way: many were apathetic.[1690] Only 57.2 of the electorate per cent voted in the midst of a post-war crisis, many abstaining because of a lack of interest, distrust in Parliament, private concerns or bad weather. Over eighty per cent had voted in 1910, and nearly ninety per cent would vote in the German election only a month later.[1691]

Prime Minister Lloyd George wanted the electorate to vote so early in order to prevent the Labour Party from benefiting from a longer campaign. Labour had adopted a socialist agenda, breaking the party truce in June, leaving the coalition in November and declaring 'Hands Off Democracy!' in its election manifesto which welcomed 'the extension of liberty and democracy in Europe', the advancement of 'world-democracy' through the Workers International and building by constitutional means 'a new world' based on 'permanent democratic principles'. It was implying that the ministry opposed 'the young democracies of the Continent' and rejected a British intervention in Russia, which reinforced associations between its demands for socialist democracy and the Bolshevik notion of the dictatorship of the proletariat, even though it had denounced Bolshevism in favour of parliamentary democracy. In domestic politics, 'the immediate

---

[1690] *The Manchester Guardian*, 'The Real Issues of the Election', 1 December 1918; 'The Real King', 14 December 1918. Press sources are used here as the the British reform had already been passed.
[1691] Ball 1991, 246; Turner 1992, 329, 332; Pugh 2002, 161.

nationalisation and democratic control of vital public services' was demanded. In foreign policy, a call for 'democratic diplomacy' might sound like flexibility with Germany.[1692] To counter socialist advances and expected Liberal losses, Lloyd George allied himself with the Conservatives, making an advance agreement with them on the distribution of seats. He also turned in his election campaign propaganda from reconstruction and social reforms to Germanophobic declarations of the need to punish the Germans collectively.[1693] The joint election manifesto of Lloyd George and Bonar Law made no mention of democracy but emphasised how 'the hosts of freedom' had crushed 'military autocracy' on the Continent for ever, appealed to the patriotism and unity of 'our people', 'our nation' and 'our Empire' and promised a further parliamentary reform based on direct contract with the people'.[1694] The supposedly universal cause of democracy was in actual fact taken over by chauvinistic and party-political interests and tended to be discursively constructed as a socialist project.

Lenin's declarations about the necessity of civil war as the proper form of class struggle in a revolutionary epoch[1695] and the fate of Kerensky's government in the Russian Bolshevik Revolution suggested that the risk of a socialist government obtaining power existed, and it was feared that this would to lead to a take-over by even more radical revolutionaries – especially so as revolutionary movements were growing in the Central Powers. The British electorate did not generally care much about constitutional developments on the Continent; the systems there were regarded as fundamentally different from the British one, and hence domestic and imperial perspectives dominated the debate. However, the Home Office reported that there were more Bolsheviks per capita in Britain than in Russia at the time of the Revolution and that British 'Bolshevism' was supported not only by Russian but also by German and Swedish 'Bolsheviks'. The election nevertheless showed overwhelming support for continued cooperation between the Conservatives and Lloyd George's Liberals. The winners were backed by the predominant Germanophobic feeling in the country and the inclination of women on the home front to vote against the Germans and the Kaiser and in favour of the Conservatives.[1696] The Conservatives had played a visible role during the ultimately victorious war and mostly supported the enfranchisement of women in 1917–18, partly because they expected that women would favour their party and partly to obviate any female hostility that might rise from continued opposition. Those soldiers who bothered to vote probably also supported the coalition. As the electoral support for Labour was much lower than expected, resulting in just 63 seats, the election

1692 *Labour's call for the people*, 1918.
1693 *The Manchester Guardian*, 'The Labour Appeal', 28 November 1918, 'Mr. Arthur Henderson', 2 December 1918; Cowden 1984, 26, 30; Wrigley 1990, 1–2; Smith 1997, 66–7; Cook 1998, 73; McCrillis 1998, 35, 38; Thorpe 2001, 39–40; Cunningham 2001, 239; Pugh 2011, 122–3; Dutton 2013, 68, 70.
1694 *The Manifesto of Lloyd George and Bonar Law*, 1918.
1695 *The Manchester Guardian*, 'Bolsheviks Busy', 17 November 1918.
1696 Suggested also in *The Manchester Guardian*, 'The Real Issues of the Election', 1 December 1918.

demonstrated the restored strength of the Conservatives and lent support for their increasingly optimistic visions. At the same time, the election revealed divisions within the Liberal Party, in which concerns caused by the possible consequences of universal suffrage, and also the still modest rise of Labour, began to materialise.[1697] The hurried election and Lloyd George's steering of the result caused opposition Liberals to argue that the Prime Minister was not following the ways of 'democracy, as in England at least it is understood'. Thus not even all Liberals were happy about the way that democracy had been implemented: H. H. Asquith said that 'the democracy of this country' should have been free to send its spokesmen to the Commons.[1698] Lloyd George's rival candidate Austin Harrison suggested that the Prime Minister had replaced 'free democracy' with 'autocracy'.[1699]

Nevertheless, the British Conservatives had successfully adapted to the transition to universal suffrage and majority democracy, as some of their reformist MPs had optimistically foreseen: it had paid off to trust the people and to move towards what *The Manchester Guardian* characterised as 'Tory democracy'[1700]. In Germany, Sweden and Finland, the right would be less successful in recruiting electoral support to retain their pre-reform positions. In these countries, the reformation of the attitudes of the right with regard to democracy and parliamentarism was only beginning; the decisive turn to democracy would, or would not as the case may be, follow in the early 1930s. One explanation for the successful transfer to the era of universal suffrage in Britain, in addition to the steered election result, may be the fact that there existed no previously established group that would lose its power or felt its interests violated as a result; hence there was no necessity to challenge democracy. Continuity rather than change remained a characteristic of the British political system, with the same political elite continuing to run politics. This made the British aristocracy readier to accept the compromises of evolutionary democratisation and remain supportive of the system – in contrast to the deeply reactionary and antidemocratic Prussian nobility,[1701] and the partly doubtful right in Sweden and Finland. In Britain, the Conservatives launched a ten-year project to attract support under universal suffrage[1702] and did quite well in the new circumstances.

Was the implementation of nearly universal suffrage understood to constitute 'democracy' then? On the pages of *The Times* in late 1918, the understanding of the reformed British electoral system as a 'democracy' was rather limited. The paper had used the term to justify the early election, insisting: 'Once the Reform Bill was carried, a prompt appeal to the country

---

1697 Wrigley 1990, 14; Turner 1992, 330, 332; Ball 1995, 61–4; Rose 1995, 31; Smith 1997, 69–70; McCrillis 1998, 16; Pugh 2002, 161–2; Bogdanor (ed.) 2003, 724–5; Charmley 2008, 97; Harris 2011, 267.
1698 *The Manchester Guardian*, 'Mr. Asquith's Speech' and 'Mr. Asquith's Election Policy', 19 November 1918.
1699 *The Manchester Guardian*, 'The Premier's Seat', 12 December 1918.
1700 *The Manchester Guardian*, 'New Food Controller', 10 July 1918.
1701 Retallack 1988, 2; Garrard 2001, 4; Retallack 2006, 11; Jefferys 2007, 16–17.
1702 McCrillis 1998, 19.

became an essential step to a conclusive and democratic victory.'¹⁷⁰³ This 'victory' referred to the achievement of the war goal internationally rather than to the establishment of a new political system at home. In this spirit, the paper lauded the 'democratic instinct' of Lloyd George for making a 'democratic decision' about an early election.¹⁷⁰⁴ On the other hand, the possibilities for democracy in India, for instance, were doubted.¹⁷⁰⁵ *The Times* denounced Labour's politicisation of democracy in the domestic debate and rather urged 'every democracy' (in the generalising sense of free states) to fight against Bolshevism, Britain being associated with 'the established democracies of the world', and more particularly with the United States.¹⁷⁰⁶ This was 'rational democracy' as opposed to the 'rapid revolution' demanded by 'Bolshevist' candidates during the British election campaign.¹⁷⁰⁷ Britain was a democracy by definition, but no reformist conclusions were to be drawn from this in the immediate post-war situation. Indeed, the only reform demanded was training for citizenship in the name of 'true democracy',¹⁷⁰⁸ which was a call typical of liberal and conservative parties at the time of the reforms of 1918–19.

Those newspapers that were inclined to Liberal views and supported Lloyd George praised the progress of democracy in British domestic politics, an editorial of *The Manchester Guardian* in July 1918 assuming that 'popular or representative government, or democracy' in its British form had been generally accepted as a model in 'Western countries'.¹⁷⁰⁹ In September, the paper asserted that '[d]emocracy in England has made a gigantic stride during the war' and called for a parliament that would represent 'the democracy as a whole' in advancing economic equality and opposing extra-parliamentary (socialist) reformers.¹⁷¹⁰ The paper also took up the need to advance the democratisation of India now that 'the contagion . . . of democracy' had, as a consequence of the war, reached Asia. Its suggestion was that the British people should thereby contribute to 'our own new era of democracy' concomitantly with 'fighting with America to make the world safe for democracy'.¹⁷¹¹ Obviously, some Liberals were ready to rethink both economic policies and the structures of the British Empire in democratic terms.

However, only rarely were interpretations of the implications of 'the new era of enlarged democracy after the war' extended to promote 'the welfare,

---

1703 *The Times*, 'A Patriotic Programme', 1 August 1918.
1704 *The Times*, 'Towards a Programme', 14 November 1918, 'The Voter's Choice', 12 December 1918.
1705 *The Times*, 'The Indian Report', 10 July 1918.
1706 *The Times*, 'The Labour Party's Manifesto', 29 November 1918.
1707 *The Times*, 'Bolshevist Candidate', 28 November 1918.
1708 *The Times*, 'Educational Issues', 13 December 1918.
1709 *The Manchester Guardian*, 'The Government of India', 6 July 1918.
1710 *The Manchester Guardian*, 'Trade Unionism and Democracy', 2 September 1918.
1711 *The Manchester Guardian*, 'The Government of India', 6 July 1918, 'A New Epoch in India', 7 July 1918, 'Indian Reforms', 12 July 1918, 'The New Era in India', 18 August 1918.

progress, status, and power of the people'.[1712] When such proposals were made, they often ended up with suggestions combining the brotherhood of mankind, British patriotism, imperial unity and 'progressive democracy'[1713] with calls for devolution as a way to advance the functioning of democracy[1714] or with demands for reforming the educational system to support democracy.[1715] In mid-September one theoretical contribution concluded that modern democracy stood not only for elections and the parliament as instruments of human progress and brotherhood between nations but also for 'equality of opportunity for all, freedom of conscience, the maximum of individual liberty that is consistent with the good of the whole, a relation of mutual confidence between the governors and the governed'. The author, aware of his idealism, listed several problems involved in the practice of democracy but concluded that it should be given a chance, for the first time, to demonstrate what it was capable of.[1716] On the election day, *The Manchester Guardian* claimed that the voting was a test of the value of elections and Parliament as instruments of democracy – something that was self-evident in Britain but not in Bolshevik Russia or Germany, or indeed in the programme of Labour.[1717]

The rhetoric of democracy was most pronounced in demonstrations of alliance with the Americans, as in Asquith's flattering talk about America as 'a great democracy' and his inclusion of Britain in a reference to 'these great democracies'.[1718] 'Democratisation' or 'parliamentarisation', however, remained something that the Allied leaders (and the German opposition) were calling for Germany. At the same time, the promises of the German government to democratise the political system were treated with scepticism.[1719] When the war was over, the conclusion was that it had 'justified democracy' since the Western democracies, which represented systems based on the will of the people, had won. Furthermore, it was 'the democratic element' within these democracies that had won.[1720] When the election result was known, *The Manchester Guardian* declared it to be the voice of 'the new democracy'.[1721] For Liberals, democracy had thus become a vague but overwhelmingly positive concept which could be used to legitimate the established British system and possible minor reforms of it.

During the election campaign, Labour had called not only for support for the democracies of the Continent but also for 'the completion of political democracy' at home with further electoral reforms and the abolition

---

1712 *The Observer*, '"Clear the Line"', 21 July 1918.
1713 *The Observer*, 'Hope and Unity', 11 August 1918.
1714 *The Observer*, '"The Round Table"', 8 September 1918.
1715 *The Manchester Guardian*, 'Election News', 14 October 1918.
1716 *The Manchester Guardian*, L.S., 'Democracy', 14 September 1918.
1717 *The Manchester Guardian*, 'The Election and After', 14 December 1918.
1718 *The Manchester Guardian*, 'League of Nations', 13 July 1918.
1719 *The Manchester Guardian*, 'Unrest in Germany', 7 September 1918, 'Lord Grey on the League of Nations', 11 October 1918, 'Press Comments on the German Reply', 22 October 1918. The quoted *Daily Chronicle* was supportive of Lloyd George.
1720 *The Manchester Guardian*, H., 'It Never Shall Happen Again', 16 November 1918.
1721 *The Manchester Guardian*, 'Britain's Voice', 29 December 1918.

of the Lords. Furthermore, it had demanded 'such far-reaching social, economic, moral, and political reforms as will make our country worthy of democracy';[1722] in this respect it differed little from Continental revisionist Social Democratic parties. *The Herald*, representing the far left, had little constructive to write about democracy or parliamentarism as practised in Britain. Its writers advocated 'a democratic or Republican Europe', supported American endeavours 'to democratise Europe' and opposed polities based on imperialism or nationalism. They called for the democratisation of education and welcomed labour activism in promoting the realisation of 'the democratic ideal'.[1723] With the approach of peace, *The Herald* complained that it had not been concluded much earlier in 'fair, honest, democratic terms' as opposed to demanding an unconditional surrender from Germany now that a victory was expected; this was 'a repudiation of democracy'. If these tough terms failed to produce peace, British soldiers had died 'not for democracy' but 'for the blood-lust of the Northcliffe Press', i.e. *The Times*, *The Daily Mail* and other papers that supported the government, and 'the reactionaries of Britain' who, *The Herald* claimed, thought like 'the reactionaries of Germany'.[1724] The paper attacked Lloyd George's Liberals by accusing them of having 'boasted [their] belief in democracy – and denied the democratic rights of half the people'.[1725] After the election, *The Herald* questioned the legitimacy of the new parliament: the hasty election made it 'no true representative of the people'. As the prevailing antiquated constitution gave the people no political power over the Commons, the workers should be prepared to put extra-parliamentary pressure on the government to secure 'political democracy'.[1726] The British far left was thus in line with its continental brethren. As for Labour politicians, Ramsay MacDonald was reported to have said that he remained 'a believer in Parliamentary action' albeit supported with industrial action.[1727]

While Liberal public discourse was turning more favourable towards democracy in Britain – though it was still cautious about using the term to characterise any detailed reform programme – the left was far from convinced that any noticeable advances in democracy had taken place. Democratisation in Germany was an even more complicated matter from the British point of view. Soutou has claimed that Lloyd George was confident that Germany would be quickly transformed into a trustworthy member of the family of Western liberal democracies.[1728] Some other researchers have suggested that he encouraged democracy in Germany but did not insist on

---

1722 *The Manchester Guardian*, 'Labour's Policy', 26 November 1918.
1723 *The Herald*, Austin Harrison, 'The Better "Ole"', 31 August 1918.
1724 *The Herald*, 'Get On With Peace', 2 November 1918; Lord Northcliffe had indeed influentially used his papers to support or criticise politicians and generals during the war. Thompson 1999, vii–viii, 238.
1725 *The Herald*, 'An Appeal to Liberals', 5 October 1918.
1726 *The Herald*, 'The Dud Parliament', 21 December 1918.
1727 *The Herald*, 'Up the International', 7 December 1918.
1728 Soutou 2014, 537.

a regime change.[1729] However, support for German democratisation was not so straightforward. In mid-October 1918, *The Manchester Guardian* reported that Max von Baden's dedication to democracy and parliamentarisation was not a genuine one.[1730] During the Reichstag debates on a new parliamentary constitution in late October, the paper summarised President Wilson's demands, which included the democratisation of the Prussian franchise, the abolition of the Prussian veto in the Bundesrat and the granting to the Reichstag of the initiative in legislation.[1731] The November Revolution in Germany appeared to the paper to be a manifestation of the potential advancement of Bolshevism at the cost of Social Democratic attempts to democratise Germany. This non-parliamentary revolution seemed to be progressing in all too radical a direction, recalling the Russian Revolution. Any counter-revolutionary foreign policy was to be avoided, however, in order not to encourage extremism in Germany.[1732] The Conservatives were known to be sceptical about the fruitfulness of making an alliance with 'the democracy of Germany', i.e. with the Social Democrats, in the search for peace.[1733] *The Times* doubted the sincerity of the German talk about democratisation and parliamentarisation.[1734]

The public debate seems to have been in line with Douglas Newton's suggestion that Lloyd George's government was hostile to the revolution in Germany and the emerging Weimar Republic and that this attitude contributed to the bad name that 'democracy' would gain in Germany in the course of 1919. Newton challenges interpretations which claimed that German democracy failed because of an overreaction from the moderate German socialists to the danger of Bolshevism and their consequent attack on the far left. Newton demonstrates the complex dynamic of the transnational discourse on democracy; in particular he considers that the British far left became radicalised as a reaction to the actions of the German SPD. Lloyd George's election campaign expressed strongly anti-German views and fears of international socialism, both of which led him to call for harder peace terms with Germany. He emphasised the collective war guilt of the Germans, denied the possibility of Germany becoming democratised

1729 Fry 2011, 145, 147, who does not really discuss Lloyd George's concept of democracy even though he calls him 'the first democratic statesman'.
1730 *The Manchester Guardian*, 'Toward Parliamentarisation', 14 October 1918, and 'Prince Max's Sincerity', *The Manchester Guardian*, 15 October 1918. Against the background of Max von Baden's previous attacks on Western democracy and parliamentarism this was the correct conclusion. Seils 2011, 625.
1731 *The Manchester Guardian*, 'Our London Correspondence', 25 October 1918.
1732 *The Manchester Guardian*, 'Turmoil in the Central Powers', 5 November 1918, 'The German Government's Plight', 8 November 1918, 'Germany and Bolshevism', 26 November 1918.
1733 *The Manchester Guardian*, 'Mr. Balfour & Peace', 9 August 1918.
1734 *The Times*, 'Truth About the "Crisis"', 25 September 1918, 'The German Crisis', 4 October 1918, 'Fluttered German Scribes', 1 October 1918, 'President Wilson's Reply', 10 October 1918, 'Need for Joint Allied Action', 25 October 1918, 'German "Democratization"', 31 October 1918, reviewing an answer by Robert Cecil, Assistant Secretary of Foreign Affairs. These news were again reviewed in Berlin papers. Seils 2011, 638.

and declared that his leftist opponents in Britain were pro-German and pro-Bolshevist. He rejected all suggestions for a more moderate policy on Germany. In Germany, these relentless policies further demonstrated to many on the right that Western 'democracy' had indeed been a mere delusion, that it was rightfully associated with the national humiliation of Germany and that the rightist opposition to wartime suggestions about democracy from both home and abroad had been well-founded.[1735]

The Herald, a major opponent of Lloyd George, was undeniably pro-German. It firmly believed in the democratisation of Germany through legislation: ministers had been made responsible to the Reichstag and the military placed under civilian control. 'Democratic procedures' in the nomination of a 'parliamentary government' were observed better there than recently in Britain. The paper 'proved' the change in Germany by citing the Conservatives' opposition to the constitutional reform and leftist demands for the abdication and punishment of the Kaiser.[1736] The British far left clearly overestimated the degree of parliamentarisation that had taken place in Germany since summer 1917,[1737] using these interpretations and idealising the activities and popular support for the German left to pressurise domestic political rivals.

The Swedish reform of late 1918 also gained some attention in the British Liberal press.[1738] The Social Democratic leader Hjalmar Branting, who had good contacts in Britain and France, was allowed to explain the Swedish position with regard to the war. According to Branting, Swedish neutrality did not arise from the mere search for an economic advantage or from a lack of democratic ideals. The Swedish government was actually pursuing a 'revolutionary' reform that would create 'a firmly democratic Sweden' resembling 'a Western democracy'. Sweden had kept a distance from 'the Finland troubles', which had provided 'an example which none of the northern nations can fail to regard with understanding eyes'.[1739] Branting spoke for 'a democratic peace' and suggested an international labour conference in support of democracy as soon as Prussian militarism was crushed.[1740] At home he reported about 'the free democratic spirit' of the armies of the Entente, who were fighting for freedom against German

---

1735 Shipway 1988, 62; Wrigley 1990, 8; Newton 1997, 1, 10–11, 415, 417, 424–5; also McCrillis 1998, 39, 42, and Fry 2011, 184–5.
1736 *The Herald*, 'Towards German Democracy', 28 September 1918, 'The Coming Peace!', 5 October 1918, 'The New Germany', 12 October 1918, 'Raising the Terms', 26 October 1918, and 'Get On With Peace', 2 November 1918, all evidently authored by H. N. Brailsford.
1737 *The Herald*, H. N. Brailsford, 'Is It a New Germany?', 9 November 1918.
1738 *The Manchester Guardian*, 'Swedish Reforms', 16 November 1918, 'Sweden and a Republic by Referendum', 18 November 1918.
1739 *The Manchester Guardian*, 'Abroad', 26 July 1918, 'Sweden and the Allies', 8 September 1918.
1740 *The Times*, 'M. Branting's Tribute to British Army', 22 July 1918; *The Manchester Guardian*, 'M. Branting's Visit', 28 July 1918, 'Socialist Appeal to Mr. Henderson', 17 November 1918.

hegemony.¹⁷⁴¹ Ludvig Nordström, a journalist, further explained the Swedish rightist fears of democracy as a reaction to the rising trade unions and Bolshevism; it was not to be regarded as a pro-German attitude (which was not true). Indeed, an Allied victory would liberate Sweden from German domination.¹⁷⁴² Sweden also figured as a general spokesman for democracy when President Wilson arrived in Europe. Branting then declared that 'the entire democratic world' hailed Wilson and that the Swedish working class totally supported his plans.¹⁷⁴³

The news from Finland was much more negative as far as democracy was concerned. The country was criticised in the aftermath of its civil war for 'the Germanisation of Finland'.¹⁷⁴⁴ The Germanophile Fennomans seemed prepared for the complete German domination of their country, by imposing policies that were supportive of Germany, restricting civil liberties, treating the Reds (or 'Finnish Bolsheviks') with mercilessness, denying equal constitutional rights to Swedish-speakers¹⁷⁴⁵ and aiming at a Prussian-style monarchy. Finland had been going backwards 'at a furious pace since the proclamation of a democratic republic at the end of 1917'. As a result, 'the most democratic country in the world, as the Finns were accustomed to boast, has become a stronghold of frantic reaction', in which the Russians, British, Americans and Swedes were all hated.¹⁷⁴⁶ *The Times* concluded that '[a] democratic Finland . . . does not suit German policy', which wished to deny the principle of national self-determination and impose a limited monarchy or German military rule on the Finns.¹⁷⁴⁷ The Germans were making Prussian cultural propaganda in the country, and dubious German methods were being used in Finnish politics.¹⁷⁴⁸ Foreign Secretary Arthur Balfour took up the Finnish case in a Commons debate as an example of ideologically driven German power politics.¹⁷⁴⁹ After the Finnish election of a German king, *The Times* wondered about the sense of destroying possibilities for understanding with the Entente, particularly as the Finns were 'too democratic in spirit to love [Germans] or their ways'. Nevertheless, the Finns would 'probably be the last people in all Europe, including Germany, to abandon belief in the intellectual pre-eminence and material invincibility of the Germans.'¹⁷⁵⁰ There was no uncertainty about Finland having turned into another Prussia at the decisive stages of the Great War.

1741 *The Times*, 'M. Branting with the Allied Armies', 16 August 1918.
1742 *The Manchester Guardian*, 'The Position of Sweden', 15 December 1918.
1743 *The Times*, 'Greetings from Sweden', 17 December 1918.
1744 *The Manchester Guardian*, 'Preparing for the Future', 17 August 1918.
1745 *The Times*, 'Racial Oppression in Finland', 3 July 1918.
1746 *The Manchester Guardian*, 'Reaction in Finland', 20 July1918, 'The Fate of Finland', 26 July 1918, 'Lenin's Work for Germany', 11 August 1918.
1747 *The Times*, 'German Dictation to Finland', 2 August 1918.
1748 *The Times*, 'Kultur Ideals for Finland', 20 August 1918, on the basis of *Vorwärts*, and 'Finland Learning from the Germans', 6 September 1918.
1749 *The Manchester Guardian*, 'Mr. Balfour & Peace', 9 August 1918.
1750 *The Times*, 'Finland under the Germans', 11 October 1918.

The Herald further recalled that the Finnish bourgeoisie had crushed a revolution with terror and German support and suggested that the appeal of the White government for British help to keep that revolution down might be successful unless the Labour Party set out to oppose this.[1751] A leftist Finnish correspondent reported how Finnish democrats (referring to the socialists as 'the Finnish democracy') were hoping for the advance of Labour in the British election and the formation of a government that would not recognise Finland until there had been a free election. The Finnish socialists had, under the influence of Bolshevism, renounced parliamentarism, but the White government (amongst whose supporters admiration of the Kaiser still continued) was practising postwar terror, using courts formed on the basis of class to punish all socialists and oppressing the workers both in and out of prison camps. The only hope was that the British democracy would save the Finns from both Bolshevism and the current reaction to it.[1752] This was all far-left discourse on democracy but not very far removed from critical non-socialist views about what was going on in Finland.

6.2 Germany loses the war, introduces parliamentary government and experiences a revolution

6.2.1 The course of the German Revolution up to the fall of the Kaiser

German politics in autumn 1918 was conditioned by the final war efforts after the losses of the summer. From the beginning of August, the leading generals were already looking for ways out of a war that would no longer be won. Among the parliamentarians, the Inter-Party Committee readdressed the possibilities for the parliamentarisation of the Reich from 12 September onwards. When the military finally announced the likelihood of a defeat on 28 September, the general public, used to optimistic news about the fighting, was totally surprised. The legitimacy of the Prussian state, which now appeared as unable to respond to the expectations and sacrifices of the people, began to deteriorate rapidly. Once Bulgaria agreed on an armistice, Field Marshal Erich Ludendorff asked for a ceasefire in order to save the army. Without consulting either the Kaiser or the leading politicians, he demanded that peace negotiations should be opened and the constitution parliamentarised. Ludendorff's evident intention was to persuade the Americans to offer better peace terms for this new 'democratic nation' on the basis of Woodrow Wilson's Fourteen Points of January 1918. This was not as such intended to advance the cause of German parliamentarism, even though the appeasement of German popular opinion was also a goal: the people should blame the political system rather than the military for the defeat. The monarchy and the politicians, particularly the Social Democrats, should accept the responsibility for it and carry out

---

1751 *The Herald*, 'The Way of the World', 30 November 1918. *The Herald* itself was subject to official censorship regarding its news on Russia. Rise 1995, 69.
1752 *The Herald*, 'The Facts About Finland', 28 December 1918.

a constitutional revolution from above. The problem was that neither the government, the Reichstag, the press nor the public had been prepared for a defeat and a sudden constitutional reform: after all, even in the spring there had still been a general belief in victory. The Kaiser and the majority parties, despite their amazement and disappointment, agreed to the suggested policy: on 30 September, the Kaiser issued a decree promising not a system change but continued parliamentarisation on the basis of the German model. On 3 October, he appointed Prince Max of Baden to the leadership of the new government. On 5 October, the new Chancellor made a government declaration that was endorsed by various parties, although the Reichstag was not allowed to discuss this programme. This unexpected parliamentarisation from above without the involvement of the people implied that responsibility for the defeat and its political consequences had indeed been attributed to the emerging parliamentary government. This, together with hostile Western attitudes, would be fatal for the emerging new political system named 'parliamentarism' or 'democracy',[1753] which tended to be viewed as a foreign import supported by domestic traitors, as the reformist parties were dubbed.

This constitutional change was, as in summer 1917, linked to the peace effort so that the national debate on the future polity became confused with relations with the Entente. The goal of the military leaders was to demonstrate to the Entente that the political changes they had demanded were happening and that flexibility in the negotiations for a truce was hence needed. The German proposal for a truce of 3 October 1918 explicitly referred to Wilson's Fourteen Points as the starting point for negotiations.[1754] The initiative to parliamentarise Germany had not this time originated from the Reichstag as in summer 1917, which weakened this body's legitimacy further.[1755] The Inter-Party Committee had renewed the demands for a reform, but the Reichstag did not convene between 5 and 22 October, when the new constitution was formulated.[1756] Nor did the public expect much from a parliament that had already failed in this respect in 1917. It was well known that many politicians accepted the reform only to obtain more favourable peace terms,[1757] not to change the German political system as such, just as the Western press had suspected. The left may have been enthusiastic about the transformation, but the right was never committed to it. The limited role of the Reichstag and the pragmatic if not downright reluctant attitude of many politicians give reason to treat interpretations of a gradual parliamentarisation (discussed in section 3.2) with caution.[1758]

1753 Verhandlungen, Max von Baden, 5 October 1918, 6154; Gusy 1997, 6–8; Pohl 2002, 9–10; Bruendel 2003, 247; Becker 2014, 30; Smith 2007, 187–8; Dahlmann 2014, 49–50; Bessel 2014, 131; Mick 2014, 162; Soutou 2014, 530–1; Leonhard 2014, 877. Cf. Grosser 1970, 149, which emphasises the activities of the opposition parties in the transition to parliamentary government.
1754 Winkler 2005; Leonhard 2014, 808, 877.
1755 Llanque 2000, 208.
1756 Leonhard 2014, 878.
1757 Mergel 2002, 42; Seils 2011, 624.
1758 This connection has been recently pointed out in Leonhard 2014, 739, 763, 876.

The constitutional transformation proceeded rapidly, the only extensive parliamentary debate taking place from 22 to 26 October. Suffrage in Prussia was democratised, and by 28 October Germany had been transformed into a constitutional parliamentary monarchy. The chancellor was made responsible to the Reichstag, but universal suffrage was not yet adopted. The new constitution became obsolete within two weeks, however, as a result of a search for more radical constitutional solutions by revolutionaries who were unhappy with what they considered to be the slow pace of democratisation.[1759] For this obvious reason, previous German research has paid modest attention to the conceptualisations of their future polity by German MPs in October 1918. They are, however, of particular interest both for an understanding of democratisation and parliamentarisation in Germany and for comparative purposes.

6.2.2 Comparing the German Revolution with the Bismarckian system and the Finnish counterrevolution

On one issue the parties of the left and centre were agreed, as might be expected from the debates of spring 1917: the war had demonstrated the imperative need for immediate democratisation. As the German people had made such far-reaching sacrifices, they deserved to be awarded a clearer say in both domestic and foreign policy matters.[1760]

In the discourse of the Social Democrats, now that the party had suddenly risen from being an object of political discrimination to leading the emergence of a new polity, the proposed reform constituted a regulated revolution by the people. According to Friedrich Ebert, it did indeed entail 'a system change of great consequences' that created a 'new Germany' while removing the need for more radical (Bolshevik-style) upheavals.[1761] Ebert's rhetorical choice to contrast this positive development in Germany – in probably the most important parliamentary speech he ever made – with the frightening events in Finland in the aftermath of a civil war that had begun as an uprising of radicalised Social Democrats is significant. The same kind of thing would not happen in Germany. As Marjaliisa and Seppo Hentilä have shown, Finnish Social Democrats and other republicans had informed the German parliamentary left on circumstances in Finland, which had made them criticise German intervention as an instance of a capitalist class war already in March. German Social Democratic papers had likewise published critical news on the German presense in Finland.[1762] Ebert now condemned the treatment of Social Democratic parliamentarians in Finland, reporting that six of them had been sentenced to death and others to lifelong imprisonment, which in his view constituted 'undoubtedly brutal class verdicts'. He did not directly accuse the Prussian system of pursuing the same kind of policies as the Finnish government, but he suggested

---

1759 Gusy 1997, 8–9; Bessel 2014, 131; Soutou 2014, 531.
1760 Bollmeyer 2007, 104–105.
1761 Verhandlungen, Friedrich Ebert, 22 October 1918, 6061.
1762 Hentilä & Hentilä 2016, 102–103, 222–3, 299.

that von Baden's ministry should use its influence to bring this violence in Finland to an end.[1763] This repeated previous Social Democratic criticism of interventions in the eastern border states. The continuing German involvement with the Finnish government clearly appeared as a problem particularly now that the international Social Democratic movement had brought the situation of the country to public knowledge.

Gustav Noske used socialist discourse in referring to the election of a German prince to the Finnish throne as illustrative of the dynastic aims of the Prussian monarchy and as an example of a militarism that disregarded the interests of the people and was planning a civil war against them.[1764] He implied that the German presence in Finland had enabled the upper classes to elect a German king without the people proper being heard. He went on to describe how the supporters of democratisation in Germany were at the same time constantly being attacked by reactionary forces who were plotting revenge.[1765]

Ebert's and Noske's speeches, as well as simultaneous criticism in *Vorwärts* of mistaken attempts to use German forces to 'create order' against the will of the peoples concerned[1766] and news about the death sentences passed on Finnish Social Democrats,[1767] are illustrative of the extent of transnational awareness in late 1918 – especially among Social Democrats – and the significance of even a minor nation as a warning example at a moment when a great power was about to make a turn towards democracy. The German Social Democrats did not want to see anything like the Finnish situation taking place in their country, at the instigation of either the far left or the right, which meant that their party would cooperate peacefully in the parliament, denounce radicalism and avoid offering any justification for revolutionary or counterrevolutionary actions against Social Democracy.

The concerns of Hugo Haase of the Independent Social Democrats bear witness to the different perspectives on the transnational revolution and the

---

1763 Verhandlungen, Friedrich Ebert, 22 October 1918, 6164. *Social-Demokraten* had described the exclusion of the Finnish Social Democratic MPs from parliamentary work as an 'International Scandal'. *The Manchester Guardian*, 'Disappearance of Finnish Social Democrats', 7 September 1918. Hjalmar Branting had proposed a protest against their imprisonment at the Inter-Parliamentary Congress in Copenhagen, which rapidly gave international prominence to the matter just before the German debates. *The Manchester Guardian*, 21 October 1918. This was a reaction to a report introduced by Väinö Tanner during his visit to Sweden and Denmark in August. Hentilä & Hentilä 2016, 229.

1764 *The Manchester Guardian*, '"A War of Conquest"', 16 July 1918 (on the leftist politicians, see 'Beyer's', [probably Gustav Bauer's] speech at the Reichstag) 'Scheidemann & the German Dynasts', 22 October 1918, originally published in *Vorwärts* on 10 September 1918.

1765 Verhandlungen, Gustav Noske, 24 October 1918, 6215.

1766 *Vorwärts*, 23 October 1918.

1767 *Vorwärts*, 24 October 1918. The paper reported that Hjalmar Branting had taken an appeal for clemency signed by 118 MPs to the Finnish Embassy in Stockholm, which demonstrates the international prominence given to the Finnish measures of repression after the Civil War. The issue was brought into the German constitutional debates as well, through *Vorwärts*.

contingent significance of the Finnish case for the German left. Haase took the German transformation as part of 'the world revolution initiated by this war' and employed natural metaphors (possibly inspired by the autumn season) for the unavoidable transformation in talking about 'profound upheavals' characterised by 'a stormy development' and 'a hurricane sweeping across the world. The revolution had not only toppled the Russian Tsar, the Austrian-Hungarian Emperor and the King of Bulgaria from their thrones, but also the minor crowns of Finland, Kurland and Lithuania – which the Germans thought they already had in their possession – would soon fall. Republican regimes were advancing everywhere, which made it impossible to maintain the monarchy in Germany too.[1768] Coming as he did from Königsberg and being an advocate of the small landowners, Haase was particularly interested in the affairs of the Baltic region. He questioned the future of the Kingdom of Finland two weeks after the election of Friedrich Karl, a son-in-law of the Kaiser, to that throne. This illustrates the highly controversial nature of the measure of the Finnish Rump Parliament. In the eyes of the German left, all this appeared as just a manifestation of the desperate throes of the Hohenzollern dynasty. The Finnish polity, which imitated and was supported by the Prussians, had lost all credibility: it was 'a regime of terror of a kind that has never been experienced in the world before', having slaughtered thousands of workers after forcing them to dig their own graves. Haase was informed that 80,000 Finnish revolutionaries had been imprisoned and 50,000 had become victims of 'the the Finnish government's orgy of blood'. The figures were exaggerated, but the point was clear: It had become necessary for German politics and for the sake of humanity and the Finnish workers that Germany should immediately withdraw its troops from Finland.[1769]

For Haase, the acts of the Finnish bourgeois government and also the Prussian support for it exemplified counter-revolutionary forces of the worst kind. They offered a topical transnational argument for preventing the same from happening in Germany and for demanding the abolition of a monarchy that was potentially leading the way to such disasters. Haase, previously known for his sympathies for the Russian Revolution, distanced himself from the Bolshevik attempts to create a socialist order, however, emphasising that his parliamentary group did not agree with all the measures of 'the revolutionary labour government in Russia'.[1770] The German far left would consistently maintain its distance from Soviet power. For Haase, the German transformation was, nevertheless, about a revolution to advance the cause of the workers and a republic, not so much about changing the

---

1768 Verhandlungen, Hugo Haase, 22 October 1918, 6185.
1769 Verhandlungen, Hugo Haase, 22 October 1918, 6189. The number of the dead would rise to 13,446, in addition to the 7370 Reds executed during the war. 1914–22 War Victims in Finland, http://vesta.narc.fi/cgi-bin/db2www/sotasurmaetusivu/results. Haase also referred to the arrest of the former Social Democratic minister Väinö Tanner, which is a further instance of transnational contacts between German and Finnish Social Democrats.
1770 Verhandlungen, Hugo Haase, 22 October 1918, 6189.

system through democratisation and parliamentarisation as it was for the Social Democrats.

For the liberals, too, the German transition constituted a revolution to a more limited extent. The Progressivist Friedrich Naumann, while recognising the value of the Bismarckian 'mixed dictatorial-parliamentary system' at the time of German unification together with its economic and cultural achievements, greeted the transition to a new system with pleasure. However, he stressed that the constitution should be altered rather than completely overturned,[1771] which reflects a higher degree of continuity in the attitudes of the German liberals than among their Swedish counterparts and finds parallels among contemporary monarchist Young Finns. Gustav Stresemann (National Liberals) recognised the role of his party as a key supporter of the Bismarckian system but, 'after the experience of the biggest revolutionising [*Revolutionierung*] that the world has ever seen' saw no reason to stick to its solutions,[1772] which made the left-liberal *Berliner Tageblatt* satirically claim that Stresemann had misjudged everything.[1773]

The attitudes of Count von Westarp, described as a typical 'Junker from east of the Elbe', had not altered.[1774] He viewed the reforms as constituting 'a fatal change' that removed the 'invaluable foundations' of the German fatherland and endangered its future. They introduced no less than 'a state ruled by parliamentary means according to the principles of the Western democracies', something that the Conservatives had consistently opposed in their party manifesto and in public speeches. The party asserted that they would make no concessions in their opposition to the 'radicalisation, democratisation and one-sided mass rule' that was threatening the country and rejected all suggestions by the government that they represented the 'dark forces of counter-revolution'.[1775] The contrast between what the right saw as the proper constitutional monarchical order and perverted Western parliamentary democracy could not have been presented more clearly. The gap remained irreconcilable, and so did the contrast between the moderate reformist Social Democrats and the left-liberals on the one hand and the right on the other. The centre took no distinct stand. The Reichstag also witnessed a violent clash between anti-Semitic and Polish members, protests against the speakers of the rival socialist party and conservative objections to anti-monarchical statements, all reflecting the highly confrontational atmosphere of the assembly.[1776] Would this turn into a democracy recognised by one or two parties only?

1771 Verhandlungen, Friedrich Naumann, 22 October 1918, 6167; also *Berliner Tageblatt*, 23 October 1918.
1772 Verhandlungen, Gustav Stresemann, 22 October 1918, 6174.
1773 *Berliner Tageblatt*, 23 October 1918.
1774 *Berliner Tageblatt*, 23 October 1918.
1775 Verhandlungen, Kuno von Westarp, 22 October 1918, 6177–8.
1776 *Berliner Tageblatt*, 24 October 1918.

6.2.3 Divergent understandings of German democracy

Chancellor Max von Baden recognised that the system change implied the implementation of new ideas such as democracy,[1777] although he avoided the use of such a term in his public speeches. For the Social Democratic Party, sensing that it was capable of influencing the course of politics for the first time, the constitutional reform – with a government approved by the Reichstag, broad circles of the people and 'the trusted men of the workers' as Friedrich Ebert put it – stood for no less than the longed-for breakthrough of democracy. Ebert was ready to declare that 22 October 1918 was 'the birthday of German democracy', which ended the alliance between the civil service and the Junkers – although he said nothing about the monarchy here. Democratisation had, according to him, become a necessity. It enabled the mobilisation of the people and guaranteed the security of the Reich. This democracy, he maintained, had arisen out of the initiative of the Germans themselves and hence could in no way represent a betrayal of the German people as the right tended to suggest. At the same time, Ebert emphasised that safeguarding 'the new democracy' against 'military power' required further constitutional reforms. His socialist call for 'economic democracy' through the removal of class differences and economic exploitation must have been controversial with the bourgeois parties.[1778] *Neue Preußische Zeitung* would immediately react to such suggestions by associating democracy with socialism.[1779] The fact that only the Social Democrats applauded what Ebert had to say about democracy and the new political role of the people reflects the limits of this reformist cause. The party was also in a difficult position in trying to please its supporters, who desired further reforms, while cooperating with non-socialist parties and countering radicalisation on the far left. Its organ *Vorwärts* nevertheless declared confidently that 'the bankrupt Junker regime, the failed system of Prussian feudalism' had now been buried[1780] and that the Reichstag had made 'a decision for democracy'.[1781]

The representatives of the far left, while welcoming the revolution, did not speak much about democracy in this context. After the government declaration, their chairman had protested against the continued closure of the Reichstag at the very moment of the democratisation of Germany. Using Marxist language, Hugo Haase associated a 'democratic peace' with the involvement of the international proletariat.[1782] Otto Rühle, who sympathised with Soviet Russia and would join the council movement in a few weeks' time, rejected 'this so-called democracy [granted] by the grace of Hindenburg' together with parliamentarism as a deception that should be replaced with the democracy of socialism created by a revolution.[1783]

1777 Bruendel 2003, 249.
1778 Verhandlungen, Friedrich Ebert, 22 October 1918, 6160–2, 6165; Seils 2011, 633.
1779 *Neue Preußische Zeitung*, 24 October 1918.
1780 *Vorwärts*, 23 October 1918.
1781 *Vorwärts*, 27 October 1918.
1782 Verhandlungen, Hugo Haase, 5 October 1918, 6154.
1783 Verhandlungen, Otto Rühle, 25 October 1918, 6270.

The left-liberals were clearly supportive of the constitutional change. Their leader, Friedrich Naumann, said that traditional theories about the strengths of monarchy over democracy had been proven wrong by the war: the monarchy had not succeeded any better in maintaining national unity. The Prussian regime had failed to facilitate the kind of development in political liberty that had taken place in Britain and France, even though demands had already been presented in the Frankfurt Parliament.[1784] The old order was responsible for the peculiar course of German history vis-à-vis the 'democratic countries', which, he implied were worthy of imitation. This ignored the doubts about Western democracy that had been typical of German political theory and public discourse. Naumann did not hesitate to defend the democratic system,[1785] and *Berliner Tageblatt* also demanded 'democratic administrative personnel' at all levels in 'a democratic era'.[1786] The National Liberals and the Catholic Centre did not join this discourse, however, so that only a part of the political centre was involved.

When the left-liberals made comparisons with the West, the Conservatives immediately reacted: in their view, 'the German democracy' (in the sense of the reformist groups of the left and the centre, from which the rightists expressly disassociated themselves) had now allied themselves with 'the desire of our enemies'.[1787] No conservative redescriptions of the existing system as 'democracy' emerged, but there were instead denouncements of the supporters of democratisation as traitors; in other words, an early form of the stab-in-the-back myth was emerging. The constitutional discourses of the reformists and the supporters of the old Prussian order were moving in completely opposite directions from the very beginning. *Neue Preußische Zeitung* condemned 'our democracy' with its 'democratic criticism' as harmful to the army and nationalism, complaining that it produced untried ideas that were immediately taken to the parliament without proper preparation. A major constitutional monarchy was being transformed into 'a modern democracy' in accordance with Wilson's guidelines by socialist enthusiasts of a supposed democratic breakthrough;[1788] in other words, this was all a socialist plot. Reporting the debates, the organ of the Prussian right contrasted Max von Baden's recognition of the rightist opposition to democratisation with Friedrich Ebert's suggestion that such opposition was 'playing with fire' and continued by sneering at highflying descriptions of 'the democratic El Dorado in which we may now live'. *Neue Preußische Zeitung* attacked Naumann's 'glorification of democracy' as being 'in strong contrast with the experiences of history'. Besides, the Western democracies were equally involved in the war, and 'the German democracy' had never established itself and was only opportunistically carrying out demands that had been made by the enemy. The paper wondered how even the National

---

1784 Verhandlungen, Friedrich Naumann, 22 October 1918, 6167–8.
1785 Verhandlungen, Friedrich Naumann, 22 October 1918, 6169.
1786 *Berliner Tageblatt*, 23 October 1918.
1787 Verhandlungen, Kuno von Westarp, 22 October 1918, 6173.
1788 *Neue Preußische Zeitung*, 21 October 1918. Interestingly, on the same day the paper printed a pledge by Berlin professors to serve the new political order.

Liberal leader had been able to reject Bismarck's glorious system. According to the paper, only Count von Westarp had called in a manly way for 'devotion to God and blood' in a continued fight against the enemy.[1789] The mouthpiece of the Junkers implied that the left was cooperating with the Russians to launch a German and thereby a worldwide revolution, while the liberals were fraternising with the West in their glorification of democracy.[1790] Both had let the war-faring fatherland down.

Democracy had been introduced as a programmatic concept in the process of the constitutional transformation, but this was done almost exclusively by the Social Democrats. The left-liberals used the concept more cautiously, and it was not employed by the other parties. Since express support for democracy from the centre had not really widened, the Social Democrats were nearly alone in their enthusiasm for a democratic breakthrough. In 1917 doubts had arisen among the right about the patriotism of the left and the centre, and this was even more the case in autumn 1918. 'Democracy' was condemned as a party-political term in a way unknown in Britain, Sweden and Finland. There were also many more conservatives in Germany who denied the existence of a national tradition of democracy on which to build.

6.2.4 The German people as a political agent

In principle, the transition of October 1918 implied the involvement of the German people in political decision-making processes for the first time. Heiko Bollmeyer has shown how during much of the war the terms 'the will of the people' (*Volkswille*) and 'the sovereignty of the people' (*Volkssouveränität*) had been seldom mentioned, while the concept of *Volk* (people or nation) as such was frequently used in war propaganda. After, the initial phase of constitutional rethinking in 1917, too, the words 'the people' and 'the German people' rather than more explicit terms for popular sovereignty had been in use, and they were used mostly in senses that supported the maintenance of the established imperial order.[1791]

During the constitutional negotiations of autumn 1918, the parties continued to hold divergent views on the connection between the Reichstag and the *Volk*: liberal and centrist parliamentarians equated the Reichstag with the *Volk*, while the Social Democrats maintained that, because of the unequal suffrage, which excluded women, the Reichstag was not yet a direct reflection of the views and conceptions of the entire population. Chancellor Max von Baden stressed that his policy was rooted in 'the sympathy' and 'the will of the majority of the people'.[1792] The Speaker, Constantin Fehrenbach (Catholic Centre), expected the ministry to maintain constant contact with the people and work for the people's best.[1793] In October 1918, however, it was only the far left that urged the Germans to adopt 'the sovereignty of the

---

1789 *Neue Preußische Zeitung*, 23 October 1918.
1790 *Neue Preußische Zeitung*, 24 October 1918.
1791 Bollmeyer 2007, 91.
1792 Verhandlungen, Max von Baden, 5 October 1918, 6151; Bollmeyer 2007, 104.
1793 Verhandlungen, Constantin Fehrenbach, 5 October 1918, 6150.

people';¹⁷⁹⁴ even the Social Democrats remained cautious about using the phrase in order to avoid associations with a radical revolution.

Max von Baden presented 'the political maturity of the German people' as 'the goal' of the new constitution. This illustrates his patronising aristocratic attitude to popular government and the divided political elite. Von Baden chose to use a metaphor which, albeit based on an over-estimation, reflected a noble optimism about the power of the people being derived from local self-government, universal male suffrage, the budgetary power of the Reichstag and the activation of the parliamentary groups since 1917: 'The German people has for a long time sat in the saddle, it should now just ride.' The point was that the people had until 1917 lacked 'the political will for power' but had, as a result of the war (and not because of any external pressures) changed its attitude.¹⁷⁹⁵

Friedrich Ebert, in line with Social Democratic ideology, stressed a positive connection between the people and the government: the German people were creating a new German state. According to Ebert, revolutions like the one at hand (a moderate Social Democratic revolution) emerge when constitutions remain stagnant while the position of the people progresses. What was happening in Germany was 'a transition to a new political system in which the people would shape its future through its freely elected representatives'. These should also include women: their wartime contributions had already been recognised by awarding suffrage to them in enemy countries such as Britain and Russia, as well as in Finland, and female suffrage was being prepared in the USA.¹⁷⁹⁶ *Vorwärts* declared that an election would allow 'the people itself to speak out', possibly in favour of socialism,¹⁷⁹⁷ and would leave future progress dependent on universal suffrage and parliamentary work.

Ebert presented the influence of 'the will of the people' on decision-making in 'the German people's state' (*der deutsche Volksstaat* – a concept that emphasised the unity of the people and a specifically German alternative to the old regime¹⁷⁹⁸ and was used by liberal and Social Democratic reformists to translate the concepts 'democracy' or 'republic') as an antidote to the danger of Bolshevism.¹⁷⁹⁹ This concept had been used by the left-liberals already in spring 1917 in order to play down the implications of transforming a monarchical state into a more republican one.¹⁸⁰⁰ Ebert's use of the concept reflects a patently revisionist strategy shared by the British Labour Party and the Swedish Social Democrats. However, an understanding of popular government resembling the unifying concept *Volksgemeinschaft*

1794 Verhandlungen, 5 October 1918, 6154; 22 October, 6189.
1795 Verhandlungen, Max von Baden, 22 October 1918, 6158–9.
1796 Verhandlungen, Friedrich Ebert, 22 October 1918, 6161, 6164; Verhandlungen, Gustav Noske, 24 October 1918, 6218; Bollmeyer 2007, 90.
1797 *Vorwärts*, 27 October 1918.
1798 Cf. Emil Nestor Setälä's suggestion in June 1919 that the Finnish Republic be called *kansanvaltio* (a people's state); Müller 2014, 43; Llanque 2015, 75.
1799 Verhandlungen, 22 October 1918, 6161; Llanque 2000, 307.
1800 Bollmeyer 2007, 131.

(a community of the people) is readable in Ebert's insistence that in the future 'only one will, that of the government of the people carried out by the trustees of the people'[1801] would prevail – as opposed to allowing the military to intervene in politics. Popular government did not necessarily stand for a democratic process characterised by a plurality of views; the people as a collective unit would decide.

The left-liberals welcomed such popular government. According to them, the imperial system had not constituted 'any complete people's state'. It had not achieved 'the embodiment of the national notion of unity';[1802] this notion also suggests a commitment to political unity – a value that could be problematic from the point of view of political pluralism. A further noteworthy feature is Naumann's stereotypical description of the Germans as 'a people of order' rather than one of 'liberty' despite the shortcomings of the old system that he was criticising.[1803] Carl Herold from the Catholic Centre did not have anything against 'the broadest masses of the people' participating in affairs of state and the government becoming 'the executive body of the popular will'.[1804] Nor would Gustav Stresemann of the National Liberals doubt the political maturity of the German people in comparison with that of other peoples.[1805]

For Kuno von Westarp of the Conservatives, by contrast, the reform still represented nothing but contempt for the great achievements of the German people in the war.[1806] Only after the November Revolution would the Prussian Conservatives replace the Kaiser and the fatherland with 'the people' in their political manifestos and rename themselves a 'people's' party (the German National People's Party).[1807] Their basic conceptions about the people would not change, however, as the final debates on the Weimar constitution in July 1919 would demonstrate. They held a pessimistic conception that many conservatives in Sweden and Finland readily shared.

6.2.5 Crypto-parliamentarism comes into the open

The Prussian elite had traditionally been unashamedly anti-parliamentary, and in 1917 calls for parliamentarism had also been qualified among most other political groups. Despite his task to parliamentarise the polity of Germany, Max von Baden continued to hold the view that, although his government had been formed with the cooperation of the Reichstag, it remained responsible to the Kaiser. He did imply, however, that governments would never again in peacetime be created without the support of the

---

1801 Verhandlungen, Friedrich Ebert, 22 October 1918, 6160–6; Bruendel 2003, 106.
1802 Verhandlungen, Friedrich Naumann, 22 October 1918, 6168.
1803 Verhandlungen, Friedrich Naumann, 22 October 1918, 6168.
1804 Verhandlungen, Carl Herold, 22 October 1918, 6159.
1805 Verhandlungen, Gustav Stresemann, 22 October 1918, 6176.
1806 Verhandlungen, Kuno von Westarp, 22 October 1918, 6173–7; *Neue Preußische Zeitung* likewise complained about contempt for 'the people's army' on 23 October 1918.
1807 Smith 2007, 196–7. Cf. the Swedish People's Party in Finland, which was at that stage equally critical of democracy.

parliament and without leading parliamentarians being nominated as ministers.[1808]

The concept of parliamentarism was thus rapidly entering German political discourse in October 1918. In his introductory speech on the constitutional proposal on 22 October, von Baden emphasised contacts, cooperation and mutual trust between the Reichstag and the executive. This would 'open new ways to reach a responsible leadership of the affairs of the Reich: the parliamentary way' and engage 'the previously inactive forces of the people'. While any express reference to the concept of governmental responsibility to the parliament was missing, the leading minister did emphasise 'the independence of the parliament' and made the important promise that in questions of war and peace the Reichstag as 'the appointed representative of the people' would decide together with the government.[1809] *Berliner Tageblatt* interpreted this speech as a criticism of the parliament for not having previously curbed executive power through the use of budgetary power.[1810]

The Social Democrats were not satisfied with von Baden's formulations of ministerial responsibility and insisted that 'the future of the parliamentary form of government' would only be ensured when the chancellor was nominated and deposed according to the will of the Reichstag. They also considered it of the utmost importance that foreign policy, especially on the use of military force and the conclusion of international treaties, should take place in agreement with the Reichstag. Finally, the Prussian 'parliament of classes' was to be replaced with 'the parliament of the people'.[1811] Such further parliamentarisation of both the Reich and Prussia, forcefully echoed by *Vorwärts*,[1812] would soon also be implemented.

The representatives of the far left remained sceptical about the proposed kind of parliamentarism. Georg Ledebour criticised the proposal for not parliamentarising the government and the Reichstag procedure properly. What should be done was to institute 'a parliamentary combat', by which he meant pro et contra debate,[1813] which, in principle, demonstrates a far-going adoption of a parliamentary ideal. Ledebour even saw a federal state of Europe governed in a parliamentary way by 'a European parliament', created by 'a process of revolutionising' as the solution to economic tensions in Europe.[1814] This was a visionary view of parliamentarism rising from the Wilsonian plans for a league of nations.

For the Catholic Centre, the involvement of leading parliamentarians in the government sufficed to create 'the closest connections between the government and the representation of the people', and to produce 'a new Germany with a free constitution'.[1815] 'Parliamentarism' was not the right

1808 Verhandlungen, Max von Baden, 5 October 1918, 6150–2.
1809 Verhandlungen, Max von Baden, 22 October 1918, 6156.
1810 *Berliner Tageblatt*, 23 October 1918.
1811 Verhandlungen, 22 October 1918, 6062; also *Berliner Tageblatt*, 23 October 1918.
1812 *Vorwärts*, 27 October 1918.
1813 Verhandlungen, Georg Ledebour, 24 October 1918, 6228; Grosser 1970, 158.
1814 Verhandlungen, Georg Ledebour, 24 October 1918, 6235–6.
1815 Verhandlungen, Carl Herold, 22 October 1918, 6159.

term to describe this arrangement. This can be contrasted with the consistent support for parliamentarisation by the liberal leaders, including those of the National Liberal Party, which had initially been created to oppose such a system. Friedrich Naumann (Progressivists) recognised 'the logic of the mechanism of the parliamentary system' provided that the people could sometimes intervene in decision-making.[1816] This hinted at the institution of the referendum that would be introduced in the Weimar constitution. *Berliner Tageblatt* interpreted the vote of confidence of 25 October as 'the first technical use of the parliamentary system in the Reichstag',[1817] an expression of left-liberal satisfaction with what they viewed as parliamentarism making a breakthrough.

The right-liberals were divided over this issue. Gustav Stresemann referred to the fact that Bismarck himself had in 1892, after his resignation, regretted his failure to reach a balance between the parliament and the government with a sufficiently strong parliament being able to criticise and control the government. This view of the 'parliamentary' stance of the leading authority in German politics of the past, together with the experiences of the war, which had proved previous conceptions of the weaknesses of decision-making in parliamentary systems in comparison with the Prussian order to be wrong, allowed Stresemann to speak for parliamentarisation despite opposition within his party and to head the Constitutional Committee in the introduction of a parliamentary system in 1917. Stresemann stuck to his argument despite the lack of 'political education' among the people and the gentry, which Bismarck (presented consistently by Stresemann as an alternative authority to political theory) had considered a precondition of parliamentarism. Stresemann accepted the fact that the new constitution made the Reichstag more clearly the source of governmental power.[1818] Thus the leader of the right-liberals, if not the party as a whole, expressly supported 'parliamentarism' albeit not 'democracy' in a wider sense. A month earlier, in an interview with the Swedish conservative paper *Aftonbladet*, Stresemann had nevertheless still listed a number of obstacles to parliamentarism in Germany, which reflect his remaining doubts about the system.[1819]

The Conservatives interpreted such parliamentarisation as synonymous with the rejection of the leadership of the Kaiser and the Bundesrat in favour of parties standing behind a 'committee of the people' (*Volksausschuss*) that constructed occasional parliamentary majorities (probably referring to the

---

1816 Verhandlungen, Friedrich Naumann, 22 October 1918, 6171; Grosser 1970, 165–6.

1817 *Berliner Tageblatt*, 23 October 1918, 25 October 1918.

1818 Verhandlungen, Gustav Stresemann, 22 October 1918, 6174, 6176. Stresemann referred to his speech in the plenary on 27 March 1917, but he had then only discussed taxation. In the plenary of 29 March 1917 (2853–4), he reacted to debates in the Herrenhaus, alluding to the need arising from the experiences of the war to reform Prussian suffrage and to strengthen the parliamentary system. Bismarck was quoted to the same end by Ernst Müller-Meinigen (Progressivist) in Verhandlungen, 26 October 1918, 6279. Mommsen 2002, 76; Grosser 1970, 115.

1819 Grosser 1970, 171–2.

abominated Inter-Party Committee). The creation of 'the new parliamentary system' endangered the war effort. For Kuno von Westarp, the new constitution also entailed 'the parliamentarisation and politicisation of the independent civil service', making this particular strength of the German state dependent on the 'party life of the parliament' and leading simply to the 'one-sided rule of the masses' (*Massenherrschaft*).[1820] This argument in favour of an independent civil service summed up many of the prevailing fears of the right not only in Germany but also in Sweden and Finland and possibly also in Britain: the established power of elite experts would be replaced by that of parties plotting in the name of the gullible people. In criticising the way in which the government had acted by referring to violations of 'the practices and principles of the parliamentary system', von Westarp recognised in passing the existence of such rules,[1821] albeit only for the sake of argument. In late September, he had still seen military dictatorship as the only way out of the crisis,[1822] and in late October he continued to oppose the advocates of democracy by attempting to obstruct the new constitution with procedural points.[1823] Likewise, Graf Arthur von Posadowsky-Wehner, a representative of the Prussian nobility and a civil servant, whose exploits included implementing laws against Social Democracy, was deeply disturbed by the fall of the Bismarckian order. He saw 'crypto-parliamentarism' (a term used by the opponents of parliamentarism before the war as secret or concealed) as having already made progress in the Reich with the legislative power interfering in the affairs of the executive power (probably referring to parliamentary questions and interpellations as well as the foreign policy initiative of 1917) and the ministry now suggesting complete parliamentary government. In von Posadowsky-Wehner's view, the objections to parliamentary government in federal states were undeniable; the constitution of the United States illustrated this[1824] – the new circumstances of autumn 1918 made the USA a relevant object of comparison even for the German right (as it was for the Finnish right in summer 1919). Parliamentarism remained a notion condemned by the right, welcomed without enthusiasm by the centre, celebrated by the liberals, advocated by the Social Democrats and viewed positively even by some within the revolutionary far left. Processes of democratisation and parliamentarisation had started as administrative orders but come to dominate parliamentary debate in late October 1918. The views of the parties had changed little in comparison with those they had expressed in spring 1917, but the arguments for parliamentarism in particular had become stronger than those for democracy.

1820 Verhandlungen, Kuno von Westarp, 22 October 1918, 6177–8.
1821 Verhandlungen, Kuno von Westarp, 22 October 1918, 6179.
1822 Grosser 1970, 179.
1823 *Berliner Tageblatt*, 27 October 1918.
1824 Verhandlungen, Arthur von Posadowsky-Wehner, 23 October 1918, 6199.

6.2.6 THE RADICAL PHASE OF THE REVOLUTION IN NOVEMBER AND DECEMBER 1918

Social tensions, strikes and mutinies had constituted a fertile ground for far-left agitation in Germany in 1918. Few Independent Social Democrats were content with parliamentarisation as it took shape during October. Some radicals were uncompromising in their demands that the Prussian political order be overthrown and set out to launch a revolution in late October. Opposition in the Navy to the Army General Staff began to rise on 28 October, soon after the constitutional debates analysed above. On 7 and 8 November the Bavarian monarchy fell after a council of workers, soldiers and farmers assumed control. The rhetoric of these councils sounded radical to those who feared a Bolshevik-type revolution even though their measures remained quite moderate.[1825]

By 9 November 1918, the revolution[1826] had reached Berlin and led to the fall of the imperial monarchy, an unprecedented event in German constitutional history. The Kaiser's known resistance to parliamentarism had become irreconcilable with the goals of the new regime, as had been suggested by some in the debates, after the US government declared on 23 October that no peace with such an autocratic ruler would be concluded. The Kaiser was therefore simply forced to abdicate.[1827] Max von Baden proposed that Friedrich Ebert should be made Chancellor and that a national constituent assembly be convened to legislate on a future constitution. Philipp Scheidemann (SPD), however, proclaimed without any wider authorisation, a 'German Republic' and the formation of a government by 'all socialist parties', which ruled out the continuation of the monarchy. The Independents, led by Karl Liebknecht, who was believed to be a Bolshevik, set out strict conditions for participation in the new government, demanding a 'social republic' in which all executive, legislative and judicial powers would be given into the hands of the working people. Various councils seemed to be attempting to take over. In the Council of the People's Deputies, the provisional cabinet, only Majority and Independent Social Democrats were represented. Instead of a soviet system of the Russian type, however, this council decided to move towards a parliamentary system based on universal suffrage for both sexes. Lacking support from the Majority Social Democrats, the far left thus failed to radicalise their revolution. The Independents, too, accepted that the future polity be formulated in a national constituent assembly, although they did not give up their calls for a 'socialist democracy'.[1828]

1825 Gusy 1997, 9–12.
1826 Armin Burkhard has concluded that this was no real revolution, as the political change was already taking place. Burkhardt 2003, 38. However, this revolution had much more radical aims than that of October. According to Christoph Gusy, the November revolution was a real one as far as constitutional law is concerned. Gusy 1997, 17.
1827 Gusy 1997, 14; Gusy 2008a, 421.
1828 Gusy 1997, 15–16; Pohl 2002, 17, 26; Bollmeyer 2007, 187; Geyer 2011, 191, 218; Gerwarth & Horne 2013, 68; Dahlmann 2014, 50; Leonhard 2014, 890, 892.

The socialist parties saw the constitutional changes of October in very different terms. The Social Democrat leader Friedrich Ebert maintained that a central constitutional aim had been reached with parliamentarisation. Having distanced themselves from revolutionary methods of societal change, the Majority Social Democrats were unwilling to engage in revolutionary activity, preferring to maintain law and order.[1829] Rejecting the Bolshevik Revolution, they feared such a dictatorial political order and prioritised cooperation within bourgeois forms of democracy,[1830] just like the Swedish Social Democrats. Democracy in this general sense became a common denominator for cooperation between the Social Democrats and the bourgeois parties of the centre and distinguished them both from the far left, who sympathised with the Bolshevik Revolution,[1831] and certainly from the right. Though by no means a decisive factor, the Finnish experience of a failed revolution in the name of Social Democracy, debated on 22 and 23 October, perhaps reinforced revisionist stands in the party. In German historiography the relevance of such a marginal case has been bypassed.

The Independent Social Democrats rejected royal prerogatives, still part of the October constitution, as incompatible with the principle of popular sovereignty and parliamentarism as they understood it.[1832] Their calls for the removal of the monarchy and the extension of democracy put pressure on the Social Democrats and, for instance, provided a model for the Swedish far left. Some Independents saw the direct democracy of council rule as an alternative to parliamentary democracy despite its obvious associations with Bolshevism. It has been suggested that the German councils were not Bolshevist but rather a form of political organisation launched by local activists.[1833] Nevertheless they represented examples of undesirable radical political and social change.[1834] Especially for the Spartacus League (a Marxist revolutionary movement), the revolution was to be continued through the work of the councils or by other revolutionary means.

The bourgeois parties, too, were ideologically and conceptually divided after this revolution. Some liberals were enthusiastic supporters of the reforms, while many only accepted democratisation in the lack of any better alternatives, hoping for the survival of the old political order in an updated form.[1835] Those who had believed in an evolutionary transition were deeply disappointed with the outbreak of an openly socialist revolution with

---

1829 Pohl 2002, 14; Bollmeyer 2007, 112, 118. See, however, Grosser 1970, 162, on the failure of the party leaders to communicate their new, more positive understanding of 'bourgeois' parliamentarism to many of their supporters.
1830 Llanque 2000, 207.
1831 Llanque 2000, 307.
1832 Bollmeyer 2007, 108, 114.
1833 Llanque 2000, 313–14; Bessel 2014, 131; Leonhard 2014, 937.
1834 Leonhard 2014, 888, 937. The potentially radical nature of the councils has been played down and their democratic nature emphasised in German historiographical interpretations that aim at a reconciliation between the different ideological camps; this may correspond with Finnish historians emphasising the non-Bolshevik intentions of the Red regime. See also section 5.4.
1835 Llanque 2000, 307.

demands going beyond the gradual democratisation that had been planned in October. Once the ferment of November was over, many saw the National Constitutive Assembly as the only sensible way to move forward.[1836] The Conservatives, already doubtful about the October reforms, regarded the November Revolution as totally unnecessary, and many supporters of the Catholic Centre remained sceptical about democratisation.[1837] The revolution appeared for them as a demonstration of the confusion to which democratisation and parliamentarisation would lead. The political change then turned violent after the Provisional Government began to use military force to prevent the revolutionary goals of the far left.[1838]

On 15 November 1918, Ebert appointed Hugo Preuß, an independent constitutional thinker, to prepare a draft for a republican constitution that would reconcile the conflicting demands. In 1915 Preuß had demanded the 'politicisation of the people' to facilitate a transition from the system of an authoritative state to a modern system of a 'people's state' (*Volksstaat*, not 'democracy', which like 'parliamentarism' sounded 'Western' and therefore objectionable;[1839] this was relevant also for Swedish and Finnish conceptualisations of the future polity as it led to what Jörn Leonhard has called 'imitating translations').[1840] Preuß aimed at a democratic republican constitution based on power derived from the people and including a parliament, although he avoided referring to 'popular sovereignty'. The vernacular terms he favoured emphasised the specifically *German* nature of the new polity, maintaining a distance from 'Western' democracies. Preuß favoured the concept 'will of the people' (*Volkswille*), a favourite term also with traditionalists during the war. Another authority participating in the preparatory work was Max Weber, whose notion of a presidency elected by the people as counterbalance to the parliament likewise challenged 'Western' parliamentarism. Both Preuß and Weber, in addition to being members of the German academic elite, who were traditionally sceptical of British and French 'parliamentary absolutism' (*Parlamentsabsolutismus*), had been influenced by Robert Redslob's book *Die parlamentarische Regierung in ihrer wahren und in ihrer unechten Form* (1918), which, recycling notions of the duality of government, defined parliamentary democracy as a 'system of balance between the executive and the legislative power'. Weber argued, in line with the prevailing scepticism about parliaments, for the limitation of their power.[1841] The republican compromise between popular presidency, the parliament and the referendum suggested by Preuß and Weber on the basis of German and international theoretical debates provided a model or point of comparison for many other republican constitutions. The situation in 1917 had been and would again in spring 1919 be rather similar in Finland.

1836 Llanque 2000, 308.
1837 Llanque 2000, 309.
1838 Bessel 2014, 132.
1839 Llanque 2000, 68; Bruendel 2003, 105–107.
1840 Leonhard 2012, 256.
1841 Mergel 2002, 75; Pohl 2002, 58, 64, 84, 86; Bollmeyer, 2007, 220, 222, 224, 228–9; Wirsching 2008, 10.

In the meantime, the bourgeoisie regrouped themselves according to their constitutional views. The German Democratic Party was founded by members of the left-liberal Progressives and the republican National Liberals to support the emerging new polity, their aim being a democratic republic in which political power would be used by representatives acting according to the will of the people.[1842] The Catholic Centre supported the introduction of parliamentarism and democracy[1843] but did so mainly in name only. The German People's Party was based on the traditions of the National Liberals revamped by Gustav Stresemann.[1844] The conservative German National People's Party continued to oppose parliamentarisation and promised to work for the fatherland by defending the monarchical elements of the democratic constitution.[1845] There were no politicians in this party who were ready to adapt their views to accept democracy. Its stance resembled that of the right in Sweden and the Swedish People's Party in Finland, among whom it found keen followers.

The 'democrats' in Germany continued to entertain different understandings of what democracy stood for, often using 'democracy' as a mere slogan in order to obtain favourable terms of peace and giving it meanings that served particular interests. This loose use of the term 'democracy' is particularly understandable in the discursive circumstances of late autumn 1918; it was indeed typical in all the countries studied here. President Woodrow Wilson had explicitly demanded the introduction of democracy as a precondition for peace, setting the concept of democracy as the norm to which the Germans should bend themselves. On the other hand, the Russian Bolshevik Revolution and its consequences in Russia and other countries with their very different claims for 'democracy', had convinced the German bourgeois parties to accept parliamentary democracy as a tolerable form of government in comparison with the councils advocated by the far left.[1846] In Germany, as elsewhere, democratisation and parliamentarisation were products of party-political compromises, but they were enforced by external pressures more clearly than in the other countries, a factor that made these concepts even more disputable. The Germans did not spend so much time negotiating on the nature of their compromise and searching for common denominators for their competing concepts of democracy as the British, Swedish and Finnish parliamentarians did, though the debates were equally confrontational in Sweden and Finland. In any case, democracy continued to appear for many Germans an externally imposed concept that did not inspire devotion or even sophisticated pro et contra debate beyond the Social Democrats and the left-liberals.

1842 Pohl 2002, 28, 31.
1843 Pohl 2002, 32.
1844 Pohl 2002, 32.
1845 Boden 2000, 39; Pohl 2002, 37.
1846 Pohl 2002, 39–41, 45.

6.3 Sweden introduces an electoral reform: No revolution like those in Russia, Finland or Germany

6.3.1 A RELUCTANT RIGHTIST OPPOSITION GIVES IN AFTER THE FALL OF THE GERMAN MONARCHY

Sweden was not yet a universal model for democracy even within the country itself in the late 1910s, like in later times. Furthermore, its transition to democracy was moulded by transnational influences to a greater extent than has usually been recognised. Political upheavals that changed political constellations in nearby countries – especially the Russian and German Revolutions, the victory of the Entente and the Finnish Civil War – affected the course of the Swedish constitutional debate and set the timetable for the realisation of the reform. The British example of extending suffrage, as well as the opportunity to bring a long struggle to an end once parliamentary government had been established and a desire to avoid the fate of Finland encouraged the reformists in 1918, but it was the German defeat that finally made the Swedish monarchy and The Right ready for a compromise – reluctantly and without really giving up their scepticism. The logic of this resistance and its transnational background, as well as those of reformism, deserve further consideration.

The transition to parliamentary government in autumn 1917 had, despite complicated negotiations and opposition from the King, taken place fairly smoothly. There were problems caused by the war and some extra-parliamentary calls for a revolution, but no major political grouping expected one to take place in Sweden. The leading Social Democrats, after seeing what the Bolshevik Revolution and the Finnish Civil War had brought about, finally rejected revolution as a goal and opted for democracy obtained by legal means and in cooperation with the Liberals.[1847] The reform attempt of the new coalition in spring 1918, however, had resulted in increased frustration as a result of continuous rightist opposition. The King had continued to oppose such democratisation, and The Right with its majority in the upper chamber had easily blocked the proposals. The constitutional confrontation thus remained unresolved. The only concession which The Right had made was to call for an examination of the issue, which could be interpreted as a readiness to consider some kind of reform instead of just categorically rejecting any.[1848]

By autumn 1918, the state of international affairs had changed, and these circumstances led to a reassessment of the situation by the King and The Right. It had become clear that Germany would not win the war and was reconsidering its political system as a way out. It was rather the Western democracies that were likely to prevail in the future. Germany was in transition towards constitutional monarchy, the parliamentarisation of its administration and the democratisation of suffrage. A period of constitutional upheaval and demonstrations led to the abdication of the Kaiser on 9 November 1918 and to the rise of the council movement.

1847 Olsson 2000, 121–2.
1848 Gerdner 1946, 31.

Prussia, the model polity of the Swedish royal family and The Right, no longer existed in its old form and, what was even worse, seemed to be sliding towards a socialist revolution.

Indeed, a revolution in Sweden had become, once again, a possible scenario after Germany experienced one and the domestic constitutional debate heated up once more.[1849] Although the Social Democrats had rejected revolutionary methods, some far leftists continued to entertain revolutionary ideas.[1850] However, the Russian Revolution hardly offered an encouraging example, the failure of the revolution in Finland had kept socialist radicalism within bounds, and the German revolution with its councils was not that promising either, even if transnational ideological influence continued to be transmitted from Germany.

German demonstrators were calling for universal suffrage and the abolition of the monarchy. King Gustav V felt that revolutionary tendencies were endangering his throne just as they had led to the fall of the Kaiser, his wife's cousin. Aware of this and related concerns on The Right, the Liberal-Social Democratic ministry decided to force through a reform proposal based on previous Liberal motions. The revolutionary atmosphere was increased by calls by the far left, encouraged by the German revolutionary process, for a national constitutive assembly, a republic, universal suffrage and the abolition of the First Chamber. Not even the possibility of a revolution of the Russian type was out of the question given that the far left continued to oppose suffrage reform in the form proposed by the government.[1851] However, all sides were persuaded to moderation by the warning example of not only Germany but also Finland, where a failed socialist revolution had turned into the misery of prison camps.

By late summer and early autumn, the Swedish debate on constitutional issues had changed somewhat as a reflection of the course of the war. Politicians were reconsidering their relationship with Germany and the Entente and their attitude to the respective constitutional models. This happened earlier and more clearly than in Finland, where the majority of the Rump Parliament continued to believe in a German victory or stuck to the possibility of introducing their favoured constitution no matter how the war might end. In Sweden, the British model was increasingly seen as worth emulating, some historical research having found resemblances between the two political systems from the eighteenth century on. It has been suggested that the proposal by a commission led by Viscount Bryce to reform the House of Lords, even if it did not lead to constitutional changes in Britain, had a transnational impact in Sweden, where the Liberal press took it up during August. Conservative papers reacted by defending the First Chamber and called for the reinforcement of its traditional status, questioning the Liberals' idealisation of the British model. At the same time, the more radical Social Democrat leaders Gustav Möller and Per Albin Hansson were revising their conceptions of a political and social revolution, concluding that socialisation

---

1849 Gerdner 1966, 104.
1850 Olsson 2000, 157–8.
1851 Gerdner 1966, 97; Stjernquist 1993, 139–40.

could take place gradually and by parliamentary means. Such ideological rethinking, already visible in the discourses analysed in previous chapters, increased unity within the Social Democratic Labour Party and further distanced it from socialist radicalism.[1852] It reinforced the parliamentary and revisionist message of the party and perhaps to some extent facilitated a rightist willingness to experiment with universal suffrage. The Social Democratic leaders spoke for the continuing participation of the party in the government at times of a major crisis in international politics, the goal being to prevent a Bolshevik upheaval in Sweden, to maintain 'democratic government' and to gain a suffrage reform.[1853] Both the Social Democrats and The Right were thus becoming readier for a partial and gradual reform of the Swedish constitution, something that the Liberals had long advocated.

The debate on a new constitution could well have been postponed further if the German Western Front had not been folding and the German leaders had not contacted the US government about the possibility of peace negotiations. After this turn, the Prussian political order was expected to fall, with obvious consequences for Sweden. The Social Democrats took the initiative and persuaded the coalition government to summon an extraordinary parliamentary session to discuss some minor political questions. After this session met on 30 October 1918, in the rapidly changing international circumstances (with the German constitution based on a parliamentary monarchy just adopted) and pressures from the press, it placed constitutional questions on its agenda[1854] – which The Right complained about, claiming that it was an illegitimate procedure.

Late October and early November 1918 marked a period of major rethinking for the Swedish political elite, linked transnationally to the fall of the Prussian political order and to the expected universal victory of parliamentary democracy. As Björn von Sydow has put it, the Swedish suffrage reform saw the light of day as a direct consequence of the German defeat and the revolution there. Reforms were considered necessary to stop a socialist revolution.[1855] A readiness for constitutional reform was rising within the previously sceptical royal family, the King and the Crown Prince hoping that the political parties would reach a compromise on the issue. Some postponement was, nevertheless, still in the air: it was proposed that resolution of the suffrage question should be put off until the ordinary parliamentary session of spring 1919. This, too, changed with news of the revolution in Germany on 9 November.[1856] King Gustav V changed his mind when it became clear that the German monarchy would also be abolished and started to urge the rightist leaders Arvid Lindman and Ernst Trygger, who had consistently opposed all concessions, to accept some sort of suffrage reform.[1857] The Swedish monarchy thus adapted itself to the democratisation

---

1852 Gerdner 1946, 31; Andræ 1998, 243–6, 271.
1853 Gerdner 1946, 30.
1854 Gerdner 1966, 92; Olsson 2000, 132–3.
1855 von Sydow 1997, 59; Nilsson 2004, 145.
1856 Gerdner 1946, 32; Gerdner 1966, 93.
1857 von Sydow 1997, 118.

of suffrage once this seemed unavoidable after the fall of the polity that had served as a model for the duality of government. For many members of the bourgeoisie in Sweden and Finland, imperial Germany had set the norm for an established political order. They wanted to see Swedish and Finnish monarchies stand as firmly as the German monarchy; now both were wavering.

For Swedish socialists, too, the revolution in Germany constituted a more fundamental ideological turn than the preceding upheavals in Russia and Finland. Transnational ties with Germany were much stronger: the views of the German far left were directly relevant for the Swedish left-wing Social Democrats, who had also traditionally looked to Germany for ideological models. Encouraged by what really seemed to be becoming an international revolution, they called for a socialist republic based on councils or soviets and attacked the majority Social Democrats over the country's economic problems and the delayed reforms. In a draft manifesto, their leaders represented Sweden as one of the backward countries of an old Europe, possessing a 'medieval' system of representation in the First Chamber, and demanded its immediate abolition. Like their German ideological brethren and the Finnish Social Democrats in autumn 1917, these left-wingers also called for the summoning of a national constituent assembly. A minority led by Zeth Höglund indeed questioned the potential of bourgeois democracy and parliamentarism to produce true liberty and were ready to turn to violence, in the spirit of classical Marxism if not Bolshevism. However, they failed to win support among their party comrades, who were concerned about the brutality of the Bolshevik system and the consequences of the Red rebellion in Finland. MPs such as Ivar Vennerström rather sought cooperation with the Majority Social Democrats in order to obtain a radicalised parliamentarism and shunned extra-parliamentary action, thus rejecting the German example. Utopians such as Carl Lindhagen and anti-bureaucrats such as Fabian Månsson represented yet other alternative lines within this small and fragmented parliamentary group.[1858]

Despite the marginality of revolutionary fervour among the far left, the Liberal-Social Democratic coalition and especially the majority Social Democrats made deliberate use of the looming fears of revolution to force The Right to finally accept the extension of suffrage. Hjalmar Branting had tried to introduce the issue during the extraordinary parliamentary session, but the motion moved forward only after the fall of the German monarchy. Prime Minister Nils Edén contacted the leaders of The Right, urging them to work for an immediate solution to the suffrage question. They – aware of the revolutionary events in Finland and Germany and of the royal family's reconsideration – recognised the necessity of reform to avoid further radicalisation of the left. After this concession by The Right, the members of government coalition just needed to reach a compromise among themselves,[1859] and to face parliamentary debates in which the relentless rhetorical opposition would continue.

1858 Andræ 1998, 13–14, 208, 221–5, 228, 233.
1859 Gerdner 1946, 31–2; Andræ 1998, 13–14, 211; Olsson 2000, 134–5, 137.

The majority of the government wanted to solve the situation by bringing a reform proposal immediately before the parliament. In the meantime, extra-parliamentary measures were employed, which added to the revolutionary atmosphere: the Social Democrats organised a hunger demonstration in Stockholm on the day following the revolution in Germany. Some demonstrators shouted out, calling for a republic as they passed the Royal Palace. The Social Democrat leaders used the demonstrations, popular demands for reform and the risk of extended revolutionary action to put pressure on the Liberals to get the proposal dealt with already during the extraordinary session. They aimed at universal and equal suffrage in both local and national elections as well as the extension of parliamentary government; these would satisfy the majority of the workers, who generally wished to avoid an open conflict. A plebiscite on a republic and the First Chamber could wait until universal suffrage took effect. They held to the view that all democratisation measures should take place through legal means.[1860] This caution may well have been vital for the success of the Swedish reform: demands for the abolition of the monarchy might have made the First Chamber once again vote the proposal down.[1861]

The coalition reached a compromise on 14 November: a proposal on universal suffrage in local elections would be brought before the extraordinary parliamentary session while one on national elections and female suffrage would wait until the ordinary session of spring 1919.[1862] A committee was nominated to prepare the new election system. The proposal was introduced before the parliament on 22 November and approved by the Special Committee after minor technical compromises on electoral practices were agreed. Extra-parliamentary pressurising continued in public meetings and the press, with 'democratic citizens' and 'the democratic masses' urging 'the democratic coalition' and 'the entire Swedish democracy' to unite in forcing through a development towards a 'Sweden ruled by the people' (*folkstyrt Sverige*). The Prime Minister presented the proposal as the minimum demand, talking about a universal democratic movement that made fundamental political reforms unavoidable in neutral states as well. Hjalmar Branting, when speaking to the crowd, described the Swedish movement as being carried by 'the democratic wave that rushes forth over the world'. News from Germany reported a socialist revolution by 'Berlin Bolshevism' calling for democracy and the takeover of power by a national constituent assembly.[1863] Per Albin Hansson hinted that the Swedish Second Chamber might also declare itself a national constituent assembly if the reform was

1860 Gerdner 1946, 32–4, 36; von Sydow 1997, 118; Andræ 1998, 248–57; Olsson 138.
1861 Olsson 2000, 170.
1862 Gerdner 1946, 33.
1863 *Social-Demokraten*, 'Väldig anslutning till söndagens demokratiska medborgarmöte i Stockholm', 'Tyska riksregeringen i händerna på Berlins arbetar- och soldatsråd' and 'Den stora författningspropositionen', 25 November 1918; 'Starkt motstånd i Tyskland mot Berlinbolsjevismen', 26 November 1918; The liberal *Dagens Nyheter* also reported on 'Den samling för fullt folkstyre' [the meeting for full people's rule], 25 November 1918, using a vernacular term for the concept of democracy at this key moment.

stopped, which provoked rightist protests about what they claimed to be extra-parliamentary measures. Nevertheless many in the parliament opted for a reform to avoid any German-like acerbation of the crisis. The Right seemed to be giving up its opposition to equal voting and female suffrage,[1864] but, as the analysis of the actual contents of the debates below will show, this was far from a clear or easy change of mind.

The more moderate leaders of The Right were moving towards a compromise despite their continued reluctance. They considered it unlikely that a rightist minority government would last or that new elections would produce a rightist majority, given the prevailing reformist and downright revolutionary atmosphere.[1865] The former prime minister Carl Swartz, who had expressed some vague readiness for reform in 1917 and had been in contact with the current prime minister about such a possibility,[1866] caused a sensation by speaking in the parliament in favour of the democratisation of the constitution[1867] – this makes for an interesting parallel with H. H. Asquith, a former opponent of reform who spoke for it when he deemed its time had come. In Sweden, however, Swartz was one of the very few rightists to do so, and his motives were suspected.[1868] Swartz's point was that the Swedes were equally capable of living under a democratic constitution as surrounding peoples, though a sufficient amount of time would (again) be needed to deliberate the nature of the reform. Other rightist leaders rather played down the danger of a revolution. The ministry, by contrast, viewed an immediate reform as quintessential. According to Stefan Olsson, both the monarch and business interests were ready for concessions by November, suggesting that The Right should give in.[1869] As we shall see, however, rightist businessmen still continued to obstruct the reform in parliament.

Several scholars have argued that now that German military strength and economic power were withering away, the business world welcomed constitutional reforms that would make Sweden resemble the Western powers (like Britain, an old trading partner) and distance the country from the allegedly autocratic Prussianism with which Sweden had been predominantly associated both home and abroad. Leading entrepreneurs did not fear a socialist takeover and were hence ready to give democracy a chance since the public demanded it so persistently. In a world in which Western democracies would prevail, it would be advantageous to have a democracy in Sweden, too.[1870] The American Ambassador had proclaimed: 'One common bond united us all – Democracy.'[1871] And Hjalmar Branting

---

1864 Gerdner 1946, 36–7; Andræ 1998, 259–60. News from Britain reported about women voting more actively than men in the election of mid-December. *Social-Demokraten*, 'En stor dag för England kvinnor', 17 November 1918; *Aftonbladet*, 17 December 1918.
1865 von Sydow 1997, 118.
1866 Gerdner 1966, 91.
1867 Palmstierna 1953, 27 November 1918, 248.
1868 *Social-Demokraten*, 'Förpostfäktningen', 27 November 1918.
1869 Olsson 2000, 142, 144–5.
1870 Söderpalm 1969; Carlsson 1985, 86; Hadenius 2008, 44–5; Olsson 2000, 147.
1871 *The Times*, 'The Bond of Democracy', 19 August 1918.

had already assured the British press that a 'Western' democracy was in the process of being formed in Sweden. Thus economic opportunism and the optimistic reception of the transnational discourse on democracy both supported the Swedish turn from Prussian to Western democratic models. This had not been a purely domestic evolutionary long-term development towards representative democracy, as contemporary rightist discourse and much of later nation-state-centred historiography suggested: its course and timing were determined essentially by international events and transnational interaction. Furthermore, opposition to the transition among The Right was still deep-rooted.

While the Special Committee, led by Branting, was still working, much of the leftist press greeted the reform as a breakthrough of democracy, although some disappointment about the compromise was also expressed.[1872] The parliamentary debates inspired little enthusiasm either in- or outside the parliament,[1873] and the vote of 17 December 1918, which sealed the reform, has been often represented as a mere formality.[1874] In the Second Chamber, only the far left openly rejected the proposal, while some rightist members abstained. The First Chamber approved it although opposing arguments from The Right continued with no indication of a surrender from that part. According to *Aftonbladet*, all this was a mere coup carried out using extra-parliamentary agitation to which even members of the government had resorted.[1875] As we shall see, the discursive battles on democracy, the political role of the people and parliamentarism continued irrespective of any party-political compromises that had been made.

6.3.2 The war and revolution as agents of domestic reform

Sweden seemed to be on the point of experiencing a revolution produced by external impulses as the introduction of the proposal to the parliament on 26 November 1918 was accompanied with demonstrations that intimated a more serious confrontation should the proposal be rejected.[1876] From a Liberal perspective, international events seemed to have made the members of right change their minds.[1877] Even the *Aftonbladet* of the day reported from 'the Germany of the revolution' about 'the disintegrated Habsburg monarchy', asking whether France would also soon experience a revolution.[1878] Hjalmar Branting presented the reform bill to the parliament in the spirit of Social Democratic internationalism as 'part of the great global settlement after the war'. The international situation implied that even countries that had not directly participated in the war were being influenced

---

1872 Andræ 1998, 264–5.
1873 Palmstierna 1953, 18 December 1918, 262; *Social-Demokraten*, 'Den stora reformen i hamnen' and 'Den stora dagen', 18 December 1918.
1874 Andræ 1998, 265, 288; Olsson 2000, 149–52.
1875 *Aftonbladet*, 'Kuppen har lyckats. Vad skall nu ske?', 18 December 1918.
1876 Palmstierna 1953, 27 November 1918, 247.
1877 *Dagens Nyheter*, 'Förspelet till författningsrevisionen', 27 November 1918.
1878 *Aftonbladet*, 'Står det segrande Frankrike inför revolution?', 'Från revolutionens Tyskland' and 'Den sönderfallna Habsburgska monarkien', 26 November 1918.

by 'the great events out in the world'.[1879] Natural metaphors of currents and winds coming into Sweden from outside and forcing change were again used to emphasise the unavoidable nature of the reform and the dangers involved in any opposition to it: if The Right prevented this reform, the parliamentary Social Democratic Labour Party would no longer be able 'to restrain a storm that must then spontaneously rise everywhere in the country'.[1880] Extra-parliamentary opinion was used to pressurise the opponents of the reform but in much more moderate terms than in Finland a year before.

This was not an open threat of revolution but was based on a strategy typical of moderate Socialists elsewhere as well: should the compromise on reform be obstructed, the moderates would not be able to prevent the radicals from proceeding to a revolution. Per Albin Hansson – a critic of the coalition, which in his opinion was not radical enough – simplified the meaning of the war for Sweden, claiming that The Right had fought for the imperial armies while the left had joined 'the democratic people's army'.[1881] The internationally oriented Minister of Naval Defence, Erik Palmstierna, rejoicing over the restoration of peace in Europe and confident about the final breakthrough of democracy, envisaged a future where democratic states would contribute 'to the future of culture and the duration of peace in the world community of nations',[1882] referring here to plans to found the League of Nations. Another description of the turn towards 'a new Sweden' was presented by Minister of Finance Fredrik Vilhelm Thorsson, according to whom the world war had 'revolutionised perceptions far beyond the circles of the working class' and there was hence no going back to the old economic and political order.[1883]

Liberal ministers concentrated on proving to The Right and their supporters that no revolutionary change would follow from universal suffrage[1884] and that no threats of revolution had been used to force through the reform.[1885] Jakob Pettersson, the chairman of the Law Committee, conceded that 'a quite profound transformation of society' could be expected, but that The Right should nevertheless contribute to the construction of a new political system like many supporters of the old regime in Germany (which of course was not a correct description of the German situation). Leftist calls for more radical solutions were unfounded owing to the fundamental differences that existed between Sweden and Soviet Russia.[1886] The Finnish case demonstrated to Erik Röing, an inter-parliamentary activist, that rightist opposition might lead to unpredictable internal strife. The Swedes should continue to avoid involvement in the war 'out there in the world' by adopting the reform.[1887]

1879 AK, Hjalmar Branting, 26 November 1918, 9:23.
1880 AK, Hjalmar Branting, 26 November 1918, 9:24.
1881 AK, Per Albin Hansson, 26 November 1918, 9:46.
1882 AK, Erik Palmstierna, 26 November 1918, 9:14–15.
1883 FK, Fredrik Vilhelm Thorsson, 26 November 1918, 5:44.
1884 AK, Axel Schotte, 26 November 1918, 9:10.
1885 FK, Nils Edén, 6 November 1918, 5:18.
1886 AK, Jakob Pettersson, 26 November 1918, 9:32–4.
1887 AK, Erik Röing, 26 November 1918, 9:31.

Suggestions about an unavoidable uprising in case of continued opposition were interpreted as threats of revolution by the spokesmen of The Right. Karl Hildebrand referred to an extra-parliamentary speech by Hjalmar Branting, which contained visions of 'a complete revolution'.[1888] Such intimidation was, in Hildebrand's view, unjustified as The Right had already conceded that the war had initiated a global movement aiming at making the people at large directly responsible for political affairs. They were already participating in legislating constitutional changes despite the potentially 'revolutionising' consequences of these.[1889] The German experiences with councils demonstrated what revolutionary constitutional change might produce.[1890] The Right recommended postponement in ways that recalled the actions of the British Conservatives in spring 1917 and the Finnish bourgeois parties in summer 1917: a new elections could be called to find out 'if the number of supporters of a radical upheaval has grown or whether hesitation has grown in the country'.[1891]

David Norman, the chairman of an anti-socialist propaganda organisation, was even more condemnatory of Branting's suggestion about unstoppable international revolutionary movements spreading to Sweden, implying that popular opposition to them might also rise.[1892] Such visions of extra-parliamentary movements emerging on both the left and the right suggested the possibility of a major confrontation. Therefore, according to Norman, the 'revolutionary spirit amongst the people' should not be agitated and abused in order not to arouse conservative forces too (like in Finland). Both extremes would be avoided by dropping the reform. Norman also referred to the dynamics of revolution: the Russian and German revolutions demonstrated how the more rightist Social Democrats tended to lose power to radicals, which would ultimately present a challenge to Social Democracy as well.[1893]

Reflective of the inter-party compromise was the aforementioned speech made by the former prime minister Carl Swartz. In 1917 Swartz had implicitly recognised the necessity of having a parliamentary government. Now he conceded that democracy was making very fast progress 'around us' (presumably in Germany) and that he had heard no one oppose a similar development in Sweden.[1894] Karl Ekman, a rightist lawyer who had participated in the planning of extended suffrage, likewise conceded that the time for the old political order was over and hoped that a new one would be built through consensus based on universal suffrage rather than by a revolution.[1895] Discursively, these two rightist politicians had moved over to the side of democracy, whereas the majority of the party carried on its rhetorical opposition.

1888 AK, Karl Hildebrand, 26 November 1918, 9:25.
1889 AK, Karl Hildebrand, 26 November 1918, 9:25.
1890 AK, Karl Hildebrand, 26 November 1918, 9:32.
1891 AK, Karl Hildebrand, 26 November 1918, 9:28.
1892 AK, David Norman, 26 November 1918, 9:39.
1893 AK, David Norman, 26 November 1918, 9:49.
1894 FK, Carl Swartz, 26 November 1918, 5:30.
1895 FK, Karl Ekman, 26 November 1918, 5:45.

On the far left, disappointment with the proposal gave rise to speculations about the possibility of a revolution even among those who favoured parliamentarism. Ivar Vennerström asserted that the Swedes were capable of creating a democratic society without turning to violent revolutionary means, but they would nevertheless decide on the need for a revolution themselves.[1896] The policies of The Right increased the threat of even moderate Swedes turning to revolutionary measures. The Right seemed to want to control voting even when the German Junkers and industrialists were ready to accept a national constituent assembly elected by universal suffrage.[1897] Fredrik Ström emphasised the importance of the international context in an era 'when we see how thrones fall and how houses of lords founder everywhere'.[1898] The situation of late 1918 corresponded with Marxist predictions of the conditions for revolution:[1899]

> We are now in the middle of a world revolution without a counterpart in history. This world revolution, which is going to fill the following years and probably decades with its events, is increasingly taking the form and character of a duel between the world of capital and the working class.

Revolutionary language of the kind used in the Finnish parliament in 1917 had entered the Swedish upper house as well. Ström hardly facilitated changes in rightist attitudes as he went on to depict the fall of 'capitalist humbug'.[1900] The world war had been initiated by capitalism, while the ongoing world revolution had been made by the working class and socialism. The future would be one of a socialist social and political order – not only in Russia but also in Austria, Hungary and Germany, and by implication in Sweden as well. The German precedent was, as a result of the transnational links of the Swedish monarchy and The Right with Germany, of particular importance: Bismarckian militarism had been replaced by a combination of workers' and soldiers' councils and a socialist government.[1901] Ström went on with his predictions, suggesting that the revolution would next affect the countries of the Entente: the British election campaign suggested this (which was a very optimistic estimate); the Social Democrats would gain power in Italy; and the leftists would take over the Socialist Party in France. The only choice for Swedes to make was whether they preferred a violent or a peaceful 'social revolution'; 'the red flag of the International and Social Democracy' would in any case also be flying 'over Stockholm, over this house and over the Royal Palace'.[1902] This was all socialist revolutionary rhetoric. Such a revolution was, however, only taking place in the minds and speech of the far left.

By 17 December 1918, when the time for a final vote had come, the arguments remained much the same and awareness of a transnational

1896 AK, Ivar Vennerström, 6 November 1918, 9:15, 18.
1897 AK, Ivar Vennerström, 26 November 1918, 9:17–18.
1898 FK, Fredrik Ström, 26 November 1918, 5:35.
1899 FK, Fredrik Ström, 26 November 1918, 5:32.
1900 FK, Fredrik Ström, 26 November 1918, 5:32.
1901 FK, Fredrik Ström, 26 November 1918, 5:32–3.
1902 FK, Fredrik Ström, 26 November 1918, 5:33, 36.

change high. Hjalmar Branting presented the war as having 'revolutionised the world', destroying those who had initiated it. The global transformation had started with the Russian Revolution in spring 1917 but had been accelerated with the German Revolution, which had direct implications for the Swedish political system:[1903]

> But now that one sees the German Revolution, sees how it is growing in strength with this total upheaval of everything that has previously been exalted and highly esteemed there, yes, then one understands that no country which is as closely in contact with Central Europe as Sweden, owing to its location, has always been and must always be, can remain as before.

The common mission was the building of 'the new Sweden'[1904] now that the revolution in Germany had convinced The Right about the inevitability of reform. For the Social Democrats, the new Germany offered a convenient model for transnational change, perhaps one that The Right would accept in the name of the old cultural ties:[1905]

> When we see how, south of the Baltic Sea, a social republic is proclaimed, since the Social Democratic Party seems to be the leading one there, and is undertaking the necessary measures of socialisation at an unexpected pace but with prudence and moderation, then one understands that our people indeed will not want to delay in following when the great nations make progress in social reforms.

Sweden needed to follow the German model of introducing Social Democracy moderately but without delay. Branting's transnational Social Democratic revolution was a compromise between retaining the formal constitution and proceeding to further the reforms aspired to by the socialists.

The party secretary Gustav Möller stated that never since the rise of the workers' movement had Sweden been closer to a revolution but that the Social Democrats, willing to introduce democracy without open conflict, had no intention of launching an actual revolution. The proposal would turn Sweden into a majority democracy surpassing in that respect Switzerland or the unicameral parliamentary polities of Norway and Finland, which were limited by provisions for minorities.[1906] Harald Hallén emphasised that this transformation would happen in Sweden, unlike in many other countries, without outbreaks of violence.[1907] The transnational connections of the revolution were self-evident for Arthur Engberg, too, who saw the spread of its ideas across borders as unavoidable.[1908] Transnational influences from Germany were at their strongest at the time of the German revolutionary

1903 AK, Hjalmar Branting, 17 December 1918, 17:21–2.
1904 AK, Hjalmar Branting, 17 December 1918, 17:24; 17 December 1918, 18:57.
1905 AK, Hjalmar Branting, 17 December 1918, 17:30.
1906 AK, Gustav Möller, 17 December 1918, 17:45, 47.
1907 AK, Harald Hallén, 17 December 1918, 17:56; also Arthur Engman, 17 December 1918, 17:79.
1908 AK, Arthur Engberg, 17 December 1918, 17:72.

experience in late 1918, when they were manifested by the Swedish left and indeed by some of the right as well.

Liberal descriptions of a Europe transformed by war, civil strife and revolution from a continent of imperialism and militarism into one of democracy and peace were equally optimistic and deterministic. Their persuasive rhetoric built on claims of the nation's unanimity and its ability to surpass other nations in the degree of popular involvement.[1909] The coalition partners were thanked (and advised for the future) about 'a continuous battle against revolutionary propensities for violence'.[1910] Prime Minister Nils Edén emphasised the fact that it was question of a peaceful Swedish adaptation to the global transformation and denied all accusations of a coup.[1911] He talked about 'this age revolutionising the world', when a new foundation for the future of Sweden, too, was being laid.[1912] 'A trying and globally regenerating time' had rapidly changed the prevailing views in Sweden as well.[1913] According to Edén, 'the enormous break in European and Swedish societal life' had initiated a legislative process in which the coalition government had no alternatives.[1914] He expressed this using a natural metaphor typical of the Swedish reform discourse, talking about 'this gust of the stormy season from the shaking world around'[1915] that had left the government no alternative but to act.

Unanimity may have been proclaimed by the left, but it was not exhibited by The Right. David Norman saw the proposal as challenging the limits of legality, being against the spirit of the constitution and tantamount to a coup. This conservative politician rejected the way that the German Revolution had been used by the left 'to enforce a fast and forceful radicalisation of our entire social order through reckless agitation'.[1916] The Social Democrats seemed ready to proceed 'by all possible means' (*med all gewalt*, derived from the German word *Gewalt* [power, force or violence], thus insinuating that extra-parliamentary methods might also be used) to the edge of an abyss should The Right oppose their demands. Norman questioned claims that the Swedish reform was a necessary part of a pan-European transformation; the left was merely 'violently' exaggerating the shortcomings of the Swedish constitution and threatening the parliament with open violence.[1917] This vocabulary of violence demonstrates the seriousness with which some of The Right viewed the confrontation. According to David Pettersson, too, 'threats of revolution, a general strike and other violent measures' had been used mischievously to 'instil an atmosphere of panic among the Swedish

---

1909 AK, Raoul Hamilton, 17 December 1918, 17:33.
1910 AK, Minister of Justice Eliel Löfgren, 17 December 1918, 18:38.
1911 AK, Nils Edén, 17 December 1918, 18:53.
1912 AK, Nils Edén, 17 December 1918, 18:6.
1913 AK, Nils Edén, 17 December 1918, 18:7.
1914 FK, Nils Edén, 17 December 1918, 10:11.
1915 FK, Nils Edén, 17 December 1918, 10:10.
1916 AK, David Norman, 17 December 1918, 17:35, 38.
1917 AK, David Norman, 17 December 1918, 17:35, 37.

people'.[1918] It was a dangerous precedent to introduce constitutional reform 'under the threat of a revolution'.[1919]

Edvard Lithander, a cosmopolitan businessman who showed no reformist views that have been claimed to have been typical of Swedish entrepreneurs, denied the validity of arguments derived from foreign revolutions: the Russian Revolution was 'not comparable with circumstances in our country' and the German Revolution had been caused by an unexpected defeat in a war that did not concern Sweden.[1920] Ernst Trygger's interpretation of the global trends also continued to differ drastically from those of the Prime Minister. This conservative lawyer saw nothing abnormal in the age that would require the Swedes to reject their old customs: even if relations between states and political systems had changed as a consequence of the war, contingent world events had not changed the norms according to which Swedish politicians should act. Transformations in countries that had lost the war such as Russia, Germany and Austria had resulted from revolutions that were 'contrary to law and justice and the ordered societal order'.[1921] Such revolutions were not the model for Swedes to follow as no violent attempts to change the political order had emerged from circles other than the current government, which had 'through violence or a failure to prevent violence' pushed through the reform.[1922] This repeated association between the unconventional manoeuvres of a reformist government with potential revolutionary violence, suggesting that the constitution and established parliamentary order had been violated and questioning the legitimacy of governmental action, is familiar to us from the rhetoric of opposition conservatives in Britain in spring 1917[1923] and from Finnish debates throughout 1917 and 1918. Trygger suggested that the government had rejected the historical principle of building the country in accordance with the law and now regarded 'the opinion of the day' as 'sovereign'.[1924] Indeed, open violence in the form of 'mutual strife between different social classes' threatened as the government's policy diminished the Swedes' obedience to the law.[1925] There was no sign of commitment to a constitutional compromise in the speech of this rightist leader. Edén felt compelled to respond to such claims, stating that the reform was a result of a long domestic reform movement and not of temporary demonstrations connected with the German Revolution.[1926]

1918   AK, David Pettersson, 17 December 1918, 17:57.
1919   AK, David Pettersson, 17 December 1918, 17:57.
1920   AK, Edvard Lithander, 17 December 1918, 17:39–40.
1921   FK, Ernst Trygger, 17 December 1918, 10:11–12.
1922   FK, Ernst Trygger, 17 December 1918, 10:12–13; see also Ollas Anders Ericsson, 17 December 1918, 10:23.
1923   The similarity with British conservatives can also be found in the claim that the current parliament was not formally competent to decide on constitutional change. FK, Ernst Trygger, 17 December 1918, 10:14. Noteworthy is the late stage at which these legalistic arguments were introduced – as a last possible means to stop the reform.
1924   FK, Ernst Trygger, 17 December 1918, 10:13.
1925   FK, Ernst Trygger, 17 December 1918, 10:13.
1926   FK, Nils Edén, 17 December 1918, 11:18.

The Right continued to express their reservations on a broad front; defenders of the compromise resolution remained rare. According to August Bellinder, the Swedish political order was much further developed than those of Russia or Germany; indeed, he asked, whether the soviets of those countries were compatible with 'true and full democratism' demanded by the left.[1927] Many were highly pessimistic about the prospects of a future Sweden should the reform come. Ernst Lindblad suggestively lamented the fact that the Social Democrats were taking over all power just when the Finnish Civil War had shown the Swedes where 'a Social Democratic conception can take us in the future'.[1928] Lieutenant General Herman Wrangel insisted that the French Revolution had already demonstrated how a reaction would always follow revolutionary excesses.[1929] References from The Right to the possibility of violence arising suggest that the risk of a civil war still loomed in their minds. The Swedish constitutional crisis of November and December 1918 was a deep and transnational one, not a mere formality.

The rightists were still fiercely opposed to the reform in their words if not in their voting. Karl Hildebrand was a rare exception when he conceded, despite his previous doubts, that foreign revolutions had changed opinions in Sweden. Hildebrand, previously a most consistent opponent to reform, employed natural metaphors for the inevitable political change, revealing his rightist adaptation to the reform through the (possibly unintended) imitation of initially leftist language: '[A] mighty wind of revolution blows over countries and has demonstrated its power to overthrow thrones and to revolutionise constitutions.' Such a revolution still involved risks, however, since it had provoked 'the atrocities of Bolshevism' as well.[1930] The concerns of The Right remained unchanged despite the compromise. Nevertheless, to counterbalance the extensive discourse of crisis, Ernst Trygger concluded his final speech by declaring that he was ready to meet what the new electoral system would bring and to adapt to it.[1931] The Right had, however, made it clear that it was still in principle opposed to the reform.

Nor was the far left happy with the Social Democrats' claims of having avoided a revolution despite the rise of 'a revolutionary flood' from Germany. The government had failed to introduce social equality of the kind that existed in Belgium or France or even political equality to the extent of that now existing in Germany, where 20-year-olds would be allowed to vote.[1932] Fredrik Ström reinforced the rightist fears of a revolution, declaring (like the Social Democrats in the Finnish parliament one year earlier) that age limits for suffrage would not stop 'revolutionary socialism'.[1933] Ivar Vennerström suggested that more could have been demanded by the reformists without it leading to a civil war – even though the workers would have been ready

---

1927 FK, August Bellinder, 17 December 1918, 10:41.
1928 FK, Ernst Lindblad, 17 December 1918, 10:37.
1929 FK, Herman Wrangel, 17 December 1918, 10:28–9.
1930 AK, Karl Hildebrand, 17 December 1918, 18:45.
1931 FK, Ernst Trygger, 17 December 1918, 11:22.
1932 AK, Ivar Vennerström, 17 December 1918, 17:61, 65.
1933 FK, Fredrik Ström, 17 December 1918, 10:44.

to launch one anyway.[1934] The Swedish revolutionaries could not accept this compromise, but their claims were countered with references to the violent nature of radical socialism in Finland, Russia and Germany, which had only led to civil wars.[1935]

6.3.3 Optimistic and pessimistic visions of a democratic Sweden

The very meaning of democracy still was a topic of heated dispute between the Social Democrats and The Right at the time of the extension of suffrage. What had changed in comparison to the previous debates of 1917 and 1918 was that once democracy had been increasingly set as the goal of the future polity in Germany (mainly by the Social Democrats), the postponing of democratic reforms in Sweden began to appear impossible.

Confrontational ideological understandings of democracy were visible in that in Sweden, as in Germany, the Social Democrats had a tendency to monopolise the concept. They could do so now that they were confident of their ultimate victory: if the German Social Democrats had managed to force through democratisation, why would the Swedish party fail? The negotiations between the coalition and The Right had already led to decisive concessions by the opposition, and the parliamentary phase was expected to merely confirm this historical compromise. Erik Palmstierna expressed his happiness at Sweden 'taking its place among the democratically governed countries of the world'.[1936] He continued to exclude The Right from the collective of democrats owing to their 'lack of democracy which is the spirit of the very essence of The Right'. The Right continued to talk in ways that did not represent 'sincere democracy' but merely covered their undemocratic aims 'in democratic attire'.[1937] The arguments used by the Swedish right indeed demonstrate the existence of such a dual policy. The inclusion of the Swedish right in the democratic front did not seem discursively possible on either side of the political divide.

The Social Democrats built on their internationalist approach, emphasising external pressures (the global progress of Western democracy and the German example of a democratic breakthrough), in addition to internal ones, that forced Sweden to change. Arthur Engberg saw democracy as the system 'where peoples now search for protection against the forces of dissolution' and 'ideas of dictatorship'.[1938] Hjalmar Branting, who was internationally well connected within the Social Democratic movement, presented the government's proposal as being based on 'the minimum demands of the democratic expressions of the people' and emphasised that the Swedish people demanded 'complete democratisation'. The proposal was not negotiable: The Right had to choose whether it would allow Sweden to follow 'democratic opinion in the world' (Branting was here employing

---

1934 AK, Ivar Vennerström, 17 December 1918, 17:68.
1935 FK, Carl Gustaf Ekman, 17 December 1918, 11:13.
1936 AK, Erik Palmstierna, 26 November 1918, 9:14.
1937 AK, Erik Palmstierna, 26 November 1918, 9:30.
1938 AK, Arthur Engberg, 26 November 1918, 9:53–4.

Wilsonian rhetoric) and finally become a democracy. It had become impossible to continue protecting the privileges of a plutocracy that was irreconcilable with 'the democratic era in which we live'.[1939]

As for the democracy that would follow, Branting defined it with attributes such as 'mature' (*mogen*) and 'informed' or 'enlightened' (*upplyst*), promising that democracy would proceed with caution and respect the common good,[1940] i.e. reassuring The Right that that they had no reason to fear the expected rise of the Social Democrats so much. The nationalised 'Swedish democracy' would be able to solve all future problems in accordance with the will of the people.[1941] Branting concluded that democratisation was required by the historical process – narratives of a thousand years of Swedish democracy and Marxist theories both supported this interpretation – and the 'old democratic struggle'.[1942] Whether this referred to the early twentieth century reform movements or actually to a thousand years of supposedly democratic tradition was deliberately left unclear.

The Social Democrats were so sure about the success of the reform that they almost neglected to attend the upper house in November – implying thereby that parliamentarism would in the future be realised mainly through the lower chamber. They did this again in December, despite continued attacks on democracy in the upper house. They let the rightists complain among themselves, knowing that the composition of the chamber would change as soon as universal suffrage was implemented, and focused on the lower chamber, where they did not hide their expectations of further progress after the victory that was at hand. Hjalmar Branting again used natural metaphors to describe the situation:[1943]

> A new wave, more forceful than ever, of the democratic swell has arrived. Already in spring 1917 this swell set all minds on fire and showed already then that this was something new, making it clear that the old could not remain as it had been before.

There was no way of stopping the pan-European wave: it would be a 'humiliation' for the Swedish people if the country remained backward in the realisation of popular power when progress was being made everywhere else.

Addressing those Social Democrats who were disappointed about the extent of the reform, Branting conceded that the proposal was a compromise that postponed some aspects of further democratisation[1944] but saw no limits to later progress. The democratic breakthrough would be so clear that privileged minorities could no longer bypass the popular will; future policies would be based on the principles of democracy; and the democratisation would be 'so radical, so thorough' that the rule of the privileged would

1939 AK, Hjalmar Branting, 26 November 1918, 9:19, 24.
1940 AK, Hjalmar Branting, 26 November 1918, 9:22.
1941 AK, Hjalmar Branting, 26 November 1918, 9:24.
1942 AK, Hjalmar Branting, 26 November 1918, 9:24.
1943 AK, Hjalmar Branting, 17 December 1918, 17:20.
1944 AK, Hjalmar Branting, 17 December 1918, 17:22.

completely disappear.¹⁹⁴⁵ Socialism, rarely publicly proclaimed in the parliament, was openly stated as the goal: the struggle for 'our socialist and democratic ideals' would continue.¹⁹⁴⁶ The Social Democratic vision of a future democracy, as formulated in the manifesto of the party, even included a 'democratic republic', which might soon become the established polity but could be postponed for the time being. Democratic government might be possible without a unicameral parliament as well.¹⁹⁴⁷

Here Branting was bargaining with dissatisfied supporters, whom he counselled to patiently wait for further democratic and socialist reforms and not join the radicalism of the far left, whom the Social Democratic organ *Social-Demokraten* had dubbed 'domestic Bolsheviks'.¹⁹⁴⁸ Gustav Möller emphasised the fact that the Social Democrats had been fighting for both democracy and socialism, believing that the latter was to be achieved through democracy rather than revolution. A 'true democracy' was now at hand.¹⁹⁴⁹ A notion of Sweden as more democratic than other countries was already being constructed, and this would be a particularly favoured myth for the Social Democrats during their later ascendancy.¹⁹⁵⁰

Harald Hallén, an old radical and 'a democratic representative of the people',¹⁹⁵¹ defined the reform as the advancement of the cause of 'Swedish democracy' against its enemies on the right.¹⁹⁵² As Per Albin Hansson put it, The Right still seemed to be fighting for the cause of Prussian order against Western democracy, despite the German defeat.¹⁹⁵³ Even if the compromise left further reforms to be hoped for, it already entailed the introduction of 'Social Democracy' in that the Social Democrats would soon gain power at all levels.¹⁹⁵⁴ In the Social Democratic discourse on democracy, the concepts of democracy and socialism were now constantly associated and reconciled with the realities of the compromise in order to unite all socialists: 'the old reactionary and oligarchically governed Sweden' would be brought to an end, and 'plutocracy', too, would disappear once the capitalist order was crushed.¹⁹⁵⁵

The Social Democratic expectations for democracy began to diversify somewhat as soon as the realisation of the reform seemed certain. Oskar Sjölander, a teacher by profession, remained a little doubtful about the potential of democracy: 'full democracy' called for the adoption of virtues such as a nobility of soul, a sense of responsibility and dedication to one's

---

1945 AK, Hjalmar Branting, 17 December 1918, 17:24.
1946 AK, Hjalmar Branting, 17 December 1918, 17:32; also *Social-Demokraten*, 'Den stora dagen', 18 December 1918.
1947 AK, Hjalmar Branting, 17 December 1918, 17:29.
1948 *Social-Demokraten*, 'Regeringens program', 26 November 1918.
1949 AK, Gustav Möller, 17 December 1918, 17:44–5.
1950 See Linderborg 2001 for later Social Democratic historiography.
1951 AK, 17 December 1918, 17:53.
1952 AK, 17 December 1918, 17:52.
1953 AK, Per Albin Hansson, 26 November 1918, 9:45–6.
1954 AK, Harald Hallén, 17 December 1918, 17:52–3.
1955 AK, 17 December 1918, 17:55.

mission in life.[1956] These were quite traditional values, but Sjölander was speaking for the strengthening of the people through education which would allow them to attain these qualities. Per Albin Hansson, repeating arguments from the party organ, called for the democratisation of foreign policy in the aftermath of the experiences of the First World War in accordance with a general Social Democratic goal, the question being how 'the influence of democracy on foreign policy should be organised'. The planned government reports to the parliament on foreign policy did not suffice to constitute 'democratic control' of this field 'in a democratic period'; the parliament should be allowed to participate in decision-making on war and treaties with foreign powers and a committee established to constantly control the running of foreign policy.[1957] Even the Liberal Prime Minister recognised that the democratisation of foreign policy would be an essential part of 'the democratic reorganisation', but he considered that more concrete measures were to be decided later.[1958]

The Right simply refused to give in despite the crumbling of the German type of monarchical polity: old opponents of excessive democratisation continued to list their preconditions. As Karl Hildebrand put it, The Right was indeed ready to accept 'a far-reaching democratisation of our constitution and society, [though] they realised that this can lead to an upheaval of a revolutionary nature'. However, they wished for guarantees against 'a democratic degeneration' (*demokratisk urartning*) and 'its perversions' (*averter*).[1959] Western democracy, in particular, continued to have its problems. Hildebrand, who had published a book on democracy in 1913, found evidence in the United States, France, Germany and South American republics to demonstrate the double-edged nature of democracy as either strengthening or weakening the nation state:[1960]

> Should not everyone understand that the fruit of democracy has both good and bad sides? The democratisation of society can in certain situations and in certain periods imply a rise in the power and strength of the people, but such a development can also lead to the ruin of the country if the pernicious powers in democratic development are allowed to exert an influence unhindered.

1956 AK, 17 December 1918, 17:60.
1957 AK, Per Albin Hansson, 17 December 1918, 18:34–5; Hansson's *Social-Demokraten* had written about 'Kontroll över utrikespolitiken' on 25 November 1918.
1958 FK, 17 December 1918, 10:9.
1959 AK, Karl Hildebrand, 26 November 1918, 9:25, 27. Minister of Naval Defence Erik Palmstierna immediately challenged the use of such expressions, pointing to the degeneration of social circumstances under the current electoral system. 26 November 1918, 9:29–30. This made Hildebrand repeat his point and add: 'It is not so simple to remove the fears of the degeneration of democracy from the world.' 26 November 1918, 9:32.
1960 AK, Karl Hildebrand, 26 November 1918, 9:26; extended in 26 November 1918, 9:32.

Economy was a sector that was potentially endangered: 'a developed democratic Riksdag' might become 'violently experimental' in industrial policies, for instance.[1961]

Hildebrand tried to explain exactly what The Right was concerned about: they feared that democracy would not be built on 'the mature will of the people based on understanding' but instead on 'a primitive and immature one that makes unjustified use of the name of the will of the people'. Democracy as such could be welcomed, but the degeneration that it threatened had to be prevented. Hildebrand warned about the risk that recently gained power tended to be abused, especially by the masses.[1962] Democracy remained in Hildebrand's understanding a tree that yielded both good and bad fruit: the recent war had demonstrated that it could strengthen a people in times of crisis, but it could also split and thereby weaken a people. The fruit of democracy was dependent on education and the organisation of the democratic system, and these remained to be arranged in satisfactory ways.[1963] Hildebrand's statement of his readiness for democracy caused Prime Minister Nils Edén to express his understanding with an equally compromise-seeking metaphor, demonstrating his own readiness to carry on negotiations about the nature of the future polity:[1964]

> Let us then help each other to tend the new tree and nurse it so that the bad fruit will be increasingly pushed aside by the good ones. Let us be agreed on all that can be done so that this Swedish democracy will fulfil its task when it sets to work.

Some leaders of The Right and the Liberals were able to find consensual ground in the field of education – a topical issue in many contemporary debates on democracy – despite their remaining disagreements on democracy. Branting of the Social Democrats, too, turned in his final speech to the rhetoric of reconciliation, suggesting that everyone should have a share and responsibility in the democratisation of the Swedish constitution.[1965] The transition would finally be discussed in the lower house in fairly conciliatory terms, which recalls the Finnish compromise in June 1919 but differs from the German vote of July 1919.

Doubts about democracy had been presented rather modestly by The Right of the lower chamber in November, partly owing to mere frustration. In December, the rightist hardliners expressed their continuous scepticism about democracy, and 37 of them opposed the proposal in the final vote. Edvard Lithander condemned Branting's deliberations on a democratic republic and questioned the argument that changes abroad made democratisation in Sweden necessary, reiterating the rightist interpretation

---

1961 AK, Karl Hildebrand, 26 November 1918, 9:27–8.
1962 AK, Karl Hildebrand, 17 December 1918, 18:44.
1963 AK, Karl Hildebrand, 17 December 1918, 18:45.
1964 AK, Nils Edén, 17 December 1918, 18:55.
1965 AK, Hjalmar Branting, 17 December 1918, 18:57.

that democratisation had already taken place. Such a 'rule by the masses' (*massvälde*) was being created with 'the hasty democratisation' that the people could not accept it. At the very least, 'democracy' demanded a new election before the enactment of the reform.[1966] David Pettersson expressed similar doubts by reporting how 'the Swedish common people in the countryside' – the members of the old peasant estate – were dumbfounded by democratisation and rejected it.[1967] Through his experience of working in Britain and Germany as well as via his British wife, Lithander may have been informed about British opposition Conservative discourse and calls for a new election. His German business contacts, too, were probably suspicious of democratisation.

David Norman, an old anti-socialist, was alarmed about suggestions that the Social Democrats aimed at further democratisation in the future.[1968] Erik Räf, a Junker-like landowner, was provoked by claims that Sweden was about to become the most democratically governed country in the world. Defining himself as a 'democrat', he viewed the reform of 1918 rather as an attempt to introduce Social Democracy and indeed socialism.[1969] Alexander Thore, a high-ranking military officer, likewise presented himself as a 'democrat' but was doubtful about 'the unlimited democracy' or 'the mass democracy which they now aim to establish'.[1970] The Swedish rightists presented themselves as democrats with the same purpose as the British Conservative opponents to universal suffrage and the Finnish monarchists of 1918: to stop the reform by claiming that the current system already constituted democracy. For the representatives of the traditionalist values of The Right, the proposed change in the constitution stood for the destruction of 'democracy' in a nineteenth-century sense, which would limit parliaments to being forums of informed debate. These rightist critics were bitter not only towards the leftist reformists but also towards the leaders of their own party, who seemed to them to be compromising this tradition. However, such opponents within The Right – in line with similar sceptics among British and Finnish conservatives – were unable to prevent the party from assenting to the reform. They nevertheless wished, and were allowed, to express their dissent without anyone bothering to counter their arguments. They were excluded from the mainstream discourse on democracy, which proceeded on leftist terms.

The conception of democracy of Ernst Trygger, the rightist leader of the upper house, had not really changed: he deplored the fact that society could be subverted through the introduction of democratisation by seemingly legal means. Such a transformation could only be allowed because the alternative, 'violent agitation' leading to 'attempts to overthrow the established social order by illegal means', was even worse.[1971] In December, Trygger was still

---

1966 AK, Edvard Lithander, 17 December 1918, 17:40–2.
1967 AK, David Pettersson, 17 December 1918, 17:57.
1968 AK, David Norman, 17 December 1918, 17:36–7.
1969 AK, Erik Räf, 17 December 1918, 18:1–2.
1970 AK, Alexander Thore, 17 December 1918, 18:19.
1971 FK, Ernst Trygger, 26 November 1918, 5:9.

reiterating general rightist concerns about democratisation, complaining about the haste and insisting on a higher age limit for the election of the upper chamber. He found it difficult to believe that democratisation would really strengthen the people so as to allow them to fulfil their responsibilities to the fatherland.[1972] Trygger was unhappy about how 'the democratic principles as embraced by the left' had been used to prevent real compromises with The Right and about the fact that the full democratisation of the First Chamber was also intended.[1973] The implication was that The Right had not really been heard and that the leaders of the party were hence not to blame for the consequences of the unhappy reform.

Even the Deputy Speaker of the First Chamber, Theodor Odelberg, put forward a procedural point against the reform, asking whether there was really 'such a hurry to democratise our country' that the proposal could not be postponed to the next ordinary parliamentary session. His suggestion, not unlike those of Conservative opponents to the suffrage reform in Britain in 1917, was that the members had not known when they had been summoned to the extraordinary parliamentary session that such a consequential constitutional proposal would be introduced 'a few days before Christmas and after the report has been tabled for one day'.[1974] The Swedish constitutional debate did not give rise to so many procedural disagreements as the Finnish one, but in Sweden, too, the opponents of the reform expressed their unhappiness by questioning the legitimacy of the entire procedure.

Samuel Clason, with his authority as a professor of history, vacillated between compromise and scepticism: in November, this old anti-reformist, too, recognised metaphorically that 'a strong democratic wave is currently going across the world' and considered it necessary for The Right to make sacrifices in allowing this process of democratisation to proceed in Sweden. At the same time, he could not avoid reminding the chamber of historical precedents in which 'an unrestrained power of the masses has only too soon led first to anarchy and then to despotism'.[1975] The Right carried on its warnings about democracy, placing responsibility for the consequences of the reform on the shoulders of the left. In December, Clason warned about the risk of the degeneration of democracy into 'demagogy', so that 'the rule of the masses dependent on the moods of the moment, of daily opinion' would rule without there being any constitutional counter-balance[1976] in a strong upper chamber. Karl Ekman feared the consequences of the left continuing to engage in 'constitutional battles' after the reform to take 'democratisation' further.[1977] Harald Hjärne had great difficulty with the entire concept of democratisation: he was positive that many of its advocates would change their minds as soon as they saw the consequences of democratisation

1972 FK, Ernst Trygger, 17 December 1918, 10:15–18.
1973 FK, Ernst Trygger, 17 December 1918, 11:20–1.
1974 FK, Theodor Odelberg, 17 December 1918, 11:16.
1975 FK, Samuel Clason, 26 November 1918, 5:40–1.
1976 FK, Samuel Clason, 17 December 1918, 10:60.
1977 FK, Karl Ekman, 17 December 1918, 11:2.

in Sweden and internationally. Hjärne was uncompromising in his condemnation: appeals to the will of the people in the name of democracy were as unreal as appeals to divine providence had been in autocracies, i.e. democracy in no way advanced modernity. The will of the people produced by 'democratic' elections was a product of manipulation – so the classical accusation against democracy went – and democracy tended to turn into plutocracy or oligarchy or even back to monarchy.[1978] The leading academic ideologists of The Right, whose political theory was closely connected to German thinking, had by no means changed their minds about the character of democracy.

At the same time, several ultra-conservative rightists expressed their anxieties about universal suffrage regardless of the fact that their counter-arguments were unlikely to affect the result. Their arguments included the old rightist contention that democratisation had already taken place. Johan Östberg insisted that previous reforms had already led to democratisation and allowed radicals to gain power at the local level and could not accept the inclusion of what he saw as 'purely Bolshevik features' and 'a democratic autocracy' in the government's proposal.[1979] Herman Wrangel insisted that full equality violated the principles of nature and could never be achieved and that attempts to realise it only led to a barren land and an enslaved people.[1980] Major Aaby Ericsson rejected the future 'rule by the masses', which was likely to lead to a 'forest of barbarians', where all values would be neglected.[1981] Hugo Hammarskjöld, a former minister for ecclesiastical affairs, did not hesitate to declare: 'I am no democrat and am too old to convert. I do not believe in the ability of democracy to make a people happier, and least of all in the type of democracy which is being discussed here and which is likely to soon lead to the rule by the masses.' History had shown the intolerable nature of tyranny from below even in comparison with tyranny from above, and there was a threat that this would happen again if power were given 'into the hands of those who are the least capable of dealing with it.'[1982] Numerous examples show that considerable principled opposition to democracy – and downright anti-democratic ideas – continued to appear in the ranks of the Swedish right; by no means its members had converted to democracy.

The only notable exception within the rightist upper chamber opposition was the former prime minister Carl Swartz. In November 1918 this former opponent of reforms was given the task of conceding on behalf of The Right (as its only clearly positive voice in the First Chamber) that 'the time for the change of our constitution in a purely democratic direction has come' as 'the Swedish people are just as capable as many other peoples of taking care of their affairs under a democratic constitution.'[1983] Swartz had studied in

1978 FK, Harald Hjärne, 17 December 1918, 11:9–10.
1979 FK, Johan Östberg, 26 November 1918, 5:19, 22–3.
1980 FK, Herman Wrangel, 17 December 1918, 10:28.
1981 FK, Aaby Ericsson, 17 December 1918, 10:21.
1982 FK, Hugo Hammarskjöld, 17 December 1918, 10:68–9.
1983 FK, Carl Swartz, 26 November 1918, 5:30.

Bonn, which had made him transnationally informed about developments in Germany – including an understanding of the significance for Sweden of the German transition to democracy after the fall of the Kaiser. Again in December, Swartz was the only rightist in the upper chamber to point out that no one denied the arrival of 'a democratisation of our type of society'.[1984] Other recognitions of the inevitability of the transition were rather half-hearted. Ernst Lindblad, who had played a role in the suffrage compromise of 1907, emphasised the readiness of The Right to award universal suffrage and to welcome 'the victory of democracy' but challenged all endeavours to establish 'Social Democratic omnipotence'.[1985] For Baron Richard Hermelin, 'full democracy' might be acceptable but a 'Social Democratic victory, a Social Democratic majority' that was being prepared with the extension of suffrage was not 'the really genuine democracy' and thus remained unacceptable.[1986] August Bellinder, while recognising that it was impossible to stop the progress of democracy, considered it essential to direct 'the democratic torrent that is roaring on' along lines that it would allow it to benefit and not harm the country. The suggested solution of this conservative, who employed natural metaphors to describe the unavoidable nature of the reform, was the creation of a stronger upper house.[1987] Carl Boberg engaged in word play by referring to 'full citizens' (*fulla medborgare*) and 'full democracy' (*full demokrati*) as they appeared in the proposal, the Swedish adjective *full* meaning both 'complete' and 'intoxicated' or 'drunken'. His hackneyed conservative suggestion thus was that democracy was likely to lack both sense and moderation.[1988] The ability to joke, on the other hand, reflects a recognition among some rightists that the reform would take place in any case and that the best course might be to ridicule it by the means of humour rather than with more serious counter-arguments.

The Liberals, despite being one of the coalition parties and long-term campaigners for reform, were left on the sidelines in these debates. They spoke in principle for a dynamic, progressive and process-like concept of democracy but it was one that had little concrete content. Prime Minister Nils Edén presented his ministry as being in the lead of 'the democratic movement',[1989] while Raoul Hamilton saw 'the great step towards democracy' that was at hand as transferring Sweden 'into a new era, the era of democracy'.[1990] According to the Minister of Public Administration, Axel Schotte, democratisation was to be seen as a medium for further transformation 'which has everywhere and in all times been essential for a society that wishes to live'.[1991] The coalition with the Social Democrats made the Liberals emphasise the common cause and downplay their concerns about the party-political implications of the reformed system.

1984 FK, Carl Swartz, 17 December 1918, 10:25.
1985 FK, Ernst Lindblad, 17 December 1918, 10:37.
1986 FK, Richard Hermelin, 17 December 1918, 10:76.
1987 FK, August Bellinder, 17 December 1918, 10:41.
1988 FK, Carl Boberg, 17 December 1918, 10:80.
1989 FK, Nils Edén, 26 November 1918, 5:14.
1990 AK, Raoul Hamilton, 17 December 1918, 17:33–4.
1991 AK, Axel Schotte, 17 December 1918, 17:8.

Erik Röing, a businessman, welcomed the search for extended democracy within the reformist coalition.[1992] Jakob Pettersson used natural metaphors in a hackneyed way to describe 'the storm wave of democracy that surges all over Europe' and which was impossible to stop.[1993] He advised The Right to accommodate itself to popular demands for democracy while accusing the leftists of idealising Bolshevik rule and its system of soviets.[1994]

On the second round in December, the Prime Minister tried to persuade the upper chamber by emphasising 'the maturity of democracy' which the Swedes had already reached. It could now be realised in 'the gust of this tempestuous time' originating 'from the shaking world around us' (natural metaphors again).[1995] The crisis that threatened from outside would be solved by creating a 'Swedish democracy' at both the national and the local level that would enable the construction of consensus.[1996] The Prime Minister apparently thought that using nationalistic discourse of this kind in defining democracy might persuade The Right:[1997]

> It is only in this way that Sweden can provide space for all of its human forces to present their justified claims and will also have an opportunity to unite all of them into a common effort for the good of the fatherland, . . . On this great and simple truth we base our trust that Swedish democracy will become a medium that will allow Sweden to endure the troubled time which we like other peoples find before us.

Otherwise Liberal members contributed to the debate on a rather general level. Otto von Zweigbergk suggested ironically that for The Right democratisation continued to be 'a veritable Pandora's box containing all the world's ills', whereas the Liberals, as democrats, had been consistently campaigning for a suffrage reform since the 1860s.[1998] Johan Bergman was exceptional in that he saw the abolition of poverty as one of the duties of a democratic state,[1999] thus extending the meaning of 'democracy' in bourgeois circles as well. Carl Gustaf Ekman, the editor-in-chief of *Aftontidningen*, stood out as a defender of bourgeois democracy as opposed to 'the pure line' of democratisation of the far left that had been manifested in foreign examples. Ekman saw good prospects for 'the development of a bourgeois democracy which is ready to realise what it considers to be right' independently of the consequences for its own interests.[2000] This contrast between socialist and bourgeois concepts of democracy is illustrative of the compromise that Liberals in all the countries studied here were searching for.

1992 AK, Erik Röing, 26 November 1918, 9:31.
1993 AK, Jakob Pettersson, 26 November 1918, 9:33.
1994 AK, Jakob Pettersson, 26 November 1918, 9:34.
1995 FK, Nils Edén, 17 December 1918, 10:10.
1996 FK, Nils Edén, 17 December 1918, 10:11.
1997 FK, Nils Edén, 17 December 1918, 10:11.
1998 FK, Otto von Zweigbergk, 17 December 1918, 10:47.
1999 FK, Johan Bergman, 17 December 1918, 10:67.
2000 FK, Carl Gustaf Ekman, 17 December 1918, 11:13.

The leftists did not hide their unhappiness with the democracy that the government had to offer; it would not allow Sweden to reach the degree of democracy of countries which were 'in these days proceeding towards a complete democratic transformation'.[2001] This referred essentially to Germany, where the formation of councils was under way; the German example also questioned the inclusion of monarchy in a future democracy.[2002] In addition to the parliamentary struggle for democratic reforms, the realisation of democracy called for the mobilisation of the Swedish people against the continued resistance from The Right;[2003] this was a further hint at direct action in the name of democracy. Ivar Vennerström attacked the Social Democratic promises of societal development and peace that would result from the reform and called for an extension of the concept of democracy. The proposal did not offer just solutions to 'fundamental democratic problems' as it failed to give everyone (especially the young) equal rights to participate in decision-making; no 'full democracy' would thus be achieved. The constitution should rather have been wholly rethought and made an instrument for achieving a 'socialist republic'.[2004] Fredrik Ström saw the new era as calling for progress 'towards a far more distinct and complete democracy' than the one that the government proposed. Democracy should be realised in Sweden through a constituent national assembly – as the intention had been in revolutionary Russia, as had been demanded in Finland in autumn 1917 and as was expected to happen in revolutionary Germany. Such an assembly would introduce a unicameral parliament and proceed to political, social and economic reforms that would extend democracy beyond mere suffrage.[2005] Ström also complained that The Right had prevailed over the Social Democrats at a moment when real advances in democracy could have been made, calling not only for 'constitutional democracy' instead of monarchy but also for 'social and economic democracy';[2006] here he was possibly motivated by similar calls from the German Social Democrats and especially the council movement as well as by universal expectations among the radicals that the revolution would be carried further. However, the Social Democrats would win the vote and would dominate the discourse on democracy and Swedish politics more generally in the decades to come, and the other parties would accept their interpretation of democracy, which would be extended to practically all areas of societal life.

2001 AK, Ivar Vennerström, 26 November 1918, 9:15.
2002 AK, Ivar Vennerström, 26 November 1918, 9:16.
2003 AK, Ivar Vennerström, 26 November 1918, 9:18.
2004 AK, Ivar Vennerström, 17 December 1918,17:61, 71; 17 December 1918, 18:36. Arthur Engberg responded by pointing out that the basic problems of democracy would indeed be solved with the introduction of universal suffrage. 17 December 1918, 17:76.
2005 FK, Fredrik Ström, 26 November 1918, 5:35.
2006 FK, Fredrik Ström, 17 December 1918, 10:42, 45.

6.3.4 THE RELATIONSHIP BETWEEN THE WILL OF 'THE PEOPLE' AND THE INTERESTS OF 'THE REALM' IS PROBLEMATISED

A special feature of the Swedish reform debates of late 1918 was the contrasting use of the collective concepts of the people and the realm. The parties of the left had long been calling for a clearer engagement of the people in politics via universal suffrage and possibly referenda, but their endeavours had been thwarted by the rightist majority in the upper house using arguments that the real people were already represented. Even after the fall of the old order in Germany, idealised by many members of the Swedish right, they remained unwilling to redefine the concept 'the people', which reflects continuities in conceptions of estate representation as opposed to democratic parliamentary one.

For leftists such as Ivar Vennerström, the people were the agent that should decide about the future form of government. The Right should trust the Swedish people and give them full civic rights since the people would take those rights for themselves anyway.[2007] Fredrik Ström declared that 'the great, deep mass of the people' would soon liberate themselves and establish a new social order,[2008] a prediction that sounded very revolutionary in the ears of The Right.

Hjalmar Branting of the Social Democrats was equally clear about the relationship between the people and political power. According to him, the Swedish people as a whole were considering whether they were[2009]

> ready to really take the final determined step and let democracy prevail and reject privileges which have all too long restrained the wide layers of the people from enjoying the right which they can justifiably demand: a proper influence on the formation of the political community.

Extra-parliamentary popular means were used by the Social Democrats to put pressure on The Right during the process of persuasion, and Branting declared: 'Now it is *demanded* outside among the people' (*nu vill man ute bland folket*, original emphasis) that the reform be implemented.[2010] Branting argued that the government and the parliament were only allowing 'the Swedish people in these circumstances to take the decisive step forward towards democratisation' which they had demanded for a long time, a transition that was also prompted by external pressures;[2011] the point here was that internal forces were more important than external ones. More far-sighted Social Democratic visions were also presented: for Harald Hallén, 17 December 1918 meant that 'the politically and morally thinking people' of Sweden 'are lifted onto a higher level and obtain a lasting accretion of power that is of invaluable importance'.[2012] Party Secretary Gustav Möller talked about a future when the Social Democratic Party would have a majority

---

2007 AK, Ivar Vennerström, 26 November 1918, 9:16–17.
2008 FK, Fredrik Ström, 26 November 1918, 5:36.
2009 AK, Hjalmar Branting, 26 November 1918, 9:19.
2010 AK, Hjalmar Branting, 26 November 1918, 9:24.
2011 AK, Hjalmar Branting, 17 December 1918, 17:22.
2012 AK, Harald Hallén, 17 December 1918, 17:56.

in the parliament and be able to make the goals of the party a reality.[2013] The party was already seen as victorious even though the debates on the reform were still going on. When Arvid Lindman of The Right maintained that 'allowing the people to state their opinion' through new elections would be the correct way to proceed,[2014] this produced an ironic response from Arthur Engberg, who referred to this recognition of the need to subject the political balance of power to the determination of the people as a whole in the future.[2015]

Liberal contributions to the subject of the political role of the people were extensive in comparison with the other themes studied here. Jakob Pettersson turned to patronising irony in criticising the negative attitude of The Right towards 'popular movements': The Right had simply held political and administrative power for so long that they could not accommodate themselves to present-day realities. His recommendation was that they should attempt to recognise the strong reform demands of 'the mighty popular movement' that was changing Sweden and contributing to the common good of the entire country.[2016] Petterson's analysis may well have been accurate: even stronger suggestions about the right defending the inherited privileges of the civil service were heard in Finland, and the two countries had a lot in common (also with Prussia) as far as the central role of administrators in politics was concerned.

In the argumentative battle over suffrage reform in December 1918, Axel Schotte, the Liberal minister responsible for public administration, defined the constitutional reform as realising 'the will of the people' so that 'the Swedish people may henceforth have full possibilities to shape their destinies on their own'.[2017] According to other leading Liberals, too, 'power has been given into the hands of the people', and the Swedish people deserved this transition of power just like many other European peoples.[2018] From a Liberal point of view, the Swedish people were mature enough to use power responsibly, respecting law and justice and were ready to reject all attempts to contravene justice with violence.[2019] The Right could appeal to old traditions of representation, but the fact was that they did not serve the needs of modern times. Some reservations were nevertheless expressed: Johan Bergman believed in the superiority of democracy even though he could not regard the people as 'perfect or flawless' and consequently called for 'an intensive and increased general instruction of the people' through the reformation of school education.[2020] According to Edvard Alkman, editor-in-chief of *Göteborgs-Posten*, the reform finally reconstructed the Swedish

---

2013 AK, Gustav Möller, 17 December 1918, 17:44.
2014 AK, Arvid Lindman, 17 December 1918, 17:18.
2015 AK, Arthur Engberg, 17 December 1918, 17:74.
2016 AK, Jakob Pettersson, 26 November 1918, 9:33–5.
2017 AK, Axel Schotte, 17 December 1918, 17:8.
2018 AK, Raoul Hamilton, 17 December 1918, 17:33; Nils Edén, 17 December 1918, 18:55.
2019 AK, Raoul Hamilton, 17 December 1918, 17:33; FK, Carl Fredrik Holmquist, 17 December 1918, 10:36.
2020 FK, Johan Bergman, 17 December 1918, 10:67.

constitution to include the people: 'The Swedish people want to move into this house in a such way that they cannot anymore be set aside or ousted.'[2021] Minister of Justice Eliel Löfgren was assured that, as a consequence of the reform, 'the great mass of our people . . . has a more secure foundation for their hopes in the future.'[2022] In Sweden, Liberal optimism about the people was more considerable and united than was the case in Germany, Finland or even Britain.

The final debate saw a further semantic battle over what 'the people' stood for. The Liberal Prime Minister, redefining the relationship between the realm and the people, challenged the traditionalist rightist conceptions of the nature of the political community as a *realm*, a concept that had been extensively used in the November debate. According to Nils Edén, 'the Swedish realm depends nevertheless on the Swedish people', and the two needed to be conceptually united so that 'the existence and future of the realm is placed on the shoulders of the entire people.'[2023] Edén thus succinctly expressed the very core of the spirit of the reform.

Whether Arvid Lindman of The Right agreed with such a definition remained far from clear: he did hope that the reform would benefit 'the people of Sweden and the realm of Sweden'[2024] but this suggested no explicit connection between the two concepts; he preferred to retain their conceptual distinction. MPs from The Right were generally displeased about continuous pressurising with references to the extra-parliamentary popular will – particularly as the party had already decided to capitulate and accept constitutional changes that could make 'broad layers of the people directly responsible for the fates of countries.'[2025]

Even Karl Hildebrand, the leader of the lower house opposition, continued to express doubts about the political consequences of 'a rise in the power and strength of the people.'[2026] He did not mean 'the elimination of the will of the people in decisions on the fate of the country' but rather called for 'aspirations to produce a more mature popular will.'[2027] Particularly irritating for him was Ivar Vennerström's suggestion that the people would rise against The Right, a use of the concept of the people that appeared to Hildebrand to refer to only a particular section of the people (the workers) and not necessarily to the majority; it seemed to exclude the peasants and the merchant class (the burghers) – the traditional non-noble estates of the realm – from 'the people.'[2028] The suggestion was that the street demonstrations of the workers mobilised by the left did not provide sufficient evidence of the will of the people and that extraordinary parliamentary elections were

2021 FK, Edvard Alkman, 17 December 1918, 10:62.
2022 AK, Eliel Löfgren, 17 December 1918, 18:41; see also Carl Gustaf Ekman, FK, 17 December 1918, 11:12.
2023 AK, Nils Edén, 17 December 1918, 18:55.
2024 AK, Arvid Lindman, 17 December 1918, 18:56.
2025 AK, Karl Hildebrand, 26 November 1918, 9:25.
2026 AK, Karl Hildebrand, 26 November 1918, 9:26. David Norman, too, was concerned about 'a spirit of revolt among the people', 26 November 1918, 9:49.
2027 AK, Karl Hildebrand, 26 November 1918, 9:27.
2028 AK, Karl Hildebrand, 26 November 1918, 9:28.

needed. This rightist argument built on a very traditionalist concept of the people, indeed on that of 'the common people' in an early modern sense of estate representation.

Edvard Lithander, chairman of the conservative cultural association *Götiska Förbundet*, tried to redescribe the state of affairs on the basis of this traditionalist concept by suggesting that the Prime Minister himself was not respecting 'the will of the people' by not ordering new elections.[2029] David Norman questioned the validity of appeals to the will of the people in the proposal as being based on a concept deliberately constructed by the left:[2030]

> [W]hat is then this Swedish people or the great layers of the Swedish people that is referred to here? Is it all the Swedish people? Is it a genuine representation of the people of Sweden that has demanded these profound constitutional reforms? I can only imagine that this demand has received its expression partly in the radical press and partly in statements made in popular meetings.

Only the workers and not the peasantry, the largest class, had been consulted, and there was thus no question of the genuine voice of the people being heard. This claim, which was based on a long native tradition of appeals to the people, would be elaborated by the rightist opposition in the upper house in December. In late November, Ernst Trygger bypassed the concept of the people in his speech, while Carl Swartz, a former prime minister, was again the only rightist leader to express his trust in the Swedish people being able to govern themselves under a democratic constitution.[2031]

The Social Democrats interpreted the rightist demands for new election as an unwillingness to bend before the will of the majority of the people and as a desire to reject the reform once again. The Right, or ironically 'the legal guardians of the people', seemed willing to simply ignore what the people had said in the election of autumn 1917 despite the limitations to suffrage that had then been in force.[2032] The Right also seemed to be misusing warning examples from abroad in order to frighten the people away from attempting to create a 'people's state' (*folkstat*)[2033] – this term was an obvious literal translation from the contemporary German discourse on democracy as a *Volksstaat* (which appeared in subsections 6.2.4. and 6.2.6 above and the connotations of which are discussed in subsections 7.2.3 and 7.4.4; see also the discussion of the Finnish word *kansanvaltio* in subsection 7.4.4).

Most speakers of The Right continued to criticise leftist definitions of the people. David Norman could not accept suggestions that Sweden lacked popular freedom,[2034] whereas David Pettersson accused the government of agitating panic among the people.[2035] Karl Hildebrand was the only one to

2029 AK, Edvard Lithander, 26 November 1918, 9:37.
2030 AK, David Norman, 26 November 1918, 9:37.
2031 FK, Carl Swartz, 26 November 1918, 5:30.
2032 AK, Per Albin Hansson, 26 November 1918, 9:45; Arthur Engberg, 26 November 1918, 9:53; FK, Ernst Klefbeck, 26 November 1918, 5:27.
2033 AK, Arthur Engberg, 26 November 1918, 9:51.
2034 AK, David Norman, 17 December 1918, 17:37.
2035 AK, David Pettersson, 17 December 1918, 17:57.

recognise that the social groups which The Right represented were about to 'relinquish their status as political leaders'.[2036] He conceded at the same time that there were plenty of good forces 'in the great mass of the people of Sweden'.[2037] However, he challenged the government's use of the concept 'the will of the people' as a motivation for the reform, suspecting that only the class interests of the workers had been allowed to define 'the will of the people', which he described as 'a phrase of popular meetings' (*folkmötesfras*). Class interests threatened to characterise democracy. The Right agreed that 'the people should be the lord in its own house', but it remained unclear what exactly the ministers meant by 'the popular will'. From the point of view of The Right, the risk of 'the primitive and immature popular will' taking over remained, and this made Hildebrand doubt whether democracy would strengthen the people in the end.[2038]

Ernst Trygger complained in the upper house about 'a strongly overexcited popular mood', which complicated the solution of constitutional issues.[2039] A conceptual contrast with the Prime Minister's speech became evident when he presented the future of 'the realm' as the key issue and called on the Swedish people to 'fulfil their duties to the fatherland' – the concepts 'the realm' and 'the people' being kept distinctly separate. In Trygger's view, the Swedish people could only benefit from the reform if the considerable power that was placed in the hands of 'the broad layers of the people' was used 'under a living feeling of love of the fatherland and duty to the common good'.[2040] All of these formulations suggest that the traditionalist conceptual world of the rightist leader had not been modified under the pressures of constitutional reform: in conservative ideology, the people remained subordinate to the realm and the fatherland, the interests of which were primary and those of individual social groups secondary.

Some highly conservative ideas continued to be expressed in the final debate as many rightists wanted to have their dissenting opinion recorded at the end of a legislative process the result of which they viewed with considerable doubt. Professor Harald Hjärne unashamedly insisted that the extension of suffrage 'to large new masses of the people' threatened the Swedish polity as a whole.[2041] For this leading historian, 'the will of the people' was no more than 'a mere metaphysical' concept with no obvious equivalent in political reality.[2042] Hjärne's rejection of the popular will as a foundation for political power illustrates that no fundamental transition to democracy had taken place in the mental world of the Swedish right – academic or not – withstanding the compromise which would be soon approved in the upper chamber.

2036 AK, Karl Hildebrand, 17 December 1918, 18:43.
2037 AK, Karl Hildebrand, 17 December 1918, 18:45.
2038 AK, Karl Hildebrand, 17 December 1918, 18:44.
2039 FK, Ernst Trygger, 17 December 1918, 10:13. Agitators were accused also by FK, Jöns Jesperson, 17 December 1918, 11:15.
2040 FK, Ernst Trygger, 17 December 1918, 10:18.
2041 FK, Harald Hjärne, 17 December 1918, 11:9.
2042 FK, Harald Hjärne, 17 December 1918, 11:10.

Baron Richard Hermelin challenged the use of the concept 'the people' in the government's arguments for its proposal and its earlier employment by Carl Swartz of The Right as well: their 'people' only stood for the Swedish working class, and even the Swedish workers and the Social Democrats were not the same thing. Hermelin, a factory-owner, claimed that many workers associated themselves with the common people, the peasantry, who had been completely ignored and 'sacrificed' in the preparation of this bill.[2043] Nils Åkesson, a farmer and thus a spokesman for those people who had not been heard, joined the debate, insisting that only tax-payers constituted the people in a political sense: civic rights should be dependent on the performance of civic duties. This connection would no longer be realised under 'the rule of the masses'.[2044] The same view was heard from Adolf Lindgren, a representative of the rising class of successful entrepreneurs (at least three of whom appear as anything but democrats in this discussion, which questions the claim about industrialists having converted to support the reform); he claimed that the majority of the Swedish people would have rejected the removal of tax limits had they been asked in elections. In Lindberg's rhetoric, 'the century-old constitution of the country' was 'such an invaluable property of the people' that 'their representatives in the parliament' had no right to discard it 'without listening to the people and receiving their consent'.[2045] Indeed, from this agrarian and entrepreneurial conservative perspective, the entire reform appeared to be a parliamentary violation of the rights of the Swedish people rather than an extension of them. The only solution which the rightists regarded as legitimate was to hold new elections under the old suffrage system.

Aaby Ericsson likewise continued to emphasise 'the daylight-clear right of the Swedish people' to have new election when 'their representatives are sacrificing the true and future good of their native land'.[2046] Ericsson could see a positive future only in what he considered to be the likely continuity of old peasant values: 'the Swedish tribe is healthy and based on that section of the Swedish people with landed property'. According to Ericsson, the peasantry would once again draw together the other sections of the people who wished to preserve the political community,[2047] ensuring the continuity of the established political order against the questionable masses. Alexis Hammarström, Governor of the County of Kronoberg, likewise insisted that the peasantry, always ready to consider the common good, formed 'the core of the people' and that their wishes differed from those of the group that the left meant when talking about 'the people'.[2048]

Interestingly, even Carl Swartz, who had clearly recognised the necessity of the reform, agreed with Ericsson that the Swedish people were exceptionally

---

2043 FK, Richard Hermelin, 17 December 1918, 10:77.
2044 FK, Nils Åkesson, 17 December 1918, 11:11.
2045 FK, Adolf Lindgren, 17 December 1918, 11:14.
2046 FK, Aaby Ericsson, 17 December 1918, 10:21.
2047 FK, Aaby Ericsson, 17 December 1918, 10:22.
2048 FK, Alexis Hammarström, 17 December 1918, 10:57.

well prepared to meet the consequences of the reform[2049] – either because he genuinely thought so or to persuade fellow members of The Right to accept the compromise anyway. Karl Ekman by contrast, combined an expression of his appreciation of the Swedish people with a protest on power being given to only one group of the masses, i.e. the workers, without first asking the 'people' proper in an election.[2050]

The Right continued to defend the established political order using the term 'the people' as applicable to an estate society. On the side of the Social Democrats, their suggestions that only the peasantry could be counted on were received as defamatory of the workers. Ernst Söderberg asserted that the latter, too, were aware of their responsibilities to their country. Allowing the workers to 'be full participants in their native land' would only increase their sense of responsibility.[2051] Mauritz Hellberg lamented the unwillingness of The Right to rethink their policy, which had, according to him, been characterised throughout by 'distrust of the lower layers of our people' and had been counter-productive in that it had only caused negative reactions among the excluded.[2052]

The oft-repeated agrarian and estate-based understanding of the Swedish nation was a manifestation not only of the Swedish conservatives' desperate opposition but also of the continuing early-modern conception of society that prevailed among them. The fact that the Swedish constitution dated from 1809 and that subsequent parliamentary reforms had maintained a considerable peasant element in the parliament had contributed to the continuity of this agrarian conception of the political community, one which can hardly be seen as consistent with democracy in any twentieth-century sense. Similar ultra-traditionalist views were also held among the representatives of the Finnish right, as can be seen in the notion of a peasant king advocated by the monarchists in summer and autumn 1918 and among some Swedish-speaking traditionalists still in summer 1919.[2053] This notion was mostly rejected by Finnish-speaking farmers as represented by the Agrarian League. It needs to be added, however, that there were also individual Swedish rightists, such as the former foreign minister Knut Agathon Wallenberg, who had 'an unwavering belief in the good sense of the Swedish people and their love of their country' and who were ready to support the proposal without qualification.[2054] However, surprisingly few rightists were able to voice an unreservedly positive attitude to universal suffrage aloud, Swartz and Wallenberg being the only exceptions in the upper chamber.

2049 FK, Carl Swartz, 17 December 1918, 10:26.
2050 FK, Karl Ekman, 17 December 1918, 11:4.
2051 FK, Ernst Söderberg, 17 December 1918, 10:75.
2052 FK, Mauriz Hellberg, 17 December 1918, 11:8.
2053 In the royal election, the motion was proposed by a Finnish-speaking farmer, which was supposed to demonstrate that both the intellectual elite and the *whole* peasantry supported a monarchy. *Hufvudstadsbladet*, 'Inför avgörandet', 8 October 1918, 'Regeringsform och konungaval', 10 October 1918.
2054 FK, Knut Agathon Wallenberg, 17 December 1918, 10:40–1.

6.3.5 Parliamentarism under democratised suffrage

The reform debates of autumn 1918 concerned democracy and the political role of the people rather than parliamentarism as such. No particular need to discuss the concept was felt: it had become difficult for The Right to openly dispute its principles once a parliamentary government had been in office since autumn 1917, parliamentary democracies had won the war, and even Germany was being transformed into a parliamentary democracy. The victory of the reformists, both internationally and nationally, was so undeniable that the rightist opposition did not question parliamentarism to the extent that its counterparts had done in Finland and continued to do so in Germany and they themselves had done on previous reform rounds.

The Swedish Social Democrats willingly presented themselves as dedicated defenders of parliamentarism – not only in comparison with other countries and in relation to The Right but also among socialists in Sweden. In spring 1917 and again in spring 1918, Branting had suggested that a delay in passing the reform might lead to the adoption of extra-parliamentary means by radical forces, at the same time emphasising that his party only opted for parliamentary means. In November 1918, this 'communist card' was used by Minister of Finance Fredrik Vilhelm Thorsson, a former radical agitator. According to Thorsson, two varieties of socialism coexisted in Sweden: one group was more than prepared to 'go the extra-parliamentary way forward in order to reach the goal which they have set for themselves'. The other line wanted 'to increase their influence in the municipalities, the regions and the parliament, and to try to construct [a new society] by making decisions one at a time'.[2055] It went without saying that the former line was Bolshevism as represented by the far left, while the latter was parliamentary democracy as represented by the Social Democrats. As for The Right, they had to choose between these alternatives: if The Right were to say 'no' again, that might give a decisive push to those who were enamoured of the extra-parliamentary alternative, leading to a much worse scenario than the one provided by the well-organised and moderate Social Democrats, who had demonstrated their capacity to engage in parliamentary work.[2056] In the circumstances of late November 1918, few among The Right disputed this analysis. Many knew, after all, that it was not only in Russia that Bolshevism had taken over and that leftist radicalism had made an unsuccessful attempt in Finland and was making progress in Germany as well. In these circumstances, it might indeed make sense to give in to the Social Democratic and Liberal proposal if that would halt any further radicalisation – although of course there was no certainty that it would do so. No speaker questioned the existence of a Bolshevist threat, but some continued to be concerned about the possibility of extra-parliamentary measures or to question the legitimacy of the observed parliamentary procedure.

The reactions of the far left to the compromise reached between the left and the right served as evidence that they were tending to become increasingly

---

2055 AK, Fredrik Vilhelm Thorsson, 26 November 1918, 5:42.
2056 AK, Fredrik Vilhelm Thorsson, 26 November 1918, 5:42–3.

radicalised[2057] and work outside the parliamentary system. Fabian Månsson attacked the academics of The Right for their 'doctrine of minority rule' by referring to German academic literature, which was supposedly highly regarded by the professors and which argued that 'parliamentarism is mere humbug, that the power of the people is a mere joke – that the power of the minority is the only one that is good enough!'[2058] Fredrik Ström said that the planned watered-down reform was likely to benefit the anti-parliamentarian syndicalist movement. He foresaw an increased struggle both in- and outside the parliament to rectify the lack of social and economic democracy, as these were issues that were likely to divide parties in the parliament and as the workers would shift the emphasis of their struggle to the labour market once the parliament had proved unable to solve their problems.[2059] The extra- and even anti-parliamentary tendencies of the far left came into the open, recalling the theoretical debate among German Socialists[2060] and radicalised Social Democracy in Finland in 1917.

Most majority Social Democrats considered it best to live with the compromise, in spite of its shortcomings. Per Albin Hansson wanted to proceed further by calling in an internationalist Marxist fashion for the parliamentarisation of foreign policy. Hansson wanted to see an institution that would not only be informed about what had already been done or what was being prepared but a parliament that would actually decide on foreign policy. A permanent committee for foreign affairs taking part in decision-making would not suffice: the parliament should be allowed to control foreign policy and the people allowed to control the parliament. This could only be done by extending the public discussion of foreign policy matters. The goal was to bring secret diplomacy, as experienced during the war, to an end.[2061] Hansson's views represent an idealism that appeared in all the parliaments studied here in the aftermath of the First World War. It was shared not only by internationally oriented Social Democrats but also by some Liberals. However, while standing committees were introduced in many countries, little was done to properly parliamentarise foreign policy.[2062] Attempts to transnationalise foreign policy through the League of Nations would have equally modest results.

Conservative concerns about parliamentarism had not entirely withered away as a result of the experiences of parliamentary work after autumn 1917 or the outcome of the First World War. Karl Hildebrand, although the voice of the compromise-willing rightists in the parliament, still had his suspicions that a democratically elected parliament might adopt economic measures that could lead to disastrous consequences.[2063]

2057 Ivar Vennerström forecast that the shortcomings of the reform would only lead to the rise of anti-parliamentarism. AK, 17 December 1918, 17:66.
2058 AK, Fabian Månsson, 17 December 1918, 18:27.
2059 FK, Fredrik Ström, 17 December 1918, 10:44, 46.
2060 Jörke & Llanque 2016.
2061 AK, Per Albin Hansson, 17 December 1918, 18:35–6.
2062 See Ihalainen & Matikainen 2016.
2063 AK, Karl Hildebrand, 26 November 1918, 5:27.

Some other members continued to raise procedural points, questioning the legitimacy of introducing the reform in this particular session. Per Andersson claimed that the rapid procedural actions after mid-November had failed to provide sufficient time for deliberation and could not hence be regarded as 'parliamentary'.[2064] Ernst Trygger claimed that the introduction of the proposal differed from what constitutional changes demanded and questioned 'the so-called parliamentarism' of the parties of the left, which aimed at pushing the reform through without allowing the people to vote about it first in an election.[2065] The worst kind of rightist scenario was presented by Ollas Anders Ericsson, who warned the Swedes of 'extra-parliamentary adventures' that would have the disastrous consequences that had been seen in revolutionary Russian and were expected to soon follow in Germany as well.[2066]

Noteworthy in the comments of the opposition right is that parliamentarism as a principle was no longer attacked. However, disagreements between the Swedish right and left about the proper form of parliamentary government had by no means been resolved by the compromise of November and December 1918; these would need to be negotiated in the years to come. In Finland, the right and the centre were in even deeper disagreement in autumn 1918.

6.4 The monarchist majority of the Finnish Rump Parliament in search of a stable polity

6.4.1 THE STRANGE LOGIC OF FINNISH CONSTITUTIONAL POLITICS IN LATE SUMMER AND AUTUMN 1918

The attempts of the monarchist majority of the post-Civil-War Finnish Rump Parliament to introduce a reformulated monarchical constitution during summer 1918 were prevented by a republican parliamentary minority on 7 August under minority provisions, which stipulated that a constitutional proposal could only be declared urgent with a 5/6 majority and accepted with a 2/3 majority; that was not the case, and a new election was needed instead. Since the monarchist ministry did not want a republican victory in such an election, it started preparations for the election of a king on the basis of paragraph 38 of the Swedish Form of Government of 1772. This constitutional law had already been used by the bourgeois parties in November 1917 to justify parliamentary sovereignty, although the republicans had remained sceptical about its applicability. When the Rump Parliament decided on the election on 9 August 1918, it was clear that a German prince was being sought, regardless of a major setback in the German war effort on the preceding day. News of developments in the West (and on the constitutional changes

---

2064 AK, Per Andersson, 17 December 1918, 18:34.
2065 FK, Ernst Trygger, 17 December 1918, 10:12–14.
2066 FK, Ollas Anders Ericsson, 17 December 1918, 10:23.

in Germany in early October[2067]) were simply disregarded. The German General Staff understandably remained supportive of the project. After the parliament did not pass the constitutional proposals to establish a monarchy, a legalistic approach was adopted and stubbornly followed regardless of the course of international affairs. Even difficulties in finding a suitable candidate during the rising military and domestic crisis in Germany did not stop the monarchists. In early September, Friedrich Karl of Hesse, the brother-in-law of Kaiser Wilhelm, gave his consent to the election, ignoring claims from the German left and the Finnish republicans that the election procedure was questionable and that he risked never enjoying the support of the majority of the Finnish people. After the postponement of a further monarchical proposal, which would have included ministerial responsibility to the parliament, the election took place. The monarchists paid no heed to Santeri Alkio of the Agrarians appealing to constitutional changes in Germany and declaring that republicanism rather than monarchism was the true connection between Finland and the new Germany, which now had a centre-left government. Nevertheless, as late as 9 October 1918, after a vote (64 to 41) on whether or not to proceed, the election took place. In a secret session, after a heated debate and a republican boycott, the Finnish parliament was nominally unanimous in choosing Friedrich Karl King of Finland with merely 64 MPs out of 200 attending.[2068]

The election was forced through regardless of the fact that the German army leaders had informed the Reichstag that the war would not be won and that the German government had declared its readiness to negotiate on the basis of Wilson's demands.[2069] Even the nomination of Max von Baden and the expected constitutional rearrangements did not stop the monarchists, while the republicans were encouraged by the German liberals and left to carry on their opposition in the expectation of major domestic and foreign

---

2067 *Helsingin Sanomat*, 'Waltiollinen pula Saksassa', 4 October 1918. On 5 October 1918, an article 'Tyska regeringskrisens avveckling' in *Hufvudstadsbladet*, reported about 'a new political development in German political life', but without making any connection with the coming Finnish royal election. On the following day, summaries of items in German papers in an article entitled 'Krisens avveckling i Tyskland' suggested that parliamentarism had been introduced in Germany but that more was demanded by democratic forces of the left and the centre. See also 'Regeringskrisens avveckling i Tyskland', 8 October 1918. There was thus clearly sufficient information in Finland about constitutional developments in Germany. *Suomen Sosialidemokraatti* had already argued in 'Monarkistit huolissaan' on 4 October 1918 that the German reforms removed the basis for a monarchy in Finland and suggested on 5 October 1918 in 'Waikutelmia Saksasta' that the German intervention in the constitutional question had been initiated by Finns and that the majority in the Reichstag were opposed to the candidacy of Friedrich Karl.

2068 Aspelmeier 1967, 69–70, 72; Huldén 1989, 180; Sihvonen 1997, 12–13, 30; Jussila, Hentilä & Nevakivi 1999, 124; Vares 2006, 123, 126–8.

2069 Sondhaus 2011, 433.

policy changes.²⁰⁷⁰ Republican opposition was not allowed to obstruct the nominally legal process, which aimed at the establishment of a strong monarchy following the Swedish Gustavian and German imperial traditions. The eighteenth-century constitution was to be commended precisely because of its permanence and its ability to develop increased parliamentary participation.²⁰⁷¹ Nevertheless, the stubbornness of the Finnish right in proceeding to a royal election at a time when Reds, vanquished in the Civil War, languished in prison camps, provoked amazement in the Entente and protests by the German left against the German government, which was supporting the White Finnish government (see subsection 6.2.2 above).

6.4.2 A CONTROVERSY OVER THE EXCESSIVE TRANSNATIONAL INFLUENCE OF GERMANY

The international situation continued to be interpreted by the monarchists in ways that supported their constitutional goals. Speaking to the parliament on 7 August 1918, Prime Minister J. K. Paasikivi (Finnish Party) rejected republican suggestions about the unavoidability of democratisation, quoting constitutional comparisons made by Professor Gustav von Schmoller, a social reformist and a leading figure of the German historical school of economics, who sat in the Prussian Herrenhaus. Schmoller had concluded that states that combined a hereditary monarchy with a free constitution and institutions were the most likely to prosper thanks to the moderation of class confrontations – which certainly existed and needed to be addressed in Finland. According to the Prime Minister, conservative, centralising and state-strengthening currents (like those in Germany before the collapse of the Western Front on the same day) would dominate after the war, and Finland should adapt itself to such a world. The German example demonstrated, furthermore, that democracy was entirely reconcilable with constitutional monarchy, whereas in the leading republics – France and the United States – it had been eclipsed by plutocracy.²⁰⁷²

The Speaker of the Rump Parliament, Paavo Virkkunen (who was not in the chair at the time), a member of the same Finnish Party, associated the internationalist character of socialism with republicanism and rejected both. The Bolsheviks and their Finnish collaborators had aimed at establishing 'a Red reign of terror and a branch of the Russian Revolution'. The idea of a republic had been imported into Finland by the Russian Revolution, the assumption of the revolutionaries being that the Finnish republic would be both revolutionary and socialist.²⁰⁷³ Virkkunen claimed

---

2070 Huldén 1989, 180; Vares 2006, 126; in article column entitled 'Från kammare och kuloar', *Hufvudstadsbladet* ridiculed the Agrarians for being simple-minded in their interpretations of German domestic and foreign policies and accused them of abusing the contingency of politics, 10 October 1918.

2071 *Hufvudstadsbladet*, 'Tärningen är kastad', 10 August 1918.

2072 VP, Juho Kusti Paasikivi, 7 August 1918, 1815–17. Plutocracy in the American republic was also rejected by VP, Anshelm Sjöstedt-Jussila (Finnish), 7 August 1918, 1841; Bruendel 2003, 187, 242–3.

2073 VP, Paavo Virkkunen, 7 August 1918, 1821.

that neither socialism[2074] nor republicanism had any national basis but were mere imports and implied that the republicans were advancing the cause of socialism – or were actually socialists in disguise, as *Hufvudstadsbladet* frequently claimed.[2075] Finnish independence had been achieved through a struggle against the Russian Revolution and its Bolshevik ideas in the Civil War, Virkkunen argued.[2076] According to Wilhelmi Malmivaara, the Red rebels continued to claim in the Russian and Swedish press that Finland's revolution was still continuing.[2077] For these Old Finns, Finland was located in the nexus of great power interests and forced to choose sides; for them that meant pro-German monarchism. Virkkunen viewed a thousand years of monarchy in Germany and the current supremacy of the country as the proper model for solving the Finnish constitutional situation and insisted that the Finns stood united in alliance with Germany. The Entente provided no relevant constitutional models; instead it was preparing an intervention in Finland by plotting to introduce a republican constitution and thereby distance Finland from Germany.[2078] The implication was that all republicans were advancing the cause of Western republicanism. Other Old Finns echoed related views: according to Oswald Kairamo, Otto von Bismarck had been right when he had supposedly proclaimed that 'the fate of the world will be solved with blood and iron' and not with parliamentary procedures. The world war had been such a battle between cultures, ideologies, eras. In contrast to the old cultural and ideological links with Germany as well as concrete help from there, Britain and France were trying to prevent the establishment of a monarchy supported by Germany, 'our only reliable friend in the world'.[2079] For Waldemar Bergroth, too, the adoption of a republican constitution implied the rejection of German help, dependence on the Entente and the restoration of Russian oppression. No republic, furthermore, was capable of providing the kind of welfare for the lower orders that was ensured by monarchical Germany.[2080] The Finnish Party was uncritically pro-German, just as the British press claimed, and its conservative views were frequently articulated by Lutheran clergymen (three of the preceding speakers were vicars).

In the midst of this pro-German and monarchist rhetorical offensive, the republicans lacked convincing foreign examples because republics were generally fighting on the side of the Entente. Germany was hence the source of arguments for them as well. Eero Hahl of the Agrarians suggested that

---

2074 Cf. Santeri Alkio's point on the un-Finnish origins of Social Democracy in the same debate: VP, 7 August 1918, 1849.
2075 *Hufvudstadsbladet*, 'Brådskande afgörande', 7 August 1918; 'Politisk nihilism', 9 August 1918; 'Agrarerna och frågan om statsskicket', 6 October 1918.
2076 VP, Paavo Virkkunen, 7 August 1918, 1822–3.
2077 VP, Wilhelmi Malmivaara, 7 August 1918, 1837.
2078 VP, Paavo Virkkunen, 7 August 1918, 1822–3.
2079 VP, Oswald Kairamo, 7 August 1918, 1824–5. Essentially the same pro-German views were presented by Pekka Paavolainen (Young Finns) on 7 August 1918, 1832, and Wilhelmi Malmivaara (Finnish Party) on 7 August 1918, 1837. On Entente plotting, see Tekla Hultin, 8 August 1918, 1867.
2080 VP, Waldemar Bergroth, 7 August 1918, 1840.

the development in Germany was towards increased democracy as could be seen in wartime promises for the extension of suffrage there.[2081] Antti Juutilainen insinuated that it was Finns rather than the Germans themselves that were behind the wishes expressed by Germany concerning the Finnish constitution.[2082] One solution might be to hold a referendum on the form of government, as had been done in Norway, with Switzerland providing another example of frequent use of the referendum.[2083] The Young Finns referred to republican examples from the Entente as well. K. J. Ståhlberg presented the Finnish situation as analogous with that of France in 1871: the country had been declared a republic during a revolution but had not yet received a republican constitution.[2084] Such a claim was dismissed by R. A. Wrede with the authority of a former rector of the University of Helsinki educated in the spirit of German constitutional theory.[2085] These men had both contributed to the preparation of the original republican proposal but in the circumstances of 1918 they were clear political opponents.

The republican arguments intensified with the changing international and German domestic situation. For the monarchists, neither the German war troubles nor the announcement of a constitutional reform there made any difference other than causing them to avoid ostentatious admiration of the German monarchy. Ernst Nevanlinna, the Chairman of the Finnish Party, instead insisted that Finland could not afford the 'bankruptcy' of a republican constitution: it would lead to constant agitation, repeated elections and endless disputes at a time when the affairs of the whole of Europe and the world were in the process of being resettled.[2086]

On the day of the election, the republicans were nevertheless determined to challenge the monarchical polity. The Agrarians insisted that no clear German demand concerning the introduction of a monarchy had been heard and that mere monarchical manipulation was behind such suggestions.[2087] Moreover, the Bulgarian monarchy had just fallen despite support from the Central Powers.[2088] Antti Rentola foresaw the current constitutional changes in Germany leading to strengthened parliamentarism over a weakening monarchy and to the renunciation of the export of German princes. It followed that good relations with Germany would be guaranteed by advancing parliamentarism rather than by adding to dynastic problems.'[2089] Artur Vuorimaa was informed about the German press rejecting the idea of a German king for Finland as being against the German national interest.

2081 VP, Eero Hahl, 7 August 1918, 1844.
2082 VP, Antti Juutilainen, 9 August 1918, 1889.
2083 VP, Artur Wuorimaa, 9 August 1918, 1880.
2084 VP, Kaarlo Juho Ståhlberg, 8 August 1918, 1860.
2085 VP, Rabbe Axel Wrede, 8 August 1918, 1862.
2086 VP, Ernst Nevanlinna, 8 October 1918, 68.
2087 VP, Antti Juutilainen, 4 October 1918, 28. On the denial of such manipulation, see Pekka Ahmavaara (Young Finns), 8 October 1918, 61.
2088 VP, Antti Juutilainen, 5 October 1918, 40; Lindman 1968, 275.
2089 VP, Antti Rentola, 4 October 1918, 29; also Bertta Pykälä (Agrarians), 8 October 1918, 84, and Kalle Lohi (Agrarians), 9 October 1918, 118.

According to him, it did not serve Finnish interests either, as a British recognition of Finnish independence was still lacking.[2090]

Without questioning the common interests and intimate cultural connections between Germany and Finland,[2091] the Agrarians maintained that the connections would still be cherished under a republican constitution. Once the Social Democrats and the centrists had been incorporated in the German government, the focus would be on relations between the two peoples rather than between the monarchies. Santeri Alkio foresaw the German left and centre soon recommending a parliamentary system, 'which they have already now been able to realise in their country', for Finland as well;[2092] this illustrates a high transnational awareness of the course of the German constitutional reform and the dependence of Finnish solutions on it. According to Alkio, however, it was rather time for the Finns themselves to formulate their constitution independently of all foreign powers.[2093] The transnational comparisons were extended to intertextuality: Vilkku Joukahainen quoted Max von Baden's governmental declaration, emphasising its appeal to support by the majority of the people, the workers included, which he thought should demonstrate to the Finnish monarchists the value of popular principles.[2094] The Agrarian republicans studied every available utterance of the new leaders of Germany to find arguments to oppose the royal election. Such transnational awareness served current political interests rather than being based on any established contacts with German party politicians. It was facilitated by the generally held conception of the cultural similarity of the two countries and the tendency of both sides in the Rump Parliament to regard Germany as a leading constitutional model. German developments were in 1918 generally considered to be directly relevant for the Finnish constitution. Matti Paasivuori, the only Social Democrat attending the debate, was even more explicit in the knowledge that his ideological brethren were about to take over in Germany: he called the Finnish monarchists 'our Junkers' and advised them to enquire from the new leftist German government whether it was still willing to deliver a monarch to Finland.[2095] The parallel between the constitutions of Germany and Finland was thus emphasised by both of the largest republican groups in Finland, just as it had been by the monarchists previously. In its editorial on the day of the royal election, *Hufvudstadsbladet* responded by attacking the Social Democrats for still holding notions about a dictatorship of the

---

2090 VP, Artur Vuorimaa, 5 October 1918, 37.
2091 VP, Artur Vuorimaa, 5 October 1918, 37. Vuorimaa used the German constitution as an object of comparison in calling for changes in the proposed Finnish one. 8 October 1918, 86; Santeri Alkio, 5 October 1918, 46; This united the Agrarians with Young Finns such as Pekka Ahmavaara, 8 October 1918, 61.
2092 VP, Santeri Alkio, 5 October 1918, 47; 8 October 1918, 56. For a denial of Germany calling for parliamentarism in Finland, which already had a parliamentary government, see Pekka Ahmavaara, 8 October 1918, 61.
2093 VP, Santeri Alkio, 8 October 1918, 59.
2094 VP, Vilkku Joukahainen, 8 October 1918, 79–80. Antti Rentola repeated the point with reference to Kaiser Wilhelm on 9 October 1918, 102; Lindman 1968, 275.
2095 VP, Matti Paasivuori, 8 October 1918, 72; 9 October 1918, 99.

proletariat and by questioning its appeals to a democratic development in Germany. It recommended to Finnish Social Democrats the kind of patriotism demonstrated during the war by their German brethren.[2096]

Once the Prussian monarchical order began to waver, the monarchists turned to anti-Entente rhetoric. Pekka Pennanen (Young Finns) contrasted the tendency of the United States to intervene in Finnish internal affairs rather than helping it with the actions of 'the mighty Germany', the only friend of Finland.[2097] Ernst Nevanlinna played down republican claims about the German constitutional changes affecting Finland, emphasising that the democratisation of Prussia was being carried out by a prince and that it was merely bringing Prussia to the same level of democracy that Finland already enjoyed.[2098] What was happening in international relations or within the German polity was not to be allowed to prevent the reinforcement of a monarchical constitution in Finland. However, the continued dependence of Finnish political discourse on German developments is visible in detailed reports in the press of the Reichstag debates in late October;[2099] by comparison, news of the Swedish reform was inconspicuous.[2100] The two sides of the Finnish constitutional dispute made use of international comparisons and transnational points as best served their current domestic political goals, but there was no denying their major importance.

6.4.3 Monarchical vs. republican democracy

Two very different notions of 'bourgeois democracy' manifested themselves as the monarchist majority set out to prepare the election of a king, not least because a ministry that had initially aimed at a republic now seemed to be demolishing democracy.[2101] The Agrarians responded by arguing consistently in favour of a 'rule by the people' of the kind they had demanded throughout 1917. Artur Wuorimaa urged the government to bring to the parliament a proposal for a new democratic constitution that distanced itself from the 'autocratic principle' that dominated the monarchical proposals.[2102] 'Real' democracy would reject both the mistaken democracy of 'the Reds' and the proposed bureaucratic and aristocratic system that was being hypocritically described by the conservatives as 'the most democratic constitutional

---

2096 *Hufvudstadsbladet*, 'Agitationen mot regeringen och lantdagen', 9 October 1918. This was a heated response to a reasonably moderate editorial entitled 'Suomi hengittää yhdellä keuhkolla' published in *Suomen Sosialidemokraatti*, 8 October 1918.
2097 VP, Pekka Pennanen, 5 October 1918, 39.
2098 VP, Ernst Nevanlinna, 8 October 1918, 68–9.
2099 *Helsingin Sanomat*, 'Saksan waltiopäiwät', 25 and 27 October 1918. *Suomen Sosialidemokraatti* concluded after the German debates that the Finnish ministry was no longer supported by the German extreme right. 'Nykyisen hallitusjärjestelmämme wararikko', 29 October 1918.
2100 *Helsingin Sanomat*, 'Ruotsin waltiosääntökysymys', 28 November 1918; 'Perustuslakiuudistus Ruotsissa', 19 December 1918; *Suomen Sosialidemokraatti*, 'Hallitusmuotokysymys Ruotsissa', 19 December 1918.
2101 *Helsingin Sanomat*, 'Pakotus hallitusmuotokysymyksessä', 7 August 1918.
2102 VP, Artur Wuorimaa, 8 August 1918, 1861.

monarchy'.[2103] Antti Juutilainen suggested that the monarchists had let the people down by working against and not in favour of a 'democratic society'. It was outrageous to claim that the people were tired of democracy and to promote monarchy, aristocracy, bureaucracy and plutocracy when the majority of the Finnish people were known to abhor these.[2104]

The rightist response to accusations of betraying democracy was to turn to rhetorical redescriptions of their constitutional proposal as representing popular power. Against the background of the debates of 1917 and the advances that democracy might make (despite contrary signs during the preceding year), the Finnish-speaking conservatives, who had long had a reformist agenda, saw it as unthinkable to plan a new political order without appealing to democratic ideals. Their spokesman Lauri Ingman accused the Agrarians of having themselves prevented 'a more democratic constitution' than that of 1772 being passed.[2105] Pekka Pennanen (Young Finns) conceded that the monarchists were ready to democratise the constitution as far as was rationally possible.[2106]

In early October, Santeri Alkio, encouraged by the ongoing political changes in Germany, which could be interpreted as 'the complete victory of democracy' and supportive of rule by the people in Finland as well,[2107] spoke strongly in favour of democracy from the point of view of a centrist republican. He saw it as senseless for the government to try and stop 'the shock waves of democracy' (a Wilsonian metaphor emphasising the irresistible nature of the change) by maintaining monarchy and oligarchy. In applying a natural metaphor resembling those of the German and Swedish reformists later in the autumn of 1918, Alkio foresaw such stubborn conservatism as productive of nothing but the reactivation of class struggles.[2108] According to Antti Rentola, too, the government was introducing a monarchy 'in an undemocratic way' on the basis of misleading claims about the decline of democracy at a time when even the right already knew that true democracy would prevail.[2109] Antti Juutilainen urged the ministry 'to return to the road of the rule by the people,'[2110] to recognise that democracy was making a breakthrough internationally and more particularly in Germany, to realise that all Finnish supporters of democracy abhorred monarchy and to understand that only a democratic republic would unite the people after the crimes of the Social Democrats.[2111] Kyösti Kallio interpreted the republican constitutional proposal of December 1917 as having already recognised a transnational development towards democracy[2112] and considered that

---

2103 VP, Artur Wuorimaa, 9 August 1918, 1880.
2104 VP, Antti Juutilainen, 9 August 1918, 1889.
2105 VP, Lauri Ingman, 8 August 1918, 1872; 9 August 1918, 1878; Juho Erkki Antila, 9 August 1918, 1888.
2106 VP, Pekka Pennanen, 9 August 1918, 1884.
2107 *Suomen Sosialidemokraatti*, 'Monarkistit huolissaan', 4 October 1918.
2108 VP, Santeri Alkio, 4 October 1918, 24–6.
2109 VP, Antti Rentola, 4 October 1918, 29; 8 October 1918, 76.
2110 VP, Antti Juutilainen, 4 October 1918, 28.
2111 VP, Antti Juutilainen, 4 October 1918, 40–1.
2112 VP, Kyösti Kallio, 8 October 1918, 77.

there was no way of turning the clock back. Ivar Lantto expressly defined the Agrarian League as a democratic party, demanding that the voice of the people should be heard in the preparation of the constitution 'in this so-called democratic country'.[2113] The Social Democrats went further: their organ cited *Vorwärts*, according to which democracy was from now on to be the basis of both constitutions and international relations.[2114] In the parliament, Matti Paasivuori ordered the monarchists to stop their 'mockery of democracy' and renounce their attempts to establish a reactionary political order that would delay the breakthrough of democracy in Finland. The Rump Parliament lacked the legitimacy to solve the constitutional issue in a way that would satisfy 'democratic opinion' outside.[2115] Only after the return of the Social Democrats to the parliament could a satisfactorily democratic constitution be adopted.

The monarchists stubbornly continued to describe the government's proposal as 'democratic'[2116] or 'liberal, democratic',[2117] which had been the consistent claim of *Hufvudstadsbladet*, for example: a constitutional monarchy was needed to advance the common good in the spirit of democracy as opposed to the special interests of party leaders in a republic.[2118] The proposal was more 'democratic' than any in force in another monarchy, including the new Germany,[2119] while the 'democratic' nature of the republican obstruction in the parliament was questionable.[2120] Annie Furuhjelm (Swedish People's Party) asserted that she was not afraid of 'the democratic spirit' of the proposal.[2121] For Kyösti Haataja (Finnish Party), the monarch was a guarantor of 'real democratic reforms' and the maintenance of 'a constructive democratic spirit'.[2122] Pekka Pennanen of the Young Finns presented the proposal as advancing democracy to an exceptional degree,[2123] even though some liberals continued to doubt whether the people's rights vis-à-vis the king had been sufficiently considered.[2124] All the monarchist groups

---

2113 VP, Ivar Lantto, 8 October 1918, 83; see also Santeri Alkio, 8 October 1918, 85.
2114 *Suomen Sosialidemokraatti*, '"Vorwärts", uusi hallitus ja rauhankysymys', 8 October 1918.
2115 VP, Matti Paasivuori, 4 October 1918, 28; 8 October 1918, 72; 9 October 1918, 99. *Suomen Sosialidemokraatti* wrote on 8 October 1918 in an article entitled 'Suomi hengittää yhdellä keuhkolla' that global events were heading towards democracy and that the Finns should join this trend.
2116 VP, Ernst Nevanlinna, 4 October 1918, 26; Pekka Ahmavaara, 8 October 1918, 59; Tekla Hultin, 8 October 1918, 64.
2117 VP, Rabbe Axel Wrede, 4 October 1918, 35.
2118 *Hufvudstadsbladet*, 'Brådskande afgörande', 7 August 1918; 'Gårdagens landtdagsbeslut', 8 August 1918.
2119 *Hufvudstadsbladet*, 'Tärningen är kastad', 10 August 1918; 'Inför avgörandet', 8 October 1918; 'Agitationen mot regeringen och lantdagen', 9 October 1918.
2120 *Hufvudstadsbladet*, 'Frågan om regeringsformen', 5 October 1918; 'Regeringsform och konungaval', 10 October 1918.
2121 VP, Annie Furuhjelm, 9 October 1918, 116; Wilhelm Roos, 9 October 1918, 118.
2122 VP, Kyösti Haataja, 8 October 1918, 89.
2123 VP, Pekka Pennanen, 4 October 1918, 38.
2124 *Helsingin Sanomat*, 'Hallitusmuotokysymys nykyisessä waiheessaan', 5 October 1918; 'Kuninkaanwaali toimitettu', 10 October 1918.

thus recognised democracy as a concept that was needed to legitimate even a monarchical mixed constitution, although it was a democracy defined by themselves. Prime Minister J. K. Paasikivi insisted with irony that Bolshevik democracy was the only type not satisfied by the proposal – if indeed the people really wanted democracy, about which he was not so sure:[2125]

> And hence it is not possible to maintain that democracy [*demokratia, kansanvaltaisuus*], unless it is understood to stand for an ultra-socialist people's commissariat, . . . could not freely develop if it has support among the people and in the parliament.

Paasikivi remained a man of tradition in that he viewed democracy as no more than one element in a traditional mixed constitution; the entire system could not be called a democracy. As for the socialist democracy experienced at the beginning of 1918, it had been a project in which a radical minority of two per cent had misled the citizens while the majority had condemned the rebellion – the implication being that the Finns as a whole were not to blame. The Prime Minister conceded that a democratic constitution might be possible but doubted the readiness of the people for it, democracy presumably meaning that 'the views of the majority of citizens who are enlightened and thinking and who have defended and support the legal social order must be decisive'.[2126] Majority democracy was possible provided that the supporters of the established order constituted that majority, and regulation was needed to ensure this.

For the Agrarians, 'the rule by the people' had become such a sacred concept that Paasikivi's representation of 'the Red terror' as a type of democracy made Artur Wuorimaa denounce the Red uprising as 'a rebellion against the rule by the people'.[2127] Democracy was to be saved from associations with socialism as it was peasant democracy that constituted real democracy. The Agrarians, encouraged by the increasingly probable reforms in Germany, carried on their deterministic interpretation that the advent of democracy was unavoidable. While the historical development was proceeding internationally and irresistibly towards 'humanity, fraternity, equality', the monarchists were plotting a totally opposite future for Finland.[2128] The Agrarians refused to recognise any democracy in the proposal.

A few ultra-conservatives of the Finnish Party and the Swedish People's Party remained openly sceptical about democracy. Oswald Kairamo characterised 'belief in the power of unlimited democracy to make people happy' as 'unwavering amongst the left' (i.e. the centre in the Rump Parliament), who would do better to understand that not everyone might hold such a belief in the aftermath of a civil war.[2129] R. A. Wrede saw the

---

2125 VP, Juho Kusti Paasikivi, 8 October 1918, 53.
2126 VP, Juho Kusti Paasikivi, 8 October 1918, 54.
2127 VP, Artur Wuorimaa, 8 October 1918, 85.
2128 VP, Artur Wuorimaa, 8 October 1918, 87.
2129 VP, Oswald Kairamo, 8 October 1918, 65.

republicans as mistaken in advocating this supposed democracy.[2130] Ernst Nevanlinna, a professor of political economy whose learning was linked to German scholarship, concluded that 'a wave of so-called democracy' could be expected after the end of the war; the news from Germany had made that clear. But Finland did not need to follow such a movement as independence had already entailed a democratic breakthrough; here the Fennoman leader was representing national self-determination and democracy as identical. No need to strive for the extension of democracy existed as there were no political forces that opposed it, not even among the old civil service class (which hardly was true). Right to the end of the constitutional struggle of 1918, Nevanlinna insisted that the proposed monarchical constitution would be one of the most democratic polities in contemporary Europe, surpassing those in Sweden or the Netherlands, for instance. The Socialists' demands for further democracy were to be ignored since nothing would satisfy them anyway.[2131]

The argument of the Finnish right was thus that Finnish democracy (as an element of the constitution) would be secured by the monarchical constitutional proposal. Republican understandings of democracy were ignored and a monarchical polity implemented in mid-October. The fall of the German monarchy in November, described by *Hufvudstadsbladet* as 'democratic constitutional changes in Germany',[2132] redefined the situation, however, removing any possibilities for the implementation of a monarchy in Finland. The Swedish reform might still be interpreted in line with the Swedish right as resulting from threats of a revolution by the government.[2133] The German defeat in the war nevertheless made a new election a precondition for the recognition of Finnish independence by the Anglo-American Entente powers. These international developments thus had major transnational impacts in Finland, giving republican understandings of democracy a new chance to influence the formation of the constitution. A compromise between the monarchical and republican understandings of democracy just needed to be found in order to end the frustrating constitutional interregnum.

6.4.4 'The will of the people' interpreted for and against a republic

Notwithstanding the prevailing disappointment with the socialist segment of the population, appeals to the will of the people remained a major argumentative strategy for both the monarchists and the republicans of the Rump Parliament. Both claimed to be better aware of the true will of the people and to be promoting its realisation. However, the degree of trust in the political potential of the Finnish people varied dramatically, with

---

2130 VP, Rabbe Axel Wrede, 8 October 1918, 88.
2131 VP, Enrnt Nevanlinna, 8 October 1918, 67–9.
2132 *Hufvudstadsbladet*, 'Kejsar Wilhelm har avgått', 10 November 1918.
2133 *Hufvudstadsbladet*, 'Sverges författningsfråga inför riksdagen', 20 December 1918.

the conservatives in particular doubting the ability of the people to grasp constitutional questions.[2134]

Prime Minister J. K. Paasikivi maintained that the suitability of diverse constitutional solutions was determined not only by the needs of the people but also by the international standing of the country. The tendency of Old Finns to both trust and to suspect the people can be seen in how Paasikivi urged the parliament to 'trust the people as they will find leaders from among themselves', on the other hand adding that 'we ... have a sad experience of what kind of leaders can rise from among the people'.[2135] This was a reference to the continued support for the Social Democrats and the risk that the Finns might again vote for such 'public enemies'. The Prime Minister doubted whether the Finns had demonstrated such political abilities as would allow a monarchy to be replaced by a republic, concluding that no further demonstrations of the immaturity of the people could be permitted if independence was to be retained.[2136] The exclusion of the Reds from the parliament was justified as they had committed 'the biggest of crimes known in the history of our people'; they had 'no moral right to demand the postponement of the issue until their representatives can again attend'; and these 'mentally ill' people should first recover before they could return to the parliament.[2137] The rebels were to blame for the current crisis of the Finnish people: 'The respect enjoyed by our people has, as a consequences of the horrendous crime of the socialists, decreased to a frightening extent. In internal affairs, divisions are spreading and trust diminishing day by day.'[2138] There was no way in which 'Red Finland' could be allowed to decide about the constitution; it remained 'for White Finland to decide'.[2139] The winners of the Civil War, and more particularly its healthiest elements, had the sole authorisation to construct the kind of polity they considered best.

The Prime Minister's pessimistic descriptions of the state of the nation were aimed to endorse the immediate adoption of the controversial constitutional proposal of his ministry. To describe the future of the Finns, Paasikivi employed a conventional conservative organic analogy: 'We all, of course, hope and believe that the Finnish people can be again joined together as a strong people and that the mental illness that has corrupted great parts of them will be healed.'[2140] The interpretation that a section of the people was mentally deranged called for authoritative political healing by the monarchy, not for democracy or parliamentarism.

Paasikivi's pessimistic views on humanity had evident consequences for the formation of the constitution: it could not be based simply on

2134 *Helsingin Sanomat*, 'Pakotus hallitusmuotokysymyksessä', 7 August 1918.
2135 VP, Juho Kusti Paasikivi, 7 August 1918, 1815.
2136 Paavo Virkkunen echoed the point on the immaturity of the Finnish people in politics in VP, 7 August 1918, 1822, and Emil Nestor Setälä advised the parliament to demonstrate the contrary by approving the new proposal, 7 August 1918, 1830.
2137 VP, Juho Kusti Paasikivi, 7 August 1918, 1817–18.
2138 VP, Juho Kusti Paasikivi, 7 August 1918, 1819.
2139 VP, Juho Kusti Paasikivi, 7 August 1918, 1846.
2140 VP, Juho Kusti Paasikivi, 7 August 1918, 1818.

popular rule. Many in his party – including several Lutheran clergymen – shared a gloomy conception of the Finnish people and the future of the polity, concluding that the strengthening of the monarchy was imperative. Waldemar Bergroth, a vicar by calling, justified a strong executive power with the argument that the people had abandoned God and turned to selfishness, party animosities, hatred of their brethren and illegality. For him, a republic was incapable of bringing about a spiritual reform that would enable 'the real rule by the people'.[2141] The Speaker of the Parliament, Paavo Virkkunen, another clergyman, considered that the people were seeking security from a monarchy.[2142] The Minister of Education Professor E. N. Setälä, spoke derisively about republicans who 'solemnly appeal to the majesty of the majority of the people', implying that they would allow the former rebels to decide about the structures of the polity. The involvement of the people in the process through referenda hence remained out of the question.[2143] Wilhelmi Malmivaara nevertheless asserted that the right trusted the people and were aiming at a proper rule by the people as opposed to 'popular mischief' (*kansanvallattomuus*, a coinage that could even be construed as 'anti-democracy') and lack of respect for law and order.[2144] Juho Erkki Antila, a farmer who would put the motion for the election of a king, further denigrated a republic as something that the Finns had already experienced when 'the people through their parliament wielded supreme power for some time' in 1917. The results of the people ruling 'directly through their parliament' had made the food shortage worse, which demonstrated to Antila the failure of 'the rule by of the people' or 'a people's republic' (*kansan tasavalta*).[2145]

This Fennoman rightist attack on popular politics provoked equally uncompromising reactions from the centre. Santeri Alkio considered a monarchy without responsibility as a direct threat to the people and the state.[2146] The right's questioning of a republic and the rule by the people on the basis of 'a dreadful revolt of the people' was unfounded.[2147] In ignoring the rule by the people, the monarchists forgot that[2148]

> this country has been liberated by the people, that the blood of the people has been shed for this liberty and that the will of this people must be heard when a constitution is formulated for the state, which has been created by the force of the people.

2141 VP, Waldermat Bergroth, 7 August 1918, 1840; also Leonard Typpö, 7 August 1918, 1842.
2142 VP, Paavo Virkkunen, 7 August 1918, 1823–4.
2143 VP, Emil Nestor Setälä, 7 August 1918, 1828–9. *Helsingin Sanomat*, 'Eduskunnan eilinen merkkipäiwä', 8 August 1918.
2144 VP, Wilhelmi Malmivaara, 7 August 1918, 1856.
2145 VP, Juho Erkki Antila, 7 August 1918, 1835.
2146 VP, Santeri Alkio, 7 August 1918, 1820.
2147 VP, Santeri Alkio, 7 August 1918, 1848.
2148 VP, Santeri Alkio, 7 August 1918, 1849. A related point on 'the feeling of the people's own power' was repeated by Kyösti Kallio, 8 October 1918, 77.

Popular sovereignty reinforced by the fight of the White Guards against Russian and Red forces in the Civil War spoke for democracy, and a republican constitution made a monarchy unsustainable. Antti Juutilainen carried on, lamenting the fact that the opinion of the people who had liberated the country was distrusted and ignored and that 'the merit, abilities and trustworthiness of our people' in the eyes of its German allies had been questioned by the Finnish Party,[2149] a supposed defender of the cause of the people. Juho Kokko foresaw that nothing but hatred from the people could be expected as a result of such monarchist policies.[2150] Alkio further added that the natural development of the rule by the people would be prevented by the monarchical proposal, which would leave nothing but revolution as the only method of changing the constitution.[2151] The rightists themselves were committing a coup d'état by electing a king on the basis of outdated legislation.[2152]

Lauri Ingman of the Finnish Party responded by maintaining that the Finnish people stood behind the right.[2153] Other MPs reasserted that they trusted the people and that that people wished for a monarchy.[2154] Ingman questioned not only Alkio's suggestion about a coup but also the constitutional position of the republicans, disputing the legitimacy and validity of the constitutional decisions at the time of the declaration of independence (when he himself had spoken for democracy) as 'revolutionary', i.e. made in extraordinary circumstances and ways.[2155] Both the Red rebels and the non-socialist republicans were thus accused of attempting a revolution that had failed.[2156]

The views of the Young Finns were divided and overshadowed by the confrontation between the Finnish Party and the Agrarians. *Helsingin Sanomat*, their organ, had still complained in early August about the monarchists deliberately misinterpreting 'the will of the people' to enforce that of their own, just as the socialists had done in 1917, and suggested that the people itself should decide through a referendum.[2157] By early October the party's stance had become ambivalent: a monarchy might do provided that 'the basic prerequisites of the rule by the people' were ensured,[2158] although it was believed that the majority of the people remained opposed

---

2149 VP, Antti Juutilainen, 9 August 1918, 1889–90.
2150 VP, Juho Kokko, 8 August 1918, 1866.
2151 VP, Santeri Alkio, 7 August 1918, 1848.
2152 VP, Santeri Alkio, 8 August 1918, 1865; see also Matti Paasivuori (Social Democrat), 8 August 1918, 1871; 8 October 1917, 52, 72; 9 October 1918, 100. Alkio was returning to an analogy he had made between the Red rebellion and the monarchist project when talking about 'the Social Democratic class coup' on 8 October 1918, 55; see also Kalle Lohi, 8 October 1918, 70.
2153 VP, Lauri Ingman, 8 August 1918, 1868.
2154 VP, Iida Yrjö-Koskinen, 9 August 1918, 1888.
2155 VP, Lauri Ingman, 9 August 1918, 1877–8.
2156 VP, 9 August 1918, 1878; also Juho Kusti Paasikivi, 9 October 1918, 96.
2157 *Helsingin Sanomat*, 'Pakotus hallitusmuotokysymyksessä', 7 August 1918.
2158 *Helsingin Sanomat*, 'Hallitusmuotokysymys nykyisessä waiheessaan', 5 October 1918.

to monarchy.²¹⁵⁹ Some republicans believed in the people being able to unite themselves again, restore mutual understanding and make 'democratic progress' if only they were given a republican constitution,²¹⁶⁰ while the monarchists believed that the people would still retain their political influence under a king.²¹⁶¹

As attempts to reach a compromise failed, the royal election approached and the German polity was already experiencing a constitutional transformation, the monarchical and republican conceptions of the people became increasingly militant. On the republican side, Alkio lamented the unwillingness of the monarchists – at a decisive moment in European history – to listen to complaints from abroad and to let the people decide about their constitution through a new election or a referendum.²¹⁶² In a republic, power would remain in the hands of the people itself, whereas a monarchy allowed a single family to decide about the fate of the people, which was contrary to the fundamentally democratic and parliamentary character of the Finnish people:²¹⁶³

> This form of government would require a contented, humble and lowly people. But the Finnish people are a discontented, demanding and proud people. The last Russian ruler during his reign made them hostile to all use of power that is not based on the sense of justice of the people themselves. The political education of the past decades has to an overwhelming extent aroused among this people the will to decide on their laws and institutions through their parliament.

It was unacceptable that the people who had liberated themselves were denied the right to make its voice heard when the Finnish constitution was formulated. Such a violation of civic rights could only be healed with a new election; this would restore the lacking consensus between the people, the parliament and the government.²¹⁶⁴ Alkio urged the old elite to trust the people and to respect 'the sacred will of the people' as the 'the sole arbiter'. The elite and the people should negotiate so that '[t]he people will feel they are participating again in the running of affairs and no longer being excluded as they now are'.²¹⁶⁵ Without such cooperation in the spirit of popular sovereignty, the constitution might again become an object of class struggles, and confrontations would become a permanent feature of politics and potentially lead to renewed civil strife.²¹⁶⁶

Fellow Agrarians likewise emphasised the right of the people as an entity to influence its fate.²¹⁶⁷ Antti Rentola cited Woodrow Wilson on the necessity

---

2159 *Helsingin Sanomat*, 'Kuninkaanwaali toimitettu', 10 October 1918.
2160 VP, Augusta Laine and Emil Linna, 7 August 1918, 1839.
2161 VP, Pekka Pennanen and Tilda Löthman, 9 August 1918, 1884–5.
2162 VP, Santeri Alkio, 4 October 1918, 24–5; 8 October 1917, 57.
2163 VP, Santeri Alkio, 4 October 1918, 25.
2164 VP, Santeri Alkio, 4 October 1918, 26; also Ivar Lantto, 8 October 1918, 83.
2165 VP, Santeri Alkio, 5 October 1917, 47; 8 October 1917, 59.
2166 VP, Santeri Alkio, 8 October 1917, 57.
2167 VP, Artur Wuorimaa, 5 October 1918, 36–7; Antti Rentola, 8 October 1918, 72.

for politicians to follow the will of the people if they wanted to survive,[2168] thereby making a transnational reference to the declared principles which the Entente was now imposing on Germany and the prospective change in the German constitution. Vilkku Joukahainen likewise spoke about 'the great rising of the people' taking place around Europe and in Finland, where, however, 'the people threw themselves as one man into the battle against the Red rebellion' only to find themselves passed over in preparations for the constitution. This had made them lose much of their previous political enthusiasm.[2169] Rentola and Antti Juutilainen ridiculed rightist doubts about the political maturity of the people, suggesting that the monarchical project reflected a spirit of 'national distrust' and even a mentality of 'a vassal people' that was incapable of independence.[2170] A social and geographical division had emerged: whereas 'the healthy forces of the people' had performed 'a healthy operation on our national body politic' (a republican organic metaphor for the Civil War), reactionary circles in Helsinki abhorred the activities of the people and planned to take over the state. The only antidote was the restoration of a regular parliament representing the Finnish people and uniting its classes; this would stop the rightist coup, which was no better than the Red uprising.[2171]

Monarchist responses were equally unbending. Kyösti Haataja (Finnish Party) stigmatised Juutilainen's conception of the will of the people as socialism, arising out of 'that Red spirit which has departed from this parliament'.[2172] Ernst Nevanlinna claimed that the current parliament remained legitimate as it had been elected by the people and consisted of 'the healthy layers of the people who support legal social order'. Here he turned to a tendentious interpretation of parliamentary sovereignty, viewing the attending MPs as the only legal and 'healthy' representatives of the Finnish people in a sick world:[2173]

> The people themselves . . . , the healthy layers of the Finnish people, those who have retained their mental balance during this upheaval of the world, they are now assembled in this house, and it is precisely they and no one else who will make the decision.

The Swedish *People's* Party, which despite its name, was overwhelmingly monarchical and sceptical about extended popular government by the Finnish-speaking majority after the Civil War, left the parliamentary debate in this respect to the Finnish-speaking rival sides, although its organ criticised the Finnish people for its 'lack of political culture' (corresponding to the German word *Kultur* as it was used in German wartime propaganda in contradistinction to the 'civilisation' of the Western powers).[2174]

2168 VP, Antti Rentola, 8 October 1918, 73.
2169 VP, Vilkku Joukahainen, 8 October 1918, 80.
2170 VP, Antti Juutilainen, 5 October 1918, 39; Antti Rentola, 8 October 1918, 74.
2171 VP, Antti Juutilainen, 5 October 1918, 41–2, 46.
2172 VP, Kyösti Haataja, 5 October 1918, 42.
2173 VP, Ernst Nevanlinna, 8 October 1918, 66.
2174 *Hufvudstadsbladet*, 'Frågan om regeringsformen', 5 October 1918.

R. A Wrede did not rate the role of the Finnish people in the political process very highly: Finnish independence was a result of favourable international trends rather than of the activities of the Finns themselves. This achievement was now jeopardised by the corruption of 'the moral make-up of the people',[2175] something that a monarchy would heal. By contrast, Tekla Hultin, a monarchical Young Finn, continued to assert that a new monarchical constitution would award the will of the people a greater influence than in any other monarchy or most republics.[2176] The degree of trust in the people was used to justify both republican and monarchical constitutional solutions: the optimism of the republicans was inspired by a positive interpretation of the contribution of the people to the Civil War, constitutional changes in Germany and a belief in national reconciliation, while the pessimism of the monarchists found support in the shock caused by the Civil War and was reflected in a desire to maintain constitutional continuity.

6.4.5 PARLIAMENTARISM REDEFINED OR ENDANGERED BY THE MONARCHISTS?

It has become clear by now that parliamentarism, too, was understood in conflicting ways by the two sides of the constitutional struggle depending on the extent to which popular representation was valued. Complete rejections of parliamentarism were, however, just as much out of the question as full denials of democracy would have been. The conservative response was to define parliamentarism with qualifications that suited a monarchical constitution and in a way that resembled the relationship between the executive and the parliament in Prussia before the reforms there.

In August, once it had become obvious that the parliament would pass no new monarchical constitution and that late eighteenth-century provisions for a royal election might be applied instead, monarchist suspicions of parliamentarism came increasingly into the open. Prime Minister J. K. Paasikivi asserted, with references to German authors and experiences, that a monarchy would diminish 'parliamentary and party problems' and introduce reforms that would be beneficial to the lower orders of the people.[2177] Parliamentary procedures appeared to be incapable of producing the required reforms and to be rather a source of domestic political strife; this comment reflects a sceptical if not hostile attitude to parliamentarism within the government. In October, after Germany had declared its aim to parliamentarise its government, nervousness within the Finnish Party began to rise.[2178] Paasikivi insisted that a monarchical constitution would realise 'the parliamentary way of government' by guaranteeing 'the influence of the parliament on the course of affairs' provided that 'the parliament with its party divisions is able to realise this – which may admittedly be questionable'.[2179] The Prime Minister was speaking in favour

---

2175 VP, Rabbe Axel Wrede, 5 October 1918, 35.
2176 VP, Tekla Hultin, 8 October 1918, 63.
2177 VP, Juho Kusti Paasikivi, 7 August 1918, 1816.
2178 *Suomen Sosialidemokraatti*, 'Monarkistit huolissaan', 4 October 1918.
2179 VP, Juho Kusti Paasikivi, 8 October 1917, 53–4.

of parliamentary government in principle while denying its potential in the political process in practice. Even if the ministry continued to declare its readiness for compromise, its measures and rhetoric questioned the basic premises of a new parliamentary republic. The Finnish constitutional debate was again approaching an impasse. Paasikivi wanted to bring the dispute to an end, emphasising the preparations for peace. This could happen only if the republican minority joined the majority.[2180]

Other hard-liners in the Finnish Party attacked parliamentarism by directing blame for the Red rebellion on the current republican opposition, especially the Agrarians. Oswald Kairamo, an estate owner embittered by the Civil War, claimed that the war had been caused by the extension of parliamentarism:[2181]

> [B]ut also that kind of unlimited parliamentary power, which the Social Democrats with the help and support of the Agrarian League tried to realise last winter, that must also be absolutely rejected as it is not only technically impossible but will also certainly lead to national weakness, misery and anarchy, as it has already done in this country.

According to Ernst Nevanlinna, the current parliament as an institution was a sufficient guarantee of the realisation of democracy. Changes in Germany altered nothing in Finland: the reconcilability of monarchy and parliamentarism was demonstrated by the fact that the German government was led by *Prince* Max von Baden.[2182] Pekka Ahmavaara (Young Finns), the First Vice-Speaker, maintained that parliamentary government had already been established in Finland in 1917, so the need for reform that Germany was experiencing did not exist.[2183] He believed that reformist Germany was coming into line with the Finnish polity rather than the Finnish polity sticking to the Prussian political order.

The Agrarians consistently rejected calls for a monarchy as endangering both democracy and parliamentarism. Pekka Hahl foresaw the election of a king as implying further constitutional changes, perhaps limitations to suffrage and parliamentary power, which differed from what he regarded as a pan-European trend to let all layers of the people participate more directly in government. According to Hahl, the Finnish government seemed to be willing 'to exclude the vast majority of the people from administering the affairs of the state. They would not be allowed to participate in the building of the new Finland which we hopefully thought would be built once the Red rebellion had been suppressed.'[2184] This statement made *Hufvudstadsbladet*

2180 VP, Juho Kusti Paasikivi, 8 October 1917, 54–5. For Santeri Alkio's response suggesting a compromise on the constitution for the same purpose, see 8 October 1917, 59.
2181 VP, Oswald Kairamo, 8 October 1918, 65.
2182 VP, Ernst Nevanlinna, 8 October 1918, 68–9.
2183 VP, Pekka Ahmavaara, 8 October 1918, 61. The unwillingness of *Helsingin Sanomat* to write clearly in favour of parliamentarism is visible in 'Parlamentaarinen hallitusjärjestelmä', 4 October 1918.
2184 VP, Pekka Hahl, 7 August 1918, 1844–5.

accuse Hahl of socialist agitation and ridicule Agrarian rhetoric in general.[2185] According to Santeri Alkio, too, a monarchy with extensive prerogatives meant limitations to democracy, which might be followed by the introduction of a bicameral system, a decrease in the political education of the people and give rise to widespread discontent among them.[2186] Antti Juutilainen was positive that the preparations for a royal election were irreconcilable with parliamentarism.[2187]

In October, Alkio considered that preparations were being made for the installation of a monarchical power that would bypass the opinion of the parliamentary majority and prioritise the protection of its oligarchic privileges over democracy and parliamentarism.[2188] Rightist lawyers seemed ready expunge the principle of ministerial responsibility from the constitutional proposal.[2189] Parliamentary government was in danger of losing its contact with the people: parliamentary debates and legislation would no longer be related to prevailing trends of thought or organise the polity in a satisfactory manner if the parliament failed to appeal to the people and cooperate with them.[2190] Antti Rentola could not understand this tendency to reduce parliamentarism in Finland at a time when that principle was making progress in much of Europe. In Germany, the allies of the Finnish monarchists were being displaced. The only way for future progress was to allow the Finns to engage themselves in parliamentary activities and end violent extra-parliamentary pressurising.[2191] The Agrarians insisted on 'the elevated road of parliamentarism' being followed. According to Antti Juutilainen, parliamentarism was the only consensual method to contain the socialism which remained in Finnish society:[2192]

> But if socialism is suppressed and forced to go underground, there is the danger that it will rise from there embittered and uncontrollable and that it will be much more difficult then to direct it onto the path of parliamentarism and consensual cooperation than it is now.

The re-engagement of the people in the running of public affairs was the way forward: Antti Rentola disagreed with attempts to prevent the people from voting as long as the 'Bolshevik contagion' might exist; indeed, the monarchist project itself was likely to provoke such radical reactions. If Germany was to be taken as a model, its experiences of socialist laws should demonstrate to the right the inefficiency of trying to confine revolutionary ideologies by limiting the political rights of the people to take part in politics through parliaments.[2193]

2185 *Hufvudstadsbladet*, 'Politisk nihilism', 9 August 1918.
2186 VP, Santeri Alkio, 7 August 1918, 1849.
2187 VP, Antti Juutilainen, 8 August 1918, 1869.
2188 VP, Santeri Alkio, 4 October 1918, 25.
2189 VP, Santeri Alkio, 4 October 1918, 27.
2190 VP, Santeri Alkio, 8 October 1917, 58.
2191 VP, Antti Rentola, 4 October 1918, 29; see also Santeri Alkio, 8 October 1917, 56, 73, 76.
2192 VP, Antti Juutilainen, 5 October 1918, 46.
2193 VP, Antti Rentola, 8 October 1918, 75.

The Agrarian calls for reconciliation were reinforced by the ideological interpretations of Matti Paasivuori, the sole voice in the parliament of the 'parliamentary Social Democrats', who were aiming at cooperation with bourgeois supporters of parliamentarism.[2194] Paasivuori concluded, ignoring the Speaker's explicit request to use a 'parliamentary' way of speaking[2195], that 'some of the bourgeoisie want to use the current class parliament to do as much harm to the Finnish working class as possible and to deprive it of all the benefits which the working people have achieved through parliamentary activity.'[2196] According to Paasivuori, the workers saw the current institution as no more than a 'rump' or 'residue parliament'. When the Rump Parliament had assumed the role of representing the people, ignoring protests from the workers, many members of the working class had adapted themselves. But this was no longer the case now that the aims of 'the class parliament' or 'half parliament' had been revealed and appeared from the perspective of the workers to constitute no less than a fight against the majority of the people. The actions of the current parliament had shown it to be illegal and unrepresentative of the people and no better than the main Red soviet during the Civil War.[2197] Paasivuori warned the representatives that the royal election and the further postponement of a new general election would lead to a deepening crisis of parliamentary legitimacy, particularly in view of the punishment of the Red rebels that was being practised in the background:[2198]

> You condemn the violent methods of the workers and expect a labour party that will focus on parliamentary activity to rise in this country. But at the same time you do all you can to turn the minds of the workers away from parliamentarism. For what value do you think that the workers give to a parliamentarism that provides benefits only for the bourgeois classes and oppresses the working class, leaving it without representation? Such parliamentarism will have no success, and if the current state of affairs continues for some time, it will be useless in this country for any worker to try to explain to the masses the good sides of parliamentarism.

Paasivuori thus summarised the key problem in the Finnish crisis of legitimacy of parliamentarism that had existed since spring 1917 and was continuing and deepening again in autumn 1918: the restoration of trust in parliamentarism among the left and the centre called for major a rethinking of the policies of the right.

It remained to be seen how the new polity would be able to solve this major crisis of parliamentary legitimacy as long as only one of the

---

2194 *Suomen Sosialidemokraatti*, 'Suomi hengittää yhdellä keuhkolla', 8 October 1918.
2195 See also VP, Matti Paasivuori, 10 October 1918, 124.
2196 VP, Matti Paasivuori, 8 October 1918, 71.
2197 VP, Matti Paasivuori, 9 October 1918, 99–100.
2198 VP, Matti Paasivuori, 9 October 1918, 100. The Social Democrats were supported in their endeavours by news that parliamentarism had obtained a decisive victory in Germany. *Suomen Sosialidemokraatti*, 'Monarkistit huolissaan', 4 October 1918; 'Waikutelmia Saksasta', 5 October 1918; 'Saksan suurin woitto', 7 October 1918.

parliamentary parties (the Agrarians) was unquestionably in favour of parliamentary government while another potentially parliamentary party (the reformed Social Democrats) remained excluded owing to its having previously abandoned parliamentary means. International pressures were also growing: American and British recognition of independence could not be expected under a German king, and even France would state that it did not regard the Finnish form of government as a legal one.[2199] The British were also unhappy about the royalist majority in the new government.[2200] In Swedish, German and British public and parliamentary discourse, the leaders of the Finnish regime had received a very bad name as extreme reactionaries. How would the Finnish political elite tackle the internal and external crisis of the legitimacy of its 'parliamentary' government? That – together with German and Swedish transitions to parliamentary democracy – is one of the issues we shall explore in the last chapter of this book.

2199 Also reported in *Neue Preußische Zeitung*, 22 October 1918.
2200 *The Manchester Guardian*, 'Finland's New Government', 30 November 1918.

7. The spring of 1919: The beginning of an era of democracy and parliamentarism?

7.1 Britain: Parliamentary democracy established or a bureaucratic state reinforced?

In spring 1919, when the other three national parliaments were still deliberating about the details of their constitutional reforms, the British wartime coalition had already extended suffrage and applied it in an election. As the public debates of autumn 1918 demonstrated, the democratic character of the British parliamentary system was increasingly taken for granted (except by the far left). However, the strongly steered nature of the reform, which had mobilised only half of the voters in December 1918 and produced a parliament in which the same coalition dominated, gave rise to criticisms about the existence of what was only seemingly a new type of parliamentary democracy in which little had actually changed. The old elite continued to hold power. The victorious Conservatives and their Liberal allies were happy about the results of the reform and did not hesitate to speak favourably about the updated parliamentary system.

The continued rule of the Coalition certainly smoothed the transition to an extended parliamentary democracy. There had been no socialist breakthrough of any significance in Britain. Despite all the seeming continuity, however, the war and the election had changed British party politics. While the immediate post-war period was favourable for the Conservatives, the party was affected by the new situation. Local party organisations needed to address a widened electorate, and many younger Conservative MPs had acquainted themselves with the ways of thinking of the working class during the war,[2201] and this potentially caused them to articulate their political views in a more reconciliatory manner.

Liberal ministers wished to introduce ambitious plans for reconstruction and social reforms. They found support from many Conservatives in the post-war atmosphere of national unity and a determination to stop Bolshevism. The common goal was to prevent radicalisation amongst the working class and unemployed former soldiers. The Liberals had been divided during the war and they became increasingly so as the government lost and opponents

---

2201 Ball 1995, 63–4.

won seats in by-elections. As the press debates on democratisation during 1918 had already suggested, the Conservatives would oppose Liberal policies on India. Conservative support for the Coalition would also diminish as a consequence of harder economic times, increasing social unrest and the growing bureaucratisation of government. Most of the planned reforms had to be rejected because of economic problems. Neither the Conservatives nor the Liberals were, in the end, ready to create a new centre party through a fusion of the government parties, as Lloyd George had envisioned when manipulating the election result of 1918.[2202]

Elsewhere in Europe, the future of democracy appeared far from secure, and fears about the spread of the Bolshevik Revolution to Western Europe continued to exist. Such fears were strengthened as a result of uprisings by radical socialists in several countries, particularly Germany, and by the activities of the British far left. Old fears of democracy as the class rule of the working class only – and thus as a way to socialism – had not withered away among the old elite,[2203] and they were constantly reinforced by revolutionary discourse among the far left in Russia, Britain and other countries. Ways to counteract the feared repercussions of the extension of suffrage and the potentially connected spread of Bolshevism remained high on the agendas of both domestic and foreign policy.

There was some unhappiness among the electorate with the Conservative Party as a counterweight to socialism but support for the far-right wing remained marginal in Britain.[2204] Public discourse was changing, with democracy becoming an increasingly usable concept for Conservatives as well. *The Times*, too, wrote about 'these democratic days' when the people were 'the real principals' both nationally and internationally.[2205] The Marquess of Salisbury recognised his belief in 'Tory democracy' in the sense of showing 'sympathy with the hopes, fears, and interests of the wage-earning classes'.[2206] For young academics, the parliamentary system had been sufficiently reformed, as can be seen in the Oxford Union, a university debating society that provided a training ground for politicians, voting against the motion that it 'had ceased to be effective and should be remodelled upon a popular and democratic basis'.[2207] Ideas about 'democratising the educational system' and making schools 'safe for democracy'[2208] were published in *The Times*, and the paper advised Britain to lead the world in evolutionary political and social change,[2209] though it was hardly an advocate of extensive democratic reforms.

2202 Ball 1991, 246; Ball 1995, 64–5; Pugh 2002, 157, 182.
2203 Cunningham 2001, 252.
2204 Webber 1986, 16.
2205 *The Times*, 'Peace and Publicity', 17 January 1919, 'Wanted – a Policy', 19 February 1919.
2206 *The Times*, 'Peers and the Rent Bill' (quoting the Marquess of Salisbury), 28 March 1919.
2207 *The Times*, 'The Parliamentary System', 31 May 1919; Haapala 2012.
2208 *The Times*, 'National Education', 26 March 1919.
2209 *The Times*, 'Giving the World a Lead', 5 March 1919.

The Liberal Prime Minister Lloyd George argued in the aftermath of the victorious election that the historic event 'afforded the democracy an opportunity of showing its confidence in the Government to change the face of the country',[2210] in other words by the public and Parliament giving the executive a full mandate. As for socialist direct action, he denounced it as Bolshevism and 'a complete subversion of every democratic doctrine'.[2211] *The Manchester Guardian* was assured that this prime minister was the best man to lead 'British democracy' and was capable of appealing directly to the people.[2212] The paper warned the Conservatives not to forget that 'the nation has never been so truly, keenly, and impatiently democratic in its every nerve' in the expectation of reforms.[2213] As for democracy and parliamentarism in international relations, issues discussed 'in the world-parliament in Paris' (i.e. the negotiations on the Treaty of Versailles) would continue to be subordinated to the British parliament, which constituted 'British Democracy'.[2214] National sovereignty would not be diminished in the face of international idealism.

The relationship to representative democracy of the Labour Party, which was accused of harbouring sympathies for Bolshevism, also remained an issue of some dispute. For the mainline party, despite its poor election results, parliamentary rather than extra-parliamentary activities were to be prioritised '[i]n a democratic country like ours, where democracy possesses political power'.[2215] Labour MPs readily used appeals to democracy to advance 'industrial democracy' and 'economic democracy',[2216] while a leading politician pointed out that democracy did not only belong to the workers.[2217] J. Ramsay MacDonald, outside Parliament, saw democracy as being in danger of becoming a farce[2218] and challenged the labour movement to discuss 'the position of Parliament in a system of democracy' as well.[2219] In his *Parliament and Revolution*, he did not see parliamentary means as sufficient for achieving socialism, although he admitted, like the majority of the party and the Social Democratic parties on the Continent, that there were hardly other ways to advance the interests of the working class. In the meantime, more radical Marxists had concluded that, after the Russian Revolution, the time of parliamentary methods was over.[2220] According to MacDonald, the people had been unhappy with Parliament, representative government and representative democracy 'as the means of expressing the

---

2210 *The Manchester Guardian*, 'Premier & Government Promises', 2 January 1919.
2211 *The Times*, 'The Prime Minister on Direct Action', 11 July 1919.
2212 *The Manchester Guardian*, 'The Premier and the Future', 20 April 1919.
2213 *The Manchester Guardian*, 'The Task of Parliament', 9 February 1919.
2214 *The Manchester Guardian*, 'Scenes at St. Stephen's', 20 April 1919.
2215 *The Manchester Guardian*, 'Labour in the New Parliament' (interview with J. H. Thomas), 1 January 1919.
2216 *The Manchester Guardian*, 'Labour's Policy of Reconstruction', 16 March 1919; *The Times*, 'Labour Memorandum', 27 March 1919.
2217 *The Times*, 'Brighter Prospect for Labour' (quoting J. R. Clynes), 31 March 1919.
2218 *The Manchester Guardian*, 'The New House of Commons', 6 January 1919.
2219 *The Times*, 'The Soviet System', 23 April 1919.
2220 Macintyre 1980, 194–5.

popular will' before the war and the election of December 1918 had not removed this dissatisfaction. This was particularly true with regard to Lloyd George's abuse of his power to call an immediate election in order to halt Labour. For MacDonald, the election had been an instance of 'an exploitation by political leaders moved by unusually low standards of honour, of the emotions of a country just released from the horrible stress of the war and intoxicated by the delight of victory'. As a consequence, MacDonald argued, anti-parliamentary movements were making progress, new political theories on parliamentary government were being introduced, and the Soviet system was spreading 'a totally new conception of political control, and of political democracy',[2221] though this was not something that MacDonald favoured.

Challenges to parliamentarism, which had been heard in Sweden and Finland in 1917, remained part of the British socialist conscience as well. 'To-day we are in revolutionary times' that touched 'Parliamentary government' as being 'a capitalist institution', wrote MacDonald. Lenin had taught that only revolution would create democracy for the working class, and in a real revolution 'representative democracy' was out of the question as Parliament was 'an ineffective thing' for the workers.[2222] For MacDonald, it was also disappointing that 'surrounded by democratic reforms, the "governing classes" have maintained their authority and have used democracy to maintain it.'[2223] As our analysis on Liberal and Conservative discourse and action has shown, this had undoubtedly happened in Britain. In some circles, it inspired a readiness for industrial action as a form of 'direct action' that might bring wage increases if nothing more.[2224] MacDonald, under whose leadership the Labour Party would rise in a few years' time, did not denounce direct action but declared himself a reformist anyway. In his vision, representative government should not be destroyed but radically reformed through devolution, a new electoral system that would produce MPs who really represented their constituencies. The goal was to combine socialism and democracy in a British, not a soviet, manner.[2225] This represented the mainline Social Democratic policies that then prevailed in Germany, Sweden and Finland, too.

Despite worries among some Conservatives and Liberals that the power of Parliament was deteriorating and support for Labour and widespread leftist disappointment with the practical effect of the extension of suffrage rising, only marginal extremist groups questioned the relevance of Parliament and sought alternative models.[2226] A relatively small group of 'council' communists were among these extremists, but they were unhappy with the 'nationalist' and 'capitalist' way in which the Russian Revolution had progressed. Hence, they preferred to continue working for a world revolution as they understood it. The anti-parliamentarism of former

---

2221 MacDonald 1919, 1–2.
2222 MacDonald 1919, 11, 13–14, 28, 56–7.
2223 MacDonald 1919, 58.
2224 Pugh 2002, 188.
2225 MacDonald 1919, 64–5, 103–104.
2226 Ball 1991, 247.

suffragists, on the other hand, had deepened as a result of inspiration from Russia. In June 1919 the Worker's Suffrage Federation (WSF) adopted an anti-parliamentary policy, with Sylvia Pankhurst contacting Lenin and allegedly moving towards revolutionary Marxist anarchism. Disputes on whether or not to use parliamentary elections for propaganda purposes continued among the far left: the Bolsheviks encouraged 'revolutionary parliamentarism', which aimed at replacing parliaments with soviets. At the same time, the WSF rejected elections and instead distributed revolutionary propaganda. According to them, parliamentary speaking was an inefficient way to talk to the people because of the distilling role of the capitalist press. Furthermore, once he was an MP, a communist might become a reformist, something that Labour MPs were generally accused of. Nevertheless even some communists concluded that the majority of the working classes considered Parliament legitimate and that it was necessary to participate in parliamentary work just to destroy such an illusion.[2227]

The transition to democracy was even more complicated in Germany, Sweden and Finland. From the point of view of British public discourse, dominated by debates on the terms of peace, there was little in German democratisation that was promising. *The Times* initially wrote more optimistically about 'German democracy' than *The Manchester Guardian*, recognising the German 'revolutionary' franchise reform as being based on 'the principles of democracy' advocated by the Allies[2228] and the election as 'an overwhelming verdict on the side of ordered democracy'.[2229] Though there was concern about possible Bolshevist advances at the cost of democracy[2230] and therefore a tendency to declare the entire assembly a failure in early March,[2231] *The Manchester Guardian* was assured that the new German Constitution was 'strictly democratic'.[2232] German reactions to the peace terms, on the other hand, manifested the 'weakness of the people' as opposed to being demonstrations of 'a manly democratic spirit',[2233] and in late June the paper concluded that the foreign policies of 'democratic Germany' had not really changed from those of 'reactionary Germany'. Hence, Germany did not deserve trust on the part of the Allied 'democracies'.[2234]

Comments in the Liberal press about the Weimar Constituent Assembly were sceptical: 'The Parliament of the German nation . . . has gone a long way towards the restoration of the old regime' and did not really distinguish itself from the former Reichstag, it was suggested. One reporter wondered about 'the complete absence of anything to indicate the advent of a radically new era and a new spirit'.[2235] Another writer could not believe that Prussia would change her temperament and predicted: 'the kind of democracy being

2227 Macintyre 1980, 195, 197; Shipway 1988, x, 6–9, 18–20, 62.
2228 *The Times*, 'Responsible German Representatives', 24 January 1919.
2229 *The Times*, 'The Struggle in Germany', 28 February 1919.
2230 *The Times*, 'The German Government and its Rivals', 3 March 1919.
2231 *The Times*, 'Failure of Weimar Assembly', 8 March 1919.
2232 *The Times*, 'The German Counter-Proposals', 29 May 1919.
2233 *The Times*, 'The Progress Towards Peace', 16 May 1919.
2234 *The Times*, 'German "Faith"', 23 June 1919.
2235 *The Manchester Guardian*, 'German Government', 20 February 1919.

forged under the Republic is very different from that which Europe would recognise as a guarantee of peace.'[2236] One experienced observer did see the National Constituent Assembly as seriously trying to create a democratic constitution and advised the British not to disrupt the process with excessively severe peace terms.[2237] All the same, for *The Manchester Guardian*, the Weimar Parliament was a mere 'hapless assembly'[2238] that lacked a parliamentary spirit in the eyes of a 'westerner'.[2239] The adoption of the Weimar Constitution brought no welcoming comments in British papers – rather expressions of superiority.

Swedish democratisation no longer attracted any attention in Britain during spring 1919. Sweden mainly appeared in discussions surrounding the founding of the League of Nations, with Hjalmar Branting featuring as a spokesman for the neutral countries and for extended democracy in international relations. In this context, he took up the dispute over the Åland Islands with Finland, implying just before the Finnish election that the Finnish government remained 'only the Government of half the people'.[2240] Indicative of the reorientation in Scandinavian political cultures from Germany to Britain is Branting's address to the British Labour Conference, in which he stated that Swedish socialism had been initially influenced by the German labour movement but had 'turned more and more for guidance to the democracies of the West'. Indeed, the fall of the Hohenzollern monarchy 'had given a great impetus to democratic forces in Sweden'.[2241] The only worrying news from Sweden was that the far left there seemed to be aiming for the 'true democracy of the Soviet system', i.e. a dictatorship of the proletariat through class war.[2242] Branting ostentatiously denounced Bolshevism – as seen in Finland and in Petrograd by the Swedes – as the negation of socialism. For Branting, socialism stood for the 'organisation' of democracy.[2243]

The Finns, too, had started to rethink their pro-Prussian political culture, at first with the founding of an Anglo-French Club that welcomed members 'who appreciate the culture of the West'.[2244] There was also the counterproductive news that some MPs had opposed 'Finnish humility before the Entente, and declared that their sympathies would always remain with Germany'.[2245] Widespread Bolshevik propaganda was reported to be hampering the internal situation in the country,[2246] and the promises of the

---

2236 *The Observer*, '"The Round Table"', 2 March 1919.
2237 *The Manchester Guardian*, George Saunders, 'The Situation in Germany', 20 April 1919.
2238 *The Manchester Guardian*, 'The Treaty and After', 4 May 1919.
2239 *The Manchester Guardian*, 'How Germany Agreed to Sign', 25 June 1919.
2240 *The Manchester Guardian*, 'Neutrals and League of Nations', 19 February 1919.
2241 *The Manchester Guardian*, 'Labour Conference', 27 June 1919.
2242 *The Manchester Guardian*, 'The Soviet Idea', 23 July 1919.
2243 *The Times*, 'M. Branting's Denunciation of Bolshevism', 22 April 1919.
2244 *The Manchester Guardian*, 'Anglo-French Club in Finland', 14 January 1919.
2245 *The Times*, 'Germany's Finnish Friends', 24 January 1919; see also Hentilä & Hentilä 2016, 371.
2246 *The Manchester Guardian*, 'Bolshevism Spreading in Finland', 11 April 1919.

socialists to use only parliamentary methods were regarded with suspicion.[2247] A republican majority in the new election[2248] and progress in plans for a republican constitution, and especially Finnish support for British anti-Bolshevik measures, earned Finland British recognition of its independence as a 'counter-revolutionary country'. This happened despite continuous complaints about the White terror in the British public debate.[2249] *The Times* reported via Sweden that that there was an unparalleled class war between the Whites and the Reds going on in a country which 'belongs more to the East than the West' and had 'the forms without the traditions of democracy and freedom'. Not even Russia had yet seen anything corresponding to the Finnish hostilities.[2250] In a report from Helsinki, William T. Goode concluded that this previously democratic country had turned to a ferocity in its treatment of the Reds that was only likely to provoke more support for Bolshevism.[2251] Considerations related to great power politics rather than the advancement of democracy would seem to have dominated the change in British policy towards Finland. An interesting detail is that the Finnish Eduskunta continued to be called 'the Diet' rather than 'the Parliament' in a more progressive sense;[2252] this obviously arose from its previous Swedish name 'Lantdag', a word that associated it with regional estate assemblies in Prussia and elsewhere, rather than the contemporary 'Riksdag'. Clearly, the status of Finland as a democratic policy remained doubtful in the British public debate, and only the implementation of a new republican constitution would gradually start to change these reserved conceptions.

7.2 The construction of a democratic and parliamentary Germany in the Weimar National Assembly

7.2.1 Expert planning for a new constitution

After October 1918, Germany experienced the most dramatic of the constitutional upheavals in the four cases studied here. First the Prussian political order, which had despised parliamentarism and prioritised executive power, was transformed into a parliamentary monarchy in October 1918, then the monarchy collapsed on 9 November 1918, and the far left attempted to introduce council rule at the local level. This attempt failed in the face of what was to be known as the Weimar Coalition, formed by the Social Democrats and the centre parties – the Catholic Centre had also moved over to the side of parliamentarism.[2253] 'Democracy' had

---

2247 *The Times*, 'Finnish Coalition', 21 April 1919.
2248 *The Times*, 'Finnish Republican Majority', 13 March 1919.
2249 *The Manchester Guardian*, 'Recognition for Finland', 7 May 1919, 'British Squadron off Helsingfors', 14 May 1919.
2250 *The Times*, 'Class War in Finland', 11 February 1919.
2251 *The Manchester Guardian*, 'The White Terror in Finland', 14 July 1919.
2252 *The Times*, 'Class War in Finland', 11 February 1919; *The Manchester Guardian*, 'Finland and British Recognition', 8 May 1919, 'Finland a Republic', 24 June 1919.
2253 Grosser 1970, 158.

been almost a party slogan of the Social Democrats in autumn 1918, and parliamentarism had been defended by some liberals as well, but the rejection of both remained categorical among the right. There had been neither the time nor the willingness for the kind of rethinking which the right in many other countries was forced to undertake in these years.

A solution to the constitutionally awkward situation after the German Revolution was to be sought by a national constituent assembly. Convening a special assembly to discuss the constitution was nothing new in German history: the Frankfurt Parliament of 1848–49 had already tried to find a solution for all of Germany but had failed to do so owing to a Prussian intervention. The idea of convening a national constituent assembly was supported by most political groups – including the liberals, members of the old elite and most socialists. The starting point seemed promising in that the assembly constituted a legitimate sovereign body supported by a large number of the people and elected on the basis of universal suffrage.[2254] However, this was not the whole truth: parliamentary traditions, such as ministerial responsibility to the parliament, or allowing parliamentary decisions to govern policies, were weak and trust in the parliament as an institution low. The dissatisfaction of the right resulting from the German Revolution was reinforced by the strengthening myth that Germany had lost the war as a result of the left plotting with the enemy and the consequent deterioration of the situation on the home front after 1917.[2255] The right, too, had been ready for some concessions that would allow the people better involvement in politics and for the appeasement of the Western powers with demonstrations of reforms. But once the Western powers proved inflexible on the terms of peace – at a time when the constitutional debates were approaching a conclusion in Germany – all readiness to advance parliamentary government evaporated among the right. Their attitudes would not move towards democracy like the majority of the right in Britain, Sweden and Finland – though there was a considerable delay in these countries, too.

Despite the rightist doubts, constitutional reforms proceeded with speed once the war was over. The general election of 19 January 1919 was already based on universal suffrage and proportional representation. The turnout (83%) suggests a high degree of political mobilisation. The SPD was successful, winning 37.9 per cent of the votes and 165 seats, which increased the self-confidence of their parliamentary argumentation. The Independent Socialists received just 7.6 per cent of the votes and 22 seats,[2256] while the Communists boycotted the election,[2257] which removed the far left to the margins of the assembly. The German Social Democratic Party had avoided radicalisation of the kind experienced in Russia or Finland, and it had even earned a reputation as a patriotic party that supported the war effort, albeit hardly among the right.

2254 Bollmeyer 2007, 196.
2255 Leonhard 2014, 916.
2256 Bollmeyer 2007, 216.
2257 Gusy 1997, 59.

Republican, anti-monarchical and parliamentary feelings were strong among the voters. The election result led to the creation of the Weimar Coalition, which was formed by the SPD, the liberal German Democratic Party (DDP) and the Catholic Centre,[2258] the supporters of parliamentarisation and democratisation now being joined by the Catholics. The chances for a successful adoption of a republican and democratic constitution were there. However, deepening economic problems, depressing news about the peace negotiations and the looming threat of a civil war[2259] prevented the realisation of such a possibility. Thomas Mergel has concluded that the election of January 1919 was the only occasion when the emerging parliamentary system won the support of the majority of the German people.[2260] Later in the spring, the moment had passed.

Outside Germany, these developments found a mixed reception: the British did not really believe that their former enemy was learning from the Western powers and adopting parliamentary government; the doubts were deep. On the other hand, the Swedish Liberal-Social Democratic government pointed to Germany when asserting to the right that the parliamentarisation of government and the democratisation of suffrage had become inevitable. In Finland, the German election suggested not only to republicans but also to most monarchists (apart from the Swedish People's Party) that the time for a Prussian-type of monarchy was over. If Germany, the principal protector of Finland in 1918, was turning into a parliamentary democracy, the same should happen in Finland, particularly when the pressures in that direction from the West were so obvious.

Previous research on the German constitutional debates of spring 1919 has been more extensive than that on the British, Swedish or Finnish reforms. Particularly noteworthy are Heiko Bollmeyer's discussions of the uses of the concepts of the people and democracy by various political groups.[2261] Tina Pohl has explored 'democratic thought' in the Weimar National Constituent Assembly from the legal point of view, problematising the use of the concepts of the people and the state in the debates, though not always with complete conceptual historical sensitivity.[2262] For Thomas Mergel, the National Constituent Assembly constituted a precursor of parliamentary culture in the Weimar Republic.[2263]

On 6 February 1919, the elected members of the National Constituent Assembly convened in Weimar – symbolically not in the Prussian capital but in a capital of German *culture*, a place where this had taken shape during the age of National Romanticism – to adopt a democratic constitution for the new republic. However, the representatives wanted to discuss everyday problems rather than the basic values of the future German polity, a trait that, of course, had been typical of the reform debates in Britain, Sweden and

---

2258 Bollmeyer 2007, 218.
2259 Gusy 1997, 39–40.
2260 Mergel 2002, 38.
2261 Bollmeyer 2007, esp. 368–73.
2262 Pohl 2002, 116.
2263 Mergel 2002.

Finland as well. Political bitterness had intensified under non-parliamentary government, and the Revolution had affected the views of the representatives. They were confronted with a major challenge in replacing the Prussian political order with a democratic parliamentary republic. This was not going to be easy as a result of the continuing prevailing attitudes and the rightist view that the entire process had been imposed from outside. Would the will of the people now be recognised as the basis for the new political order, as had been vaguely suggested by the Chancellor and the Kaiser in spring 1917, demanded in Western war propaganda and envisioned in the reforms of October 1918? And what would popular sovereignty possibly imply?[2264]

While 'the people' were indeed generally regarded as the source of political authority,[2265] understandings of the implications varied dramatically. Given the contested meaning of democracy in any polity, ideological differences and the somewhat imported nature of the key notions, the representatives held heterogeneous understandings of democracy, popular sovereignty and parliamentarism.[2266] None of the seven parties had a coherent conception of what the constitution should be like either,[2267] which complicated the negotiations.

At the opening of the Assembly on 6–7 February 1919, the strongest expressions in favour of parliamentary democracy were again heard from the Social Democrats, who had since autumn taken the lead in attempts to transform the polity of the Reich. Their interpretations were consistently disputed by the right – if not always in speeches then at least in pejorative interjections. Many members of the right made no contribution, excluding themselves from the process of negotiation and reconciliation on democracy, as some speakers in October 1918 had already suggested. The first reading of the constitutional proposal took place between 28 February and 4 March 1919 – at a time when the British electoral reform had already been put into force, the Swedish electoral reform was waiting for an extension to the national level and to women, and the Finns were voting in their first parliamentary election after the Civil War. During the committee stage between 4 March and 18 June, publicity was limited and prevented transnational transfers to Sweden and Finland, both of which were making constitutional decisions at the time, their parliaments assuming that Germany was on the way to extensive parliamentary democracy. Tina Pohl has suggested that the lack of publicity facilitated cooperation between committee members and the search for pragmatic solutions to a greater extent than the plenary debates, which more easily led to the politicisation of issues,[2268] especially given the confrontational political culture of the old Reichstag. But the key issues were later taken up in the plenaries as well, often in a radicalised form that

---

2264 Bollmeyer 2007, 9.
2265 Bollmeyer 2005, 113.
2266 Pohl 2002, 3.
2267 Bollmeyer 2007, 214.
2268 Pohl 2002, 103–104, 146. This interpretation may have arisen out of a tendency in German research to play down the significance of plenary debates on the basis of the issues having been settled elsewhere; Bollmeyer 2005, 119.

reveals the ideological differences between the parties. An important factor that decreased parliamentary publicity was a general strike in early March, which prevented the publication of non-socialist papers and subsequently caused them to focus on strike-related unrest.

The last two phases of the legislative process between 2 and 22 July 1919 and 29 and 31 July 1919 were complicated because of the tense international relations after the conclusion of the Treaty of Versailles and a domestic political crisis. The passage of the constitution received very modest attention in the press, since the parliament was rather expected to provide solutions to acute everyday problems (as had been the case in Britain and Finland and to a great extent in Sweden as well).[2269] The second reading began on 2 July 1919, just four days after the Treaty of Versailles had been signed and at a time when the economy was rapidly deteriorating. The peace terms had led to the replacement of Philipp Scheidemann's (SPD) government with that of Gustav Bauer (SPD) supported only by the Social Democrats and the centre, but no longer by the left-liberals. Awareness of the hard terms of the treaty captured the attention of the parliamentarians, and unavoidably affected the course of the debates on the constitution.[2270]

The July debates in Weimar could no longer affect constitutional decisions in the Swedish and Finnish national parliaments. With the major ideological importance of Germany for both monarchists and republicans, interest in the German constitution had nevertheless remained considerable. Many of the central issues of the republican constitutions, not least the question of the duality of government and the role of the president, were common to the debates in Germany and Finland, although there were also major differences arising from the federal nature of the German polity. Federalism was an important feature of Germany but secondary for the more uniform nation-states, so that our attention will next focus on the common issues discussed in the other national parliaments as well.

7.2.2 A REVOLUTION AGAINST DICTATORSHIP

The opening of the National Constituent Assembly was an emotional moment, 'like a dream', for the Social Democrats.[2271] A prominent role was played by their leader Friedrich Ebert, who had already been in a key position in the transition of power first from the General Staff to the government of Max von Baden and then in a government led by Ebert himself. Ebert advocated the summoning of a national constituent assembly and suppressed the radical plans of the Independents, which made his policies appear as a betrayal of the working class in the eyes of the far left. In his opening speech in Weimar, Ebert now defended the limited 'revolution' as an alternative to both the Russian Revolution and the council movement of November 1918. According to Ebert, 'the German people' had made a revolution against an old, declining 'dictatorship' (*Gewaltherrschaft*) – an interpretation of the former political order that was shared by the Social

---

2269 See, for instance, *Berliner Tageblatt*, 30 July – 1 August 1919.
2270 Pohl 2002, 210.
2271 *Vorwärts*, 7 February 1919.

Democrats and most liberals, while the right protested with heckling.[2272] Bourgeois circles criticised Ebert afterwards for having spoken from an excessively socialist point of view.[2273] The far left remained unhappy with what they regarded as an incomplete revolution. The division in views of the Revolution implied that the project of building a parliamentary polity was in danger of remaining one of the Social Democrats only.

The Social Democrats did not mind monopolising the ideologically central concept of revolution:[2274] the term 'revolution' seemingly allowed them to absolve themselves of any responsibility for the miserable state into which 'the German people' had been taken by 'the mistaken politics of the old powers'.[2275] By implication, the right was responsible for the crisis of autumn 1918 and hence also for the Revolution. The Social Democrats wanted to represent their revolution in a way that distinguished it from the less fortunate ones in Russia in 1917 and in Germany by the far left in late 1918. From the rightist point of view, of course, the Social Democrats and their allies remained guilty of the fall of Germany.

In the second plenary, after he had been elected Speaker, Eduard David (SPD) set out to define the mission of the new representative body. Once the war and the Revolution had 'demoralised and broken' the old system of government, it was the duty of the Assembly to construct a new constitution that would better serve the needs of the polity.[2276] David's general description of the state of affairs in the aftermath of the war and the Revolution was easy to accept for many, but he went further and argued that the Revolution had not only been a political coup but should also be seen as an economic and social turning point,[2277] which brought in a socialist agenda. David's argument was needed in order to challenge the Independent Social Democrats, who were demanding further revolutionary measures. It also appeased the left wing of his own party. However, such goals were not supported by the bourgeois parties.[2278] In the other three countries studied here, leading Majority Social Democrats were usually careful not to associate constitutional alterations with instant changes in economic and social structures, although in Sweden the Social Democrats had begun to move in that direction once the suffrage reform was secured. Among the parties of the far left (and the Finnish Social Democrats before the Civil War) such views were openly entertained.

The left-liberal allies held a slightly different concept of revolution. Hugo Preuß (German Democratic Party), who was a Professor of Law, had previously argued in favour of popular government and, as the Minister of Interior Affairs, had drafted a proposal aiming at a balance between

---

2272 Verhandlungen, Friedrich Ebert, 6 February 1919, 1; *Berliner Tageblatt*, 7 February 1919.
2273 *Berliner Tageblatt*, 6 February 1919; *Neue Preußische Zeitung*, 7 February 1919, quoting *Berliner Tageblatt*. Even *Vorwärts*, 7 February 1919, recognised that Ebert had emphasised socialism.
2274 *Vorwärts*, 6 February 1919.
2275 Verhandlungen, Friedrich Ebert, 6 February 1919, 1.
2276 Verhandlungen, Eduard David, 7 February 1919, 8–9.
2277 Verhandlungen, Eduard David, 7 February 1919, 9.
2278 *Berliner Tageblatt*, 8 February 1919.

parliamentarism, presidentialism, government and the referendum. He now likewise suggested that any opposition by the monarchists to the realisation of popular sovereignty (a term not used as such in the draft) had been eliminated 'by the fact of the Revolution'.[2279] Now the revolutionary era, too, had come to an end; it was time for the Assembly to merely confirm the new legal order.[2280]

Such 'attempts to declare the Revolution over' were strongly opposed by the Independent Social Democrats, who considered themselves losers in the Social Democratic-centrist settlement and consequently wanted to carry on the struggle. For Dr. Oskar Cohn, it was unacceptable that the 'Revolution' should be declared finished and the entire term excluded from the draft constitution. 'Revolution', after all, meant that the entire German state needed to be recreated.[2281]

Very different views on the Revolution were voiced by the right. Konrad Beyerle, a Bavarian Professor of Law, insisted that the 'revolutionary confusion' had already established a sufficiently democratic and parliamentary order and that no further measures in that direction were needed.[2282] Rudolf Heinze of the new German People's Party, a former Minister of Justice of Saxony, ignored any redefinition of the polity and instead defended the old Bismarckian constitution.[2283] Still further to the right, Clemens von Delbrück of the German National People's Party, who had participated in the parliamentarisation of the constitution in October 1918, maintained that the November Revolution had been totally unnecessary as the reforms of the preceding month had already created a new German polity.[2284] The rightist view was that Germany should remain a parliamentarised constitutional monarchy and reject radical reform. Adelbert Düringer consequently urged the Social Democrats to finally give up 'the illusion of a world revolution'.[2285]

International comparisons and reflections on an ongoing transnational transition to parliamentary democracy remained few and far between, which reflects a German tendency to nationalise the debate after uncomfortable external interventions. Many members, especially lawyers, had studied only in German universities, which decreased the number and depth of their international contacts in comparison with the rather more cosmopolitan (or at least German-oriented) Swedish and Finnish lawyers. The British, for their part, although lacking Continental perspectives, often had common-law examples from the dominions or the United States in mind. The members of the Assembly thus tended to see the German situation in 1919 as unique in comparison with the circumstances of the other great powers: Britain and France had created their parliamentary democracies earlier and retained them in wartime, and at the time of the peace negotiations in

2279 Verhandlungen, Hugo Preuß, 8 February 1919, 12.
2280 Verhandlungen, Hugo Preuß, 8 February 1919, 13; also *Berliner Tageblatt*, 11 February 1919.
2281 Verhandlungen, Oskar Cohn, 10 February 1919, 22.
2282 Verhandlungen, Konrad Beyerle, 3 March 1919, 464.
2283 Pohl 2002, 123.
2284 Pohl 2002, 119.
2285 Verhandlungen, Adelbert Düringer, 30 July 1919, 2090.

Versailles they did not seem to be likely sources of inspiration. Russia had gone its revolutionary way, one rejected by a great majority of Germans, and the United States – even if a republic with a president preaching the gospel of democracy – was seen by many as too different (or too upstart) to offer an applicable model. Only Oskar Cohn, an Independent Social Democrat and Jewish internationalist, argued that the possibilities for 'a democratic culture and tradition' were much better in republican France and the United States because of the different attitudes that prevailed among the bourgeoisie there. In line with his radical argument, Cohn also questioned the relevance of previous German constitutions as starting points for what the German republicans should create.[2286] This irritated those who continued to regard the nineteenth-century tradition of constitutional monarchy as one that ensured stability and strength. A particular reason for Cohn to view the American and French constitutions so positively may have been their recognition of Jews as equal citizens.

According to Christopher Gusy, the US model did play a role in the formulation of the German constitution thanks to its presidential nature. One initial intention had been, after all, to formulate a constitution that would induce the Americans to grant milder terms of peace. To a more limited extent, the French, British and neighbouring Swiss models were relevant in theoretical debates, although they were interpreted selectively according to traditional German ways of thinking.[2287] What was going on in minor powers such as the Netherlands, Sweden or Finland was not considered to have any significance. The Swiss model counted because of that country's cultural proximity and perhaps to a limited extent also because of international socialist interest in its use of direct appeals to the people and its committee-like government, which distinguished it from Western European parliamentarism. For many, however, the Frankfurt National Constituent Assembly of 1848 was the only point of comparison with the one in Weimar in 1919.

7.2.3 Defining 'the most democratic democracy in the world'

Vorwärts characterised the opening of the National Constituent Assembly as a fight for 'the idea of democracy as always represented by Social Democracy' against both rightist and leftist extremes, the Assembly being represented as the very 'bearer of democracy'.[2288] Friedrich Ebert, who as Chairman of the Social Democratic Party had been directing the constitutional transition since November, set the establishment of the new democracy in Germany as a goal. However, a wide variety of understandings of democracy obviously continued to coexist within the reformist coalition. In the debates, the members used the term pragmatically, aiming at solving concrete problems,[2289] but 'democracy' did not constitute a simple answer to

---

2286 Verhandlungen, Oskar Cohn, 10 February 1919, 23.
2287 Gusy 1997, 63.
2288 *Vorwärts*, 6 February 1919.
2289 Gusy 2000a, 23–5; Kühne 2000, 116.

these. The meanings that the members associated with the word reflected prevailing political opinions among sections of German society, and these varied a lot as no real tradition of democratic thought or historical experiences of democracy extending beyond broad male suffrage in Reichstag elections existed. Because of the wartime challenge of 'Western democracy', the concept continued to have pejorative associations with foreign intrusion. The peculiar nature of the Revolution of November 1918, with both the right and the far left remaining dissatisfied with the result, accusations that the war had been lost as a result of the activities of socialist traitors, the abuses of the councils created by the far left, a state of latent civil war during the sessions of the Assembly and the lack of economic relief with the transition to parliamentary democracy all made the concept of democracy a negatively charged one in the German context.[2290] There were numerous similarities with the Finnish constitutional crisis, but the Finns had a longer national tradition of representation, had already experienced their worst confrontations in 1917–18 and succeeded in bringing most of the Social Democrats and the Finnish-speaking right over to the side of limited democracy during the constitutional debates of spring 1919.

Without emphasising 'democracy' very extensively in these circumstances, Friedrich Ebert defined the new constitution in vernacular terms, expressing its premises in parlance that might be easier to reconcile with the traditions of German politics. Ebert talked about 'our free people's republic' (*Unsere freie Volksrepublik*)[2291] rather than 'democracy' in any sense recommended to Germany by Allied war propaganda. Eduard David, who possessed a doctorate in German and thus had a highly sophisticated sense of the semantic associations of the words, talked about *Volksherrschaft* (rule by the people) as a vernacular alternative to the foreign term, though he also sometimes referred to 'democracy' becoming central in the new political system, which he described as a 'democratic republic'.[2292] There was a longer tradition in Northern Europe of replacing 'democracy' with vernacular terms that referred to popular government (*volksregeering* in Dutch, *folkstyre* in Swedish, *kansanvalta* in Finnish). Such coinages derived from words for 'the people' often recalled ethnic and organic understandings of the state as a community of a uniform or consensual people. In Germany more clearly than elsewhere, the war had strengthened notions of the existence of a classless *Volksgemeinschaft* (community of the people), within which the people shared a common 'organic' spirit and were identical with their state. Such a polity thus could not be considered a pluralistic society suffering from conflicts of interest. Historians agree that this concept actually constituted a powerful alternative to Western parliamentary systems and Western political theory. In the context of 1919, *Volksgemeinschaft* provided a basis for conceptualising democracy in a positive, ethnic, initially enlightened and seemingly apolitical way.[2293] However, the fact that it was also able to

---

2290 Gusy 2000a, 27; Kühne 2000, 117.
2291 Verhandlungen, Friedrich Ebert, 6 February 1919, 2.
2292 Verhandlungen, Eduard David, 4 March 1919, 498, 500.
2293 See Grosser 1970, 219; Llanque 2000, 322; Bruendel 2003, 259; Leonhard 2006, 210.

provide an argument for dictatorship would become obvious towards the end of the Weimar Republic.

During and after the Weimar Assembly, *Volksgemeinschaft* was, according to Thomas Mergel, a favourite concept for most German political groups, who regarded it as expressing the prevailing wishes of the people concerning the German political culture and as characterising a harmonious community in which societal conflicts of interest had come to an end.[2294] *Volksgemeinschaft* could be interpreted in nationalist, socialist, conservative or *völkisch* (popular) terms, so that both Social Democrats and Conservatives were able to identify with it.[2295] Whether the yearning after a harmonious ethnic community was realistic and reconcilable with pluralistic democracy seems questionable in hindsight, but this was not always apparent to the people of the time. In this kind of collectivistic thinking, the concept 'the people' included more than just the majority, and the will of the people was more than just the current majority opinion. It followed from such an understanding of a community of the people that a parliament alone could not possibly be regarded as a trustworthy indicator of the will of the people,[2296] an interpretation that supported the solutions of the constitutional proposal drafter by liberals.

Volksgemeinschaft thus tended to make the concept of the people in a nationalistic sense dominate over democracy and parliamentarism in senses that referred to active political participation by the citizens and pro et contra debate. Such a way of thinking was by no means influential in Germany only: many rightist MPs in Sweden and Finland also entertained notions resembling the concept of a *Volksgemeinschaft*, as we saw in the debates of 1918. In Finnish, the customary vernacularisation of democracy was *kansanvalta*, which could be understood to refer to the totality of the people rather than mere majority opinion (the Social Democrats had monopolised the concept of the will of the people in 1917), though the extent of the concept was limited by the bilingual nature of the country and connected notions of two peoples (Finnish- and Swedish-speakers) within one nation. As we have seen, the Finnish term carried connotations derived from ethnicity (*kansa* = folk) and social difference, not only from 'the people' in a political sense. The constitutional conclusions that were drawn in Finland were similar to those in Germany: a counter-force to the parliament was called for, a presidency being seen particularly by the right as another and even more genuine representative of the will of the people. As section 7.4 will show, monarchist theorists and linguists in Finland therefore preferred to translate 'republic' with the word *kansanvaltio* (state of the people), which comes very close to contemporary German translations.

Wilhelm Pfannkuch (SPD), the most senior of the German MPs, saw no reason to avoid 'democracy' but preferred to give it a national connotation by emphasising the particular 'German democracy' which the

---

2294 Mergel 2002, 54; The nobility did not share this view, however. Malinowski 2003, 603.
2295 Bruendel 2003, 140.
2296 Gusy 1997, 64.

National Constituent Assembly itself constituted. This implied that some suspect Western democracy was not simply being imposed on Germany and that German socialists were not merely associating themselves with a transnational democratic moment. It suggested that there existed democratic traditions on which to build, at least within the Social Democratic movement in Germany. Like parliamentarism, democracy should be seen as the result of a *national* process leading to a fundamentally *German* political system, not one imported from abroad. Anyone who dared to oppose this democracy was, according to Pfannkuch, a 'counter-revolutionary'.[2297] This tendency to nationalise democracy, understandable in the context of constant accusations of betrayal by the right, was stronger among German than Swedish Social Democrats, while the Finnish Social Democrats acted in essentially the same manner.

Eduard David (SPD) was in a position, first as Speaker of the Assembly, to define 'democracy' and then, as the Minister for Internal Affairs, to direct the process of constructing the new polity. Clearly happy about the proposed constitutional reform, he turned to superlatives in declaring it to be productive of 'the most democratic constitution in the world'. For a Social Democrat, democracy was based on the complete equality of the rights of the citizens. David recognised that democracy had not so long ago been rejected in Germany as 'a concept with a rather evil reputation' and that many still longed for the so-called good old days. These opponents of democratisation should learn that 'democracy' expressed 'the highest political ideal' of the day. In democracy as defined by David, the people possessed the right of self-determination but were also responsible for demonstrating 'political self-denial' with respect to democratic majority decisions: 'the democratic rights of an individual are limited by the democratic rights of others.'[2298] These principles still seemed to be something that had to be taught to the supporters of the old regime. Advising the members of the Assembly in his role as Speaker, David applied the principles of democracy to parliamentary procedure: 'In this house, too, the responsibilities of democracy must be observed.' When David revealingly declared that the house should be 'a site of free democratic subordination of the individual to the will and work of the collectivity', the implication was that the right might not be ready to recognise decisions made by the parliamentary majority (which had not held such decisive power under the Prussian political order).[2299] This meant that pre-war traditions of confrontation should be given up and majority opinions and votes respected, though there was also a hint of the *Volksgemeinschaft* included. The goal for parliamentary work and individual MPs was to demonstrate that 'Germany is a country mature enough for democracy'.[2300] Doubts among the German right about the maturity of

---

2297 Verhandlungen, Wilhelm Pfannkuch, 6 February 1919, 4.
2298 Verhandlungen, Eduard David, 7 February 1919, 8.
2299 Verhandlungen, Eduard David, 7 February 1919, 8.
2300 Verhandlungen, Eduard David, 7 February 1919, 8. See also Friedrich von Payer's similar suggestion on successful parliamentary work as a demonstration of the breakthrough of 'the democratic idea' on 10 February 1919, 21.

the people for a democracy found a parallel in rightist sceptics in Sweden and Finland. In the British political culture, on the other hand, similar conservative doubts had become more difficult to express. The British were rather observing whether or not the Germans were mature enough.

David next elevated democracy into the position of a programmatic concept, arguing further that the constitution would create 'a democratic republic, a republic in which the supreme state power rests with the people, in which the representation of the people is the source of political power.' The use of this power of the people would, furthermore, be based on the most 'democratic' suffrage in the world.[2301] In the final debates he asserted, as a reaction to claims that the constitution was a mere 'comedy of democracy in the world', that this 'most democratic democracy in the world' would ensure peaceful development through legislation,[2302] the repetitive nature of the attribute reflecting the continuously highly contested meaning of 'democracy'. Responding to rightist criticism about how democracy was understood by the government, David now explained, employing conservative language, that democracy was needed to support 'the national feeling of a state',[2303] nationalising the concept discursively as a concession to the discourse of the opposition. David actually assigned senses of a 'community of the people' in an ethnic sense to democracy, reinforcing its essentially German rather than universal nature. Many leading Social Democrats had supported the national effort during the war, and they, too, continued to see democracy in more nationalist terms than was the case in most other countries, especially in Sweden.

David's advice to the supposedly non-democratic – or even 'anti-democratic' as *Vorwärts* more abrasively put it[2304] – minority and nationalistic redefinitions of democracy hardly convinced the parliamentary right. Their reaction was often to see 'democracy' as a concept which the Social Democrats were defining to serve merely party-political ends and the interests of the victors in the war. It remained difficult for many on the right to reconcile themselves with the victors of the German constitutional struggle no matter how moderate the German Majority Social Democratic discourse was by international standards. Interesting is the collectivistic attitude reflected by David's 'democratic subordination of the individual' in a majority democracy: Would such a democracy tolerate a plurality of views and respect minorities?

Social Democratic speakers, now in influential political positions, talked willingly about 'the democratic construction of our country' in 'the spirit of democracy'.[2305] *Vorwärts* asserted that the provisional constitution was 'purely

---

2301 Verhandlungen, Eduard David, 4 March 1919, 498. The formulation resembles that of the beginning of the Finnish republican constitution of July 1919.
2302 Verhandlungen, Eduard David, 31 July 1919, 2194–5.
2303 Verhandlungen, Eduard David, 4 March 1919, 500.
2304 *Vorwärts*, 11 February 1919.
2305 See for instance Verhandlungen, Paul Löbe, 10 February 1919, 20. Löbe had been deeply engaged in Social Democratic discourse and activism since his early youth and had in November 1918 proclaimed the opening of 'a cathedral of Democracy' in Breslau.

democratic' and guaranteed 'the democratic development of Germany'.[2306] But did the Social Democrats manage to persuade the representatives of other parties with this discourse? Their organ did recognise the left-liberals as equal 'democrats'.[2307] In practice, though the left-liberals should have had no reason to avoid the concept and had already used it positively in the autumn, they nevertheless did not mention democracy very often. There were some exceptions, to be sure: Friedrich von Payer – a dedicated defender of democratisation and parliamentarism, a former Vice Chancellor of the Reich and a leader of the German Democratic Party – did not hesitate to characterise the new Germany as a 'democracy',[2308] voicing the long-term goal of many liberals from the southern German states. The liberal organ, *Berliner Tageblatt*, also welcomed the provisional constitution as the first building block of a democratic Germany.[2309]

Indicative of the limits placed on 'democracy' in the new constitution is that its formulator Hugo Preuß (German Democratic Party), an advocate of the *Volksstaat* (state of the people), did not talk about the content of the concept before the Assembly. Preuß merely stated that in the future 'democratically recognised power' would be exercised and implied that democracy required a strong central power as opposed to particularistic tendencies;[2310] democracy was more about the centralisation of structures than about political culture in the future polity. Preuß furthermore stated that the power of the Assembly was democratically legitimate,[2311] but otherwise he left the term 'democracy' undefined. Some left-liberals nevertheless joined in the discourse on democracy: Erich Koch-Weser emphasised the democratic foundations of the constitution, accusing the far left of 'anti-democratic' ideas and the right of their inability to recognise that there existed no other ways to govern than democratic ones in the post-war world.[2312] It is noteworthy, however, that Bruno Ablaß, while accusing the far left of 'working against democracy' and declaring himself a 'democrat' and a supporter of 'real democracy', insisted that democracy called for 'powerful men who are active in the enforcement of the rights of freedom for the purpose of democracy',[2313] a formulation that indicated support for a strong presidency. Anton Erkelenz declared his belief in 'democratic progress' derived from the realisation of full civic rights and welcomed 'the democratisation of industrial relations', while emphasising that further experiments leading to increased democratisation were to be avoided.[2314] There was clearly a discursive tendency among German liberals to speak for the creation of a stable polity constructed around a constitution prepared by liberals rather than to envision further societal progress. Their enthusiasm

2306 *Vorwärts*, 11 February 1919.
2307 *Vorwärts*, 6 February 1919.
2308 Verhandlungen, Friedrich von Payer, 10 February 1919, 20.
2309 *Berliner Tageblatt*, 11 February 1919.
2310 Verhandlungen, Hugo Preuß, 8 February 1919, 13.
2311 Verhandlungen, Hugo Preuß, 8 February 1919, 12–13.
2312 Verhandlungen, Erich Koch-Weser, 28 February 1919, 391–2.
2313 Verhandlungen, Bruno Ablaß, 4 July 1919, 1309.
2314 Verhandlungen, Anton Erkelenz, 21 July 1919, 1776, 1778.

for democracy was modest in comparison with Swedish and many Finnish liberals.

Gustav Stresemann, the chairman of the right-wing German People's Party, joined in the criticism of the far left, accusing them of a 'mockery of democracy' and of advocating 'the absolutism of a minority',[2315] but he had little to add in favour of further democratisation. He viewed democracy as a partisan concept rather than a common goal, and suggested that 'the side of democracy' had long been active in criticising Bismarckian politics.[2316] While democracy of this kind could be understood as the oppositional power of the Reichstag in relation to the executive power, the audience probably understood Stresemann as referring to the Social Democratic and liberal front that since 1917 had been demanding reforms and was now ruling the country. Stresemann's own party was not part of the current coalition, and it maintained an attitude that was basically critical of democratisation. On the last day of the debate, the leader of the parliamentary group of the People's Party, Rudolf Heinze, outspokenly rejected the constitutional proposal as being based on 'the spirit of an extreme democracy'. The right-liberals (DVP) saw the proposal as an attempt to make everyone equal; it would lead to mistrust between democratic institutions, populism and the rejection of the reason of state argument.[2317] The German right-liberals clearly did not support the new democracy.

Most German reformers in 1919 no longer viewed themselves as participants in some pan-European wave of democratisation: their interest only concerned Germany. Downright traditionalist understandings of democracy also appeared in the speeches of Peter Spahn, the Deputy Chairman of the Constitutional Committee and the spokesman for the Catholic Centre, which had already been less enthusiastic about reforms in 1917. The traditional values of the party were still there: the new German polity should be democratic, no doubt, but also social and inspired by a truly Christian (Catholic) spirit. A constitution alone could not guarantee that such values would be achieved: formal political institutions informed by a Christian spirit were needed. Spahn still doubted the positive effects of female suffrage as well,[2318] even though it had already been implemented and female MPs were sitting in the same chamber. There were evident limits to the democratic attitudes of the different parties within the Weimar coalition, a factor that differs from the reformist attitudes of the ministries that had carried through corresponding reforms in Britain and Sweden (and in Finland with the exception of the Swedish People's Party).

The particularistic interests of the federal states as opposed to Preuß's centralised democracy also received expression in a speech by Konrad Beyerle, a Professor of Law representing the Catholic Centre. According to this member of the Constitutional Committee, the Revolution of autumn 1918 had already led to the introduction of a sufficiently 'democratic-

---

2315 Verhandlungen, Gustav Stresemann, 4 March 1919, 491.
2316 Verhandlungen, Gustav Stresemann, 4 March 1919, 491.
2317 Verhandlungen, Rudolf Heinze, 30 July 1919, 2093.
2318 Pohl 2002, 117–18.

parliamentary form of government', which only needed minor adjustments and no new definitions of the character of the polity. Beyerle did not question the legitimacy of the new state as such. What the 'Socialist cabinet' was proposing, however, was not just democratic but constituted an attempt to include the old leftist goal of a unitary state in the constitution, which was inacceptable. This was being done in the name of democracy, disregarding what the socialists otherwise said about democracy as the realisation of the will of the people in the state.[2319] The federalists thus linked the discourse on 'democracy' with the problematic concept of a unitary state, which diminished its legitimacy among many in the audience.

In addition to a member who explicitly questioned the form of democracy proposed by the ministry, a number of officers, judges, professors and civil servants who did not hold democratic views continued to see the restoration of an autocratic system as a possibility.[2320] Politically active professors in Germany (and in Sweden and Finland, and sometimes in Britain as well) were almost always supporters of the right.[2321] In the atmosphere of the early Assembly it was not easy to question democracy, though *Neue Preußische Zeitung* did not hesitate to warn its readers about the risk of both democracy and socialism now making a breakthrough.[2322] The rightist leader Clemens von Delbrück attempted a rhetorical redescription of democracy first by suggesting that the constitutional proposal of October 1918 had already created a sufficiently 'democratic monarchy' and that going any further entailed 'endangering democracy itself',[2323] democracy being used here in a completely conservative sense. Albrecht von Graefe declared without qualification that democracy had been imposed on the majority of the German people against their will.[2324]

Ultra-conservatives in Britain, Sweden and Finland expressed their doubts about excessive democracy even more frequently and often rhetorically constructed a 'democracy' that was to their own liking, while the majorities of rightist parties actually reconciled themselves, albeit with some delay, to the new democratic order. In Germany, the abstention of most of the right from discussing democracy and occasional denouncements of it reflected the unwillingness of the old elite to reconsider its political attitudes, which did not bode well for the future.[2325] They had been traumatised, even temporarily paralysed, by the fall of the imperial throne, but maintained their anti-democratic and anti-parliamentary principles at least until 1945. Their reactionary policies were at first realised through a strong, nearly monarchical, presidency within the political structure of the republic.[2326] Their mouthpiece *Neue Preußische Zeitung* concluded after the adoption

2319 Verhandlungen, Konrad Beyerle, 28 February 1919, 464–5.
2320 Mergel 2002, 38–9.
2321 Mommsen 2002, 116.
2322 *Neue Preußische Zeitung*, 9 February 1919.
2323 Verhandlungen, Clemens von Delbrück, 28 February 1919, 383.
2324 Mergel 2002, 56.
2325 Cf. Mergel 2002, 59, on readiness among the right and left for cooperation and compromises.
2326 Trippe 1995, 13, 194; Leonhard 2002, 32, 35.

of the Weimar constitution that 'democracy has not been implemented so categorically anywhere'.[2327] This reflects the rejection of the new polity by the German right from the very beginning.

The representatives of the far left were also dissatisfied with the degree of democracy offered by the draft constitution but for very different reasons. Oskar Cohn called for the democratisation of all aspects of the lives of the German people instead of submission to authority. Another reaction was heard when Eduard David repeatedly referred to 'economic democracy', 'social democracy' or 'labour democracy' as necessary complements to 'political democracy'. For the radical Marxists, the reform of the mere superstructures of the German political system would not suffice: they took 'democracy' as a primary principle which should lead to the abolition of all differences between the governing and the governed, with the German state being constituted by all of its citizens.[2328] Alfred Henke, a former leader of a council, contrasted the 'democracy' supported by the Social Democrats and liberals as 'the covert domination of capitalism' with 'real democracy' in the Marxist sense,[2329] which was something that the coalition parties did not want. According to Wilhelm Koenen, another council activist, this 'power of the people falsified by capitalism' and mere 'political democracy' should be replaced with 'proletarian democracy' and real 'social democracy';[2330] this sounded like Lenin's understanding of democracy. The Social Democratic response was to reject dictatorship as a means for obtaining socialist democracy[2331] and to defend political democracy in Germany as 'a democracy of the new era' that would constitute, in the longer term, a road to socialism and 'economic democracy'.[2332] Hans Vogel of the Bavarian Social Democrats, a member of the Constitutional Committee, called for the democratisation of factories and companies.[2333] However, the German Social Democrats did not dare to be too insistent in this respect in 1919: they considered it safest to guarantee a democratic constitution first and to postpone economic and societal reforms, just as the Swedish Social Democrats had chosen to do in 1918. Even many left-liberals were not ready to support them, rejecting the basic rights included in the constitution as an 'economic council system'.[2334]

Demands for the extension of democracy beyond politics resembled those put forward by the Swedish far left in this period. The German example encouraged them (and later the Social Democrats) to continue calling for more extensive democratisation in economic and social matters. In Finland, many members of the far left who had put forward radical demands in 1917 had either been killed in the Civil War or jailed or had fled to Russia and formed the Finnish Communist Party in Moscow, where

2327 *Neue Preußische Zeitung*, 1 August 1919.
2328 Verhandlungen, Oskar Cohn & Eduard David, 28 February 1919, 408–409; 4 March 1919, 500–501; 31 July 1919, 2194; Pohl 2002, 125.
2329 Verhandlungen, Alfred Henke, 10 July 1919, 1472.
2330 Verhandlungen, Wilhelm Koenen, 21 July 1919, 1780.
2331 Verhandlungen, Hugo Sinzheimer, 21 July 1919, 1796.
2332 Verhandlungen, Simon Katzenstein, 29 July 1919, 2075.
2333 Verhandlungen, Hans Vogel, 3 March 1919, 460.
2334 *Berliner Tageblatt*, 1 August 1919; see, however, Pohl 2002, 135.

they denounced 'bourgeois' democracy. In 1919 the demands for economic and social democracy in the Finnish parliament were modest in comparison with Germany and Sweden, although some Social Democrats continued to emphasise the existence of economic and social inequality.

In the aftermath of the Treaty of Versailles, any enthusiasm for *international* or *transnational* democracy would have appeared out of place in Germany: democracy was a German national issue that simply needed to be reasserted by adopting (or rejecting) the constitution. This attitude was caused by the fact that the Western democrats seemed to have 'committed a grave betrayal of democracy by assenting to this treaty'.[2335] Germany's note to the Entente had emphasised that '[t]he new constitution of the German Empire and the composition of its People's Government correspond with the strictest principles of democracy',[2336] which revealingly emphasised both the *German* nature of the new system as a *Volksstaat* and its correspondence with Western democracy. *The Manchester Guardian* had reported that both German socialists and liberals looked 'to the progressive and democratic thought of Western nations as the sole hope for the future of Europe' although the paper foresaw the risk of oppressive Western policies leading to the revival of a nationalistic spirit in Germany.[2337] Labour leaders and a commentator in *The Observer* had also wondered whether the peace had been concluded in the spirit of democracy[2338] and whether it was sane 'in this twentieth century of all the democratic movements, of the nation-knitting intercourse, and the broadening ideas'.[2339] The contradictions between the rhetoric of democracy in wartime propaganda and the realities of the peace treaty were thus widely recognised on both sides.

The project of democratising Germany clearly already ran into major trouble in the first half of 1919. Little development towards a process-like concept or beliefs in the future potential of democracy are visible in the Weimar debates, especially outside the Social Democratic group. There was no successful negotiation that would have produced compromises on democracy. Most speakers either affirmed that Germany was already a democratic republic based on popular sovereignty or questioned this claim. Reactionary views were becoming more open than in autumn and early spring, when even the right had supported democracy by staying quiet in the hope of better terms of peace. Clemens von Delbrück – a Prussian nobleman and a representative of the German National People's Party in the Constitutional Committee – had merely stated that consenting to the proposal was a major sacrifice for the right.[2340] In summer 1919 he was already openly in favour of a 'democratic' monarchy or at least a strong

---

2335 *The Manchester Guardian*, 'Government's Attitude Endorsed', 14 May 1919, on the basis of what 'Hausmann' (the left-liberal Conrad Haußmann, Chair of the Constitutional Committee) had said.
2336 *The Manchester Guardian*, 'German Reply to Draft Treaty', 28 May 1919.
2337 *The Manchester Guardian,* 'German Appeals for Moderation', 30 May 1919.
2338 *The Manchester Guardian*, 'Labour Conference', 27 June 1919; *The Times*, 'Labour and Peace Terms', 27 June 1919.
2339 *The Observer*, 'First Steps to the Real Settlement', 18 May 1919.
2340 Verhandlungen, Clemens von Delbrück, 10 February 1919, 21.

presidency and rejected the radical republic that was about to be created.²³⁴¹ The yearning for a constitutional monarchy lived on. In Britain and Sweden, the survival of the monarchy certainly helped rightists to adjust their attitudes to the circumstances of democratised suffrage.

Once the republican constitution was finally adopted on 14 August 1919, its proponents among the government parties, mainly Social Democrats, expressed their satisfaction in highly laudatory terms. It remained to be seen, however, how a constitution so eagerly defined as democratic by some Social Democratic and a few liberal advocates would function in practice. The degree of optimism surrounding democracy remained modest in the German debates in comparison with the British and Swedish ones. It resembled the atmosphere in Finland, where only the centre parties were strongly committed to the compromise which the parliament was compelled to accept in the aftermath of a civil war and under pressure from the Entente. Despite their similarities, the Finnish republican constitution proved to be much longer-lasting than that of the Weimar Republic – thanks to factors such as the long estate and parliamentary tradition, the commitment to the rule by the people by the great majority already in 1917 and the gradual turn of many on the right to the side of democracy by the early 1930s.

7.2.4 'Power in the state belongs to the people'

While 'revolution' and 'democracy' were part of the vocabulary of the left and some liberals in Germany, 'the people' was a concept cherished by all political groups in the sense of a community of the people. The long tradition of male suffrage, wartime promises to take the will of the people better into account, the slogan 'To the German People' on the pediment of the parliament building since 1916, and even the right willingly talking about the achievement of the people in the war all suggested that 'the people' was a positive term for all, though of course it had very different associations

Chancellor Friedrich Ebert left no doubt as to the popular legitimacy of political power after the free election: 'The German people is free, will remain free and in the future will always govern itself.'²³⁴² The goal was now to create 'a strong German popular state',²³⁴³ something that had never really existed. Ebert emphasised the liberty of the German people after the Revolution and – revealingly – their readiness to fulfil the demands of US President Woodrow Wilson concerning the reorganisation of the German political system.²³⁴⁴ Such a statement, in an opening speech addressing Western diplomats and negotiators in Versailles, was risky in the heated domestic setting as it could be interpreted as recognising the imported nature of popular government.

The Social Democratic Father of the House, Wilhelm Pfannkuch, took up the revolutionary slogan 'All for the people and all by the people' – to emphasise intertextually the huge revision which was taking place. He was

---

2341 Pohl 2002, 210–13.
2342 Verhandlungen, Friedrich Ebert, 6 February 1919, 1.
2343 Burkhardt 2003, 41.
2344 Verhandlungen, Friedrich Ebert, 6 February 1919, 3.

addressing the liberals as well, presenting 'the people' as both the object and the agent of future political decision-making in Germany. The fate of 'the German nation' had changed dramatically as 'the German people' had become 'the master, its own supreme power'. The rulers would no longer bypass the clear will of the majority of the people: even 'the majesty of the German people' had thus been established.[2345] *Vorwärts* declared likewise that popular sovereignty had been established.[2346] While much of this could have been heard from a leftist or centrist democrat in any country, Pfannkuch's argumentative emphasis on popular agency prepared the way for the referendum and a presidency as alternative means of popular rule side by side with the parliament.

Eduard David viewed the beginning of the Assembly as a moment when 'the people as a whole, free from all dictation, becomes the master of its fate'. Such a breakthrough of popular sovereignty meant that the will of the majority would prevail in all conflicts of opinion and interests.[2347] At the end of the legislative process, David stated that 'the will of the people is from now on the highest law.'[2348] In his vision of majority democracy, the people appeared both as an active agent and as an object of the actions of the Assembly. Overinterpreting the will of the German people, David argued that there existed 'a new, vast national will' which demanded the reorganisation of the political system and the enforcement of the rights of the people – this change in the national mood had emerged endogenously, independent of any transnational trends. The duty of the Assembly was to express this will and to work in a way that would increase the satisfaction of the German people with their institutions.[2349] Later David viewed the constitution as creating an entirely new, natural and moral relationship between the government and the people based on free elections and parliamentary representation, making the government responsible to the people via a functioning parliament.[2350]

The views of the Social Democrats – as one might presume from their party manifesto, wartime demands, reactions to the October resolutions and leadership in the Revolution of 1918 – were optimistic about the new constitution. It could be viewed as a reflection of a rapid transition of the German people from an autocratic to a republican political system, for the first time in history.[2351] The Social Democrats saw themselves as winners in a long constitutional confrontation with the monarchy, the right of the old elite and the far left. The last-mentioned group, admittedly, declared that everyone was now 'part of the *Volksganzen*' (the people as a whole) and 'the

---

2345 Verhandlungen, Wilhelm Pfannkuch, 6 February 1919, 3–4. Interestingly, the very same claim about majesty being transferred to the people was used by a Finnish conservative in June 1919, when the republican constitution was adopted.
2346 *Vorwärts*, 11 February 1919.
2347 Verhandlungen, Eduard David, 7 February 1919, 8.
2348 Verhandlungen, Eduard David, 31 July 1919, 2194.
2349 Verhandlungen, Eduard David, 7 February 1919, 10.
2350 Verhandlungen, Eduard David, 4 March 1919, 499; Bruendel 2003, 106.
2351 Pohl 2002, 114.

state'[2352] and welcomed 'the politicisation of broad layers of the population,'[2353] while simultaneously criticising the limited degree of democracy in the proposal, as was noted above.

Some left-liberals referred to the parliament as a medium when talking about the political role of the people. Hugo Preuß, the Minister of Interior Affairs, who had drafted the proposal, defined the Assembly as the representative of 'the will of the sovereign people'.[2354] Having recognised the popular origins of political power, he proceeded to talk about 'this sovereign Assembly' which exercised 'democratically acknowledged power' on behalf of 'the entire German people'.[2355] For the first time in history, the German people was applying the principle that 'the power of the state is located in the people'.[2356] This had become necessary as the failure in the war had followed from 'a lack of political leadership and political understanding among the people themselves'.[2357] Friedrich von Payer also emphasised that 'sovereignty' was 'due to the German people' and that the Assembly was commissioned to exercise that sovereignty.[2358] This liberal from Wurttemberg saw the German people as actively liberating itself from its present deplorable state.[2359] Bruno Ablaß, too, vindicated the principle of popular sovereignty exercised through the Reichstag, believing in the ability of the people to secure the rights gained in the Revolution, although he also recognised the presidency as another 'organ of control' originating from the people.[2360] The left-liberals prioritised this sense of democracy being realised through various instruments over 'the sole rule of the parliament' (*Alleinherrschaft des Parlaments*),[2361] although many of them set store by the parliament as well. An alternative interpretation held by many majority Social Democrats was that the will of the people was to be realised through a strong parliament.[2362]

Only the socialists and left-liberals talked extensively about the people. The centre, the right-liberals and the right did not engage themselves in the debate on the rising political role of the people. Such a lack of participation in the discursive process would prove to be a fatal for the political system as it only served to reinforce the view that there now existed a new *Social Democratic* political order to which the right and even many centrists were not committed. In the other studied countries at least, minor adjustments in the political argumentation of the right took place during the reform debates of 1917–19. In Germany, on the other hand, the right did not recognise the parliament as a forum in which to constructively debate the key principles

2352 Verhandlungen, Oskar Cohn, 28 February 1919, 404.
2353 Verhandlungen, Oskar Cohn, 7 July 1919, 1356.
2354 Verhandlungen, Hugo Preuß, 8 February 1919, 12.
2355 Verhandlungen, Hugo Preuß, 8 February 1919, 13; see also *Berliner Tageblatt*, 11 February 1919.
2356 Pohl 2002, 112.
2357 Verhandlungen, Hugo Preuß, 29 July 1919, 2072.
2358 Verhandlungen, Friedrich von Payer, 10 February 1919, 20.
2359 Verhandlungen, Friedrich von Payer, 10 February 1919, 21.
2360 Verhandlungen, Bruno Ablaß, 4 July 1919, 1309–10.
2361 Verhandlungen, Erich Koch-Weser, 7 July 1919, 1356; Bollmeyer 2005, 130.
2362 Pohl 2002, 199; see also Gusy 1997, 64.

of the polity: they left it to the Social Democrats and the left-liberals to take all responsibility. The seemingly strong, but in reality solitary, position of the German Social Democrats distinguishes them from their counterparts in the other three countries and added to the fallacy of the Weimar Constitution having turned Germany into a polity with popular government. No general turn to parliamentary democracy in that sense happened at a conceptual and discursive level during the constitutional debates in Weimar.

Earlier research has produced similar interpretations. Heiko Bollmeyer has pointed out how challenging it was to define the relationship between the concepts of the *Volk* and the *Reichstag*. This was frequently done by emphasising the concept of *Volkswille* (the will of the people), which had been used every now and then since 1917 by spokesmen for constitutional reform, and from autumn 1918 on also by speaking about *Volkssouveränität* (the sovereignty of the people), which had previously been a rare concept in German parliamentary discourse.[2363] The final version of the new constitution stated that all state power was derived from the people and was exercised by representative institutions.[2364] The concept of popular sovereignty, which Hugo Preuß used in the sense of both 'the sovereignty of the nation' and 'the sovereignty of the people' when introducing the draft,[2365] was not used in the actual text. The basis of the legitimacy of political power was transferred to the people to such an extent that monarchy no longer came into the question,[2366] though a tendency to make the presidency monarchical survived. Thomas Mergel concludes that the institution of Reichspräsident meant the continuation of the monarchical constitution in republican circumstances[2367] at a time when monarchism proper was losing credibility.[2368]

Mergel has shown how the argumentation of the republicans continued to focus on the concept of the people and the community of the people, the aim being agreement but with conflicting group interests dividing the discourse of the different republican groups in reality. Politicians addressed both a presumably unified community of the people and the groups whose particular interests they represented. Confrontations could be heard in the plenary sessions of the Reichstag, as parliamentarians tried to demonstrate to their supporters outside that their interests were being cared for.[2369]

Christoph Gusy has pointed out that the idea of the people as the origin of political power was by no means necessarily democratic, as the Weimar

---

2363 Bollmeyer 2007, 260, 267.
2364 Pohl 2002, 150–5, 162–70. In the Constitutional Committee, this had been seen by the Social Democratic lawyer Max Quark as the principal idea of the entire constitution and the foundation of the democratic form of government. Kühne 2000, 117.
2365 See his speech on 'the sovereign people', Verhandlungen, Hugo Preuß, 8 February 1919, 12–13.
2366 Bollmeyer 2007, 308.
2367 Mergel 2002, 40.
2368 Mergel 2002, 37.
2369 Mergel 2002, 56–7.

experience shows: every political ideology could appeal to this principle and yet draw radically divergent conclusions regarding it. Neither the anti-democratic thinkers on the right nor the advocates of the council movement completely denied popular sovereignty.[2370] In constitutional debates after 1919, it was often assumed that the people were capable of forming *one* will independently of elections and democratic proceedings in general. Such a concept of the popular will presupposed a united collective will rather than a collection of differing opinions. 'The will of the state', on the other hand, was seen as subordinate to this popular will. The people and the state were considered identical, which meant that the state had been organised by the people in the spirit of a *Volksstaat* (state of the people), a concept that some debaters in Weimar favoured. This way of thinking also led to the concepts of the state and society being used to refer automatically both to each other and to an emphasis on national unity.[2371] Swedish and Finnish ways of thinking, especially among conservatives, were not radically different from this.

The anti-democratic forces of the Weimar Republic – which had had little to say in the debates on democratisation – would also base their ideologies on the concepts of the people and the will of the people, even though they often qualified these concepts by talking about *das wahre Volk* (the real people) and *der wahre Volkswille* (the real will of the people), thus challenging the democrats. Strong ideas about the political unity of the German people (as opposed to the notion of a pluralistic people, which was more obvious in Britain and may have strengthened somewhat in Sweden during the suffrage strife and in Finland as a consequence of the Civil War) led to the conclusion that the people itself was capable of acting politically as a whole,[2372] something that Social Democratic and liberal references to the people during the Weimar debates reasserted rather than challenged. Nevertheless, different understandings of the German people coexisted in Germany as well, which made it one of the most contested concepts of the Weimar Republic.[2373]

Wolfram Pyta has emphasised that the concept *Volksgemeinschaft* (community of the people), references to which were noted above, was distinguished from more pluralistic parliamentary democracy in a Western sense, which explains some later political developments in Germany. The concept was favoured in the Weimar Republic not only by rightist movements but also by many Social Democrats and liberals, who liked to talk about a *Volksstaat* (state of the people)[2374] or *Volksherrschaft* (rule by the people) or *Volksrepublik* (republic of the people) in conceptualising popular sovereignty. Nevertheless, the notions 'community of the people' and 'state

---

2370 Gusy 2000b, 647.
2371 Gusy 2000b 648–9, 652, 658. Such an identity of the state and society can also be found in Finnish political discourse. German influences had played an important role in its formulation there; Bruendel 2003, 106.
2372 Gusy 2000a, 26, 30.
2373 Gusy 2000a, 36.
2374 Pyta 2008, 93; Pyta 2011, 32.

of the people' were merely slightly differently formulated variations of the same basic idea.[2375]

A further feature distinguishing Germany from the other three countries is that the German polity continued to live in a state of civil war so that politics tended to be conceptualised in military terms, and the war experience continued to influence parliamentary politics, moulding political mentalities and actions.[2376] This was more so than in Sweden and probably Britain, though in the Finnish case the scars of the Civil War and confrontation with the Russians would remain sore points for decades to come.[2377] Wartime concepts such as *Burgfrieden* (party truce), *Schütengraben* (trenches) and *Volksgemeinschaft* (community of the people) remained useful metaphors in everyday German political debate.[2378] Metaphors of war had entered parliamentary discourse in the other three countries as well, military confrontations being reproduced in domestic political debates, though return to peacetime discourse was quicker in Britain, for instance.[2379] Thomas Mergel has also emphasised a tendency to see politics heroically as a matter of life and death, which contributed to the rejection of the kind of compromises that are typical of multi-party democracies. The prevailing conception supported the view that parliamentary politics and its inter-party compromises represented feebleness and an inability to really lead.[2380] This may well have been one of the longer-term explanations for the weakness of the Weimar constitution, particularly as the parties of the pre-war Reichstag had also been unwilling to make compromises and had turned to violent polemics instead. On the other hand, the readiness to make compromises was not much better in the British, Swedish or Finnish parliaments in the period 1917–19: in Britain parliamentary politics remained confrontational and had contained references to a potential civil war; the Swedish right was unhappy with the constitutional compromise there to the very end and had suggested the possibility of armed resistance against revolutionaries; and in Finland ideological confrontations led to a civil war, which was only followed by a gradual restoration of constructive debate from 1919 onwards.

7.2.5 Extolling, limiting and ignoring parliamentarism

Parliamentarism had been generally despised in the Prussian political culture. The goal of the October reforms in 1918 had been to create a parliamentary government, and contemporaries had mostly also conceptualised it in that way. This kind of parliamentarism was implemented in spring 1919, though its nature was still debated.

Vorwärts emphasised how millions were looking to see 'parliamentarism in Weimar' when the National Constituent Assembly was opened[2381] and

---

2375 Pyta 2008, 93.
2376 Mergel 2002, 52; cf. Bessel 1993, 258–9 on the general rejection of militarism as opposed to right-wing propaganda.
2377 See Virtanen 2015 on Vihtori Kosola's political rhetoric.
2378 Mergel 2002, 52.
2379 Müller 2002, 356 and 365, for Britain and Germany.
2380 Mergel 2002, 55–6.
2381 *Vorwärts*, 6 February 1919, 7 February 1919.

viewing the representative institution as a sovereign parliament.[2382] Friedrich Ebert, the Social Democratic leader of the Provisional Government, described the procedure of adopting a new constitution as a parliamentary realisation of the power of the people. The Germans had embarked on 'the broad road of parliamentary consultation and decision-making', he argued, and this road would allow them to carry out inevitable economic and social reforms as well. This was a very Social Democratic promise.[2383] Parliamentarism meant that the provisional government considered the Assembly to be 'the highest and only sovereign in Germany', the power of which would never again be challenged by a monarch.[2384] For Ebert, the process of transition to parliamentarism had only begun, but his expectations for it were high.

Wilhelm Pfannkuch's definition of the emerging political system likewise focused on the National Constituent Assembly. He emphasised the responsibility and unquestionable authority of the Assembly to create conditions that would be favourable to democracy and parliamentary rule. His definition of the representative institution as the embodiment of democracy is remarkable in the light of the German tradition of seeing parliamentarism and democracy as separate. Challenging both rightist authoritarian ideals and direct democracy as advocated by some of the far left in their council movement, Pfannkuch argued that 'German democracy' by a German parliament with a republican majority expressed 'the will of the German nation'. This meant that the Assembly was not a mere symbol of German democracy but actually constituted it.[2385] Eduard David likewise emphasised the status of the National Constituent Assembly, denouncing the pre-revolutionary Reichstag as 'a pretence parliament' (*Scheinparlament*), which could speak freely but had no say when decisions were made.[2386] On the other hand, Simon Katzenstein, while insisting that the German method of realising democracy would be essentially parliamentary,[2387] pointed out that the new constitution certainly did not mean a 'system of unlimited parliamentarism' thanks to the established role of the president and the referendum.[2388]

A key position in the definition of the powers of the German parliament was held by Hugo Preuß, whose proposal distanced itself somewhat from the dualism between the executive and the parliament that had been typical of imperial Germany and much of northern Europe.[2389] Preuß insisted instead that the constitution made the political position of the Reichstag inviolable in German political life.[2390] The problem was that Germany lacked the traditions 'of the politically leading countries', which would have provided a basis for building 'democratic parliamentarism', and hence the planners had

2382 *Vorwärts*, 11 February 1919.
2383 Verhandlungen, Friedrich Ebert, 6 February 1919, 1.
2384 Verhandlungen, Friedrich Ebert, 6 February 1919, 1.
2385 Verhandlungen, Wilhelm Pfannkuch, 6 February 1919, 4.
2386 Verhandlungen, Eduard David, 4 March 1919, 498–9.
2387 Verhandlungen, Simon Katzenstein, 29 July 1919, 2075.
2388 Verhandlungen, Simon Katzenstein, 3 July 1919, 1263.
2389 Pohl 2002, 114.
2390 Verhandlungen, Hugo Preuß, 4 July 1919, 1285.

had to combine new elements of both democracy and parliamentarism in the draft constitution.[2391] From the point of view of Preuß – influenced by Robert Redslob's theory of the 'genuine' parliamentarism of the British and the 'ungenuine' parliamentarism of the French type[2392] – the Reichstag should not be the only dominant organ of the state, however: a balance between the executive and legislative powers was needed, thereby embodying a degree of duality of government. As a compromise, Preuß advocated a presidential democracy in which a nonpartisan president would execute the assumed 'true' will of the people. The role of the parliament was to represent the 'empirical' will of the people as expressed through elections. The problem with this parliamentary expression of the will of the people was that it could always be manipulated by factions and particular interests. Preuß and other left-liberals, like many of the parliamentary elite, remained sceptical about extensive forms of parliamentarism. Friedrich Naumann, for instance, referred to the British form of parliamentarism as a warning example of politicians rather than ideologies ruling the government.[2393]

Other liberals, too, viewed parliamentary powers as essentially limited: the parliament alone was insufficient to represent the will of the people in a democratic republic, they argued. Erich Koch-Weser, an expert in law and political science and a member of the Constitutional Committee, represented the principle of parliamentary support for the government as 'the best form to express democracy' and, despite the inconveniences of agitation and procedural debates, for instance, as essential for the political system. However, a fear of extreme forms of parliamentarism was also to be heard in his desire for a counterweight: the new president, elected directly by the people, should act as a balance between the government and the parliament.[2394] Koch-Weser's point in contrasting representative democracy with popular participation was: 'We do not think that the parliament is the only form of expression of democracy. We rather believe that the more pillars are created in the structure of a democratic state, the more securely established the will of the people will be.'[2395]

Gustav Stresemann of the right-liberals presented himself as a consistent spokesman for a parliamentary system of the British type: Britain was for him 'the political educator in the field of parliamentarism'.[2396] Rudolf Heinze of the same party expressed the views of the majority of the party as being critical of parliamentarism, however, condemning the new constitution for creating 'extreme parliamentarism' without the necessary counterweights. As a consequence, 'parliament is seizing the state administration' and the end result would be *Parteiherrschaft* (rule by the parties).[2397] Like reform-minded constitutionalists before, he distinguished between 'parliamentarisation' as

2391 Verhandlungen, Hugo Preuß, 29 July 1919, 2072.
2392 Gusy 1997, 64; Mergel 2002, 40.
2393 Pohl 2002, 155–62, 200.
2394 Verhandlungen, Erich Koch-Weser, 28 February 1919, 392.
2395 Bollmeyer 2005, 128, 133.
2396 Verhandlungen, Gustav Stresemann, 4 March 1919, 496.
2397 Verhandlungen, Rudolf Heinze, 30 July 1919, 2094; Grosser 1970, 115–16.

a positive increase in the power of the parliament and 'parliamentarism' as the 'Western' rule by political parties.[2398] The right, when criticising parliamentary domination, still wished to see the executive power rather than the people or the special interests of the parties as its counterweight.[2399] These views were in line with what most Swedish and Finnish conservatives also argued.

Leading Social Democrats and left-liberals remained the only MPs to speak explicitly in favour of parliamentarism during these debates, although the latter, too, wished to set limits to parliamentarism. The prevailing mistrust in parliamentarism meant that a strong presidency and national referenda were viewed as counter-weights to the parliament. Even many Social Democrats called for institutions that would counter-balance parliamentary power,[2400] which differs from the far-reaching parliamentary rule favoured by Swedish and Finnish Social Democrats. The liberals accused the conservatives of being 'inwardly enemies of parliamentarism' and the far left of a desire to replace the parliamentary system and democracy with the representation of mere workers and outright far-left dictatorship.[2401] Clemens von Delbrück of the right, though recognising certain positive characteristics in ministerial responsibility, recalled that he had always opposed the parliamentary system.[2402] There were those among the far left, too, who remained highly sceptical about 'parliamentary possibilities'. Parliamentary debates and decisions were not, according to Oskar Cohn, the way to advance the necessary social development; parliamentarism in its current form should rather be demolished.[2403] In the crossfire of such views, express support for parliamentarism certainly remained modest in the Assembly when compared to that of leading political groups in Britain, the Social Democratic-Liberal coalition in Sweden, and the Social Democrats and the centrist parties in Finland. Accusations of political opponents lacking democratic and parliamentary ideals were commonplace in Weimar. Outspoken opposition to the adopted model of parliamentarism survived among the right and the far left, and many members of the centre did not commit themselves to extended parliamentarism either.

Long before the new constitution came into force on 14 August 1919, the German general public, struggling with the everyday problems of the transition from the wartime to the post-war situation, had lost interest in constitutional issues like democracy and parliamentarism.[2404] Indeed, many had not been interested in such abstract and foreign sounding notions in the first place. The legislative process of the bill had received some publicity thanks to the strong tradition to reviewing parliamentary debates selectively in newspapers, though detailed discussions in the National Constituent

---

2398 Bruendel 2003, 246.
2399 Bollmeyer 2005, 131.
2400 Bollmeyer 2005, 130–1.
2401 Verhandlungen, Conrad Haußmann, 29 July 1919, 2082–3.
2402 Verhandlungen, Clemens von Delbrück, 4 July 1919, 1297.
2403 Verhandlungen, Oskar Cohn, 30 July 1919, 2098.
2404 Bessel 1993, 255.

Assembly were of little interest to a public overwhelmed with severe practical problems. Even though the predominance of violence in post-war German society should not be exaggerated, extra-parliamentary circumstances (including physical attacks on far-left politicians) differed dramatically from what was being debated in the Assembly.[2405] The lack of wider publicity and public interest was typical of other constitutional reforms of the period, too: the British audience was rather more interested in the practicalities of warfare and the wartime economy in 1917 and 1918. In Sweden, on the other hand, the media continued to report and comment on the reform debates, and the interest of the public was mostly maintained. In Finland, the issue of the form of government had in principle played a key role in the election of 1917, but ideological confrontations, severe economic realities and extra-parliamentary violence had led to violent rhetoric entering the parliament as well. In 1919, the election in Germany was about the constitution, and the constitutional process was discussed in the press, but most of the public clearly just wanted to have the old dispute solved.

For the formulators of the Weimar Constitution, its achievement was the completion of the Revolution of 1918 and the expected transition to ordered politics.[2406] A republican and parliamentary democracy had been created in Germany as a result of a process of constitutional reform initiated by outside pressures in autumn 1918 rather than having been the initial goal.[2407] In consequence, the project of constructing the constitution would remain, discursively at least, a partisan affair carried out by the leading Social Democrats and left-liberals. This was partly due to the fact that the German parliamentary culture emphasised the role of the spokesmen of the parliamentary groups. Even these spokesmen continued to entertain reservations about parliamentarism and to advocate alternative ways of expressing democracy. In the other three countries studied here, the participation of all parties, including their back-benchers, in the 'negotiations' over the constitution was considerably more extensive than in Germany. True government by discussion engaging the entire political spectrum was not achieved in Germany in spring 1919. In that sense, the doubts of the British press about the extent to which parliamentarism had been adopted in Germany were not unfounded.

The German political system would not be moulded in the way the new constitution promised, particularly in the minds of the right. This conclusion corresponds with social historical studies that note that the Prussian aristocracy had played a key role in preventing the influence of Social Democracy and the rise of democratic liberalism in German society and that this influence continued.[2408] It considered it necessary to exclude the masses from broader political participation.[2409] Nor did it want to contribute to the democratic state in any constructive manner and continued to vehemently

2405 Bessel 1993, 258, 261; Gusy 1997, 77.
2406 Gusy 1997, 78.
2407 Gusy 2008a, 421.
2408 The historiography has been summarised in Smith 2007, 5.
2409 Müller 2002, 351.

oppose it. Reformist conservatism of the type existing in Britain – and to a lesser extent in Sweden and Finland – did not emerge in Germany.[2410]

7.3 Sweden: Adjusting the principles of a future democracy

7.3.1 Swedish parties after the suffrage reform

Prime Minister Nils Edén had gathered the Liberals and Social Democrats around a further reform proposal in the immediate aftermath of the German Revolution in November 1918 and persuaded the reluctant right not to vote the proposal down again. However, the reform still needed to be passed in spring 1919, and its passage entailed new challenges to the parties and turns in political discourse inspired by changing national and international circumstances.

The Social Democrats seemed to have tackled the domestic crisis of late 1918 in a reasonably united way, although some wished for the reform to go further. They had, after all, finally achieved their most important goal, universal suffrage, and hence looked optimistically towards the future without needing to care too much about the far-left radicals, who had already quitted the party. The Liberals, by contrast, were divided after the decisions of late 1918 since many felt that the prime minister had acted too independently in solving the crisis, failing to negotiate sufficiently with his party and making excessive concessions to the Social Democrats. The Liberals had not confronted Edén in the debates, being consistently supportive of the government cause (unlike some of their British, German and Finnish counterparts), but their enthusiasm for the reform had nevertheless been limited. As soon as the bill passed the preliminary stage, disputes emerged within the coalition, and its foundation began to crumble.[2411] The Liberals in Sweden, as elsewhere, had a major party-political problem: they expected to be on the losing side in future elections, and in these circumstances many started to question the sense of continuing in a coalition with the Social Democrats, a major rival for votes. Liberal idealism in favour of the extended political participation of the people, democracy and parliamentarism also found its limits in Sweden.

All local representative bodies were re-elected at the beginning of 1919 in accordance with the new legislation, whereas the First Chamber would not be re-elected until the autumn of 1919 and the Second Chamber in 1921. In principle the lengthy 'constitutional battle' had come to an end with the settlement of late 1918. However, in late spring and early summer 1919, the same parliament needed to pass related legislation in both chambers to complete the reform. In practice, this appeared to many to be a counter-productive repetition of arguments that had been heard in numerous previous suffrage debates, particularly as it was now obvious who were the winners (the Social Democrats) and the losers (The Right and possibly the Liberals) in the reform issue. Nevertheless, expressions of views after the

---

2410 Malinowski 2003, 602, 604–607.
2411 Gerdner 1946, 39–40.

disputed passage of the reform bill deserve attention, not least because of the highly inter- and transnational nature of the Swedish debates during the preceding two years. Would this continue, or would the Swedish debate turn internal?

The Social Democrats, too, debated the issue among themselves after what seemed to be their greatest political victory thus far. By early April 1919, when no more than a formal approval of the proposal by the parliament was needed to complete the reform, a discussion on the past achievements and the future goals of the party was activated. Some on the left of the party regretted that the reform had not gone beyond the goals of the ministry's proposal; from their point of view, the Social Democratic leaders' peaceful revolution had failed, and promises of extended reforms in the future did not change this fact. This disappointment was reinforced by the fact that in many European countries constitutions were still being reformed during spring 1919 in a much more democratic direction: in Germany and Austria, in particular, which were key countries for the purpose of international comparison and especially relevant to Social Democracy in Sweden, the Social Democrats had become major political agents, which was not necessarily the case yet in Sweden. Socialist demands for social and economic reforms together with political ones had been activated internationally – as the far left claimed in the German and Swedish parliaments. Reflecting on the powerful status of the Social Democrats in the German government and the National Constituent Assembly, some Swedish Social Democrats were disappointed to see that their party had not gone further in its reform demands during the revolutionary moment of 1918 and hence called for a more radical approach. The leaders of the party maintained their moderate line,[2412] but these tensions would nevertheless create pressures within the Liberal-Social Democratic coalition.

The Social Democrats and Liberals had campaigned both jointly and separately for parliamentary government and universal suffrage for decades. The Social Democrats had adopted a self-confident discourse on democratic reform in confronting The Right and the monarch before and during the war, and the Liberals had mostly supported them in their demands. Only in November 1918 – after the revolutionary events in Russia, Finland and, most importantly, Germany – had the monarch and the leaders of The Right considered it necessary to accept a reform introducing universal suffrage. As this decision needed to be extended in the parliamentary session of 1919, other suggested changes in the constitution also became subject to debate. In practice, the fierce constitutional debate of the preceding two years was already calming down: The Right seemed to have given up its previously consistent resistance to the reform,[2413] although the continuing appearance of counterarguments every now and then reveal the existence of a broader dissatisfaction. Some opponents of the reform simply remained silent without having changed their minds, a lot like the German right. Torbjörn Nilsson has shown that the Swedish right would continue to emphasise the

2412 Gerdner 1946, 66–7.
2413 Möller 2007; Hadenius 2008.

weaknesses of democracy and parliamentarism throughout the twenties and into the early thirties. The supporters of The Right still did not defend formal democracy but rather wished to redescribe 'true democracy' in conservative terms; following an international conservative pattern, they emphasised the suffrage qualifications (or the lack thereof) of citizens. Women voters were nonetheless, welcome to join The Right in Sweden,[2414] as they were for conservatives everywhere.

7.3.2 Internationalism after war and revolution

The wartime revolutionary heat of the Swedish constitutional debate was calming down by early June 1919, as all knew that the suffrage reform would pass the parliament. The Social Democrats, rejoicing in their victory, were highly optimistic about the prospects for future progress. The advances of democratisation abroad remained objects of interest for leftist reformists, though the need for appealing to foreign examples had decreased.

Oscar Olsson offers an example of this universalist socialist optimism. He was convinced that 'the general revolutionary movement out there in the world' had not yet peaked. Further reforms remained on the agenda in Sweden and not merely in former autocratic monarchies (such as Germany and Austria).[2415] While the left of the party is known to have been dissatisfied with the extent of the 'revolution' of late 1918, this was not articulated in the debates.

The spokesmen of the Liberals also remained outspokenly reformist despite rising pressures within the party. Mauritz Hellberg argued, in line with the government's policy, for peaceful reforms aimed at removing societal injustice and the grounds for revolution[2416] – events that had been seen in neighbouring countries like Russia, Finland and Germany. Otto von Zweigbergk pointed out that the Germans and Austrians had given up monarchy and realised a transition to a republic without the complicated procedures of changing the constitution.[2417] The German Revolution continued to inspire not only Swedish Social Democrats but also Liberals – sometimes to the extent of that they speculated about the abolition of the monarchy. However, the republicans of the Swedish left would refrain from taking any concrete measures to that direction.

Among The Right, doubts about the claimed positive effects of the suffrage reform and the applicability of what they continued to regard as 'foreign' constitutional models imported to Sweden had not withered away. The monarchy, in particular, should be left untouched. Ernst Trygger insisted that the abolition of monarchies and the introduction of republics had had no positive effects[2418] – referring implicitly at least to Germany, Austria and Finland. Trygger also responded to Hellberg's suggestion concerning the continuing risk of an ensuing revolutionary development by pointing

---

2414 Torstendahl 1969, 212–13; Nilsson 2004, 81, 145.
2415 FK, Oscar Olsson, 5 June 1919, 53:39.
2416 FK, Mauritz Hellberg, 5 June 1919, 53:32.
2417 FK, Otto von Zweigbergk, 5 June 1919, 53:37.
2418 FK, Ernst Trygger, 5 June 1919, 53:36.

out that any revolutionary attempt would be effectively suppressed by law-abiding citizens.[2419] The Right had already made its concessions and would forcefully resist any further leftist attempts to revolutionise the political system. At the same time, Trygger denied the existence of 'any kind of fear of revolution' on the part of The Right as having led to their concessions.[2420] The concessions had been made because they had been considered necessary in the international situation of the time; they should not be regarded as opening a door for further reforms or as a licence for blackmail with threats of revolution. Aware of the remaining doubts among the German right concerning democracy and parliamentarism and of the opposition of the Finnish right to extended parliamentarism, Trygger's party chose to stand firm in its opposition to the further radicalisation of the reforms. The revolutionary moment was over for all the major parties. Society would from now on be changed through Social Democratic electoral support. Swedish politicians would employ foreign examples to hasten belated domestic reforms less, view reform from the perspective of a nation-state and increasingly start to see their way to accepting democracy as universally valid and as a model for the rest of the world.

7.3.3 Further prospects for democracy and parliamentarism

The Swedish constitutional debates of spring 1919 contained little substantial discussion on either democracy or parliamentarism. This is no surprise given that the concepts had already been debated pro et contra, defined and redefined on four occasions in two chambers during the preceding two years. The contributions that were made merely recycled previously heard arguments. The far left did, however, take the chance to elaborate on their critical arguments made in autumn 1918 against Social Democratic moderation. They were inspired in this by international radical leftist discourse not only in Russia and Germany but also among the Western left more generally.

Ivar Vennerström, for instance, emphasised that 'complete political democracy' had not been achieved with the reform. What 'the Swedish democracy' (democracy was here also being nationalised by the far left) needed was progress towards 'social and economic democracy'.[2421] Such extensions of democracy had been called for in socialist discourse that was unhappy with what bourgeois parliaments had to offer.[2422] Especially the German far left were demanding these in Weimar, and the Social Democrat leaders were giving promises in that direction to appease the left wing of their party. The reform demands of the Swedish far left also included the introduction of the referendum, an instrument that was strongly present in the German constitutional proposal. They carried on using Marxist discourse by questioning the justification of the prevailing societal order

---

2419 FK, Ernst Trygger, 5 June 1919, 53:36.
2420 FK, Ernst Trygger, 5 June 1919, 53:45.
2421 AK, Ivar Vennerström, 24 May 1919, 54:16.
2422 See MacDonald at the beginning of this chapter.

after the reform. Fredrik Ström doubted whether even referenda would increase democracy since 'in a bourgeois democracy and a capitalist society it is the money that governs'; they would merely give rise to unfounded beliefs in a 'pseudo-democracy' (*skendemokratien*),[2423] again a term recalling recent German Social Democratic discourse. Such ideologically motivated and obviously transnationally inspired discourse continued in Sweden in the aftermath of the German Revolution.

The Social Democrats no longer saw reason to carry on preaching the gospel of democracy. 'Democracy' in the sense of universal suffrage, for which they had been primarily campaigning, was already about to be achieved; other aspects of democratisation were expected to follow with the increase in Social Democratic representation at all levels. While the ministers themselves were careful not to promise too much, many backbenchers pressed for further reforms – the response from the Social Democratic leaders being to wait patiently. Arthur Engberg called on 'this new democracy' (referring to the next parliament) to decide on the proper system of representation 'in a democratic state',[2424] suggesting (provocatively for The Right) that further adjustments were needed. Viktor Larsson referred to the referendum as part of this 'democratic order'.[2425] For the Swedish Social Democrats, the transition to parliamentary democracy would be a rapid but smooth one, leading as it did to four single-party governments in the 1920s. Jussi Kurunmäki has pointed out that their revisionism and rising responsibilities did not mean giving up the old Marxist emphasis on the class struggle or the ultimate goal of socialism. Parliamentary democracy continued to have an instrumental value for them rather than being the goal in itself.[2426] It was just used very effectively.

Some Liberals, too, were unhappy with the extent of the reform, while others did not wish for more: the 'so-called democratic reform' had remained 'all too primitively democratic', as could be seen from the willingness of The Right to agree to it, as Anders Olsson claimed.[2427] Most MPs of The Right kept their concerns about the nature of any future democracy to themselves, applying 'the rhetoric of silence' as a party newspaper aptly put it.[2428] Ernst Trygger, who had reluctantly led The Right to accept the reform, only said that democracy as such was not the party's goal; what was most beneficial for the country was of the essence;[2429] this could be interpreted by a well-intentioned audience as an implicit recognition of the need for the transition to democracy in the sense of universal suffrage. Such accommodation had its limits: instead of recognising democracy in appreciative terms, the rightists continued to differentiate between good and bad democracy, associating parliamentarism with the latter. At the same time, news about

---

2423 FK, Fredrik Ström, 5 June 1919, 58:20.
2424 AK, Arthur Engberg, 24 May 1919, 54:6.
2425 AK, Viktor Larsson, 24 May 1919, 54:12.
2426 Kurunmäki 2014, 179–80.
2427 AK, Anders Olsson, 24 May 1919, 54:17.
2428 *Aftonbladet*, 'Författningsdemokrati och tilllämpning', 25 May 1919.
2429 FK, Ernst Trygger, 5 June 1919, 58:36.

the Bolsheviks questioning 'democracy in the best meaning of that word' and the idea of parliamentarism associated with it – the alternative being the dictatorship of the proletariat – caused The Right to reassess democracy as the lesser evil.[2430] *Aftonbladet* consequently recognised that the time of 'constitutional democracy' had begun.[2431] Democracy was thus creeping into conservative discourse, though the Swedish right of the interwar period would prefer to talk about 'the rule by the people' and 'the government of the people' rather than about 'democracy' or 'parliamentarism',[2432] the vernacular phrases supporting the national and even nationalist senses of democracy with connotations that approach those of the Finnish concepts (and possibly those of the German ones as well).

David Norman, a prominent anti-reformist of The Right, nevertheless continued to criticise the Social Democrats and warn about the severe consequences of the expected democratisation. Now that Finland was returning on the road towards representative democracy, the warning example from the east could be more openly discussed than in 1918, when similar radicalisation had been seen as a risk in Sweden. According to Norman, the fall of Finnish democracy illustrated the potential consequences of universal suffrage in Sweden as well:[2433]

> Finland ought to be for us a sufficiently telling and warning example of the fact that the most extensive suffrage, the most developed democracy by no means constitutes a shield against the spirit of illegality or stands for an increase in social solidarity.

Norman taunted the Social Democrats with having lost some of their enthusiasm about democracy since Hjalmar Branting's return from Petrograd on 14 April 1917 – which demonstrates the significance of that revolutionary moment in the discursive process of reform. Norman also made a further intertextual reference to Harald Hallén's suggestion in spring 1917 that full democracy might be introduced in Sweden with foreign help if the Swedish upper house did not opt for a reform.[2434] Arthur Engberg of the Social Democrats responded with derisive humour, thanking Norman for his sensitivity to the rise and fall of the international democratic spirit. Norman's remark was to be interpreted as reflecting an international rise of anti-democratic thought. This reveals socialist concerns about a counter-reaction to democratisation in Germany and elsewhere (though hardly really in Sweden, where only a few Prussian-minded ultraconservatives continued to expressly resist; in Finland the organ of the Swedish People's Party also made similar suggestions):[2435]

2430 *Aftonbladet*, 'Bolsjevismens frukter', 5 June 1919.
2431 *Aftonbladet*, 'Författningsdemokrati och tilllämpning', 25 May 1919.
2432 Kurunmäki 2014, 180.
2433 AK, David Norman, 8 June 1919, 72:9.
2434 AK, David Norman, 8 June 1919, 72:9.
2435 AK, Arthur Engberg, 8 June 1919, 72:18.

Anti-democracy and the powers of autocracy have wind in their sails, and why then should not Mr Norman from Läckeby hoist the sails on his little boat and, to please the public, try to show that he is the bold Achilles who can oppose Swedish democracy?

Harald Hallén rejected the comparison between Swedish and Finnish democracy[2436] and did not comment on the insinuation about imported revolution. His message was that The Right was just continuing to employ misleading characterisations of democracy.[2437]

Parliamentarism had been established in Sweden with the nomination of the Liberal-Social Democratic government in October 1917, but the attitudes surrounding it changed only gradually. During the reform struggles, some reformist academics had claimed that the Swedish political system had been based on parliamentarism at least since the mid-eighteenth century (if not even from the times of the *ting*s around the year 1000). This interpretation was widely adopted by the left and, in a rhetorically redescribed form, by The Right as well.[2438] As the time to reinforce the extension of suffrage was at hand, Arthur Engberg of the Social Democrats emphasised the organic development of a parliamentary practice that had not been foreseen when the constitution of 1809 had been formulated,[2439] here suggesting that modern parliamentarism was a more recent innovation and not so much part of some immemorial native heritage.[2440] Once universal suffrage had become a reality, historico-political theories based on political history claiming a thousand years of developing democracy and parliamentarism were no longer so eagerly cited; the modernity of parliamentarism was recognised. But theories about the age of reform emphasising mythical continuities nevertheless remained part of the Swedish historiographical tradition and national identity to an extent that still calls for rethinking.[2441]

7.3.4 POLITICS OF THE PEOPLE IN A DEMOCRATIC SWEDEN

The suffrage reform, once realised, was expected to redefine the political participation of the Swedish people. Women's suffrage in parliamentary elections, in particular, was viewed as a turning point. Proposals on referenda, a unicameral parliament and a republican constitution were also placed on the agenda, but most attention was paid to the completion of female suffrage. By now, it was welcomed by all contributors to the debates, former opponents considering it best to stay silent in order not to provoke future voters. Nevertheless, the effects of women's suffrage on the political system were interpreted in interestingly differing ways.

Reform initiatives and analyses of the consequences of the reform mostly originated from the far left. They had not become as ostracised as their counterparts in Finland and Germany after unsuccessful revolutionary

---

2436 AK, Harald Hallén, 8 June 1919, 72:26.
2437 AK, Harald Hallén, 8 June 1919, 72:34.
2438 Ihalainen 2015.
2439 AK, Arthur Engberg, 5 June 1919, 66:21.
2440 Also FK, Mauritz Hellberg, 5 June 1919, 53:31.
2441 See Ihalainen 2015 for an historico-political analysis of these debates.

attempts in those countries, and their claims were not particularly militant either, but they nevertheless remained alone in their criticism. Ivar Vennerström wished for a future with 'a complete political reorganisation, a complete political democracy' in which the people would participate in major decisions through popular initiatives and referenda. Universal suffrage would make it possible for 'the Swedish democracy' (a nationalised term) to remove political injustices and to introduce not only 'political democracy' but also the left's longed-for 'social and economic democracy', implying the replacement of the 'formal democracy' of universal suffrage with 'real democracy'.[2442] Socialist demands for further-going reform had been heard in late 1918, but the Liberal-Social Democrat government had prioritised the suffrage reform and continued to do so. Calls for extended democracy by the Swedish far left resembled those of the British, German and Finnish radical left, with the exception that Swedish beliefs in gradual progress towards socialist democracy were stronger than in the countries of comparison. Carl Lindhagen, for instance, presented women's suffrage as productive of major shifts in power relations that would benefit the country and the people. When 'women are involved in all ways in the whirl of party politics', a just government for all would follow.[2443] Politics in the future would stand essentially for the participation of a larger number of people in the activities of the parties that represented the workers.

The Social Democrats, despite their obvious enthusiasm over the successful reform, were rather more cautious in drawing conclusions about the political momentum. Illustrative of their understanding of politics in the future are the associations they postulated between democracy and politics. The combination was talked about in a very positive way, and it was used to define an idealised political system of the future.[2444] Party Secretary Gustav Möller characterised the extension of suffrage as the 'democratisation' of Sweden, using a concept that was common when changes in the German political system were discussed but which was unknown among British debaters. Möller also envisioned the 'political education' that universal suffrage would provide for women and its potential for changing the country.[2445] Oscar Olsson emphasised the principle of the will of the people within the new democratic constitution and insisted that in a democratic society *all* political institutions should be 'manifestations of the popular will',[2446] which left the door open for future reforms.

It is noteworthy that the Liberal ministers argued that the reform would extend popular participation, envisioning a better society resulting from it and without the reservations that some British, German and former Finnish Liberals might have expressed. They did so, perhaps in order to appear as competent rivals to the Social Democrats as reformists, despite

---

2442 AK, Ivar Vennerström, 24 May 1919, 54:16. On the extension of this discourse to the Social Democratic Party, see Friberg 2012, 92–4.
2443 FK, Carl Lindhagen, 24 May 1919, 43:2–3, 5–7.
2444 See Möller 2007, 92, for the use of the concept *folkhemmet* (the people's home) in the election campaign of the autumn of 1919.
2445 AK, Gustav Möller, 24 May 1919, 54:12–13.
2446 FK, Oscar Olsson, 5 June 1919, 58:39.

the obvious party-political risks involved. Eliel Löfgren, the Minister of Justice, saw women's suffrage and the participation of women in political parties optimistically as opening up an entirely new era, changing 'the so-called masculine culture' in such a way that humanity and understanding in politics would increase.[2447] While 'the sovereignty of the will of the people in politics' was emphasised,[2448] some doubted the ability of 'the masses themselves or the people as a whole' to decide on minor issues as so many people 'are from a political point of view completely illiterate.'[2449] Hence, instead of referenda, 'the people have a right to rule themselves and arrange their own house' through representation in the parliament,[2450] which was an old argument for 'bourgeois' democracy. In such a system, Liberal trust in the people was strong. Carl Fredrik Holmquist, the former chairman of the Committee for Suffrage Reform, extolled 'a truly constitutional culture, which exists deep in the history of the Swedish people, its experiences and its ... deep political maturity.' The reform caused Holmquist to argue for a unique 'Swedish democracy',[2451] nationalising the concept in a way resembling the discourse of the Social Democrats in Sweden and reformist liberals in Finland. The reform was thus viewed by both the Socialists and the Liberals as a national achievement enabling progress within a nation-state. References to a transnational wave of democracy, which Liberal politicians had also favoured in 1917 and 1918, were set aside as the process of reform was discursively nationalised.

For The Right, it continued to be difficult to view future politics as such an inevitable success story. Enthusiasm was perhaps dying away among other political groups as well, given the length of the reform process, which should already have been finalised. When the constitutional reform was finally approved in the parliament, a major newspaper with rightist sympathies took the half-empty strangers' and press galleries in the parliament as evidence of the indifference of the public. The calmness of the debate was interpreted as a lack of enthusiasm among the politicians.[2452] Samuel Clason nevertheless conceded in the parliament somewhat later that there was no getting around appeals 'to the mass of the people' in the new political system,[2453] which reflects an incipient adaptation to extended popular participation in politics also among the Swedish right.

7.3.5 A glance across the Gulf of Bothnia

The separation of the Swedish and Finnish polities and the inclusion of Finland in the Russian Empire in 1809 had by 1919, despite the same

---

2447 AK, Eliel Löfgren, 24 May 1919, 54:20, 24–5.
2448 FK, Mauritz Hellberg, 5 June 1919, 58:31–3.
2449 AK, Per Johan Persson, 5 June 1919, 66:12.
2450 AK, Ulrik Leander, 5 June 1919, 66:22; FK, Otto von Zweigbergk, 5 June 1919, 53:14.
2451 FK, Carl Fredrik Holmquist, 24 May 1919, 43:9–10, 16.
2452 *Aftonbladet*, 'Författningsreformen godkänd av riksdagen', 24 May 1919, 'Författningsdemokrati och tilllämpning', 25 May 1919, 'Författningsreformen slutförd och lagfäst', 26 May 1919.
2453 FK, Samuel Clason, 5 June 1919, 58:17–18.

constitutional heritage of the eighteenth-century Gustavian constitution, led to different constitutional circumstances and political cultures and practices, all visible in divergent conceptualisations of constitutional principles.[2454] Despite continued connections with German and Swedish academic and ideological debates, the political link with Russia and the traumatic experience of a civil war in 1918 had given rise to different, both more conservative and more radically republican, understandings of the key political notions in Finland. In the Finnish debates, the linguistic difference – even if the key terms were often originally borrowed from German or Swedish and then vernacularised – led to conceptualisations that differed from those in Sweden. The parliamentary process of negotiation and debate had failed to solve the constitutional and other political problems in 1917 and 1918. The majority of the political elite were nevertheless capable of reaching a constructive compromise in 1919, being forced to reconsider their positions after the traumatic experiences of the Civil War and under external pressures arising from the outcome of the world war. In Sweden, a compromise on constitutional reform was achieved through a complex parliamentary process, albeit only after similar external impulses. In Germany, the external impulses were strong, too, but the turn in political values less fundamental and lasting than in Finland or Sweden, no matter how radical some of the party-political discourse on democracy and parliamentarism there may have been.

During the constitutional debates in the Swedish and Finnish parliaments in spring 1919, the national contexts were more divergent than probably ever before or even later in the history of the two countries. The Swedes, who had avoided the war despite the sympathy for Germany among the royal family and The Right, were about to confirm the introduction of universal suffrage, which their both chambers had initially approved in the aftermath of the fall of the German monarchy. It was generally expected (or feared) that the victory of reform after a long struggle would open the gates for further constitutional reforms. Optimism over future politics was dominant among the socialist and Liberal speakers, and even The Right had begun a process of rethinking their position.

After an unparalleled national calamity, visions for the future were far less optimistic in Finland. The Finns had experienced a radical parliamentary reform with universal suffrage in 1906 but had generally become disillusioned with parliamentary politics after the parliament had proved to be unable to advance reforms either under tsarist rule or after being liberated from it. Together with deep social and ideological confrontations and a radical political discourse, further radicalised through transnational contacts with Russia, this had led to a civil war in spring 1918 and a monarchical experiment as a counter-reaction in autumn 1918. In spring 1919, the Finnish parliament convened after a new election, in which the losers of the Civil War had mostly participated, and the republicans gained a landslide victory. The major mission of the new parliament was to overcome the deep ideological differences to finally agree on a republican constitution. The

---

2454 Jansson 2009; Ihalainen & Sundin 2011; Ihalainen 2015.

situation gave little reason for optimism given the traumatic experiences of the Civil War and its aftermath, but the Finnish government and parliament made a serious (and in the long term successful) attempt to transform an open conflict in the form of a civil war into a confined parliamentary confrontation. In the end, parliamentary democracy won out, albeit in a confined presidential form.

In terms of foreign policy, too, Sweden and Finland were further apart in 1919 than in any other period. Most Swedes had wanted to avoid any ideological confrontation resembling the Finnish Civil War. Swedish attempts to annex the Åland Islands during that war had led to the deepest mutual foreign policy crisis that the two countries have ever experienced. News about the threatened status of the Swedish language in Finland was also commonplace in the Swedish press.[2455] This confrontation nearly removed the neighbouring country as the usual object of comparison from parliamentary debates: Finland did not exist for the Swedes to the same extent after the Civil War as during the suffrage campaign. Nor did contemporary Sweden really exist for Finns, if we look at press reports, for instance. This was exceptional in Finnish political culture, which customarily uses explicit and implicit comparisons with Sweden in all areas of life and has discursively integrated[2456] much of Swedish political culture. Although interpretations of the immemorial native roots of democracy and parliamentarism were common to both countries at that time, references to the shared constitutional past differed considerably: in Sweden, continuing progress rather than the tradition of representative government or the inheritance of the long eighteenth century was emphasised after the reform was achieved, whereas Finnish conservative circles called for the preservation of elements of the eighteenth-century Swedish constitution, and these were transferred to the new republican one as well. Finnish politicians went back much more readily to the experiences of a common history to argue for and against democracy and parliamentarism,[2457] which illustrates the rather more historically oriented nature of Finnish political discourse.

7.4 Finland: Moving towards a compromise on a presidential parliamentary republic

7.4.1 RE-ORIENTING THE POLITY AFTER THE WAR

In Finland, as in much of the rest of Europe, many republicans had realised by early October 1918 that Germany would lose the war and reform its constitution, and that this would have implications both for its international affairs and for transnational constitutional development. The republicans correctly foresaw that the German alliance and the election of Friedrich Karl to the Finnish throne would cause foreign political problems for the newly independent country and also delay the constitutional settlement. The

---

2455 *Aftonbladet*, 'Hur länge hava svenskarna bott i Finland', 24 May 1919.
2456 Leonhard 2011, 257.
2457 Ihalainen 2015.

monarchical majority of the Rump Parliament had nevertheless proceeded to the royal election on 9 October 1918, dismissing the evident political turn in Germany, which was expected to lead to the creation of a parliamentary democracy, Allied calls for a democratic government for Finland and continuing republican protests in the national parliament. The leaders of the conservative Finnish and Swedish People's Parties as well as many liberal Young Finns, ignoring news from the surrounding world, were unwilling to give up the chance to carry through their monarchical scheme, which was designed to save both the nation and the old elite from the excesses of democracy and parliamentarism. When updates to the eighteenth-century monarchical constitution as concessions to the republicans did not convert the opponents, the monarchists went for a legalistic application of the provisions of the 1772 constitution and got their king – though only nominally and only for two months.

Not only did Germany lose the war as expected, but the German monarchy also fell in early November. These two facts – as well as the lacking recognition of independence by the Anglophone powers – forced the monarchists into profound reconsiderations of foreign policy and the constitution and to concede that a new election was needed.[2458] The Finnish situation was in some respects parallel to that of both Sweden and Germany, though it was even more complicated and there was a time lag in its evolvement: in the new state of international affairs, it had become hopeless to carry on opposition to domestic reform demands as transnational trends were so obviously in favour of democracy and parliamentarism and indeed explicitly demanded it. Friedrich Karl abdicated from the Finnish throne in December after it had become clear that Britain would not accept any combination of a German monarch with a Western parliamentary system in Finland.[2459] The Finnish monarchy ceased to exist, and even a modified version of it had no chance of surviving given the questionable legality of the monarchists' actions in electing a king. For the great majority of the political nation, monarchy had become associated with opposition to democracy and parliamentarism, which added to an age-old popular hatred of the ruling classes.

In the changed international circumstances, the Finns had once again started to search for a constitutional solution in January 1919. They needed to find a compromise that would stabilise the polity after two years of fruitless and destructive controversy, during which proposals ranging from extreme parliamentarism rejecting the division of power to a presidential parliamentary republic and a constitutional monarchy of the Prussian type had been the major alternatives. A solution was urgently needed: the international and domestic situation was dangerous in that it was not out of the question that a new revolutionary attempt might be made – by either the left or the right. A Bolshevik government had, despite the continuing civil war in Russia, established itself in Petrograd, and the Bolsheviks had allied themselves with exiled survivors of the Finnish Red government,

---

2458   Jyränki 2006, 39.
2459   Paasivirta 1961, 111; Polvinen 1987, vol. 2, 112–13.

including former Finnish MPs such as Kullervo Manner (the Speaker of the first parliament of 1917), Otto Wille Kuusinen and Yrjö Sirola, who had all criticised bourgeois parliamentarism in the debates of November 1917 and had been founding members of the Finnish Communist Party. This party openly denounced democracy and parliamentarism and strove for a dictatorship of the proletariat established by an unavoidably violent revolution that would destroy the bourgeois state. Kuusinen concluded that the Kautskyist parliamentary class struggle had failed by diminishing the workers' belief in an armed struggle.[2460] It is unlikely that these views only emerged after the failed revolution; these men had already challenged bourgeois democracy and parliamentarism in earnest in 1917.

Finnish relations with the Entente could not have been worse. A civil war was going on in Russia, and some Finnish activists were considering an intervention on the White side. Britain and the United States were reluctant to recognise Finnish independence as long as the country remained a loyal ally of Germany – this was manifested in the application of a monarchical constitution of the Prussian type, the election of a German prince to the throne and the anti-Western attitudes expressed during the constitutional struggles of 1918. Germany itself provided a contrary constitutional model in January 1919: it had abolished monarchy after losing the war and, after the revolutionary council experiment by the far left, was moving towards a republican constitution based on universal suffrage and parliamentary democracy, though parliamentarism would remain limited by strong presidential exceptional powers and the possibility to appeal directly to the people through referenda. The German constitutional model nevertheless remained from a Finnish perspective more valid than any provided by the Entente or Sweden: this can be seen in extensive reports on the Weimar debates in newspapers of every major party.[2461] Even if it remained unclear whether political attitudes had changed in Germany as fundamentally as the constitutional rearrangements suggested, transnational influence from there continued to involve both the republicans and the monarchists.[2462] Sweden, the old constitutional mother country, had also chosen a reformist path after the right agreed to an electoral reform, mainly to stop the spread of revolutionary tendencies resembling those in Germany. However, Sweden remained an odious object of imitation for conservative and nationalist

---

2460 Polvinen 1971, 66–8; Kettunen 1986, 90; Hyvärinen 2003, 86, 90.

2461 *Hufvudstadsbladet*, 'Krisens utveckling i Tyskland', 4 March 1919; *Suomen Sosialidemokraatti*, 'Saksan hallitusmuotokysymys', 5 March 1919; 'Johdonmukaisuutta', 10 March 1919; *Helsingin Sanomat*, 'Waikutelmia Weimarista', 25 April 1919.

2462 The Swedish and Finnish Ambassadors, together with those of Denmark, Lithuania and Norway, were the only major diplomats to attend the opening of the German National Assembly on 6 February 1919. Edvard Hjelt, who had signed the agreement with Germany in March 1918, continued to represent Finland in Berlin. *Neue Preußische Zeitung*, 7 February 1919; *Berliner Tageblatt*, 7 February 1919. On the other hand, *Hufvudstadsbladet* obviously wanted to postpone decisions on the Finnish constitution until Germany had decided on its new polity. 'Samhällets självbevarelseplikt', 14 June 1919.

Finnish MPs – despite the shared constitutional tradition – as long as it continued its attempt to annex the Åland Islands, its domestic politics were run by the Social Democrats and their obedient Liberal allies, who had been unwilling to openly help the Whites during the Civil War, and the Swedish People's Party in Finland demonstrated signs of separatism. As for the Finnish Social Democrats, they too had been disappointed by the lack of sympathy from Sweden during the Civil War but were reconsidering whether the revisionist Swedish strategy of reform through the parliament might not lead to better results after all. Even Karl Kautsky, whose teachings they have been supposed by many Finnish historians to have followed, had denounced their previous policies as sheer Bolshevism. Väinö Tanner, a moderate Social Democratic leader, travelled around Scandinavia to create new contacts with sister parties. Hannes Ryömä, a member of the new Constitutional Committee and also the editor-in-chief of *Suomen Sosialidemokraatti*, described the revolutions of late 1918 as a breakthrough of democracy in a parliamentary sense rather than any advancement of Bolshevism.[2463] Both Tanner and Ryömä had been looking for contacts to German Social Democracy already during 1918.[2464] The fact that these leaders wanted to direct Finnish Social Democracy towards Western European revisionism is visible in positive statements about the policies of the German SPD as opposed to Bolshevism and the failed Finnish Revolution.[2465]

Constitutional questions had been far from merely domestic issues in 1917 (under Russian influence) or in 1918 (under German influence), and they would continue to be influenced by transnational connections in 1919. Britain had required the Finns to hold a new election as a demonstration of their renunciation of pro-German policies and as a precondition for the recognition of Finnish independence. To the British and Americans, the Finnish monarchists appeared as uncritical admirers of Germany, whereas the republicans were believed to support Western democracy.[2466] Not all republicans or reformists were Anglophiles, however, as connections with Germany had long been dominant in most areas of culture. Russian transnational involvement in Finnish constitutional debates had been nearly extinguished by the Civil War, Sweden was excluded because of its alleged expansionism (in the Åland Islands), Germany concentrated on solving its own constitutional and socio-economic challenges, and the United States was divided by a dispute on whether or not to commit itself to the League of Nations. In the meantime, victorious Britain had become the most important transnational actor on the constitutional scene and a model that could no longer be simply ignored.[2467]

Back home, the wounds of the Civil War remained sore with the incarceration of the defeated Reds in prison camps with death tolls that were higher than the casualties in the actual war. The treatment of the

---

2463 Soikkanen 1975, 315, 319, 324.
2464 Hentilä & Hentilä 2016, 221–3.
2465 *Suomen Sosialidemokraatti*, 'Johdonmukaisuutta', 10 March 1919.
2466 Vares 2006, 130.
2467 See also Pekonen 2014.

prisoners had provoked concerned publicity in the Western media and among leftist groups in particular. The exiled Reds in Soviet Russia were assumed to be eager for revenge, and the left at home was bitter about its previous exclusion from political life. The republican Whites who had been represented in the Rump Parliament were sour about the uncompromising constitutional dictation of the monarchists in autumn 1918 and unwilling to make concessions towards anything resembling a monarchy. The monarchists, too, were disappointed because their favourite polity of an updated Gustavian[2468] or applied Prussian monarchical type had proved to be unachievable. Many found it difficult to believe in the political potential of the people after the masses had let the ruling classes down by rejecting representative government and joining the Red rebellion.

That rebellion had been crushed and traditionalist monarchism had received a major transnational blow, but no one knew whether the revolutionary period was over. The revolutionary language of class confrontation might well re-enter the parliament after a new election. And, in fact, verbal strife would only gradually die out of constitutional debates, as a reflection of reconsideration within the Social Democratic Party and also among some of the right. Radical Social Democrats nevertheless admonished the bourgeoisie to renounce the policies they had followed in the first ten years of the reformed parliament if they wanted the Social Democrats to prevent a new revolutionary bid.[2469] Non-socialist members, for their part, did not hesitate to remind the left about the lawless rebellion against a parliamentary majority that had taken place.

The weariness with constitutional strife had nevertheless increased a readiness for compromise in most parties. International examples also contributed to this: if the Swedish right had given in after over a decade of opposition, and if the German left and bourgeoisie could be expected to agree on a new constitutional settlement soon, why should the Finns demur – especially as the dangers arising from continued controversy for a newly independent state next to Russia were so grave? A constitutional compromise was known to be a precondition for the recognition of Finnish independence by Britain and the United States. Without this, the survival of the country in the post-war situation would remain precarious. Even so, the discursive process towards a compromise would not be an easy one: all parties would need to reconsider their old stands and possibly redefine their key political concepts in order to be able to negotiate and agree on a compromise on the polity. All but the leaders of the Swedish People's Party would turn out to be ready for such a reassessment in spring 1919, with the Swedish-speaking conservatives refraining for both ideological and language-policy reasons (in order to gain a stronger status for Swedish, a minority language, as

---

2468 The Swedish People's Party did not give up its idealisation of the duality of government in Gustav III's eighteenth-century constitution. *Hufvudstadsbladet*, 'Samhällets självbevarelseplikt', 14 June 1919; 'Regeringsformen antagen', 22 June 1919.
2469 See VP, Jonas Laherma, 25 April 1919, 132; Mikko Ampuja, 25 April 1919, 134–5.

a 'national' one). Ideological closeness to the Prussian right can be seen in quotations from its representatives published in the organ of the party.[2470]

The constitutional debates of spring 1919 were preceded by major changes in the Finnish party system. The overwhelmingly monarchist Swedish People's Party, suspicious of the Finnish people at large after the Civil War, won 22 seats in the election of March 1919. Many of the spokesmen of the party continued to hold political views and theories that resembled those of the German or the Swedish right; the party stood against extended democracy or parliamentarism and for the protection of minority rights. The Finnish-speaking conservatives had reorganised themselves into the monarchist National Coalition Party, based on a union between the former Finnish Party and monarchist Young Finns, and calling for the safeguarding of 'the legal societal order inherited from forefathers'.[2471] This party opposed extreme forms of parliamentarism as proposed by the Power Act of 1917 and looked for a counterbalance in a strong presidency resembling a monarchy, a polity recalling German counterbalances to parliamentarism. Its electoral support proved modest: the party won a mere 28 seats, which reflected the unpopularity of the monarchical project of 1918. The National Progress Party created by the republican Young Finns, by contrast, gained 26 seats, which demonstrated the strong support for republicanism among liberal voters. The victory of the Agrarian League, the most consistent defender of republicanism, democracy and parliamentarism in the Finnish parliament throughout the constitutional disputes of 1917–18, was also important for the victory of parliamentary democracy. Ideologically this party was distinct from the German conservative Catholic Centre and the predominantly conservative Swedish peasant parties. The voters recognised its contribution with 42 seats. All in all, the republicans had an undisputable majority of almost three fourths, with only the National Coalition and Swedish People's Party representing the lost monarchical cause.

The Finnish Social Democratic Party was completely reorganised after the Civil War: armed revolution was denounced, previous links with the Bolsheviks were cut and the moderate German and Swedish Social Democratic Parties were adopted as models. The revolutionary Finnish Communist Party was declared illegal in Finland and remained so throughout the interwar period.[2472] The Finnish left was thus divided only after a failed violent revolution and significantly later than the Social Democrats in Sweden and Germany; a comparable division and the lack of links with Russian revolutionary discourse in 1917 might well have saved Finland from a civil war. Even though the Social Democrats lost 12 seats in 1919, they remained the largest group in the parliament with 80 seats. An openly far left party was lacking, but some radicalism remained within the Social Democratic Party and would be revived in the Finnish Socialist Labour Party in 1922.

2470 *Hufvudstadsbladet*, 'Krisens utveckling i Tyskland', 4 March 1919.
2471 *Kansallisen Kokoomuspuolueen vaalijulistus*, 1919.
2472 Kettunen 1986, 90; Jussila, Hentilä & Nevakivi 1999, 126–7; Vares 2006, 132.

During the election campaign, the need for a proper constitution was widely discussed, and thus the mandate of the new parliament to solve the issue was undeniable. The choices to be made were between a limited democracy maintaining the duality of executive and legislative powers and an extended parliamentary democracy that would award the people, the parliament and the parties rather than the head of state the key role in the political system. As Vesa Vares has pointed out, the international situation of early March 1919 – in contrast to 1918 – favoured the republican alternative: three empires had fallen and many European countries were actively searching for democratic and parliamentary constitutional solutions.[2473] The implications of the changed international context and the transnational links of the Finnish parliamentarians need to be taken into account since they indicate that the formation of the Finnish republican constitution, too, was a partly transnational and not merely a national discursive process.

After the election, the republicans formed a minority government supported by the Agrarians and the Progress Party and including the monarchist Swedish People's Party – to avoid any escalation of the language issue. The ministry was led by Kaarlo Castrén, a rightist Progressivist. The new parliament, which convened on 1 April, voted down two proposals for a monarchical constitution conditionally approved in 1918, and on 13 May 1919 it received a new proposal for a republican constitution, produced after considerable disagreement within the ministry.[2474] A republican constitution was not easy to accept for the monarchist majority of the Swedish-speakers, and the party would continue to oppose it to the end. This opposition was motivated by the language provisions, which they saw as corroding the status of the Swedish language, but the speeches of the party members show that their stands were also influenced by ideological factors. The party would leave the coalition in August as a result of disagreements on language policy,[2475] and possibly also in protest against the republican constitution.

The republican turn had immediate effects on relations with the Entente: Britain and the United States recognised Finnish independence in early May once they saw a parliamentary democracy emerging.[2476] The British based this recognition on their view of the ongoing Russian Civil War and the potential construction of a new anti-German alliance: they believed that the recognition would reduce German influence in the Baltic and win a trustworthy opponent to the Bolsheviks over to the British side.[2477] The Finnish election result suggested that no more than a third had supported the monarchical project of 1918. Crypto-monarchism survived, of course, in the form of a presidency, the power of which continued to be negotiated between the republicans and the National Coalition Party until the final passage of the bill on 21 June.

2473 Vares 2006, 137.
2474 Sihvonen 1997, 15.
2475 Vares 2006, 140.
2476 Sihvonen 1997, 15; Jussila, Hentilä & Nevakivi 1999, 127–9.
2477 Sundbäck 1994, 371–5.

The formulation of the republican bill corresponds with the proposal that had been debated by the Weimar National Constituent Assembly since late February. Even though the Finnish proposal had been prepared to a great extent during 1917, old cultural contacts with Germany were kept alive by republicans and monarchists alike. The old model polity had turned into a parliamentary democracy, as the republicans had foreseen in autumn 1918. The Finnish right still followed the stances of the German right at least as far as political theory was concerned. The Germans, furthermore, faced similar challenges in reconciling parliamentarism with a presidency authorised by a popular vote. The issue of transnational influence from Germany has not been much explored in Finnish historical research. Sven Lindman argued in 1937 (at a time when the Weimar Constitution had already failed and all associations with it were avoided) that the premises of the Finnish constitution had been formulated in 1917, well before the other constitutions that were adopted after the First World War, and that it was not influenced to any considerable extent by the debates of those states that needed to decide on a new constitution – despite some manifestations of influence in the parliamentary debates of spring 1919. Lindman thus conceded that there may have been something that we could call transnational influence but doubted the relevance of the German example, 'even if the German proposal was probably known in Finland before the new form of government was accepted'.[2478] The republican turn in the Finnish parliamentary debates on the constitution nevertheless remained transnationally connected with Germany – as the parliamentary turn in spring and summer 1917 and the monarchical reaction in summer and autumn 1918 had been. The Finnish press at least remained interested in German developments. The comparative and transnational analysis of parliamentary debates below also suggests that connections continued to exist even though the changed political situation made the speakers more selective in their references to German models.

However, the new international set-up by no means predetermined the decisions of the Finnish parliamentarians. There were still several options available: the republic could be based on the kind of far-reaching parliamentarism demanded by the Social Democrats and approved by the Agrarians as fellow proponents of the Power Act of 1917, or it could include a strong presidency as a counterbalance to the parliament as suggested in the republican proposal of late 1917. The latter alternative, which resembled the German plans with a strong Reichspräsident, was favoured by many republicans and former monarchists alike. After negotiations, which partly took place in conjunction with the parliamentary debates themselves, a compromise was found on a presidential republic combining parliamentary democracy with a strong presidency with veto rights. This would become a lasting polity that would be gradually parliamentarised only after 1981. Full parliamentarism would be introduced in the constitution of 2000 and further extended in 2012.

The constitutional compromise was supported by an increasing readiness among the left and centre (both traumatised by the failure of

---

2478 Lindman 1937, 12.

radical parliamentary rule in 1917 and the Civil War) to allow the president some independent executive power provided that legislative power would remain concentrated in the parliament. The German presidential model and the maintenance of the Swedish monarchy, accepted by their sister parties, may also have supported this readiness. The Finnish-speaking right, too, appeared to be increasingly prepared to go back to a slightly more optimistic conception of the people and to accommodate themselves to a republic provided that the president remained independent of the parliament and had a suspending veto in legislation – a model that was to be followed in Germany as well. The republicans, too, understood the necessity of compromise – unless they wished to take the risk of a further postponement through the right using minority provisions (with just 1/6 of the votes being enough to force a postponement).[2479] This provision was, in fact, used by the National Coalition Party in the next to final vote on 14 June 1919. As hardly anyone wanted the constitutional strife to continue, a final compromise was sought and the National Coalition Party, too, voted for a presidential republic on 21 June, after obtaining some further additions to presidential power.

The alternatives in the Finnish debates were in many ways parallel to those in Weimar; this was particularly true of the status of the president as a counterbalance to the feared extreme parliamentarism. In both countries, the right campaigned for a strong 'monarchical' president deriving his power directly from the people, whereas the left and some of the centre preferred a more parliamentarised polity. Lindman recognised that constitutional dualism connected the German and Finnish constitutions and distinguished them from other polities of the time (though a degree of dualism was retained in Sweden as well).[2480]

Many members of the Finnish-speaking right, unlike the German right, were moving towards the acceptance of the republican constitution. Vesa Vares suggests that many of them were unwilling to appear as opponents of democracy and parliamentarism. They were also concerned about extra-parliamentary measures by the left and centre that might produce another revolution and civil war supported by the Bolsheviks in the east.[2481] The right was drawing the same conclusions that the leaders of the Swedish right had drawn in November and December 1918: there was no way of halting an evidently Europe-wide transition to parliamentary democracy after Britain had won the war and both Germany and Sweden had chosen that path. At the same time, the Swedish People's Party remained an advocate of the traditional political order, trying to retain as much of the special status of the linguistic minority and the administrative elite as possible – even at the cost of appearing reactionary in its opposition to democracy and parliamentarism. Vares adds that the Social Democrats were not happy about the constitutional proposal in comparison the Power Act of July 1917. Nevertheless, the newly organised party considered it necessary to accept a compromise that allowed a degree of parliamentarism, as its leaders did not

---

2479 Vares 2006, 141–2.
2480 Lindman 1937, 13–14.
2481 Vares 2006, 144.

want radical socialists to take over the party again and to lead it into another civil war. A feared rightist coup was also to be prevented.[2482] These then were the different party-political reasons for the overwhelming majority support for the republican constitution.

Noteworthy are the rather rapid disappearance of the most uncompromising Social Democratic references to a class struggle challenging bourgeois democracy and parliamentarism and the prominent roles given to a few moderate leaders in the constitutional debates. The party leaders had evidently decided to keep the process under control and to prevent the radicals from repeating the militant discursive attacks of 1917: the moderates could speak for compromise, while other Social Democrat MPs could carry on using socialist rhetoric to appease the party's supporters (and to keep open an alternative option should the constitution fail). The German and Swedish models of successful constitutional reform carried out by Social Democrats supported belief in this strategy. However, it was not easy to persuade the majority of the Finnish workers to place their trust in the parliamentary system again, and even the more moderate of the Social Democrats recalled the injustices committed by the 'half-parliament' of 1918.[2483] Bourgeois doubts about the ability of the Social Democrats to respect parliamentarism in a bourgeois or Western sense had not died out either,[2484] though these doubts decreased in the course of the debate as the left turned out to be more constructive than had been expected.

The constitutional compromise in its entirety was acceptable to few. The rightist members still protested against the definition of the powers of the presidency by using minority provisions[2485] on 14 June and thus delayed the adoption of the constitution. The consequent anti-right reaction in the parliament and the press was fierce,[2486] which may be explained by the tendency of the rightist parties to (ab)use parliamentary procedure in 1917 and 1918 as well[2487] and the continuous obstruction of the Swedish People's Party. The general weariness of the public with the never-ending constitutional strife played a major role. A compromise was reached around an earlier proposal, to a great extent identical with the postponed bill but including a few persuasive concessions to the right. Thereafter the constitution was accepted by 165 votes against 22 on 21 June 1919.[2488] It was signed by the Regent, C. G. E. Mannerheim, on 17 July 1919, and a parliamentary republic with a monarchical presidency was established.

2482 Vares 2006, 145, 147; see also *Suomen Sosialidemokraatti*, 'Hallitusmuoto hywäksytty', 22 June 1919.
2483 VP, Väinö Tanner, 25 April 1919, 135–6.
2484 VP, Santeri Alkio, 25 April 1919, 132; see Mikko Piitulainen (Agrarian) on the non-existent parliamentary basis of 'the so-called People's Delegation' (*kansanvaltuuskunta*) of the Reds during the Civil War, 25 April 1919, 134.
2485 Cf. the flexibility of the British unwritten constitution, which had allowed the introduction of the Representation of the People Act with a simple parliamentary majority.
2486 Vares 2006, 145.
2487 Ihalainen 2017.
2488 Sihvonen 1997, 16; Jussila, Hentilä & Nevakivi 1999, 129.

7.4.2 Rethought international comparisons and transnational connections after the war and the revolutions

As Prime Minister Paasikivi had argued during the constitutional conflict of 1918, a small newly independent state had to design its constitution to correspond with the state of international affairs. The awareness of foreign powers observing the Finnish parliament and deciding on their future relationship with the country on the basis of the ability of the Finns to settle their constitutional disputes was high in spring 1919 as well.[2489] However, the instability of the international situation was also used by the right to maintain that it was best to just stick with the constitution inherited from eighteenth-century Sweden.[2490]

The most obvious shift in international comparisons was a drastic decrease in direct references to Germany. In the circumstances of spring 1919, further references to German models by former monarchists would have been out of place; it was more helpful to refer to Scandinavian and British monarchical models instead.[2491] Bourgeois republicans, regretting their equally uncritical admiration of Germany during 1918,[2492] did not wish to be associated with German models any more either. The Minister for Social Affairs, Santeri Alkio, rather used general European examples to justify parliamentarism. Though he expected the new German polity, too, to be built on far-reaching democracy, he preferred to take Switzerland and the United States as positive examples of republicanism.[2493] Even the American system appeared in a positive light once US recognition of Finnish independence had been received.

The monarchical adventure of the Rump Parliament of 1918 had not merely discredited the Form of Government of 1772;[2494] it had also made transnational links with Germany appear as unpatriotic scheming. The constitutional debates of the new parliament hence opened with mutual recriminations about the degree of commitment of the opposing parties in serving German interests and the abuses of German contacts in attempting to enforce a monarchical constitution. Georg Schauman, of the Swedish Left (a minority group within the Swedish People's Party), who had actively tried to persuade Friedrich Karl to turn down the invitation to the throne, attacked the monarchist ministry of 1918 for having asked the Germans to issue statements intended to induce the Finnish republicans give up their

---

2489 VP, Matti Helenius-Seppälä, 25 April 1919, 142; Oskari Mantere (Progressivists), 14 June 1919, 903; Rafael Erich, 14 June 1919, 918; Juho Kaskinen (Progressivists), 14 June 1919, 1025–6.
2490 VP, Ernst Estlander, 25 April 1919, 131.
2491 VP, Emil Nestor Setälä, 25 April 1919, 133.
2492 See Tekla Hultin's reminder of this, VP, 25 April 1919, 137, as well as Santeri Alkio's explanation, 25 April 1919, 138.
2493 VP, 24 May 1919, 511. The more conservative section of the Agrarians suggested that Finland had acted like David in the Old Testament, forgetting God and turning to external powers, which had led to famine, war and plagues. Frans Kärki (a clergyman), 14 June 1919, 888.
2494 For more on this, see Ihalainen 2015.

resistance to a monarchical constitution. Schauman cited the German Foreign Minister Paul von Hintze as having stated in the Main Committee of the Reichstag on 24 September 1918 (two days before the final breakthrough of the Entente on the Western front) that while the Germans had told the Finnish government that they considered the constitutional question an internal affair to be decided by the Finns themselves, a wish expressed by the Finnish government had caused the Germans to 'semi-officially' express their sympathy for the institution of a constitutional monarchy.[2495] The Finnish government was now accused of having contacted the Kaiser to ask his son to become a Finnish king *before* the constitutional issue had been settled in the parliament.[2496] When Professor E. N. Setälä (National Coalition Party) reacted by questioning the reliability of von Hintze's information about the issue and declaring Schauman's claims about contacts with Germany to be unfounded,[2497] Schauman added that von Hintze's statement had been published in German papers and also in the Finnish paper *Hufvudstadsbladet* (which Schauman was citing).[2498] Ernst Estlander, an even more fervent monarchist, consequently described Schauman's activities in Germany, including his attempts to dissuade Friedrich Karl from taking the crown, as 'disloyal' and aiming at influencing the legal decision of the Finnish parliament via Germany.[2499] Both conservative monarchists and liberal republicans had, it seemed, abused their German connections in 1918, thereby transnationalising the constitutional dispute, and now the argument was about who had been more traitorous in their transnational connections.

Schauman resolutely defended his negotiations in Germany in autumn 1918 as having been based on a mandate from the republican parties of the Finnish parliament.[2500] He had reported in September that the German left encouraged the Finnish republicans to continue their opposition to monarchy and to wait for a change of regime in Germany.[2501] Antti Juutilainen (Agrarian) confirmed this, conceding that such information from Germany had helped the republicans to hold on to their views. Schauman had later informed the republicans about the political changes in Germany after they started in early October, which had strengthened their determination to block the monarchical scheme. He had also told the Germans about the limited support which the monarchical project of the Rump Parliament enjoyed.[2502] Hjalmar Procopé (Swedish People's Party), an activist who had recruited Finnish volunteers for the German army, further accused the republicans of having become 'secret forces that played their game in Berlin' at a decisive moment in September 1918, and called to

2495   VP, Georg Schauman, 25 April 1919, 128–9.
2496   VP, Georg Schauman, 25 April 1919, 129. For a related accusation, see Väinö Tanner, 25 April 1919, 135.
2497   VP, Emil Nestor Setälä, 25 April 1919, 129.
2498   VP, Georg Schauman, 25 April 1919, 130.
2499   VP, Ernst Estlander, 25 April 1919, 131; 25 April 1919, 133.
2500   VP, Georg Schauman, 25 April 1919, 131.
2501   Vares 1998, 248.
2502   VP, Antti Juutilainen, 25 April 1919, 137.

account their claims that the Finnish parliament then did not represent all of the people of Finland.²⁵⁰³ Juho Vennola (Progressivist), the Minister of Commerce and Industry, for his part, declared that the right had given up the country's independence in turning so one-sidedly to Germany to achieve its national political goals.²⁵⁰⁴ Thus both sides of the constitutional struggle of 1918 had clearly been exploiting transnational connections with Germany to win a domestic political battle, and the pernicious consequences were now recognised. Generally, however, the debate tended to exclude Germany and other foreign countries from comparisons, and emphasised the national character of the constitutional reform in a way that was typical of other countries, too. While 1917 and 1918 had been years of transnational debate, 1919 was one of increasingly nation-state-centred perspectives.

Russia had been totally excluded from constitutional references as a consequence of the Civil War. Only the alliance of the Reds with the Bolsheviks was taken up in the heat of the debate in reactions to any continued use of the language of class struggle by the Social Democrats. Santeri Alkio accused the Social Democratic leaders of 1917 of having allied themselves with the Russian Bolsheviks and allowing Lenin to challenge the republican constitution of Finland. The risk of a further Bolshevik revolution remained present in the minds of several non-socialist members,²⁵⁰⁵ which in turn offended some socialists.²⁵⁰⁶ Others asserted that the threat of Bolshevism was, given the result of the Civil War, no greater in Finland than elsewhere.²⁵⁰⁷ Some centrists suggested rather that the right might be equally inclined to launch an extra-parliamentary coup,²⁵⁰⁸ which was indeed a possibility until the promulgation of the constitution.

The Social Democrats, in seeking new models, were in principle re-orienting themselves towards the Swedish²⁵⁰⁹ rather than the German SPD and could see the Entente in positive terms as well,²⁵¹⁰ though their willingness to replace revolutionary radicalism with parliamentary methods were still generally doubted.²⁵¹¹ However, the moderates offered alternative visions. Väinö Voionmaa, a professor of history, used Britain, Sweden and

2503 VP, Hjalmar Procopé, 25 April 1919, 140.
2504 VP, Juho Vennola, 25 April 1919, 141.
2505 VP, Santeri Alkio, 25 April 1919, 132; 2 June 1919, 654; 14 June 1919, 900. The point was repeated by Kalle Lohi (Agrarian), 25 April 1919, 134, Ernst Estlander, 25 April 1919, 140, and Juho Vennola (Progressivist), 25 April 1919, 141. The National Coalition Party, furthermore, called for international cooperation against international Bolshevism in its party manifesto. *Kansallisen Kokoomuspuolueen ohjelma*, 1918.
2506 VP, Olga Leinonen, 25 April 1919, 136.
2507 VP, Matti Helenius-Seppälä (Christian Labour Union), 25 April 1919, 142.
2508 VP, Kalle Lohi, 14 June 1919, 903.
2509 For an indirect suggestion that this was so, see VP, Rafael Erich (National Coalition), 25 April 1919, 138.
2510 For a positive view of British parliamentarism and the political system of the United States, see VP, Väinö Voionmaa (Social Democrat), 24 May 1919, 518–19.
2511 *Aftonbladet*, 'Finsk politik just nu', 26 May 1919, reported on 'the inflammatory, intemperate language' used against the bourgeoisie and in favour of the Reds in the Finnish Social Democratic press and public meetings.

Norway (to a lesser extent the United States and Australia) as points of reference when commenting on the practices of parliamentary government. The parliamentarised Norwegian Constitution of 1814 – based 'on a longer political experience than ours' – in his view contained restrictions to executive power that could be copied in Finland as well. For instance, in Norway the king could not dissolve the Stortinget before decisions on the budget were made. The British political system appeared to Voionmaa as the most developed model for control of the executive,[2512] which was a daring suggestion in a country where Britain had just recently been looked down on as an enemy. Jonas Laherma of the Social Democrats provocatively went back to the Swiss constitution, recalling Kuusinen's controversial arguments in 1917, but then turned to Austria and Estonia as examples in arguing for democratised supreme executive power.[2513] The transnational process of formulating democratic constitutions offered Finnish speakers a variety of examples from which to choose in supporting their own particular arguments. Norway appeared as particularly applicable because of its cultural affinity; moreover, Norway was not Sweden, which served as a less attractive model in the circumstances of the ongoing dispute about the possession of the Åland Islands.

The Swedish-speaking minority did maintain the link with Sweden to some extent. Swedish practices of the parliamentary control of government, for instance, were something that Georg Schauman of the Swedish Left, an expert on the Swedish Age of Liberty, would have liked to adopt.[2514] However, Ernst Estlander of the majority Swedish People's Party explained why such Swedish examples were not applicable: the dispute over the Åland Islands had inflamed relations between the two countries. Estlander's hope was that the territorial question would be soon solved and good relations restored. In the meantime, other Scandinavia countries worked better as constitutional examples.[2515] Estlander himself rejected France as being a failed republic and saw the United States and Switzerland as unique and hence inapplicable cases. This leading lawyer continued to warn about the risks of a democratic republican constitution, advising Finland not to join countries (like Germany and implicitly Sweden) where 'radical and revolutionary upheavals' were leading to forms of government that were unlikely to provide secure foundations for the future of these states.[2516] Estlander's argument was that the Swedish constitutional tradition as safeguarded in Finland continued to provide an ideal form of government in times of transnational constitutional ferment.

Professor Rafael Erich (National Coalition Party), a specialist in constitutional law and a former pro-German monarchist who had invited

2512 VP, Väinö Voionmaa, 24 May 1919, 520–2; 2 June 1919, 650.
2513 VP, Jonas Laherma, 24 May 1919, 538. On the continuity of the Swiss model but movement towards parliamentarism among Social Democrats, see Lindman 1968, 373, 376.
2514 VP, Georg Schauman, 24 May 1919, 535–6; 3 June 1919, 699–700; Lindman 1968, 386; cf. Georg von Wendt (also Swedish Left), 3 June 1919, 725.
2515 VP, Ernst Estlander, 2 June 1919, 668.
2516 VP, Ernst Estlander, 2 June 1919, 667–8, 670.

the German troops to Finland in spring 1918, also turned to the familiar debate on the deficiencies of the constitution of the Third Republic to argue against the excessive democracy and parliamentarism that, in his view, were being proposed by the Finnish ministry.[2517] He considered that British parliamentarism was inapplicable outside that country,[2518] and he doubted the applicability of the German plans for a presidency as well,[2519] wishing to see an even stronger executive power. This exemplifies the Finnish conservatives' disappointment with the radical course of the reforms in Germany. The French republican example was likewise rejected by the monarchist Paavo Virkkunen (a vicar by calling), who found support for a strong presidency in 'the mighty United States of the west', with which 'wide circles of our people have made contact',[2520] mainly through emigration. This is revealing of the opportunism of the monarchists in Finland, given that Virkkunen had in the preceding year spoken for a Germanic 'democratic monarchy'. Until 1918, conservatives like Virkkunen had tended to despise the USA as an upstart nation, but the monarchical elements of its presidency now paradoxically provided politically correct arguments for them. E. N. Setälä, while also recognising the American example, nevertheless preferred to emphasise the positive experiences of monarchy in Britain and Norway,[2521] in this way keeping the monarchical alternative alive.

Väinö Voionmaa of the Social Democrats could not help ironising these conservative turns from Prussian to American constitutional models. He himself rejected the American presidential model as being based on eighteenth-century practices.[2522] Matti Helenius-Seppälä (Christian Labour Union) warned of copying the American system, which, he claimed, might soon be changed;[2523] this was an over-interpretation of the consequences of the introduction of women's suffrage in the United States. Helenius-Seppälä encouraged the Finnish Social Democrats to look rather to Germany, which was governed by one of their brethren, President Friedrich Ebert. A *moderate* Social Democrat was ruling Germany in an exemplary way after a successful revolution made by *parliamentary* means under Social Democratic leadership. The German example demonstrated how the Finnish constitutional proposal opened access to power even to socialists and should hence be supported by them.[2524]

Hjalmar Procopé, a pro-German attorney from the Swedish People's Party, which opposed parliamentary democracy, found positive precedents in the Norwegian constitution, which had been disparaged previously by his party colleague R. A. Wrede for being excessively republican, and rejected British parliamentarism as inapplicable to any other country. Having worked in 1918 for the invitation of a German king, Procopé now painted a gloomy

2517 VP, Rafael Erich, 24 May 1919, 526–7; 3 June 1919, 726.
2518 Lindman 1968, 362.
2519 VP, Rafael Erich, 4 June 1919, 749.
2520 VP, Paavo Virkkunen, 2 June 1919, 642; 2 June 1919, 658.
2521 VP, Emil Nestor Setälä, 2 June 1919, 665; 3 June 1919, 729; 4 June 1919, 738.
2522 VP, Väinö Voionmaa, 3 June 1919, 720.
2523 VP, Matti Helenius-Seppälä, 3 June 1919, 729.
2524 VP, Matti Helenius-Seppälä, 14 June 1919, 911.

picture of a future parliamentary republic that resembled South American 'nigger republics'.²⁵²⁵ Georg Schauman of the Swedish Left countered his claim by emphasising the successful extension of parliamentarism in Britain, France, Germany and the Scandinavian states. The Swedish experience since autumn 1917 demonstrated to him how unfeasible non-parliamentary government had become in the modern world. The German Revolution, again, had invalidated older German constitutional theory, a favourite source of argumentation for Finnish conservatives.²⁵²⁶ This transnationally connected liberal thus recommended the Finns to become part of the northwest European cultural area of parliamentarism and not hold on to the outdated institution of monarchy. For many bourgeois republicans, too, Western European parliamentary democracies had become models to follow, in much the same way as they had for Swedish Liberals previously. The Chairman of the Constitutional Committee, Heikki Ritavuori (Progressivist), whose proposal would finally be adopted, saw Britain, France and Switzerland as precedents that were applicable to Finland.²⁵²⁷ And as for the election of a president and his right of veto, the United States could be added to the list of models²⁵²⁸ – to please the monarchist National Coalition Party.

Although Anglophile republicanism had existed to a limited extent before in the minds of the Finnish political elite, it had come into the open after the war, which reflects an incipient turn from German to Anglo-American models among them. This turn is illustrative of the highly contingent nature of international comparisons and transnational links in parliamentary debates on constitutional issues. The process of formulating the Finnish constitution between spring 1917 and summer 1919 belonged to the course of international events and the transnational debate on constitutional reform to a greater extent than was the case in Britain or even in Germany and Sweden, although the implications of the history of events and turns in the transnational discourse on constitutions were considerable in these countries, too. The insecure international standing of a small nation aiming at maintaining its independence made Finland particularly dependent on contingent transnational factors and developments: first on the inherited Swedish constitutional tradition, second on the radicalising course of the Russian Revolution, third on the last phase of Prussian political culture and the German Revolution, and fourth on the symbolic victory of British parliamentarism and American presidentialism in the war.

The transfers of influence from Russia were curtailed as a result of the Finnish Civil War, those from Germany decreased with Germany's defeat in the war, those from Sweden were temporarily obstructed by the Åland Islands crisis, and those from Britain and especially the United States opened up by the result of the First World War, although Britain had

---

2525 VP, Hjalmar Procopé, 3 June 1919, 712; 4 June 1919, 741.
2526 VP, Georg Schauman, 4 June 1919, 744. For Rafael Erich's response, see 4 June 1919, 745.
2527 VP, Heikki Ritavuori, 24 May 1919, 537.
2528 VP, Heikki Ritavuori, 3 June 1919, 708, 724.

sometimes provided a parliamentary model before.[2529] The internationalism of the radical socialists derived from Russia in 1917 was replaced by the monarchists' and the republicans' transnational influences from Germany in 1918, while selective transnational comparions of all political groups based on various versions of Western parliamentary democracy began to develop from spring 1919 onwards. At the same time, the constitutional debate tended to be increasingly nationalised and seen as a uniquely Finnish issue rather than one that was dependent on transnational constitutional debates. This was the predominant way of thinking in the other studied countries as well, with the transnational dimension being easily forgotten. On the other hand, the new or updated constitutions of the late 1910s, it has been argued in this book, are fully understandable only in the contemporary transnational context of their adoption.

7.4.3 Searching for a compromise between Socialist, centrist and rightist democracy

The Finnish MPs simply had to find a compromise on the constitution after over two years of unproductive constitutional strife, a new election that had produced an overwhelming republican majority, and a general realisation that Finland would need to turn to republicanism and Western forms of democracy and parliamentarism to gain recognition of its independence from the Anglophone great powers. Parliamentary suffrage had been democratic in that it had been unique in its extent when implemented in 1907, but the polity had not really been democratised, and the parliamentarisation of government had also stopped half-way. Disagreements over the methods and the implications of further reform had not gone away, but a compromise was nevertheless needed to rectify the precarious situation of the state.

The Social Democrats had to reconcile their previous radical Marxism and involvement in a failed armed uprising against a bourgeois parliamentary majority with the necessity of cooperating with the winners of the Civil War to solve the constitutional strife through a compromise. The most radical leaders of the pre-war parliamentary party had either been killed or fled to Russia. The more moderate members rejected the use of extra-parliamentary force and demonstrated a willingness to redefine socialist 'democracy' to fit a multi-party polity based on parliamentary principles of the kind already exemplified by Sweden and Germany. The redefinition was so fundamental that the pre- and post-Civil-War parties would resemble each other only in name and in their future goal of socialism. The Marxist rhetoric of class struggle was replaced with a more positive attitude towards parliamentary cooperation with 'the peasant democracy' and 'the bourgeois democracy',[2530] though that took time and did, of course, not apply to all MPs.

Indeed, at the beginning of the session some Social Democratic MPs still continued the international left-wing tendency to monopolise 'democracy' for the Social Democrats. Jonas Laherma viewed the whole bourgeoisie, including the centre, as being united in the oppression of the workers and

---

2529 See Pekonen 2014.
2530 *Suomen Sosialidemokraatti*, 'Hallitusmuoto hyväksytty', 22 June 1919.

hypocritical in their cant on democracy: bourgeois 'democracy' was only intended to fool the people.[2531] Väinö Hupli lamented what he saw as the lack of a truly liberal and democratic bourgeoisie in Finland, ignoring the struggle of the Agrarians for a parliamentary democracy in 1917 and in the Rump Parliament.[2532] According to Mikko Ampuja, the new election had not produced legitimate parliamentary representation owing to the fact that suffrage continued to be denied to the Red prisoners. If 'all the power of the workers, all the power of democracy, is not represented in this parliament',[2533] the legitimacy of the parliament to legislate on the new constitution remained questionable. This recalled the uncompromising Social Democratic definition of democracy in 1917, which had associated it with the rule of the workers and presented the Social Democrats as its sole advocates. Ampuja argued that the spread of Bolshevism could only be stopped by passing 'as democratic a constitution as possible' – 'democratic' in the sense of parliamentarism as defined by the Social Democrats. In Ampuja's view, the Civil War had not been caused by the concentration of power in the parliament but by a departure from proper democracy by the bourgeois parties. Now a constitution facilitating a transition to parliamentary democracy like that in neighbouring countries was needed.[2534] Such a continuation of pre-war discourse did not make for an easy compromise.

Even MPs known for their moderation such as Väinö Voionmaa were at first uncompromising. According to Voionmaa, the bureaucrats of the right had responded to the attempt of the Finnish people to liberate themselves by constructing barriers to the realisation of democracy. The bureaucrat class – which evidently stood for the National Coalition Party and the Swedish People's Party here – was still fighting against the recent and consequently unstable democracy of the country, ready to 'toll the bells of false democracy'. Consequently, Finland had seen nothing but 'seeming democracy' thus far. With their continuous rhetorical redescriptions of 'a real, genuine, authentic, parliamentary democracy', the monarchists were now campaigning for the extension of presidential powers. In Voionmaa's view, future democracy and parliamentarism should rather be given the means to prevent the bureaucrats from abusing their power against the interests of democracy.[2535] The Agrarian League, a party in the present government, was also accused of sacrificing its 'fine democratic principles' and causing 'sad consequences for democracy' with the current constitutional proposal. From the Social Democratic point of view, the Agrarians appeared to be

2531 VP, Jonas Laherma, 25 April 1919, 132.
2532 VP, Väinö Hupli, 25 April 1919, 137.
2533 VP, Mikko Ampuja, 2 June 1919, 662. He further claimed that the left and the defenders of democracy were identical.
2534 VP, Mikko Ampuja, 2 June 1919, 663.
2535 VP, Väinö Voionmaa, 24 May 1919, 516–20; see also VP, Georg Schauman (Swedish Left), 24 May 1919, 536. The point about the bureaucrats resisting democracy was taken up by Jonas Laherma, 3 June 1919, 704. On the other hand, Rafael Colliander (Swedish People's Party) pointed out ironically that the more democratic a country became, the more civil servants it needed. 3 June 1919, 755.

betraying 'the most important foundations of common democracy' and were no longer standing 'fraternally in the ranks of democracy', no longer joining the Social Democrats in demanding the 'pure democracy' and 'proper democratic principles' of the Power Act of July 1917.[2536] The purpose of this was to persuade the Agrarians to join again in leftist demands for extended democracy.[2537] To the same end, Voionmaa presented the right with its claims that 'real democracy consists in a divided democracy' and its advocacy of 'pseudo-democratic forms' of presidency as the common rival of both parties. He was nevertheless positive that Finland would in the future, against all the odds, be democratic.[2538] As Väinö Tanner's criticism of rightist attempts in 1918 to curb democracy also shows,[2539] the Social Democrats continued a discursive struggle to extend democracy. It helped the ongoing negotiations that the socialist radicals stayed quiet (possibly owing to group pressure) and the moderates cut down their oppositional rhetoric in the debates of June, allowing the new leaders to finalise the constitutional compromise with the bourgeois parties.

The most prominent among these moderate Social Democrats was Hannes Ryömä, the editor of the party organ and a member of the Constitutional Committee. His discourse aimed at bridging the gap between the Social Democrats and the centre parties, and his appeals to democratic forces in the parliament included bourgeois politicians, unlike Social Democratic discourse before the Civil War. Ryömä was even ready to distinguish between socialism and democracy, explaining that the motives of the Social Democrats in their criticism of the proposal were 'in no way socialist but purely democratic'. Their goal was to create 'a constitution that would allow the democratic majority of the people to act within it and advance social development',[2540] i.e. democracy appeared as a procedural concept resembling the one adopted by the moderate Swedish left. Ryömä's compromise-oriented statement suggested that his party now aimed at majority democracy in cooperation with other democratic forces. The party recognised – albeit only through the voice of Ryömä – that despite all its remaining shortcomings, the proposal 'makes a democratic system of government possible'.[2541] The only other compromise-seeking speech was made by Leo Hildén, who urged 'every democrat' to accept this constitutional compromise.[2542] The compromise-seekers were few but – evidently with the support of the party leadership – they managed to unite their party and the bourgeois republicans in a collective redefinition of Finnish democracy. Leaving the defence of the compromise to a few members did not commit the entire party to it should the bourgeois republican constitution fail; this may have been a conscious strategic choice aimed at satisfying those supporters

2536 VP, Väinö Voionmaa, 24 May 1919, 521–2; 2 June 1919, 649–50.
2537 VP, Väinö Voionmaa, 2 June 1919, 650.
2538 VP, Väinö Voionmaa, 2 June 1919, 651; 3 June 1919, 721.
2539 VP, Väinö Tanner, 25 April 1919, 135.
2540 VP, Hannes Ryömä, 24 May 1919, 510.
2541 VP, Hannes Ryömä, 14 June 1919, 927.
2542 VP, Leo Hildén, 24 May 1919, 534.

who were still bitter about the outcome of the Civil War and not necessarily ready to give in. However, the organ of the party would later – under Ryömä's guidance – declare the compromise, despite its shortcomings, to be 'a victory for the rule by the people'.[2543]

The constitutional compromise was not easy for the Agrarians, either. Their leader Santeri Alkio was provoked by Social Democrat insinuations and suggested that some of the socialists were still looking for a new Bolshevik rebellion. He viewed ironically the demand to concentrate all power in the parliament from a party that had abolished democracy in favour of dictatorship in the Civil War. The proposed republican constitution would 'establish democracy here, and it would weaken class power whether this originated from the right or the left',[2544] the goal being that 'all class interests must be subordinated to democracy: democracy must be established'.[2545] The Agrarian conception of democracy continued to be essentially procedural, resembling that of the Swedish Liberals: 'the rule by the people' would increase in the future in such a way that the people would advance and take power increasingly into their own hands.[2546] Disregarding Social Democratic criticism that they were compromising the constitution, the Agrarians followed the principle of 'the rule by the people' most consistently of all parties, the others being forced to modify their conceptions of democracy more radically so that they would able to vote for the new republican constitution.

The Progressivists, who had separated themselves from the monarchist faction of the Young Finns to become resolute republicans, and who even referred to 'the democratisation of economic life' in their manifesto of 1918,[2547] were another group that continued to express their pre-war demands. Bruno Sarlin emerged as a major spokesman for bourgeois democracy. Sarlin challenged former monarchists by defining the rule by the people as the very force that had produced a victory in the 'War of Liberation' (as the Civil War was called by non-socialists). In his view, gradual steps towards the rule by the people since 1906 had significantly added to the political conscience, love of liberty and patriotism of the Finnish people,[2548] and democracy had hence significantly contributed to the formation of an independent nation. The Declaration of Independence had already stated that a democratic and a parliamentary republic was the sole form of government suitable for 'the democratic worldview of our people and our national character'.[2549] It was, indeed, the regard for the rule by the people as primary that had enabled the Finns 'to trample down the poisonous head of Bolshevism to astonishment of the great powers of the world'.[2550] The Civil War had been fought together by the different social groups of the White side 'for the rule by the people, for

---

2543 *Suomen Sosialidemokraatti*, 'Hallitusmuoto hywäksytty', 22 June 1919.
2544 VP, Santeri Alkio, 25 April 1919, 132–3; 2 June 1919, 651, 653.
2545 VP, Santeri Alkio, 2 June 1919, 654; also Mikko Piitulainen, 25 April 1919, 134.
2546 VP, Pekka Saarelainen, 14 June 1919, 908.
2547 Hyvärinen 2003, 87.
2548 VP, Bruno Sarlin, 14 June 1919, 884.
2549 VP, Bruno Sarlin, 14 June 1919, 884.
2550 VP, Bruno Sarlin, 14 June 1919, 884.

democratic equal rights in the state and society and the liberty of the people [the nation].[2551] This association between democracy, equal civic rights, national self-determination[2552] and the national character – based on the fact that the Finnish word *kansa* means both the people and the nation, with the word for citizen (*kansalainen*) also being derived from it – went further in Sarlin's rhetoric than in that of any other Finnish MP, except perhaps Santeri Alkio. Other centrists, too, saw a republican constitution as the only one suited to 'such a democratically inclined people as the Finns'.[2553] The final draft could be described by the liberals as 'democratic in the full sense of the word', entailing the achievement of full 'democratic independence' and enabling the introduction of reforms in all fields of societal life in the future,[2554] which again associated democracy with nationalism and the progress that the political process would produce. The Finnish centrist republicans evidently held a concept of democracy resembling that of the Swedish Liberals.

However, the former monarchists of the National Coalition Party had to be won over before the constitutional issue could be settled. It took time before this party would include references to democracy in its manifestos.[2555] Even when a constitutional compromise aimed at healing the wounds of civil strife was in sight, Hugo Suolahti, the chairman of the party and a professor of German philology and Vice-Rector of the University of Helsinki with obvious connections with German conservatism, still referred to 'the class hatred which the Social Democratic Party has used as its weapon in a fight against the so-called bourgeoisie' as the worst kind of party fanaticism, to which a republican constitution might once again lead.[2556] Not unlike the Swedish right in late 1918, the National Coalition Party distanced itself from the constitutional compromise to the very end, keeping thereby open an option to criticise it afterwards should it fail. It would take time before the party would finally adapt itself to parliamentary democracy, indeed until its denouncement of the far-right activism of the early 1930s by mainstream conservativism in both countries.[2557]

Rafael Erich and E. N. Setälä, a professor of Finnish language and literature, who had authored the original Declaration of Independence, reiterated in mid-June that the goal of the National Coalition Party in 1918 had been a 'democratic ... monarchy'[2558] and that such a monarchy would have enabled the realisation of democracy just as well as a republic.[2559]

2551 VP, Bruno Sarlin, 14 June 1919, 884.
2552 Cf. *Hufvudstadsbladet*, 'Betänkliga riktningar inom regeringen och riksdag', 15 June 1919, which saw this principle as leading to the rule of the least capable elements of every society.
2553 VP, Oskari Mantere, 14 June 1919, 904.
2554 VP, Juho Kaskinen, 21 June 1919, 1026.
2555 Hyvärinen 2003, 86.
2556 VP, Hugo Suolahti, 21 June 1919, 1021.
2557 Nilsson 2002a, 101; Kurunmäki 2010, 76.
2558 VP, Rafael Erich, 14 June 1919, 917; also Paavo Virkkunen, 2 June 1919, 641, and Hedvig Gebhard, 14 June 1919, 918.
2559 VP, Emil Nestor Setälä, 25 April 1919, 133.

Making use of his authoritative academic position as the leading expert on the Finnish language, Setälä problematised the semantics of the key concepts of the constitution and concluded that the proposal failed to fulfil the criteria of 'real democracy'. His conservative scepticism was reflected in his statement that the power of the parliament was 'democracy if the parliament can be regarded as realising the will of the people'.[2560] However, as the will of the parliament and the people might differ – a point accepted even by Liberals and Social Democrats in the Weimar debates – Setälä found in a presidency 'the highest trustee of the people', who should be given the right of veto and powers to supervise and dissolve the parliament as the way to curb the potential 'oligarchic dictatorship' that it threatened to become.[2561] This point resembled the German justifications for the powers of the Reichspräsident, although it was of course common anti-parliamentary discourse and had been heard with reference to the Third Republic as well. So were complaints about democracy as the 'adulation of incompetence'.[2562] Setälä's and Erich's doubts about far-reaching democracy realised through the parliament were also reflected in attempts to translate 'republic' with the coinage *kansanvaltio* ('state of the people') and to thus distinguish the Finnish term semantically not only from the Greek original but also from the established egalitarian vernacular term *tasavalta* (literally 'the equality of power'),[2563] which for the conservatives implied a leftist understanding of the form of government. This rightist discourse found a transnational source in the German Liberals' aim to call the new form of government a *Volksstaat* (state of the people, a coinage favoured not only by Hugo Preuß but even by some Social Democrats) and to thereby nationalise the political system and distinguish it from Western models. This term was not far away from *Volksgemeinschaft* (community of the people), reflecting an organic rather than pluralistic understanding of the state. But the professors of the Finnish National Coalition Party failed in their rhetorical redescription of the new form of government.

Even more uncompromising opponents to democratisation stood up from the ranks of the Swedish People's Party, for whom the connotations of the rule by the people meaning the rule by the *Finnish* people, the *common* people or the workers were all to be rejected. The party represented a linguistic minority, and its spokesmen consisted mainly of members of the old elite,[2564] which to some extent explains their tough line. According to the party organ *Hufvudstadsbladet*, the entire revolutionary age was characterised

---

2560 VP, Emil Nestor Setälä, 24 May 1919, 500.
2561 VP, Emil Nestor Setälä, 24 May 1919, 500. Jonas Laherma violently rejected the notion of the dictatorship of a democratic parliament. 24 May 1919, 538; 3 June 1919, 707; 14 June 1919, 897.
2562 VP, Emil Nestor Setälä, 24 May 1919, 504.
2563 VP, Emil Nestor Setälä, 24 May 1919, 524. See a reaction in *Suomen Sosialidemokraatti*, 'Hallitusmuotokysymyksen käsittely eduskunnassa', 25 May 1919; 3 June 1919, 707; 14 June 1919, 896. See also Artturi Hiidenheimo, 2 June 1919, 669, who regarded *kansanvaltio* as expressing the idea of 'a real democracy'.
2564 Hyvärinen 2003, 86, 99. Its party manifesto of 1917, unlike those of the other bourgeois parties, did not refer to 'citizens' either. Stenius 2003, 351.

by an uncritical and opportunistic use of the catchword 'democracy' to persuade the masses to wreck states and to destroy everyone who opposed them.[2565] When the constitutional proposal came before the parliament, the paper wrote about 'a purely anarchical democracy' like that of the Age of Liberty that was threatening the country with demagogical politics, party dictatorship of the socialist type, the degeneration of democracy, bad government, the destruction of the European forms of culture that had been preserved in the Civil War and violations of individual freedoms and poverty. In demanding a republic, 'the bourgeois left' seemed to be overwhelmed by a 'superstitious' belief in democracy. But history demonstrated that such a 'dominion of everyone' (*allhärskarmakt*) would soon come to an end: once this 'the rule by the people' had done enough damage to the nation it would be replaced with a more sensible system, just as Gustav III had once saved the realm by introducing the constitution that was currently in force.[2566] Ernst Estlander remained convinced that excessively democratic societies (like the one now in the making) increased human weaknesses and hence endangered civic liberty.[2567] The Social Democrats were not to be forgiven: they would just continue to abuse parliamentary government to establish their ultimate goal, the class rule of the workers.[2568] Emil Hästbacka saw the Finns as not mature enough for a democratic state: the experiences of the unicameral parliament and the Civil War demonstrated that the radicals of the left would never be satisfied with 'a democratic republican constitution' and still aimed at a socialist political order.[2569] These spokesmen of the Swedish-speaking minority, concerned to ensure its linguistic and property rights but also ideologically opposed to democracy, had no sympathy for majority democracy in summer 1919, a stance that tended to marginalise the party and contributed to its exit from the government two months later. The ranks of the enthusiastic defenders of democracy remained limited in Finland as well, consisting mainly of the centrist and liberal republicans and Social Democrats, with even many of the latter continuing to question the true democracy of the new constitution. The Swedish-speaking right in the meantime continued to put forward openly anti-democratic views, concluding that the republican constitution did not provide a necessary counterweight to universal suffrage and 'unbalanced democracy'.[2570]

The conservative counterarguments caused Santeri Alkio to emphasise the fact that the democratic moment was at hand, defend the potential for progress that would be created by the power of the people and challenge the elitism of the conservatives' attitudes. Democracy, would despite all

---

2565 *Hufvudstadsbladet*, 'Betänkliga riktningar inom regeringen och riksdag', 15 June 1919; 'Regeringsformen antagen' and 'Från kammare och kuloar', 22 June 1919.
2566 *Hufvudstadsbladet*, 'Från kammare och kuloar', 25 May 1919; 'Köpslagandet om regeringsformen', 4 June 1919; 'Samhällets självbevarelseplikt' and 'Inför avgörandet i dag', 14 June 1919.
2567 VP, Ernst Estlander, 3 June 1919, 675, 699; 5 June 1919, 811.
2568 VP, Ernst Estlander, 14 June 1919, 893.
2569 VP, Emil Hästbacka, 2 June 1919, 638.
2570 *Hufvudstadsbladet*, 'Regeringsformen antagen', 22 June 1919.

its visible shortcomings, inevitably prevail, and the old elite had better recognise that in time:[2571]

> The rule by the people is a recent newcomer. It is easy to mock. It does a lot of stupid things. But it contains a promise for the future! And if 'the qualified' remain entirely devoid of enthusiasm for the rule by the people, if they remain strangers to the factors and goals at which the rule by the people in its ineptitude aims, we can with good reason expect that the qualified will gradually be displaced. The people must through bitter experiences teach themselves to realise those aims to the realisation of which the people at large are right now invited by historical progress.

Few non-socialist politicians in the parliaments studied here voiced such optimistic descriptions of the democratic process in the aftermath of the First World War. Alkio warned both the Swedish- and Finnish-speaking intellectual elites of the risk of finding themselves redundant if they should refrain from understanding the will of the people, moving onto the side of the rule by the people and thereby earning the respect of the nation.[2572] This challenge to both the Svecoman and Fennoman elites (and separately to the Social Democrats) and the consistent defence of the rule by the people by the Agrarians combined with the new revisionism of the Social Democrats explains to a great extent the ability of the Finns to reject extremes and to find a middle ground on bourgeois democracy.

7.4.4 Popular sovereignty recognised by all but one parliamentary party

While 'the rule by the people' remained a contested concept in the Finnish parliament in spring and summer 1919, the notion of popular sovereignty had undoubtedly established itself. Understandings of this sovereignty varied but even the National Coalition Party advocated a 'state of the people', as we have just seen. Despite the disappointment of the Civil War, the party was returning to the predominantly positive notions of the people they had held in 1917.

The republicans of the ministry, as consistent spokesmen for the rule by the people, denounced the ways in which 'the will of the majority of the people' had been ignored both by the Red rule during the Civil War and by the monarchist campaign of 1918.[2573] Their notion of the rule by the people was tightly connected with a conception of the nation state as a self-determining entity. This was not least due to the confused semantics of the Finnish terms for the concepts of the people, nation, citizen and even the state: they declared that they were aiming at 'the political [*valtiollinen*, derived from word *valtio* (the state)][2574] liberty of the people'.[2575] Especially

---

2571   VP, Santeri Alkio, 24 May 1919, 513.
2572   VP, Santeri Alkio, 24 May 1919, 512–13.
2573   VP, Juho Vennola (Progressivist), 25 April 1919, 140–1.
2574   On the special connotations of this attribute, which was derived from the word for 'the state' and weakened the parliamentary dimension of the polity, see Pulkkinen 2003, 251.
2575   VP, Santeri Alkio, 25 April 1919, 132.

the Agrarians spoke for the political involvement and honouring of the will of the people, seeing the realisation of the concept of the rule by the people as a necessary process in the construction of the nation state. Pekka Saarelainen criticised rightist politicians who 'still do not want to submit themselves to the express will of the majority of the people' and to the inevitable progress of the rule by the people.[2576] Professor Juho Vennola (Progressivists) denounced the way in which the Prime Minister Paasikivi in 1918 had questioned the ability of Finnic peoples to form states. On the contrary, Vennola considered it the mission of the Finnish parliament to formulate a new constitution based solely on 'the character of this people', disregarding foreign influences[2577] and the transnational involvement of the Russians in 1917 and the Germans in 1918. He thus nationalised the process of legislating a constitution in a manner that was typical in all the studied states in the post-war period. Bruno Sarlin of the same party was optimistic about the political potential of the Finnish people to build a democracy thanks to its high political awareness, which had been growing since the parliamentary reform. It was, indeed, the duty of the Finns to demonstrate to the world that they possessed the political maturity to form an independent state.[2578] In the end, as Juho Kaskinen put it, 'this people through their parliament' had formulated a constitution to their liking.[2579] Georg Schauman of the Swedish Left likewise called for a demonstration of the ability of the Finns to learn from hardships and to raise the level of their 'political culture' by approving the proposed republican constitution.[2580] The liberal republicans were capable of turning the traumatic experiences of the Civil War into a source of progress for a better political culture.

A willingness to rethink their position was not so evident among the Social Democrats, who continued to attack the right for their patronising attitude towards the people during the Rump Parliament of 1918. According to Väinö Tanner, 'disregard of the will of the people' had dominated that 'half-parliament', in which even the prime minister had questioned the political maturity of his people and had been ready to disregard their will on constitutional issues.[2581] Hannes Ryömä sought compromise and tried to explain the constitutional goals of the Social Democrats: they wanted 'the people to feel that they were living under the rule of law in a state governed in accordance with the will of the people',[2582] a demand that most bourgeois MPs as well could easily associate themselves with. At the constitutional level, this implied for the Social Democrats that 'the supreme power in the state will belong to the people, which is represented by the parliament'[2583]

2576 VP, Pekka Saarelainen, 14 June 1919, 908.
2577 VP, Juho Vennola, 25 April 1919, 141. Ernst Estlander protested against Vennola's characterisation of Paasikivi, 25 April 1919, 143.
2578 VP, Bruno Sarlin, 14 June 1919, 884–5.
2579 VP, Juho Kaskinen, 21 June 1919, 1026.
2580 VP, Georg Schauman, 14 June 1919, 894. Noteworthy is the use of the phrase 'political culture' which only emerged in social scientific research in the 1950s.
2581 VP, Väinö Tanner, 25 April 1919, 136; Hannes Ryömä, 24 May 1919, 508.
2582 VP, Hannes Ryömä, 24 May 1919, 507.
2583 VP, Hannes Ryömä, 24 May 1919, 508.

– a formulation that brought the bourgeois republicans and the Social Democrats together and was included in the proposal for the republican constitution. Ryömä went on to reinterpret the origins, course and implications of the transnational trend of democratisation after 1917, connecting the Social Democratic rising in Finland with this trend: the pre-war concentration of political power in the hands of 'qualified' oligarchies had everywhere given rise to discontent and led to 'a global crisis, a general cultural bankruptcy'. Since the rising masses had had no chance to participate in politics, they had turned to Bolshevism, with evident pernicious consequences, especially in Finland. Having explained away the Civil War, Ryömä envisioned a turn for the better: when the people got used to active political participation and were allowed to make 'the qualified' understand their will, they, too, would learn to appreciate political qualifications as opposed to political agitation. It was essential for this prospective transition to mutual understanding that the educated elite should approach the people rather than distance themselves from the masses[2584] – a point that Santeri Alkio endorsed and developed further, thereby reconciling the constitutional discourses of the Social Democrats and the Agrarians. Ryömä's vision of societal consensus in a parliamentary democracy, built on increased interaction and understanding between different social groups, was exceptionally optimistic by Finnish standards, and it recalled Swedish revisionist Social Democratic optimism as well as some arguments heard from members of the British Labour Party. This was a prognosis that would eventually come true in the Winter War (1939–40), by which time the Social Democrats had been integrated into the polity and joined the bourgeois parties in defence of the country against a new Soviet challenge.

Such a transition was by no means an easy one, and it was only beginning in 1919. Väinö Voionmaa pointed out the unwillingness of the Social Democrats to contribute to the 'transfer of the current system of oppression into the new political era', by which he meant the establishment of a bourgeois political order. Instead, a new 'political direction for the entire people' was needed. In Voionmaa's analysis, the problems of Finnish society followed from the administration of the state having been run by small privileged classes. This had produced 'a deep class division within the state' and the submission of the Finnish people to the patronage of the bureaucrats.[2585] All this should change: the Finnish people had reached a level of political development that simply demanded that their supreme power be recognised. While the people would still need to delegate their power to professionals, the constitution should provide guarantees against abuses of this power. Quoting Anton Menger, an Austrian socialist legal theorist, Voionmaa urged the masses of the Finnish people, who were still about to enter politics for the first time, to preserve their political liberty by carefully scrutinising the use of political power.[2586] One instance of the abuses of

2584 VP, Hannes Ryömä, 24 May 1919, 512–13.
2585 VP, Väinö Voionmaa, 24 May 1919, 515–16.
2586 VP, Väinö Voionmaa, 24 May 1919, 517.

'our credulous and politically so inexperienced people' was, in Voionmaa's view, the rightist claim that a strong presidency was reconcilable with true parliamentary democracy.[2587] Despite its pessimism, Voionmaa's vision, too, saw a possibility of the Finns growing together politically provided that the people demonstrated a sufficient degree of political activism.

The rightist doubts about the people had been undeniable in 1918 and could not be fully concealed in 1919 either. Most representatives of the National Coalition Party refrained from taking a clear stand, but their party manifesto defined citizenship in a way implying that not all members of the working class deserved citizenship.[2588] Some rethinking of popular sovereignty was nevertheless taking place: Rafael Erich, a spokesman for a constitutionalist line within the party, recognised that in a modern state 'the people are the foundation and source of all political [*julkinen*] power', that the people in this role were above both the parliament and the government and that no form of government other than 'a state of the people' (*kansanvaltio*, the favourite Germanic concept of the conservatives) was thinkable.[2589] The will of the people expressed in the election had unquestionably been in favour of a republic, even though their change of mind was, according to Erich, caused by global trends,[2590] a statement that made republicanism appear as a transnational rather than a native phenomenon. This conservative adaptation to popular sovereignty and republicanism was spurred by the constitutional changes that had already been realised in Sweden and were being prepared in Germany as well as by related cautious re-evaluations in political theory. Trying to explain the policies of the conservatives in 1918, Erich insisted that the monarchists, too, had aimed at 'the realisation of the permanent will of the people',[2591] but they did not believe that a parliament necessarily expressed this will.[2592] Conservative reservations about the implications of popular sovereignty had not gone away, to be sure, and a republican form of government with 'an advocate of the people' in the form of a strong president to counter party interests was called for.[2593] This reflects a conception of executive power that was inherent in the Gustavian constitutional tradition and was reinforced by the proposal for a new German constitution.

Professor E. N. Setälä, who had participated in drafting the previous version of the constitution, also recognised popular sovereignty and defined

---

2587 VP, Väinö Voionmaa, 24 May 1919, 517, 520.
2588 Stenius 2003, 351.
2589 VP, Rafael Erich, 25 April 1919, 138; 24 May 1919, 524.
2590 VP, Rafael Erich, 14 June 1919, 917.
2591 VP, Rafael Erich, 25 April 1919, 139; 24 May 1919, 524.
2592 For a radical Social Democratic response, see Mikko Ampuja who accused the former monarchists of trying to hide their opposition to democracy with the reactionary term 'the permanent will of the people'. The conservatives had, he claimed, bought the press and persuaded it to echo reactionary views about what 'the holy will of the people is even if the people have not this time managed to understand it'. Reactionary clergymen presented conservative solutions, appealing to divine will, for the same purpose. VP, 3 June 1919, 713.
2593 VP, Rafael Erich, 24 May 1919, 526.

a 'state of the people' as a political system in which 'power originates from the people and is in the last instance in the hands of the people themselves'.[2594] However, he was not so certain about the parliament being 'the sole omnipotent advocate of the cause of the people': the parliament might not always observe the will of the people, and this called for a president who would be elected by the people to supervise on their behalf that their will was respected by the parliament and would be empowered 'to appeal to the people' by calling a new parliamentary election if necessary. Setälä's conservative thinking did not include the referendum as an extension of the popular state as in his opinion it would have required the common people to possess higher levels of education and dedication to public affairs than was the case in Finland.[2595] The ideas coming from the new Germany were not to be imitated uncritically.

At the same time, an even more conservative branch of the National Coalition Party, while recognising the principle of popular sovereignty, carried on the argumentation of the monarchist project. Paavo Virkkunen defended the duality of legislative and executive power, since both were legitimated by 'the free authorisation of the people' as expressed in elections.[2596] A second political power was needed and could be found in a strong executive power authorised by the people and independent of the parliament.[2597] Popular monarchy was to be replaced with a popular presidency: the president should be 'most closely connected with the people'.[2598] Erkki Kaila, a theologian in favour of democracy, also argued for a balance between 'a democratic parliament' and a president representing 'the will of the people' as a solution suitable for the Finnish people in the midst of the Europe-wide ferment.[2599] This was in fact the kind of presidency that the former monarchists and bourgeois republicans succeeded in introducing. At the same time, some members of the National Coalition Party still questioned the ability of 'those classes of the people who now together constitute the majority and have little political experience' (the centrist parties and the Social Democrats) to prevent the unavoidable degeneration of parliamentary sovereignty, as Professor Theodor Homén claimed. He could not believe that the Finns were more rational, better and wiser than all other peoples[2600] and thus capable of ruling a republic.

The majority of Finnish-speaking conservatives did nevertheless participate in the construction of a new popular government. Once the National Coalition Party had managed – with a combination of rhetoric and obstruction – to get through a sufficiently strong presidency, their chairman, Professor Hugo Suolahti, began to speak optimistically about the people in a traditional Fennoman spirit: the remaining weaknesses of

---

2594 VP, Emil Nestor Setälä, 24 May 1919, 500.
2595 VP, Emil Nestor Setälä, 24 May 1919, 500.
2596 VP, Paavo Virkkunen, 2 June 1919, 641.
2597 VP, Paavo Virkkunen, 3 June 1919, 719; 21 June 1919, 1018; Hugo Suolahti, 21 June 1919, 1020.
2598 VP, Paavo Virkkunen, 3 June 1919, 730.
2599 VP, Erkki Kaila, 14 June 1919, 914–15.
2600 VP, Theodor Homén, 14 June 1919, 912.

the republican constitution would be remedied by 'the common sense of the people and their growing maturity'. In the Civil War, the Finns had reached the lowest point of degradation, but Suolahti asserted that his party had always counted on the capability of the Finnish people.[2601] Rafael Erich emphasised the responsibility of the people for maintaining legal order and spoke positively about 'a common political conscience' in the current parliament of the Finnish people, who had together planned 'a democratic, parliamentary republic'.[2602] E. N. Setälä, too, mitigated his previous criticism, emphasising the need for the legislators to trust the Finnish people again. He believed that 'a people that can create and form a state can retain its political existence with this constitution'. It was better to accept this as a new starting point than allow the interregnum to continue.[2603] The discursive process of negotiation and the concessions of the republicans, together with the changed inter- and transnational circumstances, had persuaded the National Coalition Party to accept a parliamentary *and* presidential republic – and in the end this acceptance was voiced in much clearer terms than was the case with the right in Sweden or Germany. The Finnish parliament had succeeded in constructing a compromise acceptable to the majority.

A similar turn is not visible in the Swedish People's Party, however. Its spokesmen continued to express monarchical views and were sceptical about popular involvement in politics – partly out of a rightist ideology that resembled Swedish and Prussian conservatism, partly as a rhetorical tool to increase pressure on the majority to accord language-political concessions. *Hufvudstadsbladet* ridiculed the optimistic belief in the good intentions of the people, regarding it as too immature to take responsibility for governing the realm in a new 'popular rule'. These 'orgies of popular rule' (*folkväldesorgierna*), were likely to lead on the one hand to the degeneration of the polity but on the other also to a healthy transnational reaction that would cut equal suffrage, establish new political procedures and restore a strong state power. In fact, the paper claimed, confidence in democracy and parliamentarism was already declining.[2604] There was a tendency for such views to be marginalised in the debates of early summer 1919: they could be dismissed as reflections of a class-based defence of privilege and the status of a minority language by a group that belonged to the victors of the Civil War, but they also gave rise to considerable concern. The opposition of the Swedish People's Party to democracy and parliamentarism was compared with the anti-parliamentary methods of the Bolsheviks, and its obstruction appeared as a fruitless prolongation of the constitutional strife.[2605]

Ernst Estlander, as a representative of aristocratic elitism, painted a pessimistic picture of the Finnish people in the aftermath of the Civil

2601 VP, Hugo Suolahti, 21 June 1919, 1021.
2602 VP, Rafael Erich, 21 June 1919, 1021–2; also Juhani Arajärvi, 21 June 1919, 1025.
2603 VP, Emil Nestor Setälä, 21 June 1919, 1028.
2604 *Hufvudstadsbladet*, 'Från kammare och kuloar', 15 June 1919; 'Från kammare och kuloar', 22 June 1919.
2605 *Suomen Sosialidemokraatti*, 'Porwari-bolshewismi', 25 May 1919; 'Eduskunnan lehteriltä', 3 June 1919; *Helsingin Sanomat*, 'Totuuksia poliittisesta keinottelusta', 5 June 1919; 'Ratkaisu käsissä', 19 June 1919.

War as not having 'reached maturity in culture or politics'. For such a 'small and politically weak nation' that 'lacked political traditions' and was prone to political agitation, a republic remained a very dangerous form of government.[2606] Estlander spoke ironically about 'those who believe that they represent the absolute will of the people'[2607] and proposed the representation of interests of different sections of society in the parliament, but he failed to win support even from his own party.[2608] Estlander claimed that extended parliamentarism endangered the rights of the people and even 'democracy'.[2609]

Emil Hästbacka went even further, seeing the Finns as too immature to understand 'the life of the state' or 'to form a state'. As they lacked 'a sense of political connectedness', they could not be given unbounded political power. A threat from those elements of the people whose parliamentary representatives had been ready to lead an anarchical uprising (i.e. the Social Democrats) continued to exist: 'the people of Manner and Tokoi' would renew calls for a new societal order. Such a will of the people had, according to Hästbacka, been only 'temporarily constructed through agitation'[2610] – implicitly of the Finnish-speaking lower classes – and thus could not be trusted. For Hästbacka, only a monarchy based on the inherited Swedish constitution would ensure stable politics that would benefit all social classes.[2611] Artur Eklund further suspected that the republicans were merely abusing a temporary 'democratic high tide' to pass a constitution to their liking[2612] and that transnational trends were again being used to the detriment of the nation. Such anti-popular government discourse excluded the Swedish People's Party from the compromise on a presidential republic, to which even the National Coalition Party had finally agreed.

These sceptical attitudes towards majority rule were linked with the language question, i.e. the rights of Swedish-speakers in an independent Finland, which had become an issue after the Civil War in both the Finnish-Swedish and the Swedish press. While a single nation-state was being built, the people of the time were careful to distinguish between the different ethnic groups, one of which was constituted by Swedish-speaking Finns. Georg von Wendt, who represented the Swedish Left, when talking about the language provisions of the constitution, made a division between 'the Finnish people' (*suomalainen kansa*) and 'the Swedish people' (*ruotsalaiskansa, det svenska folket*) and referred to the 'nationality solution' (*kansallisratkaisu*) for each of these 'brother peoples' (*veljeskansat*),[2613] the ethnic epithets being used with reference to linguistic groups in Finland. Such an understanding of the existence of two peoples within one state demonstrates the strong feeling of separateness among the Swedish-speakers at the time of the formulation

2606   VP, Ernst Estlander, 2 June 1919, 668.
2607   VP, Ernst Estlander, 2 June 1919, 668.
2608   Vares 2006, 141.
2609   VP, Ernst Estlander, 24 May 1919, 505.
2610   VP, Emil Hästbacka, 2 June 1919, 638.
2611   VP, Emil Hästbacka, 2 June 1919, 639.
2612   VP, Artur Eklund, 14 June 1919, 917.
2613   VP, Georg von Wendt, 24 May 1919, 514.

of the republican constitution and goes a long way to explaining why constitutional formulations about power belonging to the people (which possibly meant only Finnish-speakers) were not welcome to many Swedish-speaking Finns. Opposition to republicanism and the advocacy of the monarchical tradition was thus related to concern about the equal standing of the two linguistic groups. Hjalmar Procopé asserted that the Swedish-speakers were not aiming at any violent 'revolution' even though they would vote against the proposal because it lacked any provisions for national languages, for which the Swedish-speakers had been campaigning.[2614] These provisions would form the basis of the Language Act of 1922. Opposition to the constitutional proposal by the Swedish People's Party was taken by the Agrarians as provocation, which illustrates the heated nature of the confrontation: Simson Pilkka threatened that the voters of the Finnish people would soon bring down such opposition to the will of the majority of the people.[2615] The Swedish People's Party voted in any case against the final compromise and left the government soon afterwards.

The process of passing a constitution based on political power derived from the people as represented in the parliament was still a vexed one in the summer. However, an overwhelming majority finally voted for the proposal on 21 June. Lauri Kristian Relander (Agrarians), the Speaker, declared that this approval was a positive act of state (*valtioteko*) of the entire people and aimed at a happier future, and he thanked the parliament for having been able to overcome party divisions that tore the people apart.[2616] *Helsingin Sanomat* saw the resolution as increasing trust in both the Finnish people and in their parliament.[2617] While these comments still sounded to many as overly optimistic in June 1919, the goals would be achieved over the longer term: the constitution would unify most of the Finnish people.

7.4.5 THE REMAINING LIMITS ON PARLIAMENTARISM

The implications of the introduction of parliamentarism to the Finnish constitution had been debated during 1917 especially in connection with a revision of the parliamentary procedure and the adoption of the Power Act in July. In the Rump Parliament of 1918, parliamentarism as a principle had been treated with suspicion by the monarchical majority, while the republicans had defended it fiercely. A degree of parliamentarism had generally become understood as indispensable for the future Finnish constitution even then. However, the conceptions of parliamentarism still varied greatly in 1919, and some open opposition to the entire principle surfaced: there was no agreement about some *Western* notion of parliamentarism being applied as such to the Finnish constitution.

The centrist governmental parties remained the most enthusiastic advocates of the principle. Kalle Lohi of the Agrarians depicted the Finnish

---

2614 VP, Hjalmar Procopé, 2 June 1919, 661. On the depth of the language division, see Rinta-Tassi 1986, 37–9, and Ihalainen 2015, 16.
2615 VP, Simson Pilkka, 14 June 1919, 932.
2616 VP, Lauri Kristian Relander, 21 June 1919, 1029.
2617 *Helsingin Sanomat*, 'Suuriarwoinen saawutus', 22 June 1919.

people, after their miseries caused by the lack of parliamentarism, as practically unanimous in their determination to establish a parliamentary polity.[2618] Heikki Ritavuori, a Progressivist lawyer who, as the Chairman of the Constitutional Committee, formulated the final compromise for the republican constitution, likewise regarded it as impossible to oppose parliamentarism 'in an era when the parliamentary form of government prevails in all leading European realms'.[2619] Santeri Alkio shared this interpretation of an ongoing process of parliamentarisation throughout Europe and pointed out that domestic conflicts had frequently arisen out of tendencies by governments to pursue policies that differed from the prevaling views held by parliaments.[2620] For Alkio, parliamentarism should, however, be of the regulated American kind, a view that ignored the lack of actual parliamentarism in the United States and nurtured the ideal of a presidential republic resembling one that existed in a victorious great power. As Juho Vennola also conceded, the Finnish constitution would continue to be based on the duality of government rather than on any concentration of power in the parliament.[2621] It should hence be seen as a compromise to appease the National Coalition Party and a polity that was distinct from Western European versions of parliamentarism.

The Social Democrats had much rethinking to do with regard to parliamentarism. Their willingness to accept parliamentarism of a Western European type or in any bourgeois sense had become subject to serious doubt as a consequence of the events of 1917 and 1918. But the party had changed its course after the Civil War, aiming at parliamentary cooperation and criticising the monarchists of 1918 for their utterly 'indecent' violations of 'the parliamentary life of this country'.[2622] In the course of the debates of 1919, the Social Democratic approach to parliamentarism became increasingly constructive. Speaking on behalf of his group, Hannes Ryömä consistently emphasised the principles of majority parliamentarism, by which he meant that the country would be governed according to the will of the majority of the people so that the views of *all* groups would be taken into consideration on an equal basis and all actions of the executive would be subjected to parliamentary scrutiny. The holders of the executive power should be elected by the parliament (a requirement that had not changed since 1917), should be accountable to it and would not be able to limit the legislative power of the representative institution. However, majority parliamentarism certainly did not stand for 'parliamentary dictatorship', as its opponents claimed.[2623] Parliamentarism implied that the government should have no policy other than one supported by the parliament; it should hence search for concord between itself and the representative institution.

2618 VP, Kalle Lohi, 4 June 1919, 743.
2619 VP, Heikki Ritavuori, 3 June 1919, 708.
2620 VP, Santeri Alkio, 24 May 1919, 511–12.
2621 VP, Juho Vennola, 14 June 1919, 922.
2622 VP, Väinö Tanner, 24 April 1919, 136.
2623 VP, Hannes Ryömä, 24 May 1919, 508–9; 3 June 1919, 727; 5 June 1919, 814; 14 June 1919, 927.

Such a principle would change the course of European history, which had previously been characterised by confrontations between parliaments and governments arising from the tendency of the latter to reserve autocratic powers for themselves and to disregard policies advocated by parliaments, thereby forcing these to fight for their rights.[2624] Ryömä's analysis placed the Finnish constitutional crisis of the preceding two years in a broader European context and helped to relativise it in the eyes of both the left and the right: the Finnish transition to parliamentarism was part of a global change; it was only distinguished by having been a particularly violent one. A further issue which the Social Democrats brought to the agenda and continued to express their demands concerning it in 1917 and 1918 was the parliamentarisation of foreign policy; this also entailed the abandonment of secret diplomacy as practised by governments before and during the war.[2625] This was a goal that their ideological brethren and some liberals pursued in other countries as well. At the same time, the Social Democrats expressed their frustration over the extent of parliamentarism that they could expect: despite the inclusion of the principle of political power belonging to the people as represented by the parliament, the presidency was in actual fact going to constitute another nub of power that was capable of bypassing the parliament. Future parliaments would hence need to ensure the realisation of parliamentary government in practice;[2626] in other words, the constitutional process could not stop at this stage.

Väinö Voionmaa was another Social Democratic MP who analysed the prospects for parliamentarism. Like many Swedish socialists, this professor of history based his argument on Fredrik Lagerroth's thesis of a thousand years of democratic and parliamentary progress in Sweden and Finland.[2627] The thesis justified the claim that most Finns regarded it as 'unthinkable that the parliament could act against the people, that the parliament as an institution could turn against the people, as it has itself grown and been formed out of the people'.[2628] This understanding of the organic development of the Finnish people and their representative institution through four-estate diets to the current unicameral parliament was intended to persuade former monarchists and current supporters of presidential powers to accept an extension of parliamentary power. Both the parliament of 1917 and that of 1918 appeared as having acted against the will of the majority of the people. Voionmaa also compared the Finnish situation with Western European parliamentarism, suggesting that ministerial responsibility would decrease class conflicts and create 'strong feelings of responsibility towards the wide layers of the people' within the bureaucracy. This Social Democratic criticism of the civil service, heard from them and the Agrarians many times before, was directed against the old elite class represented by the conservatives. It culminated in Voionmaa's suggestion that 'Western bureaucracy does

2624 VP, Hannes Ryömä, 24 May 1919, 511.
2625 VP, Hannes Ryömä, 24 May 1919, 509; also Jonas Laherma, 24 May 1919, 538.
2626 VP, Hannes Ryömä, 14 June 1919, 926–7.
2627 Ihalainen 2015.
2628 VP, Väinö Voionmaa, 24 May 1919, 517.

not see its interests to be in conflict with the interests of the people as the bureaucracy in our country always does'.[2629] This implied that a sense of responsibility and common interests with the people were lacking among the elite, as the legalistic manoeuvres of the right had demonstrated in 1917 and 1918. Western European parliamentarism, although by no means perfect, should be set as the goal[2630] and native and Prussian traditions of administration thereby challenged.

With the compromises between the centre and the right that seemed to be cutting parliamentary powers and producing 'a parliament that is not the master of itself',[2631] Voionmaa lamented what he viewed as an international tendency to replace parliamentarism – which was claimed to be obsolete – with the direct rule of the people as voters.[2632] This was an implicit reference to the role of the presidency and the referendum in the future German constitution. The election of a president by a popular vote weakened parliamentarism in Finland before the principle had 'had time to take root and strengthen itself, and there is really nothing in it that could be reduced or decreased,' Voionmaa claimed.[2633] The National Coalition Party appeared to be abusing the will of the people in order to create a political institution that would 'upset parliamentarism, which is still at such a tender phase of growth'. In Voionmaa's view, the parliament, as a democratic institution, should elect the president 'on behalf of the people' and subject him to 'popular control via the parliament'.[2634] Without such a solution, 'our parliamentarism is in danger': there was the risk of 'some unknown unparliamentary forces . . . playing their dark games here and carrying through sudden amendments that appear to be in no way parliamentary'.[2635] The analysis was pessimistic but well informed with regard to both developments in Germany and the stance of the remaining rightist opposition in Finland. Despite such pessimism, the Marxist militancy of 1917 aiming at the rule of a socialist majority in the parliament as the only alternative had been renounced. Although over twenty amendments proposed by the Social Democrats were voted down by the bourgeois majority, the Social Democrats finally acceded to the compromise.[2636]

The National Coalition Party was still not sure about the extent of parliamentarism either. Within this leading party of the right, there was a tendency to downplay parliamentarism by dismissing differences between the government on the one hand and the parliament with its problem-causing parties on the other by combining the two – a way of thinking that was also typical of Finnish political culture more generally.[2637] Rafael Erich, as a specialist in constitutional law, proposed a concept of the state that was

2629 VP, Väinö Voionmaa, 24 May 1919, 518.
2630 VP, Väinä Voionmaa, 24 May 1919, 521.
2631 VP, Väinö Voionmaa, 2 June 1919, 650.
2632 VP, Väinö Voionmaa, 3 June 1919, 719.
2633 VP, Väinö Voionmaa, 3 June 1919, 721.
2634 VP, Väinö Voionmaa, 3 June 1919, 721.
2635 VP, Väinö Voionmaa, 3 June 1919, 722.
2636 Jyränki 2006, 41.
2637 Pulkkinen 2003, 234, 238, 251.

in line with traditional political theory and was critical of the French version of parliamentarism in particular. According to this concept, democracy was not to be applied beyond the election of the parliament.[2638] Erich could recognise the responsibility of ministers to the parliament as a 'political principle' and was not opposed to references to parliamentary government in the constitution, but he rejected any judicial principle of constitutional parliamentarism as extreme and unproductive, resembling the notorious Power Act. In his view, 'correctly understood and healthy parliamentarism' required a balance between the parliament and the government so that the parliamentary control of the government was kept 'within proper limits'; it required a president as a moderator between the government and the people and between the people and the parliament.[2639] Without the presidential right to dissolve the parliament, 'no parliamentary system can function in the first place, and then we are taken to an entirely different level and leave parliamentarism for good'.[2640] Léon Duguit, a leading French expert in administrative law, had taught that '[a] parliamentary system is not possible unless we have, side by side with a parliament based on universal suffrage, a head of state who personifies executive power'.[2641] This lesson from the Third Republic was now relevant to Finland as well and was reinforced by the proposal for the Weimar constitution. Tekla Hultin, who was also knowledgeable about France, likewise called for an independent presidency under 'a parliamentary form of government'.[2642] This in fact represented the National Coalition Party's demand before voting for any republican constitution, and the party could found its demands on a considerable body of international theoretical debate.

However, Erich's conservative political theorising also enabled the National Coalition Party to recognise parliamentarism as a valuable element within the tradition of the duality of government as long as it did not take the form of simple majority parliamentarism. Erich certainly cited examples from France and Germany as indicative of the inevitability of parliamentarism in a modern state (unlike Paasikivi in 1918), but he also mentioned the various forms of parliamentarism existing in different countries. The ability of the parliament to cooperate with and scrutinise the actions of the government was valuable, but the parliamentary control of all state activities would lead to mock-parliamentarism and constant governmental crises. The government should possess expertise, influence and authority in the eyes of both the parliament and the people. This could be achieved with a president who regulated and balanced parliamentarism. Moreover, governments were unlikely to abuse their power vis-à-vis the parliament as long as governmental power was no longer understood as contrary to the people and democracy.[2643]

2638 Pekonen 2003, 144.
2639 VP, Rafael Erich, 24 May 1919, 1, 524–7; 2 June, 658, 661; 4 June 1919, 742, 745.
2640 VP, Rafael Erich, 24 May 1919, 526.
2641 VP, Rafael Erich, 24 May 1919, 526.
2642 VP, Tekla Hultin, 3 June 1919, 724.
2643 VP, Rafael Erich, 2 June 1919, 658–60.

Once the National Coalition Party had managed to negotiate a sufficiently strong government and presidency, Erich welcomed the compromise as 'functional parliamentarism', a polity that had been prepared with the parliamentary reform of 1906 and the decisions of late 1917.[2644] This was one more rhetorical conservative description of parliamentarism. Juhani Arajärvi, the chairman of the parliamentary group, even declared the MPs to be 'the representatives of the majesty of the nation',[2645] a speech act that is illustrative of the turn from the monarchism of 1918 to the presidential republicanism of 1919. At the same time, opposition to the 'parliamentary dictatorship' of the type of 1917 continued to be voiced by former monarchists.[2646] Theodor Homén referred to the history of every country where the parliament had received all political power – including the Swedish realm in the eighteenth-century Age of Liberty – as revealing the abuses that resulted from this, whereas the cooperation between the government and the parliament when the Estates of Finland convened between 1863 and 1906 had, in his view, produced good results. The experiences of parliamentary supremacy after 1917 provided a further warning instance of an omnipotent parliament that was characterised by 'the adulation of incompetence', the waste of public funds and the degeneration of all administration.[2647] Homén would consequently join the Swedish People's Party in voting against the urgent adoption of the proposal, but the leaders of the National Coalition Party managed to persuade the majority of Finnish-speaking conservatives to join the side of limited parliamentarism.

Even after it had achieved many of its language-policy goals, the Swedish People's Party chose not to be reconciled with a form of parliamentarism limited by a presidency. In fact, it challenged the national parliament concretely by holding meetings of the Swedish Folktinget, of which many of the party's MPs were also members, and having its debates reported in *Hufvudstadsbladet* as if it was another parliament.[2648] The organ of the party wrote about parliamentarism with a degree of hostility not paralleled in Swedish papers of the right, viewing it as a catchword that the majority of the parliament abused in order to weaken the power of the state by introducing the rule of a 200-headed assembly divided by parties.[2649] It claimed that the proposal made the parliament 'autocratic' so that 200 members of 'the most ignorant parliament in the world', possessing less than average intelligence and a tendency to follow all extreme theories, would determine all the affairs of the state on a weekly basis. This meant that 'the fickle mass' and 'the mob' became the king (with the role of the president being played down)

2644 VP, Rafael Erich, 21 June 1919, 1022–3.
2645 VP, Juhani Arajärvi, 21 June 1919, 1025. The same expression in German had been used in the Weimar debates earlier in the spring.
2646 VP, Paavo Virkkunen, 2 June 1919, 641.
2647 VP, Theodor Homén, 14 June 1919, 912.
2648 *Hufvudstadsbladet*, 'Svenska folktinget' and 'Svensktinget', 25 May 1919.
2649 *Hufvudstadsbladet*, 'Betänkliga riktningar inom regeringen och riksdag' and 'Från kammare och kuloar', 15 June 1919; 'Regeringsformen antagen', 22 June 1919.

and that as a result there would be constant government crises just as in there had been Italy and France and in Sweden in the Age of Liberty. The speeches made by the Agrarians and Social Democrats in the parliament were excoriated as mere agitation.[2650]

In the Eduskunta (the national parliament), Ernst Estlander used his academic expertise to consistently oppose parliamentarism and to deplore cuts in the power of the president as a return to the Power Act, which had led to 'the Red treason and its democratic ideals about the state and society'. In Estlander's view, the republican Agrarians, too, held the same pernicious ideals.[2651] He claimed that 'the so-called parliamentary principle' would lead to a deplorable loss of governmental independence and authority to the parliament,[2652] producing 'an omnipotent representation of the people'.[2653] Majority parliamentarism would endanger the most important legal rights of the citizens,[2654] and particularly those of the speakers of a minority language. Hjalmar Procopé saw the new Finnish constitution as the establishment of parliamentary despotism run by 'a collegium of autocrats'.[2655] According to him, 'utterly rampant parliamentary rule' (*lantdagsvälde*), potentially supportive of the extension of Bolshevism, was to be expected.[2656] This parliamentarism would not advance democracy but rather endanger the realisation of the power of the people. Swedish theorists (discussed in the subsections on Sweden) had shown that parliamentarism was a specifically *British* system, the applicability of which was questionable unless a monarchy, strong parties and the governmental management of the parliament of the British kind were also introduced. The experiences of the preceding two years demonstrated that the formation of parliamentary government of a Western European type would not succeed in Finland.[2657] This was quite a provocative statement for Finnish-speaking republicans and recalls the views of the German right. Emil Hästbacka gave further expression to the fears of many Swedish-speakers over their minority status and the safety of private property by arguing that proportional representation in the parliament gave power into the hands of 'people who are more or less illiterate in the fields of economy and politics'. The proposal would produce 'a ruling parliament' based on 'the notorious ideals of the Power Act', which Hästbacka, speaking in Swedish, disparaged by using the Finnish word *valtalaki-idealet* rather than translating it into Swedish, thereby implying

---

2650 *Hufvudstadsbladet*, 'Från kammare och kuloar', 25 May 1919; 'Köpslagandet om regeringsformen', 4 June 1919; 'Regeringsformen antagen' and 'Från kammare och kuloar', 22 June 1919.
2651 VP, Ernst Estlander, 24 May 1919, 505.
2652 VP, Ernst Estlander, 24 May 1919, 505–506.
2653 VP, Ernst Estlander, 3 June 1919, 722.
2654 VP, Ernst Estlander, 24 May 1919, 506.
2655 VP, Hjalmar Procopé, 2 June 1919, 648. Väinö Voionmaa responded by pointing out that parliamentarism was the opposite of dictatorship. 2 June 1919, 651. Santeri Alkio likewise rejected the term as inappropriate. 2 June 1919, 652.
2656 VP, Hjalmar Procopé, 14 June 1919, 930.
2657 VP, Hjalmar Procopé, 4 June 1919, 741–2.

that such radicalism flourished among Finnish-speakers only.[2658] Clearly the Swedish People's Party remained opposed to any extended form of parliamentarism, even to a greater extent than the Swedish right.

Liberal circles were provoked by such opposition. Georg Schauman of the Swedish Left could not sympathise with opponents of parliamentary government in an era when parliamentarism was making a breakthrough in Germany as well as in Western Europe and Scandinavia. The time of parliamentary government had come: it had become impossible to govern without parliamentary support in any modern democracy.[2659] It was unjustified to talk about parliamentary dictatorship as no concentration of power in the parliament of the type envisaged in the Power Act would ensue.[2660] Bruno Sarlin, a Progressivist, also lamented the fact that opposition to the results of the parliamentary reform of 1906 was still being waged with dreams of limiting suffrage, instituting a bicameral system and obstruction of the adoption of a parliamentary republic.[2661] The government parties together with the Social Democrats and some Swedish-speaking liberals had clearly opted for Western parliamentarism and brought the Finnish-speaking right on board with the presidential compromise.

Even after the approval of the proposal by an overwhelming majority, there was a risk that the Regent C. G. E. Mannerheim, the commander of the Whites and an old monarchist, might not promulgate the republican constitution. As it was generally assumed that the Swedish Instrument of Government of 1772 was still in force – a reflection of the truly long-term trajectories that prevailed in Finnish political life – no law would enter into force without ratification by the regent. Mannerheim, who was close to the Swedish People's Party, was far from enthusiastic about the new constitution, which in his view reduced the political impact of the presidency, and he therefore postponed the ratification to mid-July. Plans for a coup d'état, an invasion of Petrograd (possible for a monarch under the Swedish Constitution of 1772) and the rejection of the new constitution, all proposed by rightist activists during this postponement, did not, in the end, win his support. Neither were the leaders of the National Coalition Party, many of whom had already made a rhetorical turn in favour of regulated parliamentarism, ready to challenge the parliamentary majority again or to encounter the international reactions that would follow. They had the failure to establish a monarchy in the previous autumn in mind. The former prime minister J. K. Paasikivi pessimistically warned that 'all sorts of democracies would attack us' if the republican constitution was rejected, which shows how unhappy this devout monarchist was about the

---

2658 VP, Emil Hästbacka, 5 June 1919, 881. Otto Wrede condemned 'economic democracy' even before the term had really entered Finnish debates; Germany, he claimed, provided a warning example of democracy, having demolished the best ordered state in the world. *Hufvudstadsbladet*, 'Betänkliga riktningar inom regeringen och riksdag', 15 June 1919.
2659 VP, Georg Schauman, 4 June 1919, 744.
2660 VP, Georg Schauman, 14 June 1919, 894.
2661 VP, Bruno Sarlin, 14 June 1919, 884.

'democratic' line to which the National Coalition Party had been forced to bow. According to this constitution, the supreme power belonged to the Finnish people as represented by the parliament. Legislative power was divided between the parliament and the president. The president also had a role in the use of executive power side by side with the government. The government was responsible to the parliament, but the president also had a role in its appointment. He further had the right to call new parliamentary elections.[2662] Even this kind of balance between legislative and executive powers remained unacceptable to some former monarchists: R. A. Wrede saw the republican constitution as a representative of a trend towards 'a half-anarchical parliamentary power' characterised by ignorance and tending to destroy morality and cultural values.[2663] Despite this constant opposition to parliamentarism, the constitution turned out to be a lasting one that, much later, enabled the establishment of a truly parliamentary polity.

2662 Sihvonen 1997, 16; Jussila, Hentilä & Nevakivi 1999, 129; Vares 2006, 143, 147–8.
2663 Vares 2006, 147.

8. The entangled parliamentary revolutions of 1917–19: Comparison, discussion and conclusion

Recent surveys on the First World War suggest that the discrepancies between the sacrifices that the war demanded from the people and their possibilities for political participation made them call for reforms from 1916 onwards and increasingly after the Russian Revolution broke out in March 1917. I have argued in this book that consequently several political cultures – both great powers and smaller states not directly involved in the war – almost simultaneously entered new cycles of nationally multi-sited and transnationally interconnected debates on constitutional reform. The entangled discourses concerned the political implications of the war, the possibilities opened and the threats posed by the Russian Revolution and ideologically motivated competing conceptualisations of democracy, the people and parliamentarism. These concepts were becoming objects of constant debate, redefinition and contestation within – and to some extent also between – European political cultures. While the discursive processes of constitutional reform took place primarily at the level of nation states, they were transnationally connected to a greater extent than national historiographies have previously recognised, thanks to existing transnational personal connections between the political elites, interlinked media debates and alternative ideological transnational networks of professionals and politicians linked by theory and ideology that facilitated the transfer of ideas at many levels.

I have reconstructed and analysed the dynamics of these simultaneously national and transnational discursive processes in their national, comparative and transnational contexts, focusing on four national parliaments – those of Britain, Germany, Sweden and Finland – and selected conservative, liberal and socialist party newspapers, in seeking an understanding of the logic of the competing conceptualisations of the political actors and groups involved in defining the proper nature of a future polity. Debates have been contextualised in order to show which discursive constructions of each concept the participants entertained, how they defined and rhetorically redescribed related terms by employing them in specific arguments to achieve particular goals and why certain processes of rethinking took place and the political consequences of these. At the same time, I have explored how and why obvious transnational transfers occurred or were blocked and what their political implications were.

8. The entangled parliamentary revolutions of 1917–19: Comparison, discussion and conclusion

This study offers a contribution to the comparative and transnational history of political discourse based both on comparisons between parallel nation-state-level debates as recorded in parliamentary and press sources and on an examination of the mutual links between these debates. Such research reveals and explains similarities and differences in attitudes and ideologies between national contexts and, by pointing out contemporary comparisons and transnational discursive transfers, increases our awareness of the entangled nature of national pasts. Though building on existing national historiographies and reasserting some of their findings, this analysis gives us reason to modify some earlier nation-state-centred interpretations: similar or alternative outcomes in other national contexts challenge the exceptional, self-evident or self-sufficient nature of the national reform processes. While exceptional in some respects, the national processes had a lot in common and were often transnationally connected. Even some of their particular features only become visible through this kind of transnational comparison focusing on discourse, textual content and concepts.

For instance, exceptionally consensual wartime attempts to strengthen the legitimacy of parliament and limited reformulations of British 'democracy' become visible in international comparative contexts, including uses of 'democracy' and 'Prussianism' in Allied propaganda and some contemporary international comparisons in the British parliament. The pressures of Western propaganda played a role in attempts to democratise and parliamentarise the Prussian political order, turning the key concepts party-political, potentially treasonous or in need of nationalisation, emphasising the unity of the people in ways not found in the other countries. There was no such complex parliamentary negotiation on democracy and parliamentarism in Germany as in Sweden and Finland. Though Swedish and Finnish constitutional solutions depended to a great extent on the course of the war and on German debates, they differed from them as for the readiness of at least some of the right to experiment with democratisation. Sweden moved from German to Western political models after major ideological confrontations over democracy. In Finland, radical political discourses adopted from Revolutionary Russia and legalist responses contributed to a fiercer confrontation on democracy and parliamentarism than in the other countries and to the rise of a crisis of independence: the legitimacy of parliamentary government deteriorated, a cycle of violent parliamentary discourse, civil war and Prussian reaction followed, and finally a republican compromise was made under external pressures. While Finland became internationally a warning example of a failed democracy in spring 1918, foundations for what would much later be called a 'very sustainable' polity were nevertheless laid in spring 1919.

Politics has been understood here as consisting of discursive and related physical processes that took place on different potentially interlinked levels and in different forums simultaneously – as well as at different times – with political actors constructing, reproducing and contesting policies in interaction with each other and with the political process. Parliamentary debates have been analysed as nexuses of multi-sited political discourses, including connected academic and public debates, so that the previous and simultaneous activities of the parliamentarians in other national and transnational forums, historical spaces, their mobility between these spaces and connected physical experiences and possible discursive transfers have been taken into consideration whenever traceable and interpreted as relevant for the understanding of a speech act. This methodological approach, focusing on the evolving meanings of the concepts in use in political arguments, integrates discourse-oriented methods ranging from language policy studies to the study of the history of political discourse, thereby widening the repertoire of conceptual history beyond the historical semantics of *Begriffsgeschichte* or the analysis of speech acts in the history of political thought. It is applicable to any corresponding comparative and transnational study of political discourse.

The analysis of the parliamentary reform debates was organised into four national contexts, five half-year periods of evolving national and international contexts and four broad topics: (i) national debates on the political implications of the First World War and national revolutions together with international comparisons and the transnational connections of these debates; (ii) competing ideologically motivated conceptualisations of democracy; (iii) alternative arguments concerning the political role of the people; and (iv) rival understandings of parliamentarism. In the rest of this conclusion, the central findings of these four categories are summarised in their national contexts in a generalising manner, related causal explanations discussed and the consequences for our understanding of the political history of the late 1910s explicated. The relative importance of the transnational aspects for the national discursive processes of reform is also discussed.

The First World War was the major transnational force that changed polities: the simultaneity and entanglement of reform pressures and related debates arose to a great extent from the realities and experiences of the war. In early 1917, political leaders on both sides of the Western Front shared an understanding that the people's sacrifices for the war effort had made it necessary to look for new ways to take the will of the people into consideration and to counteract a threatening crisis of legitimacy. Universal suffrage and parliamentary representation were seen not only in Britain but also increasingly in Germany as the best method to reconnect the people and the government.

In Britain, the War Cabinet proceeded with a previously prepared proposal on a suffrage reform shortly after the outbreak of the Russian Revolution, in the expectation that the U.S.A. would soon enter the war. The American emphasis on 'democracy' in war propaganda increased the pressure for reform, requiring that political realities should better correspond with the rhetoric of the Entente, although in the British domestic wartime context the concept of democracy was politicised late in comparison with the other countries and mainly by opposition forces. The common war experience that had united classes and parties was generally seen as enabling the political nation to move forward with the reform, the government presenting it as mobilising the power of the people for victory and reconstruction, creating a new Britain in the new world. As elsewhere, the rightist opposition wished to concentrate on the war effort and postpone the reform, questioning its legitimacy. The majority of the Conservatives, however, adapted themselves; in this they were influenced by their new conceptions of the lower classes arising from the shared war experiences and by optimistic prospects of obtaining party-political support from them. This adaptation, justified with talk about power being 'derived from the people' – which led to conceptualisations of democracy not so different from those voiced on the Continent – allowed the British reform process to take place earlier and made it more consensual than in the countries of comparison. Britain thus provided a model that reformists in Germany, Sweden and Finland used to persuade the right in those states, as the comparison shows. The relatively consensual nature of the process is also explained by the moderation of the Labour Party, which had been successfully integrated into the wartime government. As part of a national front, this party avoided in wartime the kind of labour internationalist argumentation that was typical of Social Democratic parties, striving to bridge class differences, saving further reform demands for later and rejecting revolution.

In Germany, dissatisfaction over the marginalisation of the Reichstag came into the open from late 1916 onwards. As in Britain, the impetus for reform was a reflection of the pressures caused by the war and the influence of war propaganda. Even the Chancellor recognised a certain need to rethink how the popular will could be taken into consideration when, in the aftermath of the Russian Revolution and the inception of the British suffrage reform and with the threat of the U.S.A. joining the Entente, the opposition openly challenged him about the postponed Prussian suffrage reform. I have shown how the British and German reform processes became discursively intertwined in ways that lent support to German rightist theories that the defeat in the war had been caused by domestic treason, with the Social Democrats being inspired by the British example. While the reformist left and centre emphasised that the war had changed Germany and the entire world, the right rejected all reform as a violation of the constitutional monarchy at a time when all forces should be concentrated on winning the war.

The Swedish reform process was likewise dependent on the course of the war even though the country was not directly involved in the fighting. The war forced the political elite to reconsider which constitutional model to follow: whereas The Right, supported by academics, continued to favour the Prussian example, the Liberal and Social Democratic left tended to turn towards Western European models and especially that of Britain. The implications of interconnections between the constitutional strife of the 1910s and historical writing for the long-term national grand narrative on the rise of Swedish democracy have not been previously considered to a sufficient degree. This study challenges teleological historiography on the rise of 'democracy' in the eighteenth century, above all,[2664] and strengthens the consideration of transnational aspects as for the reforms of the early twentieth century. The Russian Revolution, the British reform, the German reform debates and the American entry allowed the Swedish left to argue

[2664] Discussed in Ihalainen 2010 and Ihalainen 2015.

that the entire world was changing and that Sweden must therefore join this transnational reform. This was an argument that The Right still refused to accept.

Finland, though still part of the Russian Empire, had experienced the hardships of the war only indirectly and remained discursively outside it – in rather misleading ways. However, the different stages of the Russian Revolution (in March, July and November 1917) brought to the fore postponed reforms and disappointment with the results of the radical parliamentary reform of 1906 and provided evolving revolutionary models for new reformist and anti-reformist cycles of discourse. While the Finnish right counted on the Prussian model of a well organised polity prevailing in a new Europe, and thus also in Finland, after a German victory, the left in 1917 adopted a parliamentary discourse that was at times indistinguishable from Bolshevist revolutionary rhetoric. The importance of this discursive confrontation for the rise of a concrete violent conflict have not been considered sufficiently in older Finnish research. Discursive transfers from Revolutionary Russia remained limited in Britain and Germany, but Sweden and Finland were affected more concretely, the former owing to the mobility of internationalist socialists and the latter by way of a rail connection with Petrograd, the centre of the Revolution, although the Finnish socialists had difficulties in understanding the divisions and dynamics of the Russian revolutionary movement. The Revolution at first intensified national debates on democracy, inspiring the left, but it soon turned into a yardstick for the definition of democracy by all political groups. The Revolution also brought about redefinitions of parliamentarism as its Bolshevist version challenged 'bourgeois' and 'Western' parliamentarism.

British MPs were unenthusiastic about the Revolution, prioritising the continuity of the alliance with Russia. The concept was nevertheless politicised by the right to oppose the reform as an illegitimate 'revolution' introduced in the midst of a war. Some reformist Conservatives and Liberals, on the other hand, shared the suggestion of Labour MPs that the reform in fact would prevent a revolution by redefining the relationship between the people, Parliament and the government. At the end of 1917, the Representation of the People Bill became conceptualised as a parliamentary revolution in a positive sense, as a substitute for a socialist revolution.

In Germany, the Russian Revolution could be presented as a challenge to the Prussian order. Even in autumn 1918, however, it was still only the far left that spoke about an unavoidable transnational revolution and aimed at a socialist revolutionary democracy, which differs from Finland in 1917. The Social Democrats consistently emphasised reform, and from autumn 1918 onwards their moderate revolution was tailored to the circumstances in Germany: a revolution against the old Prussian order had been made, but it was not to be radicalised in the ways suggested by the far left. Even this restricted revolution was rejected by the right, and the tendency to extend the revolution to socio-economic issues was disliked by many liberals as well, which left the Social Democrats and their left-liberal allies alone in their revolutionary project, which differs from cooperation across the bloc lines in Sweden, for instance.

Stockholm, as a meeting place for international socialists, experienced the Revolution through cross-national mobility. The transnational revolutionary moment received its most concrete expression when the Social Democrat leader Hjalmar Branting participated in the reform debate on 14 April 1917, having just arrived from a visit to revolutionary Petrograd, and in interventions by far leftists who had on the preceding days hosted Lenin on his way to Petrograd. The left, including the Liberals, took the Revolution and the promises by the Kaiser on a future reform as evidence of a transnational constitutional change that Sweden was bound to join. However, the Social Democrats distanced themselves from direct action, prioritising reform through universal suffrage and parliamentary cooperation and opposing the Bolsheviks in late 1917, while at the same time pressurising The Right with insinuations about a possible popular rising. The far left conceptualised the constitutional confrontation in Sweden as part of a transnational revolution, supported a more revolutionary constitutional reform and sympathized with the radicalised discourse and related action of the Finnish Social Democrats. The split among the socialists marginalized support for the revolutionary cause in Sweden. The Right nevertheless attacked all reformists for their alleged 'revolutionary' scheming.

The analysis shows that the Finnish Civil War of early 1918 made the Swedish Social Democrats argue all the more consistently that a revolution should be executed through parliament, not by violent means. However, in order to force through a reform after the German Revolution in late 1918, they raised the possibility of a more radical revolution in case their moderate version was not approved by The Right and supported their argument with street demonstrations and emphasising the dictate of an irresistible transnational constitutional change. Their Liberal allies presented the reform as a way to prevent the progress of Bolshevism and hence to counter a possible revolution – a lot like in Britain. The Right still denied the legality of foreign revolutions and their relevance for Sweden, implying that the reformist coalition was importing a revolution by 'violent' extra-parliamentary agitation that might lead to civil strife of the kind seen in Finland. The suffrage reform was by no means a mere matter of course: most rightist MPs carried on their anti-reformist discourse to the end, and in summer 1919 some were still asserting that revolutionary activities would be answered with force. Only a few joined the leftists, using similar natural metaphors to describe an inevitable constitutional change. The far left, on the other hand, was disappointed with the Social Democrats' limited revolution and did not exclude the possibility of a civil war to advance democratic socialism. There was not yet a shared 'Swedish democracy' inherited from the eighteenth century, and the ideological confrontations reminded to a great extent those in Finland.

In Finland, the revolution was creeping in even more concretely. During the spring and summer of 1917, Finnish socialists received news of revolutionary developments not only in Petrograd but also in Berlin and Stockholm. I have shown how the concept of revolution became highly politicised in the parliament, the alternative interpretations being either that an international revolution had already entered Finland and was spreading to Sweden, Germany and Britain or that the Social Democrats were trying to import a Russian phenomenon through agitation. By the time of the introduction of a bill on parliamentary sovereignty in July 1917, the Social Democrats were applying the language of irreconcilable class antagonism to interpret the Finnish situation, building on previous radical discourse of their own and inspired by the Russian revolutionary discourse transferred through the mobility of revolutionaries between Petrograd and Helsinki. When the Bolsheviks – the only foreign socialist group supporting the aims of the Social Democrats, who seemed to be promoting the Bolshevist goal to internationalise the revolution – were believed to be taking over in Russia, parliamentary cooperation tended to be replaced with increasingly radical interpretations of the class struggle, revolution and civil war as the means to establish the rule of the working classes. This differs drastically from the avoidance of associations with Bolshevism in mainstream socialist discourse in Sweden, Germany and Britain – and from claims that the Bolsheviks had little influence on Finnish Social Democrats who rather looked at Germany. Risto Alapuro, among others, has argued that the Finnish Social Democrats wished to prevent a socialist revolution by introducing reforms still in November 1917 – that there was a revolution but no leaders or participating masses.[2665] I have shown how the sovereignty of the Finnish parliament, as advocated by the leading minister, the head of the Constitutional Committee and the Social Democratic parliamentary majority, was to be seen as part of the international 'last fight' between the proletariat and the capitalists, while a compromise with the bourgeoisie as counter-revolutionaries was discursively excluded. When the right responded with a class-based and legalistic discourse, the revolutionary class division of the Russian type became discursively established.

The breakthrough of revolutionary discourse and related extra-parliamentary action was even more obvious in the second parliament of 1917, which had a bourgeois majority and convened immediately after the October Revolution in Russia. The Social Democrats talked constantly about an unavoidable revolution of the Bolshevik type leading to violence, and a class war and a civil war being needed for the destruction of capitalist society, monarchies, parliaments and the press. They presented the bourgeoisie as counterrevolutionaries belonging to an international alliance that had used the same sinister methods in all revolutions throughout history. Thanks to their capitalist injustices and conspiracies, the Finnish and international bourgeoisie were to blame for the rise of a revolution which the Social Democrats were unable to stop. It appeared to the Social Democrats that it was their world-historical duty to make a revolution as opposed to carrying on the use of parliamentary means. This parliamentary vituperation, even hate speech, was reinforced by the party press and implemented in extra-parliamentary violence. The radicalisation of the Finnish Social Democratic discourse two months before the actual outbreak of the Civil War went far beyond anything heard in revisionist or even far-left socialist

---

2665 Alapuro 1988, 167–9; Liikanen 1993, 577, commenting Alapuro's thesis; Alapuro 2003, 541; Haapala & Tikka 2013, 109, 111, Hentilä & Hentilä 2016, 98.

discourse in the British, German or Swedish parliaments. Consequences for political events should be considered: radical discourse was leading to an attempted revolution against a parliamentary majority and also to an armed conflict when the right and the centre questioned the justification of what they saw as an imported revolution and the use of extra-parliamentary violence. This revolution failed, and the government of the White victors would see it as identical with the Bolshevik Revolution. Indeed, even the decision on a republican constitution in connection with the Declaration of Independence in December 1917 would be presented as an illegitimate revolutionary measure to be countered with a monarchy. Anthony D. Upton's concept of the 'Finnish Revolution' thus finds a lot of support in the analysis of parliamentary discourse: it was how the contemporaries understood the development.[2666]

The collective experiences and propagandistic discourses of the First World War and the Russian Revolution brought democracy, too, to the centre of the political debate around Europe and among nearly all ideological groups, even ones with authoritarian goals. Democracy (in contradistinction to Prussianism, against which the Entente claimed to be fighting) was becoming the norm for organising post-war political systems, though endless debate on the proper form of democracy ensued. I have demonstrated that the course of the national debates on democracy everywhere was greatly influenced by the state of international affairs constituted by an intensifying dispute between Germany and the Entente on what democracy stood for, Woodrow Wilson's successful importation of the rhetoric of democracy to Europe, the Russian Revolution opening entirely new visions for the future, and the outcome of the war. Typical of the debate in all countries was an emphasis on equal voting rights for both sexes and (with the exception of the far left) on the parliamentary representation of the people as constitutive of democracy.

Britain was the forerunner in constitutional reform in 1917–18 but not really in the rhetoric of democracy, despite pre-war examples: the analysis shows that few British politicians conceptualised the suffrage reform as a step in the advancement of democracy in spring 1917, their stance being that, while there was no need to democratise the British political system, the reform was needed to strengthen the people's morale in wartime. The anti-reformist opposition nevertheless tactically redescribed the established system as democratic and themselves as its defenders against the 'Prussian' methods employed by the government. Some reformists viewed democracy in Britain as essentially regulated, but only a few Liberals described the entire political system as democratic. Democracy was not a programmatic concept even for the Labour Party at this stage; this differs from continental Social Democracy and finds an explanation in the desire of the coalition partners to avoid associations with the Russian Revolution and the Marxist concept of democracy as the rule of the proletariat. It is illustrative of the

---

2666 Cf. Liikanen 1993, 576, on the unwillingness of Finnish historians to refer to a 'revolution'.

isolationist attitudes of the British parliamentary elite that the use of the word 'democracy' reproduced the war propaganda claim about fighting the war for democracy rather than expressing any vision of a transnational democratic breakthrough that would change the world and Britain with it.

In autumn 1917, when the legislative process was still under way, some reformists began to redefine the British political system through a normative concept of democracy. The Irish Nationalists attacked the government for its 'Prussianism' and used 'democracy' in a positive sense to engage in politicking. Identifying oneself and one's party with democracy became increasingly common towards the end of 1917, but even so the references to democracy remained few in comparison with continental Social Democratic and Liberal reformist discourses. Awareness of the diversified uses of 'democracy' to defend a variety of policies was nevertheless rising. After the Bolshevik Revolution, fears of socialist revolutionaries taking over democracy and turning it into class rule were common. They were reinforced by far-left publicity that questioned the reality of democratisation in Britain in comparison with Germany. Some critics of mass democracy appeared in both Houses in early 1918, but downright anti-democratic views were not articulated as they were in the other countries of comparison. On the contrary, some explicit parliamentary speech acts showed the British Conservatives were moving over to the side of the democratic masses – honestly or for tactical reasons. For many peers, a transition to a democratic constitution seemed unavoidable, and some saw democracy as a way to diminish class confrontations and to advance societal progress. Such readiness among the old elite to adapt to democracy in the exceptional wartime circumstances would be decisive for the success of the British reform.

From spring 1918 onwards, the Entente was demanding the democratisation of Germany as a precondition of peace. In the British press, the constitutional debate was taken over by the focus on the war being fought for democracy. Only some Labour activists conceptualised the suffrage reform as the democratisation of British society and implying further reforms, while the far left continued to criticise the British system for its lack of democracy in comparison with Germany. In autumn 1918, the mobilisation of 'the new democracy' for an election remained modest by international standards. While the Labour Party urged Britain to support the progress of democracy on the Continent, denounced Bolshevism and called for reforms at home, the Conservatives and Liberals suspected Labour of advocating socialist democracy. The Conservatives wished to avoid any fuss about democracy, viewing Britain as already being a democracy and rejecting reform demands based on the advancement of democracy. Liberal papers defended the policies of the War Coalition as democratic, emphasised democratic progress and spoke for reforms designed to stop the advance of socialism. Prime Minister Lloyd George himself, on the other hand, defined his government as a representative of democracy more distinctly after he had secured an election victory. The opposition, on the left but also within the Liberal Party, responded by challenging Lloyd George's foreign and domestic policies as incompatible with the advancement of democracy.

A debate, both theoretical and political, on the implications of democracy for domestic politics was activated as soon as peace had been restored.

In 1919, the discourse of the British Conservatives began to see the prevailing political system as democracy in a positive light, especially as the rise of 'Tory democracy', sympathetic towards the working classes and believing in the construction of democracy through education, had been rewarded with electoral success. The Liberal press described Parliament as 'British Democracy' and Lloyd George's reformist government as the realisation of that democracy. The Labour Party, despite its unhappiness about the manipulated election that had enabled the old elite to retain power under the rhetoric of democracy, profiled itself as a supporter of representative as opposed to direct democracy as the way to achieve socialism. It denounced the notion of democracy as the rule of the workers and challenged Lenin, who had rejected parliamentary methods in favour of democracy produced by a revolution. The far left carried on using a discourse on democracy as the rule of the working class, but it remained a marginal force.

If the British reform could be turned into a source of optimism and disputes about democracy saved until the post-war period, in Germany democracy became a concept of open dispute that inflamed the political debate during and after the war. Spring 1917 already saw the reactivation of an older debate on 'Western' democracy that was critical of the American, British and French political systems. This debate was provoked by the attacks of the war propaganda on Prussianism as an opponent of democracy, the Russian Revolution, the British reform and the US entry into the war. As a reflection of their dissatisfaction with the running of wartime policies, some socialists and liberals pointed to the strengths of 'democracies' in order to challenge the Prussian political order. Whereas official Germany denied the Western accusations about the lack of democracy in Germany and emphasised the popular elements of the constitution, left-liberals demanded democratisation as compensation for military service. The Social Democrats, while recognising certain strengths in the German polity in comparison with the West, deplored the delayed democratisation of its institutions, calling for a suffrage reform in Prussia and hoping for a reform of the federal constitution as well. However, the other parliamentary parties did not share the socialist and left-liberal views: the right rejected all democratisation as treason and defended the monarchical political order. Outside Germany, the challenge to the Prussian order was overinterpreted and the ability of the established political system to stop reform underestimated. In Sweden and Finland, it encouraged both Social Democratic and Liberal reformism, whereas rightist anti-reformism continued to trust the stability of the Prussian system. The same happened in summer 1917, when the German left called for democracy with universal suffrage as the first step and spoke enthusiastically about the advancement of democratic ideas. The reform process came to a standstill as a result of an intervention of the military leaders, for whom democratisation was associated with a readiness to give up fighting the war produced by Western propaganda. The false impressions abroad were also inspired by the fact that *Vorwärts* and *Berliner*

Tageblatt nevertheless published overoptimistic news about the progress of democratisation in Germany and internationally. The conservative press, by contrast, mocked the leftist 'Reichstag democracy' and encouraged foreign opponents of similar reforms to stand firm against Western democracy in the expectation of a German victory.

When no such victory was won, a legitimacy crisis broke out. In late September 1918, the General Staff advised the politicians to respond positively to Woodrow Wilson's call for democratisation in order to achieve better peace terms. The right responded by rejecting all reform as the importation of 'Western democracy' and mass rule by the opportunistic and treasonous 'German democracy', and most other parties, too, were hesitant to talk about democratisation. Since the Social Democrats did not hesitate to monopolise the concept, 'democracy' took on a party-political connotation not known in the three countries of comparison. For the SPD, the reform stood for the crushing of Prussianism and the realisation of some of the party's main goals, which went on to call for 'economic' together with political democracy; this strengthened the associations between democracy and socialism, particularly as the left-liberals spoke only very generally about the advent of 'a democratic era'. The Social Democrats were left practically alone with their 'democracy'.

A similar division was established in the Weimar Assembly, the Social Democrats using majority democracy as a normative concept that defined proper political behaviour and as a programmatic concept directing future policies, their leaders being roused by their own rhetoric, which talked about making Germany the 'most democratic democracy in the world'. The comparative analysis shows, however, that they also tried to sell the concept to its critics by nationalising it as 'German democracy' or vernacularising it by using the ethnic, organic, collectivistic and seemingly apolitical term 'rule of the people' (*Volksherrschaft*), which came close to the popular word *Volksgemeinschaft* (community of the people), and the notion that the collective popular will was more than the mere will of a parliamentary majority. The German right did not participate in such deliberations about democracy beyond some rhetorical redescriptions and oppositional interjections. This differs from the readiness of the right in the other national cases to argue about the nature of democracy. The right-liberals denounced the project, and the Catholic Centre continued to recycle traditionalist and federalist views, needing time to accommodate itself to the new system. Even the left-liberals set limits to democratic progress and replaced 'democracy' with terms such as *Volksstaat* (state of the people), calling for a strong presidency and referenda as expressions of the popular will as opposed to parliament. The far left saw the constitution as not going far enough in the direction of 'proletarian democracy'. All these stands were relevant also for contemporary Swedish and Finnish constitutional debates which cannot be fully understood without knowledge of them.

An even more extensive debate on democracy took place in Sweden, where the suffrage reform was postponed until after the German Revolution. Immediately after the Russian Revolution, the left launched a campaign proclaiming that the time of irresistible democratisation had come – even referring to the breakthrough of *demokratism*, a term used positively by the Social Democrats and pejoratively by the right. Unlike Germany, all of the left, from the liberals to future communists, adopted 'the democracy of Sweden' as the denomination of their joint reformist bloc. Only the right remained outside in leftist discourse, which deepened the opposition between the reformists as democrats and the anti-reformists as anti-democrats but implied that the socialists recognised bourgeois reformists as equal democrats. This inclusiveness differed decisively from the Finnish Social Democratic understanding of themselves as the only democrats and facilitated discursive and other kinds of cooperation across the ideological divide.

In the Swedish constitutional debates, democracy nevertheless became a key term for all political groups from the right to the far left. I have shown that this has to do with a widely adopted but ideologically interpreted nationalist narrative of ancient Swedish democracy. Not unlike their counterparts in Britain and Finland, the theorists of The Right consistently claimed that the prevailing system already constituted a democracy in comparison with all foreign models and was evolving towards an even more democratic character without the need for further reforms; indeed, the extension of suffrage would even make Sweden excessively democratic by international standards. Democratisation required an advanced political maturity among the people at large, and hence a constitutional change would only become possible with further political education. Though anti-reformist and motivated by political theories shared with German academia, the Swedish rightist understanding of democracy did include an evolutionary element that was supported by an historiographical myth of native Swedish democracy and parliamentarism.

The Liberals in Sweden believed to a greater extent than their brethren in Britain, Germany or Finland in the democratic process as productive of a better society. This enabled them to join the socialist left in criticising The Right. In spring 1917 they agreed with Woodrow Wilson on the necessity of replacing Prussianism with democracy as the way out of the war, and in spring 1918 they already viewed Sweden as a Western democracy. This facilitated the change of sides with regard to political models. Cooperation with the Social Democrats was easy in that the latter had clearly turned to revisionism in their understandings of democracy, rejecting the tenets of an irreconcilable class struggle. For them the concept of democracy was essentially processual: universal suffrage would produce Social Democratic majorities, and consequent reforms carried out by the parliament would lead to the goal of democracy. They shared a leftist historiographical interpretation according to which Swedish political culture had been democratic for nearly a thousand years. Their leader Hjalmar Branting defined democratisation as 'democratic equality with respect to the public affairs of the state and the community'. He welcomed a *revision* towards Western democracy and denounced Russian and Finnish revolutionary versions of democracy. This democracy would be much more moderate than that of the far left, for whom democracy stood for a new socialist political order achieved through immediate constitutional reforms that would abolish the monarchy and the upper house and implement direct democracy. However, even the far left generally prioritised reform over revolution as the way to achieve democracy. They shared with the Finnish socialists a critical attitude to Western varieties of democracy, and an idealisation of the Swiss system as an alternative to the shortcoming of 'Western' democracy. They also entertained an understanding of the first Finnish parliament of 1917 as a 'complete democracy' and voiced expressions of support for the Finnish radical Marxist concept of democracy during the Finnish Civil War.

The practical parliamentarisation of the Swedish government in autumn 1917 supported conceptions of the First World War and the constitutional struggle at home as a battle between Prussianism and democracy, with the Liberal-Social Democratic coalition, which wished to see Sweden move over to the democratic Western side. It also increased Social Democratic optimism about achieving reforms and democracy in a parliamentary way. The Social Democrats consequently denounced the Red rising in Finland as a violation of the principles of democracy, which caused the far left to accuse them of capitulating to 'bourgeois' democracy. For the Social Democrats, democracy realised through equal parliamentary representation remained the key concept of their reformist discourse. Even in spring 1918, The Right still sought support against the reform from classical political thought and the situation in other European countries (especially Finland), where democracy seemed to be on the retreat. The cases of Finland as another Sweden and Sweden as another Germany should clearly be considered more profoundly in Swedish historical research.

Towards the end of 1918, the surrounding reality changed dramatically as a result of the German Revolution. The Swedish reform was brought forward with an extensive extra-parliamentary campaign for *folkstyre* (rule by the people, cf. *Volksherrschaft*). This reflected the revolutionary development in Germany, and it emphasised, again, the irresistibility of the ongoing pan-European transition. A party-political compromise was reached between the reformists and The Right, but I have demonstrated how the discursive battles over democracy continued in the parliament. The Social Democrats, encouraged by the success of their brethren in Germany, tended to monopolise democracy and went on excluding The Right as an undemocratic force that merely cynically abused the term. The reform had its limits but these would be compensated for by future progress towards Social Democracy; even the ultimate goal of socialism was proclaimed more openly now that a breakthrough was at hand. The Right, on the other hand, emphasised the mature nature of 'Swedish democracy' as being capable of solving national problems. Some Liberals also liked to nationalise the concept, while others favoured a processual and dynamic concept that might include connected social reforms.

Few rightists moved discursively to the side of democracy; most continued to obstruct the reform with procedural points, redescribe Sweden as a democracy and themselves as democrats, distinguish between good and bad democracy, express doubts about the 'democratic' future, put forward downright anti-democratic ideas or just remain silent. Even the few spokesmen for compromise preferred nineteenth-century informed democracy to what they saw as a degeneration resulting from easiness by which the masses could be manipulated. It was only the need to oppose Bolshevism that encouraged them to envisage concessions, and they stipulated that these should be accompanied with education of the people to wield 'the rule by the people' in senses not so different from those attached to the concept by their counterparts in Germany and Finland. The radicalised far left, by contrast, profiled themselves as opponents of 'bourgeois democracy' and, motivated by German examples, proponents of the radical Marxist notion of complete political, economic and social 'real' democracy. Their socialist republic would now be created outside the parliament and through revolution if necessary.

The comparative analysis shows that the intensity and confrontational character of the Finnish debate on democracy was unique in comparison with the other three parliaments, which suggests that the Civil War which the country experienced in spring 1918 is partly explained by the heat of this ideological confrontation. While the Germans and Swedes sometimes used vernacular translations for democracy, the Finnish word *kansanvalta* was more widely used and could convey particular connotations such as the community of the people or the rule by the Finnish-speaking majority, the common people or the proletariat. The Finns did not generally view the First World War as a battle for democracy; instead, they conceptualised their internal constitutional strife as one concerning the proper nature of democracy.

The findings of this study, opening the logic of socialist parliamentary discourse in Finland, question interpretations of the Finnish Social Democratic Party as having held a purely Kautskyist concept of democracy and being driven into a civil war unwillingly only by prevailing socio-economic circumstances and the radicalisation of the masses. The consideration of the discursive aspect of parliamentary politics demonstrates that the party tended to increasingly adopt the Russian revolutionary, even Bolshevist-like, understanding of democracy, which emphasised class divisions and saw democracy and the bourgeoisie as necessarily opposite forces. Social Democrat MPs frequently defined parliamentary democracy, social democracy and the rule by the proletariat as identical and excluded all non-socialist groups from cooperation in the construction of democracy. In the other three national parliaments, by contrast, the majority socialists typically aimed at cooperation with liberal reformists, recognising them as democrats. The concept of democracy used by the Finnish Social Democratic Party during 1917 was exceptionally exclusive and divisive, resembling that of Russian revolutionary discourse, which to a large extent explains the ideological confrontation leading to the Civil War, particularly as the centre and the right concluded that the Social Democrats had adopted the Bolshevik concept of revolutionary democracy. The non-socialist Agrarians spoke enthusiastically for the rule by the people but wished to retain the duality of government; the liberals feared that democracy had been hijacked by the socialists; and the conservative Finnish Party saw limitations to parliamentarism as a condition for the establishment of the rule by the people. The Swedish People's Party refrained from expressing its scepticism about democracy at the time of the declaration of independence.

In the aftermath of the Bolshevik Revolution, the confrontation on democracy deepened further. While the Social Democrats endeavoured to monopolise the concept, some bourgeois speakers defended alternative understandings. The Social Democrats insisted that the bourgeoisie had launched a class war aimed at destroying the rule by the people (or of the proletariat) and were only abusing the concept of democracy in their claims. Themselves, they demanded the immediate democratisation of society at all levels, represented Bolshevik rule as 'genuine democracy' and rejected defences of parliamentary democracy as generally understood in Western Europe: only a parliament with a socialist majority and a constitution based on socialist principles deserved to be called democratic. In rightist responses, the established system and the proposed new constitution were typically presented as democratic, and the bourgeois coalition set democracy as its constitutional goal, defining itself as an opponent of socialist policies of terror and envisioning a bourgeois democracy in which parliamentary power would remain regulated. However, the centre and the right held different conceptions about what constituted proper democracy: the centre considered that democracy lay in the Finnish people, while the right remained committed to the eighteenth-century constitutionalist tradition, which regarded excessive popular power with suspicion. Finding a common discourse on democracy with the socialists turned out to be impossible, and a civil war followed. During the hostilities, the Red government issued a constitutional proposal built on the notion that the rule by workers constituted democracy and denounced 'bourgeois' or 'Western' democracy.

This wartime propaganda of the defeated Reds, together with the political process that had led to the civil war, supported the association of democracy with socialist extremism among the centre and the right. German support for the White regime offered a chance to restore the traditional monarchical political order as a reaction to what was seen as extreme democracy. In the post-war situation, even many liberals favoured the German constitutional model over that of the Entente. Socialist views did not count as nearly all Social Democrats were excluded from the parliament. Even so, there followed fierce disputes between the monarchists and the republicans over the proper extent of popular power. The conservatives and some liberals redescribed the existing state of affairs as constitutive of democracy and asserted that a monarchy, too, would be reconcilable with democracy. This reflects the fact that they accepted democracy in the sense of universal suffrage as necessary for a modern polity even if their intention was to limit it into a mere formality. The conservative prime minister actually doubted the desire of the Finns to establish democracy, and MPs from the Swedish People's Party opposed parliamentary democracy as practised in the Finnish unicameral form. The Agrarians and some liberals, by contrast, demanded the rule by the people, claiming that it was justified by the national character, the nation's developed political culture, a civil war fought to defend democracy and an international trend of democratisation that was unstoppable. They contrasted the perverted democracy of Bolshevism with the Nordic tradition of peasant democracy and rejected monarchy as being opposed to the principles of the rule by the people. This confrontation ended with a further impasse when the monarchical project failed along with the German Revolution, the Finnish debate remaining dependent on the course of international politics and competing political groups making opportunistic use of chances opened by it.

In spring 1919, however, the Finnish parliament managed to discover a spirit of reconciliation under external pressures. Class-based arguments were gradually replaced by views searching for a compromise with representative democracy limited by a strong presidency. Centrists who denounced both leftist and rightist class interests, moderates among the Social Democrats and compromise-minded politicians within the National Coalition Party played a key role in the process. The centrists continued to emphasise the democratic awareness of the Finns as demonstrated in their will for independence and their readiness to defend democracy in the Civil War and referred to an international democratic moment that Finland was compelled to join, envisioned progress towards a more advanced democracy and challenged the rightist anti-democratic attitudes as outdated elitism. The Social Democratic Party – or at least its prominent spokesmen in the parliament – rethought its attitude towards 'peasant' and 'bourgeois democracy', recognising the possibility of cooperating with those who held different understandings of democracy under a constitution that appeared to be democratic at least as far as procedures was concerned. Many Finnish-speaking conservatives who were also academics (ab)used their authority to express doubts about democracy, which reflected continuity in conservative transnational ways of thinking, but nevertheless voted for the compromise once it included a sufficiently strong presidency. The Swedish People's Party, by contrast, remained relentlessly anti-democratic. This party would become an advocate of liberal values only much later.

Divergent conceptions about the people were used to motivate different views about their political role everywhere. Not all conservatives were equally sceptical about the political potential of the people: many members of the British Conservative Party viewed the contribution of the lower classes to the war positively and expressed respect for the political capabilities of the people, arguing for a reform in response to popular expectations. They believed that redefining the relationship between the people and the state through universal suffrage would maintain and help to restore the diminished legitimacy of the parliamentary system.[2667] They could even find a common goal with the Labour Party, with whom they had cooperated in the War Cabinet, in calling for 'a Parliament of the people', as well as with the Liberals, some of whom expressed a vision of 'government for the people and by the people'. This was a unique crossing of the ideological divide in comparison with the German, Swedish and Finnish conservatives, and also

---

2667 Müller 2002, 359, has drawn a similar conclusion when comparing nationalistic wartime discourse in Britain and Germany.

in British history. It was built on the exceptional wartime notion of the unity of the nation, some Conservatives using nationalist rhetoric to persuade their party fellows and ignoring the potentially radical implications of democracy. Even though gendered descriptions of the political system remained dominant, a readiness to allow women to vote prevailed in the Lords as well, which set an important example for Continental bicameral parliaments deliberating the same question.

Wartime patriotism had revived traditional appeals to the people as an authority in Germany as well. The reformist parties in the Reichstag and indirectly even the Chancellor recognised the contributions of the people to the war, emphasising the need to increase their opportunities for participation. Despite the weaknesses of the Reichstag, parliamentary debates deserve more attention in reconstructions of prevalent views than has been the case in German historiography; in them we can find links between British and German reform debates that the German right would later abuse against democracy. From March 1917 onwards, the Social Democrats recalled the role of the Reichstag as the voice of the German people, emphasising that rising popular discontent could be appeased only by reforming the Prussian suffrage system. The far left, inspired by the Russian Revolution, pointed more openly to the readiness of the people for action to advance their rights. The centrist parties, too, joined in the argumentation for the political mobilisation of the people for the war effort, although they avoided open advocacy of popular sovereignty. The right, while strongly cherishing a concept of a community of the people, prioritised the monarchy as the way to express the popular will.

With the monarchical polity already in decline in autumn 1918, arguments for a government based on the will of the majority of the people strengthened, especially in Social Democratic discourse. A peculiar conceptualisation of democracy – one that was transferred to contemporary Swedish and Finnish discourses as well – was provided at this time by the expression *der deutsche Volksstaat* (the German state of the people), which emphasised the unity of the people and the state. Even reformist socialists and liberals used this to nationalise democracy as a kind of *Volksgemeinschaft*, a community of the people, as opposed to Western democracy (something that the Nazis would later exploit). The right interpreted all vindications of democracy as contempt for the heroic German people, but the prevalent notion of a *Volksgemeinschaft* tended to make the concept of the people in a nationalistic sense dominate over democracy and parliamentarism to an extent not seen in Sweden and Finland. The idea of popular power remained an object of constant dispute in the Weimar Republic. In the Weimar Assembly, only the Social Democrats and the left-liberals emphasised popular sovereignty as being expressed by the parliamentary majority, often with vocabulary distinguishing the German popular government from the Western type, and introducing alternative expressions of the popular will, including the referendum and a strong presidency.

Germanic conceptions of the people found their way to the north as well. However, one feature distinguishing Swedish and Finnish political concepts of the people from the British and German ones is the politicisation of the notion of the ancient liberty of the peasant estate. The Swedish right denied the need for reform by arguing that the people proper (the common people, the peasantry in the sense of the early modern estate society) did not call for one, that 'the people' of the Social Democrats only represented the interests of the working class and that extended suffrage did not serve the interests of the 'realm', to which the interests of the people remained subordinated. The people were regarded as subject to leftist abuse, and women were not included in the Swedish people in a political sense. Nevertheless, some rightist suggestions about the need for concessions to save the state were heard, which reflects a gradual rethinking on the right that entertained the possibility of reform. The left, by contrast, called for the restoration of the ancient peasant liberty and emphasised the identity of the people and the realm, employing the German term 'state of the people' (*folkstat*) to make this point. The far left spoke for the activation of the people and emphasised the popular readiness for mass action, whereas the Social Democrats wanted to make the parliament a more accurate voice of the people, hinting occasionally at the possibility of an extra-parliamentary popular rising should the upper chamber obstruct the reform. At the time of the breakthrough of the reform, the Social Democrats described 'the informed democratic will of the people' as the hope of the Swedish state and the world and emphasised the universal right of the people to participate in the administration of the state. The Liberals, too, prioritised the sovereignty of the people over that of the state and welcomed the political activation of the people – to a greater extent than in the countries of comparison.

Nearly all the Swedish parties rejected the Finnish Red concept of the people as being a Bolshevist notion, standing for the dictatorship of the proletariat. I have shown how the discourse of the Finnish Social Democrats had tended to monopolise 'the people' in 1917, regarding only their party as voicing the wishes of the lower classes, the core of the Finnish people; this created a division between the people proper and the educated classes resembling the use of the concept of *narod* in Russian revolutionary discourse which had more impact on Finland than has been generally recognised. Such a definition was consistently questioned by the centre and the right, who, having ensured a bourgeois parliamentary majority, emphasised the role of the parliament as the representative of the Finnish people, while the Social Democrats questioned this after losing their majority. At the time of the declaration of independence, however, all political groups except the Swedish People's Party were overwhelmingly optimistic about the Finnish people as a wielder of power and praised its political maturity. After the Civil War, especially clerical MPs of the Finnish Party and many members of the Swedish People's Party questioned the political maturity or the political culture of the Finnish people with regard to the introduction of democracy, parliamentarism or a republic. The religious castigation of the people as an argument against democracy in the Finnish Rump Parliament of 1918 was exceptional in comparison with the other studied parliaments. Both the monarchical right and the republican centre used organic analogies to refer to a mentally deranged socialist segment of the people to either justify a monarchy or to explain away the guilt of the people as a whole by claiming that the rebellion had been imported by Russian Bolsheviks and their Finnish followers, who had led the people astray. The Agrarians and some liberals reiterated their trust in the Finnish people, interpreting the Civil War as the defence of the rule by the people and demanding a role for the sacred will of the people in the formulation of the constitution. They emphasised the potential of political education for preparing the people to participate in the government of the state and rejected monarchy as totally opposed to the political character and experience of the Finns. I have suggested that the ability of the Finnish-speaking conservatives to re-find their trust in the Finnish people and to recognise their supremacy in a modern state more openly than The Right in Sweden or Germany was decisive in the formulation of the republican compromise in 1919. The parliament found a compromise in which the popular will was expressed through both the parliament and a presidency. The Swedish People's Party, by contrast, emphasised the existence of Swedish-speakers as a separate people in order to advance the status of the minority language and continued to entertain doubts about the excessive involvement of the Finnish masses in politics.

Were then parliaments capable of expressing the will of the people? Even if the status of Parliament in British political culture was stronger than in any other state and no MP problematised parliamentarism (the far left being left outside Parliament), the British political elite found a common wartime goal in the creation of a parliament that could be trusted by the people, who should not be allowed to reject parliamentary government and turn to direct action. The Conservatives were particularly concerned about the deterioration of the legitimacy of Parliament, and this concern offers a further explanation for their support for the reform. The War Cabinet consequently proclaimed its unreserved optimism about the future of parliamentary government, implying that the unity produced by the war effort would be perpetuated. Some Conservatives saw in a stronger parliament a counterbalance to the growing power of the executive, others tried to obstruct reform by questioning the legitimacy of the process on the basis of the prolonged legislative process and the lack of a public debate. The Bolshevik Revolution increased awareness of the political changes that universal suffrage implied, but Parliament was generally viewed as adaptable and capable of preventing a revolution in Britain. Many Conservatives spoke positively about the potential of popular government and emphasised the need to ensure that Parliament would maintain its dominant role in the future democratic system. This Conservative strategy proved successful, guaranteeing a gentler transition to parliamentary democracy than in Germany, Sweden or Finland, where the right was more sceptical. In Britain, the reform gradually won the support of a large majority of the old elite, maintaining the essence of the old constitution while democratising it to a degree sufficient to absorb post-war societal pressures. The parliamentary process proved able to handle ideological eruptions without them turning into cycles of mutual provocation.

The story of German parliamentarism would be very different, despite the strengthening role of the Reichstag in the pre-war political culture. All political groups continued to have their doubts about parliamentarism, especially in its 'Western' form, with even Social Democratic discourse traditionally distrusting the parliament as opposed to the people as a democratic political agent. For most non-socialist parties, the duality of government was a dominant *sine qua non*. The idea of introducing the parliamentary responsibility of the government was nevertheless brought to the agenda by the Social Democrats, the far left and some liberals in order to challenge Prussian anti-parliamentary views. A distance from the British and French types of parliamentarism was maintained even though the strength of those systems was admired by some Social Democrats. The centre parties were unclear as to what they meant by parliamentarisation: the right-liberals said that the German people had been trained politically by the war, while the left-liberals suggested intensified inter-parliamentary cooperation between the Central Powers as a way of mobilising public opinion transnationally. All such speculation was taken by the Prussian right as using parliamentarism, which according to them was declining in the West, to challenge the monarchy. The opposition demands and the vague reform promises made by the executive have sometimes been overinterpreted in German research as silent democratisation or parliamentarisation,[2668] particularly as the contemporary opposition press was enthusiastic about them, but this comparative study suggests that they did not really parliamentarise the conceptual world of the German political elite.

From October 1918 onwards, the government adopted parliamentarisation as its official goal in the hope of gaining better terms of peace. However, owing to previous doubts, war propaganda and wartime confrontations, parliamentarism remained a concept of fundamental contestation. The Social Democrats emphasised their belief in parliamentary democracy, increasingly in spring 1919, when they had a strong parliamentary presence, whereas the centre parties were not so certain about the applicability of the 'Western' concept: the left-liberals wished to retain a notion of democracy being constituted by popular and presidential interventions side by side with parliament, while the right-liberal leader lacked the backing of his party when he extolled British parliamentarism. The right refrained from all cooperation, regarding parliamentarism as a shameful replacement of the well-organised constitutional monarchy with the rule of the masses misled by political parties. Some on the far left also wished to demolish parliamentarism, but for very different reasons. Like 'revolution' and 'democracy', 'parliamentarism' remained a partisan concept in Germany held by Social Democrats and a few left-liberals; it did not become a concept shared by liberals and conservatives – to some extent at least – as would be the case in the countries of comparison.

Sweden and Finland turned to parliamentary government in the studied period, but the debate on its pros and cons continued with arguments drawn from the rival Prussian and British models just as the timing depended on the result of the world war. At the same time, the rise of the Bolshevik

---

2668 Müller 2014, 47–8; Leonhard 2014, 739, 763, for instance.

alternative made all sides clarify what they meant by parliamentarism and in the case of the right move gradually to its side. The theorists of the Swedish Right, echoing German political theory, consistently condemned Western parliamentarism as productive of an excessive concentration of power, rule by the masses and party abuses; they considered the established political system in Sweden a better version of parliamentarism. Leftist agitation had made people expect too much of parliamentarism, the weaknesses of which had been demonstrated in history and which was in decline internationally. As in the case of democracy, the left responded with the theory of an ancient native parliamentary tradition that just needed to be revived. The Liberals were ostentatiously in favour of British parliamentarism and eager to accuse The Right of anti-parliamentarism. The socialists were divided over direct versus representative democracy. The majority Social Democrats favoured parliamentarism as a political process productive of reforms once universal suffrage was introduced and the power of the lower chamber asserted, which caused the far left to accuse them of surrendering to bourgeois parliamentarism and to voice occasional calls for mass action. The Social Democrats profiled themselves as defenders of parliamentarism in Sweden, seeing it as a way to reform the international system as well. They opposed far-left anti-parliamentarism, implying that the rejection of their alternative might lead to the rise of Bolshevist extra-parliamentary activities. The division of socialists, parliamentarisation of government and connected promises of democratic reforms took place in Sweden at a decisive moment, preventing the escalation of the constitutional debate into violence, as happened in Finland. The Right continued to question the positive effects of parliamentarism and warned about extended suffrage leading to increased anti-parliamentarism. Their criticism decreased gradually, however, as a result of the outcome of the war, parliamentarisation in Germany and, perhaps, demonstrations from the Swedish left that they indeed favoured parliamentary methods.

The Finnish government was in principle parliamentarised in spring 1917, but the all-party ministry did not work in practice. There was no split of the socialists into supporters of parliamentarism and advocates of direct action, as there was in Germany and Sweden, and this led to the radicalisation of the entire party. A socialist parliamentary majority strengthened doubts about majority parliamentarism among non-socialists. The right idealised the duality of power in the inherited eighteenth-century constitution and the contemporary German and Swedish models. Mutual recrimination about breaking parliamentary rules tended to diminish the legitimacy of parliamentary procedures. In the aftermath of the Russian Revolution, the Social Democrats challenged the authority of the national parliament by calling their revolutionary organisation a 'parliament' and by presenting the soviets in Petrograd and the Finnish parliament as parallel institutions. Parliamentary work in a chamber with a socialist Speaker was affected by extra-parliamentary politics manifested in crowd demonstrations. This, together with a tradition of confrontational socialist agitation and constant revolutionary impulses from Petrograd, led to the further deterioration of parliamentary legitimacy. The Social Democrats attacked the bourgeoisie for the failure of parliamentary government, citing the frustration of their supporters with an unproductive parliament, emphasising their exclusive understanding of parliamentary democracy and social democracy as identical, and suggesting that further extra-parliamentary measures would follow. The deterioration of the parliamentary legitimacy was further acerbated when the Speaker of the parliament reconvened it after its dissolution. The dynamics of parliamentary discourse and the intentional deconstruction of parliamentary legitimacy during 1917 have not been previously much considered in Finnish research.

After the Social Democratic idea of a socialist-dominated parliament ruling the country came to nothing, the supporters of a parliamentary strategy were driven out of the parliamentary group for the new election or were not allowed to voice their opinions. The Social Democrats disputed the legitimacy of the new parliament, prioritising revolution over parliamentarism, since, according to them, the proletariat had given up their trust in the parliament and the party was not capable of, or responsible for, preventing the consequent extra-parliamentary action. The bourgeoisie was to blame: its policies had initiated a revolution, and it was accused of aiming at the destruction of all parliamentary activity. Moreover, bourgeois parliamentarism was declared to be an institution that was incapable of producing any reform and hence due to be destroyed by the masses in a revolution that would produce a socialist society. Crowd violence and a civil war against the parliament were presented as likely if the parliament failed to subordinate itself to socialist democracy. In autumn 1917, Finnish Social Democrat MPs contributed to the normalisation of violent political discourse by attacking all non-socialists as counterrevolutionaries and communicating their message to a larger audience through party papers which they themselves edited. No matter what has been maintained in much previous research, any Kautskyist conceptions of the parliament[2669] were taken over by more radical Marxist view of parliaments as mere forums for agitation.

The centre and the right in Finland, like many theorists and politicians in Germany and France, called for alternatives to extended parliamentarism as a way to express the will of the people. Some were sceptical about parliamentarism, using what they regarded as the unfortunate eighteenth-century Swedish experience of a ruling 'parliament' (the Diet) as a counterargument, wishing to retain the constitution that had emerged as a reaction to such rule and redescribing it as sufficiently parliamentary. Challenges by 'the workers' parliament' and demonstrators were denounced. When the legitimacy of the new parliament with its bourgeois majority was challenged by the socialists, even many members of the right defended the institution despite their remaining reservations about the proper extent of parliamentarism, an indication of an ongoing change of attitudes among them. Since, in parliamentary discourse, a civil war started to appear as possible and even inevitable, bourgeois MPs, too, began to give up hopes

---

2669 Kettunen 1986, 87–8, for instance.

of solving the crisis by parliamentary means, seeing the organisation of the White Civil Guards as necessary. All this facilitated a transition to the concrete use of violence.

After the Civil War, considerable limitations to parliamentarism were included in the monarchical constitutional proposals, the process that had led to the Civil War being interpreted as a demonstration of its detrimental character. While not completely questioning parliamentarism, most monarchists emphasised that a monarchy would counterbalance parliamentarism while still allowing it to exist; others, like Prime Minister J. K. Paasikivi, were openly hostile. The centre rejected monarchy, emphasised international progress towards parliamentary government and saw parliamentarism as the only way for the government to keep contact with the people and to reintegrate the socialists into the political system. In 1919, they stressed the progress of parliamentarism in Western Europe but proposed a presidency as a check on it in order to appease the right, who continued to oppose far-reaching parliamentarism of the type of the Third Republic, citing foreign literature that was critical of parliamentarism, although in the end they did accept a 'functional parliamentarism' – even quasiparliamentarism – regulated by a presidency. The Social Democrats were moving towards the acceptance of majority parliamentarism in the Western sense, distancing themselves from direct democracy but still opposing a strong presidency. To persuade the right, they referred to national traditions of popular representation and to the more trusting relationship between the people and the administration that Western parliamentarism would create. The Swedish People's Party remained openly anti-parliamentary, arguing against parliamentarism and organising a rival parliament to defend the interests of the linguistic minority and thereby challenging the national parliament.

It is time to assess the relative importance of international comparisons and transnational connections for the national processes of constitutional change in the late 1910s. It has become clear that foreign models were always selected, often tendentiously interpreted and deliberately applied in order to win arguments and extend political power at home. Nevertheless, alternative ideological transnational networks contributing to discursive transfers existed, on both the left and the right, and to some extent among liberals, too. Politicians from smaller countries were typically more transnationally connected and readier to use foreign examples in arguments than those of the more self-sufficient great powers.

The significance of interrelations between Germany, Sweden and Finland (and increasingly also Britain from late 1918 onwards) found much support in primary sources and biographies of the actors: comparisons between Sweden and Germany and Finland and Germany were particularly frequent in the smaller national parliaments. The international events of early 1917 increased transnational thinking everywhere. For Finland, eighteenth-century rather than contemporary Sweden was a major focus of comparison owing to the continuation of the old Swedish constitution there; for Sweden, the failed Finnish democratic parliament provided an essential warning example. Both countries turned increasingly to British models after the Entente won the war. In 1919, however, national debates interconnected by the war and revolutionary impulses faded away when the war was over and connections with Bolshevist Russia cut. Comparisons with other parliamentary democracies also decreased, the debates and the concepts used were increasingly nationalised, which left the mistaken long-term impression (also in national historiographies) that each reform had been a national affair only marginally influenced by what was happening at the same time elsewhere. This assumption clearly needs to be reconsidered and the interaction between the national and the transnational aspects and the temporal variation in their relative importance recognised, with the transnational predominating in 1917 and 1918 and the national again in 1919.

The British debates tended to be insular, ignoring any possible transnational connections even in late 1917, when constitutional debates had been going on in several other European countries for some time. British internationalism focused mainly on the Empire and on Britain as a universal model nation, although American influence is visible in the extension of discourse on democracy during 1917. Continental examples were rarely used, attempts by the supporters of proportional representation and women's suffrage to refer to Sweden and Finland being overshadowed by the opponents' use of warning examples. The transnational aspect nevertheless mattered. The prevailing attitude among the British Conservatives and Liberals towards democratisation in Germany was sceptical if not downright hostile, its honesty being doubted and an inclination to Bolshevism feared. Critical reports presented the Weimar Parliament as being different from Western parliamentarism and questioned the ability of the Germans to become a democratic nation, which only served to reinforce the anti-democratic stand in Germany. Doubts about the ability of the Finnish right to distance themselves from Prussianism, the socialists to denounce Bolshevism and Finnish society to survive its unprecedentedly violent class war were still strong in early 1919, although progress towards a republican constitution and support for British foreign policy interests restored some of the lost confidence later on.

Germany was subject to external pressures for reform arising out of Allied war propaganda, which, like German propaganda previously, emphasised the contrasts between the political systems. Germany remained a centre of rival transnational networks: that of the Prussian monarchical order as a model of a stable polity and that of Social Democracy – either in the sense of reformist parliamentary socialism or the establishment of the rule of the working class through a class struggle and revolution. Nordic liberals were also highly interested in German developments. In Sweden and Finland, the left and the centre (quite correctly) maintained that socialist internationalism was being countered by a transnational network of rightist capitalists, academics and bureaucrats, professors playing prominent roles. These networks have not been very extensively explored in previous research. Significant for German history would be the daringly open Social Democratic and liberal recommendations of the British system as a model for reform, which provoked the right to develop a conspiracy theory. Transnational awareness also figured interestingly in autumn 1918, when the parliamentarisation of the German government was at hand: the German left raised the issue of the persecution of workers in Finland, implying that the time for such Prussianism was over in Germany and suggesting that its application in Finland should likewise be brought to an end. The course of international affairs also famously directed the course of debates on the Weimar Constitution during 1919, the outer world being excluded from the nation-state-centred debates and the terms of the Treaty of Versailles decreasing German enthusiasm for a political change towards 'Western' democracy and parliamentarism.

The dependence of the Swedish constitutional debate on the course of the war and transnational debates became equally evident. Parliamentary debates and the press contain both insinuations and evidence of the existence of transnational connections between the Prussian and Swedish right; likewise the left, emphasising the inevitability of the transnational constitutional transformation, were inspired by the different stages of the reform demands of the German left to a greater extent than by the Russian Revolution. The Social Democrats even occasionally implied that foreign support for a reform initiated by the united left would be available. Finland provided a model of reform mainly for the far left, whereas the Social Democrats avoided all association with the Finnish socialists, and The Right used the Finnish development as a warning example. The Swedish Liberals, too, were more reformist and internationalist in their rhetoric than their brethren in the other studied countries. The Right, by contrast, denied the existence of transnational trends of reform and comparability with other countries, pointing out the problems in foreign systems and condemning the internationalism of the left with its inclination towards revolutionary or Anglo-American models. Rightist opposition to reform in Germany and Finland supported the continuation of the Swedish Right's anti-reformist stands.

The Swedish reform debates also referred to Finland, especially during the Civil War there. The bourgeoisie and the Social Democrats were to some extent united in defence of a 'parliamentary' and 'democratic' Finnish regime against 'Bolshevism', The Right moving rhetorically to the side of Finnish democracy, while the Social Democrats viewed the bourgeois Finnish government as based democratically on a parliamentary majority and saw the Finnish Social Democrats as promoting 'anti-democracy'. The far left saw the Finnish Civil War as a class struggle between the have-not working class and the haves, revolutionaries and counter-revolutionaries. When Prussia intervened in the fighting, the Civil War became part of an international ideological conflict. The defeat of the Reds made Finland an uncomfortable object of comparison for the left, the Social Democrats looking to Norway, Denmark and Germany for instances of democratisation and The Right exploiting the Finnish case to argue against universal or female suffrage. By this time, Hjalmar Branting had become an exceptionally well-connected transnational actor, and when talking to the Western press, he was able to redefine the course of Swedish politics from German influences towards

'Western democracy'. The change of sides over to Western democracy took place gradually and more distinctly in Sweden than in Finland.

Until the recognition of Finnish independence at the end of 1917, Finnish transnational links to Russia were strong, as visible in previous research. The participation in revolutionary assemblies by Finnish MPs and visits by Kollontai, Lenin and Stalin to Helsinki demonstrate their intensity. Lenin, who saw the Russian and Finnish revolutions as interconnected, was hiding at the home of a Social Democrat MP and was in contact with MPs who opposed bourgeois democracy and Western parliamentarism, sending letters to them calling for a revolution. Transnational links with Sweden, Germany and Britain existed among the socialists, but they were overshadowed by the links with Petrograd. The present analysis shows how the right presented Prussia as the model for building an ideal society, while the Social Democrats attacked Prussianism and overestimated the success of the reformist initiatives in Berlin as a demonstration of an international revolution in which they themselves were participating. In socialist parlance, the workers appeared as the defenders of global democracy against the bourgeoisie, who were part of a reactionary international. After the Bolshevik Revolution, these transnational discourses were further strengthened, the socialists looking for support from Russia and the bourgeoisie from Germany. Constitutional debates became transnational to an exceptional degree, and accusations of malicious transnational alliances for and against the Revolution and democracy were commonplace. The Social Democrats associated themselves with an international and more particularly a Russian class struggle and revolution, arguing that membership in the Zimmerwald International obliged them to take part in this 'last fight'.

In 1918 and 1919, alleged Swedish indifference towards the Finnish Civil War, the occupation of the Åland Islands and the deepening of language disputes in Finland reduced international comparisons and transnational connections between Sweden and Finland in an exceptional way. Sweden existed for the Finnish monarchists only in its eighteenth-century form. A strong consciousness of the significance of international developments prevailed in the Rump Parliament, but very different conclusions were drawn about the implications for the future constitution. Under the dominant influence of Germany and a one-sided public debate that favoured Germany, both the Western Powers and the Bolsheviks were rejected as models by the government. For the monarchists, Germany constituted the model polity in all areas of political life: the government justified its constitutional proposal with references to German political theory on constitutional monarchy and used anti-parliamentary quotations from Otto von Bismarck. Transnational interference from Germany was at times requested, and news about the German defeat and the initiation of parliamentarisation there were disregarded. Republicanism was associated with international socialism and rejected as a foreign import. At the same time, the republicans emphasized the republican, parliamentary and democratic features of the German polity and its likelihood to soon reform itself. They also defended the strengths of the French republican constitution, denying associations between republicanism and democracy on the one hand and Bolshevism on the other.

In spring 1919, the formation of the republican constitution as a compromise was discussed through international comparisons and was pushed forward by external pressures: the need to prevent a new Bolshevist revolution, the German example of constructing a democratic republic with a strong presidency, other examples of transnational democratisation and the readiness of the Anglophone great powers to recognise Finnish independence only after the Prussian alliance had been given up and a republican constitution adopted. While previous transnational connections were condemned and explicit references reduced, interest in the Weimar Assembly remained high and led to further conceptual transfers. Links with Bolshevist Russia were limited to underground communists. With regard to parliamentarism or a monarchical presidency, Britain, the Scandinavian countries (though preferably not Sweden) and the United States now served as sources of examples for all sides, and France and Switzerland for the republicans, even though there was a growing tendency to nationalize the constitutional question, just as in other countries.

Previous research in political history has mainly focused on the course of events at national, and especially governmental, levels without analysing interconnected discursive processes in parliaments and the press or making international comparisons between thematically, synchronically and ideologically parallel constitutional debates in various national parliaments or considering concrete transnational links between the national debates. Transitions to parliamentary governments based on democratic suffrage have consequently been seen as nation-specific, even if in the period 1917–19 such transitions took place simultaneously in several northwest European polities as a consequence of a total war that touched everyone and were evidently interdependent. The above analysis, while specifying the common and distinctive features of debates on constitutional reforms that were primarily nation-state-centred, has demonstrated the significance of transnational connections for the reform processes in all the studied countries and shown that competing transnational networks were of the utmost importance in smaller states such as Sweden and Finland and indeed also mattered in more self-sufficient great powers like Britain and Germany.

In Britain, the suffrage reform was to a great extent conceptualised as the evolution of the existing form of popular government to make it better able to respond to popular expectations in the post-war situation and to counteract any revolutionary developments. Imperial perspectives and conceptions of Britain as a universal model meant that there were few transnational transfers from continental Europe. The wider politicisation of 'democracy' during the war was avoided by the government through definitions of the war effort as a defence of democracy, which included the established domestic political order, but after the restoration of peace democracy tended to become politicised in domestic political contexts as well. Such special features of the British polity only become visible through comparison.

In Germany, the war propaganda of the Entente definitely affected debates on democracy, deepening party-political divisions in understandings of the concept. There seems to be no reason to claim that there was a process of wartime parliamentarisation in Germany despite the rise of reform demands during 1917: the demands were unspecific as to what parliamentarisation might mean and were accompanied with reservations from reformists of all parties. After the war, too, democracy, the political role of the people and parliamentarism were conceptualised in specifically German ways with both the reformists and their opponents delimiting the legitimacy of parliamentary democracy. Comparisons with Sweden and Finland – rather than with Britain only – are particularly enlightening here.

German wartime calls for reform affected discourses on democratisation and parliamentarisation in Sweden and Finland to a greater degree than has been previously acknowledged, which supports the impression of a transnational revolution. This study has shown that we cannot fully understand Swedish and Finnish constitutional history, especially in the late 1910s, without studying it side by side with German constitutional debates. German historiography, too, would benefit from comparisons with political systems that were in many ways similar to the German one, such as those of Sweden and Finland, rather than only with those of the other great powers with their rather different polities and traditions of political debate.

In Sweden, the First World War was experienced concretely as a constitutional battle that divided the ideological field to the very end. The victory of the reformist alliance, which was much stronger discursively than in the other three countries, also implied the victory of their interpretation of the national constitutional past and their vision of democracy as a parliamentary process leading inevitably to (social) democracy. However, it is important to keep in mind the contingency of the Swedish reform process as well as the influence of foreign powers such as Britain, Germany and Russia – and even Finland – in the formation of 'Swedish democracy'.

Parliaments such as the German and the Finnish ones, based on nearly universal suffrage but lacking real power, easily turned into forums of uncompromising and violent political debate, which – instead of solving societal problems through the parliamentary process of deliberation – added to the heat of the public debate, and thereby exacerbated the crisis. The Finnish parliament saw an exceptionally confrontational debate throughout the studied period but especially in 1917. This study has shown that the radicalisation of the Social Democratic parliamentary *discourse* – and the parliamentary politics of the Finnish left in general – as well as the discursive links of the right to Swedish and German debates have not been sufficiently considered in previous research together with other factors. While the path to the Finnish Civil War has been customarily explained from the point of view of social history by economic difficulties and class divisions,[2670] and while the Finnish case still appears problematic in international comparisons in the lack of a direct link between engagement in the war and the outbreak

---

2670 Kirby 1976, Alapuro 1988, Haapala 1992 and Haapala 2014, for instance. Reviewed in Liikanen 1993.

of a civil war, an emphasis on transnational links and the dynamics of political discourse offers an alternative, overlooked, explanation. The Finnish case evidently deserves more attention in comparative research given the exceptional degree to which the concepts of democracy, the people and parliament became subject to dispute there, as part of international constitutional and ideological debates applied to the Finnish context. On the other hand, the course of Finnish political history can be explained better in transnational contexts and with the consideration of the different justifications for their political actions which the rival sides expressed in the parliament. The impact of transnational revolutionary discourses was strongest of all in Finland, particularly as they reinforced an already existing Marxist discourse that was exceptionally confrontational. Transfers of revolutionary language from Petrograd and especially the Bolsheviks to the Finnish Social Democrats (as opposed to links between the latter group and revisionists in Germany and Sweden or rival Russian groups) deserve more attention in the analysis of the Finnish road to a civil war. The fierceness of the discursive class struggle in the Finnish parliament was unique in comparison with the debates in Britain, Germany and Sweden.

A consideration of the discursive dimensions of the debates in the Finnish parliament and the press leads to conclusions that differ from those drawn by above-cited scholars who have emphasised differences in Finnish Social Democratic and Bolshevik goals and support conclusions on the interconnectedness of Russian and Finnish radical discourses in the revolutionary situation of 1917 – though not denying longer-term ideological differences between the parties.[2671] I have shown in this study that, discursively, the Finnish Civil War already started in the aftermath of the October Revolution in November 1917. There is no reason to ignore this discursive confrontation as mere talk designed to put pressure on the bourgeois parties as the same violent discourse was heard from most Social Democrat MPs and was reinforced in the extensive socialist press. Furthermore, instead of comparisons with Eastern European countries, ones with states that shared legal and representative traditions of the Swedish and Finnish kind are needed – even though they may reveal some 'eastern' features in Finnish political developments.

This is not the place for an epilogue on the inter-war or post-Second World War crises of democracy and parliamentarism. Yet disappointments with the post-First World War rise of 'an age of democracy' and its consequent fragility remain evident. Parliamentarism became under attack by Carl Schmitt and others in a few years' time, and many new democracies were transformed to autocracies during the following two decades. Yet despite all the contestedness and fragility of democracy an evident change had taken place as a consequence of the First World War: even within autocratic

---

[2671] See Soikkanen 1961, Upton 1980, Kettunen 1986, Rinta-Tassi 1986, Zetterberg 1992, Hyvärinen 2003 and Siltala 2009, for instance.

regimes there was an increased need to construct political legitimacy through appeals to the people and to contest the meaning of democracy.[2672]

Whereas connections between war experiences and calls for reform and revolution have been pointed at in previous research,[2673] a more systematic interpretation of the post-war situation of 1919 in national and transnational debates on democracy, the people and parliamentarism offered in this book contributes to our understanding of the long-term pan-European conceptual histories of these key concepts of modern political cultures. It demonstrates both decisive breaks with predominantly conservative nineteenth-century constitutional debates and important continuities in the contestability and fragility of parliamentary democracy.[2674] The comparative and transnational perspectives reveal the particular dynamics of national discursive processes and their entanglements across borders. Diversified and competing understandings of democracy, the political involvement of the people and parliamentarism as the way of realising this remain decisive factors in present-day national, international and transnational debates as well, both in Europe and globally. In the years 1917–19 an evolutionary reform succeeded in countries where the conservatives concluded that mass democracy might serve their interests (in Britain and to a limited extent in Finland and Sweden) and where socialists and liberals were capable of cooperation at the decisive stages of reform (in Britain and Sweden, in Germany to a limited extent and in Finland from 1919 onwards). It failed where a readiness to adapt or cooperate across the ideological divide did not exist.

2672 Eley 2002, 3; Müller 2011, 3–5, 47.
2673 Müller 2011; Bessel 2014; Leonhard 2014.
2674 See Grotke & Prutsch 2014, Sellin 2014 and Stråth 2016.

Appendix: Selected key events in national politics

Year	Britain	Germany	Sweden	Finland	other countries
1905			Norway leaves the union	general strike	Russo-Japanese War ends with a Russian defeat; Revolution in Russia
1906				parliamentary reform: unicameral parliament and universal suffrage, including women; no parliamentary government	State Duma in Russia; Russian socialist parties struggle to control key concepts
1907			extensions of male suffrage	1st parliamentary elections produce a Social Democratic victory	
1909	People's Budget		universal male suffrage for the lower chamber; unequal suffrage for the upper chamber retained		
1910	general elections; Liberal ministry; threat to create new peers	proposal for the reform of Prussian suffrage withdrawn			
1911	Parliament Act		Social Democratic cooperation with reformist bourgeois groups	Social Democrats aim at seizing power from the bourgeoisie and carrying out a revolution	
1912		elections with high attendance; Social Democrats become the largest parliamentary group; warnings about *Kryptoparlamentarismus*			
1914	war against Germany; constitutional confrontations on the Irish Home Rule Bill left aside; party truce	war against Britain; *Burgfrieden*	monarchical intervention in politics; extraordinary parliamentary elections with constitutional disputes; pro-German neutrality; *borgfreden*	war economy; increasing Russian troops	
1915	War Coalition formed; debates on electoral reform in the Commons	some Social Democrats protest on the war; Preuß writes on *Volksstaat*			female suffrage in Denmark; Zimmerwald International formed
1916	preparations for extended suffrage	calls for suffrage reform in Prussia		elections produce a Social Democratic parliamentary majority after an election campaign reflecting class antagonism	February-December: Battle of Verdun

Appendix: Selected key events in national politics

1917	March: the 1st reading of the Representation of the People Bill
May: 2nd reading
June-November: committee stage
November-December: 3rd reading and Lords debates	February: unrestricted submarine warfare
March: intensified calls for reform of the Prussian suffrage
April: imperial promises for reform
July: Reichstag intervenes in foreign policy; anti-reformist reaction	April-June: demands for suffrage reform with increasing extra-parliamentary pressure
June: reform postponed
September-October: reformist election victory; parliamentarisation of government with a Liberal-Social Democratic coalition; reconsideration of pro-German policies	March: restoration of autonomy within the Russian Empire; constitutional strife begins
April: all-party government with a Social Democratic first minister
June-July: parliamentary sovereignty forced through by the Social Democratic majority
October: new elections produce a bourgeois majority
November: general strike; parliamentary sovereignty in a bourgeois form
December: declaration of independence and republican constitutional proposal to parliament; recognition by the Bolshevik government	March: abdication of Nicholas II and the nomination of the Provisional Government in Russia
April: Woodrow Wilson's speech on making the world safe for democracy and US declaration of war on Germany; Lenin's return to Russia
July: Bolshevik uprising
November: Bolshevik Revolution
1918	January-February: Lords debates and final amendments by the Commons; debate on democratisation focuses on Germany; politicisation of 'democracy' in the domestic context by the left
November: ceasefire
December: 1st elections with extended suffrage lead to a Conservative victory	September: defeat of the German army appears as likely; call for the parliamentarisation of government
October: parliamentarisation of the monarchical constitution
November: ceasefire; Revolution; abdication of Wilhelm II	February: debates on the Finnish Civil War
April: reform proposal voted down by the First Chamber
November-December: increasing extra-parliamentary pressure for reform after the German defeat; reform passed in both houses	January: German and Swedish recognitions of independence
January-April: Civil War between the Reds and the Whites ends with a White victory and prison camps
June-October: monarchical constitutional proposals in the Rump Parliament
October: election of Friedrich Karl of Hessen to the throne
December: abdication of Friedrich Karl	January: Woodrow Wilson's Fourteen Points
March: peace between Bolshevik government and Germany
1919	disputes on the implications of democracy at home; doubts about Finnish and German democracy	January: elections lead to a republican majority and the formation of the Weimar Coalition
February-July: the Weimar National Assembly debates the republican constitutional proposal
June: the Treaty of Versailles discredits democracy further
August: the Weimar Constitution comes into force	May-June: completion of the suffrage reform	March: elections produce a republican majority
April: British and US recognitions of independence
May-June: debates on a republican constitution end with a presidential compromise
July: republican constitution comes into force	

Bibliography

Primary sources

Allmänna Valmansförbundets valupprop, 1917. Retrieved from snd.gu.se/sv/vivill/party/m/manifesto/1917.
Bondeförbundets valprogram, 1917. Retrieved from snd.gu.se/sv/vivill/party/c/manifesto/1917.
Dokumente zur Deutschen Verfassungsgeschichte. Bd. 3, Deutsche Verfassungsdokumente 1900–1918. 1990. Ernst Rudolf Huber (ed.). Kohlhammer, Stuttgart.
Frisinnade Landsföreningens valprogram, 1917. Retrieved from snd.gu.se/sv/vivill/party/fp/manifesto/1917.
Hansard 1803–2005. Retrieved from http://hansard.millbanksystems.com and House of Commons Parliamentary Papers database.
Kansallisen Kokoomuspuolueen ohjelma, 1918. Retrieved from Pohtiva – Poliittisten ohjelmien tietovarasto at www.fsd.uta.fi/pohtiva/ohjelmalistat/KOK/52.
Kansallisen Kokoomuspuolueen vaalijulistus, 1919. Retrieved from Pohtiva – Poliittisten ohjelmien tietovarasto at www.fsd.uta.fi/pohtiva/ohjelmalistat/KOK/105.
Kautsky, Karl 1906: *Yhteiskunnallinen vallankumous*, translated by Väinö Tanner. Osuuskunta Kehitys, Pori.
Kautsky, Karl 1907: *Parlamentarismi, kansanlainsäädäntö ja sosialidemokratia*, translated by Erl. Aarnio. Arbetaren'in kirjapaino, Helsinki.
Kautsky, Karl 1918a: The Bolsheviki Rising. In *Weekly People*, March. Retrieved from https://www.marxists.org/archive/kautsky/1918/03/bolsheviki.htm.
Kautsky, Karl 1918b: *The Dictatorship of the Proletariat*. Retrieved from https://www.marxists.org/archive/kautsky/1918/dictprole/ch04.htm.
Kautsky, Karl 1919: *Terrorism and Communism*. Retrieved from https://www.marxists.org/archive/kautsky/1919/terrcomm/ch08b.htm.
Labour's call for the people. 1918 Labour Party General Election Manifesto. Retrieved from http://labourmanifesto.com/1918/1918-labour-manifesto.shtml.
Lords: House of Lords Hansard. House of Commons Parliamentary Papers database.
MacDonald, J. Ramsay 1919: *Parliament and Revolution*. In *The Socialist Library*, vol. 12. [S.n., s.n.].
Maalaisliiton ohjelma, 1914. Retrieved from Pohtiva – Poliittisten ohjelmien tietovarasto at www.fsd.uta.fi/pohtiva/ohjelmalistat/MAAL/270.
Mallock, W.H. 1918: *The Limits of Pure Democracy*. Chapman & H., [s.l.].
The Manifesto of Lloyd George and Bonar Law. 1918 Conservative Party General Election Manifesto. Retrieved from http://www.conservativemanifesto.com/1918/1918-conservative-manifesto.shtml.
Palmstierna, Erik 1953: *Orostid. Politiska dagboksanteckningar*, vol. 2: 1917–1919. Tiden, Stockholm.

Riksdagens protokoll vid lagtima riksmötet år ..., Första kammaren (FK). Riksdagen, Stockholm.
Riksdagens protokoll vid lagtima riksmötet år ..., Andra kammaren (AK). *1867–1948*. Riksdagen, Stockholm.
Sosialidemokraattisen puolueen ohjelma, 1903. Retrieved from Pohtiva – Poliittisten ohjelmien tietovarasto at www.fsd.uta.fi/pohtiva/ohjelmalistat/SDP/445.
Suomen kansanvaltuuskunnan ehdotus Suomen valtiosäännöksi. Esitetty työväen pääneuvostolle tarkastettavaksi ja päätettäväksi yleistä kansanäänestystä varten. 1918: [S.n.], Helsinki.
Till Sverges arbetande folk!, 1917. Retrieved from https://snd.gu.se/sv/vivill/party/s/manifesto/1917.
Till Sverges valmän!, 1917. Retrieved from https://snd.gu.se/sv/vivill/party/v/manifesto/1917.
Valtiopäiväasiakirjat (VP). 1908–1975. Eduskunta, Helsinki.
Verhandlungen des Deutschen Reichstags. Reichstagsprotokolle. Stenographische Berichte. www.Verhandlungen des Deutschen Reichstags.de/index.html.
Wavrinsky, Edvard 1917: *Den svenska riksdagens interparlamentariska grupp 1892–1917.* [S.n.], Stockholm.

Newspapers

Aftonbladet
Berliner Tageblatt
Dagens Nyheter
Freiburger Zeitung
Helsingin Sanomat
The Herald
Hufvudstadsbladet
The Manchester Guardian
Neue Preußische Zeitung [*Kreuz-zeitung*]
Social-Demokraten
The Times
Työmies/Suomen Sosialidemokraatti
Vorwärts

Literature

Adams, Jad 2014: *Women & the Vote: A World History.* Oxford University Press, Oxford.
Alapuro, Risto 1988: *State and Revolution in Finland.* University of California Press, Berkeley.
Alapuro, Risto 1990: Vallankumouskausi 1917–1918 vertailevalta kannalta. In *Väki voimakas, vol. 4: Suomi 1917–1918.* Juha Hannikainen, Markku Hyrkkänen & Olli Vehviläinen (eds). Työväen historian ja perinteen tutkimuksen seura, Tampere.
Alapuro, Risto 2003: Vallankumous. In *Käsitteet liikkeessä: Suomen poliittisen kulttuurin käsitehistoria.* Matti Hyvärinen et al. (eds.). Vastapaino, Tampere.
Andræ, Carl Göran 1998: *Revolt eller reform. Sverige inför revolutionerna i Europa 1917–1918.* Carlsson, Stockholm.
Anderson, Margaret Lavinia 2000: *Practicing Democracy: Elections and Political Culture in Imperial Germany.* Princeton University Press, Princeton.
Anon. *Seddon Cripps, 2nd Baron Parmoor. In* Parmoor and the Cripps family, 1970, http://www.friethhistory.org/Parmoor/020_ParmoorCripps.html. Accessed 26 June 2014.

Armitage, David 2004: Is There a Pre-History of Globalization? In *Comparison and History: Europe in Cross-National Perspective*. Deborah Cohen & Maura O'Connor (eds). Routledge, New York & London.

Aspelmeier, Dieter 1967: *Deutschland und Finnland während der beiden Weltkriege*. von der Ropp, Hamburg-Volksdorf.

Baldwin, Peter 2004: Comparing and Generalizing: Why All History Is Comparative, Yet No History Is Sociology. In *Comparison and History: Europe in Cross-National Perspective*. Deborah Cohen & Maura O'Connor (eds). Routledge, New York & London.

Ball, Stuart 1991: Parliament and Politics in Britain, 1900–1951 – *Parliamentary History* 10(2) 1991, 243–76.

Ball, Stuart 1995: *The Conservative Party and British Politics 1902–1951*. Longman, London.

Bavaj, Riccardo & Martina Steber 2015: Germany and 'the West': The vagaries of a Modern Relationship. In *Germany and 'the West': The History of a Modern Concept*. Riccardo Bavaj & Martina Steber (eds). Berghahn Books, New York & Oxford.

Becker, Jean-Jacques 2014. Heads of state and government. In *The Cambridge History of the First World War*, vol. 2. Jay Winter (ed.). Cambridge University Press, Cambridge 2014.

Berger, Stefan 1994: *The British Labour Party and the German Social Democrats, 1900–1931*. Clarendon Press, Oxford.

Bessel, Richard 1993: *Germany after the First World War*. Clarendon Press, Oxford.

Bessel, Richard 2014: Revolution. In *The Cambridge History of the First World War*, vol. 2. Jay Winter (ed.). Cambridge University Press, Cambridge 2014.

Beuerle, Benjamin 2018: Concepts of Democracy from a Russian Perspective: Debates in the late imperial period (1905–1917). In *Democracy in Modern Europe: A Conceptual History*. Jussi Kurunmäki, Jeppe Nevers & Henk te Velde (eds). Berghahn Books, New York & Oxford.

Beyme, Klaus von 1999: *Die parlamentarische Demokratie: Erstehung und Funktionsweise 1789–1999*. 3rd edition. Westdeutsche Verlag, Opladen.

Biefang, Andreas & Andreas Schulz 2016: From Monarchical Constitutionalism to a Parliamentary Republic: Concepts of Parliamentarism in Germany since 1818. In *Parliament and Parliamentarism: A Comparative History of a European Concept*. Pasi Ihalainen, Cornelia Ilie & Kari Palonen (eds). Berghahn Books: New York & Oxford.

Biewer, Ludwig 1994: Rudolf Nadolny und Ernst von Hülsen und die deutsche Patenschaft bei der Geburt des souveränen Finnland 1917/18: Eine bisher unbekannte Aufzeichnung vom Mai 1923 – *Jahrbücher für Geschichte Osteuropas* 42(4) 1994, 562–72.

Birgersson, Bengt Owe, Stig Hadenius, Björn Molin & Hans Wieslander 1984: *Sverige efter 1900. En modern politisk historia*. Bonnier fakta, Stockholm.

Blackburn, Robert 2011: Laying the Foundations of the Modern Voting System: The Representation of the People Act 1918 – *Parliamentary History* 30(1) 2011, 33–52.

Boden, Ragna 2000: *Die Weimarer Verfassung und die deutsche Außenpolitik*. Lang, Frankfurt.

Bogdanor, Vernon (ed.) 2003: *The British Constitution in the Twentieth Century*. Oxford University Press, Oxford.

Bogdanor, Vernon 2003a: Introduction. In *The British Constitution in the Twentieth Century*. Vernon Bogdanor (ed.). Oxford University Press, Oxford.

Bogdanor, Vernon 2000b: Conclusion. In *The British Constitution in the Twentieth Century*. Vernon Bogdanor (ed.). Oxford University Press, Oxford.

Bollmeyer, Heiko 2005: Repräsentative Partizipation? Parlamentskonzeptionen in den Verfassungsberatungen von Weimar 1919. In *Inklusion und Partizipation. Politische Kommunikation im historischen Wandel*. Christoph Gusy & Heinz-Gerhard Haupt (eds). Campus-Verlag, Frankfurt & New York.

Bollmeyer, Heiko 2007: *Der steinige Weg zur Demokratie. Die Weimarer Nationalversammlung zwischen Kaiserreich und Republik*. Campus-Verlag, Frankfurt & New York.

Borisova, Tatiana & Jukka Siro 2014: Law between Revolution and Tradition: Russian and Finnish Revolutionary Legal Acts, 1917–18 – *Comparative Legal History* 2(1) 2014, 84–113.

Borthwick, Robert 1979: Questions and Debates. In *The House of Commons in the Twentieth Century: Essays by Members of the Study of Parliament Group*. S. A. Walkland (ed.). Clarendon Press, Oxford.

Botzenhart, Manfred 1974: *Deutscher Parlamentarismus in der Revolutionszeit 1848–1850*. Droste Verlag, Düsseldorf.

Botzenhart, Manfred 1993: *Deutsche Verfassungsgeschichte 1806–1919*. Kohlhammer, Stuttgart.

Brandt, Hartwig 1998: *Der lange Weg in die demokratische Moderne: deutsche Verfassungsgeschichte von 1800 bis 1945*. Wissenschaftliche Buchgesellschaft, Darmstadt.

Brandt, Peter 2008: Vom endgültigen Durchbruch der parlamentarischen Demokratie bis zu den Anfängen des sozialdemokratischen Wohlfahrtsstaats – Nordeuropa in der Zwischenkriegszeit. In *Demokratie in der Krise. Europa in der Zwischenkriegszeit*. Christoph Gusy (ed.). Nomos, Baden-Baden.

Bruendel, Steffen 2003: *Volksgemeinschaft oder Volksstaat. Die „Ideen von 1914" und die Neuordnung Deutschlands im Ersten Weltkrieg*. De Gruyter, Berlin.

Brusewitz, Axel 1964: *Kungamakt, herremakt, folkmakt. Författningskampen i Sverige 1906–1918*. Prisma, Stockholm.

Burkhardt, Armin 2003: *Das Parlament und seine Sprache: Studien zu Theorie und Geschichte parlamentarischer Kommunikation*. De Gruyter, Berlin.

Carlsson, Sten 1985: *Den svenska historien, vol. 14, Från storstrejken 1909 till folkhemspolitik*. Bonnier, Stockholm.

Charmley, John 2008: *A History of Conservative Politics since 1830*, 2nd edition. Palgrave Macmillan, Basingstoke.

Chickering, Roger 2004: *Imperial Germany and the Great War. 1914–1918*. Cambridge University Press, Cambridge.

Childers, Thomas 1990: The Social Language of Politics in Germany: The Sociology of Political Discourse in the Weimar Republic – *The American Historical Review* 95(2) 1990, 331–58.

Close, David H. 1977: The Collapse of Resistance to Democracy: Conservatives, Adult Suffrage, and Second Chamber Reform, 1911–1928 – *The Historical Journal* 20(4) 1977, 893–918.

Cohen, Deborah & Maura O'Connor 2004: Comparative History, Cross-National History, Transnational History – Definitions. In *Comparison and History: Europe in Cross-National Perspective*. Deborah Cohen & Maura O'Connor (eds). Routledge, New York & London.

Cohen, Deborah 2004: Comparative History: Byer Beware. In *Comparison and History: Europe in Cross-National Perspective*. Deborah Cohen & Maura O'Connor (eds). Routledge, New York & London.

Collette, Christine 1998: *The International Faith: Labour's Attitudes to European Socialism*, 1918–39. Ashgate, Aldershot.

Colley, Linda forthcoming: *Wordpower: Writing Constitutions and Making Empires*.

Congleton, Roger D. 2011: *Perfecting Parliament: Constitutional Reform, Liberalism and the Rise of Western Democracy*. Cambridge University Press, Cambridge.

Cook, Chris 1988: *A Short History of the Liberal Party 1900–1997*, 5th edition. Macmillan, Basingstoke.
Cowden, Morton H. 1984: *Russian Bolshevism and British Labor 1917–1921*. East European Monographs, Boulder.
Crossick, Geoffrey 1996: And what should they know of England? Die vergleichende Geschichtsschreibung in heutigen Großbritannien. In *Geschichte und Vergleich. Ansätze und Ergebnisse international vergleichender Geschichtsschreibung*. Heinz-Gerhard Haupt & Jürgen Kocka (eds). Campus-Verlag, Frankfurt & New York.
Cunningham, Hugh 2001: *The Challenge of Democracy: Britain 1832–1918*. Longman, Harlow.
Fredrickson, George M. 1995: From Exceptionalism to Variability: Recent Developments in Cross-National Comparative History – *The Journal of American History* 82(2) 1995), 587–604.
Dahlmann, Dittmar 2014: Parliaments. In *The Cambridge History of the First World War*, vol. 2. Jay Winter (ed.). Cambridge University Press, Cambridge 2014.
Dodd William E. 1923: Wilsonism. – *Political Science Quarterly* 38(1) 1923, 115–32.
Dutton, David 2013: *A History of the Liberal Party since 1900*, 2nd edition. Palgrave Macmillan, Basingstoke.
Ehrnrooth, Jari 1992: *Sanan vallassa, vihan voimalla. Sosialistiset vallankumousopit ja niiden vaikutus Suomen työväenliikkeessä 1905–1914*. Suomen Historiallinen Seura, Helsinki.
Eley, Geoff 2002: *Forging Democracy: The History of the Left in Europe*. Oxford University Press, Oxford.
Endemann, Helen 1999: *Das Regierungssystem Finnlands. Die finnische Regierungsform von 1919 im Vergleich mit der Weimarer Reichsverfassung*. Peter Lang, Frankfurt.
Epstein, Klaus 1960: Der Interfraktionelle Auschuß und das Problem der Parlamentarisierung 1917–1918 – *Historische Zeitschrift* 191(3) 1960, 562–84.
Eskola, Seikko 2011: Suomi 1917 Ruotsin silmin – *Tieteessä tapahtuu* 29(4–5) 2011, 12–18.
Evans, Eric J. 2000: *Parliamentary Reform, c. 1770–1918*. Longman, Harlow.
Figes, Orlando & Boris I. Kolonickij 1999: *Interpreting the Russian Revolution: The Languages and Symbols of 1917*. Yale University Press, New Haven.
Friberg, Anna 2012: *Demokrati bortom politiken. En begreppshistorisk analys av demokratibegreppet inom Sveriges socialdemokratiska arbetareparti 1919–1939*. Atlas, Stockholm.
Friberg, Katarina, Mary Hilson & Natasha Vall 2007: Tankar kring komparation ur ett svenskt-engelskt perspektiv – *Historisk Tidskrift* 127(4) 2007, 717–37.
Fry, Michael Graham 2011: *And Fortune Fled: David Lloyd George, the First Democratic Statesman, 1916–1922*. Peter Lang, New York.
Fuchs, John Andreas 2008: Zu den deutschen Reaktionen auf die russischen Revolutionen von 1917 – Einblicke in Politik und Presse – *Forum für osteuropäische Ideen- und Zeitgeschichte* 12(1) 2008, 29–45.
Galembert, Claire de, Olivier Rozenberg & Cécile Vigour 2013. Faire parler ou faire taire le Parlement ? Les débats en assemblées politiques, des objets paradoxaux. In *Faire parler le Parlement : Méthodes et enjeux de l'analyse des débats parlementaires pour les sciences sociales*. Galembert, Claire de, Olivier Rozenberg & Cécile Vigour (eds). LGDJ, Paris.
Garrard, John 2001: *Democratisation in Britain: Elites, Civil Society and Reform since 1800*. Palgrave, Basingstoke.
Garrigues, Jean & Eric Anceau 2016: Discussing the First Age of French Parliamentarism (1789–1914). In *Parliament and Parliamentarism: A Comparative History of a European Concept*. Pasi Ihalainen, Cornelia Ilie & Kari Palonen (eds). Berghahn Books, New York & Oxford.

Gerdner, Gunnar 1946: *Det svenska regeringsproblemet 1917–1920: från majoritets- koalition till minoritetsparlamentarism.* Almqvist & Wiksell, Uppsala.
Gerdner, Gunnar 1954: *Parlamentarismens kris i Sverige vid 1920-talets början.* Almqvist & Wiksell, Uppsala & Stockholm.
Gerdner, Gunnar 1966: Ministären Edén och författningsrevisionen. In *Kring demokratins genombrott i Sverige.* Stig Hadenius (ed.). Wahlström & Widstrand, Stockholm.
Gerwarth, Robert & John Horne 2013: Kuvitelmien bolševismi: Vallankumouksen pelko ja vastavallankumouksellinen väkivalta 1917–1923. In *Sodasta rauhaan. Väkivallan vuodet Euroopassa 1918–1923.* Robert Gerwarth & John Horne (eds), trans. Tatu Henttonen. Vastapaino, Tampere.
Gerwarth, Robert 2014: The continuum of violence. In *The Cambridge History of the First World War*, vol. 2. Jay Winter (ed.). Cambridge University Press, Cambridge 2014.
Geyer, Michael 2011: Zwischen Krieg und Nachkrieg – die deutsche Revolution 1918/19 im Zeichen blockierter Transnationalität. In *Die vergessene Revolution 1918/19.* Alexander Gallus (ed.). Bundeszentrale für Politische Bildung, Bonn.
Gorham, Michael S. 2003: *Speaking in Soviet Tongues: Language Culture and the Politics of Voice in Revolutionary Russia.* Northern Illinois University Press, DeKalb.
Gottlieb, Julie V. & Richard Toye (eds) 2013: *The Aftermath of Suffrage. Women, Gender, and Politics in Britain, 1918–1945.* Palgrave Macmillan, Houndmills.
Götz, Norbert 2001: *Ungleiche Geschwister. Die Konstruktion von nationalsozialistischer Volksgemeinschaft und schwedischem Volksheim.* Nomos, Baden-Baden.
Götz, Norbert 2005: On the Origins of 'Parliamentary Diplomacy': Scandinavian 'Bloc Politics' and Delegation Policy in the League of Nations – *Cooperation and Conflict* 40(3) 2005, 263–79.
Green, Nancy L. 2004: Forms of Comparison. In *Comparison and History: Europe in Cross-National Perspective.* Deborah Cohen & Maura O'Connor (eds). Routledge, New York & London.
Grew, Raymond 2006: The Case for Comparing Histories. In *Modes of Comparison: Theory and Practice.* Aram A. Yengoyan (ed.). University of Michigan Press, Ann Arbor.
Grigg, John 2003: *Lloyd George: War Leader 1916–1918.* Penguin, London.
Gronow, Jukka 1986: *On the Formation of Marxism: Karl Kautsky's Theory of Capitalism, the Marxism of the Second International and Karl Marx's Critique of Political Economy.* Finnish Society for Sciences and Letters, Helsinki.
Grosser, Dieter 1970: *Vom monarchischen Konstitutionalismus zur parlamentarischen Demokratie. Die Verfassungspolitik der deutschen Parteien im letzten Jahrzehnt der Kaiserreiches.* Nijhoff, Den Haag.
Grotke, Kelly L. & Markus J. Prutsch 2014: Constitutionalism, Legitimacy, and Power: Nineteenth-Century Experiences. In *Constitutionalism, Legitimacy, and Power: Nineteenth-Century Experiences.* Kelly L. Grotke & Markus J. Prutsch (eds). Oxford University Press, Oxford.
Gruhlich, Rainer 2012: *Geschichtspolitik im Zeichen des Zusammenbruchs. Die Deutsche Nationalversammlung 1919/20. Revolution – Reich – Nation.* Droste, Düsseldorf.
Gullace, Nicoletta F. 2002: *"The Blood of Our Sons": Men, Women, and the Renegotiation of British Citizenship During the Great War.* Palgrave Macmillan, New York.
Gusy, Christoph 1991: *Weimar – die wehrlore Republik?* Mohr, Tübingen.
Gusy, Christoph 1993: *Die Lehre vom Parteienstaat in der Weimarer Republik.* Nomos, Baden-Baden.
Gusy, Christoph 1994: Die Entstehung der Weimarer Reichsverfassung – *Juristenzeitung* 49(15) 1994, 753–63.
Gusy, Christoph 1997: *Weimarer Reichsverfassung.* Mohr Siebeck, Tübingen.

Gusy, Christoph 2000a: Einleitung: Demokratisches Denken in der Weimarer Republik – Entstehungsbedingungen und Vorfragen. In *Demokratisches Denken in der Weimarer Republik*. Christoph Gusy (ed.). Nomos, Baden-Baden.

Gusy, Christoph 2000b: Fragen an das „demokratisches Denken" in der Weimarer Republik. In *Demokratisches Denken in der Weimarer Republik*. Christoph Gusy (ed.). Nomos, Baden-Baden.

Gusy, Christoph (ed.) 2008: *Demokratie in der Krise. Europa in der Zwischenkriegzeit*. Nomos, Baden-Baden.

Gusy, Christoph 2008a: Auf dem Weg zu einer vergleichenden europäischen Verfassungsgeschichte der Zwischenkriegzeit – Ein Tagungsbericht. In *Demokratie in der Krise. Europa in der Zwischenkriegzeit*. Christoph Gusy (ed.). Nomos, Baden-Baden.

Gusy, Christoph 2008b: Verfassungsumbruch bei Kriegsende'. In *Demokratie in der Krise. Europa in der Zwischenkriegzeit*. Christoph Gusy (ed.). Nomos, Baden-Baden.

Haapala, Pertti 1992: Valtio ja yhteiskunta. In *Itsenäistymisen vuodet 1917–1920, vol. 3 Katse tulevaisuuteen*. Ohto Manninen (ed.). Painatuskeskus, Helsinki.

Haapala, Pertti 1995: *Kun yhteiskunta hajosi: Suomi 1914–1920*. Painatuskeskus, Helsinki.

Haapala, Pertti 2010a: Jakautunut yhteiskunta. In *Sisällissodan pikkujättiläinen*. Pertti Haapala & Tuomas Hoppu (eds). WSOY, Helsinki.

Haapala, Pertti 2010b: Vuoden 1917 kriisi. In *Sisällissodan pikkujättiläinen*. Pertti Haapala & Tuomas Hoppu (eds). WSOY, Helsinki.

Haapala, Pertti 2010c: Sota ja sen nimet. In *Sisällissodan pikkujättiläinen*. Pertti Haapala & Tuomas Hoppu (eds). WSOY, Helsinki.

Haapala, Taru 2012: *'That in the opinion of this House': The parliamentary culture of debate in the nineteenth-century Cambridge and Oxford Union Societies*. University of Jyväskylä. Jyväskylä.

Haapala, Pertti & Marko Tikka 2013: Vallankumous, sisällissota ja terrori Suomessa vuonna 1918. In *Sodasta rauhaan. Väkivallan vuodet Euroopassa 1918–1923*. Robert Gerwarth & John Horne (eds), trans. Tatu Henttonen. Vastapaino, Tampere.

Haapala, Pertti 2014: The Expected and Non-Expected Roots of Chaos: Preconditions of the Finnish Civil War. In *The Finnish Civil War 1918: History, Memory, Legacy*. Tuomas Tepora & Aapo Roselius (eds). Brill, Leiden.

Hadenius, Stig, Torbjörn Nilsson & Gunnar Åselius 1996: *Sveriges historia. Vad varje svensk bör veta*. Bonnier Alba, Borås.

Hadenius, Stig 2008: *Sveriges politiska historia från 1865 till våra dagar. Konflikt och samförstånd*. Hjalmarson & Högberg, Stockholm.

Halonen, Mia, Pasi Ihalainen & Taina Saarinen 2015: Diverse discourses in time and space: Historical, discourse analytical and ethnographic approaches to multi-sited language policy discourse. In *Language Policies in Finland and Sweden: Interdisciplinary and Multi-sited Comparisons*. 2015. Mia Halonen, Pasi Ihalainen & Taina Saarinen (eds). Multilingual Matters: Bristol.

Harris, Robin 2011: *The Conservatives: A History*. Bantam, London.

Harvard, Jonas 2016: War and 'World Opinion': Parliamentary Speaking and the Falklands War – *Parliamentary History* 35(1) 2016, 42–53.

Häupel, Beate 1993: *Karl Kautsky. Seine Auffassungen zur politischen Demokratie*. Lang, Frankfurt.

Haupt, Heinz-Gerhard & Jürgen Kocka 2004: Comparative History: Methods, Aims, Problems. In *Comparison and History: Europe in Cross-National Perspective*. Deborah Cohen & Maura O'Connor (eds). Routledge, New York & London.

Haupt, Heinz-Gerhard 2006: Historishe Komparastik in der internationalen

Geschichtsschreibung. In *Transnationale Geschichte. Themen, Tendezen und Theorien*. Gunilla Budde (ed.). Vandenhoeck & Ruprecht, Göttingen.

Haupt, Heinz-Gerhard 2007: Comparative history – a contested method. – *Historisk Tidskrift* 127(4) 2007, 697–716.

Heikkilä, Jouko 1993: *Kansallista luokkapolitiikkaa. Sosiaalidemokraatit ja Suomen autonomian puolustus 1905–1917*. Finnish Historical Society, Helsinki.

Hentilä, Seppo 1979: *Den svenska arbetarklassen och reformismens genombrott inom SAP före 1914. Arbetarklassens ställning, strategi och ideologi*. Suomen Historiallinen Seura, Helsinki.

Hentilä, Seppo 1980: *Veljeyttä yli Pohjanlahden*. Gaudeamus, Helsinki.

Hentilä, Seppo 2015: Sosialismi tuli Suomeen Saksasta. In *Pro Finlandia. Näkökulma: Saksa, Iso-Britannia, Itävalta ja Unkari*. Jussi Muorteva & Pertti Hakala (eds). Kansallisarkisto, Helsinki.

Hentilä, Marjaliisa & Seppo Hentilä 2016: *Saksalainen Suomi 1918*. Siltala, Helsinki.

Hewitson, Mark 2001: The *Kaiserreich* in Question: Constitutional Crisis in Germany before the First World War – *The Journal of Modern History* 73(4) 2001, 725–80.

Hirschman, Albert O. 1991: *The Rhetoric of Reaction: Perversity, Futility, Jeopardy*. The Belknap Press of Harvard University Press, Cambridge (MA).

Hobsbawm, Eric 1994: *Age of Extremes: The Short Twentieth Century 1914–1991*. Michael Joseph, London.

Hornberger, Nancy & David Cassels Johnson 2007: Slicing the onion ethnographically: Layers and spaces in multilingual language education policy and practice – *Tesol Quarterly* 41 (3) 2007, 509–32.

Huldén, Anders 1989: *Finlands kungaäventyr 1918*. Söderström, Helsinki.

Hyvärinen, Matti 2003: Valta. In *Käsitteet liikkeessä: Suomen poliittisen kulttuurin käsitehistoria*. Matti Hyvärinen et al. (eds.). Vastapaino, Tampere.

Ihalainen, Pasi 2005a, *Protestant Nations Redefined: Changing Perceptions of National Identity in the Rhetoric of English, Dutch and Swedish Public Churches, 1685–1772*. Brill, Leiden & New York.

Ihalainen, Pasi 2005b: Lutheran National Community in 18th-Century Sweden and 21st-Century Finland – *Redescriptions: Yearbook of Political Thought and Conceptual History* 9(1) 2005, 80–112.

Ihalainen, Pasi 2009: Patriotism in Mid-Eighteenth-Century English and Prussian War Sermons. In *War Sermons*. Gilles Teulie and Laurence Lux-Sterritt (eds). Cambridge Scholars Press, Newcastle-upon-Tyne.

Ihalainen, Pasi & Kari Palonen 2009: Parliamentary sources in the comparative study of conceptual history: methodological aspects and illustrations of a research proposal. *Parliaments, Estates & Representation* 29 2009, 17–34.

Ihalainen, Pasi 2010. *Agents of the People: Democracy and Popular Sovereignty in British and Swedish Parliamentary and Public Debates, 1734–1800*. Brill, Leiden & New York.

Ihalainen, Pasi 2011: La Finlande de 1809 : une autre Suède – Le langage politique à la Diète de Porvoo à la lumière de l'éducation d'Alexandre Ier et du gouvernement representatif à la suédoise Alexandre. In *Frédéric-César de La Harpe 1754–1838*. Olivier Meuwly (ed.). Bibliothèque historique vaudoise, Lausanne.

Ihalainen, Pasi & Karin Sennefelt 2011: General Introduction. In *Scandinavia in the Age of Revolution: Nordic Political Cultures, 1740–1820*. Pasi Ihalainen, Michael Bregnsbo, Karin Sennefelt & Patrik Winton (eds). Ashgate, Farnham.

Ihalainen, Pasi & Jonas Sundin 2011: Continuity and Change in the Language of Politics at the Swedish Diet, 1769–1810. In *Scandinavia in the Age of Revolution: Nordic Political Cultures, 1740–1820*. Pasi Ihalainen, Michael Bregnsbo, Karin Sennefelt & Patrik Winton (eds). Ashgate, Farnham.

Ihalainen, Pasi, Michael Bregnsbo, Karin Sennefelt & Patrik Winton (eds) 2011: *Scandinavia in the Age of Revolution: Nordic Political Cultures, 1740–1820*. Ashgate, Farnham.

Ihalainen, Pasi 2013: From a Despised French Word to a Dominant Concept: The Evolution of 'Politics' in Swedish and Finnish Parliamentary Debates. In *Writing Political History Today*. Willibald Steinmetz, Ingrid Holtey & Heinz-Gerhard Haupt (eds). Campus-Verlag, Frankfurt & New York.

Ihalainen, Pasi 2014: Prospects for Parliamentary Government in an Era of War and Revolution: Britain and Germany in Spring 1917. In *The Politics of Dissensus: Parliament in Debate*. Kari Palonen, José María Rosales & Tapani Turkka (eds). Cantabria University Press, Santander.

Ihalainen, Pasi 2015: The 18th-century traditions of representation in a new age of revolution: History politics in the Swedish and Finnish parliaments, 1917–1919 – *Scandinavian Journal of History* 40(1) 2015, 70–96.

Ihalainen, Pasi & Taina Saarinen 2015: Constructing 'Language' in Language Policy Discourse: Finnish and Swedish Legislative Processes in the 2000s. In *Language Policies in Finland and Sweden: Interdisciplinary and Multi-sited Comparisons*. Mia Halonen, Pasi Ihalainen & Taina Saarinen (eds). Multilingual Matters, Bristol.

Ihalainen, Pasi, Cornelia Ilie & Kari Palonen 2016: Parliament as a Conceptual Nexus. In *Parliament and Parliamentarism: A Comparative History of a European Concept*. Pasi Ihalainen, Cornelia Ilie & Kari Palonen (eds). Berghahn Books, New York & Oxford.

Ihalainen, Pasi 2016a: European Parliamentary Experiences from a Conceptual Historical Perspective. In *Parliament and Parliamentarism: A Comparative History of a European Concept*. Pasi Ihalainen, Cornelia Ilie & Kari Palonen (eds). Berghahn Books, New York & Oxford.

Ihalainen, Pasi 2016b: 'Läntinen demokratia' Euroopan sisäisenä jakolinjana ensimmäisen maailmansodan lopulla. In *Länsi. Käsite, kertomus ja maailmankuva*. Jukka Jouhki & Henna-Riikka Pennanen (eds). Finnish Literature Society, Helsinki.

Ihalainen, Pasi & Satu Matikainen 2016: The British Parliament and Foreign Policy in the 20th Century: Towards Increasing Parliamentarisation? – *Parliamentary History* 35(1) 2016, 1–14.

Ihalainen, Pasi 2018: The First World War, the Russian Revolution and Varieties of Democracy in Northwest European Debates. In *Democracy in Modern Europe: A Conceptual History, European Conceptual Histories*. Jussi Kurunmäki, Jeppe Nevers & Henk te Velde (eds). Berghahn Books, Oxford & New York.

Ikonen, Kimmo 1995: Politiikan on palveltava sotilasjohtoa: Ludendorff ja Suomi 1917–1918. In *Niin tuli sota maahan! Sotien ja sotalaitoksen vaikutus suomalaiseen yhteiskuntaan*. Jari Niemelä (ed.). Turun historiallinen yhdistys, Turku.

Ilie, Cornelia 2016: Parliamentary Discourse and Deliberative Rhetoric. In *Parliament and Parliamentarism: A Comparative History of a European Concept*. Pasi Ihalainen, Cornelia Ilie & Kari Palonen (eds). Berghahn Books: New York & Oxford.

Innes, Joanna & Mark Philp (eds) 2013: *Re-imagining Democracy in the Age of Revolutions: America, France, Britain, Ireland 1750–1850*. Oxford University Press, Oxford.

Innes, Joanna, Mark Philp and Robert Saunders 2013: The Rise of Democratic Discourse in the Reform Era: Britain in the 1830s and 1840s. In *Re-imagining Democracy in the Age of Revolutions: America, France, Britain, Ireland 1750–1850*. Innes, Joanna & Mark Philp (eds). Oxford University Press, Oxford.

Jakobsen, Uffe & Jussi Kurunmäki 2016: The Formation of Parliamentarism in the Nordic Countries from the Napoleonic Wars to the First World War. In *Parliament and Parliamentarism: A Comparative History of a European Concept*. Pasi Ihalainen, Cornelia Ilie & Kari Palonen (eds). Berghahn Books. New York & Oxford.

Jansson, Torkel 2009: *Rikssprängningen som kom av sig. Finsk-svenska gemenskaper efter 1809*. Atlantis, Stockholm.

Jefferys, Kevin 2007: *Politics and the People: A History of British Democracy since 1918*. Atlantic, London.

Jörke, Dirk & Marcus Llanque 2016: Parliamentarism and Democracy in German Political Theory since 1848. In *Parliament and Parliamentarism: A Comparative History of a European Concept*. Pasi Ihalainen, Cornelia Ilie & Kari Palonen (eds). Berghahn Books, New York & Oxford.

Junila, Marianne & Charles Westin (eds) 2006: *Svenskt i Finland – finskt i Sverige*. Svenska litteratursällskapet i Finland, Helsinki.

Jussila, Osmo, Seppo Hentilä & Jukka Nevakivi 1999: *From a Grand Duchy to a Modern State: A Political History of Finland since 1809*. Hurst & Company, London.

Jyränki, Antero 2006: Kansanedustuslaitos ja valtiosääntö 1906–2005. In *Suomen Eduskunta 100 vuotta*, vol. 2. Edita, Helsinki.

Kaelbe, Hartmut 2001: *Wege zur Demokratie. Von der Französischen Revolution zur Europäischen Union*. Deutsche Verlags-Anstalt, München.

Kan, Aleksander 1999a: Hjalmar Branting, ryska demokrater och bolsjeviker år 1918 mellan den ryska oktober- och den tyska novemberrevolutionen – *Kungl. Humanistiska Vetenskaps-Samfundet i Uppsala Årsbok* 1999, 127–48.

Kan, Aleksander 1999b: Lenin, Branting och Höglund. Vad visste man inom svensk arbetarvänster om bolsjevikerna före Lenins sista Stockholmsbesök? – *Scandia* 65(1) 1999, 97–111.

Kan, Aleksander 2005: *Hemmabolsjevikerna. Den svenska socialdemokratin, ryska bosjeviker och mensjeviker under världskriget och revolutionsåren 1914–1920*. Carlsson, Stockholm.

Kekkonen, Jukka 2016: *Kun aseet puhuvat. Poliittinen väkivalta Espanjan ja Suomen sisällissodissa*. Art House, Helsinki.

Ketola, Eino 1987: *Kansalliseen kansanvaltaan. Suomen itsenäisyys, sosialidemokraatit ja Venäjän vallankumous 1917*. Tammi, Helsinki.

Ketola, Eino 1990: SDP:n itsenäisyyspolitiikka 1917. In *Väki voimakas, vol. 4: Suomi 1917–1918*. Juha Hannikainen, Markku Hyrkkänen & Olli Vehviläinen (eds). Työväen historian ja perinteen tutkimuksen seura, Tampere.

Kettunen, Pauli 1986: *Poliittinen liike ja sosiaalinen kollektiivisuus. Tutkimus sosialidemokratiasta ja ammattiyhdistysliikkeestä Suomessa 1918–1930*. Suomen Historiallinen Seura, Helsinki.

Kirby, David 1974: Stockholm—Petrograd—Berlin: International Social Democracy and Finnish Independence, 1917 – *The Slavonic and East European Review* 52(126) 1974, 63–84.

Kirby, David 1976: The Finnish Social Democratic Party and the Bolsheviks – *Journal of Contemporary History* 11(2/3) 1976, 99–113.

Kirby, David 1986a: 'The Workers' Cause': Rank-and-File Attitudes and Opinions in the Finnish Social Democratic Party 1905–1918 – *Past & Present* 111(1) 1986, 130–64.

Kirby, David 1986b: *War, Peace and Revolution: International Socialism at the Crossroads, 1914–1918*. Gower, Aldershot.

Kluxen, Kurt 1985: Britischer und Deutscher Parlamentarismus im Zeitalter der industriellen Massengesellschaft. Ein verfassungsgeschichtliche Vergleich. In *Deutscher und Britischer Parlamentarismus. British and German Parliamentarism*. Adolf M. Birke & Kurt Kluxen (eds). Saur, München.

Kocka, Jürgen 1996: Historische Komparastik in Deutschland. In *Geschichte und Vergleich. Ansätze und Ergebnisse international vergleichender Geschichtsschreibung*. Heinz-Gerhard Haupt & Jürgen Kocka (eds). Campus-Verlag, Frankfurt & New York.

Kocka, Jürgen 2003: Comparisons and Beyond – *History and Theory* 42(1) 2003, 39–44.

Kocka, Jürgen & Heinz-Gerhard Haupt 2009: Comparison and Beyond: Traditions, Scope, and Perspectives of Comparative History. In *Comparative and Transnational History: Central European Approaches and New Perspectives*. Heinz-Gerhard Haupt & Jürgen Kocka (eds). Berghahn Books, New York & Oxford.

Kolbe, Laura 2008: Helsingin valtaus 1918 ja muistamisen politiikka: vapaussota vai kansalaissota? In *Helsinki 1918. Pääkaupunki ja sota*. Laura Kolbe & Samu Nyström (eds). Minerva, Helsinki & Jyväskylä.

Koselleck, Reinhart 1972: Einleitung. In *Geschichtliche Grundbegriffe. Historisches Lexikon zur politisch-sozialen Sprache in Deutschland*. Reinhart Koselleck, Werner Conze & Otto Brunner (eds). Vol. 1. Klett-Cotta, Stuttgart.

Koselleck, Reinhart 1992: Volk, Nation, Nationalismus, Masse. In *Geschichtliche Grundbegriffe. Historisches Lexikon zur politisch-sozialen Sprache in Deutschland*. Reinhart Koselleck, Werner Conze & Otto Brunner (eds). Vol. 7. Klett-Cotta, Stuttgart.

Koselleck, Reinhart, Urike Spree & Willibald Steinmetz 2006: Drei bürgerliche Welten? Zur vergleichend Semantik der bürgerlichen Gesellschaft in Deutschland, England und Frankreich. In Reinhart Koselleck, *Begriffsgeschichten*. Suhrkamp, Frankfurt.

Krause, Hartfrid 1975: *USPD. Zur Geschichte der Unabhängigen Sozialdemokratischen Partei Deutschlands*. Europäische Verlagsanstalt, Frankfurt am Main.

Kühne, Jörg-Detlef 2000: Demokratisches Denken in der Weimarer Verfassungsdiskussion – Hugo Preuß und die Nationalversammlung. In *Demokratisches Denken in der Weimarer Republik*. Christoph Gusy (ed.). Nomos, Baden-Baden.

Kühne, Thomas 2005: Demokratisierung und Parlamentarisierung: Neue Forschungen zur politischen Entwicklungsfähigkeit Deutschlands vor dem Ersten Weltkrieg – *Geschichte und Gesellschaft* 31(1) 2005, 293–316.

Kujala, Antti 1989: *Vallankumous ja kansallinen itsemääräämisoikeus. Venäjän sosialistiset puolueet ja suomalainen radikalismi vuosisadan alussa*. Finnish Historical Society, Helsinki.

Kurunmäki, Jussi 2000: *Representation, Nation and Time: The Political Rhetoric of the 1866 Parliamentary Reform in Sweden*. University of Jyväskylä, Jyväskylä.

Kurunmäki, Jussi 2008: Different Styles of Parliamentary Democratisation in Finland and Sweden: An Analysis of Two Debates over Parliamentary Reform in 1906. In *The Parliamentary Style of Politics*. Suvi Soininen & Tapani Turkku (eds). Valtiotieteellinen yhdistys, Helsinki.

Kurunmäki, Jussi 2010: 'Nordic Democracy' in 1935: On the Finnish and Swedish Rhetoric of Democracy. In *Rhetorics of Nordic Democracy*. Jussi Kurunmäki & Johan Strang (eds). Finnish Literature Society, Helsinki.

Kurunmäki, Jussi 2012: The Lost Language of Democracy: Anti-rhetorical Traits in Research on Democratisation and the Interwar Crisis of Democracy – *Res Publica: Revista de Filosofía Política* 27 2012, 121–30.

Kurunmäki, Jussi 2014: Rhetoric Against Rhetoric: Swedish Parliamentarism and the Interwar Crisis of Democracy. In *The Politics of Dissensus: Parliament in Debate*. Kari Palonen, José María Rosales & Tapani Turkka (eds). Cantabria University Press, Santander.

Kurunmäki, Jussi 2015: How Women's Suffrage Was Devalued: The Burden of Analytical Categories and the Conceptual History of Democracy. In *Parliamentary and Democratic Theory: Historical and Contemporary Perspectives*. Kari Palonen & José María Rosales (eds). Barbara Budrich Publishers, Opladen, Berlin & Toronto.

Kurunmäki, Jussi, Jeppe Nevers & Henk te Velde (eds) 2018: *Democracy in Modern Europe: A Conceptual History*. Berghahn Books, New York & Oxford.

Lenman, Bruce 1992: *The Eclipse of Parliament: Appearance and Reality in British Politics since 1914*. E. Arnold, London.
Leonhard, Jörn 2001: *Liberalismus: zur historischen Semantik eines europäischen Deutungsmusters*. Oldenbourg, München.
Leonhard, Jörn 2002: Anatomies of failure? Revolutions in German history: 1848/49, 1918 and 1989/90. In *Ten years of German unification: transfer, transformation, incorporation?* Jörn Leonhard (ed.). Birmingham University Press, Birmingham.
Leonhard, Jörn 2006: 'Über Nacht sind wir zur radikalsten Demokratie Europas geworden'. Ernst Troeltsch und die geschichtspolitische Überwindung der Ideen von 1914. In *„Geschichte durch Geschichte überwinden": Ernst Troelsch in Berlin*. Friedrich Wilhelm Graf (ed.). De Gruyter, Berlin.
Leonhard, Jörn 2007: Politik – ein symptomatischer Aufriss der historischen Semantik im europäischen Vergleich. In *«Politik». Situationen eines Wortgebrauchs im Europa der Neuzeit*. Willibald Steinmetz (ed.), Campus-Verlag: Frankfurt & New York.
Leonhard, Jörn 2008: *Bellizismus und Nation. Kriegsdeutung und Nationsbestimmung in Europa und den Vereinigten Staaten 1750-1914*. De Gruyter, München.
Leonhard, Jörn 2011: Language, Experience and Translation: Towards a Comparative Dimension. In *Political Concepts and Time: New Approaches to Conceptual History*. Javier Fernández Sebastián (ed.). Cantabria University Press, Santander.
Leonhard, Jörn 2014: *Die Büchse der Pandora. Geschichte des Ersten Weltkrieges*. Beck, München.
Liebich, André 1999: The Mensheviks. In *Russia under the Last Tsar: Opposition and Subversion 1894-1917*. Anna Geifman (ed.). Blackwell, Oxford.
Lieven, Dominic 2015: *Towards the Flame: Empire, War and the End of Tsarist Russia*. Penguin, London.
Liikanen, Ilkka 1993: Skuldens långa skugga. Frihetskrigslitteraturens upprorsbild och dess senare skeden – *Historisk Tidskrift för Finland* 78(4) 1993, 562–79.
Liikanen, Ilkka 2003: Kansa. In *Käsitteet liikkeessä: Suomen poliittisen kulttuurin käsitehistoria*. Matti Hyvärinen et al. (eds.). Vastapaino, Tampere.
Linderborg, Åsa 2001: *Socialdemokraterna skriver historia. Historieskrivning som ideologisk maktresurs 1892–2000*. Atlas, Stockholm.
Lindman, Sven 1935: *Parlamentarismens införande i Finlands statsförfattning*. Almqvist & Wiksell, Uppsala.
Lindman, Sven 1937: *Studier över parlamentarsmens tillämpning i Finland 1919–1926. Med särskilda hänsyn till regeringsbildningens problem*. Åbo Akademi: Åbo.
Lindman, Sven 1968: Eduskunnan aseman muuttuminen 1917–1919. In *Suomen kansanedustuslaitoksen historia*, vol. 6. Eduskunnan historiakomitea, Helsinki.
Lindman, Sven 1969: *Från storfurstendömet till republik*. Ekenäs tryckeri, Ekenäs.
Llanque, Marcus 2000: *Demokratische Denken im Krieg: die deutsche Debatte im Ersten Weltkrieg*. Akademie Verlag, Berlin.
Llanque, Marcus 2015: The First World War and the Invention of 'Western Democracy'. In *Germany and 'the West': The History of a Modern Concept*. Riccardo Bavaj & Martina Steber (eds). Berghahn Books, New York & Oxford.
Lyon, Ann 2003: *Constitutional History of the United Kingdom*. Cavendish, London.
Machin, Ian 2001: *The Rise of Democracy in Britain, 1830–1918*. Macmillan, Basingstoke.
Macintyre, Stuart 1980: *A Proletarian Science: Marxism in Britain 1917–1933*. Cambridge University Press: Cambridge.
Malinowski, Stephan 2003: *Vom König zum Führer. Sozialer Niedergang und politische Radikalisierung im deutschen Adel zwischen Kaiserreich und NS-Staat*, 3rd edition. Akademie Verlag, Berlin.
Marjanen, Jani 2009: Undermining methodological nationalism: 'histoire croisée' of concepts as transnational history. In *Transnational political spaces: agents,*

structures, encounters. Mathias Albert et al. (eds.). Campus-Verlag, Frankfurt & New York.

McCrillis, Neal R. 1998: *The British Conservative Party in the Age of Universal Suffrage: Popular Conservatism, 1918–1929.* Ohio State University Press, Columbus.

Mergel, Thomas 2002: *Parlamentarische Kultur in der Weimarer Republik. Politische Kommunikation, symbolische Politik und Öffentlichkeit im Reichstag.* Droste, Düsseldorf.

Mick, Christoph 2014: 1918: Endgame. In *The Cambridge History of the First World War,* vol. 1. Jay Winter (ed.). Cambridge University Press, Cambridge.

Miller, Michael 2004: Comparative and Cross-National History: Approaches, Differences, Problems. In *Comparison and History: Europe in Cross-National Perspective.* Deborah Cohen & Maura O'Connor (eds). Routledge, New York & London.

Molin, Karl 1992: Historical Orientation. In *Creating Social Democracy: A Century of the Social Democratic Labor Party in Sweden.* Klaus Misgeld, Karl Molin & Klas Åmark (eds). Pennsylvania State University Press, University Park.

Möller, Tommy 2007: *Svensk politisk historia. Strid och samverkan under tvåhundra år.* Studentlitteratur, Lund.

Möller, Horst & Manfred Kittel (eds) 2002: *Demokratie in Deutschland und Frankreich 1918–1933/40. Beiträge zu einem historischen Vergleich.* Oldenbourg, München.

Möller, Horst 2002: Lassen sich die deutsche und die französische Demokratie nach dem Ersten Weltkrieg vergleichen? In *Demokratie in Deutschland und Frankreich 1918–1933/40. Beiträge zu einem historischen Vergleich.* Horst Möller & Manfred Kittel (eds). Oldenbourg, München.

Mommsen, Wolfgang J. 2002: *Die Urkatastrophe Deutschlands. Der Ersten Weltkrieg 1914–1918,* 10th edition. Klett-Cotta, Stuttgart.

Morrow, John H. 2004: *The Great War: An Imperial History.* Routledge, London & New York.

Müller, Jan-Werner 2011: *Contesting Democracy: Political Ideas in Twentieth-Century Europe.* Yale University Press, New Haven.

Müller, Sven Oliver 2002: *Die Nation als Waffe und Vorstellung. Nationalismus in Deutschland und Großbritannien im Ersten Weltkrieg.* Vandenhoeck & Ruprecht, Göttingen.

Müller, Tim B. 2014: *Nach dem Ersten Weltkrieg. Lebensversuche moderner Demokratien.* Hamburger Edition, Hamburg.

Muschick, Stephan 2001: *Für Schweden in Europa. Die diskursive Konstruktion europäischer Gemeinschaft im „Zeitalter es Nationalismus" (1890–1918).* Nomos, Baden-Baden.

Mylly, Juhani 2006: Edustuksellisen kansanvallan läpimurto. In *Suomen Eduskunta 100 vuotta,* vol.1. Edita, Helsinki.

Neunsinger, Silke 2010: Cross-over! Om komparationer, transferanalyser, *histoire croisée* och den metodologiska nationalismens problem – *Historisk Tidskrift* 130(1) 2010, 3–23.

Newton, Douglas 1997: *British Policy and the Weimar Republic, 1918–1919.* Clarendon Press, Oxford.

Nilsson, Torbjörn 1993: Forskning om svensk politisk historia 1866–1920. In *Svensk politisk historia. En kommenterad litteraturöversikt.* Britta Lövgren (ed.). Humanistisk-samhällsvetenskapliga forskningsrådet, Stockholm.

Nilsson, Torbjörn 2002a: *Guide till Sveriges historia i Europa.* Wahlström & Widstrand, Värnamo.

Nilsson, Torbjörn 2002b: Med historien som ledstjärna – Högern och demokrati 1904–1940 – *Scandia. Tidskrift för historisk forskning* 68(1) 2002, 77–107.

Nilsson, Torbjörn 2004: *Mellan arv och utopi. Moderata vägval under hundra år, 1904–2004.* Santérus, Tukholma.

Norton, Philip 2011: Introduction: A Century of Change – *Parliamentary History* 30(1) 2011, 1–18.
Nyman, Olle 1965: *Parlamentarismen i Sverige: huvuddragen av utvecklingen efter 1917.* Ehlin, Stockholm.
Nyman, Olle 1966: *Tvåkammarsystemets omvandling: från privilegievalrätt till demokrati.* Almqvist & Wiksell, Stockholm.
Nyström, Samu 2013: *Helsinki 1914–1918. Toivon, pelon ja sekasorron vuodet.* Minerva, Helsinki.
O'Connor, Maura 2004: Cross-National Travelers: Rethinking Comparisons and Representations. In *Comparison and History: Europe in Cross-National Perspective.* Deborah Cohen & Maura O'Connor (eds). Routledge, New York & London.
Olsson, Stefan 2002: *Den svenska högerns anpassning till demokratin.* Acta Universitatis Upsaliensis, Uppsala.
Palonen, Kari 2001: Transforming a Common European Concept into Finnish: Conceptual Changes in the Understanding of 'Politiikka' – *Finnish Yearbook of Political Thought* 5 2001, 113–53.
Palonen, Kari 2003: Politiikka. In *Käsitteet liikkeessä: Suomen poliittisen kulttuurin käsitehistoria.* Matti Hyvärinen et al. (eds.). Vastapaino, Tampere.
Palonen, Kari 2006: *The Struggle with Time: A Conceptual History of 'Politics' as an Activity.* LIT, Münster.
Palonen, Kari 2008: *The Politics of Limited Times: The Rhetoric of Temporal Judgment in Parliamentary Democracies.* Nomos, Baden-Baden.
Palonen, Kari 2010: Begriffsdebatten und Debattenbegriffe. Das parlamentarische Paradigma des Begriffsstreits und -wandels – *Zeitschrift für Politische Theorie* 1(2) 2010, 156–172.
Palonen, Kari 2012: *Parlamentarismi retorisena politiikkana.* Vastapaino, Tampere.
Palonen, Kari 2014: *The Politics of Parliamentary Procedure: The Formation of the Westminster Procedure as a Parliamentary Ideal Type.* Barbara Budrich, Leverkusen.
Palonen, Kari 2015: Skinner, Quentin (1940–). In *Encyclopedia of Political Thought.* Michael T. Gibbons (ed.). Wiley, Oxford.
Palonen, Kari, José María Rosales & Tapani Turkka 2014: Introduction: The Parliamentary Politics of Dissensus. In *The Politics of Dissensus: Parliament in Debate.* Kari Palonen, José María Rosales and Tapani Turkka (eds). Cantabria University Press, Santander.
Paulmann, Johannes 1998: Internationaler Vergleich und interkultureller Transfer. Zwei Forschungsansätze zur europäischen Geschicte des 18. bis 21. Jahrhunderts – *Historisches Zeitschrift* 267 1998, 649–85.
Pedersen, Susan 2004: Comparative History and Women's History: Explaining Convergence and Divergence. In *Comparison and History: Europe in Cross-National Perspective.* Deborah Cohen & Maura O'Connor (eds). Routledge, New York & London.
Pekonen, Kyösti 2003: Hallitseminen. In *Käsitteet liikkeessä: Suomen poliittisen kulttuurin käsitehistoria.* Matti Hyvärinen et al. (eds.). Vastapaino, Tampere.
Pekonen, Onni 2014: *Debating "the ABCs of Parliamentary Life": The Learning of Parliamentary Rules and Practices in the late Nineteenth-Century Finnish Diet and the early Eduskunta.* Jyväskylän yliopisto, Jyväskylä.
Peltonen, Markku 2013: *Rhetoric, Politics, and Popularity in Pre-revolutionary England.* Cambridge University Press, Cambridge.
Petrusewicz, Marta 2004: The Modernization of the European Periphery: Ireland, Poland, and the Two Sicilies, 1820–1870: Parallel and Connected, Distinct and Comparable. In *Comparison and History: Europe in Cross-National Perspective.* Deborah Cohen & Maura O'Connor (eds). Routledge, New York & London.

Philp, Mark 2013: Talking about Democracy: Britain in the 1790s. In *Re-imagining Democracy in the Age of Revolutions: America, France, Britain, Ireland 1750-1850*. Innes, Joanna & Mark Philp (eds). Oxford University Press, Oxford.

Pipes, Richard 1992 (1990): *The Russian Revolution 1899-1919*. Fontana, London.

Pohl, Tina 2002: *Demokratisches Denken in der Weimarer Nationalversammlung*. Kovac, Hamburg.

Polvinen, Tuomo 1971: *Venäjän vallankumous ja Suomi, vol. 2*: Toukokuu 1918 – joulukuu 1920. WSOY, Porvoo & Helsinki.

Polvinen, Tuomo 1987 (1967): *Venäjän vallankumous ja Suomi 1917-1920*. Vol. 1-2. WSOY, Porvoo, Helsinki & Juva.

Pombeni, Paolo 2005: Political Models and Political Transfer in the Shaping of Europe. *European Review of History—Revue européenne d'Histoire* 12(2) 2005, 223-38.

Pugh, Martin 2002 (1982): *The Making of Modern British Politics 1867-1945*, 3rd edition. Blackwell, Oxford.

Pugh, Martin 2011: *Speak for Britain! A New History of the Labour Party*. Vintage, London.

Pulkkinen, Tuija 1989: *Valtio ja vapaus*. Tutkijaliitto, Helsinki.

Pulkkinen, Tuija 2003: Valtio. In *Käsitteet liikkeessä: Suomen poliittisen kulttuurin käsitehistoria*. Matti Hyvärinen et al. (eds.). Vastapaino, Tampere.

Purvis, June & Sandra Stanley Holton 2000: *Votes for Women*. Routledge, London.

Pyta, Wolfram 2008: Antiliberale Ideenwelt in Europa bei Kriegsende. In *Demokratie in der Krise. Europa in der Zwischenkriegszeit*. Christoph Gusy (ed.). Nomos, Baden-Baden.

Pyta, Wolfram 2011: Demokratiekultur: Zur Kulturgeschichte demokratischer Institutionen. In *Demokratiekultur in Europa. Politische Repräsentation im 19. und 20 Jahrhundert*. Detlef Lehnert (ed.). Böhlau Verlag, Köln, Weimar & Wien.

Ragin, Charles C. 1987: *The Comparative Method: Moving Beyond Qualitative and Quantative Strategies*. University of California Press, Berkeley & London.

Räsänen, Iisa 1998: Järjestystä vai itsehallintoa? Vallan käsite Suomen hallitusmuotokeskustelussa 1918 – *Politiikka* 40(4) 1998, 263-72.

Rasmussen, Anne 2014: Mobilising minds. In *The Cambridge History of the First World War*, vol. 3. Jay Winter (ed.). Cambridge University Press, Cambridge 2014.

Rauh, Manfred 1977: *Die Parlamentarisierung des Deutschen Reichs*. Droste, Düsseldorf.

Recker, Marie-Luise (ed.) 2004: *Parlamentarismus in Europa. Deutschland, England und Frankreich im Vergleich*. Oldenbourg, München.

Reimann, Aribert 2000: *Der große Krieg der Sprachen. Untersuchungen zur historischen Semantik in Deutschland und England zur Zeit des Ersten Weltkriegs*. Klartext-Verlag, Essen.

Retallack, James 1988: *Notables of the Right: The Conservative Party and Political Mobilisation in Germany, 1876-1918*. Allen & Unwin, Boston & London.

Retallack, James 1996: *Germany in the Age of Kaiser Wilhelm II*. Macmillan, Basingstoke.

Retallack, James 2006: *The German Right 1860-1920: Political Limits of the Authoritarian Imagination*. University of Toronto Press, Toronto.

Rinta-Tassi, Osmo 1986: *Kansanvaltuuskunta punaisen Suomen hallituksena*. Valtion painatuskeskus, Helsinki.

Roitto, Matti 2015: *Dissenting Visions – Government, Parliament and the Problematic Anglo-American Atomic Collaboration in British Atomic Foreign Policy, 1945-6*. University of Jyväskylä, Jyväskylä.

Rose, Tania 1995: *Aspects of Political Censorship 1914-1918*. University of Hull Press, Hull.

Roussellier, Nicolas 1997: *Le parlement de l'éloquence : La souveraineté de la deliberation au lendemain de la Grande Guerre*. Presses de Sciences Po, Paris.

Rush, Michael 2001: *The Role of the Member of Parliament since 1868: From Gentlemen to Players*. Oxford University Press, New York.

Rydén, Per 2001: Guldåldern. In *Den svenska pressens historia, vol 3: Det moderna Sveriges spegel (1897–1945)*. Gunilla Lundström, Per Rydén & Elisabeth Sandlund (eds). Ekerlid, Stockholm.

Saunders, Robert 2013a: Democracy. In *Languages of Politics in Nineteenth-Century Britain*. David Craig & James Thompson (eds). Palgrave, Basingstoke.

Saunders, Robert 2013b: Tory Rebels and Tory Democracy: The Ulster Crisis, 1900–14. In *The Foundations of the British Conservative Party: Essays on Conservatism from Lord Salisbury to David Cameron*. Richard Carr & Bradley W. Hart (eds). Bloomsbury Academic, New York.

Saunier, Pierre-Yves 2013: *Transnational History*. Palgrave Macmillan, Basingstoke.

Schmidt, Gustav 1977: Effizienz und Flexibilität politisch-sozialer Systeme. Die deutsche und die englische Politik 1918/19 – *Vierteljahrshefte für Zeitgeschichte* 25(2) 1977, 137–87.

Schönberger, Christoph 2001: Die überholte Parlamentarisierung. Einflußgewinn und fehlende Herrschaftsfähigkeit des Reichstags im sich demokratisierenden Kaiserreich – *Historische Zeitschrift* 272 2001, 623–66.

Schönberger, Christoph 2009: Der Deutsche Bundestag zwischen Konstitutionalismus und parlamentarischer Demokratie. Historische und vergleichende Variationen auf ein Thema Gerhard Loewenbergs. In *Parlamentarismusforschung in Deutschland. Ergebnisse und Perspektive 40 Jahre nach Erscheinen von Gerhard Loewenbergs Standardwerk zum Deutschen Bundestag*. Helmar Schöne & Julia von Blumenthal (eds). Nomos: Baden-Baden.

Schöne, Helmar & Julia von Blumenthal (eds) 2009: *Parlamentarismusforschung in Deutschland. Ergebnisse und Perspektive 40 Jahre nach Erscheinen von Gerhard Loewenbergs Standardwerk zum Deutschen Bundestag*. Nomos: Baden-Baden.

Schuberth, Inger 1981: *Schweden und das Deutsche Reich im Ersten Weltkrieg. Die Aktivistenbewegung 1914–1918*. Ludwig Röhrscheid Verlag: Bonn.

Scollon, Ron & Suzie Wong Scollon 2004: *Nexus Analysis: Discourse and the Emerging Internet*. Routledge, London.

Seaward, Paul & Pasi Ihalainen 2016: Key Concepts for Parliament in Britain (1640–1800). In *Parliament and Parliamentarism: A Comparative History of a European Concept*. Pasi Ihalainen, Cornelia Ilie & Kari Palonen (eds). Berghahn Books: New York & Oxford.

Seils, Ernst-Albert 2011: *Weltmachtsstreben und Kampf für den Frieden. Der deutsche Reichstag im Ersten Weltkrieg* Peter Lang, Frankfurt.

Sellin, Volker 2014: *Das Jahrhundert der Restaurationen. 1814 bis 1906*. Oldenbourg, München.

Shipway, Mark 1988: *Anti-Parliamentary Communism: The Movement for Workers' Councils in Britain, 1917–45*. Macmillan, Basingstoke.

Sihvonen, Riitta 1997: *Valtaistuin vapaana. Kysymys korkeimman vallan käytöstä 1917–1919*. Eduskunnan kirjasto, Helsinki.

Siltala, Juha 2009: *Sisällissodan psykohistoria*. Otava, Helsinki.

Skinner, Quentin 2002: *Visions of Politics, vol. 1: Regarding Method*. Cambridge University Press, Cambridge.

Sluga, Glenda 2004: The Nation and the Comparative Imagination. In *Comparison and History: Europe in Cross-National Perspective*. Deborah Cohen & Maura O'Connor (eds). Routledge, New York & London.

Smith, Angela K. 2005: *Suffrage Discourse in Britain during the First World War*. Ashgate, Aldershot.

Smith, Jeremy 1997: *The Taming of Democracy: The Conservative Party, 1880–1924*. University of Wales Press, Cardiff.

Smith, Jeffrey R. 2007: *A People's War: Germany's Political Revolution, 1913–1918*. University Press of America, Lanham.

Söderpalm, Sven Anders 1969: *Storföretagarna och det demokratiska genombrottet. Ett perspektiv på första världskrigets svenska historia.* Gleerup, Lund.

Soikkanen, Hannu 1961: *Sosialismin tulo Suomeen: ensimmäisiin yksikamarisen eduskunnan vaaleihin asti.* WSOY, Porvoo.

Soikkanen, Hannu (ed.) 1967: *Kansalaissota dokumentteina. Valkoista ja punaista sanankäyttöä v. 1917-1918, vol. 1: Mielipiteiden muovautuminen kohti kansalaissotaa.* Tammi, Helsinki.

Soikkanen, Hannu 1975: *Kohti kansan valtaa. Suomen Sosialidemokraattinen Puolue 75 vuotta, vol. 1, 1899-1935.* Suomen sosialidemokraattinen puolue, Vaasa.

Soikkanen, Hannu 1990: Sosialidemokraattisen työväenliikkeen itsenäisyyspoliittinen linja. In *Väki voimakas, vol. 4: Suomi 1917-1918.* Juha Hannikainen, Markku Hyrkkänen & Olli Vehviläinen (eds). Työväen historian ja perinteen tutkimuksen seura, Tampere.

Sondhaus, Lawrence 2011: *World War One: The Global Revolution.* Cambridge University Press, Cambridge.

Soutou, Georges-Henri 2014: Diplomacy. In *The Cambridge of the First World War,* vol. 2. Jay Winter (ed.). Cambridge University Press, Cambridge.

Spenkuch, Hartwin 1998: *Das Preußische Herrenhaus. Adel und Bürgentum in der Ersten Kammer des Landtages* 1854-1918. Droste, Düsseldorf.

Steinmetz, Willibald 2007: Neue Wege einer historischen Semantik des Politischen. In «Politik». *Situationen eines Wortgebrauchs im Europa der Neuzeit.* Willibald Steinmetz (ed.). Campus-Verlag, Frankfurt & New York.

Steinmetz, Willibald 2011: New Perspectives on the Study of Language and Power in the Short Twentieth Century. In *Political Languages in the Age of Extremes.* Willibald Steinmetz (ed.). Oxford University Press, Oxford.

Willibald Steinmetz, Ingrid Holtey & Heinz-Gerhard Haupt (eds) 2013: *Writing Political History Today.* Campus-Verlag, Frankfurt & New York.

Stenius, Henrik 2003: Kansalainen. In *Käsitteet liikkeessä: Suomen poliittisen kulttuurin käsitehistoria.* Matti Hyvärinen et al. (eds). Vastapaino, Tampere.

Stibbe, Matthew 2001: *German Anglophobia and the Great War, 1914-1918.* Cambridge University Press, Cambridge.

Stjernquist, Nils 1993: Konflikt och konsensus i Sverige under skilda konstitutionella villkor. In *Politikens väsen. Idéer och institutioner i den modern staten.* Björn von Sydow, Gunnar Wallin & Björn Wittrock (eds). Tiden, Stockholm.

Stollberg-Rilinger, Barbara 2005: Was heißt Kulturgeschichte des Politischen? – *Zeitschrift für Historische Forschung* 35 2005, 9-24.

Stråth, Bo 2016: *Europe's Utopias of Peace: 1815, 1919, 1951.* Bloomsbury Academic, London.

Sulkunen, Irma, Seija-Leena Nevala-Nurmi & Pirjo Markkola (eds) 2009: *Suffrage, Gender and Citizenship: International Perspectives on Parliamentary Reforms.* Cambrige Scholars, Newcastle.

Sundbäck, Esa 1994: 'A Convenient Buffer between Scandinavia and Russia': Great Britain, Scandinavia and the Birth of Finland after the First World War – *Jahrbücher für Geschichte Osteuropas* 42 1994, 356-75.

Sveriges konstitutionella urkunder, 1999: SNS, Stockholm.

te Velde, Henk 2005: Political Transfer: An Introduction – *European Review of History* 12(2), 205-21.

Thompson, J. Lee 1999: *Politicians, the Press & Propaganda: Lord Northcliffe & the Great War, 1914-1918.* Kent State University, Kent.

Thorpe, Andrew 2001: *A History of the British Labour Party,* 2nd edition. Palgrave, Basingstoke.

Tikka, Marko & Petri Karonen 2014: Säätyjen edustajat, parlamentarismin puolustajat.

In *Kansallisten instituutioiden muotoutuminen. Suomalainen historiakuva Oma Maa -kirjasarjassa 1900-1960*. Petri Karonen & Antti Räihä (eds). Finnish Literature Society, Helsinki.

Torstendahl, Rolf 1969: *Mellan nykonservatism och liberalism. Idébrytningar inom högern och bondepartierna 1918-1934*. Svenska bokförlaget, Stockholm.

Trippe, Christian F. 1995: *Konservative Verfassungspolitik 1918-1923. Die DNVP als Opposition in Reich und Ländern*. Droste, Düsseldorf.

Tuomisto, Tero 1990: Helsinki 1917. In *Väki voimakas, vol. 4: Suomi 1917-1918*. Juha Hannikainen, Markku Hyrkkänen & Olli Vehviläinen (eds). Työväen historian ja perinteen tutkimuksen seura, Tampere.

Turner, John 1992: *British Politics and the Great War: Coalition and Conflict 1915-1918*. Yale University Press, New Haven.

Tvåkammarriksdagen 1867-1970. Ledamöter och valkretsar, vol. 5, 1985-1996. Anders Norberg et al. (ed.). Almqvist & Wiksell, Stockholm.

Ullrich, Volker 2010 (1997): *Die nervöse Großmacht 1871-1918. Aufstieg und Untergang des deutschen Kaiserreichs*. Fischer, Frankfurt.

Upton, Anthony F. 1970: *Kommunismi Suomessa*. Kirjayhtymä, Helsinki.

Upton, Anthony F. 1980: *Vallankumous Suomessa 1917-1918*, vol. 1. Transl. Antero Manninen. Kirjayhtymä, Helsinki.

van Dijk T.A. 2003: Knowledge in Parliamentary Debates – *Journal of Language and Politics* 2(1) 2003, 93-129.

Vares, Vesa 1998: *Kuninkaan tekijät. Suomalainen monarkia 1917-1919. Myytti ja todellisuus*. WSOY, Porvoo.

Vares, Vesa 2000: Rantakari Kaarle Nestor (1877-1948). In *Kansallisbiografia*, http://www.kansallisbiografia.fi/kb/artikkeli/1654/.

Vares, Vesa 2006: Kansanvalta koetuksella. In *Suomen Eduskunta 100 vuotta*, vol. 3. Edita, Helsinki.

Virtanen, Aarni 2015: 'Toimikaa, älkää odottako'. *Vihtori Kosolan puheiden muutokset 1929-1936*. University of Jyväskylä, Jyväskylä.

von Sydow, Björn 1997: *Parlamentarismen i Sverige: utveckling och utformning till 1945*. Gidlund, Hedemora.

Wade, Rex A. 2000: *The Russian Revolution, 1917*. Cambridge University Press: Cambridge.

Walters, Rhodri 2003: The House of Lords. In *The British Constitution in the Twentieth Century*. Vernon Bogdanor (ed.). Oxford University Press, Oxford.

War Victims in Finland, http://vesta.narc.fi/cgi-bin/db2www/sotasurmaetusivu/results.

Webber, G. C. 1986: *The Ideology of the British Right 1918-1939*. Routledge, London.

Weckerlein, Friedrich 1994: *Streitfall Deutschland. Die britische Linke und die 'Demokratisierung' des Deutschen Reiches, 1900-1918*. Vandenhoeck & Ruprecht, Göttingen.

Wehler, Hans Ulrich 2003: *Deutsche Gesellschaftsgeschichte. Vierter Band, Vom Beginn des Ersten Weltkriegs bis zur Gründung der beiden deutschen Staaten*. Beck, München.

Werner, Michael & Bénédicte Zimmermann 2006: Beyond Comparison: Histoire Croisée and the Challenge of Reflexivity – *History and Theory* 45(1) 2006, 30-50.

White, Isobel & Andrew Parker 2009: Speaker's Conferences, Library of the House of Commons, SN/PC/04426, 1 December 2009, www.parliament.uk/briefing-papers/SN04426.pdf.

Winkler, Heinrich August 1999: Demokratie oder Bürgerkrieg. Die russische Oktoberrevolution als Problem der deutschen Sozialdemokraten und der französischen Sozialisten – *Vierteljahrshefte für Zeitgeschichte* 47(1) 1999, 1-23.

Winkler, Heinrich August 2005: *Weimar 1918–1933. Die Geschichte der ersten deutschen Demokratie*. Beck, München.

Winkler, Heinrich August 2006 (2000): *Germany: The Long Road West*, Vol. 1: 1789–1933. Oxford University Press, Oxford.

Winter, Jay 2014: Introduction to Volume II. In *The Cambridge History of the First World War*, vol. 2. Jay Winter (ed.). Cambridge University Press, Cambridge.

Wirsching, Andreas 2007: Einleitung. In *Herausforderung der parlamentarischen Demokratie. Die Weimarer Republik im europäischen Vergleich*. Andreas Wirsching (ed.). Oldenbourg, München.

Wirsching, Andreas 2008: *Die Weimarer Republik: Politik und Gesellschaft*. Oldenbourg, München.

Wirsching, Andreas 2008: Verfassung und Verfassungskultur im Europa der Zwischenkriegszeit. In *Demokratie in der Krise. Europa in der Zwischenkriegzeit*. Christoph Gusy (ed.). Nomos, Baden-Baden.

Wolff, Charlotta 2009: *Noble conceptions of politics in eighteenth-century Sweden (ca 1740–1790)*. Finnish Literature Society, Helsinki.

Wrigley, Chris 1990: *Lloyd George and the Challenge of Labour: The Post-War Coalition 1918–1922*. Harvester Wheatsheaf, Hemel Hempstead.

Wrigley, Chris 2009: The European Context: Aspects of British Labour and Continental Socialism Before 1920. In *The Foundations of the British Labour Party*. Matthew Worley (ed.). Ashgate, Farnham.

Zetterberg, Seppo 1992: Itsenäistyvä Suomi. In *Vuosisatamme Suomi*. Seppo Zetterberg (ed.). WSOY, Porvoo.

Zetterberg, Seppo 2000 (1986): Venäjästä Neuvostoliitoksi. In *Venäjän historia*. Heikki Kirkinen (ed.). Otava, Helsinki.

Abstract

Pasi Ihalainen http://orcid.org/0000-0002-5468-4829

The Springs of Democracy
National and Transnational Debates on Constitutional Reform in the British, German, Swedish and Finnish Parliaments, 1917–1919

During the First World War, conflicts between the people's sacrifices and their political participation led to crises of parliamentary legitimacy. This volume compares British, German, Swedish and Finnish debates on revolution, rule by the people, democracy and parliamentarism and their transnational links. The British reform, although more about winning the war than advancing democracy, restored parliamentary legitimacy, unlike in Germany, where Allied demands for democratisation made reform appear treasonous and fostered native German solutions. Sweden only adopted Western political models after major confrontations, but reforms saw it embark on its path to Social Democracy. In Finland, competing Russian revolutionary discourses and German- and Swedish-inspired appeals to legality brought about the deterioration of parliamentary legitimacy and a civil war. Only a republican compromise imposed by the Entente, following a royalist initiative in 1918, led to the construction of a viable polity.

Subject and Place Index

A

academic(s), 19, 26–7, 31, 40, 110, 128, 161, 166, 168, 196, 210, 219–220, 224, 231, 235, 250–2, 278, 305, 322, 325, 330–1, 365, 388, 400, 423, 461, 464, 486, 501, 505, 507, 519, 527

Age of Liberty (Sweden and Finland), 34, 61n, 173, 210–11, 338, 478, 487, 500–501

agency, agent(s), 14n, 16, 37–41, 84, 96, 113, 138, 141, 147, 156, 165, 189, 235, 250, 302, 357, 373, 392, 446, 456, 523

Agrarian League (Finland), 54, 63–4, 182, 186, 191, 193–4, 197–198, 204, 206, 208, 264, 267, 269, 274, 277, 279–80, 284, 287–9, 319, 325–8, 331, 335–7, 398, 402, 403n, 404–10, 414–15, 418–21, 470–2, 475n, 476, 482–4, 488–90, 495, 497, 501, 517–18, 522

Åland Islands, 34, 300, 318, 323, 427, 465, 468, 478, 480, 529

amendment, 45, 75–6, 87, 104, 108, 145, 204, 222, 225, 231–3, 239, 498

American(s), *see* United States of America

Anglo-American model, 34, 124, 145, 195, 250–1, 480, 528

Anglophile(s), 34, 61, 115n, 137, 139, 173, 251, 317, 325, 468, 480

anti-reformism, 17, 59, 70, 85, 93, 121, 123, 146, 157, 176, 209, 215, 221, 223, 225, 228, 250, 298, 387, 460, 508–9, 511, 513, 515, 528

aristocracy, 52, 92–3, 98, 122, 142, 160, 220, 228, 231–2, 250, 328, 338, 342, 358, 407–408, 454, 493

army, armed forces, 47, 50, 52–3, 55, 60, 65, 67, 105, 113, 122, 131, 133, 139, 174, 214, 227, 234, 244, 250, 295, 297–8, 317, 347, 349, 356, 363, 374, 402, 476

Australia, 83–5, 221, 223, 235, 242, 303, 478

Austria, Habsburg monarchy, 14, 66, 115, 151–2, 159, 248, 353, 373, 376, 379, 456–7, 478, 490

B

Baltic states, 301, 353

Belgium, 84–5, 186n, 224, 227, 380

Berlin, 17, 57, 92, 139, 142, 146, 174, 183, 186, 196, 259, 304n, 306, 317, 321, 346n, 356n, 363, 371, 467n, 476, 509, 529

bill, 44–5, 72–6, 78, 80, 85–6, 88, 90, 92, 95–102, 104–106, 111, 115, 119, 183, 190, 192, 202, 214–15, 217, 219–222, 225–6, 228, 231–3, 236–9, 293–4, 342, 373, 397, 453, 455–6, 471–2, 474, 508, 510

Bismarckian system, 119, 126, 134, 324, 351, 354, 357, 361–2, 434, 441, 529

Bolshevik, Bolshevism, 21–2, 31, 39, 59, 68–9, 112, 178–9, 181–5, 187–9, 191–3, 197, 199–200, 202–203, 216, 218–20, 222–3, 239n, 256–61, 267–70, 273–4, 276, 278–80, 285n, 286, 288–9, 295, 298–302, 306, 308, 310, 315–23, 326–9, 335, 340–1, 343–4, 346, 348–9, 353, 363–4, 370, 380, 383, 399, 410, 422–4, 427–8, 466, 471, 473, 477, 484, 493, 501, 509, 512, 517, 519, 523, 527–30

conception(s), 16, 58, 69–70, 112, 179, 184, 186–7, 190, 198, 200, 267, 269–70, 272, 279–80, 286, 310, 312,

316, 340, 404, 460, 510, 517, 521
  influence, 17n, 29, 68, 178–9, 184,
    186–9, 191–3, 197–8, 200–203, 218,
    241, 256–61, 263, 264n, 266n, 270,
    272, 274, 278, 283, 290, 315–16, 327,
    334–5, 341, 349, 366, 369, 371, 388,
    390, 403, 419, 423, 426–7, 470, 477,
    482, 490, 508, 510, 517, 522, 527,
    529–30, 532
  October/November Revolution,
    17, 29, 65, 68, 92, 104n, 178–9, 187,
    216–20, 231, 237, 239, 254, 256–8,
    261–3, 266n, 273, 279, 283, 285, 288,
    290, 292, 298, 301, 316–17, 326, 335,
    341, 364, 366–7, 403–4, 423, 510–12,
    518, 522, 529
  uprising, 187, 190, 192, 261, 327, 484
  threat, 16, 237, 263, 290, 317, 341,
    346, 358, 399, 422, 473, 477, 524
  see also revolution: Russia
bourgeois(ie), 15, 36, 46, 51–2, 59, 60,
    64, 67–8, 70, 120, 132, 140, 143, 175–
    9, 181–4, 187–93, 194, 198, 200, 202,
    206–207, 209, 212, 216, 254, 256–79,
    282–3, 285–7, 289–91, 298–300, 302,
    304, 312–13, 316, 320, 349, 353, 366,
    370, 414, 420, 432–3, 435, 458, 467,
    469, 475, 477, 480–3, 485, 489–90,
    492, 498, 510, 517, 525, 528,
  democracy, 69, 120, 132, 145, 160,
    180, 187, 198–200, 203, 205, 210, 218,
    264, 268, 273–81, 288, 301–302, 308,
    317, 326, 329, 364, 366, 370, 390, 407,
    435, 444, 459, 463, 467, 474, 480–4,
    487–8, 515–19, 528, 529
  parliamentarism, 15, 22, 36, 51, 64,
    66, 68–9, 145, 170, 176, 180, 183,
    188n, 194, 207, 209, 212, 218, 254,
    257, 261–2, 266, 268, 270, 272, 276,
    280, 283–4, 286–90, 312–13, 317,
    364n, 370, 420, 467, 474, 480, 496,
    508, 518, 521, 524–5, 528
  party, 51, 58, 60, 66–8, 112–13, 142,
    175, 178, 180, 182–4, 189–90, 192,
    195, 198, 200, 203, 205, 207–208, 218,
    242n, 256–8, 260, 262, 269–70, 273,
    276–80, 282–3, 285n, 286, 291, 310,
    316–17, 319, 326, 355, 364, 366, 375,
    401, 433, 482–3, 486n, 490, 532
  see also class: bourgeois
Britain, British
  constitution, *see* constitution, British
  constitutional history, 29n, 30, 96,
    219

government, 46, 49, 78, 89, 93, 101,
    114, 119, 127, 136, 216, 221, 225n,
    227, 294–6
  model, 29, 32, 34–5, 83, 98, 115, 119,
    122, 127, 139, 153, 185, 253, 310, 343,
    368, 468, 481, 507, 527, 530
  political culture, 92, 103, 145, 172,
    439, 522
  political history, 88, 104, 340
  polity, 30, 34, 46, 75–6, 78, 82, 87, 98,
    102, 105, 119, 123, 214–15, 224, 232,
    235–8, 295, 530
  reform, 73, 75, 86–7, 113, 130, 132,
    140, 215, 217, 222, 233, 256, 293,
    340n, 507, 512–13
  see also British Parliament
British Parliament, 21, 32, 34, 45, 59,
    76, 83–4, 87, 108, 111, 115, 127, 146,
    172–3, 215, 217, 221, 224, 231, 239,
    253, 308, 422, 424, 505
  House of Commons, 44–7, 72–3,
    76–7, 87, 89n, 94–102, 104–5, 108,
    114, 117, 119, 125, 136, 146, 151, 167,
    214–17, 219, 220, 222, 224–5, 230–2,
    235, 239, 242, 250, 293–6, 305, 308,
    342, 345, 348, 512
  House of Lords, peer(s), 44–6, 73, 75,
    81, 87, 90, 99, 104–105, 122, 214, 217,
    219, 221–4, 228–32, 234–7, 239, 293,
    295–6, 305, 345, 368, 512, 520
  Mother of Parliaments, 83
  Parliament Act of 1911, 44–6, 72, 74,
    81, 90–1, 99, 107, 122, 169, 217, 220,
    222, 228, 232, 295
  parliamentarism, 48, 137, 284, 291,
    324, 477n, 479–80, 523–4
  Westminster, 216, 237n
Bulgaria, 349, 353, 405

C

cabinet, *see* British government
Canada, 84
Central Powers, 74n, 109–10, 127, 137,
    159, 251, 297, 318, 341, 405, 523
Centre Party (*Zentrum*) (Germany),
    53–4, 110–111, 113–16, 121, 124,
    130, 133–5, 137, 181, 196, 240–1, 243,
    245–7, 249, 297, 351, 354, 356–7,
    359–60, 362, 364–6, 402n, 406, 428,
    430, 432, 434, 441, 447, 453, 470, 473,
    507, 514, 523
centrist(s), 54, 196, 203, 240–1, 243,
    248–9, 251, 277, 281, 319, 323n, 326,
    328, 337, 357, 406, 408, 434, 446–7,

453, 477, 481, 485, 487, 492, 495, 519–20
Chancellor (*Kanzler*) (Germany), 50–1, 53, 55, 57, 111, 113, 116–23, 125, 129n, 133–4, 136, 146, 166, 240–1, 243, 245–6, 249–50, 253, 297, 305, 350–1, 355, 357, 360, 363, 431, 445, 507, 520
citizen(s), 27, 31, 97, 100–102, 104, 109, 114–15, 117, 119, 137, 142, 144, 163–4, 174n, 178, 206, 216, 221, 234, 239, 272, 311–12, 332, 343, 371, 389, 410, 435, 437–8, 443, 457–8, 485, 485n, 488, 491, 501
civil government, 53, 55
civil liberties, 46, 260, 348
civil war, 16, 45, 56, 76, 81, 185, 187, 231, 341, 352, 380, 450, 466–7, 471, 509–10, 532
   British, 305
   Finnish, 16–17, 31, 35, 63, 67, 71, 81, 184, 188, 192, 200–201, 203, 212, 214, 223, 253, 261–4, 266–71, 282, 285–6, 288–9, 291, 295, 298–302, 304–308, 310, 312, 314–17, 322–3, 326–8, 330–5, 337–8, 348, 351, 352n, 367, 380–1, 403–404, 410, 412, 414, 416–18, 420, 431, 433, 443, 445, 449–50, 464–5, 468, 470, 473–4, 477, 480–4, 487–90, 493–4, 496, 505, 509–10, 516–19, 521–2, 525–6, 528–9, 531–2
   German, 81, 430, 436, 450
   see also Reds and Whites (Finland)
class, 32, 54, 64, 66–7, 69, 72, 74n, 79, 92, 98, 108, 111, 113, 119, 122, 125, 128, 130, 147, 157, 165, 172, 174n, 192–4, 197–201, 203–204, 210–211, 216, 224, 227, 229–31, 234, 236, 239n, 265–7, 269, 271, 281, 284, 291, 298, 310–311, 315–16, 319, 328, 349, 351, 355, 360, 379, 394, 397, 403, 411, 414n, 416, 420, 425, 436, 469, 482, 484, 490, 492–4, 497, 506–507, 510, 512, 517, 519, 521, 531
   bourgeois, 36, 192–3, 199, 209, 216, 259, 269, 283, 285n, 290, 355, 420, 474
   capitalist, 191, 351
   class antagonism, hatred, 67–8, 70, 174–5, 187, 194, 201, 267, 285n, 316, 466, 485, 510
   class enemy, 191, 286, 288
   class rule, 36, 160, 283, 423, 487, 512
   class struggle, 35–6, 58, 67–8, 70,
113, 180, 185, 188–9, 192, 194, 201, 208, 257–8, 260, 265–6, 269–70, 272, 275, 299–300, 341, 408, 415, 459, 467, 474, 477, 481, 510, 515, 527–9, 532
   class war, 16, 192, 270–2, 275, 281, 427–8, 510, 518, 527
   lower, 64, 90, 122, 147, 193, 202, 206, 209, 494, 507, 519
   middle, 58
   proletariat, 191, 199, 206, 216, 269, 275, 285n, 287, 427
   upper, 63–4, 157, 193–4, 198, 300, 352
   working, 35, 56, 59, 62, 68, 82, 89n, 113, 162, 181, 188, 192, 198–9, 201, 226, 234, 263, 266, 272, 284, 286–7, 290, 292, 299–300, 308, 348–9, 374, 376, 395–7, 420, 422–6, 432, 467, 487, 491, 510, 513, 521, 527–8
Congress of Soviets, 182, 187, 189–91, 193, 199, 202, 209
consensus, 41, 49, 57, 61, 82, 193, 248–9, 375, 390, 415, 490
conservative(s), 14, 19, 21, 31, 34, 39, 50–2, 58–60, 62–3, 65, 86n, 90, 112–13, 116, 118, 123, 127, 135, 138, 141–6, 152n, 158–9, 161, 166–9, 172–3, 186, 209–11, 221, 231, 243, 245, 251, 254, 276, 280–1, 288, 293, 297–8, 300, 304, 308, 310–311, 314, 318–20, 322, 326, 328–30, 332–4, 336, 343, 354, 356–7, 359, 361, 366, 375, 378–9, 386, 388–9, 395–8, 403–4, 407–8, 410, 412, 417, 437, 439, 442, 446n, 449, 453, 457, 460, 464–7, 469–70, 475n, 476, 479–80, 486–7, 491–2, 497, 499–500, 504, 514, 517–19, 522–3, 533
Conservative Party (Britain), *see also* Unionist Party, 44–8, 58, 72–107, 121, 166, 214–15, 217, 219–20, 222–6, 228–9, 231–9, 288, 293–6, 332, 341–2, 346, 375, 386–7, 422–5, 507–508, 512–13, 519–20, 522, 527
   Tory Democracy, 90, 92, 228, 342, 423, 513
constitution, constitutional
   British, 75, 83, 86, 88, 231, 293
   change, modification, reform(s), shift, transformation(s), 13, 18, 22, 28, 29n, 33, 37, 42, 44, 47, 49, 53–4, 56, 75–6, 78–9, 82–3, 85–6, 88, 90, 95–6, 104, 108, 111, 113, 116–18, 121, 123, 128, 130–3, 138, 140, 143–5,

149, 154, 160–1, 164, 183, 190, 214,
216–17, 232, 236–7, 240, 245–6,
250–3, 280, 293–4, 298, 301, 303,
306, 308, 310, 319, 323, 325, 333, 347,
350–1, 355–7, 364, 368–9, 372, 375,
379, 393–6, 401–402, 405–407, 411,
415, 417–18, 422, 429, 438, 448, 454,
463–4, 474, 477, 480, 491, 504, 509,
511, 515, 526, 528, 530
conflict, confrontation, disputes,
tension, 27, 44–5, 60, 63, 67, 71–3,
76, 80–1, 99, 108, 167, 169, 205, 227,
253, 266, 269, 315, 328, 367, 407, 446,
470, 475–6, 509
comparison, 34, 242, 272, 403
crisis, 72, 76, 81, 99, 113, 133, 208,
241, 253, 257, 289, 315, 338, 362, 380,
436, 497, 505–506, 514, 526
culture, 27, 463
debate, 13, 18, 21–2, 24, 27–8, 30, 32,
39, 41–2, 56–7, 61–2, 71, 73, 82, 109,
111, 113–15, 122, 124, 149, 178–9,
185, 191, 195, 197, 222, 240, 245n,
253, 260, 290–1, 300, 318, 319n, 321,
324–5, 340, 352n, 363, 367–8, 387,
418, 429–30, 436, 448–9, 456–8, 464,
468–70, 474–5, 481, 512, 514–15,
524, 527–31, 533
Finnish, 31, 34, 156, 167, 175, 179,
185, 190–1, 195, 211–2, 269, 280,
283, 300, 307, 318, 320, 323–5, 340,
401, 404–407, 415, 418, 436, 467n,
468, 472–3, 479–80, 495–7, 501, 505,
514, 531
German, 18n, 32, 50, 61, 113, 115,
121–3, 129–30, 138, 196, 204, 241,
247, 252, 325, 329, 352n, 363, 369,
405–407, 416, 426, 430, 432, 435, 439,
458, 467, 480, 491, 498, 518, 531
Gustavian (Finland), 65, 196, 211,
307, 320–1, 403, 464, 469, 491
Instrument of Government of 1809
(Sweden), 60–2, 253–4
issue(s), 33, 60, 64, 68, 75, 101, 110–
111, 144, 182, 189, 207, 255, 328, 333,
368, 396, 409, 453, 476, 480, 485, 489
monarchical, 35, 91, 116, 131, 211,
320–4, 328–9, 331, 336–8, 401, 407,
411, 417, 448, 466–7, 471, 475–6, 526
republican, 31, 34, 58, 61, 106, 138,
173, 182, 250, 258, 276, 278, 289, 297,
318, 320, 323–6, 328, 332, 337–8, 365,
404–406, 408, 411, 414–15, 417, 428,
430, 432, 435, 439n, 445–6, 454, 461,
464–7, 469, 471, 473–4, 477–9, 483–
5, 487, 489–91, 493–6, 499, 502–503,
505, 511, 518, 522, 527, 529–30
revolution, 92, 350
rights, 55, 129, 229, 247, 348
Swedish constitution (Finland), 34,
65, 173, 181, 195, 278, 310, 320, 465,
478, 480, 494, 526
tradition, 27, 31, 49, 60, 63, 65–6, 85,
90–1, 126, 134, 137–8, 145, 158, 161,
167, 171–3, 185, 206, 222, 232, 239,
256, 271, 278, 283, 307, 310, 319–20,
327, 357, 368, 382, 403, 410, 429, 425,
445, 451, 465, 468, 478, 480, 491, 495,
499, 518–19
unwritten constitution (Britain), 19,
45, 474n
coup, 184, 200n, 256–7, 260–1, 263,
268–9, 283, 287, 290, 302, 312, 373,
378, 414, 416, 433, 474, 477, 502
crisis, 14–15, 26, 35, 45, 68, 72, 76–7,
81, 97, 99, 111, 113, 133, 141, 151n,
159, 177–8, 194, 200n, 201, 208, 210,
212–13, 223, 241–2, 249, 253, 256,
257, 268, 270, 282, 284, 289, 296,
304–6, 311–13, 315, 323, 333, 338,
340, 362, 369, 372, 380, 385, 390, 402,
412, 420–1, 432–3, 436, 455, 465, 480,
490, 497, 505–506, 514, 526, 531
culture (*Kultur*), 108, 133n, 153, 205n,
321–2, 416, 430

D

declaration of independence (Finnish),
258, 265, 278, 285n, 315, 317, 320,
405, 414, 484–5, 511, 518, 521
deliberation, see also parliament:
deliberation, 15, 17, 38, 49, 68, 100,
102, 172, 181, 211, 214, 224, 233, 237,
260, 276, 296, 372, 385, 401, 422, 514,
520, 531
democracy, democratic
breakthrough, turn, 146, 161–2, 251,
306, 340, 356–7, 381–2, 411, 512
centrist, 203, 277, 281, 326, 328, 337,
408, 446, 481, 485, 487, 519
debates on, 14, 19, 22, 24, 30, 87, 385,
423, 449, 508, 511, 531, 533
defenders of, 86, 90, 242, 249, 268,
482n, 487, 529
definition of, 13, 18, 19n, 27, 48, 89,
91, 156, 158, 199–200, 202–203, 213,
215, 225, 259, 274–6, 278, 280, 343,
439, 451, 482–3, 504, 508, 530

democrat(s), 13, 152, 198, 200, 225–6, 276–7, 279, 307, 349, 381, 386, 388, 390, 397, 444, 446, 449, 515–17
democratisation, 18, 29–30, 34, 46, 50, 58, 61, 74n, 86n, 108, 111, 117, 120, 124n, 125–32, 143, 146, 150, 152, 154–6, 158–60, 164, 173, 182, 196, 198, 220, 225, 232, 241–7, 249–52, 255, 274–5, 292–4, 297, 301, 304, 306, 309–10, 314, 342–3, 345–7, 351–2, 354–6, 362, 364–7, 369, 371–2, 381–2, 384–90, 403, 407, 423, 426–7, 430, 438, 440–1, 443, 449, 457, 459–60, 484, 486, 490, 505, 512–15, 518, 523, 527–8, 531
 era of, 97, 154, 159, 255, 327, 343, 389, 422
 folkstyre (rule by the people) (Sweden), *see also* people: *folket*, 154, 436, 516
 flood of, wave of, 71, 159, 293, 304, 371, 382, 387, 390, 411, 441, 463
 forces of, 74n, 90, 92, 146, 158–9, 309, 402, 427, 483
 functioning of, order, system, 17, 48, 228, 239, 279, 308, 344, 356, 385, 442, 483, 522
 international, 157, 197, 204
 kansanvalta (rule by the people) (Finland), *see also* people: *kansa*, 174, 197–8, 205, 274, 278, 410, 436–7, 517
 language of, rhetoric of, 49, 58, 74, 86, 89–91, 154, 159, 203, 268, 294, 308, 326, 344, 444, 511, 513
 mass, 92, 97, 220, 328, 332, 386, 512, 533
 modern, 220, 296, 344, 336, 356, 502
 monarchical, 35, 91, 326, 328–9, 331, 366, 411
 parliamentary, 14, 17, 22–3, 29–32, 41, 61n, 62–3, 81–2, 97, 106, 127, 197, 211, 218, 249, 273, 277–8, 290, 293, 296, 298, 310, 322, 330, 337, 339, 340, 354, 364–6, 369, 399, 421–2, 430–1, 434, 436, 448–9, 454, 459, 465–7, 470–3, 479–82, 485, 490–1, 517–18, 522–3, 525, 527, 531, 533
 principles of, 49, 105, 223, 226, 239, 276, 280, 293, 300, 307, 319, 340, 382, 387, 426, 438, 444, 482–3, 516
 politisation of, 214
 proper, true, 86, 88, 90, 154, 157, 204, 226, 229, 239, 326, 343, 383, 408, 427, 457, 482, 487, 518

republican, 407
rightist, 203, 276, 481
spring of, 17, 72, 149
socialist, 182, 340, 363, 410, 443, 462, 512, 525
suffrage, 13, 28, 50 59, 81, 129, 166, 204, 234, 291, 340, 530
undemocratic, 69, 91, 216, 218, 278–9, 306, 327, 329, 381, 408, 516
Western, 119, 124, 126–8, 130, 156, 248, 252, 292, 303, 318, 320–1, 344, 346–7, 354, 356, 367, 372–3, 381, 383–4, 436, 438, 444, 468, 514–15, 520, 529
Deutsche Vaterlandspartei (German Fatherland Party), 248
Denmark, Danish, 33, 142, 146, 149, 151, 153–4, 160, 166–7, 242, 251, 253, 303, 306, 352n, 467n, 528
dictatorship, 70, 86, 105, 112, 162, 266, 310, 317, 340, 362, 364, 381, 406, 427, 432, 437, 443, 453, 460, 467, 484, 486–7, 496, 500–2, 521
discursive processes, 13, 17–21, 26, 28, 37–40, 49, 71, 175, 277, 317, 447, 460, 469, 471, 493, 504–506, 526, 530, 533
Dolchstoß (stab in the back) (Germany), 248
domestic politics, 15, 54, 57, 74, 92, 113, 120, 144, 248, 340, 343, 468, 513
duality of power, duality of government, 31, 35, 116, 134, 138, 182, 187, 203, 209, 247, 276, 287, 365, 370, 432, 452, 469n, 471, 492, 496, 499, 517, 523–4
dynasty, *see also* monarchy, 139, 178, 318, 353

E

Eduskunta, *see* Finnish parliament
electoral reform, 29, 47–9, 60, 63, 79, 110–111, 114, 117–19, 123, 127, 130, 132–3, 140–1, 196, 225, 237, 240, 250–1, 344, 367, 431, 467
electorate, 42, 51, 58, 77, 102, 224, 239, 311, 338, 340–1, 422–3
emperor, *see also* Kaiser and Tsar, 53–4, 353
Empire (British, Russian), 14, 29n, 62–3, 65, 78, 80, 82–5, 103, 151n, 173, 179, 186, 221, 223, 227, 234–5, 237, 285n, 326, 341, 343, 463, 471, 508, 527
Entente, 21–2, 32, 55, 58, 74, 87–8, 92, 108, 127–9, 140, 156, 175, 185–6, 195, 240–1, 244, 250, 252–3, 258, 300–1, 310, 318, 322–4, 339, 347–8,

Subject and Place Index

350, 367–8, 376, 403–405, 407, 411, 416, 427, 444–5, 467, 471, 476–7, 506–507, 511–12, 518, 527, 531
estates, 64, 162, 165, 167, 173, 174n, 272, 334, 338, 386, 392, 394–5, 398, 428, 445, 500, 521
  four-estate diet, 63, 173, 497
ethnicity, 56, 140, 174n, 198, 278, 322, 436–7, 439, 494, 514
Europe, European, 13–14, 15n, 16, 19n, 22–3, 27–30, 32, 35, 40, 42, 49–51, 56, 60, 62, 65–6, 73, 82–5, 88, 97–8, 115, 117, 124, 128–30, 134, 138, 141, 144–6, 149, 151–2, 154, 156, 158, 163, 167, 172–4, 185–7, 195–6, 199, 201, 204, 208, 222, 225, 239–40, 244, 246, 253, 262–3, 269–70, 272, 280, 290, 292–4, 302–303, 307, 310–311, 313, 321–2, 325, 335–6, 339–40, 345, 348, 360, 370, 374, 377–8, 382, 390, 393, 405, 411, 415–16, 418–19, 423, 427, 435–6, 441, 444, 451, 456, 465, 468, 471, 473, 475, 480, 487, 492, 496–8, 501–502, 504, 507–508, 511, 516, 518, 526–7, 530, 532–3
executive power, *see* power
extra-parliamentary, 14, 40, 100–101, 104, 113, 168, 177, 184, 193, 283, 308, 312, 345, 367, 394, 399, 454, 524
  action, 54, 59, 67, 81, 113, 125, 141–4, 160, 168–70, 172, 177, 181, 184, 194, 255–6, 261, 264–5, 267, 284–6, 301, 308, 314–15, 370–3, 375, 378, 392, 399, 419, 424, 477, 481, 509–11, 516, 521, 524–5
  forces, 52, 76, 161, 208, 214, 314, 375

F
fatherland, 55–6, 109, 126, 248, 322, 354, 357, 359, 366, 387, 390, 396
federal elections (Germany), 50–1, 109, 121, 129, 131, 151, 436
Finland, Finnish
  autonomy, 63, 65, 173, 175, 182, 190
  constitution, *see* constitution, Finnish
  constitutional debate, 22, 27, 31–2, 73, 113, 178–9, 185, 191, 195, 222, 290–1, 300, 318, 321, 324–5, 340, 418, 436, 464, 468–70, 474–5, 481, 514
  counter-revolution, 192, 200, 268, 275, 302, 321, 353, 428, 510, 528
  Fennomans (Finnish nationalists), 66, 195, 281, 327, 329, 331–2, 348, 411, 413, 488, 492

  government, 69, 177, 179, 181–2, 209, 298, 300, 307, 317–18, 321–2, 351, 353, 403, 418, 427, 465, 476, 524, 528
  grand duchy of, 62, 173, 175
  political culture, 20, 26–7, 31, 33, 35, 173, 197, 212, 327, 427, 463–4, 465, 489, 498, 518, 521
  polity, 30, 35, 65, 82, 85, 173, 175, 177–9, 184, 188, 201, 205, 250–1, 266–7, 276, 283, 289, 308, 326, 328, 330, 333–4, 337, 339, 353, 365, 370, 401, 405, 411–13, 418–20, 465–6, 469–70, 472–3, 475, 481, 490, 493, 496, 500, 503–505, 508, 518, 520
  Russification measures, 65, 175, 202, 320
  Svecoman(s), 65, 488
Finnish parliament, Eduskunta, 26, 31, 40, 42, 63–4, 70, 73, 111, 113, 152, 171, 174, 176, 178, 181–4, 187, 190–1, 193, 195, 198, 203–205, 207, 209–10, 212, 244, 250, 253, 256, 258, 260, 262–5, 270, 273, 276–7, 283–4, 292, 302, 315, 321, 325, 330, 339, 376, 380, 402, 428, 444, 450, 464, 470, 475–7, 488–9, 493, 501, 510, 516, 519, 524, 531–2
  Grand Committee, 68, 152n
  legitimacy of, 35, 64, 66, 173, 176–8, 181–4, 192, 194, 209, 212–13, 256–7, 260–2, 265, 281–4, 287, 315–16, 409, 416, 420–1, 482, 505, 511, 524–5
  parliamentarian(s), 20, 34, 117, 180, 208, 241, 267, 281, 287, 302, 318, 335, 351, 366, 471–2
  parliamentary institutions, 31, 33, 63, 66–8, 176–7, 184, 199, 207, 209, 257, 261–2, 282–4, 287, 320, 329, 334, 339, 415, 418, 420, 476, 497–8, 524
  Parliamentary Reform Committee, 63
  Power Act, 183–5, 189–90, 198, 202, 206, 208–209, 212, 255, 257, 259–61, 264, 272–3, 277–9, 282–3, 286–7, 307, 315, 326, 470, 472–3, 483, 495, 499, 501–502
  Rump Parliament, 305, 318, 320–3, 328–9, 331, 337, 353, 368, 401, 403, 406, 409–11, 420, 466, 469, 475–6, 482, 489, 495, 521, 529
Finnish Party (Finland), *see also* National Coalition Party, 58, 63, 65–6, 186, 194, 196, 202–204,

561

Subject and Place Index

206, 210–212, 267, 269, 276, 281, 284, 287–9, 319–20, 323, 329–34, 403–405, 409–10, 412, 414, 416–18, 470, 517, 521

First World War, the War, the Great War, 13–18, 20–2, 29–32, 34, 36n, 37, 42–4, 46–50, 52–8, 60–1, 63, 65, 69, 71–83, 85–6, 88, 91–119, 121–8, 130–9, 143–7, 152–4, 156, 158–9, 163, 166–7, 169, 174–5, 177, 179, 185–6, 188, 192, 195–7, 214–23, 225, 227–9, 232–8, 240–1, 243, 245–6, 248–52, 255, 258, 264–6, 269, 292–301, 303–304, 308–11, 318–20, 322, 324, 333, 335–6, 338–41, 343–4, 346–9, 351, 353, 356–9, 362, 365, 367–8, 373–9, 384–5, 399–405, 407, 411, 422, 425, 429, 433, 436, 439, 445, 447, 453–4, 456–7, 464–7, 472–3, 480, 488, 497, 504–508, 511–13, 515–17, 519–20, 522–4, 527–8, 530–2
    defeat (Germany), 15, 58, 63, 248, 301, 349–50, 367, 369, 379, 383, 411, 429, 436, 447, 465–6, 480, 507, 529
    General Headquarters (Germany), 55
    submarine warfare, 49, 55, 109, 218, 252
    total war, 13, 47, 49, 55, 71–2, 75, 101, 108–109, 113, 133, 144, 530
    War Cabinet (Britain), 47, 73, 93–4, 96, 102, 215, 221, 227, 294–6, 340, 506, 519, 522
    war experience, 13, 15–17, 29, 73, 76, 80, 91–2, 113, 116–17, 121, 126, 138, 144, 216, 234–6, 249, 294, 303, 361, 384, 400, 450, 506–8, 511, 531, 533
    war finances, 54–5, 57, 71, 132, 240
    war propaganda, 32, 48–9, 73, 87, 106, 110–111, 119, 124, 126, 128, 132, 215, 240, 294–5, 357, 431, 436, 506–507, 512–13, 523, 527, 531

foreign policy, 29, 57, 61, 111, 120, 133, 135, 139, 144, 169, 244–6, 250, 252, 254, 259, 279, 292, 295, 299, 301, 307, 320–2, 328, 336, 341, 346, 351, 360, 362, 384, 400, 423, 465–6, 497, 527

Fourteen Points (Woodrow Wilson), 292, 294, 349–50

France, French, 14, 26, 28n, 29–31, 33–5, 39–40, 46, 49, 53, 56, 61, 66, 69, 71, 85, 89–90, 107–108, 115, 121, 123–8, 133n, 135, 137–8, 144, 146, 150, 154–5, 169–70, 172, 208, 223, 262–3, 273, 293, 305, 316, 322, 324–5, 347,

356, 365, 373, 376, 380, 384, 403–404, 421, 427, 434–5, 452, 478–80, 499, 501, 513, 523, 525, 529–30
    Revolution, 14, 71, 142, 147, 148n, 150, 231, 263, 267, 270, 306, 330, 380, 405

G

gender, 42, 44, 102, 105, 234–5, 267
    female MPs, 63, 267, 441
    female suffrage, *see* suffrage, female
    gendered language, 78, 166, 520
    gender equality, 42, 311
    male suffrage, manhood suffrage, *see* suffrage: male, manhood
    suffragette, suffragist, *see* suffrage: suffragette, suffragist

general elections (Britain), 45–7, 49, 74, 77, 89, 91–3, 220, 222, 226, 228, 234–5, 242, 295, 340–6, 349, 375–6, 386, 422–5, 512–13

general strike, 57–8, 67, 195, 261, 266, 269, 271, 273, 275, 281, 286–7, 290, 378, 432

German, Germany
    constitution, *see* constitution, German
    democracy, 118, 123, 131, 243, 346, 346–7, 355–6, 426, 437, 451, 514
    democratisation of, 46, 120, 125–7, 130–1, 160, 241–2, 246–7, 294, 304n, 346–7, 355, 367, 407, 426, 430, 443, 512–13
    government, 44, 115, 119, 124, 180, 294, 339, 344, 402–403, 406, 418, 456, 528
    Hohenzollern(s), 86n, 152, 322, 353, 427
    Imperial, *see also* federal state, 34, 108–109, 120, 132, 139, 142, 150, 197, 247, 275, 292, 317, 321, 325, 357, 359, 363, 370, 403, 442, 451
    monarchy, 35, 53, 61, 75, 92, 113, 116–17, 120–1, 125–7, 129, 131–2, 134–5, 136–9, 145, 196, 212, 245, 251, 253–4, 318, 320, 322, 324, 329–30, 349, 351–3, 355–6, 358, 363, 367–70, 391, 402, 404–405, 411, 427–8, 434–5, 444–6, 451, 457, 464, 466–7, 523
    political culture, 20, 31, 35, 50–1, 118, 131, 138–9, 197, 427, 430–1, 437, 440, 450, 454, 480, 522
    polity, 30, 50, 52, 54, 75, 108, 116–17, 124–8, 130, 139, 144, 250–1, 297,

308, 319, 324–5, 350–1, 353, 359, 363, 365–6, 368, 381, 384, 407, 415, 418, 430–4, 436, 438, 440–3, 448, 450, 467n, 472–3, 475, 481, 508, 513, 520, 527, 529
  Provisional Government, 365, 451
  Revolution, 29n, 74n, 349, 351, 367–8, 375, 377–9, 429, 455, 457, 459, 480, 509, 514, 516, 519
  Williamite Germany, 59, 126
German parliament, Reichstag, 31, 50–7, 64, 73, 108–14, 117–18, 120–1, 123, 125, 126n, 128–31, 133–5, 137–8, 140, 144, 147, 150n, 151, 167, 180, 196, 240–1, 243–50, 294–5, 346–7, 350–1, 354–5, 357–61, 402, 407, 426, 431, 436, 441, 447–8, 450–2, 476, 507, 514, 520, 522
  Bundesrat, 50, 55, 125, 346, 361
  Frankfurt Parliament, 50, 131, 197, 356, 429
  legitimacy of, 51, 122, 249, 350, 531
  Main Committee (*Hauptausschuß*), 57, 116, 241, 476
  role of the, 28n, 51–2, 110, 115, 134, 136–7, 247–8, 350, 452, 520, 522, 531
  Weimar National Assembly (*Nationalversammlung*), 106, 248, 363, 365, 368, 370, 376, 426–38, 440, 442, 446–7, 450–1, 453–4, 456, 472, 514, 520, 530
  see also Prussia
Germanophile(s), 61, 139, 144, 150, 169, 186, 250, 252, 258, 319, 321, 347–8, 404, 468, 478–9
global questions, 16, 18, 29, 78, 117, 134, 151n, 189, 218, 237, 254–5, 263, 266, 270, 303–304, 309, 325, 328, 373, 375, 377–9, 381, 409, 489, 491, 497
government
  cooperation, coalition, 47–8, 73–4, 78–9, 82, 86, 89, 96–8, 105, 143, 160, 162, 166, 180, 227, 229, 248, 252–5, 276–80, 299, 301, 309, 311–12, 318, 341, 367, 369–71, 374, 378, 381, 389, 422–3, 435, 441, 443, 453, 455–6, 471, 509, 511–12, 516, 518
  legitimacy of, 31, 35, 45–6, 99, 101, 181, 194, 213, 260, 379, 421, 505
  majority, 47, 60–1, 132, 136–7, 166, 179–80, 205, 208, 211, 252–3, 255, 257, 286, 288–9, 338, 371, 421, 496, 520, 528
  parliamentarisation of, 18–19, 29–30, 44, 50–4, 57, 61, 106, 108, 117, 122–3, 125, 134–9, 142, 146, 152, 155–6, 160, 164, 170, 173, 176, 180, 182, 195, 197, 204, 211, 215, 240–50, 254–5, 276, 294, 297, 301, 304, 339, 344, 346–7, 349–51, 354, 360–7, 430, 434, 452, 481, 496, 516, 523–4, 528–9, 531
  popular, 48, 80, 85, 127, 144, 156, 238, 334, 358–9, 416, 433, 436, 445, 448, 492, 494, 520, 522, 530
  representative, 27, 34, 40, 45, 60, 91, 97, 100, 111, 124, 155, 216, 219, 272, 280, 326, 343, 424–5, 465, 469
  see also British, Finnish, German and Swedish government
great power(s), 17, 27, 28n, 31–2, 71, 87, 108, 110, 118, 130, 135, 151, 214, 241, 248, 292, 352, 404, 428, 434, 481, 484, 496, 504, 526, 530–1
Gulf of Bothnia, 299, 463

H
Haparanda, 156
hate speech, 71, 510
Helsinki, 17, 40, 69, 92, 147, 149, 156, 176–80, 183–8, 200, 208–209, 237n, 257, 263n, 267n, 279, 283, 285, 287, 290, 318, 321, 328–9, 405, 416, 428, 485, 510, 529
historical trajectories, 27, 33, 37, 39, 168, 172, 205, 502
historiography, 30, 34n, 150, 162, 168, 364, 373, 383n, 454n, 507, 520, 531

I
ideology, 17, 19, 24, 26, 28, 32, 35–40, 54, 56, 59, 66, 74–5, 82, 87, 89, 96–7, 104, 118n, 120, 125, 127, 132, 139, 147–9, 152, 159, 160n, 162–3, 174, 185–6, 195–7, 201, 205, 213, 215, 218–19, 231–2, 241, 251–2, 255, 272, 274, 277, 286, 298–9, 301, 304, 316, 338, 348, 358, 368–70, 388, 396, 404, 406, 419–20, 431–2, 449, 452, 459, 464, 469–71, 487, 493, 497, 504–506, 511, 515, 519, 526, 530–3
  ideological confrontation, 13, 34, 54, 59, 143, 162, 192, 208, 232, 248–9, 256, 260, 268, 278, 281–2, 300, 315, 318, 326, 364, 381, 404, 450, 454, 464–5, 505, 509, 517, 522, 528
illegality, *see also* rule of law, 257, 265, 273, 284, 289, 470
Independent Labour Party (Britain), 46

Independent Social Democrats
(Germany), 112, 133, 241, 352,
363–4, 429, 433–5
international affairs, *see also* foreign
policy, 62–3, 73, 140, 217, 301, 367,
402, 465–6, 475, 511, 528
international
change, *see also* transnational,
change, 18, 93, 129, 143, 157, 164,
195, 237, 270, 282, 303, 325, 329, 335,
369, 374, 388, 405, 408, 410–11, 417,
434, 460, 498, 518, 524, 526, 529
communication, connections,
contacts, interaction, links, networks,
relations, *see also* transnational:
communication, connections,
contacts, interaction, links, networks,
15, 29, 35, 37, 51, 65, 69, 74, 120,
136–7, 140–1, 145, 147, 149, 151,
154–5, 179, 182, 203, 220, 229, 237,
251, 258, 260, 269–70, 292, 301, 303,
307, 321, 323, 329, 340, 346–7, 352,
355, 374–6, 381, 407, 409, 412, 421,
424, 427, 432, 434, 465, 477n, 502,
508–10, 527–9
comparisons, *see also* transnational,
comparisons, 20, 32, 43, 62, 87, 123,
145, 152–3, 167, 185, 197–9, 224,
272, 303, 324, 328–9, 407, 434, 439,
456, 469, 472, 475, 480, 505–506, 512,
515, 526, 529–31
context, *see also* transnational,
context, 32, 62–3, 71, 73, 93, 140, 143,
167, 217, 237, 259, 282, 294, 300, 315,
335, 367, 369, 373, 376, 399, 402–403,
405, 417, 455, 457–8, 465–6, 471–2,
480, 506, 511, 518, 526, 528–9
debate, discourse, discussion, *see
also* transnational: debate, discourse,
discussion, 30, 39, 87, 113, 238, 292,
365, 458, 499, 531, 533
democracy, *see also* transnational,
democracy, 35, 49, 127, 155, 157,
197–8, 294, 408, 444, 519
internationalism, 20, 31, 70, 74, 82–5,
137, 141, 144–5, 148, 151, 154–5,
157, 179, 189, 194, 198, 223, 238, 243,
260, 269–70, 279, 303, 373, 381, 400,
403, 435, 481, 507–508, 527–8
politics, 65, 237, 258, 360, 369, 519
revolution, *see also* transnational,
revolution, 56, 66, 69, 152, 165, 185,
187, 195, 203–204, 259, 262, 280, 370,
375, 509–10, 528–9

interpellation(s), 51, 53, 142–3, 151,
159–60, 164, 302, 362
intervention, 15, 31, 41, 60, 72, 109, 131,
139, 143, 161, 222, 225, 241, 245–6,
291, 298–300, 317–18, 321n, 323,
340, 351–2, 402n, 404, 429, 434, 467,
509, 513, 523
Irish National Party (Britain), 47–8, 74,
225–8, 512

J
journalism, *see also* newspapers and
press, 20, 49, 117, 156, 159, 193, 241,
348

K
Kaiser, *see also* Wilhelm II, 50–1, 54,
111, 113, 133, 145–7, 150, 196, 240–1,
246, 248, 253, 297, 324, 336, 341, 347,
349–350, 353, 359, 361, 363, 367–8,
389, 402, 431, 476, 509
Kautskyism, 17n, 59, 66–8, 70, 120, 149,
151, 157, 179, 197, 199–200, 268,
285–6, 467, 517, 525
Kurland, 353
Königsberg, 120, 353

L
Labour Party (Britain), 44, 46–8, 52,
73n, 74, 79, 82, 84–5, 88–9, 94–7,
102n, 106, 160n, 186, 190, 199, 215–
16, 218–19, 221, 223, 226, 228–9, 235,
237, 254–5, 294–5, 316, 340–5, 349,
358, 424–6, 490, 507–508, 511–3, 519
language policy (Finland), 65–6, 465,
469, 471, 493–5, 500–501, 506, 522,
529
League of Nations, 223, 237–9, 374, 400,
427, 468
left, leftist(s), 14, 16n, 17, 19, 22, 34–5,
46, 52, 55–6, 58–62, 69, 76, 92, 95–6,
110–13, 115, 119, 123–4, 130–5,
139–45, 147–52, 154–5, 157, 160–5,
167–72, 182, 188–92, 195–7, 199,
208–209, 212–13, 217, 223, 226,
228–30, 240–9, 251–6, 265, 267,
270, 272, 275n, 277–8, 281, 295, 298,
300–303, 305–10, 312–13, 315, 317,
328, 336, 345–7, 349–66, 368, 370,
373–6, 378, 380, 383, 386–7, 390–2,
394–5, 397, 399–403, 406, 410, 420,
422–3, 425–9, 432–3, 435–6, 440–3,
445–8, 451–8, 461–2, 466–7, 469–70,
472–6, 478, 480–1, 483–4, 486–7,

489, 494, 497, 502, 507–17, 519–24, 526–9, 531
Left-Liberals, Progressivists (Germany), 53, 57, 113, 116, 122–3, 125–6, 136, 241–8, 354, 356–7, 359, 361, 366, 432–3, 440, 443, 447–8, 452–4, 508, 513–14, 520, 523
legitimacy, 14–15, 26, 177, 232, 238, 270, 387, 397, 492
   illegitimacy, 169, 316, 369, 508, 511
   of military leadership, 71, 113
   of policy-making, political leadership, 15, 31–2, 45, 51, 60, 66, 71–3, 91, 94–5, 99–101, 113, 122, 132, 136, 232–3, 237–8, 249, 296, 298, 345, 349–50, 379, 399, 401, 414, 426, 429, 440, 442, 445, 448, 505–508, 514, 519, 522, 531, 533
   see also Finnish parliament, German parliament, government, parliament: legitimacy of
liberal(s), 13–14, 19–21, 34, 39, 50–4, 57, 61n, 63, 65–6, 115, 121–3, 125–6, 131, 135–7, 140, 150, 161, 167, 172–3, 180, 183, 199–201, 204, 209, 240, 242–9, 277, 280–1, 291, 318–19, 322, 324, 329, 334, 354, 356–62, 364, 366, 390, 394, 402, 409, 429, 432–3, 437, 440–1, 443–9, 452–4, 462–3, 466, 470, 476, 480, 486–7, 489, 497, 502, 504, 509, 513–15, 517–20, 522–3, 526–7
   democrats, 85, 87–8, 292, 303, 310, 331, 345, 378, 390, 409, 482, 485, 511
   government, 44, 46, 60, 99, 143, 166, 168, 215, 253, 311–12, 318, 370, 389, 430, 453, 456, 461–2, 516
   ministry, 45–6, 79, 254, 299–301, 368, 374, 422, 462
   reform, reformist(s), 44–5, 47, 54, 81–2, 88, 100, 107–108, 126, 146, 158, 216, 228, 231, 301, 318, 358, 369, 389, 457, 459, 462, 508, 512–13, 517, 533
Liberal Party (Britain), 39, 44–8, 53, 73n, 74–5, 77–85, 87–9, 94, 97, 99–102, 105, 107–108, 122, 154, 169, 215–7, 219, 224–6, 228–31, 233–4, 236–7, 294, 296, 303, 328, 341–5, 347, 394, 422–6, 462, 508, 511–13, 515, 519, 527, 533
Liberal Party (Sweden), 39, 54, 57–62, 122, 135–6, 140–1, 143–6, 148–50, 151n, 153, 155, 158–63, 165–6, 168, 172–3, 217, 223, 229, 246, 250–4, 277, 299–303, 306, 308–12, 328, 367–71, 373–4, 378, 384–5, 389–90, 393–4, 399–400, 430, 441, 453, 455–7, 459, 461–4, 468, 480, 484–5, 507, 509, 515–16, 521, 524, 528, 533
Lithuania, 353, 467n
London, 17, 74, 77, 115, 218, 235
Lutheranism, 31, 248, 322n 332, 404, 413

M
Majority Social Democrats (Germany), *see also* Social Democrats: German, 110, 112–13, 130, 152, 186, 199, 240, 256, 363–4, 433, 439, 447
mandate, 42, 73, 93, 106, 123, 144, 214, 290, 424, 471, 476
Marxism, 52, 67, 74, 89n, 95, 112, 120, 132, 134, 149, 154, 157, 160, 169, 174n, 179, 185–6, 188–9, 194, 198, 200, 226, 241, 251, 263, 266–7, 272, 274, 279, 286, 288, 290, 300, 303, 305–307, 312–13, 316, 335, 355, 364, 370, 376, 382, 400, 424, 426, 443, 458–9, 481, 498, 511, 516–17, 525, 532
   Spartacus League, 364
   see also Socialism
masses, 48, 68, 74n, 92, 97, 99, 102, 104, 118–21, 131–2, 146–7, 154–7, 162–4, 172, 216, 221, 231, 236, 243, 274n, 285–6, 309, 311, 328, 331–2, 359, 385–7, 394, 396–8, 420, 454, 463, 490, 510, 512, 517, 522, 533
   rule of the, 51, 157, 211, 354, 362, 386–8, 397, 514, 523–4
   mass movement, 17, 36, 56, 67, 117, 119, 134, 147, 154, 165, 168–71, 218, 266, 283, 288, 314, 371, 392, 396, 469, 487, 490, 517, 521, 524–5
Menshevism, Mensheviks, 184, 186
methodology, 23n, 25, 30, 32, 36–8, 506
   comparative history, 24–7, 30
   conceptual history, conceptual analysis, 18, 24, 28, 37, 38n, 40, 75, 506
   methodological nationalism, 36
   multi-sitedness, 13, 18–19, 37, 39–40, 505
   post-nationalist history, 26
militarism, 55, 73, 125, 134, 196, 218n, 260, 271, 275, 302, 347, 352, 376, 378
minority protection, 64, 320, 470

moderates, 16n, 51, 58, 82, 95, 141–2, 148, 168, 169n, 181, 184, 208, 218, 254, 257, 268–9, 300, 314, 323n, 346, 354, 372, 374, 376, 399, 407n, 456, 468, 470, 474, 477, 479, 481, 483, 519
monarchy, monarchist(s), 14, 29, 33–5, 53–4, 60–2, 65, 75, 91, 99, 113, 115–16, 122, 125, 129, 131–4, 137, 145, 150, 165, 167, 173, 197, 205, 210–12, 250, 252–4, 271, 276–7, 296–7, 302, 304–305, 313, 315, 317–31, 333–9, 348–9, 352, 354, 356, 358, 363–4, 366–7, 369–70, 372–3, 376, 384, 386, 388, 391, 398, 401–19, 430, 432, 434–5, 437, 442, 445, 448, 456–7, 464, 466–76, 478–82, 484–5, 488, 491–7, 500–503, 507, 510–11, 518–19, 521–2, 526, 529–30
   abdication, 109, 144, 173, 207, 254, 347, 363, 367, 466
   anti-monarchism, 65, 354, 430
   German, *see* Germany, monarchy
   majority, 320, 401, 407, 471
   royal prerogative, 45, 61, 113, 130, 181, 319, 339, 364, 419
   see also anti-monarchism

N
nation, will of the, 78, 89, 132
national
   communities, 27, 54, 76, 79, 97, 236
   context, 16, 18, 20–5, 27–8, 33–4, 42, 128, 464, 505–506
   debate, 21–2, 24, 40, 249, 350, 506, 508, 511, 527, 530
   historiographies, history, 23–7, 32, 36–7, 40, 60, 162, 504–505, 527
National Coalition Party (formerly Finnish Party) (Finland), 334, 470–1, 473, 476–8, 480, 482, 485–6, 488, 491–4, 496, 498–500, 502–503, 519
National Liberals (Germany), 114n, 121–2, 130, 135–6, 243, 297, 354, 356, 359, 361, 366
Netherlands, the, 85, 114, 153–4, 222, 253, 303, 411, 435
newspapers, *see also* press and journalism, 13, 19, 21, 34, 64, 69, 137, 142, 154, 158, 180, 233, 235, 267, 300, 338, 343, 453, 459, 463, 467, 504
New Zealand, 83, 223
Norway, 33–4, 146, 149, 153–4, 166, 223, 242, 253, 293, 303, 305, 323, 325, 329, 405, 467n, 479

Norwegian parliament, Stortinget, 63, 152n, 166–7, 306, 323, 325, 329, 377, 478–9, 528

O
old elite(s), 16, 52, 64, 160n, 234, 240, 319, 328, 331, 415, 422–3, 429, 442, 446, 466, 486, 488, 497, 512–13, 522
Old Finns (Finland), *see* Finnish Party
oligarchy, 104, 210, 241, 263–4, 274, 280, 290–1, 293, 295, 323–4, 327, 383, 388, 408, 419, 486, 490

P
parliament, parliamentary, parliamentarism
   chamber(s) of the parliament, *see* British and Swedish parliament
   concealed parliamentarism (*Kryptoparlamentarismus*), 52, 362
   cooperation, 52, 60, 140, 142, 192, 282, 481, 496, 509–10
   deliberation, 15, 17, 38, 49, 68, 102, 172, 211, 214, 233, 260, 401, 531
   democracy, 14n, 22, 29–30, 32, 41, 61n, 62–3, 81–2, 97, 106, 127, 197, 211, 218, 249, 273, 277–8, 290, 293, 296, 298, 310, 322, 337, 340, 354, 364–6, 369, 399, 421–2, 430–1, 434, 436, 448–9, 454, 459, 465–7, 470–3, 479, 481–2, 485, 490–1, 517–18, 522–3, 525, 531, 533
   dimension, 69, 488n
   discourse, 20, 27, 28n, 32, 35, 38–41, 59, 68, 74, 88n, 119, 124, 128, 181, 184, 201–202, 232–3, 236, 254, 264, 272, 281–3, 288, 303, 421, 448, 450, 505, 508, 511, 517, 525, 531
   debate, 15, 19, 21, 30, 37n, 39–41, 42n, 49, 52–3, 59, 64, 73, 74n, 88, 89n, 93, 95–6, 100, 104, 109, 116, 137, 139, 142–3, 145, 148, 165, 169, 175, 190, 252, 259, 263, 267–8, 278, 281, 289, 315, 337, 351, 362, 370, 373, 416, 419, 453, 465, 472, 480, 505, 520, 528
   government, 22, 28, 33–5, 44, 46, 48, 51–4, 57, 62, 68, 70–1, 85–6, 96, 98, 100–101, 104, 108, 127, 138, 166, 169–70, 174, 180–1, 185, 194, 208, 213, 219, 222–3, 229–30, 238, 242–3, 245, 247–51, 254, 260, 273, 276, 281–4, 286, 288, 296, 298, 312–13, 318, 327, 335, 338–9, 347, 349–50,

362, 367, 371, 375, 399, 401, 406n, 418–19, 421, 425, 429–30, 450, 456, 478, 487, 497, 499, 501–502, 505, 522–3, 525–6, 530
  group, 52, 56, 68, 114, 116, 140, 191–2, 202, 246, 256, 264, 268, 273–4, 282, 283n, 285n, 288, 334, 353, 358, 370, 441, 454, 500, 525
  legitimacy of, 15, 31–2, 35, 45, 51, 64, 66, 72, 94–5, 99–101, 173, 176–8, 181, 183n, 184, 192, 194, 209, 212–13, 233, 237–8, 249, 256–62, 281–2, 284, 315, 345, 350, 399, 409, 414, 420–1, 448, 482, 505–506, 519, 522, 524–5, 531
  majority, 60–1, 64, 66–7, 99, 118, 151n, 154, 166, 169, 174, 178–80, 182, 184, 192, 194, 200, 202, 204–205, 208, 211, 241, 244, 251, 253–4, 256–7, 261, 266, 276, 279, 282, 297–8, 308, 311–13, 318, 335–6, 419, 438, 469, 474n, 481, 502, 510–1, 514, 520–1, 524, 528
  ministry, 45–7, 60–1, 64, 76, 140–1, 172, 180, 205, 211, 215, 228, 249, 252–5, 260, 298–302, 313–14, 338, 340, 352, 357, 362, 368, 372, 389, 401, 407–408, 412, 418, 442, 456, 475, 479, 488, 524
  national, 18–19, 22, 28, 33, 39, 42, 50, 136, 175–8, 208, 224, 238, 259, 287, 297, 422, 432, 466, 500–501, 504, 517, 524, 526, 530
  powers of, 44, 51, 64, 131, 171, 192, 211, 287, 297, 320, 451
  responsibility of government, 13
  skepticism about, 48, 50–1, 75, 87, 91, 176, 208, 249, 330, 332, 337, 344, 360, 365, 367, 385–7, 410, 416–17, 426, 452–3, 486, 493–4, 518–19, 522, 525, 527
  sources, 14, 22, 25, 30, 37, 40, 505, 526
  sovereignty of, 49, 52, 64, 68, 70, 72, 98, 134, 151n, 171–2, 174, 176–7, 182, 188–91, 193, 198, 208–12, 240–1, 251, 253, 256, 258, 266, 272, 287, 312, 317, 327, 401, 416, 429, 447, 451, 492, 510
  supremacy (*Parlamentsherrschaft*), 53
  state parliaments (Germany), 50
  tradition, 82, 167, 172, 283, 429, 445, 524
  unicameral, 45, 63, 142–3, 152, 160–1, 173, 289, 306, 330, 337, 377, 383, 391, 461, 487, 497, 518
  will of the, 53, 137–8, 205, 207, 217, 244, 282, 338, 360, 486
  work, 64, 67, 125, 134, 160, 177, 183n, 280, 282, 285n, 289, 298, 352n, 358, 399, 400, 426, 438, 524
  see also extra-parliamentary
  see also British, Finnish, German, Prussian and Swedish parliament
party
  programme, 52, 57, 66–7, 89, 112, 188, 253, 344–5
  truce, 46, 54–5, 72, 78, 237n, 240, 297, 340, 450
patriotism, 46–7, 52, 54, 56, 72, 79, 85, 88, 92, 105, 114–15, 128, 130, 154, 186, 188, 208, 218, 220, 224, 236, 243, 246, 341, 344, 357, 407, 429, 475, 484, 520
Peace Treaty of Brest-Litovsk, 292, 297
Peace Treaty of Versailles, 18, 424, 432, 434–5, 444–5, 528
people
  das Volk (Germany), 55–7, 133, 357, 448–9
  folket (Sweden), *see also* democracy: *folkstyre*, 56, 251, 392, 395, 521
  kansa (Finland), *see also* democracy: *kansanvalta*, 56, 174n, 199, 413, 437, 485, 494
  narod (Russia), 199, 521
  will of the people, *see also* popular will, 13, 17, 60–1, 68, 97, 99, 108, 120, 122, 132–3, 152, 159, 161, 163–5, 170, 184, 205–6, 227–8, 231, 244, 249, 261, 281–2, 291, 295, 309, 311–12, 325, 332–3, 344, 352, 357–8, 366, 382, 385, 388, 393–6, 411, 414–17, 431, 437, 442, 445–7, 449, 451–2, 462–3, 486, 488–9, 491–2, 494–8, 506, 520–2, 525
  power of the people, 48, 182, 203, 251, 282, 289, 314, 326–7, 336, 344, 358, 387, 400, 439, 443, 451, 487, 501, 506
  Volksgemeinschaft (community of the people) (Germany), 54, 133, 174n, 358, 436–8, 449–50, 486, 514, 520
  Volksherrschaft (rule of the people) (Germany), 436, 449, 514, 516
  Volksstaat (people's state) (Germany), 358, 365, 395, 440, 444, 449, 486, 514, 520
  Volkswille (will of the people)

(Germany), 357, 365, 448-9
see also nation, will of the
Petrograd, 17, 22, 40, 69, 75, 82, 111, 141-2, 147-50, 154, 156, 174, 176-9, 181, 183-94, 196, 199-200, 202, 204, 209, 241, 256-8, 260-1, 263n, 268, 271, 274n, 279, 283, 427, 460, 466, 502, 508-10, 524, 529, 532
plenary sessions, 18, 64, 117, 216, 261-2, 305, 361, 431, 433, 448
plutocracy, 128, 161, 297, 324, 382-3, 388, 403, 408
policy decision-making, 22n, 45, 47, 57, 76, 80, 100, 115, 217, 321, 357, 361, 384, 391, 446, 451
political
   action, 15, 37-8, 40, 201n, 235, 532
   change, development, transformation, 15-17, 30, 32, 36, 38-9, 62, 103, 159, 169, 224, 231, 242, 272, 302, 350, 363n, 365, 380, 402n, 408, 449, 476, 490, 522, 528
   circumstances, conditions, 24, 27, 236
   community/ies, group(s), 13, 19, 21-2, 31, 38, 40-1, 56, 65, 90, 105, 116, 120, 134, 140, 176, 180-1, 195, 197, 206, 214, 234, 236-7, 243, 278, 290, 330, 333, 359, 367, 392, 394, 397-8, 429-30, 437, 445, 453, 463, 481, 508, 515, 519, 521, 523
   concepts, semantics, 15, 18n, 24, 33, 35, 41, 87, 124, 130, 469, 520
   conflict, tension, 16, 71
   corruption, 324, 330
   culture, *see also* Britain, Finland, Germany, Sweden: political culture, 13, 20, 22-4, 26, 27-8, 37, 38n, 92, 124, 201n, 489n, 504, 533
   deliberation, 38
   discourse, 13, 16, 19-20, 23, 25, 29n, 35, 37-40, 56, 64-5, 72, 74, 86, 88, 126, 132, 136, 144, 174, 189, 200n, 202, 210, 215, 226, 360, 407, 449n, 455, 464-5, 505-506, 525, 532
   elite(s), 16, 35, 48, 51-2, 61, 71, 81, 99, 102-104, 108, 113, 118, 124, 127, 134, 139, 162, 220, 245, 294, 303, 336, 342, 358, 369, 421, 464, 480, 504, 507, 522-3
   equality, 151, 309, 380
   event, 20-1, 201, 511
   history, 19, 28, 31, 37-8, 40, 88, 104, 147, 211, 253, 340, 461, 504, 530, 532
   influence, 52, 59, 65, 137, 201, 331, 335, 415
   mobilization, 63, 340, 429, 520
   model, 30, 34, 130, 139, 195, 250, 297, 505, 515
   movement(s), 32
   identification, 35
   order, 13, 29, 32, 51, 72, 90, 92, 95, 108, 119, 125-7, 131-2, 144, 155, 167, 173, 175, 191, 208, 220, 239, 241, 249, 269, 271, 298, 308, 319-20, 327, 356, 363-4, 369-70, 374-6, 379-80, 397-8, 408-409, 418, 428, 431-2, 438, 447, 473, 487, 490, 505, 513, 515, 518, 530
   participation, 18, 29, 42, 109, 437, 454-5, 461, 490, 504
   process, 13, 15, 18, 23, 28, 37-9, 55, 94, 114, 132, 136, 156, 169, 175, 237, 257, 268n, 333, 417-18, 485, 505, 518, 524
   question, 20, 118, 369
   reality, 41, 396, 506
   reform(s), 15-16, 50-1, 90, 118, 164, 297, 345, 371
   rights, 44, 60, 87, 102, 106, 114-16, 118, 121, 147, 156, 163-4, 205-206, 214, 216, 218, 223, 233-4, 251, 290, 297, 304, 310-2, 329, 336, 345, 391-2, 397, 415, 419, 438, 440, 446-7, 485, 511, 520-1
   rival(s), 20, 90, 298, 347
   role, 13-14, 18, 28n, 33, 42-3, 45, 53, 56, 93, 101, 114, 134, 162, 247, 259, 319, 334, 337, 355, 373, 393, 399, 447, 506, 519, 531
   science, 19, 86, 161, 452
   structures, 15, 49, 51, 122, 442
   system(s), 13, 15, 30, 35, 41, 46, 48-9, 51-2, 58-9, 63, 71, 73, 75, 79-80, 82-3, 88, 90, 94, 99, 102, 104, 107-108, 110, 113, 119, 121, 124, 126-8, 132, 134-5, 152, 161, 163, 171-2, 176, 192, 210, 215, 222, 225, 227, 232, 236, 239-40, 243, 246, 248-9, 254, 285n, 293-4, 297, 307, 324, 329, 333, 336, 342-4, 349-50, 358, 367-8, 374, 377, 379, 436, 438, 443, 445-7, 451-2, 454, 458, 461-3, 471, 477n, 478, 486, 492, 511-13, 520, 524, 526-7, 531
   tradition, 53, 82, 494
   values, 41, 307, 464
   views, 19, 83, 136, 311, 422, 470
politicisation, 29, 51, 125, 200n, 225,

310, 343, 362, 365, 431, 447, 520, 530
popular opinion, 15, 237, 349
popular will, *see also* people, will of the, 98, 123, 143, 165, 180, 205, 207, 236, 269, 359, 382, 394, 396, 425, 449, 462, 507, 514, 520, 522
post-war reconstruction, 17, 26, 77, 79, 95, 103, 107, 109, 123, 132, 214, 235, 266, 294, 341, 422, 506
power, 13, 15, 20, 30-1, 38, 44-5, 48, 51, 55, 59, 64, 68, 70, 74, 77-8, 80, 90, 98, 107, 109-10, 114, 122, 125-6, 131-3, 137-8, 154, 160, 165, 167, 169-72, 174-5, 177-8, 182-4, 187-8, 191-4, 196, 198, 201, 203, 210-12, 218, 221, 231, 242, 244, 249-51, 257-8, 260, 263, 265-6, 270, 272, 274-5, 280, 282-91, 293-5, 297, 300, 305, 308, 311, 314-16, 320, 326, 330-1, 333, 336, 342, 344-5, 355, 358, 362-3, 365-6, 375-6, 378, 380, 382-5, 387-8, 392, 394, 396, 398, 400, 408, 410, 413, 415, 418-19, 422, 424-5, 432, 438-40, 443, 445-8, 451, 462, 473-4, 479, 482, 484, 487, 489-95, 497-503, 507, 513, 518, 520-2, 524, 531
  balance of, 52, 134, 138, 171-2, 187, 205, 210-11, 244, 273, 280, 287, 290-1, 338-9, 361, 365, 393, 441, 452-3, 466-7, 471, 486, 491-2, 496, 499, 503, 522, 524
  budgetary, 55, 170, 211, 296, 358, 360
  executive, 50, 57, 77, 110-11, 113, 125, 129-30, 135-7, 182, 187, 196, 210-11, 247, 272, 280, 296, 326, 360, 362-3, 365, 413, 428, 441, 452-3, 471, 473, 478-9, 491-2, 496, 499, 503, 522
  seizing political, 55, 66-7, 93, 164, 188, 201, 259, 263n, 265, 282, 289, 296, 308, 341, 371, 380, 484
  see also people, monarchy: royal prerogative
press, 16, 20, 22, 25, 32n, 40, 42n, 51, 55, 58, 68, 75, 85, 88, 100-101, 105, 114, 131, 141-2, 145, 165, 168, 171, 173, 175-6, 186, 198, 216, 226, 233, 245-6, 248-9, 255-6, 259, 267-8, 270-1, 273, 279, 281, 283, 286, 294-5, 298-300, 305, 315, 319, 322, 325, 345, 347, 350, 368n, 369, 371, 373, 395, 407, 426, 432, 454, 463, 465, 474, 477, 491, 494, 505, 510, 513-14, 523, 528, 530, 532
  Aftonbladet (Sweden), 21, 153, 310, 315, 361, 373, 460
  Berliner Tageblatt (Germany), 21, 123, 137, 244, 354, 356, 360-1, 440, 513-14
  Dagens Nyheter (Sweden), 21, 145, 150, 158, 371n
  debates, 18, 21-2, 37, 39, 100, 109, 268, 302, 423, 505, 532
  Helsingin Sanomat (Finland), 21, 324, 338, 414, 418n, 495
  Herald (Britain), 21, 75n, 88n, 89n, 94n, 129n, 229, 232, 279n, 294-5, 345, 347, 349
  Hufvudstadsbladet (Finland), 21, 180, 204, 276, 278, 300, 339, 402n, 403n, 404, 406, 409, 411, 418, 467, 476, 485n, 486, 493, 500
  Manchester Guardian (Britain), 21, 86n, 88, 134, 217, 294, 342-4, 346, 352n, 424, 426-7, 444
  national, 18-19, 21, 74, 140, 302, 321, 373, 404-405, 454, 465, 472, 494, 512
  Neue Preußische Zeitung (also known as *Kreuz-Zeitung*) (German), 21, 135, 243, 247, 355-6, 359, 442
  Pravda (Russia), 181
  Social-Demokraten (Sweden), 21, 144n, 146, 163, 165, 255, 304n, 308-309, 314, 352n, 383
  The Times (Britain), 21, 91, 100n, 218n, 239n, 342-3, 345-6, 348, 423, 426, 428
  Työmies, later *Suomen Sosialidemokraatti* (Finland), 21, 69, 192, 198, 212, 260, 273-4, 286, 402n, 407, 409, 468
  Vorwärts (Germany), 21, 110, 112, 114, 117-18, 128, 129n, 132, 138, 180, 241, 243-4, 304, 352, 355, 358, 360, 409, 435, 439, 446, 450, 513
  see also newspapers and journalism
pre-war, 21, 52-4, 65, 67, 73, 77-8, 87, 111, 137-8, 140, 167-8, 228, 338, 438, 450, 481-2, 484, 490, 511, 522
prime minister, *see also* Chancellor, 47, 51, 61, 74-5, 77-8, 84, 88, 93, 98, 100, 102-103, 114, 119, 125, 140-1, 143, 159, 164, 182n, 190-2, 198, 205, 261, 269, 275, 289, 292, 295-6, 302-303, 311, 322, 324, 329, 340, 342, 370-2, 375, 378-9, 384-5, 388-90, 394-6, 403, 410, 412, 417, 424, 455, 475, 489, 502, 512, 518, 526
privilege(s), 21, 87, 100, 104, 122, 191,

199, 203, 235, 309, 332, 382–3, 392–3, 419, 490, 493
procedure, 33, 38, 66, 68, 149, 169n, 171, 182–4, 190, 210, 212, 221, 226, 232, 275, 285n, 315, 347, 360, 369, 387, 399, 402, 404, 417, 438, 451, 457, 474, 493, 495, 519, 524
pro-German attitude, *see* germanophile(s)
propaganda, 16, 21, 32, 48, 73, 108, 111, 119, 124, 126, 128, 187, 240, 248, 294, 375, 427, 431, 436, 444, 505, 507, 513, 523, 527, 531
  American, 49, 61, 506
  British, 48–9, 61, 87, 106, 124, 215–16, 295, 341, 426, 512
  Finnish, 316, 518
  French, 61, 124
  German, 49, 110, 131, 244, 321, 348, 357, 416, 450n, 527
proportional representation, 44, 59, 62, 73, 84–5, 88–9, 104, 106, 215, 217, 220, 222–4, 229–31, 233, 239, 241, 293, 429, 501, 527
Prussia, Prussian, 31, 35, 50–1, 58, 82n, 111, 118, 120, 125–6, 129, 133, 135, 137–9, 141–2, 144–7, 149, 166, 195–7, 210, 215, 218n, 245, 247, 251–2, 254, 259, 278, 300, 306, 315, 319, 322, 325, 346–8, 352–3, 356, 359, 368, 427, 429–30, 450, 460, 470, 480, 493, 498, 505, 507, 511, 528, 530
  autocracy, 86, 108, 155, 252, 372
  elite, 51, 58, 118, 122, 126, 132, 135, 359
  Herrenhaus, 51, 111, 117–18, 120, 122, 129–30, 134–5, 146, 150, 228, 253, 294, 297, 361n, 403
  Junkers, 31, 74n, 86n, 120, 136, 146, 148, 150–1, 158, 168, 252, 294, 354–5, 357, 376, 386, 406
  lower chamber, 116, 123, 129, 297, 305
  ministers, 51
  nobility, 109, 122, 342, 362, 444, 454
  system, 32, 50–1, 54–5, 62, 65, 73, 92, 108, 110–11, 113–23, 125–32, 136, 143, 146, 150–1, 153, 156, 196–7, 228, 240–1, 243–8, 250, 255, 292, 294–8, 304, 306, 319–20, 322, 325, 330, 336, 346, 348–9, 351, 353, 355–6, 360–3, 369, 373, 383, 407, 417–18, 426, 428, 430–1, 438, 450, 466–7, 469, 479, 498, 505, 507–508, 513, 520, 523, 527, 529

Prussianism, 32, 107, 111, 118, 122, 124, 128–30, 145–6, 150, 159, 196, 215, 227–8, 241, 254, 294, 297, 303, 326, 372, 505, 511–6, 527–9
publicity, 51, 55, 100, 104, 295, 431–2, 453–4, 469, 512

R
race, 140, 234
radicalism, radicals, 26, 46, 52, 56–9, 61, 70, 82, 89, 100, 106, 112, 140–5, 149–50, 155–7, 159–60, 162, 169, 171, 178–9, 186, 188, 191–2, 194, 199, 200n, 209, 217, 220, 226, 229, 240, 242n, 243, 250, 255, 261, 266, 268, 274, 277, 294, 300, 307–308, 318–19, 324, 326, 341, 352, 363–4, 368–9, 374, 381, 383, 388, 391, 395, 399, 443, 455–6, 462, 469–70, 474, 479, 481, 483, 487, 491n, 502, 510, 516, 525
  action, 16, 58, 141, 149–50, 157, 170–1, 178, 184–5, 188, 209, 212, 262, 264, 268, 286, 289, 298, 313–14, 346, 351, 358, 375, 391, 399, 410, 419, 423–4, 443, 464, 477–8, 481, 509, 511
  discourse, 35, 48, 64, 67, 70, 112, 156, 174, 176, 184, 192–3, 200, 205, 227, 264, 266–7, 286, 316, 458, 464, 474, 505, 510–11, 517, 531–2
  radicalisation, 15, 45, 59, 64, 67–8, 96, 112, 141–3, 151–2, 157, 164, 169, 178, 184, 191–2, 209, 211–2, 219, 222, 248, 253, 262, 264, 268–9, 276, 285n, 289, 298–9, 301, 315, 346, 351, 354, 363, 370, 378, 400, 422, 429, 431, 458, 460, 464, 480, 508–10, 517, 524, 531
  rhetoric, 13, 16, 79, 169–71, 178, 188, 264, 286, 363, 431
reactionarism, *see also* revolution: anti- and counter-revolution, 14, 16, 72, 121, 128, 129n, 146, 150–2, 154, 176, 193, 198, 219, 263, 277, 279, 304–305, 310, 326–7, 338, 342, 345, 352, 383, 409, 416, 421, 426, 442, 444, 473, 491n, 529
Reds, the (Finland), 59, 203n, 267n, 298–9, 301–302, 306–308, 317, 319, 322–3, 326, 333, 348, 353n, 403, 407, 412, 428, 468–9, 474n, 477, 518, 528
Red Guards, Workers' Guards (Finland), 17n, 67, 176–7, 185, 259, 266–8, 270–1, 273, 285n, 306
referendum, 91, 93, 138, 144–5, 154,

163, 169, 272, 296, 316, 323, 333, 336, 361, 365, 392, 405, 413–15, 434, 446, 451, 453, 458–9, 461–3, 467, 492, 498, 514, 520
Reform Act of 1832 (Britain), 220
Reich (Germany), *see* federal state, 50–1, 111–12, 115–19, 121–5, 128–30, 137–8, 196, 241–2, 244–6, 297, 349, 355, 360, 362, 431, 440
Reichstag (Germany), *see* German parliament, 31, 50–7, 64, 73, 108–14, 117–18, 120–1, 123, 125, 128–31, 133–5, 137–8, 140, 147, 151, 167, 180, 196, 240–1, 243–50, 294–5, 346–7, 350–1, 354–5, 357–61, 402, 407, 426, 431, 436, 441, 447–8, 450–2, 476, 507, 514, 520, 522
Reichspräsident (Germany), 138, 448, 472, 486
representation, 42, 50–2, 73, 82, 103, 138, 160n, 163, 173, 202, 216, 219, 233, 252, 293, 317, 321, 392, 395, 431, 453, 459, 494, 500
  proportional, 44, 59, 62, 73, 84–5, 88–9, 104, 106, 215, 217, 219–20, 222–4, 229–31, 233, 239, 241, 429, 501, 527
  representative government, 14, 27, 33–4, 40, 49, 56, 58, 60, 66, 72, 86, 91, 97, 100–101, 111, 124, 134, 145–6, 155, 169, 180, 184, 205, 210, 216, 224, 230, 239, 242, 272, 276, 280, 293, 326, 330, 343, 373, 417, 424–5, 452, 459–60, 465, 469, 513, 519, 524, 526
  representative institutions, 13, 17, 19, 29, 31, 33, 41, 51n, 59, 62–3, 67, 75, 80–1, 97–8, 101, 109, 111, 122, 131, 133, 136, 138–9, 161n, 163–4, 173–4, 176, 178, 180, 182, 204, 209–10, 217, 231, 236, 238–9, 247, 252, 261–2, 264, 276, 278, 281, 284, 287, 290, 296, 302, 314, 319, 334, 339, 345, 360, 416, 433, 446–8, 451, 455, 463, 482, 496–7, 506, 511, 516, 521
  representatives of the citizenry, people, 31, 45, 81, 94, 98–9, 114, 116, 131, 134, 138, 164, 173, 190, 203, 236, 244, 262, 264, 266, 278, 281, 288, 332, 345, 358, 360, 366, 383, 395, 397, 416, 420, 437, 439, 447, 463, 501, 511, 521
  representative traditions, 27, 30–1, 60–1, 158, 201, 327, 393, 436, 465, 532

Representation of the People Act (Britain), 292, 294, 340, 474n
republican(s), republicanism, 35, 54, 61, 65, 70, 182, 197, 318, 320–5, 328, 332–5, 337–9, 351, 353, 358, 366, 401–408, 411, 413–16, 418, 428, 430, 432, 448, 451, 464–5, 468–73, 475–6, 479–81, 484–5, 487–95, 500–501, 518, 521, 529–30
  democracy, 65, 70, 197, 276, 278, 323, 326, 328–9, 338, 345, 365, 403, 407–408, 411, 428, 430, 445, 454, 470–3, 478, 485, 487, 529
  presidential republic, 290, 452, 465–7, 472–3, 493–4, 496, 500
  see also constitution, democracy: republican
responsibility, see also parliament, 13, 30, 49–51, 56, 64, 70, 98, 121–2, 125, 171–3, 176, 207–208, 244, 250, 253–5, 273, 278, 287, 309, 313, 320, 328, 338–9, 349–50, 360, 385, 387, 402, 413, 419, 429, 448, 451, 453, 493, 497, 499, 523
revolution, revolutionary
  age of, era, period, 13, 17, 31, 33, 190, 221, 261, 434, 469, 486
  agitation, 16, 142, 149, 252, 265, 288, 320, 335, 378, 386, 509–10, 524
  anti-revolutionary, 14, 16, 301
  atmosphere, mood, 16, 69, 106, 141–2, 147, 174–5, 178, 186, 242, 287, 368, 371–2
  constitutional, 92, 350
  counter-revolution, *see also* Finland: counter-revolution, 185, 192, 200, 203, 268, 275, 302, 321, 346, 353–4, 428, 438, 510, 528
  international, 56, 69, 187, 259, 272, 370, 375, 509, 529
  Marxist, 52, 149, 364
  parliamentary, 220, 222, 504, 508
  process, 17, 29n, 149, 176, 200, 268, 368
  proletarian, 58, 262–3, 268
  Revolution of 1906 (Russia), 14, 63–4, 67, 145, 173, 192, 197, 204, 262, 283, 288, 319, 326, 335, 464, 484, 500, 502, 508
  Revolution of 1917 (Russia), 16, 18, 22, 46, 57, 61–2, 64, 74, 79, 82, 89, 92–4, 100, 106, 110–13, 115, 117–20, 122, 124, 127–8, 130, 132, 134, 140–4,

146, 149–50, 152, 154–6, 159, 161–2, 169, 173, 179–81, 185, 187–92, 194, 201–203, 208, 240, 249, 253, 260–1, 264, 266, 268–9, 276, 284, 300, 312, 320, 333, 335, 346, 353, 368, 377, 379, 403–404, 424–5, 432, 480, 504, 506–508, 511, 513–14, 520, 524, 528
Revolution of 1918 (German), 29n, 349, 351, 367–8, 375, 377–9, 429, 455, 457, 459, 480, 509, 514, 516, 519
revolutionary radicalism, 59, 285n, 477
world, global revolution, 29, 147, 197, 218, 255, 260, 263, 280, 353, 376, 425, 434
see also Bolshevism: October/November Revolution
rhetoric, 16, 21, 23n, 37n, 38, 40, 45, 48–9, 52, 58, 70, 78–9, 86, 88–90, 93–4, 99, 102–103, 107, 110, 122–3, 152–4, 158–9, 169, 171, 178, 192, 197, 199, 203, 206, 211, 216, 228–9, 232–3, 236, 241, 259, 264, 268, 271, 280, 286, 288–90, 294, 297, 307–308, 326, 328–9, 331, 336, 339, 344, 351, 363, 370, 375–6, 378–9, 382, 385, 397, 404, 407–408, 418–19, 442, 444, 450n, 454, 459, 461, 474, 481–3, 485–6, 492–3, 500, 502, 504, 506, 508, 511, 513–14, 520, 528
right, the
  right party (*Konservative*) (Germany), 34, 52–3, 89, 91–2, 97, 106, 116–19, 124, 126, 131, 134, 137–8, 221, 225, 241–3, 246, 276, 288, 304–305, 330, 332, 342, 347, 350, 354–5, 357, 362, 364, 429, 433–4, 436–40, 442–7, 449, 453–4, 456, 458, 470, 472–3, 493, 501, 505, 507–509, 513–15, 520, 522, 527
  Right (*Högern*) (Sweden), 31, 34–5, 57–62, 89–92, 97, 106, 131, 140, 142–3, 145–8, 150–1, 153–62, 165–72, 194, 196, 221, 225, 250–5, 276, 278, 288, 296–7, 299, 301–10, 312–15, 322, 330, 332, 334, 342, 362, 366–70, 372–401, 411, 430, 438, 450, 455–61, 463–4, 467, 469–70, 473, 485, 493, 502, 505, 507–508, 515–16, 521–2, 524, 528
  rightist(s), 20, 59–61, 91, 114, 119, 131, 140–1, 155, 157–8, 160, 162, 164–5, 167–8, 171–2, 174, 203, 206, 212, 225, 247, 250–3, 255–6, 267–8, 273, 276, 279n, 281, 283, 287, 298–301, 303–305, 309–15, 319, 326–8, 330, 347–8, 356, 367, 369, 372–6, 379–80, 382, 385–9, 392, 394–401, 408, 413–14, 416, 419, 429, 431, 433–5, 437, 439, 442, 445, 449, 451, 459, 463, 471, 474, 481, 483, 486, 489, 491, 493, 498, 502, 507, 509, 513, 515–16, 518–19, 521, 527–8
Riksdag, see Swedish parliament
rule of law, see also illegality, 489
Russia
  administration, 65, 284
  despotism, 55, 120
  Duma, parliament, 51n, 63, 178, 187, 283
  Provisional Government, 173, 175, 178–9, 181–4, 187–9, 191, 203, 256, 258, 261, 275, 316
  Romanovs, 65, 173, 178
  socialists, 59, 65, 69, 112, 119, 153, 156, 182, 184, 187, 199, 257, 381, 510
Russo-Japanese War, 63

S

Scandinavia, 32–6, 65, 69, 129, 159, 195, 242, 301, 320–1, 329, 427, 468, 475, 478, 480, 502, 530
Social Democrats, 22, 35, 48, 63, 65, 79, 89, 92, 114, 119, 151n, 199, 203, 345, 375–6, 424, 507
  Austrian, 66, 456
  Finnish, 16n, 35, 39, 54, 63–4, 66–70, 79, 82, 89, 92, 95, 112–13, 118, 129, 141–2, 147, 151n, 152, 154–6, 160–1, 169, 173–85, 187–95, 197–213, 219, 241, 242n, 246, 251, 255–91, 298, 300–302, 306, 308, 312–13, 315–19, 321, 327, 331, 334–5, 351–2, 353n, 370, 380, 406–409, 412, 414n, 418n, 420–1, 425, 433, 436, 438, 444, 453, 468, 470, 472–4, 477–9, 481–5, 487–92, 494, 496–8, 501–2, 509–10, 513, 515, 517–19, 521, 524–6, 528–9, 531–2
  German, see also Majority Social Democrats (Germany), 50–7, 64–5, 69, 89, 95, 110, 112–13, 115–20, 125, 129–35, 137–41, 147, 150n, 151–2, 154, 160n, 173, 180–3, 186, 189–90, 192, 196–7, 199, 219, 240–7, 249–51, 254, 278, 303, 316, 324, 346, 349, 351–5, 357–8, 360, 362–4, 366, 381, 391, 406–407, 425, 428–9, 431–5,

437–41, 443–9, 451, 453–4, 456, 458–9, 470, 497, 486, 507–508, 513–14, 516, 520, 523, 527
International, 69–70, 82, 84, 251, 260, 269, 352, 373, 381
revisionism, 35, 46, 67–70, 96, 112, 140, 162, 164, 169, 211, 229, 264, 272, 298, 345, 488, 490, 515
Swedish, Labour Party, 35–6, 39, 54, 57–62, 69, 82, 89, 95, 112, 129, 139–48, 151–2, 155–7, 159–66, 168–73, 181, 186, 189–90, 192, 197, 199, 219, 223–4, 229, 246, 250–6, 278, 298–303, 305, 307–16, 318, 347, 358, 364, 367–71, 373–4, 377–8, 380–6, 389, 391–2, 395, 397–400, 425, 430, 433, 438, 443, 453, 455–63, 468, 470, 490, 509, 513, 515–16, 521, 524, 528
socialism, socialist, *see also* Russia: socialists, 14n, 19, 21, 26, 35–6, 51–54, 57–9, 63, 66–70, 82, 89, 95–7, 106, 112–13, 119–20, 125, 129n, 140–5, 147–9, 151–2, 154, 156–7, 160–2, 168–9, 171–2, 174–6, 178–85, 187–94, 197, 208–10, 212–13, 218–19, 221, 223, 226, 230, 235, 245, 249, 251, 253–4, 256–8, 260, 262–72, 274–82, 284, 288–9, 294, 298, 300–301, 303–304, 307–308, 311–14, 317–19, 324, 326–8, 337, 340–1, 343, 346, 349, 352–6, 358, 363–4, 368–72, 374, 376–7, 380–1, 383, 386, 390–1, 399–400, 403–404, 410–12, 416, 419, 422–9, 433, 435–8, 442–4, 447, 456–60, 462–4, 470, 477, 479, 481, 483–4, 487, 490, 497–8, 504, 508–10, 512–18, 520–1, 524–9, 532–3
agenda, 340, 433, 457
agitation, 36, 67, 70, 149, 157, 168, 187–8, 200, 263, 267, 270, 281, 284, 288, 335, 363, 378, 419, 494, 509–10, 524–5
anti-socialist legislation, 50
circles, 187
society, 36, 525
see also anti-socialist legislation, Marxism, left, Reds, Social Democrats and syndicalism
South Africa, 85
sovereignty, 91, 133, 136, 173, 179
national, 16, 164, 174, 178, 182, 226, 278, 424, 448, 521
popular, sovereignty of the people, 14, 16, 24, 30, 48, 66, 120, 133, 159, 164, 174n, 178, 205, 236, 305, 309, 312, 316–17, 357–8, 364–5, 414–15, 431, 434, 444, 446–9, 463, 488, 491–2, 520–1
see also parliament: sovereignty of
Stockholm, 17, 58, 69, 82, 89, 92, 142, 144–5, 148–50, 152, 154–5, 165, 170, 177, 224, 237n, 244, 352n, 371, 376, 509
Stuttgart, 57
suffrage, 41–2, 45, 59, 62, 80, 83, 84n, 99, 122–3, 142, 146, 233, 237, 253–5, 275, 284, 291, 311, 333, 370, 380, 391, 395, 418, 457, 482, 502
anti-suffragist(s), 44, 91, 105, 107, 223, 233
debates, 72–5, 105, 111, 125, 142, 154, 222, 303, 393, 439, 449, 455, 514
democratic, democratisation of, 13, 28, 50, 59, 81, 86, 125, 129–30, 158–9, 166, 204, 234, 242, 246, 291, 314, 340, 346, 351, 367, 370, 399, 430, 439, 445, 481, 530
enfranchisement of soldiers, 48, 76
equal, 30, 50, 120, 142, 148, 151, 159, 243, 251, 255, 303, 371–2, 493
extension, extended, 13, 58, 62, 72–3, 74n, 80, 88, 90–1, 93, 97, 101, 104–106, 119, 142, 145–6, 153, 158, 162, 166, 214, 234, 241–2, 251, 253, 295, 305, 308, 311–13, 367, 370, 375, 381, 389, 396–7, 405, 422–3, 425, 461–2, 515, 521, 524
female, 34, 42, 44–5, 49n, 54, 62–3, 65, 72–3, 75, 77, 84–5, 88n, 91, 93–4, 100–102, 104–107, 114, 118–21, 130, 142, 144n, 151–3, 156, 165–6, 173, 214, 217, 220–1, 223, 234–5, 242, 251, 293, 303–304, 311–12, 329, 341, 357–8, 363, 371–2, 441, 461–3, 479, 527–8
forty tax and vote grades (Sweden), 59, 62, 128, 139
male, manhood, 44, 50, 59, 72–3, 77, 104–107, 118, 125, 128, 131, 142, 151–2, 156, 234–5, 293, 303, 358, 363, 436, 445
reform, 13, 33, 44, 47, 54, 58–9, 68, 72–3, 79, 82, 94–6, 98, 105–107, 111, 114–16, 118, 121–4, 129, 132, 139, 146, 148, 150–1, 154, 156, 160, 163, 168, 171, 176, 180, 214–15, 217, 220, 222, 224–5, 238, 241, 243–5, 249–50, 253, 293–4, 297–8, 301, 303, 318–19,

334, 342, 361n, 368–9, 374, 386–7, 390, 393, 426, 433, 455–7, 461–5, 506–507, 509, 511–14, 520, 524, 530
suffragette, suffragist, 44, 46, 88n, 160, 235, 294, 329, 426
three-class franchise (Prussia), 50, 54, 111, 113, 121, 128, 130, 147
universal, 17–18, 30, 33, 35, 50, 57–63, 66, 68, 72–3, 75, 83, 87, 89, 102, 106, 108, 118, 122, 125, 128–31, 140, 142–3, 148, 151–2, 154–6, 160, 162, 172–3, 176, 179, 186, 192, 217, 219, 221–3, 242, 249, 255, 266–7, 274, 276, 284, 293, 295–6, 302, 305–306, 308, 312, 319, 326–7, 329, 337, 342, 351, 358, 363, 368–9, 371, 374–6, 382, 386, 388–9, 391n, 392, 398, 429, 455–6, 459–62, 464, 467, 487, 499, 506, 509, 513, 515, 518–19, 522, 524, 531

Sweden, Swedish
constitution, *see* constitution, Swedish
democracy, 34, 142, 147, 157, 161, 307, 314, 371, 382–3, 385, 390, 427, 458, 461–3, 507, 509, 515–16, 531
government, 54, 57, 59–62, 138–41, 143–6, 151, 154–5, 157, 160, 163–6, 168–172, 182, 222, 249–56, 276, 300, 302, 305–8, 312–14, 347, 368–73, 375, 378–81, 384, 388, 392, 395–7, 399, 401, 411, 430, 455–7, 459–62, 465, 516, 523
political culture, 20, 27, 31, 33, 35, 139, 427, 463–4, 465, 515
polity, 30, 82, 146, 153, 162, 166, 173, 311–12, 365, 370, 381, 383, 385, 396, 481, 520
see also Swedish parliament
Swedish parliament, Riksdag, 33n, 42, 58, 61n, 111, 139, 142, 146, 156, 161, 163, 167–8, 171, 249–50, 258, 298, 301–303, 312–14, 385, 428, 456, 511
First Chamber, 57, 59–60, 62, 90, 139, 143, 148, 150, 152, 158, 162–3, 165, 168–9, 171, 214, 228, 250, 253, 301–302, 305, 309, 314, 319, 367–8, 370–1, 373, 382, 387–90, 396, 398, 455, 458, 464, 521
Second Chamber, 57, 59–60, 62, 141, 151, 158, 166, 168, 171–2, 214, 252, 302, 313–14, 319, 371, 373, 382, 385, 455, 458, 464, 524
Special Committee, 373

Swedish People's Party (Finland), 58, 63, 66, 180, 186, 194–5, 204, 210–12, 225, 267, 276, 284, 289, 296, 320, 323, 325, 329–31, 333–4, 359n, 366, 409–10, 416, 430, 441, 460, 466, 468–71, 473–6, 478–9, 482, 486, 493–5, 500, 502, 518–19, 521–2, 526
Swedish tradition (in Finland)
constitutional, 31, 63, 65–6, 138, 173, 185, 201, 256, 278, 283, 307, 310, 320, 410, 465, 468, 478, 480, 491, 495, 499, 518
cultural, 65–6, 185
legal, 31, 33, 65–6, 167, 201, 320, 532
political, 31, 33, 65, 127, 185, 205–206, 283, 307, 319, 327, 445, 473, 519, 532
Switzerland, 34, 56, 84–5, 129, 142, 145, 155, 272–3, 377, 405, 475, 478, 480, 530
syndicalism, syndicalist, 22, 143, 216, 306, 400

T
Tasmania, 85
Third Republic, *see also* France, 167, 208, 210, 479, 486, 499, 526
transfers, *see also* transnational:
transfers, 23, 25, 27–8, 37, 145, 188
cultural, 26, 35, 188
of ideas, 20–1, 24, 32, 35, 186, 189, 197, 200, 264, 480, 504, 506, 508, 510, 520, 526, 530, 532
transnational
agents, 37, 39–40, 141, 147, 156, 302, 307, 506, 528
analysis, studies, 18n, 23–4, 28–30, 36, 40, 472, 506
change, *see also* international, change, 18, 71, 75, 88, 93, 107, 129, 139–40, 142–4, 148, 153–4, 159, 229, 293, 304, 309, 376–7, 408, 434, 463, 478, 480, 490, 494, 507, 509, 512, 528
communication, connections, contacts, interaction, links, networks, *see also* international: communication, connections, contacts, interaction, links, networks, 16, 19–24, 26–8, 32–3, 37, 39–40, 42–3, 54–5, 69, 71, 73, 75, 83, 87–8, 136–7, 141, 147, 156, 173, 178, 182, 185, 188, 200, 202, 217, 222–4, 259–60, 300, 303–304, 353n, 369–70, 373, 376–7, 464, 468, 471–2, 475–7,

Subject and Place Index

480, 504–506, 526–30, 532
comparisons, *see also* international, comparisons, 13, 18, 20–8, 30, 32, 33, 37, 40, 43, 50, 75, 87, 153, 159, 197, 222–4, 302, 305–306, 323, 352–3, 368, 376–7, 380, 406–407, 467, 472, 477–8, 480–1, 504–6, 526–8, 533
context, *see also* international, context, 16, 21, 23, 25–8, 32, 37, 40, 60, 62, 73, 144, 148, 179, 259, 309, 325, 373, 406, 411, 434, 446, 463, 466, 471, 478, 480–1, 491, 493–4, 504, 528–9, 532
cultural ties, 322, 377
debate, discourse, discussion, *see also* international: debate, discourse, discussion, 14, 16–20, 22, 24–5, 27–30, 32–3, 37, 39–40, 42–3, 49–50, 54–5, 57, 60, 69–70, 73, 87–8, 111, 113, 119, 139–40, 156, 173–4, 179, 184, 193, 197, 202, 240–1, 259–60, 291–2, 302, 321, 325, 346, 373, 407, 456, 459, 468, 471–2, 476–7, 480–1, 504–506, 528–9, 532–3
democracy, *see also* international, democracy, 14, 18–19, 22, 27, 29–30, 32, 42–3, 58, 60, 70–1, 73, 87–8, 108, 129, 153, 156–7, 159, 182, 200, 229, 238n, 250, 304, 309–10, 346, 373, 408, 438, 444, 463, 466, 504, 508, 512, 529–30, 533
history, 23–8, 29n, 40, 505
influence, impact, 24, 27, 29, 32, 58, 61, 65, 73, 111, 129, 140, 217, 260, 291, 293, 321, 367–8, 377, 403, 406, 411, 465, 467–8, 472, 480–1, 486, 489, 494, 507–9, 527, 529
institution, 19, 24, 26–7, 37, 238n, 400
revolution, *see also* international, revolution, 16, 18, 22, 29, 37, 40, 46, 65, 93, 104, 144, 147, 149, 164, 167, 183–4, 190, 197, 241, 259, 352, 370, 377, 469, 508–509, 529, 531
transfers, 19–28, 32, 37, 142, 147, 156, 173, 197, 200, 406, 431, 480, 504–506, 526, 530, 532
ways of thinking, 129, 143–4, 280, 302–303, 416, 519
Tsar, 64, 68, 71, 118, 121, 128, 131, 145, 148, 154, 177–8, 202, 207, 295, 312, 353, 464

U

Union of Democratic Control (Britain), 46
Unionist Party (Conservatives) (Britain), see also Conservative Party, 47, 76–7, 80, 82, 84, 90, 98, 103–104, 114, 214–15, 217, 225, 330
United States of America, 14, 34, 49, 55, 57, 61, 71, 73–4, 80, 83–5, 88, 92, 107, 109–10, 124, 126–7, 134, 144, 150, 153–4, 217, 220, 223, 242, 247, 252, 258, 266, 271, 292, 302–303, 321–5, 329, 337, 343–5, 348–9, 362, 384, 403, 407, 421, 434–5, 467–9, 471, 475, 477n, 478–80, 496, 506–507, 513, 527, 530

V

veto, 45, 50, 55, 68, 81, 209, 319, 346, 472–3, 480, 486
vote of no confidence, 53

W

Weimar Coalition, 54, 245, 428, 430, 441
West, the, 17, 31–2, 61, 86, 110, 116, 119, 127–8, 131, 134, 136–8, 140, 152, 159, 177, 179, 218, 244–5, 247–8, 250, 252, 276, 305, 318–24, 344–5, 347, 356–7, 365, 367, 372, 401, 416, 423, 427–31, 436, 444, 467, 505, 513, 516, 523, 528–9
Western model, 22, 29, 34, 49–50, 61, 66, 86–7, 110, 116, 119, 124, 126–8, 130, 134, 139, 145, 154, 156, 167, 169, 172–3, 197, 225, 245, 248, 252–3, 257, 272, 292, 294, 297, 301–303, 307, 313, 317–18, 320, 322–3, 339, 343–4, 346n, 350, 354, 356, 365, 372–3, 381, 383–4, 404, 427, 430, 435–6, 438, 444, 449, 453, 466, 468, 474, 480–1, 486, 495–8, 501–502, 505, 507–508, 513–16, 518, 520, 523–4, 526–9
Western politicians, 29, 49, 87, 124, 128, 220, 225, 252, 292, 343, 347, 445, 515
Whites, the (Finland), 289, 299–300, 304–305, 308, 316–18, 322, 324, 412, 428, 468–9, 484, 502
White government, 295, 299–300, 307, 317–18, 349, 403, 511, 518
White Guards, 264–5, 285n, 286n, 414, 526

worker(s), *see also* class, working, 35, 48, 58, 60, 66–8, 105, 114–15, 120, 150, 157–8, 168, 176–7, 179, 181, 183, 185, 187, 193–4, 197–203, 208–209, 211, 218, 242, 258, 260, 262–4, 268–70, 272, 274n, 275, 279, 281–2, 284–7, 298, 300–302, 316, 333, 336, 345, 349, 353, 355, 363, 371, 376–7, 380, 394–8, 400, 406, 420, 424–5, 453, 462, 467, 474, 481–2, 486–7, 513, 518, 525, 528–9

Worker's Suffrage Federation (British), 426

world history, 71, 120, 303

Wurttemberg, 85, 114, 242, 447

Y

Young Finns (Finland), 63, 66, 195, 204, 206, 209, 265, 267, 273, 277, 280–1, 289, 291, 324, 326, 328–9, 334, 354, 404–409, 414, 417–18, 466, 470, 484

Z

Zimmerwald International, 56, 58, 69, 82, 155, 189, 269, 529

Index of Names

A

Ablaß, Bruno, German MP, German Democratic Party, 440, 447

Adamson, William, British MP, Labour, 48, 237

Ahmavaara, Pekka, Finnish MP, Young Finns (Liberals), 277, 281, 289, 329, 334, 418

Aho, Juhani, Finnish author, 322

Airola, Matti, Finnish MP, Social Democrat, 206, 266n, 270

Åkesson, Nils, Swedish First Chamber Member, The Right, 397

Alkio, Santeri, Finnish MP, Chaiman of the Agrarian League, Minister for Social Affairs, 63, 186, 194–5, 197, 204, 208–209, 264–5, 267, 269–70, 287, 289, 323n, 325–8, 335–9, 402, 404n, 406, 408, 413–15, 419, 475, 477, 484–5, 487–8, 490, 496, 501n

Alkman, Edvard, Swedish Member of the First Chamber, Editor-in-Chief of *Göteborgs-Posten*, 393

Amery, Leo, British MP, Conservative, Parliamentary Under-Secretary, 107–108

Ampuja, Mikko, Finnish MP, Social Democrats, 482, 491n

Anderson, Andrew, British MP, Liberal, 219

Andersson, Hans, Swedish Member of the Second Chamber, The Right, 165

Andersson, Per, Swedish Member of the Second Chamber, The Right, 401

Antila, Juho Erkki, Finnish MP, Finnish Party (Conservatives), 413

Arajärvi, Juhani, Finnish MP, Finnish Party/National Coalition Party (Conservatives), Chairman of the Parliamentary Group, 284, 500

Arffman, Kusti, Finnish MP, Agrarian League, 325, 337

Arokallio, Gustaf, Finnish MP, Young Finns (Liberals), 206, 265, 277, 324, 326, 334

Aronen, Nestori, Finnish MP, Social Democrats, 272, 282

Asquith, Herbert Henry, British MP, Liberal, former Prime Minister, Leader of the Opposition, 47–8, 75, 77, 97, 102, 342, 344, 372

B

Baden, Max(imilian) von, German Prince, Chancellor, 346, 350, 352, 355–60, 363, 402, 406, 418, 432

Banbury, Frederick, Sir, British MP, Conservatives, 94, 101

Barker, Ernest, British political scientist, 49

Bathurst, Charles, Sir, British MP, Conservative, 220

Bauer, Gustav, German MP, Social Democrats, Chancellor, 432

Bebel, August, German MP, Social Democrats, 64

Bellinder, August, Swedish Member of the First Chamber, The Right, 380, 389

Bergman, Johan, Swedish Member of the First Chamber, Liberals, 390, 393

Bergroth, Waldemar, Finnish MP, Finnish Party (Conservatives), 404, 413

Bernstein, Eduard, German Social Democratic theoretician and MP, 35, 52, 56, 67, 112, 114, 128, 188n, 211

Bethmann Hollweg, Theobald von, German Chancellor, 53, 55, 57, 111, 113, 116, 125, 133, 166, 244

Index of Names

Beyerle, Konrad, German MP, Catholic Centre, Professor of Law, 434, 441–2
Bismarck, Otto von, Prussian nobleman (Herzog zu Lauenburg), former Chancellor, 51, 119, 126, 134, 245, 311, 324, 351, 354, 357, 361–2, 376, 404, 434, 441, 529
Björk, Matts, Finnish MP, Swedish People's Party, Court of Appeal Judge, 325
Blair, Reginald, British MP, Conservatives, 85
Bonar Law, Andrew, British MP, Conservatives, the Chancellor of the Exchequer, 47, 78, 98, 103, 224, 237, 238n, 341
Brailsford, Henry Noel, British journalist, radical leftist, 295
Branting, Hjalmar, Swedish Member of the Second Chamber, Chairman of the Social Democrats, 39, 57, 60–1, 69, 89n, 140–4, 147–8, 150–1, 155–7, 159, 163–4, 171, 224, 250, 252, 254, 302, 304, 306, 308–10, 313–15, 347–8, 352n, 370–3, 375, 377, 381–3, 385, 392, 399, 427, 460, 509, 515, 528
Brück, August von, Freiherr, German Ambassador to Finland, 321
Bryce, James, 1st Viscount Bryce, British nobleman, Liberals, Professor in Law, former British Ambassador to the United States, 219–20, 223, 234–5, 296, 305, 368
Buckmaster, Stanley, Sir, British nobleman, Liberal, former Lord Chancellor, 219
Bulwer-Lytton, Victor, 2nd Earl of Lytton, British nobleman, Conservatives, 220
Burdett-Coutts, William, British MP, Conservatives, 83, 86–7, 231

C

Castrén, Kaarlo, Finnish Prime Minister, National Progress Party (Liberals), 471
Cave, George, Sir, British MP, Conservatives, Secretary of State for the Home Department, 79, 97, 220
Cavendish-Bentinck, Henry, British MP and nobleman, Conservatives, 92, 98, 102–103
Cecil, Hugh, British MP and nobleman, Conservatives, 77, 100–101, 108

Cecil, Robert, British MP and nobleman, Conservatives, 107, 239–40
Chaloner, Richard, British MP and nobleman, Conservatives (1918 1st Baron Gisborough), 93
Chamberlain, Austen, British MP, Liberal Unionist, 222
Chaplin, Henry, 1st Viscount Chaplin, British nobleman, Conservatives, 235
Clarke, George, Baron Sydenham of Combe, British nobleman, former Governor of Victoria, 221
Clason, Samuel, Swedish Member of the First Chamber, The Right, Professor of History, 151, 165, 309–11, 387, 463
Clifford, William Hugh, 10th Baron Clifford of Chudleigh, British nobleman, Conservatives, 231
Clynes, John Robert, British MP, Labour, 79
Coats, Stuart, Sir, British MP, Conservatives, 84
Cohn, Oskar, German MP, Independent Social Democrats, 434–5, 443, 453
Compton-Rickett, Joseph, British MP, Liberal, Paymaster-General, 85, 107
Courtney, Leonard, 1st Baron Courtney of Penwith, British nobleman, Liberals, Professor of Political Economy, 230–1, 237
Coyote, Colin, British MP, Liberals, 233
Craik, Henry, Sir, British MP, Scottish Unionist, 76, 85, 90, 93, 95, 103
Crewe-Milnes, Robert, 1st Marquess of Crewe, British nobleman, Liberals, Leader of the House, 234
Cripps, Charles, 1st Baron Parmoor, British nobleman, Conservatives, 223
Curzon, George, Earl Curzon of Kedleston, British nobleman, Conservatives, Leader of the House, 221, 223, 232–3

D

David, Eduard, German MP, Social Democrats, Speaker, Minister, 56, 69, 114, 118, 129, 133–4, 433, 436, 438, 443, 446, 451
Davidson, Randall, 1st Baron Davidson of Lambeth, Archbishop of Canterbury, 235
Delbrück, Clemens von, German MP and Prussian nobleman, German

National People's Party, 434, 442, 444, 453
Dernburg, Bernhard, German MP, Progressive People's Party, 247
Devlin, Joseph, British MP, Irish Nationalists, 225–6
Dickinson, Willoughby, British MP, Liberals, 87
Dillon, John, British MP, Irish Nationalists, 225n, 226, 233
Duguit, Léon, French expert in administrative law, 499
Düringer, Adelbert, German MP, German National People's Party, 434

E
Ebert, Friedrich, German MP, Chairman of the Social Democrats, Chancellor, Reichspresident, 69, 115, 241, 247, 351–2, 355–6, 358–9, 363–5, 432–3, 435–6, 445, 451, 479
Edén, Nils, Swedish Member of the Second Chamber, Chairman of the Liberals, Prime Minister, Professor of History, 144–6, 153, 155, 161, 172, 254, 302, 370, 378, 385, 389, 394, 455
Ekman, Carl Gustaf, Swedish Member of the First Chamber, Liberals, Editor-in-Chief of *Aftontidningen,* 390
Ekman, Karl, Swedish Member of the First Chamber, The Right, Court of Appeal Judge, 375, 387, 398
Eloranta, Evert, Finnish MP, Social Democrats, 209
Engberg, Arthur, Swedish Member oft he Second Chamber, Social Democrats, 304, 311, 377, 381, 391n, 393, 459–61
Engels, Friedrich, German Marxist theoretician, 70
Erich, Rafael, Finnish MP, National Coalition Party (Conservatives), Professor of Constitutional Law, 181, 317, 478, 485–6, 491, 493, 498–500
Ericsson, Aaby, Swedish Member of the First Chamber, The Right, 388, 397
Ericsson, Ollas Anders, Swedish Member of the First Chamber, The Right, 401
Erkelenz, Anton, German MP, German Democratic Party, 440
Erzberger, Matthias, German MP, Catholic Centre, 241
Estlander, Ernst, Finnish MP and nobleman, Swedish People's Party, Professor of Legal History, 212, 277n, 476, 478, 487, 489n, 493–4, 501

F
Fehrenbach, Constantin, German MP, Catholic Centre, 357
Field, William, British MP, Irish Nationalists, 226
Fisher, William Hayes, British MP, Conservatives, Parliamentary Secretary of the Local Government Board, 96
Frederick William IV (von Hohenzollern), King of Prussia, 196–7
Friedrich Karl von Hessen, Count of Hesse, German nobleman and King Elect of Finland, 402, 465–6, 475–6
Furuhjelm, Annie, Finnish MP, Swedish People's Party, 267, 323–4, 329, 409

G
Graefe, Albrecht von, German MP and Prussian nobleman, Conservatives, 131, 134, 138, 442
Gascoyne-Cecil, James, 4th Marquess of Salisbury, British nobleman, Conservatives, 228
Geijer, Erik Gustaf, Swedish historian, 152
George V (Windsor), King of United Kingdom, 47
Giffard, Hardinge, 1st Earl of Halsbury, British nobleman, Conservatives, former Lord Chancellor, 232
Goltz, Rüdiger von der, German general and nobleman, 321
Goode, William T., British reporter, 428
Gradnauer, Georg, German MP, Social Democrats, journalist with *Vorwärts,* 241–2
Gretton, John, British MP, Conservatives, 90–1
Gullberg, Wilhelm, Swedish Member of the First Chamber, Liberals, 306
Gustavus V (Bernadotte), King of Sweden, 140

H
Haapanen, Santeri, Finnish MP, Agrarian League, 337
Haase, Hugo, German MP, Chairman of the Independent Social Democrats, 55–6, 120, 147, 241, 247, 352–3, 355

579

Haataja, Kyösti, Finnish MP, Finnish Party (Conservatives), 409, 416
Hahl, Eero, Finnish MP, Agrarian League, 404
Hahl, Pekka, Finnish MP, Agrarian League, 418
Haldane, Richard, 1st Viscount Haldane, British nobleman, Liberals, 49, 229, 236
Hallén, Harald, Swedish Member of the Second Chamber, Social Democrats, 144, 146, 151, 157, 162, 164, 169, 172, 303, 305, 307, 309, 377, 383, 392, 460–1
Hallendorff, Carl, Swedish Member of the Second Chamber, The Right, Professor, Rector of the Stockholm School of Economics, 145, 161, 167
Hamilton, Raoul, Swedish Member of the Second Chamber, Liberals, Vice-Speaker, 303, 389
Hammarskjöld, Hjalmar, Swedish nobleman, The Right, former Prime Minister, 60, 139
Hammarskjöld, Hugo, Swedish Member of the First Chamber, The Right, former Minister of Ecclesiastical Affairs, 388
Hammarström, Alexis, Swedish Member of the First Chamber, The Right, 397
Hansson, Per Albin, Swedish Member of the Second Chamber, Social Democrats, editor-in-chief of *Social-Demokraten*, 308, 313, 368, 371, 374, 383–4, 400
Harrison, Austin, British journalist, 342
Haußmann, Conrad, German MP, German Democratic Party, Chairman of the Constitutional Committee, 244
Heine, Wolfgang, German MP, Social Democrats, 137
Heinze, Rudolf, German MP, German People's Party, Chairman of the Parliamentary Group, 434, 441, 452
Helenius-Seppälä, Matti, Finnish MP, Christian Labour Union, 202, 479
Hellberg, Mauritz, Swedish Member of the First Chamber, Liberals, editor-in-chief of *Karlstads-Tidningen*, 150, 153, 158, 164, 398, 457
Hemmerde, Edward, British MP, Liberals, 219, 224
Henderson, Arthur, British MP, Labour, minister, 79, 82

Hermelin, Richard, Swedish nobleman, 389, 397
Herold, Carl, German MP, Catholic Centre, 359
Hertling, Georg von, Graf von Hertling (Count Hertling), Catholic Centre, Chancellor, 249, 305
Hildebrand, Karl, Swedish Member of the Second Chamber, The Right, historian, editor-in-chief of *Stockholms Dagblad*, leader of the lower house opposition, 61, 145, 150, 153, 158, 161, 165, 168, 306, 313–14, 375, 380, 384–5, 394–6, 400
Hildén, Leo, Finnish MP, Social Democrats, 483
Hindenburg, Paul von, Prussian nobleman and general, leader of the German army, 55, 246, 355
Hintze, Paul von, Prussian nobleman, German foreign minister, 476
Hjelt, Edvard, Finnish diplomat, 317, 467n
Hjärne, Harald, Swedish Member of the First Chamber, The Right, professor of history, 305, 311, 387–8, 396
Holmquist, Carl Fredrik, Swedish Member of the First Chamber, Liberals, 463
Homén, Theodor, Finnish MP, National Coalition Party (Conservatives), professor of applied physics, 492, 500
Hope, Harry, Sir, British MP, Conservatives, 101
Hornborg, Eirik, Finnish MP, Swedish People's Party, 186, 195, 276, 284
Hultin, Tekla, Finnish MP, Young Finns (Liberals), 210, 329, 417, 499
Hupli, Väinö, Finnish MP, Social Democrats, 482
Huttunen, Evert, Finnish MP, Social Democrats, editor-in-chief of *Työ*, 182, 183n, 193, 202, 209, 257, 279n
Hyöki, August, Finnish MP, Finnish Party (Conservatives), 202
Hänninen-Walpas, Edvard, Finnish MP, Social Democrats, editor-in-chief of *Työmies*, 63–4, 69, 183n, 191–3, 206, 212, 264, 274–5, 284, 286
Härmä, Erkki, Finnish MP, Social Democrats, 263, 269
Hästbacka, Emil, Finnish MP, Swedish People's Party, 487, 494, 501
Höglund, Zeth, Swedish Member of

the Second Chamber, Leftist Social Democrats, 58, 152, 161–2, 165, 170–1, 370

I
Ingman, Lauri, Finnish MP, chairman of the Finnish Party (Conservatives), professor of theology, 210n, 276, 287, 332, 408, 414

J
Jokinen, Alma, Finnish MP, Social Democrats, 279
Joukahainen, Vilkku, Finnish MP, Agrarian League, 406, 416
Juutilainen, Antti, Finnish MP, Agrarian League, 193, 265, 404, 408, 414, 416, 419, 476

K
Kaila, Erkki, Finnish MP, National Coalition Party (Conservatives), theologian, 492
Kairamo, Oswald, Finnish MP, Finnish Party (Conservatives), botanist, 267, 289, 404, 410, 418
Kallio, Kyösti, Finnish MP, Agrarian League, minister of agriculture, 277, 337, 408, 413n
Kaskinen, Juho, Finnish MP, National Progress Party (Liberals), 489
Katzenstein, Simon, German MP, Social Democrats, 451
Kautsky, Karl, German Marxist theoretician, 17n, 35, 56, 59, 66–70, 120, 149, 151, 157, 179, 188n, 197, 199–200, 241, 261, 268, 271–2, 283, 285n, 286, 467–8, 517, 525
Kerensky, Alexander, Socialist Revolutionary Party, minister in the Russian Provisional Government, 82, 239n, 341
Key, Ellen, Swedish feminist activist and socialist intellectual, 303, 307
Kjellén, Rudolf, Swedish Member of the First Chamber, The Right, professor of political science, 61, 145, 154, 161, 166
Koch, Gerhard Halfred von, Swedish Member of the First Chamber, Liberals, 311
Koch-Weser, Erich, German MP, German Democratic Party, 440, 452
Koenen, Wilhelm, German MP, Independent Social Democrats, 443
Kokko, Juho, Finnish MP, Agrarian League, 207, 337, 414
Kollontai, Alexandra, Russian Bolshevik revolutionary, 58, 182n, 188–9, 191–2, 199, 279, 529
Kujala, Jussi, Finnish MP, Social Democrats, 266, 269, 275, 286
Kuusinen, Otto Wille, Finnish MP, Social Democrats, Marxist theoretician, 67, 69, 183n, 257, 262–3, 265, 266n, 272–5, 278–9, 282, 285, 290–1, 302, 316, 326, 467, 478

L
Lagerroth, Fredrik, Swedish historian, 61n, 168, 497
Laherma, Jonas, Finnish MP, Social Democrats, 182n, 478, 481, 482n, 486n
Laine, Augusta, Finnish MP, Young Finns (Liberals), 326
Larsson, Viktor, Swedish Member of the Second Chamber, Social Democrats, 145, 459
Ledebour, Georg, German MP, Independent Social Democrats, former London correspondent, 56, 115, 132, 134, 360
Lehokas, Vilho, Finnish MP, Social Democrats, 282
Lehtimäki, Kondrad, Finnish MP, Social Democrats, author, 193
Lenin, Vladimir, Russian Bolshevik revolutionary, 17n, 22, 56, 69–70, 89n, 112, 142, 145, 148–9, 155, 157, 160–1, 170, 179, 182, 184, 187–9, 191–2, 202–3, 257–9, 262–4, 271, 274n, 275, 278–9, 280n, 283, 291, 298, 323, 341, 425–6, 443, 477, 509, 513, 529
Levy-Lawson, Harry, 2nd Baron Burnham, British nobleman, Liberal Unionists, the owner of *The Daily Telegraph*, 220
Liebknecht, Karl, German socialist leader, chairman of the Independent Social Democrats, 57, 363
Lindblad, Ernst, Swedish Member of the First Chamber, The Right, 150, 380, 389
Lindgren, Adolf, Swedish Member of the First Chamber, The Right, 397

Lindhagen, Carl, Swedish Member of the Second/First Chamber, Leftist Social Democrats, mayor of Stockholm, 61, 144–5, 148–9, 152, 154, 157, 160, 162, 163n, 170, 370, 462

Lindman, Arvid, Swedish Member of the Second Chamber, the chairman of The Right, 58–9, 141, 172, 224, 302, 310–311, 313, 369, 393–4

Lithander, Edvard, Swedish Member of the Second Chamber, The Right, chairman of the conservative cultural association *Götiska Förbundet*, 379, 385–6, 395

Lloyd George, David, British MP, chairman of the Coalition Liberals, prime minister, 47–9, 74, 78, 88, 93, 97, 100, 102–103, 119, 292, 296, 340–3, 345–7, 423–5, 512–13

Lohi, Kalle, Finnish MP, Agrarian League, 267, 277, 495

Long, Walter, British MP, Conservatives, the Secretary of State for the Colonies, 80, 83, 91, 94

Lonsdale, John, Sir, British MP, Irish Unionist, 226

Lowther, James, British MP, Conservatives, the Speaker of the House of Commons, 73

Ludendorff, Erich, field marshal, leader of the German army, 55, 246, 295, 349

Luopajärvi, Mikko, Finnish MP, Agrarian League, 265, 277, 284

Luxemburg, Rosa, German Marxist theoretician, 36, 188n

Lvov, Georgy, Russian prince, Liberals, 204

Löfgren, Jonas Eliel, Swedish Member of the Second Chamber, Liberals, Minister of Justice, 164, 303, 309, 394, 463

Löwegren, Gunnar, Swedish Member of the Second Chamber, Social Democrats, 146, 155–6, 172

M

MacDonald, James Ramsay, British MP, former chairman of the Labour, theoretician, 84, 89, 94–5, 345, 424–5

MacKinder, Halford, British MP, Scottish Unionists, the Director of the London School of Economics, 77, 99, 216

Mallock, William Hurrell, British author, Conservatives, 293

Malmivaara, Wilhelmi, Finnish MP, Finnish Party (Conservatives), Pietist leader, 329, 330n, 404, 413

Manner, Kullervo, Finnish MP, Social Democrats, the Speaker of Eduskunta, later the Prime Minister of Red Finland, Commander-in Chief of the Red Guards and chairman of the Finnish Communist Party, 177, 183n, 206, 256–7, 266n, 274, 275, 279, 283–5, 287, 337, 467, 494

Mannerheim, Carl Gustaf Emil, Finnish nobleman (friherre), Commander-in-Chief of the Finnish White Army, Regent, 317, 474, 502

Månsson, Fabian, Swedish MP, Leftist Social Democrats, 160n, 370, 400

Marx, Karl, German Marxist theoretician, 70

Meinecke, Friedrich, German historian, 304

Menger, Anton, Austrian socialist legal theorist, 490

Mertin, Erich, German MP, German Reichspartei, also a member of the Prussian House of Representatives, 123, 138

Michaelis, Georg, German Chancellor, 246–7

Mikkola, Antti, Finnish MP, Young Finns (Liberals), Chairman of the Legal Affairs Committee, the founder of *Turun Sanomat*, 267

Molotov, Vyacheslav, Russian Bolshevik revolutionary, 179

Mond, Alfred, British MP, Liberals, 84, 108

Müller-Meiningen, Ernst, German MP, Progressive People's Party, 122, 361n

Mäkelin, Yrjö, Finnish MP, Social Democrats, Chairman of the Constitutional Committee, 183n, 185–90, 193, 198–200, 202, 206, 262, 266n

Mäkelä, Santeri, Finnish MP, Social Democrats, 271

Mäki, Jaakko, Finnish MP, Social Democrats, chairman of the parliamentary group, 198, 273–4, 283n

Möller, Gustav, Swedish MP, party secretary of the Social Democrats, 305, 368, 377, 383, 392, 462

N

Napoleon III (Bonaparte), French president and emperor, 108

Naumann, Friedrich, German MP, chairman of the Progressive People's Party, 354, 356, 359, 361, 452

Nevanlinna, Ernst, Finnish MP, chairman of the Finnish Party (Conservatives), professor of political economy, 206, 211, 329, 405, 407, 411, 416, 418

Nicholas II (Romanov), Russian Tsar, Grand Duke of Finland, 109, 144, 173, 207

Niukkanen, Juho, Finnish MP, Agrarian League, 328

Nordström, Ludvig, Swedish journalist, 348

Norman, David, Swedish Member of the Second Chamber, The Right, chairman of the antisocialist *Svenska folkförbundet*, 154, 165, 168, 267, 307, 375, 378, 386, 394n, 395, 460–1

Noske, Gustav, German MP, Social Democrats, 117–19, 128–9, 132, 352

O

Olsson, Anders, Swedish Member of the Second Chamber, Liberals, 459

Olsson, Olof, Swedish Member of the First Chamber, Social Democrats, 166n

Olsson, Oscar, Swedish Member of the First Chamber, Social Democrat, 457, 462

O'Neill, Charles, British MP, Irish Nationalists, 226

P

Paasikivi, Juho Kusti, Finnish MP, Finnish Party (Conservatives), Prime Minister, 63, 322, 324, 329, 403, 410, 412, 417–18, 475, 489, 499, 502, 526

Paasivuori, Matti, Finnish MP, Social Democrats, 288, 406, 409, 420

Palme, Olof, Swedish historian, 299

Palmer, Roundell, Viscount Wolmer, British nobleman and MP, Conservatives, 224, 233, 236

Palmstierna, Erik, Swedish nobleman (friherre), Member of the Second Chamber, Social Democrats, Minister of Naval Defence, 142, 146, 159, 164, 168, 304n, 374, 381, 384n

Pankhurst, Sylvia, British suffragist leader, 88n, 426

Payer, Friedrich von, nobleman from Wurttemberg, German MP, chairman of the parliamentary group of the Progressive People's Party/German Democratic Party, former Vice-Chancellor of the Reich, 114, 242, 247, 438n, 440, 447

Peel, William, Viscount Peel, British nobleman, Conservatives, 237

Pennanen, Pekka, Finnish MP, Young Finns (Liberals), 407–409

Persson, Daniel, Swedish Member of the Second Chamber, Liberals, Vice-Speaker, 153, 165

Pettersson, David, Swedish Member of the Chamber, The Right, 378, 386, 395

Pettersson, Jakob, Swedish Member of the Second Chamber, Liberals, chairman of the Law Committee, 374, 390, 393

Petty-Fitzmaurice, Henry, 5th Marquess of Lansdowne, British nobleman, 228

Pfannkuch, Wilhelm, German MP, Social Democrats, 437–8, 445–6, 451

Pilkka, Simson, Finnish MP, Agrarian League, 495

Pollock, Ernest, British MP, Conservatives, 98–9

Ponsonby, Arthur, British MP, Liberal/Labour, 111

Posadowsky-Wehner, Arthur von, Silesian nobleman (Graf von Posadowsky-Wehner, Freiherr von Postelwitz) and German MP, 362

Preuß, Hugo, German Minister of Interior Affairs, German Democratic Party, Professor of Law, 365, 433, 440–1, 447–8, 451–2, 486

Procopé, Hjalmar, Finnish MP, Swedish People's Party, 476, 479, 495, 501

Pykälä, Bertta, Finnish MP, Agrarian League, 327

Päivänsalo, Bror Hannes, Finnish MP, Finnish Party (Conservatives), 332

Pärssinen, Hilja, Finnish MP, Social Democrats, the editorial secretary of *Työläisnainen*, 271

R

Rahja, Jukka, Finnish Bolshevist revolutionary, 188

Rantakari, Kaarle, Finnish MP, Finnish Party (Conservatives), 53, 194, 196–7, 210
Rantanen, Frans, Finnish MP, Social Democrats, 196–7, 202, 210
Rawlinson, John, British MP, Conservatives, 107
Redmond, William, British MP, Irish Nationalists, 227
Redslob, Robert, German constitutional lawyer, 138n, 365, 452
Rees, Caradoc, British MP, Liberals, Parliamentary Secretary for Home Office, 100
Rees, John David, British MP, Unionists, 225
Reid, George, British MP, Unionists, former prime minister of Australia, 84
Relander, Lauri Kristian, Finnish MP, Agrarian League, the Speaker, 495
Rentola, Antti, Finnish MP, Young Finns (Liberals), 277, 288, 405, 408, 415–16, 419
Ritavuori, Heikki, Finnish MP, National Progress Party, chairman of the Constitutional Committee, 480, 496
Rosenqvist, Gustaf, Finnish MP, Swedish People's Party, Professor of Dogmatics, 194, 210, 331n, 333–4, 339
Russell, Frank, 2nd Earl Russell, British nobleman, Labour sympathizer, 221, 235, 237
Rühle, Otto, German MP, Independent Social Democrats, 355
Ryömä, Hannes, Finnish MP, Social Democrats, editor-in-chief of *Suomen Sosialidemokraatti*, 468, 483, 489–90, 496–7
Räf, Erik, Swedish Member of the Second Chamber, The Right, 150, 154, 165, 168, 386
Röing, Erik, Swedish Member of the Second Chamber, Liberals, 303n, 374, 390

S

Saarelainen, Pekka, Finnish MP, Agrarian League, 328, 489
Salin, Eetu, Finnish MP, Social Democrats, 191, 266, 275, 287
Salter, Arthur, British MP, Unionists, 76, 81, 83, 92, 98–9, 103
Samuel, Herbert, British MP, Liberals, former home secretary, 80, 86, 88, 101–102, 216
Sarlin, Bruno, Finnish MP, National Progess Party, 484–5, 489, 502
Schauman, Georg, Finnish MP, Swedish Left, historian, 321n, 475–6, 478, 480, 489, 502
Scheidemann, Philipp, German MP, Social Democrats, Chancellor, 147, 150n, 363, 432
Schmoller, Gustav von, Prussian nobleman, Member of the Prussian Herrenhaus, Professor of Economics, 403
Schotte, Axel, Swedish Member of the Chamber, Liberals, Minister of Public Administration, 389, 393
Schybergson, Emil, Finnish MP, Swedish People's Party, 63, 186, 194, 276
Scott, Leslie, British MP, Conservatives, 83, 103
Setälä, Emil Nestor, Finnish MP, National Coalition Party (Conservatives), Professor of Finnish, acting prime minister, Minister of Education, 63, 289, 330, 358n, 412n, 413, 476, 479, 485–6, 491–3
Simon, John, Sir, British MP, Liberals, former minister, 79
Sneidern, Axel von, Swedish Member of the Second Chamber, Liberals, 309
Sirola, Yrjö, Finnish MP, Social Democrats, 63, 69, 152, 261–3, 266n, 269–71, 274–5, 277–9, 283, 300, 467
Sivkovich, Hans, German MP, Progressivists, 57
Smith, Frederick, British MP, Conservatives, Attorney General, 219
Spahn, Peter, German MP, chairman of the parliamentray group of the Catholic Centre, chairman of the Main Committee, 116, 121, 135, 441
Staaff, Karl, Swedish politician, Liberals, former Prime Minister, 60
Ståhlberg, Kaarlo Juho, Finnish MP, Young Finns (Liberals), Professor of Law, 63, 183, 209, 273, 280, 324–6, 334, 405
Sterne, Axel, Swedish Member ofthe Second Chamber, Social Democrats, journalist writing in *Folkbladet*, 159, 304–5, 309, 312
Stresemann, Gustav, German MP, chairman of the National Liberals/

German People's Party, 121–2, 130, 132, 135–6, 243, 354, 359, 361, 366, 441, 452
Ström, Fredrik, Swedish Member of the First Chamber, party secretary of the Leftist Social Democrats, 148, 152, 157, 170, 376, 380, 391–2, 400, 459
Stuart-Wortley, Charles, 1st Baron Stuart of Wortley, British nobleman, Conservatives, 238
Suolahti, Hugo, Finnish MP, chairman of the National Coalition Party (Conservatives), professor of German philology and Vice-Rector of the University of Helsinki, 485, 492–3
Suosalo, Kalle, Finnish MP, Social Democrats, 203
Svinhufvud, Per Evind, Finnish nobleman, Prime Minister, 276
Swartz, Carl, Swedish Member of the First Chamber, The Right, former Prime Minister, 141, 143, 372, 375, 388–9, 395, 397–8
Sydenham Clarke, George, 1st Baron Sydenham of Combe, British nobleman, 221, 223n, 228, 235
Söderberg, Ernst, Swedish Member of the First Chamber, Social Democrats, 398
Söderblom, Nathan, Archbishop of Uppsala, 224
Söderholm, Karl, Finnish MP, Swedish People's Party, 210–211

T

Taimi, Adolf, Finnish Bolshevik revolutionary, 179
Takkula, Eetu, Finnish MP, Agrarian League, 327
Talas, Onni, Finnish MP, Young Finns (Liberals), Minister of Justice, Professor of Administrative Law, 195, 280, 291, 328
Thore, Alexander, Swedish Member of the Second Chamber, The Right, 386
Thorsson, Fredrik Vilhelm, Swedish Member of the Second Chamber, Social Democrats, Minister of Finance, 374, 399
Tokoi, Oskari, Finnish MP, Social Democrats, Prime Minister, workers' union leader, 179–80, 182n, 190–3, 198, 205, 207, 260–2, 259, 275, 281–2, 337, 494

Trygger, Ernst, Swedish Member of the First Chamber, leader of The Right, 158, 168, 305, 311, 315, 369, 379–80, 386–7, 395–6, 401, 457–9
Tulenheimo, Antti, Finnish MP, Finnish Party (Conservatives), Minister of Justice, 194, 204, 205n, 212

V

Vahlquist, Condrad, Swedish Member of the Second Chamber, The Right, 161, 168
Valkama, Wäinö, Finnish MP, Finnish Party (Conservatives), 281, 323
Valpas, Edvard, see Hänninen-Walpas
Vennerström, Ivar, Swedish Member of the Second Chamber, Leftist Social Democrats, 149, 152, 157, 160, 165, 302, 312–13, 370, 376, 380, 391–2, 394, 400n, 458, 462
Vennola, Juho, Finnish MP, National Progress Party, Minister of Commerce and Industry, 477, 489, 496
Victoria von Baden, Queen of Sweden, 253
Virkkunen, Artturi, Finnish MP, Finnish Party (Conservatives), editor-in-chief of *Uusi Suometar*, 331–2
Virkkunen, Paavo, Finnish MP, Finnish Party (Conservatives), the Speaker, 269, 288, 329, 403–4, 412–13, 479, 492
Vogtherr, Ewald, German MP, Social Democrats, 114
Voionmaa, Väinö, Finnish MP, Social Democrats, Professor of History, 477–9, 482–3, 490–1, 497–8, 501n
Vuoristo, Jussi, Finnish MP, Social Democrats, 266n, 270, 285

W

Waldén, Ola, Swedish member of the First Chamber, Social Democrats, 148
Wallenberg, Knut Agathon, Swedish Member of the Chamber, The Right, former Foreign Minister, 398
Walton, Joseph, Sir, British MP, Liberals, 83
Ward, Arnold, British MP, Conservatives, 84, 91, 93
Wardle, George, British MP, Labour, Parliamentary Secretary of the Board of Trade, 95–6

Wartenburg, Heinrich Yorck von, Prussian nobleman (Graf Yorck von Wartenburg), Member of the Prussian Herrenhaus, Conservative leader, 134

Watson, John Bertrand, British MP, Liberals, 84, 88, 97n

Weber, Max, German political theorist, 109, 365

Wedgwood, Josiah, British MP, independent liberal radical, 100, 216

Wendt, Georg von, Finnish MP, Swedish Left, 494

Werner, Ferdinand, German MP, German Ethnic Party, 250

Westarp, Kuno von, Graf von Westrap (Count of Westarp), Prussian nobleman and MP, National Conservatives, Councillor of the Prussian High Administrative Court, 122–3, 126, 131, 137, 354, 356, 359, 362

Wiemer, Otto, German MP, chairman of the Progressivist parliamentary group, 116–17, 125–6

Wiik, Karl Harald, Finnish MP, Social Democrats, 69, 152, 182, 183n, 186n, 188n, 191, 203, 257, 259–60, 275, 280n, 300

Wilhelm II (von Hohenzollern), German Emperor, 50–1

Williams, Aneurin, British MP, Liberals, the Treasurer of the Proportional Representation Society, 81, 84–5, 88, 102, 216

Wilson, William Tyson, British MP, Labour, a trade union activist, 226

Wilson, Woodrow, President of the United States, Democrats, 29, 73, 87, 107, 110, 124, 186, 227, 252, 292, 295, 349, 366, 415, 445, 511, 514–15

Wilson-Fox, Henry, British MP, Conservatives, 77, 102

Winnington-Ingram, Arthur, Bishop of London, 235

Wood, Edward Frederick Lindley, British MP, Conservatives 98

Wrangel, Herman, Swedish Member of the First Chamber, The Right, 380, 388

Wrede, Rabbe Axel, Finnish nobleman (friherre) and MP, Swedish People's Party, former Professor of Roman Law and Rector of Helsinki University, 63, 323, 325, 330–1, 333, 335, 405, 410, 417, 479, 503

Wrede, Otto, Finnish former minister, 502n

Wuorimaa, Artur, Finnish MP, Agrarian League, 265, 277, 284, 328, 405–407, 410

Z

Zweigbergk, Otto von, Swedish Member of the Chamber, Liberals, the editor-in-chief of *Dagens Nyheter*, 150, 158, 164, 390, 457

Studia Fennica Ethnologica

Memories of My Town
The Identities of Town Dwellers and Their Places in Three Finnish Towns
Edited by Anna-Maria Åström, Pirjo Korkiakangas & Pia Olsson
Studia Fennica Ethnologica 8
2004

Passages Westward
Edited by Maria Lähteenmäki & Hanna Snellman
Studia Fennica Ethnologica 9
2006

Defining Self
Essays on emergent identities in Russia Seventeenth to Nineteenth Centuries
Edited by Michael Branch
Studia Fennica Ethnologica 10
2009

Touching Things
Ethnological Aspects of Modern Material Culture
Edited by Pirjo Korkiakangas, Tiina-Riitta Lappi & Heli Niskanen
Studia Fennica Ethnologica 11
2008

Gendered Rural Spaces
Edited by Pia Olsson & Helena Ruotsala
Studia Fennica Ethnologica 12
2009

Laura Stark
The Limits of Patriarchy
How Female Networks of Pilfering and Gossip Sparked the First Debates on Rural Gender Rights in the 19th-century Finnish-Language Press
Studia Fennica Ethnologica 13
2011

Where is the Field?
The Experience of Migration Viewed through the Prism of Ethnographic Fieldwork
Edited by Laura Hirvi & Hanna Snellman
Studia Fennica Ethnologica 14
2012

Laura Hirvi
Identities in Practice
A Trans-Atlantic Ethnography of Sikh Immigrants in Finland and in California
Studia Fennica Ethnologica 15
2013

Eerika Koskinen-Koivisto
Her Own Worth
Negotiations of Subjectivity in the Life Narrative of a Female Labourer
Studia Fennica Ethnologica 16
2014

Studia Fennica Folkloristica

Narrating, Doing, Experiencing
Nordic Folkloristic Perspectives
Edited by Annikki Kaivola-Bregenhøj, Barbro Klein & Ulf Palmenfelt
Studia Fennica Folkloristica 16
2006

Mícheál Briody
The Irish Folklore Commission 1935–1970
History, ideology, methodology
Studia Fennica Folkloristica 17
2008

Venla Sykäri
Words as Events
Cretan Mantinádes in Performance and Composition
Studia Fennica Folkloristica 18
2011

Hidden Rituals and Public Performances
Traditions and Belonging among the Post-Soviet Khanty, Komi and Udmurts
Edited by Anna-Leena Siikala & Oleg Ulyashev
Studia Fennica Folkloristica 19
2011

Mythic Discourses
Studies in Uralic Traditions
Edited by Frog, Anna-Leena Siikala & Eila Stepanova
Studia Fennica Folkloristica 20
2012

Cornelius Hasselblatt
Kalevipoeg Studies
The Creation and Reception of an Epic
Studia Fennica Folkloristica 21
2016

Genre – Text – Interpretation
Multidisciplinary Perspectives on Folklore and Beyond
Edited by Kaarina Koski, Frog & Ulla Savolainen
Studia Fennica Folkloristica 22
2016

Studia Fennica Historica

Modernisation in Russia since 1900
Edited by Markku Kangaspuro & Jeremy Smith
Studia Fennica Historica 12
2006

Seija-Riitta Laakso
Across the Oceans
Development of Overseas Business Information Transmission 1815–1875
Studia Fennica Historica 13
2007

Industry and Modernism
Companies, Architecture and Identity in the Nordic and Baltic Countries during the High-Industrial Period
Edited by Anja Kervanto Nevanlinna
Studia Fennica Historica 14
2007

Charlotta Wolff
Noble conceptions of politics in eighteenth-century Sweden (ca 1740–1790)
Studia Fennica Historica 15
2008

Sport, Recreation and Green Space in the European City
Edited by Peter Clark, Marjaana Niemi & Jari Niemelä
Studia Fennica Historica 16
2009

Rhetorics of Nordic Democracy
Edited by Jussi Kurunmäki & Johan Strang
Studia Fennica Historica 17
2010

Fibula, Fabula, Fact
The Viking Age in Finland
Edited by Joonas Ahola & Frog with Clive Tolley
Studia Fennica Historica 18
2014

Novels, Histories, Novel Nations
Historical Fiction and Cultural Memory in Finland and Estonia
Edited by Linda Kaljundi, Eneken Laanes & Ilona Pikkanen
Studia Fennica Historica 19
2015

Jukka Gronow & Sergey Zhuravlev
Fashion Meets Socialism
Fashion industry in the Soviet Union after the Second World War
Studia Fennica Historica 20
2015

Sofia Kotilainen
Literacy Skills as Local Intangible Capital
The History of a Rural Lending Library c. 1860–1920
Studia Fennica Historica 21
2016

Continued Violence and Troublesome Pasts
Post-war Europe between the Victors after the Second World War
Edited by Ville Kivimäki and Petri Karonen
Studia Fennica Historica 22
2017

Personal Agency at the Swedish Age of Greatness 1560-1720
Edited by Petri Karonen & Marko Hakanen
Studia Fennica Historica 23
2017

Pasi Ihalainen
The Springs of Democracy
National and Transnational Debates on Constitutional Reform in the British, German, Swedish and Finnish Parliaments, 1917–19
Studia Fennica Historica 24
2017

Studia Fennica Anthropologica

On Foreign Ground
Moving between Countries and Categories
Edited by Marie-Louise Karttunen & Minna Ruckenstein
Studia Fennica Anthropologica 1
2007

Beyond the Horizon
Essays on Myth, History, Travel and Society
Edited by Clifford Sather & Timo Kaartinen
Studia Fennica Anthropologica 2
2008

Timo Kallinen
Divine Rulers in a Secular State
Studia Fennica Anthropologica 3
2016

Studia Fennica Linguistica

Minimal reference
The use of pronouns in Finnish and Estonian discourse
Edited by Ritva Laury
Studia Fennica Linguistica 12
2005

Kaisa Häkkinen
Spreading the Written Word
Mikael Agricola and the Birth of Literary Finnish
Studia Fennica Linguistica 19
2015

Antti Leino
On Toponymic Constructions as an Alternative to Naming Patterns in Describing Finnish Lake Names
Studia Fennica Linguistica 13
2007

Linking Clauses and Actions in Social Interaction
Edited by Ritva Laury, Marja Etelämäki, Elizabeth Couper-Kuhlen
Studia Fennica Linquistica 20
2017

Talk in interaction
Comparative dimensions
Edited by Markku Haakana, Minna Laakso & Jan Lindström
Studia Fennica Linguistica 14
2009

Planning a new standard language
Finnic minority languages meet the new millennium
Edited by Helena Sulkala & Harri Mantila
Studia Fennica Linguistica 15
2010

Lotta Weckström
Representations of Finnishness in Sweden
Studia Fennica Linguistica 16
2011

Terhi Ainiala, Minna Saarelma & Paula Sjöblom
Names in Focus
An Introduction to Finnish Onomastics
Studia Fennica Linguistica 17
2012

Registers of Communication
Edited by Asif Agha & Frog
Studia Fennica Linguistica 18
2015

Studia Fennica Litteraria

Aino Kallas
Negotiations with Modernity
Edited by Leena Kurvet-Käosaar & Lea Rojola
Studia Fennica Litteraria 4
2011

The Emergence of Finnish Book and Reading Culture in the 1700s
Edited by Cecilia af Forselles & Tuija Laine
Studia Fennica Litteraria 5
2011

Nodes of Contemporary Finnish Literature
Edited by Leena Kirstinä
Studia Fennica Litteraria 6
2012

White Field, Black Seeds
Nordic Literacy Practices in the Long Nineteenth Century
Edited by Anna Kuismin & M. J. Driscoll
Studia Fennica Litteraria 7
2013

Lieven Ameel
Helsinki in Early Twentieth-Century Literature
Urban Experiences in Finnish Prose Fiction 1890–1940
Studia Fennica Litteraria 8
2014

Novel Districts
Critical Readings of Monika Fagerholm
Edited by Kristina Malmio & Mia Österlund
Studia Fennica Litteraria 9
2016

Elise Nykänen
Mysterious Minds
The Making of Private and Collective Consciousness in Marja-Liisa Vartio's Novels
Studia Fennica Litteraria 10
2017

www.ingramcontent.com/pod-product-compliance
Lightning Source LLC
Chambersburg PA
CBHW081431020526
44114CB00056B/2695